EDISON

A Life of Invention

Paul Israel

John Wiley & Sons, Inc.

New York • Chichester • Weinheim • Brisbane • Singapore • Toronto

This book is printed on acid-free paper. ⊚

Published by John Wiley & Sons, Inc.
Published simultaneously in Canada

All illustrations unless otherwise noted are courtesy of Edison National Historic Site, National Park Service, Department of the Interior.

This publication is designed to provide accurate and authoritative information in regard to the subject matter covered. It is sold with the understanding that the publisher is not engaged in rendering special services. If professional advice or other expert assistance is required, the services of a competent professional person should be sought.

Library of Congress Cataloging-in-Publication Data

Israel, Paul.
    Edison : a life of invention / Paul Israel.
        p.   cm.
    Includes bibliographical references and index.
    ISBN 0-471-36270-0 (paper) .
    1. Edison, Thomas A. (Thomas Alva) 1847–1931. 2. Inventors—
United States—Biography.   I. Title.
TK140.E3187   1998
621.3'092—dc21
    [B]   98-10105

Printed in the United States of America

10 9 8 7 6 5 4

To my father, Leo, and the memory
of my mother, Esther

Contents

Acknowledgments

Thomas Edison's record of 1,093 U.S. patents and several key inventions in a variety of different technologies remains unsurpassed. The primary goal of this biography is to explain how he achieved such an extensive record of success as an inventor. An important part of the explanation lies in Edison's collaborative style of work and in the very able men he chose to assist him during his career at his shops and laboratories and in numerous business enterprises that marketed the inventions he produced. The documentary record they left behind, totaling more than five million pages, makes it impossible for any single scholar to study Edison and his work alone. Fortunately, like Edison, I have been assisted by many fine collaborators during the eighteen years that I have been editing his papers, including the last seven and a half in which I have also been working as his biographer.

My colleagues at the Thomas A. Edison Papers Project at Rutgers University and at the Edison National Historic Site have provided immeasurable support and assistance through the years and their insights into Edison have informed my own thinking about him. First among them I must thank Reese Jenkins, the first director of the project, and his successor, Bob Rosenberg, for their support and encouragement during years I spent researching and writing this book. I would never have been able to complete it without the financial assistance they helped me to obtain and the release time they gave me from the project. I am also indebted to my fellow editors at the book edition, Keith Nier and Louis Carlat, who read chapters, pointed out important resources, and offered many significant ideas of their own regarding Edison. The large microfilm edition staff—Tom Jeffrey, Terry Collins, Greg Jankunis, Leslie Fields, and Al Salerno—have all assisted me in similar ways. But I must especially thank Lisa Gitelman, who began her career with the microfilm edition after assisting me as a research assistant on the biography. Her research made my own work on the biography much easier and she has continued to be an invaluable colleague through the years. I also want to thank many other people who have been connected with the Papers Project over the years and whose work has informed my own. In particular, Martha King, who read early chapters, and Greg Field, who not only assisted me while he was connected with the project but has continued to assist me as a friend and colleague. Leonard Reich, W. Bernard Carlson, Andre Millard, Maryann Hellrigel, and Andrew Butrica are other former editors who deserve special mention for their help and insights through the years. Finally, I must give a special thanks to Helen Endick and

Grace Kurkowski, who have helped me with small and large administrative tasks, particularly in connection with the administering of my grants.

The funding for this book came from the Humanities, Science, and Technology Program of the National Endowment for the Humanities (Grant RH-21014-91), which enabled me to conduct research and begin writing the book and to hire Lisa as a research assistant. I could not have finished the writing without the generous assistance of the two grants from the Alfred P. Sloan Foundation.

Many other people have also assisted with the writing of this book. Phil Pauley, my colleague in the History Department at Rutgers University, provided me with an invaluable reading of the manuscript that helped to make it better. Several stimulating conversations with Scott Sandage helped me to conceptualize the chapters that examine Edison's fame. Peter Martland, Ray Wile, and Charles Hummel kindly made available some of their own research materials on the phonograph. At the Edison National Historic Site in West Orange, New Jersey, I have enjoyed the assistance of archivist George Tselos and his assistant Doug Tarr. Several people have assisted me through the years at the Henry Ford Museum & Greenfield Village, most notably Linda Skolarus, William Pretzer, John Bowditch, and Judith Endelman. At the Smithsonian, I have been fortunate to work with Bernard Finn, who has also been a good friend through the years. Mimi Bowling, a former archivist at the Edison National Historic Site, assisted me with the Frank Sprague Papers at the New York Public Library. The staff at the Baker Library at Harvard University provided similar help with the Henry Villard Papers. A special thanks must be given to the research seminar of the Center for the History of Business, Technology, and Society at the Hagley Museum & Library, which heard a version of Chapter 15. In particular I want to thank seminar director Philip Scranton and Richard Butsch, whose formal comments on the paper were full of helpful suggestions.

Anyone working on the history of technology must thank the members of the Society for the History of Technology, who provide such a welcoming intellectual home for us all and without whose work this book would not have been possible. In particular, I want to thank Thomas P. Hughes, who taught us all how to think seriously about Edison, and Robert Friedel, who brought me to the subject of Edison and has been a wonderful friend through the years.

I must also thank my two editors at Wiley. Roger Scholl was my original editor at the press and convinced me to undertake the daunting task of trying to encapsulate Edison's life in a single volume. His successor, Hana Lane, has been responsible for reading the manuscript and offering many suggestions that greatly improved it. A special thanks is also due to Joanne Palmer, who guided the book through the production process.

Finally, I want to thank the boys in the band—Jerry, Phil, Bob, Bill, Mickey, Vince, and Bruce—and Kali, Achilles, Athena, Rainy, and the Guys for providing me with a very special kind of encouragement and support.

CHAPTER 1

Childhood and Education

The world might never have heard of Thomas Alva Edison if his family had not been forced to leave their home in the small village of Vienna in Upper Canada (what is today the province of Ontario). The young Edison would have found a more sedate economic and industrial environment in Canada than he did in the United States, one that did not emphasize invention and innovation. "The problem of Canadian invention and technology," wrote one scholar after surveying its history, "lies not in the area of individual creativity, but in the much simpler areas of public education and means of capital formation . . . individually and in groups we resist innovation, and our institutions for the production of risk capital do not work."[1] Whatever innate abilities might have contributed to his success, even Thomas Edison could not have flourished in an environment that did not provide the intellectual and economic resources necessary for invention.

The Edison family left Canada for the United States primarily for political reasons. They had been among the early settlers in western Upper Canada when they arrived there in 1811 from Nova Scotia, where they had originally fled with other loyalist families after the American Revolution. The Edisons were drawn to Upper Canada by the mild climate and fertile land they found in the area around the northern shore of Lake Erie known as the Talbot Settlement. The provincial government encouraged settlement in this section through Colonel Thomas Talbot, who received an additional 200 acres of land for each 50 acres of his original 5,000-acre land grant that was settled by others. The Edison family, consisting of John, his wife Sarah, and their seven children with their spouses and children, were settled by Talbot in Bayham township, one of twenty-seven under his control, where they helped establish the village of Vienna. The family primarily engaged in farming and lumbering, which were the principal enterprises of the region.[2]

Edison's mother and father, Nancy and Samuel Edison.

The western section of the province also contained a large number of American settlers who were attracted by its land prices, cheap in comparison with those in the United States. Bayham was one of the many townships in the region that remained predominantly American throughout the 1830s. Although Americans in the province remained loyal to the Crown during the War of 1812, they did not have the same attachment to the empire as did the British settlers who arrived later. Indeed, as provincial politics splintered into conservative and reform factions in the 1830s, support for conservatives in the region was strongest among recent British immigrants who found the views and actions of many of those already in the province too egalitarian. Growing up in Bayham, Samuel Edison Jr. was infected by this egalitarian impulse, which was reinforced by his marriage to the American-born Nancy Elliott. Her family was among those from the United States attracted by cheap land prices and perhaps by a sense of religious ministry—her father was a Baptist minister from upstate New York. The Edisons were also nominally Baptist. Samuel's parents were both baptized into the Baptist Church when he was fifteen, although they were later excluded from the congregation for nonattendance and for refusing to obey church doctrine. Religious issues played an important role in the political life of the province where the Church of England received special privileges, including a large portion of land set aside as the Clergy Reserve.

An innkeeper by trade, Samuel doubtless participated in political debates, and his own reading included the works of Thomas Paine. Thomas Edison later said of his father that he "has always been a rebel, a regular red-hot cop-perhead Democrat, and General Jackson was his hero."[3] Andrew Jackson's rep-utation as a strong but populist and egalitarian leader who attacked entrenched privilege would have presented a striking contrast to the province's political leaders and perhaps served as a model for the young supporter of constitutional reform.

Political conflict arose in the province as the government became domi-nated by a small group known as the Family Compact. They acted to preserve their own privilege and to recreate an elite British society by maintaining the power of the appointed executive branch in opposition to the elective assem-bly; by giving the Church of England its privileged position; and, according to the reformers, by promoting such projects as the Welland Canal and the Bank of Upper Canada at the expense of local improvements such as schools and roads. American egalitarian ideology became the basis for political opposition as a reform-conservative split emerged in the province. By the 1830s the re-formers were an identifiable group who demanded constitutional reform to ex-tend political participation. According to a leading scholar, they tended "to equate democracy and prosperity" and often contrasted the "lack of popular participation in state affairs and the economic backwardness of Upper Canada with the 'popular sovereignty' and prosperity" of the United States.[4] Reformers also drew on the example of British radicalism with its political unions and calls for constitutional reform.

When the provincial governor disbanded the assembly in 1836 and helped conservatives gain an overwhelming victory in new elections, many in the re-form movement were radicalized. Led by the fiery newspaper editor William Lyon MacKenzie, who began to agitate for a new political union with reform-ers in Lower Canada (present-day Quebec province), they began to organize meetings throughout the province. Economic hardships created by a poor har-vest and the tightening of credit caused by a commercial depression through-out the Anglo-American world further exacerbated this volatile political envi-ronment. By the fall of 1837 armed meetings had taken place and MacKenzie was moving increasingly toward rebellion, although his activities were largely confined to the provincial capital of Toronto. News of rebellion in Lower Can-ada led to an ill-planned insurrection by MacKenzie during the first week of December. Although MacKenzie's troops were easily dispatched by provincial forces, early news of the insurrection seemed to indicate success, and radicals in the western part of the province led by Charles Duncombe quickly gathered to join the rebellion after hearing rumors that he and other leaders would be arrested by local officials. By December 12, news of MacKenzie's defeat finally reached the west and Duncombe's revolt dissipated as he advised his followers to return to their homes while he and rebel leaders fled to the United States. Among the rebel leaders who joined Duncombe in flight across the border to Detroit was Samuel Edison Jr. Not much is known about Samuel in the pe-riod immediately after the rebellion. He may have joined Duncombe in his attempts to organize an invasion from Detroit and perhaps in a failed attack in late February 1838 on Fighting Island in the Detroit River.

Among those who stayed behind was Samuel's brother Marcellus, who was imprisoned briefly before being released on bail on December 21. Although some of those most closely associated with the rebel leaders were treated harshly and a few executed (particularly after a series of failed invasions led by the exiled rebels), the authorities were generally lenient toward the majority of those arrested. In the London district, which included Bayham, no action was taken against most of the followers, including Marcellus Edison. Samuel, on the other hand, was indicted for high treason and his estate seized. Unable to return to Canada, Samuel spent some time in Detroit and Peru, Ohio, before settling between 1838 and 1839 in Milan, Ohio, where he was finally joined by his family.[5]

What attracted the Edison family and many others to Milan were the economic opportunities expected to follow the opening of the Milan Canal on July 4, 1839. The 3-mile canal between Milan and the navigable portion of the Huron River gave the "dull inland village" (population 600–700) an outlet on Lake Erie, and, according to the local newspaper, it soon became, after Cleveland, "probably the first town in value of its exports, between Buffalo and Detroit."[6] During the 1840s Milan was one of the leading grain-shipping ports in the world. It also became an important shipbuilding and regional manufacturing center with a population of over 1,500. Along with the growing city, during these years the Edison family prospered. Samuel, who apparently also speculated in land, supported the family as a shinglemaker; his brother Thomas operated a ship that brought shingle bolts from Canada. Although they were not one of the town's leading families, the Edisons were well-off and associated with some of Milan's more prominent citizens. In August 1841 Samuel obtained a plot of land on the bluff overlooking the canal basin on which he built the seven-room brick house in which Thomas Alva Edison was born on February 11, 1847. The last of Samuel and Nancy Edison's seven children, he was the fourth to be born in Milan, but the only one of the four who survived early childhood (the last died in 1847). His three surviving siblings—eighteen-year-old Marion, sixteen-year-old William (known by his middle name Pitt), and fourteen-year-old Harriet Ann (called Tannie)—had all been born in Vienna.[7]

In the year of Thomas's birth, Milan reached its peak as a grain port, shipping over 900,000 bushels of wheat and nearly 138,000 bushels of corn. However, grain shipments soon began a precipitous decline as farmers began to bring their products to Mansfield, which was on the newly opened rail line between Sandusky and Cleveland; wheat shipments from Milan declined by over half in 1848 and fell to under 282,000 bushels in 1849. Milan's economic decline eventually affected the Edison family, who moved to Port Huron, Michigan, in the spring of 1854.

Little is known of Thomas Edison's life in Milan, but from all accounts it was unexceptional and included typical boyhood activities. There is some evidence that young Thomas, usually called Alva or Al while growing up, was a sickly boy. One of his friends from Milan claimed that he had a catarrhal infection that bothered him at times. He also recalled that among Thomas's playmates was Mary Taylor, who lived nearby and "would go to bed with him" when he was not feeling well. Another playmate, who was born the same year as Edison, later wrote him of "things we boath remember of the old cannal whear we went boating and swimming in summer scating and playing [shinny?] in winter and of the hills we coasted down in winter and of the ships they built in Milan."[8] Edison's own recollections included a visit to Vienna to see his grandfather; the covered wagons of a Milan gold rush party that included his uncle Snow Edison, who died soon after his arrival in California in the fall of 1849; the marriage of his sister Marion to Homer Page on December 19, 1849; and the drowning death of his playmate George Lockwood. Other accounts tell of his "fondness for building little plank roads out of the debris of the yards and mills," of his learning "the songs of the lumber gangs and canal men," and of his copying store signs in the village square.[9]

Perhaps because of illness, Thomas did not attend the local public school, although his older siblings did, but his mother no doubt taught him to read and write. As a former schoolteacher she would have been well prepared to do so. There was at that time a general expectation in American society that mothers would teach their children to read before they began attending school.[10]

While Milan was Edison's birthplace and his home for the first seven years of his life, the lumber town of Port Huron was where he grew up and received most of his early education. It is not known why the Edisons came to Port Huron, but the town had a sizeable Canadian-born population and Samuel was likely aware of its booming lumber industry. It was twice the size of Milan and had a population of 3,100. Edison later recalled that "The town in its pristine youth was a great lumber center, and hummed to the industry of numerous sawmills. An incredible quantity of lumber was made there yearly until the forests nearby vanished and the industry with them. The wealth of the community, invested largely in this business and in allied transportation companies, was accumulated rapidly, and as freely spent during those days of prosperity in St. Clair County, bringing with it a high degree of domestic comfort."[11]

Although Samuel Edison's fortunes waxed and waned over the years, the family lived comfortably in a large, two-story house that had been built by the first purveyor to the Fort Gratiot military reservation in a pine grove on the north side of Port Huron. According to a later resident of the house, it had six bedrooms on the second floor (at various times the Edisons had boarders in the house) and downstairs "a wide hall ran from north to south through the house, on either side of which were two large, high ceilinged rooms with wide fireplaces."[12] From the house one could see Lake Huron and the St. Clair River, as well as the abundant woodlands. Sometime after moving into the house Samuel took advantage of its location and built a 100-foot observation tower to the south and charged twenty-five cents for the view. This apparently became a paying proposition as a tourist attraction for railroad excursions to the lake.

Most Edison biographers describe Samuel as a grain merchant, but a November 1856 credit report indicates that he operated a grocery, was a "fair bus[iness] man," and that the family had "$5000 or $6000, mainly R[eal] E[state]." However, by the following February he was "not largely engaged in business," and a December report noted he had been "indicted for selling R.E. not his own." It went on to say that "his reputation has suffered & rumor has his [property] in his wifes name," and concluded "should not like to trust largely." By February 1858 he was out of business, having "totally failed."[13] Samuel's grocery business may well have been affected by the Panic of 1857. During these years he also engaged for a time in the lumber business. To make ends meet the family took in boarders and Edison remembered helping his father with a truck garden: "After my father moved to Port Huron, he engaged in lumbering and also had a 10 acre field of very rich land which was used for truck gardening. After the field was ploughed I, in conjunction with a German boy of about my age, did the planting. About eight acres were planted in sweet corn, the balance in radishes, onions, parsnips, and beets, etc.; I was very ambitious about this garden and worked very hard. My father had an old horse and wagon and with this we carried the vegetables to the town which was $1^{1}/_{2}$ miles distant and sold them from door to door. One year I remember turning in to my mother 600 dollars from the farm."[14]

Whatever economic difficulties the Edison family experienced was probably ameliorated by assistance from the eldest son William Pitt, who operated what the local newspaper described as "one of the most commodious and spacious livery stables in the State. . . . The building is 60 feet wide and 100 feet long, with a carriage repository 25 feet wide, and extending the entire length of the building, on the north side. The main building is two stories high, and is finished externally in such good style as to render it a pleasing feature in the appearance of that prominent part of the village. The internal arrangements are on a liberal scale, and complete in every particular. Mr. Edison keeps sixteen horses, with vehicles to match, and we are glad to know that he is doing a good business."[15] Pitt's successful experience in the livery business later led to his involvement with the city's first horse-railway streetcar line.

Financial difficulties afflicting the Edison family may have affected Thomas's schooling. Standard accounts of his school career indicate that he was taken out of school by his mother because a teacher considered him to be "addled." Whether or not this story has any truth behind it, there is evidence that economic difficulties played a role in his limited school attendance. Thomas was known to have briefly attended both the private school of Reverend George Engle and the Port Huron Union School, although the exact dates of his attendance are unknown. In 1885 Reverend Engle wrote Edison to ask for financial assistance, reminding him that when he attended the school, "Your father, not being very flush with money, I did not urge him to pay the school bill."[16] In

1855 the annual tuition for Engle's school was $130, which included board, fuel, lights, and English instruction. An 1854 fee schedule indicates that an eleven-week term cost about $30. Additional annual charges included $12 per year for instruction in Latin and French and $40 for music instruction by a Miss D. Edson, from whom Thomas took music lessons while at the school (the Edisons had a piano at home).

Most biographers assume that Thomas attended Engle's school shortly after the family moved to Port Huron and that his attendance at the Port Huron Union School occurred soon after. However, the reminiscences of those who knew him as a boy in Port Huron indicate that he was twelve or thirteen when he attended the public school. P. L. Hubbard, who apparently was Thomas's teacher at the school, and N. W. King, a playmate, both recalled that he attended in 1860. Ambrose Robinson, who boarded at the Edison home in 1858–1859, remembered Thomas going to school during construction of the Grand Trunk railway line to Fort Gratiot.[17] The cost of attending the public school may well have delayed his enrollment. Although supported in part by taxes, Michigan schools also required parents to pay an additional rate bill based on the number of days a student attended, which included fuel costs and assessor's fees. While this probably did not amount to more than $5 to $10 per year, economic difficulties between 1857 and 1858 may have caused Samuel and Nancy to decide that she should teach him at home. Tannie's marriage to Samuel Bailey in June 1855 meant that none of the other Edison children were living at home and would have allowed Nancy to devote her full attention to her young son.

Thomas's attendance at the Union School in 1859–1860 may, in fact, have been a result of his growing interest in science, a subject in which Nancy could have given him little guidance. The school was noted for its teaching of mathematics, science, and drawing. Edison later stated that he first learned physical science from Richard Parker's A *School Compendium of Natural and Experimental Philosophy*, the principal science textbook used at the Union School.[18]

Whatever limited experience he had in Port Huron schools, Edison's mother was clearly his most important teacher. He later recalled, "My mother taught me how to read good books quickly and correctly, and as this opened up a great world in literature, I have always been very thankful for this early training."[19] The only specific information that we have about Edison's education is found in lists of books he was known to have read around the ages of twelve or thirteen. We can, however, speculate about the sorts of books that he might have read as a young boy. As a former schoolteacher, Nancy probably used standard primers, spellers, and readers in teaching her son to read and write. A religious woman who attended churches in both Milan and Port Huron, Nancy no doubt also taught her son with Bible readings, and Edison later remembered attending Sunday school at his mother's church in Port Huron, where he would have received additional Bible instruction.

Most attention has been focused on a select list of books that Thomas later recalled he and his mother read together. The two most commonly mentioned books are Edward Gibbon's *Decline and Fall of the Roman Empire* and David Hume's *History of England*. Neither of these difficult works would have been typical reading for a mother and her preadolescent son (they supposedly read these before Thomas was twelve), and, surprisingly, no one has thought to ask why Nancy chose these books. The most likely explanation is that these, as well as many other books they read together, were in Samuel Edison's library. Nancy's role in educating her son was the primary parental influence on his intellectual development, but Samuel clearly influenced his son's reading matter. Considered in this light, Samuel's political activities and his participation in the Canadian rebellion take on new significance for his son's intellectual development.

The books that Thomas recalled reading at home were by authors of the Enlightenment and were concerned with politics and religion. Besides Gibbon and Hume, he also recalled reading the works of Thomas Paine: "My father had a set of Tom Paine's books on the shelf at home. I must have opened the covers about the time I was 13. And I can still remember the flash of enlightenment which shone from his pages. It was a revelation, indeed, to encounter his views on political and religious matters, so different from the views of many people around us. Of course I did not understand him very well, but his sincerity and ardor made an impression upon me that nothing has ever served to lessen."[20] All three of these writers tended toward skepticism and anticlericalism and argued that natural law rather than authority or religious revelation was the primary source of true knowledge. Their works had been widely read and influential during the American Revolution and continued to have some popularity in the early republic and among radical reformers in Britain and Canada.

Paine's *Age of Reason* especially influenced both Samuel Edison and his son. Samuel was an advocate of religious free thought, which drew heavily on Paine's scientific deism and his critique of organized religion. Whether through discussions with his father or through his reading of Paine and other anticlerical works, Thomas, too, became imbued with freethinking and had little interest in his mother's more traditional religious beliefs. He would later write that "my mother forced me to attend [her church]—my father gave me Paine's Age of Reason."[21] As an adult he would become an admirer of Robert Ingersoll, the leading American freethinker of the late nineteenth century, of whom he wrote, "Some day when the veil of superstition is lifted Ingersoll will stand out as a great personality."[22] He also maintained a lifelong esteem for Paine, writing an introduction to his collected works in 1925. Edison wrote of Paine that he

suffered then, as now he suffers not so much because of what he wrote as from the misinterpretation of others. He has been called an atheist, but atheist he was not. Paine believed in a supreme intelligence, as representing the idea which other men often express by the name of deity.

His Bible was the open face of nature, the broad skies, the green hills. He disbelieved the ancient myths and miracles taught by established creeds. But the attacks on those creeds—or on persons devoted to them—have served to darken his memory.[23]

When Edison wrote those words in 1925 he could have been describing his own experience following an interview that appeared in the October 2, 1910, edition of the *New York Times Magazine* in which he denied the existence and immortality of the human soul. He explained his views by stating that "Nature is what we know. We do not know the gods of religions. And nature is not kind, or merciful, or loving. If God made me—the fabled God of the three qualities of which I spoke: mercy, kindness, love—He also made the fish I catch and eat. And where do His mercy, kindness, and love for that fish come in? No; nature made us—nature did it all—not the gods of the religions." These ideas struck many readers as atheistic, and ministers and others spoke out against him. Edison refused to be drawn into a public controversy, but defended himself privately in words that echoed his later defense of Paine: "You have misunderstood the whole article, because you jumped to the conclusion that it denies the existence of God. There is no such denial, what you call God I call Nature, the Supreme intelligence that rules matter. All the article states is that it is doubtful in my opinion if our intelligence or soul or whatever one may call it lives hereafter as an entity or disperses back again from whence it came . . . scattered amongst the cells of which we are made."[24]

As a freethinker Edison followed Paine and Ingersoll in expressing skepticism toward traditional religion and in urging that clerical authority and biblical myths be replaced by the truths of nature uncovered through scientific investigation. He argued that "Scientific men as a rule do not believe in the immortality of the soul because the more they investigate the works of nature the more firmly they reach that conclusion." At the same time for those who believed "the religion of the Bible they better not try to shake the belief as it is certainly more consoling. However if we all carry out the golden rule in this life we have little to fear from the hereafter no matter what our belief may be."[25] Edison's support for the Golden Rule followed from what a historian of American freethinking described as the belief that "Whatever truth Christianity did contain . . . had existed in the book of nature long before the coming of Christ. Therefore, the morals of Christianity were good . . . because of their harmony with nature."[26] Although attacked by religious believers for his freethinking ideas, Edison remained optimistic that the "old order of things are rapidly passing. The schoolhouse, the newspaper, and the advancement of scientific investigation, will in not many years make these beliefs seem ridiculous."[27] Nonetheless, his attachment to the Golden Rule and his own conventional moral values, as well as his adherence to the Protestant work ethic, suggest the continuing importance of his mother's moral teachings.

Just as his later religious views followed from ideas learned through his father, Edison's ideas regarding another subject that concerned him throughout his life were also influenced by Samuel. Toward the end of his life Edison wrote of his views on diet and health that "my family for three generations, have followed the teachings of Cornaro. His principles were taught me from childhood, and I have always followed them."[28] Although unknown today, Luigi Cornaro's *The Temperate Life* was reprinted in numerous British and American editions during the eighteenth and nineteenth centuries. First published in Italy in 1558, when Cornaro was ninety-four, it described how at the age of forty he rejuvenated himself by adopting an abstemious diet. After successfully regaining his health, he then set out to establish the natural laws of diet and health, which were the main subject of his treatise. Cornaro's basic rules concerning food and drink were to "take only the quantity which my stomach can easily digest and only the kinds that agree with it."[29] Edison recalled that his father and grandfather were so impressed "with the belief that the secret of long life lay in little eating that the idea was dinned into my head from my earliest boyhood. Morning, noon, and night I was told to leave the table while still hungry. I do not remember whether, in the beginning, it was hard to do this, but, in any event, I soon became accustomed to it."[30] Edison, in turn, sought to impress his own children with this idea and eventually convinced his second wife to adopt an abstemious diet.

As he aged Edison conducted irregular dietary experiments, following Cornaro's admonition "that any man may, by dint of experimenting, acquire perfect knowledge of his own constitution and of its most hidden qualities, and find out what food and drink, and what quantities of each, will agree with his stomach," and, like Cornaro, as he got older he reduced the quantity of food in his diet.[31] For many years Edison had "no special diet, I eat every kind of food, but in very small quantities, 4 to 6 oz to a meal." However, during the last decade of his life he developed a rather peculiar diet that usually consisted of a piece of toast, one or two glasses of milk, one tablespoon of cooked oats, one tablespoon of spinach, one sardine, and four Uneeda biscuits, although he varied the sardines "with a lamb chop and also I vary the vegetables."[32] In 1930 he shifted to a milk diet consisting of "about 7 glasses of milk per day divided into 7 meals—each glass 300 cubic centimeters—twice a day I eat ¹/₂ of a small orange nothing else. I do not lose weight."[33] With habits formed in boyhood, Edison continued to follow Cornaro's teachings throughout his life, striving always to maintain dietary habits that would keep his weight constant.

While the books in his father's library helped form Edison's ideas regarding religion and diet, perhaps the two most important books he read were Parker's *Natural Philosophy* and an English translation of a textbook authored by the German chemist Carl Fresenius. Richard Parker was a Boston high school principal who wrote a number of textbooks on subjects ranging from grammar to history to science. His *Natural Philosophy* was, as the full title indicated, a compendium that drew on standard scientific works of the day. Whether the young Edison read Parker as part of his course work at the Union School or on his own, he would have received basic instruction in what we would today call physics, which included, according to the title page, "mechanics, hydrostatics, hydraulics, pneumatics, acoustics, pyronomics, optics, electricity, galvanism, magnetism, electro-magnetism, magneto-electricity, and astronomy" as well as "a description of steam and locomotive engines, and of the electro-magnetic telegraph." The editions from the late 1850s, which Edison most likely read, contained an expanded discussion of telegraphy, including the Morse code, and its frontispiece illustrated the electric telegraph. He also would have learned the basics of electricity and something about batteries. Edison later recalled that when he was twelve years old, about the time he probably read Parker, he built a one-half-mile telegraph line between his house and that of his friend James Clancy.[34]

Whereas Parker had no special training or knowledge in the subject matter of his textbook, Carl Fresenius was a prominent German chemist whose textbooks were standards in the field of analytical chemistry. According to both an early magazine biography and his official biography, Edison obtained a copy of Fresenius's "Qualitative Analysis."[35] This was probably Fresenius's System of Instruction in Qualitative Chemical Analysis; but it is possible he had the less detailed Elementary Instruction in Chemical Analysis, which included both qualitative and quantitative analysis. Both of these books, as well as the System of Quantitative Analysis, were available in editions translated by the English chemist J. Lloyd Bullock.

Just what chemical experiments Thomas undertook is unknown, but Fresenius provided practice exercises and experiments in his books. These were concerned with methods of determining the chemicals found in a particular compound through precipitation and reactions with reagents (qualitative analysis) and in what proportions they were found based on weight measurements (quantitative analysis). Thomas's boyhood friend James Clancy remarked upon "what chances you and I used to take at your old home and how your good Mother used to talk to us and say we would yet blow our heads off."[36] And his former teacher P. L. Hubbard recalled how when Edison and "some other boys were trying some experiments in an old wooden telegraph office and in mixing some acids and other chemicals an explosion took place that wrecked a corner of the building and burned you and some of the other boys."[37]

Edison does seem to have had a large collection of chemicals. An archaeological study at the site of the Edison home turned up a wide variety of glass fragments, supporting evidence for his having an extensive collection of chemicals, although probably not the 200 accorded him in legend. Many of the fragments were from the crucibles, test tubes, beakers, flasks, dishes, funnels, and other equipment he would have needed to carry out Fresenius's experiments. Although it is not known what chemical apparatus Thomas had, Fresenius recommended such items as a spirit burner, blowpipe, mortar, metal spoons and pincers, and a filtration stand. Edison later said that he had apparatus made at the Pullman shops in Detroit while he was working as a newsboy on the Grand Trunk Railway. For a time he was allowed to carry out experiments in the baggage car of the train, until a bottle of phosphorus broke and set the car on fire. According to his official biography, Edison later "wondered how it was that he did not become an analytical chemist instead of concentrating on electricity, for which he had at first no great inclination."[38] Yet, when his career is seen in retrospect, what stands out is how often his researches involved chemistry, as retired chemist Byron Vanderbilt noted in 1971 when he published a study titled *Thomas Edison, Chemist.*

Books could "show the theory of things," but, as Edison noted in a 1911 *Century Magazine* interview, "doing the thing itself is what counts." In that interview he also claimed that at the age of twelve most boys were "interested in knowing how things are done."[39] This was certainly true of his own experience. The chemical laboratory and the telegraph line did not exhaust his youthful interest in science and technology. Ambrose Robinson remembered that he "used to love to get hold of a mechanical journal to study" and that after school the twelve-year-old Thomas would often make things in his workshop, often "knock[ing] it all to pieces and again mak[ing] it over until it suited [him]."[40] Among the things that he built were "water mills . . . cannon, and many other articles of experiment."[41] He also built a little steam engine railroad in one room of the family home.

Many Americans first experienced machinery on farms and in small village shops. Gristmills, sawmills, drills, clocks, and other machines were prevalent throughout the society. As a youth in Port Huron, Michigan, Edison learned about these machines—as had generations of artisans—through direct observation. The industries of Port Huron provided many opportunities for him to become familiar with the gears, cams, ratchets, escapements, bearings, and other elements of nineteenth-century mechanical technology. An 1860 description of the town noted that besides the many lumbermills and shipyards, Port Huron also contained "foundries and machine shops, with numerous mercantile and mechanical establishments."[42] The telegraph office was in a jewelry store where two watch repairers could be seen working on the intricate mechanisms of timepieces. Steam engines were also common, including, of course, the new railroad. Like many boys his age Edison "was dead set on being engineer of a locomotive." As a newsboy on the train he would sometimes "employ a substitute so that I might take the trip in the engine. Often I was permitted to handle the machinery, to shovel coal and rub up the brass and steel work." He would have been the envy of many a boy when at the age of thirteen he ran "a freight train all alone for sixty-two and a half miles."[43]

Experiences such as these led Edison's father to say that "Thomas Alva never had any boyhood days; his early amusements were steam engines and mechanical forces."[44] Yet in most ways his boyhood was quite normal, and as Anthony Rotundo points out in his recent study of nineteenth-century "boy culture" even such things as "steam engines and mechanical forces" made up part of the ordinary American boy's experience. The same technological drive that existed in the general culture affected boy culture. As Rotundo notes, "The building of toy ships that would actually float, the construction of snow forts, the performance of crude scientific experiments—these common boyhood activities taught youngsters the skills (and the habit) of mastery over nature in the service of human needs and knowledge."[45]

Edison engaged in other common forms of play as well. At the age of nine he spent "all my spare hours . . . organizing a secret service among my companions and digging in caves in which we met, suggested by my reading Sylvanus Cobb, Jr's. stories—particularly 'The Gunmaker of Moscow.' We dug a cave with a concealed trap door, and then from this dungeon, fitted up with a fireplace, table, chairs, papers, games and a stock of provender laid in from [his father's] garden."[46] Such clubs and gangs were common in nineteenth-century America, and rival groups were often divided by neighborhoods. Thomas's friends were probably the "north side boys" mentioned in a letter from his boyhood friend John Talbot.[47] Although there are no accounts of their fighting with the southsiders, Thomas was involved in at least one fight, which took place between the American boys of Port Huron and the Canadian boys of Sarnia during the visit of the Prince of Wales in 1860. Often boys would dare each other to undertake dangerous activities or to play pranks on adults, and Edison got into his share of scrapes through such activities. James Clancy recalled one incident "when we made a hole in the but[t] of a big pine tree near the Ice house, filled it with powder, drove a plug in then you told Mike Oates to put his cap over the plug and you put a match to it. Mikes cap went up to the top of the observatory and it blew the side out of the Ice house."[48] Edison himself told of a practical joke he played on the soldiers at Fort Gratiot. He and a friend imitated the sentries calling for the Corporal of the Guard and succeeded in rousing the corporal three nights in a row. However, the soldiers then set a trap that caught Edison's friend while he escaped by hiding in a potato barrel in the cellar of his house.[49]

Boy culture often existed in tension with the domestic culture of women, as mothers sought to "exert moral power" over their sons "by implanting an active conscience" through teaching, lecture, and discipline.[50] Mothers, rather than girlfriends, were the most significant female figures associated with boy culture, which often defined itself by opposition to maternal influence. Indeed, the beginning of romantic attachments often marked an important passage out of boyhood. Although it is known that during these years Edison had a girlfriend named Carrie Buchanan, this seems to have been more a childhood infatuation than a serious romance. It was Nancy Edison who clearly was the most important female influence in the life of her son. One of Edison's boyhood friends remembered "being in front of your house one day and seeing your mother standing at the door calling you to come into your lessons. We boys were just coming from the Pine Grove swimming place and I thought at the time it was pretty tough on you."[51] James Clancy also recalled how Edison's mother "used to look when she would come out on the big stoop of the house and call *Alva*."[52] Edison himself related how after pulling the prank on the Fort Gratiot sentries he "received a good switching on the legs from my father, the first and only one I ever received from him, although my mother kept a switch behind the old Seth Thomas clock that had the bark worn off. My mother's ideas and mine differed at times, especially when I got experimenting and mussed up things."[53]

Nancy may well have been overprotective of her son, particularly after the deaths of her other young children had left him as the only child in the household. Although her nurturing fostered the self-confidence that later helped him to find such great success, there is some evidence that Edison rebelled not only against her but also against female domestic culture in general. It is notable that from the time he went to work at the age of thirteen on the Grand Trunk Railway, he was largely on his own—leaving early in the morning and returning late at night. After leaving Port Huron at age seventeen, he made only brief visits back to his home.

As an adult Edison made little accommodation to the demands of domesticity. Whereas according to Rotundo most of his contemporaries "accepted willingly the confinement of clothing that had once seemed like shackles" and "wiped away the once-treasured grime of outdoor activity" from their faces and hands, Edison was most commonly described by reporters as unshaved, indifferent to dress (frequently in clothes dirtied from experiments), and needing "brushing and combing and grooming all over."[54] Edison always seemed to be more comfortable in the masculine culture of the telegraph operating room, the machine shop, the laboratory, and the mine than he did in the feminine confines of the family parlor. A desire to avoid domestic concerns may well have contributed to his famous work style with the long hours that frequently kept him away from home. During the 1890s, when his second wife might well have begun to assert greater demands on him to conform to her genteel middle-class expectations, he remained away from home for weeks in the New Jersey hills where he delighted in the simple mining life. "Talking with the boys all night, sleeping on floors, clambering in and out of the giant machinery, and surrounded by dirt and equipment on all sides," notes historian Andre Millard, "Edison was in his element."[55] It is not surprising that reporters characterized his second wife as treating him with maternal as well as spousal affection, and that the unkempt Edison could be described, as in a 1913 article, as "this big, smiling, white-haired, blue-eyed, sixty-six-year-old boy of hers."[56]

The most significant rite of passage out of boyhood was entry into the world of work. Like many youngsters, Edison's boyhood ended in his midteens when he left home to begin working full-time as a telegraph operator, but even before then he had accumulated several years of working experience. Thomas's work in his father's truck garden would not have been unusual—many boys whose fathers were not farmers maintained some kind of garden—and for the Edisons the truck garden was an important source of income. Thomas, however, tired of this work, as "hoeing corn in a hot sun is unattractive," and after the Grand Trunk Railway was extended from Toronto through Port Huron to Detroit (the line opened on November 21, 1859), by, he recalled, "a great amount of per-

Thomas Edison at age 14.

sistence I got permission from my mother to go on the local train as a newsboy."[57] Nancy was doubtless reluctant to allow her son to take a job that required him to leave home early in the morning and to stay out until late at night.

While working on the train Thomas soon demonstrated an entrepreneurial talent that he probably learned by observing his father's efforts to make ends meet through a variety of enterprises. He certainly developed entrepreneurial sensibilities similar to those later ascribed to Samuel Edison by a close friend: "a lively disposition always looking on the bright side of things" and "full of most sanguine speculation as to any project he takes in his head."[58] Thomas also exhibited his father's fondness for storytelling. Unlike his father, however, Thomas's career would be profoundly affected by a new economic institution. The telegraph and the railroad companies for whom he worked as a young man were the first great American corporations. Although Thomas retained the entrepreneurial values of his father, he would achieve his success by taking advantage of the new opportunities they afforded.

Six months after going to work for the Grand Trunk Railway, Thomas started two stands in Port Huron. One sold periodicals and the other fruits and vegetables. He employed two boys to tend these enterprises, giving them a share of the profits, but soon closed the periodical store because he could not trust the boy in charge. He continued to run the vegetable store for nearly a year and even got permission to have "two large baskets of vegetables from the Detroit market loaded in the mail car and sent to Port Huron" because they were better than the local produce. The railroad managers never asked Edison to pay freight for his produce and he later speculated that "I was so small and industrious and [had] the nerve to appropriate a U.S. mail car to do a free freight biz so monumental that it probably caused passivity." In addition to produce from the Detroit market, he bought butter and blackberries from farmers along the line, "buying wholesale and at a low price and permitt[ing] the wives of the engineers and trainmen to have the benefit of the rebate." When the railroad began running a daily immigrant train to transport Norwegians to Iowa and Minnesota, he also employed a boy to sell bread, tobacco, and candy.[59]

As news of the Civil War increased his newspaper sales Thomas decided to give up the vegetable store, and the Battle of Shiloh on April 6, 1862, proved this to be a good decision. As he later recalled:

> On the day of this battle when I arrived at Detroit, the bulletin boards were surrounded with dense crowds and it was announced that there were 60 thousand killed and wounded and the result was uncertain. I knew that if the same excitement was attained at the various small towns along the road and especially at Port Huron that the sale of papers would be great. I then conceived the idea of telegraphing the news ahead, went to the operator in the depot and by giving him Harper's Weekly and some other papers for three months, he agreed to telegraph to all the stations the matter on the bulletin board. I hurriedly copied it and he sent it, requesting the agents who displayed it on the blackboard, used for stating the arrival and departure of trains, I decided that instead of the usual 100 papers that I could sell 1000, but not having sufficient money to purchase that number, I determined in my desperation to see the Editor himself and get credit.

He explained to the editor of the *Detroit Free Press* what he had done about telegraphing the news, but indicated that he only had money for 300 papers. Taking a chance on the young entrepreneur, the editor gave him credit for the rest, and his faith was rewarded when Thomas's enterprise proved even more successful than he anticipated.

> The first station called Utica, was a small one where I generally sold two papers. I saw a crowd ahead on the platform, thought it some excursion, but the moment I landed there was a rush for me; then I realized that the telegraph was a great invention. I sold 35 papers; the next station, Mt. Clemens, now a watering place, but then a place of about 1000, I usually sold 6 to 8 papers. I decided that if I found a corresponding crowd there that the only thing to do to correct my judgement in not getting more papers was to raise the price from 5 cents to 10. The crowd was there and I raised the price; at the various towns there were corresponding crowds.

By the time he got to Port Huron he sold the few papers he had left at twenty-five cents each. Not only did he make "what to me was an immense sum of money," but he "started the next day to learn telegraphy and also printing."[60]

Edison's newspaper experiences provided valuable lessons that he later used in marketing himself and his inventions. The episode of the Battle of Shiloh taught him something of the power of the press. His father was also an avid newspaper reader, and Thomas later told of "forgetting" to bring the papers home so that his father would allow him to stay up receiving the news from his friend James Clancy over their telegraph line.[61] He learned more lessons while publishing his own newspapers.

His first paper was the *Weekly Herald*, which he published during the spring of 1862 with editorial assistance from conductor Alexander Stevenson. He printed the newspaper in a railway baggage car using discarded type and a galley proof press. It contained gossip, news, and advertisements of people and businesses in the towns along the rail line, including such items as the price of agricultural products, mail express and stage service information, and notices of births and military recruitments. He also published items about the Grand Trunk Railway and its employees, such as the account of a lost baggage swindle thwarted by a company detective. In another instance he endorsed a company engineer, recommending that he receive one of the company's premiums. The editorial tone he adopted also suggests how much his mother's moral teachings had become a part of his character. His strong work ethic is evident in an article headlined "The more to do the more to be done," which claimed that stations with only a single porter were kept in "first class order," whereas "at other stations where there is two Porters things are vise versa." He also called on Port Huron to enforce its "law requireing Saloons & Grog shops to close on Sunday . . . as they are a complete nuisance."[62] Although the paper was successful (Edison later claimed a circulation of 275 to 500 subscribers for his paper, which cost eight cents per month), he was forced to abandon it, apparently as a result of the mishap with his chemical laboratory that nearly burned the baggage car.

The accident with the chemicals may also have led to Edison's deafness. He recalled that the baggage master who put out the fire "got a bad burn and boxed my ears so severely that I got somewhat deaf thereafter."[63] But he also attributed it to another episode when a conductor helping him on to the train "took me by the ears and lifted me. I felt something snap inside my head, and my deafness started from that time and has ever since progressed."[64] Whether these episodes were coincidence or cause, Edison apparently first became aware of his hearing loss while working on the train. A doctor who treated him late in life thought that his deafness was a congenital degenerative disorder that could have been brought on early by a trauma. Throughout his life Edison would claim that his poor hearing was an advantage; that it reduced distractions by enabling him to concentrate. His private secretary during the last decades of his life believed that, although Edison "was wonderfully patient and philosophical about his affliction and seldom referred to it. . . . He also felt the loss of his hearing very much when he had visitors, and if they told funny stories among themselves and laughed hilariously, a wistful look came over his face, for he was very fond of humorous stories."[65]

Just as he continued to experiment with his chemicals in the cellar of the family house after having them removed from the train, so too Edison continued his publishing activities with the assistance of William Wright, an apprentice printer working at the *Port Huron Commercial*. Edison later called this paper *Paul Pry*, although Wright remembered it as the *Blowhard*. The paper was so filled with "hot stuff and so fixed with personalities," according to Wright, "that we knew it prudent to do the work on it quietly and at midnight" on Saturdays. He also recalled several incidents of outrage on the part of those who were the subject of the paper's stories, which caused Edison to "[run] the gauntlet of the well-deserved kicks and cuffings naturally incident to the circulation of such a sheet."[66] Edison's early experiences with the power of the press would be further reinforced by his work as telegraph operator.

Even before he went to work on the Grand Trunk, Edison had begun to learn telegraphy using the line he had built between his house and James Clancy's. It was while working on the railroad, however, that he gained new understanding of the telegraph's importance, not only for newspapers but also for its role in controlling traffic on the railroad line. A number of the telegraph operators along the line later recalled his spending time in their offices practicing telegraphy. John Thomas thought he was the first to teach Edison the rudiments of telegraphy, remembering that they used to practice at his office in the evenings. The station agent at New Baltimore, John Raper, reminisced about "the many times [Edison] came into my office to practice on my Telegraph Key and look at my specimens of Bugs Flies &c." Fred Betts, who was operator at the depot in Detroit, recalled how "Al Edison used to walk into our office and practice Telegraphy." Thus, when Edison rescued Mt. Clemens operator James MacKenzie's son from an oncoming railway car, which led to an offer of formal lessons, he probably already had some skill as an operator, a skill that MacKenzie then refined. Edison later stated that while studying with MacKenzie during the summer of 1862 he worked "about 18 hours a day" and "soon became quite proficient."[67] His ability to operate a telegraph key and sounder appears not to have been affected by the hearing difficulties he had begun to experience. This may even have proved of some benefit during his years as a telegrapher by allowing him to concentrate on the click of the telegraph sounder without distraction from other noises.

With his improved operating skills Edison obtained his first job as an operator in Port Huron. For a time he apparently operated his own telegraph line between Fort Gratiot and the train station, "but the business was small and the operator at Port Huron knowing my proficiency and who wanted to go into the US M[ilitary] Telegraph, where the pay was high, succeeded in convincing his brother-in-law (Mr. [Micah] Walker) that I could fill the position all right." The telegraph office was in Walker's jewelry and stationery store, and there Edison also had access to books and journals, as well as the tools and gear mechanisms used in clock repair. Walker recalled that the "telegraphing did not take over $\frac{1}{3}$ of Edison's time. He was no good to wait on customers, so had plenty of time to experiment and tinker. And in doing so, was a great annoyance to my workmen." Thomas often spent the night in the shop to practice taking press reports because "the goal of the rural telegraph operator was to be able to take the press."[68] After a time Edison applied for a job as operator with the Grand Trunk Railway and received a position as night operator at Stratford Junction, Ontario. This marked the beginning of his years as an itinerant telegrapher and a new period in his education as an inventor.

CHAPTER 2

Itinerant Telegrapher

Thomas Edison's education continued during his years as a telegraph operator as he cultivated his operating skills and moved into the elite ranks of well-paid press telegraphers. He also advanced his knowledge of telegraph technology and electrical science through a program of self-study that included both reading and practical experiment. Edison was not alone in pursuing such studies. They were an important aspect of the culture of ambitious telegraph operators.[1] Edison's experiences as a telegrapher also provided another sort of practical education as the naive teenager was introduced into the ways of the wider world. As he grew to manhood, Edison left behind his boyhood name, Alva, and became known as Tom.

During the years 1863 to 1868, Edison was one of many young men who joined the ranks of itinerant or "tramp" telegraphers who drifted from city to city. Tramping was a way of industrial life in the nineteenth century for many American workers, who found themselves on the move because of economic necessity. Responding to the boom and bust cycle of the economy or to seasonal employment fluctuations, the itinerant worker was drawn by the promise of higher wages and better job opportunities. For skilled craft workers itinerancy was a custom derived from European traditions in which journeymen traveled to seek employment and to complete the final stage of their training. In his study *The American Telegrapher*, Edward Gabler describes how many young operators "honed the skills of hand and ear, and then followed the way wires and trunk lines to the promise of the big city."[2] Although tramping usually grew out of economic necessity, in some crafts it was also used by those who wanted to see a bit of the world before settling down. Wanderlust rather than economic factors seems to have been the primary motive for the itinerant telegrapher of Edison's day. This was especially true during and immediately after the Civil War because of the high demand for skilled operators on commercial lines to replace those who had gone into the United States Military Telegraph. The close connection between telegraph and rail lines also encouraged operator mobility. One of Edison's fellow operators recalled that "The boys in those days had extraordinary facilities for travel. As a usual thing it was only necessary for them to board a train and tell the conductor they were operators. Then they would go as far as they liked. The number of operators was small, and they were in demand everywhere."[3]

Edison's itinerant career was typical of many of his contemporaries. Like most operators, Edison began by serving an apprenticeship with James MacKenzie, a local operator. He then developed his skills through a combination of practice instruments and handbooks for self-instruction. He obtained his first job working part-time at the telegraph table in Walker's jewelry store and then joined the large ranks of railway telegraphers when he became a night operator at Stratford Junction, a small station on the Grand Trunk Railway in Ontario, Canada. As his operating skills improved, Edison was able to move on to offices in larger cities in the United States. Little interested in settling down, the teenage Edison took advantage of the demand for skilled operators to see something of the world.

By becoming a telegraph operator Edison joined an elite fraternity of technical workers with a unique subculture that had its own lore, language, jokes, and shared attitudes toward the uninitiated. Operator culture also had a skill-based hierarchy. At the beginning of his career the inexperienced Edison was what telegraphers called a "plug," that is, a second-class or "inferior" operator. Such operators—particularly those who worked in small rural offices—had second-class status within the fraternity as well. Edison recalled that "Operators were designated as 1st class oprs & plug oprs, the latter being inefficient & there was very little association between the two classes."[4] The goal of ambitious telegraphers such as Thomas Edison was to enter the ranks of well-paid first-class operators, which included the fastest senders and receivers, the elite of whom were the press-wire operators.

Made up largely of young men, operator culture retained many of the characteristics of boy culture. As Anthony Rotundo has argued, young men formed a "male youth culture," beginning in the teen years and lasting into the twenties or even early thirties, which "combined elements of the boys' world they had left behind with aspects of the men's lives they had not yet attained."[5] Competition was an important element of youth culture, as it had been in boy culture, and among telegraphers this often manifested itself through the prestige placed on operating skill and speed. Operators engaged in both formal contests and private battles to determine who was the fastest. Although company rules required the sending operator to transmit at a speed suited to the skill of the receiver, operators often tried to force each other to "break." Inexperienced operators in particular, especially if they were newly arrived in a city, would find themselves the object of an initiation rite in which a particularly fast sender would be placed at the other end of the line to overwhelm the plug operator.

When Edison arrived in Boston in 1868, looking very much the small-town hick with his clothes wrinkled from a long journey, the Boston operators "put up a job to roast me, as they say." He was requested to take press copy from New York, and one of the fast senders from that city "started at a rapid gate," but after a few minutes "I noticed he was getting up to his limit, turning my head I found nearly every operator in the office watching me from behind." By then, Edison was a very skilled receiver who was able "to do 4 or 5 words per minute more than [the New York operator] could send." However, the New York operator began to abbreviate, while Edison was required to write out his text for the newspapers. Knowing he would soon have to break, Edison "opened the key and [signaled] 'You seem to be tired, suppose you send a little while with your other foot.' This saved me. . . . After this, I was all right with the other operators."[6]

Such pranks and practical jokes were as common to youth culture as they had been to boy culture and operator lore is full of such antics, as are stories of Edison's operating days. The son of his landlady in Louisville, for example, re-membered how Edison suffered at the hands of his fellow operators, recalling several "incidents that occurred during your stay at our home. 'The boys' Berry, Swindel and Steveson, and their pranks and capers how you went to bed with your boots on under the pretense of being asleep, and the way they pulled you out, how mother hid you in her wardrobe in order to evade *that gang*," and how when Edison moved to another boarding house "the boys moved your trunk back . . . the gall of that jolly lot was amusing."[7] Edison participated in such pranks himself. In one instance he obtained "a second hand Rhumkorff induction Coil which although it would only give a small spark would twist the arms & clinch the hands of a man so he couldnt let go of the electrodes." With a friend he connected it to the wash tank at the railroad roundhouse and then "bored a hole in the roof so we could see the men as they came in. . . . We en-joyed the sport immensely."[8]

Lacking other forms of social foundation young men developed friendships with each other that provided an important source of support. Telegraph oper-ators developed friendships not only with those at neighboring tables but also with operators along the line whom they knew by their "touch" on the tele-graph key, and they frequently "talked" to each other over the line during slack periods. Ed Gilliland, one of Edison's friends from Cincinnati, remembered how after Edison went to work in Boston, he "chatted with him occasionally over the wire, nearly always concerning some new invention he had brought out." Edison recalled that it was the practice among his fellow press operators whenever "a lull occurred to start in & send jokes or stories the day men had collected & these were copied & pasted up on the bulletin board . . . any joke originating anywhere in that area was known the next day all over."[9] Edison en-joyed telling stories and jokes throughout his life. He especially liked to collect jokes, and when he became friends with Henry Ford the two of them enjoyed trading jokes.

Operator friendships sometimes played an important role in gaining employment, and this was true for Edison as well. For example, one of Edison's friends "teleg[rap]h[e]d me that he could get me a job at Memphis Tenn. [and] as I wanted to see the country I accepted it." This may be the operator who remembered that he had wired one of the company's officials that "Edison was alright. If he had an opening for him to put him to work."[10] Milton Adams, an operator Edison had first met in Cincinnati in 1865, helped him to obtain the job in Boston in 1868.

Operators also kept in contact with each other through the pages of the *Telegrapher*, a journal begun by the National Telegraph Union (NTU) in 1864. The NTU was more a fraternal organization than a union, and self-improvement and self-help were its primary messages for telegraphers, although it did oppose Western Union's arbitrary employment and salary practices. Not surprisingly, the common indulgences of male youth culture—excesses of drink, tobacco, gambling, foul language, and sex—were concerns of those seeking reform from within the ranks of telegraphers as well as of corporate managers. To advance the professional status of operators they encouraged their fellows to practice self-control. Edison appears not to have indulged in such excesses, except in developing a taste for chewing tobacco and cigars. Although Edison did visit some of the gambling houses he found prevalent in postwar Memphis, he spoke disapprovingly of them and of the lax state of affairs he encountered in the city.

Edison's reminiscences are filled with tales of drunken operators, but he imbibed only occasionally and moderately, and then usually beer. In Louisville, the other operators even entrusted him with their money when they had their weekly picnic. This was "a matter of precaution as some were not able to gauge exactly their capacity for Liquor & as I did not drink I was used as a sort of Alcoholometer & refused to advance money when the limit was reached." He gave up this responsibility after being knocked unconscious by one drunken operator to whom he refused to advance money. Edison's reminiscences contain other accounts of drunken sprees and violence on the part of his fellow operators. This was seen as a particularly serious problem in the profession, and the president of the NTU sought to exclude from union ranks any operator "addicted to drunkenness, even should he be the finest description of an operator."[11]

Sexual activity was not discussed openly, but "gay, reckless, and fast young men" among the operating ranks were often criticized in the *Telegrapher*. Nothing is known of Edison's relations with women during this period, although his account of explaining telegraphy at a girl's school in Boston suggests that he was rather awkward around them. Edison's own reminiscences describe a predominantly male world. Women operators were rare until after the Civil War, when romances among operators began to become part of craft lore.

It was not until the 1870s that the increasing presence of women, particularly in large city offices, began to influence operator culture in more genteel directions than Edison had experienced during his career.[12]

His fellow operators usually described Edison as studious, spending his free money on books, particularly those concerned with electrical science and technology. Such study was advocated by the editors of the *Telegrapher*. In fact, one of the reasons the NTU had started the journal was to provide a place for operators to turn for such knowledge. Editors Franklin Pope and James Ashley, in particular, emphasized the importance of technical and scientific knowledge as a way to personal advancement for operators who aspired to more responsible positions as industry managers or engineers. They encouraged operators to turn such knowledge to improvements in the "art of telegraphy," noting that inventions demonstrated both technical expertise and the personal initiative necessary for such management positions as chief operator, office manager, or superintendent. Accounts of telegraph manufacturers in the journal's pages also suggested that becoming the owner of a shop offered another route of advancement for technically knowledgeable telegraphers.[13]

Edison was imbued with this ideology of self-improvement and technical self-education and was among those who contributed technical articles to the *Telegrapher*. As a boy working on the Grand Trunk Railway he had supplemented his self-study of chemistry and telegraphy with frequent visits to the library of the Detroit Young Men's Association because "money was scarce and so were scientific books." As a telegrapher he continued to frequent "the Libraries in all Cities that I worked," reading "mostly technical books."[14]

Although declining traffic and the consolidation of most important lines into Western Union following the Civil War caused opportunities and pay to decline, Edison and his generation of operators found telegraphy to be a rewarding career. It was still a young industry in which the diligent, hard-working, and intelligent operator could advance into management. Edison was typical of the ambitious operator who followed the ideology of self-improvement to move through the ranks from plug to the elite of the press operating corps. Press operators such as Edison were in a particularly good position to gain insights into other fields, especially journalism and politics, as well as to acquire knowledge of business practice, which they could use to establish successful careers outside of telegraphy. Early in his career as an inventor Edison demonstrated a sophisticated understanding of business practices learned in part from his work as an operator. Even more important, he was able to draw on his knowledge of the press, gained from his experiences as a train boy and a telegrapher, to promote himself and his inventions. But it was his interest in and aptitude for the technical side of telegraphy that led him to choose invention as the most promising route for his personal advancement.

Edison's performance in his first major telegraph job demonstrated both his strengths and weaknesses as an operator and set a pattern for his subsequent career. He discovered that the "night job just suited me as I could have the whole day to myself." This allowed him time to read and experiment, but it also meant that he did not always get sufficient sleep. Although Edison appears to have needed only four or five hours of sleep per day through most of his life, he did find it necessary to catnap to refresh himself, noting that "I had the faculty of sleeping in a chair any time for a few minutes at a time." At Stratford Junction he "taught the night yardman my call, so I would get $^1/_2$ hour sleep now and then between trains and in case the station was called, the watchman would awaken me." One of the earliest Edison biographical sketches also described an ingenious device that he supposedly constructed at Stratford for the purpose of automatically sending in his watchman's call of "six" every half hour, thus allowing him to sleep. This story was repeated in the official Dyer and Martin biography with the addition that "detection and a reprimand came in due course, but were not taken seriously."[15] Whether true or not, this story illustrates both the technical ingenuity Edison revealed during his service as a telegrapher and the lack of responsibility that on occasion led to his dismissal from a job. These traits had already been apparent during the months he worked in Walker's jewelry store, where he sometimes neglected his duties for experiments.

Edison's dismissal from his post at Stratford Junction was apparently not caused by his sleeping habits. "One night I got an order to hold a freight train and I replied that I would. I rushed out to find the signalman, but before I could find him and get the signal set, the train run past. I ran to the Telegraph Office and reported I couldn't hold her, she had run past. The reply was 'Hell.' The despatcher on the strength of my message that I would hold the train, had permitted another to leave the last station in the opposite direction There was a lower station near the Junction where the day operator slept. I started for it on foot. The night was dark and I fell in a culvert and was knocked senseless." Fortunately the trains saw each other on a straight piece of track and no accident occurred. However, the superintendent ordered Edison and the station agent to his office in Toronto:

> We appeared before the General Superintendent, W. I. Spicer who started in hauling Mr. Carter over the coals for permitting such a young boy to hold such a responsible position. Then he took me in hand and stated that I could be sent to Kingston States Prison, etc. Just at this point, three English swells came into the office. There was a great shaking of hands and joy all around; feeling that this was a good time to be neglected I silently made for the door; down the stairs to the lower freight station, got into the caboose going on the next freight, the conductor who I knew, and kept secluded until I landed a boy free of fear in the U.S. of America.[16]

How long Edison remained at home in Port Huron after this episode is unknown. He later told of an incident, never corroborated, that occurred during the winter of 1863–1864 when an ice floe damaged the telegraph cable under the river between Port Huron and Sarnia, leading him to suggest using locomotive steam whistles to transmit Morse code between the two towns. At some point Edison landed a job as a telegrapher with the Lake Shore & Michigan

Southern Railroad, working in the office of the company's division superintendent at Adrian, Michigan. The Adrian job, too, was a "night job which most
oprs disliked but which I preferred as it gave me more leisure to Experiment,"
and he "obtained from the station agent a small room [and] established a little
shop of my own" in which to conduct experiments.[17]

Edison soon had another run-in with the railway authorities that resulted
in his dismissal, and his own account again largely absolves him of any blame.
Instructed by his division superintendent to break into the busy telegraph line
to send an important message, Edison spent several minutes struggling with
another operator who turned out to be the telegraph superintendent of the
entire railroad. As Edison recalled, he became "livid with rage when he arrived
& discharged me on the spot. I told him the Genl Supt told me to break in &
send the dispatch he then turned to the Supt who had witnessed this burst of
anger & said Mr H did you tell this young man to break in & send your dispatch he repudiated the whole thing— Their families were socially close & I
was sacrificed My faith in human nature got a slight jar—"[18]

Edison next obtained a position as a day operator in Fort Wayne for the
Pittsburgh, Fort Wayne & Chicago Railroad. Finding he did not enjoy this job,
in part because he preferred night work, he soon moved to Indianapolis, where
he was working in the Western Union office at the Union Depot by the fall of
1864. Indianapolis was a growing rail center as well as the capital of Indiana
and became known as "Railroad City" when the Union Railway Company
brought several rail lines together at the Union Depot. The depot was described by the local newspaper as "a harbor for pickpockets, bounty jumpers,
thieves, &c . . . the women and children who infest the depot at all hours of the
day and night peddling apples, pies, &c . . . have become a first-class nuisance."[19] The telegraph office there was an important and busy one with extensive commercial traffic. Edison worked days on a way wire, one of the less important lines linking small town stations to the main station, but, as he later
recalled, "I was ambitious to be able to take press report." Boarding at the
nearby Macy House, only four blocks from the depot, he would come into the
office every night to practice taking press copy at a table next to the regular
press operator before heading home at one o'clock.[20]

Finding that the press report "came faster than I could write it down legibly," he devised what might be considered his first true invention, one that he
reworked many years later into a patent. At the time Edison became a telegrapher, operators usually received messages by listening to the clicking of a device known as a sounder—short intervals between the clicks for the dots and
long intervals for the dashes of Morse code—and then writing the message out
in longhand as they listened. Receiving by sounders was considered not only
faster but more accurate than the older method of indenting dots and dashes
onto paper tape with a Morse register, which recorded the dots and dashes on
a strip of paper that then needed to be translated from code before delivery to
customers. Nonetheless, sounders required operators to learn to write quickly

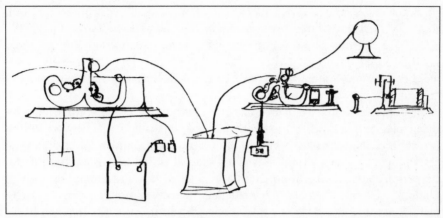

Edison's first invention was a telegraph practice instrument that used a pair of standard Morse registers to record a message at regular speed and then play it back at a slower speed.

and legibly. Although sounders had generally replaced the old Morse registers by the time Edison became an operator, many offices still had them around as surplus equipment. Obtaining a pair of registers from office manager John Wallick, Edison arranged one of them to record the incoming message at the regular speed of forty words per minute and then used the indented tape produced to operate the second register by actuating "a delicate double lever" that opened and closed a local sounder circuit "at the rate of 25 or 30 words per minute according to the speed of the clockwork, which could be varied at pleasure." A notebook used by Edison in 1867 contains his drawing of this design.[21]

Edison used this device not only as a practice instrument, but also to take press messages with fellow operator Ed Parmalee. According to Edison, they got "permission from the press man to put this in circuit & together we took press for several nights my companion keeping the apparatus in adjustment, & I copying. The reg[ular] Press opr would go to the theatre or take a sleep—only finishing the report after 1 am." Because he could take more care with his press copy, Edison's reports were neater and contained fewer errors than the regular operator's, leading the newspapers to complain about the quality of the latter's reports. This led to an investigation by the office manager, who put an end to Edison's press-wire career in Indianapolis.[22]

His fellow operators also derided Edison's budding ambitions as an inventor. George Parmalee recalled the "fun we made of your attempts to be something better than an operator." When George's brother Ed, also an operator, helped Edison to experiment with using his Morse-register practice instrument as a repeater for signals transmitted over long distances, another operator, Dick Duncan, tried to discourage Edison by telling him it would not work. Although the repeater design worked on a local wire, Duncan had so discouraged Edison that he "threw the whole business on to the sidewalk & started off up the street." Ed Parmalee, however, continued to encourage Edison and "gathered up the 'bones' & brought them up to the office." They then "gave them another trial one Sunday between S[t.] Louis & Pittsburg and they proved a success."[23]

Edison seems to have been constantly short of money while working in Indianapolis. At that time he apparently had only one suit, which he wore until it was so threadbare he had to buy another. Edison's reminiscences and those of several operators with whom he worked often describe him as caring little for his personal appearance, although by 1867 he had "a Valise containing a Lot of clothing." George Parmalee recalled that "there was nothing very attractive about you when we sat side by side as operators in Indianapolis Ind. you hadnt 50 cts then." Edison's lack of finances received the sympathy of the manager of the depot restaurant who claimed that he provided the young operator free meals. Unhappy in Indianapolis, Edison moved to Cincinnati in the late winter of 1865.[24]

Cincinnati proved to be a friendlier environment for Edison. Not only was the river city a more pleasant and cultured place, but Edison also made several friends among the operators there, including some with whom he continued to be close for many years. The "Queen City of the West" was an important port on the northern bank of the Ohio River about midway between Pittsburgh and the Mississippi River. Also known as "Porkopolis" for its extensive hog slaughtering and packing industry, which supported a large number of associated industries in leather goods, oils, candles, and soaps, Cincinnati was the major manufacturing city of the Midwest. Its manufacturing sector was quite diversified and included a large machinery industry. While Edison was there he also would have seen workers constructing John Roebling's great suspension bridge over the Ohio River to Covington, Kentucky. Culturally diversified, Cincinnati contained a large foreign-born population; most notable were its German-speaking residents, who constituted about one-fourth of the total population and congregated in a part of the city along the Miami Canal known as "Over-the-Rhine." The musicians appearing in the German beerhalls were one of many cultural attractions in Cincinnati, which had several theaters, museums, and libraries as well.

Among Edison's friends in Cincinnati were fellow operator Ezra (Ed) Gilliland, whom he had first met in Adrian, and Nat Hyams, a comedian (and later manager) at Wood's Theater, which featured burlesques. They shared a room together at the Bevis House, and Hyams remembered that the actor Harry Howard was also a roommate. Edison and Gilliland used to copy plays for the theater as a way of practicing their telegraph skills and to make some extra money, with Gilliland sending and Edison receiving. Among these plays was *The Dumb Man of Manchester*, which they copied for Hyams, who appeared in the play in June 1865. Edison was quite interested in the theater, per-

haps even acting as an extra; fellow operator "Jot" Spencer later expressed regret at "the loss suffered by dramatic arts when [Edison] turned [his] back on
tragedy."[25] Another friend and fellow operator, Milt Adams, recalled that "aside
from an occasional visit to the Loewen Garden 'over the Rhine,' with a glass of
beer and a few pretzels, consumed while listening to the excellent music of a
German band, the theatre was the sum and substance of [our] innocent dissi-
pation." They were especially fond of tragedy, and when "Forrest and John Mc-
Cullough were playing at the National Theater, and when our capital was sufficient we would go to see those eminent tragedians alternate in Othello and
Iago. Edison always enjoyed Othello greatly."[26]

Shakespeare was very popular in American theater, and Edison probably
saw one of the Cincinnati performances of *Richard III* as well. The *Operator*
later stated that the title character of this play was "said to have been his favorite character, and whenever his duties in the office permitted, he would arise
from his instrument, hump his back, bow his legs and proceed with 'Now is the
winter of our discontent,' to the great amusement of his fellow-operators."[27]
This opening line would later appear in his laboratory notebooks. Edison considered Shakespeare to be an important source of inspiration for his own creativity, later saying of the bard, "ah Shakespeare! That's where you get the ideas!
My, but that man did have ideas! He would have been an inventor, a wonderful inventor, if he had turned his mind to it. He seemed to see the inside of
everything. Perfectly wonderful how many things he could think about. His
originality in the way of expressing things has never been approached."[28]

In Cincinnati Edison worked days on a way wire to Portsmouth, Ohio, but
he "kept up the practice of coming around nights to copy press & would willingly act as a substitute for any opr who wanted to get off for a few hours The
few hours in most cases meant all night, however I didn't care, requiring little
sleep but I was bound to become proficient in the very shortest time."[29] Fellow
operator William Stanton recalled that Edison used to catch three or four
hours' sleep in the wee hours of the morning. He also stated that Edison did no
experimenting while in Cincinnati, but instead spent his time improving his
skills as a receiver.[30]

The formation of the Cincinnati branch of the National Telegraphic Union
gave Edison an opportunity to demonstrate to management his increasing skill
as a press operator. In June 1865 some of the Cincinnati operators applied to
form a local district and on Sunday, September 17, Edison was among those
who met to formally organize it. At the September meeting a number of the operators got quite drunk in celebration, and most of the night corps failed to
show up for work, including the regular press operator. Edison decided to take
the press report, believing that this would be better than nothing and "that I
couldnt see how I would be discharged for the attempt & to prevent delaying
the report by interrupting for repetitions I determined I would get what I could
& not interrupt." He took press copy until three in the morning, writing an illegible word when he had trouble receiving and "trusting to the printers to

sense it"; they apparently were able to read the frequently illegible hand of George Bloss, editor of the *Cincinnati Daily Enquirer.* Upon reading the "Sunday Night Dispatches" in the newspaper next morning Edison was delighted to discover that "the press report read perfectly." While Edison was working on his regular wire, chief operator J. F. Stevens examined the previous night's press. Coming over to Edison, he "said young man I want you to work the Louisville wire nights your salary will be 125."[31]

While Edison had achieved his ambition of becoming a first-class operator, he clearly retained a streak of wanderlust and soon decided to tramp south. Although Edison claimed in his reminiscences that he headed directly for Memphis, other evidence suggests that he may have spent the last three months of 1865 in Nashville. John Lonergan, who began working in the Nashville office in October, claimed that Edison was there when he arrived and that when Edison left in January 1866 he was asked by the superintendent of the Southwestern Telegraph Company if he would recommend Edison for a job in Memphis. The only clear evidence for when Edison was in Memphis is found in the flyleaves of books that he purchased there in March.[32]

Whenever it was that Edison arrived in Memphis, he found himself in a town that was in the midst of chaos as it moved from military to civilian control following the Civil War. Economic duress, political conflict, and racial tension were rampant in the city, as were lawlessness, violence, and vice. To Edison gambling establishments seemed especially common. He often got a midnight meal at a "gorgeously furnished Faro bank" and found that "there were over twenty keno rooms running," the largest of which was a Baptist church with the keno "wheel being in the pulpit & the gamblers in the pews." On the southern edge of the city near Fort Pickering, which was the base for several black regiments, a large numbers of freed slaves established a shantytown and competed with the primarily Irish lower-class immigrants for jobs on the wharfs and in the brickyards at the fort. This resulted in racial animosity and violent confrontations between the two groups that was further exacerbated by conflicts between the city's largely foreign-born and ill-trained police force and the black soldiers who patrolled the city. Political and racial tensions were also inflamed by the Memphis newspapers and politicians. To Edison everything seemed "wide open [and] demoralization reigned supreme. there was no head to anything." He thought "the whole town was only 13 miles from Hell."[33]

The telegraph situation in the city was also confused as control shifted from the Military Telegraph to the Southwestern Telegraph Company. Several operators were among the many men, including large numbers of soldiers, who found themselves stranded in Memphis because of the muddled postwar situation, and this caused rents to be quite high. Edison was fortunate to secure lodgings above the Delta Restaurant next door to the telegraph office, which was located in the same building as the *Memphis Bulletin,* one of the newspapers for which he took press copy on the New York wire. Amid all the chaos he also managed to continue his program of self-study, even taking up languages when he acquired a Latin grammar and a Spanish dictionary. He continued to experiment as well. George "Fattie" Stewart, who worked with Edison in Memphis and later in Boston, recalled that Edison "got into his head the idea of sending duplex dispatches [transmitting two messages simultaneously in opposite directions over a single wire] and all his spare time was devoted to experiments in the office."[34]

Edison later claimed that among his experiments in Memphis he devised a repeater that allowed New York and New Orleans to communicate directly for the first time since before the war and that an account of this transmission appeared in a local newspaper. However, an account of the first direct communication between these cities from the pages of the November 25, 1865, *Memphis Bulletin* that was reprinted in the *Telegrapher* shortly thereafter does not mention Edison or his repeater. If his account is to be believed, this also led to his dismissal because the chief operator, a protege of the Southwestern Telegraph Company's superintendent Tom Johnson, had been attempting to establish communications between the two cities and resented Edison's accomplishment. However, it is unlikely that Edison was dismissed because of this episode as he was still in Memphis at the end of March 1866. It may be that he confused his later experiments with the November transmission or exaggerated his own role. A more plausible reason for his leaving Memphis is suggested by Edison's statement that the unpleasant conditions then reigning in the city caused him to be "rather pleased than otherwise" when he was discharged. It is most likely that growing racial tensions in the city, which resulted in a race riot on May 1, were the actual cause of his leaving.[35]

Edison remembered arriving in Louisville "on a bitterly cold day, with ice in the gutters."[36] This was probably April 8 or 9, 1866, when heavy frosts were reported following the heaviest snow of the season on April 7. Edison was attracted to Louisville because the city was experiencing a shortage of telegraph operators, but he found the office there to be in a dilapidated condition and managed in an undisciplined fashion. Drunkenness was common, and on one occasion Edison claimed that a drunken operator nearly wrecked the office, which required him to use his knowledge of the switchboard wiring to rig it up so he could continue taking press copy from New York. Only after the office was moved to more sumptuous quarters in July 1867 did discipline improve.

Edison may not have found the telegraph office much of an improvement over the one in Memphis, but Louisville itself was a more prosperous city. An important commercial center on the Ohio River, Louisville boasted theaters and other entertainments, including several German beerhalls, that would have attracted Edison. He also might have attended lectures on subjects of special interest such as one on phonography (a form of shorthand for which he subsequently purchased a manual) at Myers' Commercial College or another on physics and chemistry at the English and German Academy.[37]

Although Edison worked in Louisville for nearly a year and a half, he briefly left the city in one last episode of wanderlust that became a turning point in his life. On August 1, 1866, Edison and two of his fellow telegraphers left for New Orleans via Nashville intending to take a steamer for Brazil. Interested in seeing more of the world, they were attracted by an advertisement for telegraph operators to work on the Brazilian telegraph. Edison may have been thinking about going to South America for some time. A fellow operator later remembered him "paying some attention to the spanish language with a view of going to Mexico or So. America," and in a letter to his family from Louisville, Edison noted that he was "able to Speak Spanish & Read & write it as fast as any Spaniard I can also Read French too but Cant Speak it."[38] (French and Portuguese were the official languages of Brazil.) Edison and his companions intended to take a steamer that had been chartered to take a larger number of former Confederates who were emigrating to Brazil, but the New Orleans race riot that had occurred on July 30 disrupted their plans. When they arrived, the city was in great disorder and they had to make alternative arrangements. Edison, however, changed his mind and decided to return to Louisville. According to Edison, the reason for his change of mind was the advice of an old man sitting in the steamship office, who, upon hearing his reason for going to Brazil, replied "that he had sailed the sea for 50 years & had been in every port in every country that there was no country like the US that if there was anything in a man the US was the place to bring it out & that any man that left this country to better his condition was an ignorent damned fool. I had been thinking this way myself for the last few days & the speech of the old man I considered good advice So I told my companions that I was going home."[39] This was, in fact, excellent advice for a lower-middle-class white man in midcentury America, for at the time no other country provided better opportunities for someone in Edison's position.

The treatment of a Union soldier on the streets of New Orleans rather than race riots or other issues related to the abolition of slavery produced the most profound impact on Edison's political beliefs as a consequence of the Civil War. In later reminiscences he recalled seeing

a poor devil in a blue uniform grinding an organ. He was blind in one eye. He had a big scar above the other eye. One of his legs was cut off below the knee. His other leg was severed above the knee. His left arm was cut off below the elbow. His right hand was mutilated so that only the little finger remained. With that finger he turned the organ handle and brought forth doleful tunes. A big brute of a Southerner came along and stopped in front of the organ, looking the cripple soldier all over. Then he drew a ten dollar bill out of his pocket and tossed it on the organ. As he started away the old soldier called after him to know if he had not made a mistake, saying that no man had ever given him a bill before. The Southerner turned about with a fierce look and responded that he was willing to give ten dollars any time to see a Yankee sliced up like the organ grinder, because that was the way he would like to see every blankety blanked Yankee carved up. Well, that incident made a Republican of me.[40]

Edison as a young telegraph operator. From the Collections of Henry Ford Museum & Greenfield Village (Neg. B37330).

Edison's father was a lifelong Democrat, and it is possible that this episode forced Edison to reconsider his own political allegiances. But his later support for Republican politicians had more to do with the party's role in promoting policies favorable to industrial capitalism, particularly a protective tariff.

During his stay in Louisville, Edison continued to improve his ability to receive press copy, especially as he was not a good sender. While there he developed a distinctive handwriting style that allowed him to write very small and rapidly and that two years later earned an article in the *Telegrapher*, which called Edison "about the *finest* writer we know of." The article described a 5-x-8 sheet of his press copy on which there were 647 words, each letter separate from the other, "which is one of the peculiarities of Mr. Edison's chirography, and the whole plain as print."[41] Edison's description of how he came to develop this style is indicative of both his increasing skill as a press operator and his growing technical sophistication. The wire he worked did not allow him to break in to ask the sending operator to repeat missed words or sentences. This situation was further compounded by poor reception caused by problems with the line from Cleveland and by leakage in a cable across the Ohio River between Cincinnati and Covington, Kentucky, which caused the current to fluctuate. Although Edison found a way to overcome the cable problem "by using several relays, each with a different adjustment [to work] several sounders all connected with one sounding-plate," it still "required a large amount of imagination to get the sense of what was being sent." To "write down what was coming and imagine what wasn't coming," Edison experimented with his handwriting "to find the fastest style." He improved his "imagination" by regularly reading several papers each day to keep abreast of current news. In this way he learned about "every member of Congress & what committees they were on & all about the topical doings as well as the prices of breadstufs in all the primary markets."[42] Edison supplemented his newspaper reading by listening to political and other discussions between Associated Press agent George Tyler, a Harvard graduate, and George Prentice, editor of the *Louisville Journal,* in the early morning hours after he finished taking the press. With his knowledge of current events Edison was able to supply missing words and sentences when conditions made it difficult to receive the press copy clearly.

Edison also furthered his reputation as a press operator when he spent what he later claimed to be fifteen hours "without a moments intermission for food" taking President Andrew Johnson's message to Congress as well as his "long-winded veto of the District of Columbia bill," which had failed to reach Louisville in time by post, requiring that it be sent by wire from Cincinnati. While Edison may have exaggerated his feat in taking this copy, he was rewarded with a dinner given by the newspapers. He also stated that he introduced an innovation during the taking of these messages "which was greatly appreciated by the newspaper people" and consisted in "paragraphing the copy or writing it in sections called by the printers 'takers,'" which made up three lines in the printed column. This allowed the night editor to "run his shears between these sections & these were divided up among a dozen printers," thus saving the editor work and reducing the time needed to set the type.[43]

As in his previous stops, Edison continued to experiment. One of his landladies, who called him "Hugo" Edison (a nickname he earned in Louisville by virtue of his love for the novels of Victor Hugo), told of how he closeted himself with his books and wires. One of his fellow operators recalled that he strung some of these wires between the telegraph office and the two-story brick building behind it that housed the shop of instrumentmaker W. H. Johnson, which later became a Western Union manufactory. It is possible that Edison had instruments made in Johnson's shop for his experiments. Among the telegraph apparatus that Edison did make was a battery, which seems to have been the cause of his dismissal. When he went into the battery room of the telegraph office to get some sulphuric acid for his battery, he spilled it and it leaked through the ceiling into the office of the manager. Perhaps because of the new quarters or because of irritation over Edison's experimental apparatus, the manager informed Edison "that he couldnt afford to keep me any longer."[44] Returning for a second time to Cincinnati, Edison continued to take press copy, but more important, he increasingly focused his attention on the technical side of telegraphy and began to make the transition from operator to inventor.

CHAPTER 3

From Operator to Inventor

With his return to Cincinnati in 1867 Edison rejoined one of the more sophisticated technical communities in the telegraph industry. In post–Civil War America, telegraph invention was most successfully undertaken in a few major industrial cities that included Cincinnati, New York, Boston, Philadelphia, Chicago, and the Washington, D.C., and Baltimore nexus, as well as in a few smaller but vital technical communities such as San Francisco and Cleveland. Invention increasingly concentrated in these cities because they contained both a large community of technically skilled operators and higher ranking telegraph officials and the machine shops and skilled mechanics needed by inventors to help convert their ideas into working instruments. The shops and the large operating rooms became meeting grounds that hastened the exchange of information about telegraph technology. They also served as laboratories for telegraph inventors.[1]

Prior to the Civil War, only Boston, Philadelphia, and New York had contained telegraph shops of any significance, but soon afterward telegraph manufactories began to be established in a number of other cities. Although Cincinnati apparently had no specialized telegraph manufactory during the time Edison was there, the city's many machine shops would have provided both skilled mechanics to help build experimental apparatus and a source for used machinery. Edison was able to acquire a foot-operated lathe and some tools that he set up in a rented room in the top of an office building where he could construct and alter his own experimental telegraph apparatus.[2]

The Cincinnati office was notable for its skilled operating staff, and a number of operators there showed interest in telegraph technology. Most notable were Edison's friend and fellow operator Ed Gilliland, who later established one of the first telegraph shops in the city, chief operator J. F. Stevens, who assisted Moses Farmer in his tests of a duplex telegraph system in December 1865, and E. C. Armstrong, later superintendent of the City and Suburban Telegraph Association. Charles Selden, who later became an important inventor and telegraph superintendent, also may have been in Cincinnati when Edison was there. Like Edison, Selden read scientific and technical books in the city's libraries. In addition, Western Union superintendent George Hicks, whose self-adjusting repeater was extensively used on Western Union lines, was headquartered in Cincinnati. Another significant member of the Cincinnati telegraph fraternity was Charles Summers, the telegraph superintendent of the Indianapolis, Cincinnati, and Lafayette Railroad, who gave Edison "permission to take such scrap apparatus as I desired & which was of no use to the Co." Summers was "fond of experimenting," and he and Edison worked together on a self-adjusting relay that would open the local circuit containing the battery and receiving instrument while adjusting automatically to changing electrical conditions.[3] Telegraph officials such as Summers were an important source of support for inventors, providing not only surplus equipment, but also access to telegraph lines and sometimes personal assistance in experiments. Those officials willing to support inventive work were most commonly located in the larger cities of the Midwest and Northeast.

It was during his second stay in Cincinnati that Edison began to develop a reputation for his technical expertise. Quite apart from Summers's interest in him, Edison's fellow operators from that time all remembered his interest in experiments. He also attracted the attention of a local business that asked him to install a private telegraph line for them. According to James Gamble Jr., son of one of the founding partners of the soap and candle company Proctor and Gamble, Edison installed a private line between the company's downtown office and their factory on the city's outskirts. Gamble thought that the instrument was of Edison's own design (he did work on such an instrument the following year), but it may have been one already on the market, such as the one produced by the New York inventor and manufacturer Charles Chester.[4] In the postwar era, private lines became one of many new telegraph services that began to provide improved communications within the city for a variety of purposes, most of them related to business. Another increasingly popular form of urban telegraphy was the fire-alarm system, which enabled a rapid report of a fire's occurrence and location to be sent by telegraph wire directly to a fire station when someone pulled the lever of an alarm box. By the time of Edison's return Cincinnati had installed its first fire-alarm telegraph. Although Edison's early success as a telegraph inventor would subsequently come in the field of urban telegraphs, in Cincinnati his primary interest remained long-distance telegraph improvements that might be wanted by Western Union, the company for which he worked as an operator.

Edison's continuing technical education and his experimental work can be followed in the pages of the notebook he kept while in Cincinnati in 1867. Edison was in the habit of using small pocket notebooks to make "notes and diagrams," but the Cincinnati book is the only one to survive from his itinerant telegraph years.[5] The drawings in the Cincinnati notebook are the earliest examples of Edison's fine freehand drawing style. Disproving a biographer who claimed that "Edison was handicapped by poorer-than-average hand coordination and was a primitive sketcher," his notebooks show him to be a skilled drawer.[6] What he lacked was the training to make mechanical drawings to measured scale. These he left to the skilled mechanics who worked in his shops and laboratories. There is no evidence that Edison ever had formal drawing lessons, but other members of his family also showed drawing ability, and this might have been something of a family trait. An 1883 biographical sketch of family patriarch Samuel Edison indicates that he "has also been engaged in fine copying or drafting for a house in New York," and Edison's brother William Pitt reportedly showed such talent that according to one account, "his friend wanted to send him to Paris to develop his talent."[7] Pitt's son Charles Edison also demonstrated drawing talent in the notebooks he kept while working in his uncle's laboratories, and Edison's own sons displayed artistic talents as well.

Edison's Cincinnati notebook primarily contains drawings, but there are also two lists of books that he probably made while sitting in the Cincinnati Free Library or the Mechanic's Library. The chief operator later claimed that "many times Edison would get excused from duty under pretense of being too sick to work, and various other excuses, and invariably strike a beeline for the Library, where he would spend the entire day and evening reading De La [Rive's] or Noads' Manual [of Electricity], and such other works on electricity as were to be had."[8] Among those works Edison listed were Faraday's *Researches in Electricity*, Culley's *Handbook of Practical Telegraphy*, and Walker's *Electric Telegraph Manipulation*. He also listed other works with their prices, perhaps indicating his interest in acquiring them, including Sabine's *Electric Telegraph*, the first (1867) edition of which he later cited in his laboratory notebooks. Sabine or Culley may well have been sources of information about polarized relays in which the magnetic core was arranged to respond to changes in current polarity. These proved to be effective switching devices that were extensively used on European cable and long-line telegraphs, but were not employed in American telegraphy. They would become an important element in many of Edison's telegraph designs, and his Cincinnati notebook featured drawings of polarized relays, including one of his own design, which he may have built himself or had made in a local shop. Sabine's figures for the conductivity of silver and copper also appear in a table drawn by Edison in his notebook, although he labeled this "Conductivity Metails Proc[ee]d[i]ngs Royal Society."[9]

Most of the entries in Edison's notebook are drawings of repeater and relay designs. Relays, which switched the incoming signal from the main line to the local sounder circuit, were an important element in repeaters, which transferred the weak incoming signal to a new transmitting circuit with its own battery and then forwarded it to the next station. The longer transmission distances created by Western Union's consolidation of the nation's telegraph lines, as well as its transcontinental line to San Francisco, made improvements in these devices particularly important. Because varying line conditions made it necessary for operators constantly to adjust relays, Edison, as well as other inventors, was concerned with making them self-adjusting so they would automatically respond to changing conditions. Repeaters were a subject of even greater interest to inventors. Franklin Pope, editor of the *Telegrapher*, published a series of articles about them in 1864 and 1865, and Daniel B. Grandy, who became an operator at the close of the war, later recalled that "One of the first efforts of the embryo 'electrician' in those days, used to be the invention of a new 're-peater.'"[10] Existing repeaters such as Hicks's served as models for young inventors such as Edison and Grandy. Edison drew several repeater designs in his notebook, some of which he based on patent or other published drawings of the instruments and others of which he drew from the instruments themselves. In some cases he modified the original design, as in his drawing of the Hicks repeater, which he altered to allow the repeater station to act as a terminal station. Edison also drew his own original designs. Among these was a repeater for the Phelps combination printer, which he later published in modified form in the *Telegrapher*. Another of his designs was for a type commonly known as a "button" repeater, in which the direction of transmission was manually switched. Edison's button repeater design was later described in the 1869 edition of Franklin Pope's *Modern Practice of the Electric Telegraph*. Pope, whom Edison knew personally by then, stated that Edison's repeater was "found to work well in practice" and would be "very convenient in cases where it is required to set up a repeater in an emergency, with the ordinary instruments used in every office."[11]

Another subject of growing interest at this time was the attempt to send two messages simultaneously over a single wire. Double transmission systems, which could be either the more common "duplex" (sending in opposite directions) or "diplex" (sending in the same direction), had been a subject of experimentation in Europe since the 1850s, but few Americans thought them feasible. However, noted American telegraph inventor Moses Farmer had demonstrated a system between Boston and Portland, Maine, and on a line from Cincinnati to Indianapolis in 1865. Three years later, Joseph Stearns successfully introduced a duplex on the lines of the Franklin Telegraph Company in Boston. A short notice of the 1865 experiment with Farmer's duplex on the Cincinnati–Indianapolis line was reported in the pages of the *Telegrapher*, and Edison may have heard about it from Gilliland or other operators whom he knew in those two cities. If he was aware of the test, it may have spurred his own experiments in Memphis, which had taken place soon after. After his return to Cincinnati, Edison probably discussed the test with Stevens, and Charles Summers may have been familiar with it as well, particularly if the line used was the railway's rather than Western Union's. Because relays were an important element in duplex design, Edison's and Summers's experiments on self-adjusting relays may

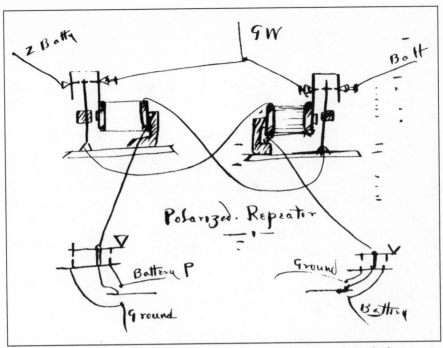

Edison's 1867 drawing of an automatic repeater design employing a polarized relay.

have involved double transmission experiments as well; Summers later assisted Henry Nicholson with experiments to send four messages simultaneously (quadruplex). The duplex designs in Edison's notebook were of the "differential" or "compensation" type, in which a sounder relay with oppositely wound electromagnets negated the outgoing signal so the sounder responded only to an incoming signal. According to Gilliland, Edison used parts from an old repeater in his Cincinnati double transmission experiments, and he may have rewired self-adjusting relays, such as those used in the Hicks repeater, in developing his duplex designs.

Edison also began working on a system of secret signaling for military use at the urging of George Ellsworth, who was then working in the Cincinnati office. As telegraph operator for the Confederate raider John Morgan, Ellsworth had tapped wires to read Union messages and send false ones, and he asked Edison to invent a secret signaling method in the hope that they could sell it to the government for a large sum of money. However, Ellsworth left Cincinnati before Edison finished developing a system. The following year, Edison attempted to interest John Van Duzer in the invention. Van Duzer was the civilian electrician of the U.S. Signal Corps and Edison had known him in Memphis where he became telegraph superintendent just before Edison left the city.

In letters to Van Duzer he described his apparatus as being contained in a one-foot-square box, weighing eighteen pounds, and costing $125 to $150 for a set of two instruments. Edison never specified his exact design, but what he did say about it suggests that it used a strong current to keep the relays along the line closed. The signaling was probably done by using increases in the current level to induce a current in an induction coil wound around an ordinary relay coil, which then worked the sounder. Edison claimed that the instruments could not be used at intermediate stations, "except by grounding the wire. This is instantly detected by both terminals, and each Terminal may allow him to receive or not just as they wish." Edison's instrument was never adopted, although he later claimed that he placed it on a private line between New York and Philadelphia.[12]

For unknown reasons, Edison decided to leave Cincinnati at the end of September and return to Port Huron, where he remained for about six months; his stay may have been prolonged by illness during the winter of 1867–1868. At the time of his return, his parents had moved to another house in Fort Gratiot, his boyhood home having been commandeered for use by the military reservation in 1864 and subsequently purchased by the reservation agent. The state of the family's financial circumstances at this time are unclear. They were again taking in boarders, and Samuel continued to speculate in land. Elected a justice of the peace in 1866, he also may have worked as a contractor. His brother Pitt clearly continued to prosper, becoming manager of the new Port Huron and Gratiot Street Railway, which opened for business in October 1866.

During his sojourn in Port Huron Edison continued to design telegraph apparatus, and he later claimed that he installed a double transmitter of his contrivance on a Grand Trunk Railway telegraph cable under the river between Fort Gratiot and Port Edward, Canada, after one of the two cables had broken. This double transmitter may be the duplex design he described in an article submitted to the *Telegrapher* in late December 1867 or early January 1868, which became Edison's first technical publication. This article was enthusiastically received by editor Franklin Pope, who published a short note in the January 11, 1868, issue telling him "Good! Come some more." However, when Pope relinquished the editorship to James Ashley in February, Edison's article was mislaid. This delayed its publication, under the title "Edison's Double Transmitter," until April, by which time Edison had arrived in Boston, where his friend and fellow operator Milton Adams had obtained a job for him in the city's main Western Union office.[13]

It was in Boston, where Edison found one of the oldest and most sophisticated telegraph communities in the country, that his inventive career began in earnest. Second only to New York City as a telegraph center in the immediate postwar era, Boston provided a stimulating environment for his ambitions as an inventor. Western Union alone had four offices in the city. The main Western Union office where Edison worked was managed by George Milliken, who had several telegraph inventions to his credit, including some he developed with the noted electrical inventor Moses Farmer. Farmer had a laboratory in the shop of manufacturer Charles Williams Jr., which was one of several innovative telegraph shops in Boston. Other telegraph companies also had message offices in the city, and the Franklin Telegraph Company, then one of Western Union's chief rivals, was based in Boston. In an effort to compete more effectively with Western Union, Franklin Telegraph president Joseph Stearns had devised a duplex telegraph that he installed on his company's lines the same year as Edison arrived in Boston. Boston also boasted the first fire-alarm telegraph system in the country (it had been developed by Farmer and William Channing in 1851), and the city's financial community provided a source of funding to develop other urban telegraph systems.

Working nights as a press-wire operator, Edison spent his days exploring this technical community. He visited the city's telegraph shops and wrote an article about them for the *Telegrapher* in which he described a number of the inventions developed or marketed by these firms. He also noted the existence of Farmer's laboratory in Charles Williams's shop, where Edison himself was soon doing experimental work as well. Williams's shop had several machinists who specialized in such work, one of whom, Thomas Watson, later became famous for his work with inventor Alexander Graham Bell, who used the shop as an experimental laboratory as well as a place to have instruments made. Edison wrote about other activities in the Boston telegraph community for the *Telegrapher*. In one article he discussed battery experiments conducted on the line of the Boston and Maine Railroad and noted that both this line and the fire-alarm telegraph line being extended to Roxbury used Milliken's and Farmer's patented steel and copper compound wire, which became the subject of still another article.

The broad range of telegraph technologies on display in the city's telegraph shops and working on its lines inspired Edison to expand the scope of his own inventive activity, and he was soon working on printing telegraphs, fire alarms, and facsimile telegraphs (for transmitting handwriting and pictures). Work on several projects at the same time would become an important element in Edison's style of invention and one of the sources of his creativity. Edison also published articles that described some of his own designs for telegraph relays and repeaters, while his friend Milton Adams wrote an article on systems for automatically transmitting and receiving Morse code that included the description of a design Edison had based on his Indianapolis practice instrument. Though Edison began to make his mark as a member of the technical elite of operators through these articles, he was still modestly signing them "E." He would adopt the initials "TAE" as he moved into the ranks of prominent telegraph inventors, and after he became famous he would develop his well-known umbrella signature.[14]

As important as Boston's technical community was for Edison's inventive career, the proximity of financiers interested in telegraph technology was equally significant. Like most young inventors Edison had technical know-how but lacked financial resources for experiments and patent expenses as well as the business connections necessary to introduce innovations. In Boston he found local capitalists and corporate officials who were willing to support his inventive efforts and fund their introduction. By turning to these investors Edison was following a pattern common to many telegraph inventors of his generation, and he later advised young inventors to follow his example when trying to find support for their first inventions.[15]

Soon after arriving in Boston, Edison began to garner support for his inventive work. In late April, fellow operator Dewitt C. Roberts agreed to "furnish or cause to be furnished sufficient money to patent and manufacture one or more of [Edison's proposed] Stockbroker Printing Instrument."[16] When Roberts left Boston in November to enter the flour business in upstate New York, he sold part of his interest in this stockprinter to stockbroker Samuel Ropes Jr. Before leaving, Roberts had become interested in another Edison invention, an electric vote recorder, and he had provided funds for Edison to have it made in Charles Williams's shop.

Roberts also provided the money for the fees involved in applying for a patent for the vote recorder, which Edison filed in October. Although it was relatively cheap in comparison to other countries, patenting in the United States was still an expensive process. Each application had to be accompanied by a $15 fee and a model and a measured drawing, both of which required additional expenses to have been made. After the application was allowed, the inventor was charged an additional $20 fee. Additional costs could be incurred if the patent was put into interference with another application or issued patent to determine which inventor had priority of invention. Most inventors relied on patent agents and attorneys, who of course charged fees for their work. Edison, for example, used Boston patent attorney Joseph Adams for his fire-alarm caveat (a kind of preliminary patent application) and the firm of Teschemacher and Stearns for his printing telegraph patent.

Edison's work on the electric vote recorder was inspired by articles that had recently appeared in the *Telegrapher* about similar devices then being considered by the New York State legislature and the Washington, D.C., city council. Edison's design incorporated an electrochemical recorder listing each of the legislator's names alongside two columns headed "Yes" and "No." The legislator would move a switch to transmit his vote to the appropriate column and to two dials on either side of it that totaled the votes. As each legislator voted, the recording clerk placed a sheet of chemically treated paper over two columns of metal type containing the legislator's name. As the clerk moved a metal roller over the name, current passed through the paper, decomposed the chemicals, and recorded the individual vote. This design was based on a common recording method used in automatic telegraphs, and Edison would spend several years in the early 1870s working on chemical-recording telegraph systems. Although Edison obtained his first patent for this invention (U.S. Patent 90,646, issued on June 1, 1869), he was not successful in having the vote recorder adopted. The greater speed and efficiency made possible by such a machine were little appreciated by legislators who used the roll call process to round up votes.[17]

Edison was more successful with his printing telegraph design. Besides Roberts, Edison attracted several other supporters for his work on printing telegraphs. In June 1868 John Lane, former president of the Franklin Telegraph Company, agreed to back Edison's work on his "Improved Automatic Printing Telegraph." The description of the instrument found in his assignment to Lane shows similarities with the printing telegraph for which he applied for a patent the following January. By that time his association with Lane apparently had ended, and the patented design was used by Samuel Ropes and two new investors, flour merchant Joel Hills and hide broker William Plummer, to start a business for reporting the prices of gold and stocks. Edison's work was supported by $1,300 Hills and Plummer advanced to Ropes for use in "perfecting and developing" the printer. They also paid all of the patent costs and agreed to give Edison an additional $250 when the instrument went into practical use.[18]

Edison's principal backer for his other inventions was another Franklin Telegraph Company official. In July 1868 E. Baker Welch, a company director whom Edison had met in late March, agreed to fund Edison's experiments on double transmitters and fire-alarm telegraphs. Welch also supported Milton Adams's efforts, with assistance from Edison, to develop a new printing telegraph design. Welch paid for the filing of Edison's patent caveat for his fire-alarm telegraph and was apparently prepared to back Edison and his fellow operators George Newton and Patrick Burns, the latter a student at Harvard College, if they succeeded in getting the contract for the fire-alarm telegraph in Cambridge. However, city officials "had no confidence" in the young inventor and instead gave the contract to the Gamewell Fire-Alarm Telegraph Company, which was the largest and most successful fire-alarm company in the country.[19] With Welch's support, Edison also began to advertise his double transmitters in the pages of the *Telegrapher*, although there is no evidence that he sold any. Welch provided further funds for Edison's test of his double transmitter on the Atlantic and Pacific Telegraph Company's line between Rochester and New York during April 1869. The following month, Welch also acquired an interest in the magnetograph, a dial telegraph instrument Edison had developed with machinist George Anders for use on private lines. Anders had been employed by the telegraph manufacturing firm of Edmands and Hamblet, whose dial telegraph Edison had described in his article on Boston manufacturers. Anders's intimate knowledge of this device, as well as Edison's own study of it, doubtless contributed to their own design, but as a result their dial instrument may have been too similar to Edmands and Hamblet's to be patentable.[20]

During this time Edison was working on another invention for which he was unable to find experimental funds. In the summer of 1868 he had conversations about a proposed facsimile telegraph with Isaac Livermore, treasurer of the Michigan Central Railroad, whose offices were at City Exchange in Boston. Livermore's brother-in-law, Anson Burlingame, was attempting to introduce a telegraph system into China, but faced problems in transmitting Chinese characters. Livermore was therefore quite interested in Edison's proposal for a telegraph capable of sending and receiving facsimiles of handwritten messages. In early September Edison also wrote to John Van Duzer about the invention in the hope that Van Duzer could interest the East India Telegraph Company in it. In that letter Edison claimed he had been working on his facsimile for three years, but that he had "done nothing with it for nearly 3 weeks: being engaged on my automatic Printers, of which four (4) have Already been made by Williams." At that time he thought it would "probably be several months before I will be able to Bring it out, as experiments are rather Costly and there is a scarcity of funds." In December he was still seeking $500 to $800, which, he told Van Duzer, was necessary "to get it perfect [because] 5 or more machines would have to be constructed in different shapes before the perfect one could be reached besides a large amount of experimenting independent of the machine itself= With sufficient Tools and supplies I could do it nearly all myself." However, his failure to find funding prevented him from continuing work on a facsimile telegraph.[21]

In describing his facsimile to Van Duzer, Edison had compared it to other patented designs and pointed out those features he considered essential to facsimile telegraphy and that he claimed his design incorporated: "Now with these systems all before me, I conceived that an apparatus for transmitting writing, 'fac simile,' to be of any practical value, must not depend upon synchronious movements, 2nd that it must be *practical* 3d simple, and 4th Rapid, 5th self acting, (ie) No operators & 6th No prepartion of messages."[22] Rather than use mechanical apparatus to achieve synchronism between transmitter and receiver, Edison sought to achieve this by electrical means through polarized relays, which would become a characteristic of much of his design work in telegraphy over the next several years. Edison's facsimile used polarized relays in the transmitter and receiver to respond synchronously to the alternating positive and negative battery currents he used to transmit the message. Edison, who had begun to explore polarized relays in Cincinnati, used them in some of his other inventions from this time on as well. Other early examples include his combination repeater and a self-adjusting relay, both of which he described in the *Telegrapher*.

Edison's most significant use of polarized relays was in his patented printing telegraph used in the gold reporting business. This machine incorporated a modified polarized relay that acted as a switch to activate either the typewheel or the printing mechanism depending on what kind of current was transmitted. Edison's printer thus could be worked by means of a single transmitting wire, a potentially important improvement over the original stockprinter invented by Edward Calahan, which employed three different wires, two to turn the two typewheels and one to operate the printing mechanism. Edison later called this

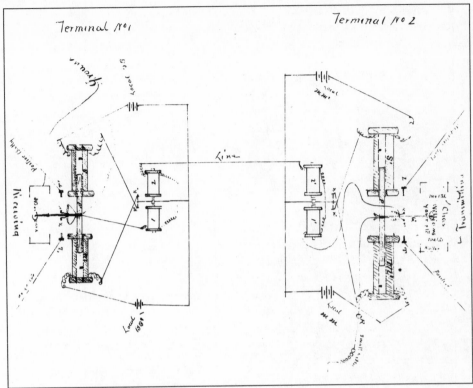

Edison's 1868 facsimile telegraph design used a polarized relay at each end of the line to synchronize the transmitter and receiver. (Courtesy American Philosophical Society)

polarized relay design "the most perfect device for producing two movements at a distance on one wire by magnetizm as it does not depend upon an even & rapid transmission of waves to effect the result but will act with the slowest as well as the most rapid pulsations."[23] Nonetheless, the relay proved inadequate because its weak permanent magnetism often prevented it from switching properly between printing and typewheel circuits, thus causing them to act simultaneously.

The introduction of Calahan's stockprinter on the New York Stock and Gold Exchanges in early 1868 had opened up a new field for telegraph inventors, which Edison was among the first to enter. Calahan's Gold and Stock Telegraph Company was soon making plans to expand its system to other cities, as was Samuel Laws, whose Gold and Stock Reporting Company, the primary competitor to Calahan's Gold and Stock, used a dial-indicating instrument to report prices from the New York exchanges to brokers' offices. At the time Edison began to introduce his printer, Laws was planning to extend his service to Boston in connection with the Bankers' and Brokers' Telegraph Company.

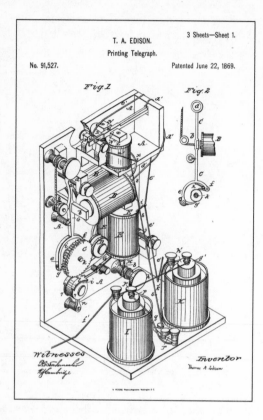

T. A. EDISON.
Printing Telegraph.

3 Sheets—Sheet 1.

No. 91,527.

Patented June 22, 1869.

Fig. 1

Fig. 2

Witnesses

Inventor
Thomas A. Edison

Edison's second U.S. patent incorporated a polarized relay (at top), which acted as a switch to activate either the typewheel or the printing mechanism of a printing telegraph depending on whether a positive or negative current was transmitted.

Edison's stock-quotation enterprise was located at 9 Wilson Lane, the same building that housed Banker's and Broker's Telegraph, and it is possible that Franklin Pope, who was Laws's general superintendent and well aware of Edison through his contributions to the *Telegrapher*, considered using the young inventor's printer for this Boston operation.

Edison's gold and stock quotation service began operation in January 1869 with funding from Hills and Plummer. Edison managed the operation with Ropes and telegraph operator Frank Hanaford; there is some evidence that Roberts may have returned briefly to assist them as well. Their first customer was the banking and brokerage house of Kidder, Peabody and Company, and they eventually had twenty-five subscribers. Edison also provided private-line service for several Boston businesses; most firms used private lines between their downtown offices and salesrooms and their factories or warehouses on the outskirts of the city. Edison and Hanaford, who may have been backed in this operation by a D. D. Cummings, initially intended to use the magnetograph and installed some lines with this instrument. However, after Welch acquired an interest in the instrument in May 1869, he objected to their using it and they had to install printers instead. According to Edison, he had a small laboratory in the building that became the "headquarters for the men and also of tools and supplies for these private lines. They were put up cheaply, as I used the roofs of houses as the W.U. did. It never occurred to me to ask permission from the owners; all we did was to go to the store, etc. and say we were telegraph men and wanted to go up to the wires on the roof and permission was always given."[24]

Edison's new enterprise enabled him to resign from his job as Western Union operator, and he placed a notice in the January 30 issue of the *Telegrapher* stating that he would now "devote his time to bringing out his inventions." This marked his formal transition from operator to inventor, a goal toward which he had been working since his arrival in Boston a year earlier.[25]

Edison and his associates found it relatively easy to establish new businesses with these inventions for the urban telegraph market. Unlike the inter-city telegraph system dominated by Western Union's national network, with which it was difficult to compete, urban telegraphs required only the limited start-up funding necessary to build instruments and string short lines within a city. More important for success was the character of the instruments, and those providing the first service or offering the most reliable and cheapest instruments were best able to achieve competitive advantage. When Edison began offering stock-and-gold quotation service in Boston, he was the first in the market with a simple, reliable instrument, although the polarized relay switch sometimes failed to operate properly and caused complaints.[26]

Edison's private-line business also depended on instruments that were both reliable and easy to use. The magnetograph had a potential advantage over competitors because it did not require a battery, an important feature in an era when batteries were not a widely used consumer good because their acid solutions had to be changed frequently. The magnetograph obviated the need for a battery by using a magneto in which an armature turning in a magnetic field generated an electric current. One potential customer in New York City was using Charles Chester's dial telegraph but wanted to replace it with Edison's and Anders's instrument because he objected to batteries. However, Edison found this sale and others frustrated by Welch's failure to push the manufacture of the magnetograph sufficiently. Welch's unwillingness to allow Edison and Hanaford to use the magnetograph in their private-line business seriously limited the instrument's success, and Edison's printer proved to be an inadequate replacement as a private-line instrument. Welch, who proved to be an inadequate source of funding for Edison's double transmitter experiments as well, may not have had the funds necessary to push the magnetograph business, although he and Anders subsequently achieved modest success selling Anders's magneto-operated dial and printing telegraph instruments. Unable to use the magnetograph and lacking sufficient funding to improve his printer, Edison decided to abandon his Boston businesses and move to New York during the spring of 1869.

Edison initially traveled to New York in April to prepare for tests of his double transmitter on a line of the Atlantic and Pacific Telegraph Company between New York and Rochester. At the time Atlantic and Pacific was a small Western Union competitor with lines from New York to Cleveland via Albany, Rochester, and Buffalo. On April 13, Edison conducted a test from Rochester that the *Telegrapher* called a "complete success" over "the longest circuit [400 miles] which has ever been practically worked by this system."[27] However, in a May 8 letter to Welch, Edison stated that after arriving in Rochester he had to wait four days before getting a line, which he did not get "until late at night, and then the wires worked very poorly on account of bad insulation, and I came to the conclusion not to wait any longer but return to New York and wait till they trimmed the line which they are doing now. . . . What delays me here is awaiting the alteration of my instruments which on account of the piling up of jobs at the instrument makers have been delayed and I will probably have to wait one week longer." Noting that other companies had also expressed interest in the invention, Edison told Welch: "So you see that there is no use letting anything stand in the way of successfully getting this apparatus perfected. Me and [Franklin] Pope have experimented considerable upon it and have several improvements only one thing stands in the way now and that is Induction, and my alterations will overcome that, so I have concluded to stick here till I am successful.[28] There is no evidence that Edison conducted another trial of his double transmitter, and he appears to have soon given up working on it.

But Edison remained in New York for other reasons than his attempts to improve the double transmitter. In the same letter to Welch, he described an offer he had received to equip a line with the magnetograph and commented that "N.Y. appears to be quite different to Boston. People here come and buy without your soliciting." In July he wrote Hanaford about his printer, noting that "it is useless for me to lay around or come to Boston, for I cannot make any money there and we should be farther than ever from the solution of this interesting problem. If I stay here I can earn enough money to fix the thing all straight within a reasonable time."[29] About the time Edison wrote to Hanaford, he succeeded Pope, who had taken Edison under his wing, as superintendent of Laws's Gold and Stock Reporting Company. Edison recognized that Boston's financial community was more conservative than the one he found in the entrepreneurial hotbed of New York, which was the headquarters for both Western Union and the gold and stock quotation business. His decision to remain there proved to be one of the most important of his career.

CHAPTER 4

A Leading
Electromechanician

In January 1871 Western Union president William Orton wrote to central division superintendent Anson Stager about his negotiations with the Gold and Stock Telegraph Company regarding their competing interests in the business of supplying financial news. In the course of that letter Orton explained the strong patent position held by Gold and Stock, aided in part by the work of a young inventor whom he called Eddison. So impressive did he consider Edison's printing telegraph inventions that he ranked him second only to George Phelps, Western Union's manufacturing superintendent, whose printing telegraph the company was using in competition with Gold and Stock. Orton also thought that Edison was "probably the best electro-mechanician in the country." Edison had achieved this reputation less than two years after arriving in New York in 1869.[1]

Edison's decision to remain in the New York City area was prompted by the city's role as the center of the U.S. telegraph industry. Western Union and most other telegraph companies had their headquarters in New York, and many of the leading members of the industry's technical community had located there to have ready access to company officials who might support their work. Furthermore, New York's entrepreneurial financial community provided the major source of support for the new urban telegraph services that offered market reports, private lines, and messenger and alarm services. Edison's growing reputation as an inventor in these markets brought him into contact not only with leading telegraph officials but also with major New York financial figures. Through these relationships he began to learn about the world of finance and venture capital and gained new insights into the business side of innovation.

Edison also learned to profit from the growing corporate context of invention as new competitive forces in the telegraph industry led companies to seek control over the work of key inventors. Taking advantage of this environment, he would secure access to the telegraph machine shops that provided such crucial resources for telegraph invention.

Edison's appointment as superintendent of Laws's Gold and Stock Reporting Company in August 1869 provided him with greater resources to develop his ideas for printing telegraphs than had the insufficiently funded gold reporting operation in Boston. Although Laws had initiated gold reporting and had an extensive business, he faced increasing competition from Calahan's Gold and Stock Telegraph Company. Recognizing that the Calahan stockprinter had advantages over his indicator, Laws designed his own printer, but his patent on it was delayed by a patent office interference with the reissue application for Calahan's printer. Edison took on the task of redesigning the Laws printer and received a patent on it before Laws's own patent was issued. Edison's redesign did more than just make the Laws instrument more patentable; he substantially improved its operation by reducing the size of the printer and the number of its moving parts, improving its mechanical operation, and replacing the ink ribbon with a wheel. He also added an electromagnet to operate the unison stop, which maintained synchronism between the printer and the transmitter.[2]

Even as Edison was improving this printer, Laws was negotiating a merger with Calahan's Gold and Stock Telegraph Company. By early September, Gold and Stock agreed to buy out Laws, and they concluded the merger a month later. The merger consolidated not only the business of the two companies but also their patents. The most important of these was H. N. Baker's 1856 printing telegraph patent (U.S. Patent 147,759), for which Laws had acquired the rights. Baker's claims for independent typewheel and printing circuits predated Calahan's patent and might have led to a costly patent infringement suit. Although Edison's improvement of the Laws printer would have been important to continued competition between the firms, it was not essential to the newly combined company, which consequently did not require his services. Gold and Stock already employed Calahan as its superintendent. Edison's brief tenure with Laws certainly added to his growing reputation, but this proved a small consolation. As he noted in a letter to his friend Frank Hanaford, "the Consolidation . . . [and] my Consequent dismissal has upset all my calculations."[3]

No doubt aware of the negotiations, Edison had been making alternative plans, including some with Laws, who was obviously impressed with Edison's technical ability and perhaps felt some responsibility for the loss of his job. Although nothing substantial came of Laws's interest in Edison's other inventions, he did offer to provide the necessary funding to develop Edison's double transmitter and also purchased George Anders's interest in the magnetograph and offered to purchase E. Baker Welch's interest in it as well.[4]

More significantly, Edison went into business with Franklin Pope, who had become something of a mentor to the young inventor. Together with James

Ashley, the editor of the *Telegrapher*, they formed the electrical engineering firm of Pope, Edison & Company. Their advertisement in the *Telegrapher* noted that "a necessity has long been felt, by Managers and Projectors of Telegraph Lines, Inventors of Telegraph Machinery and Appliances, etc., for the establishment of a Bureau of Electrical and Telegraphic Engineering in this city." At the time, the only other such firm was Chester, Partrick & Carter of Philadelphia. Pope, Edison & Company offered a variety of services, including instrument and wire testing, telegraph line construction, repair, and maintenance, and patent application and drawings preparation. They also proposed to act as purchasing agents for telegraph and electrical apparatus, to design instruments for special use, to construct experimental apparatus, and to conduct experiments "with scientific accuracy." Ashley also wrote an editorial boosting the firm and praising Pope's and Edison's technical abilities, calling Edison "a young man of the highest order of mechanical talent, combined with good scientific electrical knowledge and experience."[5]

Edison and Pope devised a new printing telegraph that became the basis for another service offered by the partners of Pope, Edison & Company. By December 1869, they had formed the Financial and Commercial Telegraph Company and began to provide gold and other price quotations to merchants and importers whose interest in these prices was "not sufficient to warrant them in employing the more expensive instruments in such general use among the brokers of Wall and Broad streets."[6] The Financial and Commercial printer they designed was simple to use and operated over a single wire, thus avoiding the necessity of a local battery, which would have to be maintained by the user. The transmitter, which consisted of a breakwheel with a dial indicating letters and numbers, sent signals of rapidly alternating current. The polarized relay of the typewheel circuit was designed to respond only to the short signals transmitted while the breakwheel was being turned. Once the proper letter was reached, a stronger current was then transmitted to activate the printing mechanism.

Dr. Leverett Bradley, a Jersey City, New Jersey, electrical manufacturer noted for his patented magnetic helices and his electrical measuring instruments, manufactured the Financial and Commercial printer and also provided space for Edison's experiments. Edison later recalled leaving Bradley's shop near the Pennsylvania Railroad Station every night and taking the 1 A.M. train to Elizabeth, N.J., where he boarded with the Pope family, and then getting up at 6 A.M. to catch the seven o'clock train back to Jersey City. "This continued all winter and many were the occasions when I was nearly frozen in the Elizabeth walk."[7]

Already aware of Edison's work on printing telegraphs from his contributions to the Edison-Laws printer, the Gold and Stock directors voted on February 8, 1870, to have the company's president, George Field, inform Financial and Commercial Telegraph that their instrument was infringing Gold and Stock's patents. This action led to protracted negotiations between the two companies, but on February 10 Field and Elisha Andrews, one of the Gold and Stock directors and a former president of the company, signed two agreements with Edison. The first of these provided for him to devise a one-wire printer "to be smaller than the Calahan instrument and the speed to be as great if not greater" for which Edison would receive $7,000.[7] The agreement also included an addendum in which Edison agreed to "include my services as C[onsulting] Electrician for one year from date of the application for Letters patent" of the printer. On May 24, 1870, Edison executed a patent (U.S. Patent 128,608) for the printer specified in the agreement. Although assigned to Gold and Stock the printer was never used, but one year after filing the patent application, Edison would sign a five-year contract to serve as the company's "Consulting Electrician and Mechanician."[8]

The second February 10 agreement was equally important to Edison's future as an inventor. Under its terms Edison agreed to develop a simple and reliable facsimile telegraph that would not require "elaborate preparation" of messages before they were sent, equal the average speed of the Morse telegraph, be faster for press messages, and transmit photographs, "hierogliphical characters, short hand, and messages in any Language." The instrument also had to be capable of dropping copies at any point along the line and allowing them to be retransmitted from chemical strips. Edison was to receive $3,000 for this device. Even more significantly, Field and Andrews agreed to "furnish a good comfortable room at a rent of not exceeding ten dollars per month, and all the necessary tools, and machinery to make experiments for and *Construct* said apparatus, the tools not to exceed a cost of four hundred $400., and to pay a first class mechanic to be employed [by Edison] until said instruments shall be completed, not to exceed six months working time, and for the stock to be used in their construction and the incidental expenses pertaining thereto."[9] Five days later, Edison and William Unger, a Newark machinist, rented a room at 15 Railroad Avenue in Newark and established the Newark Telegraph Works. By the end of April they had spent the $400 for tools and machinery, and in May began experimental work on the facsimile telegraph. Although Edison experimented on and off for several years with facsimile telegraphs he did not patent a system until 1881. The Newark Telegraph Works, however, became a thriving enterprise and marked the beginning of Edison's career as an inventor-manufacturer.

Edison had probably been the one who insisted that the contract he signed included the provision regarding shop facilities. He had learned firsthand the importance of machine shops to the inventive enterprise during the year he spent in Boston. This lesson had been reinforced when he came to New York to test his double transmitter and found himself "awaiting the alterations of my instruments which on account of the piling up of jobs at the instrument makers have been delayed."[10] Throughout the rest of his career as a telegraph inventor, Edison made sure that his contracts for inventive work included support for manufacturing or laboratory machine shops. Edison was not the only telegraph inventor to recognize the importance of the machine shop. A number of his contemporaries also engaged in manufacturing. In addition to the income from their shops, they also enjoyed a readily available machine shop at no extra cost and without the wait time for service. Jesse H. Bunnell, whom Edison had known as an operator and with whom he worked on inventions in the winter of 1873–1874, was one of the most successful operators to travel the path of inventor-manufacturer. Another leading telegraph inventor, and one of Edison's main competitors, Elisha Gray, cofounded Western Electric Manufacturing Company.[11]

Even though Gold and Stock was now supporting Edison's work, other issues involved in his partnership with Pope and Ashley remained unresolved. In mid-March, to avoid patent infringement, they began negotiations with Gold and Stock, which agreed to acquire their patents and take over Financial and Commercial Telegraph's business operations. The agreement signed on April 30 included a new "gold printer" developed by Edison and Pope. In this instrument Edison and Pope incorporated lessons they had learned from their previous printers. Like Edison's other printing telegraphs, it was designed to run on one wire and incorporated a polar relay. In this case the relay switched the current between the typewheel and printing mechanisms and the machine's unison stop. Unlike the mechanical unison Edison had designed for the Laws printer, the one in the gold printer was electrical. As in the Financial and Commercial instrument the length of the signal determined whether the typewheel or the printing mechanism was activated, but Edison and Pope improved the design by shunting the circuit around the printing electromagnet so that it responded only to the long signals. The gold printer became an important instrument for Gold and Stock, which used it to report gold sales through the 1880s.[12]

The negotiations with Gold and Stock had been conducted with the company's new president, Marshall Lefferts. Lefferts's involvement in the American telegraph industry dated to 1849 when he had introduced Scotsman Alexander Bain's automatic telegraph into the United States. Lefferts was the general manager and chief engineer of American Telegraph Company at the time of its merger into Western Union, and he continued to serve as Western Union's chief engineer. He also became superintendent of Western Union's Commercial News Department. Although he was elected president of Gold and Stock in March 1870, Lefferts did not resign from Western Union until the following January. As president of Gold and Stock he was the leading figure in the development of the company's policy "to control all improvements which may present themselves and by the possession of which we can more surely control our business, perfect our system, extend its usefulness, and render it the most complete in the world."[13] This was part of a larger strategy aimed at controlling the market reporting business, and it was one of the first significant attempts by a corporation to control inventive work. It became an influential model in the telegraph industry, especially for Western Union, and was important to Edison's

own inventive career. To ensure Gold and Stock's control of his printing telegraph inventions, Edison sent Ashley to Boston to reacquire the rights to his
Boston printer from Hills and Plummer; these were assigned to Gold and Stock
as part of the company's contract with Pope, Edison & Company.[14]

At the time they signed this contract Lefferts had not yet made private-line
telegraphs part of his company's business, and Pope, Edison, and Ashley reserved for themselves the right to use their printers for this purpose. However,
they also made Lefferts president of their private-line business, which operated
as the American Printing Telegraph Company. Two other Gold and Stock directors were also involved in the business, which was incorporated in July
1870. In May Pope and Edison had begun developing another printer especially for this business. This printer incorporated features from their other
patented designs, and as was typical of Edison's printers, it employed a polarized relay that like the one in the Boston printer switched the signal between
typewheel and printing mechanism depending on the polarity of the transmitted current. However, the relay was in an independent circuit with the printing
magnet and a local battery. Each printer had two keys connected to it that
acted as transmitters. When an operator depressed the right-hand key, positive
currents were transmitted and moved a dial on the transmitting instrument that
worked in unison with the typewheel of the receiving printer. When the correct
character was reached, the operator depressed the left-hand key, which sent a
negative current and caused the polar relay to switch the signal into the local
battery circuit of the receiving instrument to activate its printing magnet. Because the battery was used only when the printer was in operation, it required
little strength and low maintenance. These were important advantages as the
printer was often used on private lines staffed by inexperienced operators. Although "comparatively slow" compared to other printing telegraphs, the American Printing Telegraph instrument was considered exceedingly simple in
design and was awarded first prize at the American Institute fair in New York
as the "Best Electric Printing Telegraph Instrument." The American Printing Telegraph Company, which began operating in earnest in November, was
equally successful. It provided private lines for a variety of businesses throughout the New York City region and began expanding to other cities, including
San Francisco. Lefferts soon decided that it would be to Gold and Stock's advantage to take over American Printing Telegraph.[15]

The buyout of American Printing Telegraph by Gold and Stock effectively
ended Edison's relationship with Pope and Ashley. Although his career had begun to blossom under their tutelage, the relationship had become increasingly
strained. The reasons for this are unclear, but probably grew out of Edison's independent work for Gold and Stock. Edison himself later claimed that

> In the sale of the Company for printing gold quotations, I was entitled to $1200,
> but Mr. Ashley thought that amount excessive, although his part was to be 20,000
> dollars profit, for which he did absolutely nothing. Thinking that perhaps I might
> not get anything at all, I told General Lefferts. . . . He said, say nothing, do noth-

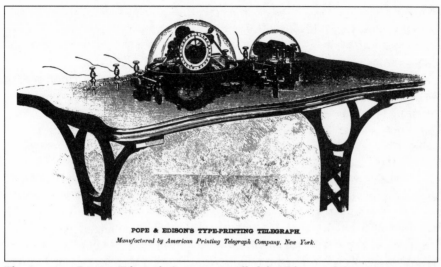

POPE & EDISON'S TYPE-PRINTING TELEGRAPH.
Manufactured by American Printing Telegraph Company, New York.

The American Printing Telegraph Company installed this Edison and Pope instrument on private lines. It had a dial indicator for use when transmitting and used a separate combined polarized and conventional relay to operate the instrument when receiving.

ing, leave it to me. When the deal went through, the General handed me $1500 and said that was my share, had saved it out when he made the payment.[16]

The actual purchase price for the gold printer was $15,000 and Edison's percentage is unclear. He also may have confused it with the buyout of American Printing Telegraph, from which Pope and Ashley each received 510 shares of capital stock in Gold and Stock while Edison received only 180. Whatever the cause of the break, it resulted in Ashley's banning Edison's name from the *Telegrapher* for several years. When he did again write of Edison, it was in a campaign of vituperation in which he denounced Edison as a "professor of duplicity and quadruplicity" who appropriated others' inventions as his own. Drawing on his own experience, Ashley claimed that "Every person who has had dealings heretofore with Edison knows that he is utterly unreliable, that it is a well known characteristic of his to systematically and deliberately 'go back' on every person who has ever endeavored to aid or cooperate in his inventions or business." Pope, too, became an opponent of Edison, frequently supporting other inventors' claims against his. Henry Van Hoevenbergh, a Gold and Stock employee, thought the rupture was caused by Edison's selling patents that were jointly owned by all three and remembered "hearing from various sources that Frank took up Mr Edison when he (Edison) was poor and even ragged and that Edison treated Frank with the grossest ingratitude."[17]

As Edison fell out with Pope and Ashley, he grew increasingly close to Marshall Lefferts, and as a former Gold and Stock employee recalled, Edison "was generally regarded" as Lefferts's protege.[18] Recognizing Edison's talents, Lefferts had encouraged his inventive work and was drawing him closer to Gold and Stock; in October 1870 he began negotiating for Edison's long-term service as company inventor. Until his death in 1876 Lefferts continued to be a primary influence in Edison's life and supported him in other enterprises as well. Lefferts was particularly important to Edison's education as an inventor, teaching him important lessons about the patent system and the role of patents as a business tool. Edison's style of patenting to "cover the field" was learned from Lefferts, whose policy of controlling the technology of printing telegraphy helped Gold and Stock to gain market dominance.

Lefferts further increased Edison's awareness of the patent system by introducing him to his patent attorney, Lemuel Serrell. An attorney for several leading telegraph inventors, Serrell had long been associated with Lefferts, and his father, William Serrell, had handled the original Bain automatic patents. The experienced patent solicitor taught the young inventor a particularly important lesson during their meeting on October 3, 1870. Under Serrell's watchful eye Edison made drawings and notes of several designs for printing and automatic telegraphs, batteries, polarized relays, and other electrical inventions on which he was working. Serrell informed him that such a record would be essential to defend his inventions in the patent office or in the courts, and Edison concluded his notebook with the statement that for "all new inventions I will here after keep a full record."[19]

Lefferts was also responsible for introducing Edison to Daniel Craig, who was becoming the principal promoter of high-speed automatic telegraph systems in the United States. Craig and other proponents of automatic telegraphs believed that these systems were faster, cheaper, and more accurate than the Morse key and sounder system. They argued that automatic machinery made it possible for them both to employ less skilled and, thus, cheaper operators, and to transmit at much higher speeds while producing a permanent recorded message that did not rely on the skill of the operator. Craig, who first became involved with automatic telegraphs in the 1850s while serving as president of Associated Press, believed that these advantages were particularly significant for the transmission of press copy. With lower labor costs and higher transmission speeds, he thought he would be able to send large amounts of news copy for significantly less than Western Union, which had helped to force him from the presidency of Associated Press in 1866. Craig hoped to use automatic telegraphy to wrest control over the transmission of press reports from Western Union and Associated Press.[20]

Craig had become interested with Lefferts in the automatic system of Englishman George Little. This was a chemical recording system based on the original 1846 design of Alexander Bain. In these systems, an operator used a specially designed perforating machine to punch holes representing Morse or other telegraph codes into a strip of paper. The transmitting operator then fed this strip into a high-speed transmitter. As the perforations passed rapidly under a metal stylus, the stylus would make electrical contact with a revolving drum,

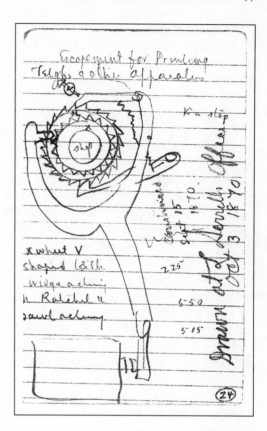

Edison drew this escapement
mechanism for printing telegraphs
at the office of his patent attorney
Lemuel Serrell in October 1870.

thus closing the circuit. This caused a series of rapid, intermittent signals to be transmitted to an automatic receiver at the other end of the line, which recorded a series of Morse dots and dashes when the electrical signals passed through a metal stylus and caused chemicals in specially treated recording paper to decompose. The receiving operator then translated the Morse code. Other automatic systems, notably the system devised by Englishman Charles Wheatstone and used extensively in Great Britain, employed ink recorders that were considerably slower than chemical recorders.[21]

Lefferts, whose association with automatic telegraphy dated to the beginnings of the telegraph industry, had become interested in Little's automatic in 1868 after Western Union refused to adopt it following a demonstration on the company's wires. However, the costs of introducing the system were greater than he could afford, and through Craig he had entered into negotiations with the National Telegraph Company, a nearly moribund rival of Western Union. Craig negotiated an agreement that would enable him to create a new competitor to Western Union to transmit press reports. Under its terms Craig became general agent of the National Company, although without salary "in regard to selling the capital stock negotiations with Editors and Proprietors of newspapers news agents." The company also agreed to make him a member of the board of directors if the system proved successful on a line between Washington and Boston that it would undertake to build. Furthermore, "the leading Editors of the Country" or their representatives would be added to the board if Craig furnished sufficient evidence to indicate that such an action would "insure the absorption by such Editors and their friends of not less than Four Millions of the Capital stock of the Company." If the Little system proved successful, Craig would have a powerful weapon to use against Associated Press and Western Union.[22]

Although both Craig's private correspondence and his public pronouncements indicated imminent success for the Little system, it was plagued by significant technical problems. The most critical problem was an effect commonly called tailing. Induced currents, set up when the circuit was broken and the line discharged, retarded and prolonged the signal. While imperceptible at moderate speeds, this effect distorted the recorded message at high speeds or long distances, as dots often appeared as dashes and dashes might cause the entire message to appear as a solid line. Another major difficulty was presented by the necessity of designing a perforator that was fast, reliable, and simple enough to be used by the unskilled operators who were considered essential for making automatic telegraphy cost-effective; Craig thought that young girls would provide the cheapest labor. Other necessary improvements included repeaters to allow for long-distance transmission and a means to enable messages to be dropped at intermediate offices. This last problem was particularly significant if the system was to service small-town newspapers.

Edison had begun working on an automatic transmitter, probably at Lefferts's behest, before he met Craig. A design for which he applied for a patent at the end of June was his first attempt to solve the tailing problem by mechanically switching in a battery as the perforated slip passed under the metal contact, thus reversing the polarity of the line current and discharging the wire.[23] Craig, however, was initially interested in having Edison develop a perforator to prepare the transmitting slips for the Little system, and on August 3 he contracted with Edison to

> devise and perfect a Perforating Apparatus, to be constructed of Iron and Steel, not to occupy a space exceeding twelve inches square, to have an extremely small number of pieces, to bring its reliability to the highest point possible with mechanism, to be capable of a speed of twenty-five words or more, per minute, according to the expertness of the writer, to space, write & punch mathematically accurate, to weigh not more than twenty pounds, to require no extraneous power, motor or force, but to work by the mere act of working. The cost, when manufactured in numbers, not to exceed fifty dollars.[24]

Meeting these specifications would prove very difficult. At the time, the fastest perforators only did ten words per minute, and only Leverett Bradley's patented design required no additional power source. For his efforts Edison was to re-

Edison's perforator for the automatic telegraph system.

ceive $1,300 in cash plus an additional $3,700 in stock of the National Telegraph Company and one-half of whatever Craig received for the sale of the invention.

Edison had a tremendous ability to gain the confidence of potential backers, and Craig was no exception. He soon began praising Edison's "superior talents" and assuring him that "your notes, like your confident face, always inspire us with new *vim*."[25] Craig's growing confidence in Edison soon led to discussions regarding additional improvements Edison might make to the Little system. On August 17 Craig agreed to furnish funds for Edison to develop a repeater design he thought suitable for the automatic system. Little himself thought there was considerable promise in Edison's repeater, which he thought worked even more rapidly than necessary, and urged him to "make the works substantial . . . so that the machine can be *relied upon* in Repeating offices."[26] Craig also proposed to Edison that he develop the "printer" (a form of typewriter) that Moses Farmer had suggested for transcribing automatic messages. Edison convinced Craig that he could develop such a machine by himself and began working on this as well. On at least three other occasions, when Craig came to Edison with printers or perforators designed by other inventors, Edison assured him that his own designs were better. Edison's self-confidence in his ability to beat out other inventors was later remarked upon by Edward Johnson, a longtime associate. As general manager of the Edison Speaking Phonograph Company in 1878, Johnson contemplated asking the company to provide him $500 for experiments to develop a standard instrument, but thought that "Edison would never allow me to pass him if he had to put every man in his employ on the Phonograph. I have seen him pushed to the wall in this way and with always one result—viz—his winning the race."[27]

More a promoter than a financier, Craig was better at putting other people's money at risk than his own and soon found a new investor to support Edison's work on automatic telegraphy. George Harrington, a former assistant secretary of the treasury under Lincoln, had become interested in telegraphy while serving as ambassador to Switzerland. Upon returning to the United States he became intrigued by Craig's vision for the future of automatic telegraphy; at the end of November he joined Craig and others in forming the Automatic Telegraph Company after agreeing to fund Edison's experiments in that line. Harrington's support for Edison came in the form of a partnership agreement signed on October 1, 1870. Under the terms of this agreement Harrington became Edison's partner in a new shop known as the American Telegraph Works, with Harrington supplying $6,000 of the shop's capital and Edison $3,000. The profits of the shop were to be divided in the same ratio. Except for inventions made for Gold and Stock, Edison bound himself "not to invent under said contract any machinery that will militate against automatic telegraphy." The status of Edison's inventions other than those for automatic telegraphy was ambiguous, although the agreement did state that "any original inventions or improvements that [Edison] may make, other than those such as may be suggested or arise from the current work in the manufactory" would entitle him to additional compensation.[28]

Edison's own investment in the American Telegraph Works included the machinery and tools of the Newark Telegraph Works, which turned over some of its manufacturing operations to the new, larger shop. Edison described his shops in a letter to his parents in late October and exulted in his improved circumstances: "I have a large amount of business to attend to. I have one shop which Employs 18 men, and am Fitting up another which will Employ over 150 men= I am now what 'you' Democrats call a 'Bloated Eastern Manufacturer.'"[29] Edison slightly exaggerated the size of the American Telegraph Works, but it was one of the larger electrical manufacturing firms in the country. By early December he was working "45 hands day and night" there on a variety of experimental and manufacturing work.[30]

Edison took advantage of the fact that he now had a backer with rather large pockets. Although the agreement establishing the American Telegraph Works called for Harrington to contribute $6,000, Edison spent rather more liberally for machinery. Hearing complaints about his heavy expenditures, Edison wrote letters of explanation to both Craig and Harrington on December 7. He told Craig that

I cannot take Ten thousand dollar contracts on Three thousand or four thousand worth of Machinery— The Manufacture of Mechanism is a Slow operation being legitimate, and all Legitimate Businesses they are slow but sure, and the *slower the more sure*. If Mr. H. feels dissatisfied, with the Expenditures (every cent which is represented in good sound solid and accurate machinery) I will sell some of my Stock coming to me from the American Printing Co and pay him for what he has spent or the excess over what he expected to pay.

To Harrington he explained that *"the money you are now paying is not for Machinery But for work on the Automatic System and on the Gold and Stock Contract of $7,500."*[31] These explanations apparently satisfied Harrington; within six months he had spent $16,000 equipping the shop and another $11,000 on Edison's experiments in automatic telegraphy.

Through the years, Edison would continue to be rather free with money supplied by his backers whenever they allowed him to spend what he believed necessary. Although they often complained about slow progress or large expenses, he seemed able to retain their confidence and to provide explanations that satisfied them. The explanations he offered to Harrington and Craig in his letters of December 7 for the inadequate performance of the perforator typified this. He explained that the machine, which had been taken apart for experiments, had not been entirely reassembled when Harrington came into the shop to inspect it. "But," he told Harrington, "it is of no consequence whether it worked or not. It was an experiment as I told you once before, not made to show but to Satisfy me that I was all right." And he furthermore explained to Craig that although "Mr H says that some of our experiments were useless . . . after he has had more experience in this business, he will find that *No experiments are useless.*"[32] Edison recognized that failed experiments often provided important insights during the research process, but Harrington and other backers were interested only in positive results.

Even if this difference in attitude created some tension between Edison and Harrington, Edison was working hard to get the shop off the ground and to make improvements in the automatic system. In his December 7 letter to Harrington he claimed that "I am attending to the shop from seven in the morning till one & two oclock next morning." The list of jobs he described to Craig was equally impressive:

Besides a thousand small details in the other room in the manufacture of 150 printing Machines= I have also in process of manufacture 12 Universal Printing Machines, a Regulating Temperature Machine Two other perforating Machines— a New screw slotting machine, A wire straightning Machine= Polishing Machine, and other things which also takes thinking.[33]

Included on this list were outside contracts, such as G. M. Sternberg's patented electromagnetic regulator for furnaces, but the important items were the experimental perforators being developed for automatic telegraphy and the printing telegraphs being manufactured for Gold and Stock.

Lefferts had just given Edison a manufacturing order for 150 "Cotton Instruments," a printer Edison was developing for the newly opened New York Cotton Exchange. Although Edison executed the patent application in January 1871, he did not begin production on the instruments until the spring. The cotton printer incorporated features from Edison's earlier designs, including a polarized relay. The instrument was briefly used on the cotton exchange, but its most important role was in further strengthening Gold and Stock's patent position as it incorporated a method that Edison had found to get around Calahan's basic patent for a two-typewheel instrument. He did this by mounting the two typewheels (one for numbers, the other for letters) on the same shaft and then using a cover over the paper strip and a sliding printing platen to shift between them when printing.[34]

The "12 Universal Printing Machines" being manufactured for Gold and Stock were experimental models of a private-line printer Edison had been working on since September. His work on this design was apparently spurred by a new private-line printer George Phelps had developed for Western Union, which included modifications for stock reporting. Western Union president William Orton was attempting to use Phelps's printer to expand the company's Commercial News Department into a potential rival to Gold and Stock. Lefferts, in turn, was hoping to use Edison's universal private-line printer to compete for commercial news as well as on circuits such as his proposed "Lawyers" line. To fend off competition from Western Union, Lefferts also began to introduce another Edison printer into Chicago to compete with lines recently opened there by the Commercial News Department. He did this surreptitiously, arranging through Edison to send Samuel Ropes to Chicago to establish a stock and grain quotation business. Within a short time Ropes had fifty subscribers, only twenty-five fewer than the Commercial News Department. Lefferts used Ropes's operation to open negotiations with Orton by telling him that Gold and Stock "had frightened Edison by representations of infringement of patents, &c, and that they could buy out what had been done at Chicago for a small sum." Lefferts then offered to sell the business to Western Union and also to discuss an arrangement between the two companies in regard to reporting business news. Orton agreed to acquire the Ropes operation from Lefferts because "it has seemed to me better that if this field [of business reports] must be occupied, the ability to control it should remain with us than to permit an alliance with the opposition."[35] By the beginning of January earnest negotiations were under way between the two companies on the rest of the market for business reports throughout the country.

It was during these negotiations with Gold and Stock that Orton became aware of Edison's rising reputation, and they may even have met in mid-January at the behest of Tracy Edson, a Gold and Stock director involved in the negotiations.[36] In Orton's view, Edison's work for Gold and Stock was an important asset to that company during the negotiations. In the same January letter in which he referred to the young inventor as a leading electromechanician,

Orton told Stager that he had learned that Edison was not only developing a new one-wire printer and new transmitter (probably the universal private-line printer) to compete with the Phelps instrument, but also that Gold and Stock

> have made a contract with Eddison, under which they are entitled to all his new inventions and improvements upon their present apparatus. It is highly probable, therefore, that the two companies do now, and will for a long time to come, control the most desirable inventions capable of performing the special service under consideration. In view of this fact, their claim to share equally with us in the profits of carrying on this business in other cities may not be unreasonable.[37]

Orton believed that Edison strengthened Gold and Stock's already strong patent position, which included all significant printing telegraph patents except Phelps's. As negotiations dragged into March, Orton also became concerned that Lefferts was pushing the Pope and Edison American Printing Telegraph instruments "in all quarters" while he began to "despair of ever getting enough" printers from Phelps "to demonstrate what we can do."[38] The two companies finally reached agreement on May 25. Western Union acquired majority control of Gold and Stock, which remained a separate company with Lefferts as president, and turned over both the Commercial News Department and Phelps's patents to its new subsidiary.[39]

With the Phelps patents, Gold and Stock now controlled all the important patents for market reporting and private-line telegraphs. To ensure its patent monopoly, the company also signed a new contract with Edison the following day. This agreement culminated negotiations that had been going on since October and formalized the arrangement that Orton believed had existed in January. The Gold and Stock committee that negotiated the contract with Edison considered it to be "a very advantageous one for the Company, receiving as it does the Co-operation and good will of Mr Edison for the future [and] acquiring the Universal Instrument for the Company for . . . all purposes at one half the price originally expected."[40] Edison and Lefferts had originally discussed a payment of $30,000 for the universal and even talked about $40,000, which is apparently the source of the story that Edison received the latter amount. Under the terms of the May 26 agreement he received $15,000 in stock for the universal private-line printer and another $20,000 in stock for all other inventions in printing telegraphs he had already made. Edison also became "consulting Electrician and Mechanician" for a period of five years at an annual salary of $2,000, with additional payments of $1,000 in any year during which Gold and Stock adopted one of his inventions.[41]

As Edison's role grew at Gold and Stock, he also became more important to the development of the automatic telegraph system. Although he was associated with Western Union, he gained additional support from its new competitor, the Automatic Telegraph Company. By March he was developing other components, including hand-cranked and power-driven transmitters and electrically and weight-driven ink recorders intended to supplement the faster chemical recorder for short lines, as well as the perforator, repeater, and copying printer (the typewriter for transcribing messages). By the end of the month, Edison's work had progressed to the point that Harrington began to plan a demonstration of the system. However, the expenses of supporting Edison's expanding efforts on automatic telegraphy soon led him to bring in other investors. Their October 1, 1870, agreement had a provision for a third partner that was initially intended for Craig. However, on May 10, 1871, Harrington instead signed an agreement bringing several other investors into the partnership. These investors included Josiah Reiff and William Mellen, who along with Harrington and Craig had incorporated the Automatic Telegraph Company on November 30, 1870. Their associates, railroad magnate William Palmer, iron manufacturer John McManus, and nurseryman Samuel Brown also joined the partnership. These new investors reimbursed Harrington $12,000 of the money he had already spent equipping the American Telegraph Works and supporting Edison's experiments, and they agreed to split half of any further expenses. Reiff would eventually become the most important of these partners, subsequently investing nearly $175,000 in automatic telegraphy and also becoming Edison's friend and advocate.[42]

Edison's jubilation over his growing stature as an inventor was tempered by the fact that he could not share it with his mother, who had died on April 9 after a long illness. The cause of her death is unclear, but her illness apparently deranged her mind. According to biographer Matthew Josephson, Thomas learned by telegram about Nancy's death on April 11 and promptly left for the funeral. Edison never talked about his mother's death, but he left no documents from the last half of April, suggesting that he did not return to work immediately. Whatever impact Nancy's death had on her son, it soon created an embarrassment for the family when Samuel began an affair with a local girl named Mary Sharlow, who eventually bore him three children.[43]

Whatever personal loss Edison may have felt, he was now well established in his professional life as the proprietor of two manufacturing shops with impressive facilities for experimental work. He also had substantial backing for his experiments from two major telegraph companies. Gold and Stock, with help from the deep pockets of Western Union, was paying him a substantial annual salary, supporting his experiments on printing telegraphs, and using his shops to manufacture printers. Perhaps anticipating increased orders, Edison and Unger moved the Newark Telegraph Works to larger quarters on Ward Street in Newark and renamed it Edison & Unger. Automatic Telegraph Company, which had taken over the lines and business of National Telegraph, provided an additional source of manufacturing contracts. In addition, investors in the company were providing Edison with both direct support for the American Telegraph Works and substantial sums for developing his own system of automatic telegraphy.

These arrangements were not without their drawbacks as Edison had to balance competing demands on his time and talents. This situation was further complicated by Western Union's takeover of Gold and Stock, which meant that he was now working for both the telegraph industry giant and one of its principal competitors. These competing interests were of particular concern to Daniel Craig, who, even before Edison signed his contract with Gold and Stock, wrote Lefferts to complain that Edison "says you keep him stirred up all the time with a sharp stick—just as though your trumpery gold reporting was of any importance along side of our operations. I respectfully *protest* against your going over the North River [to Newark], or sending a Letter in that direction for the next *four weeks*. I never have any trouble with Edison except when you stick in your oar—*keep it out*."[44] For Lefferts, whose interest in automatic telegraphy had become secondary to Gold and Stock, this was of little concern. And for Edison, any concerns over the source of his funding were overshadowed by his new opportunity to focus on what he most enjoyed—inventing.

CHAPTER 5

Competing Interests

Even though he was working under contract to corporate sponsors, Edison was able to take advantage of the competitive high tech environment of the 1870s telegraph industry to carve out a large degree of personal independence. The fact that the corporate world in which he worked was still relatively informal helped him to do so. General incorporation acts had been enacted only since the 1850s, and the nation's few large-scale corporations, primarily Western Union and a few railroads, were only starting to develop the kind of sophisticated bureaucracies that have come to characterize the modern corporation. Moreover, corporations were just beginning to develop strategies on invention and innovation. Marshall Lefferts's policy to control crucial technology for Gold and Stock was well ahead of that of most of his contemporaries. Furthermore, because invention in the nineteenth century was generally believed to be a product of the unpredictability of individual inventive genius, personal relationships between corporate managers and inventors were considered crucial to the success of any corporate strategy affecting invention. Both of these factors—competition and personal relationships—were important in Edison's career as a telegraph inventor.

Edison's ability to attract the attention of competing telegraph interests helped to bring him both independence and substantial resources. At the same time, his seeming lack of concern for conflicts of interest and a rather cavalier attitude toward the interests of his associates when they conflicted with his own caused his personal reputation to suffer even as his reputation as an inventor continued to grow. Frank Pope and James Ashley were not the only ones who found Edison "utterly unreliable" in his personal dealings. Although he had great respect for Edison's inventive talents, Western Union president William Orton also came to believe that he had "a vacuum where his conscience ought to be."[1]

During the summer following his new arrangements with Gold and Stock and Automatic Telegraph, Edison did take care to try to define both their interests and his own in a series of four notebooks that he began using between July 24 and August 5. Edison intended the entries he made in these books to be official records "to be used in any contest or disputes regarding priority of ideas or inventions." He also employed them to define the limits of his work for Gold and Stock and Automatic Telegraph. Thus, on the first page of his book devoted to Gold and Stock, Edison reserved for himself "any ideas contained in this book which I do not see fit to give said G & Stock Telegraph." Similarly, another notebook contained a "Record of Ideas as they occur day by day applicable and for the Dot and Dash system of fast Telegraphy invented for Geo Harrington and D H Craig." A third was reserved for a "Dot and Dash and Automatic Printing Translating System, Invented for myself exclusively, and not for any small brained capitalist." The last of the four notebooks, contained "ideas conceived, and experiments tried on miscellaneous Machines and things"— ideas that Edison did not specifically reserve either for himself or for his employers. However, even in this notebook, he carefully noted potential conflicts, for example, a discussion of chemical recorder designs where he indicated one "device I do not consider fast and not applicable to Automatic or fast telegraphy, but that shown in another figure is."[2]

Although Edison found it necessary to take some care in juggling his own interests and those of the investors paying for his inventive work, working on multiple projects stimulated him. Indeed, this trait became a hallmark of his inventive style as ideas and devices from one experiment or design influenced another. Furthermore, if he reached a dead end on one project he found it useful to "just put it aside and go at something else; and the first thing I know the very idea I wanted will come to me. Then I drop the other and go back to it and work it out."[3]

A related characteristic was Edison's tendency to conceive seemingly endless variations in the design for a particular device. Edward Dickerson, a Western Union attorney, later described him as possessing a "remarkable kaleidoscopic brain. He turns that head of his and these things come out as in a kaleidoscope, in various combinations, most of which are patentable."[4] This tendency was doubtless encouraged by his association with Marshall Lefferts, who appreciated the ways in which the patent system enabled Gold and Stock to control the field of printing telegraphy by acquiring all of the key patents on that technology, but it was also typical of Edison's own method of technological problem solving. His early notebooks often contain the statement "I do not wish to confine myself to any particular device." These words to Edison were not only a legalistic phrase associated with the patent system, but also corresponded to his pattern of sketching numerous alternative solutions to a particular problem. A typical example can be found in a notebook entry from the summer of 1871 that included several alternative designs for mechanical paper feeds for the system of automatic telegraphy he reserved to himself. Another entry in the same notebook not only described the device he intended to use for translating perforated or embossed automatic messages into roman letters, but also contained a comment that nicely characterizes this aspect of his inventive style. Above his sketch of one such device (which itself drew heavily on his printing telegraph designs) Edison wrote, "I do not wish to confine myself to any particular Translating Printing Machine, as I have innumerable machines in my Mind."[5]

Much of Edison's work on both automatic and printing telegraphy during this period focused on mechanical design. Because stock-tickers and private-line printers were operated by a wide range of users with little electrical know-how, they needed to be simple to operate. As a result, mechanical designs were often as important and sometimes even more crucial than electrical arrangements for ensuring the reliability of a printer. In automatic telegraphy much of Edison's work also centered on mechanical elements intended to make the machinery easy to use so that skilled telegraphers could be replaced with cheaper, unskilled operators. "You captivate my whole heart," Daniel Craig told Edison, "when you speak of making machines which will require 'No Intelligence.' That's the thing for *Telegraphers.*"[6] Although he was a former operator, Edison believed in the virtues of automatic machinery as a valuable tool for increasing corporate profits. He also assumed, as did many nineteenth-century technological enthusiasts, that it could lessen the burdens on working people by making their labor easier and increase their living standard by reducing the cost of goods.

Edison's great facility with mechanical components was an essential aspect of his technical creativity. The notebooks from this period are filled with experimental designs in which various kinds of mechanical escapements played an important role. The skill with which he manipulated these mechanical elements was a product of both hard study and native genius; for example, in February 1872 he filled a notebook with over one hundred designs.[7] This dictionary of escapements included Edison's own variations, as well as many of the standard designs reproduced in such works as the guide for inventors published by patent agents Munn and Company, who also published *Scientific American*. Further evidence of the mechanical character of Edison's telegraph designs can be found in his draft of a book on telegraphy, written during the winter 1873–1874, in which he planned to present the results of his many years of experiments in the field. One chapter (of which there are several extensive drafts) was devoted almost entirely to mechanical movements used in breakwheels, and another focused on printing telegraphs, whose designs were extensively influenced by their mechanical elements. Even chapters on the basic electrical actions of different telegraph systems and devices were titled "Electrical Movements" and "Miscellaneous Movements," suggesting that Edison, who considered "a logical mind that sees analogies" to be an essential quality of an inventor, conceptualized electrical effects as analogous to mechanical motion.[8]

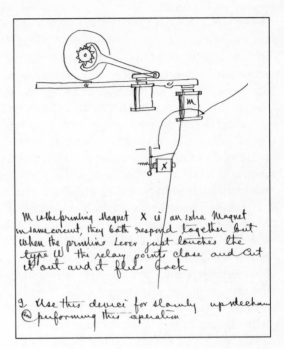

In this printing telegraph design Edison added an extra relay magnet, X, that responded when the printing magnet, M, was activated in order to more quickly cut off the current from the printing magnet.

Edison's electromechanical approach was typical of telegraph inventors. Indeed, the practice was so widespread that James Reid, a telegraph official and journalist, felt compelled to point out Elisha Gray's contrasting style in his historical account of *The Telegraph in America*: "Mr. Gray's characteristic as an inventor is in avoiding mere mechanical devices to accomplish results. . . . He seeks to make electricity do its work direct."[9] Yet even Gray devoted much of his attention to electromechanical designs for printing telegraphs and other instruments. And his inventive work took place within the confines of machine shop practice at Western Electric. The design process used by Edison, Gray, and other inventors involved a close interaction with skilled experimental machinists in constructing, testing, and altering designs. The same skilled machinists whom Edison employed in his early manufacturing shops accompanied him to his later laboratories where they continued to play a crucial role in turning his multitude of ideas into practical working apparatus. Electromechanical design factors reinforced the already extensive influence of mechanical technology and American machine shop practice in telegraph invention.

The manufacturing activities at his shops provided Edison additional insights that he used in the process of invention and innovation. Frequently new technical problems that he had not initially envisioned arose during manufacturing or when customers tried to use the products. Information from the marketplace and the manufacturing shop, therefore, were crucial for making the kind of incremental improvements that were necessary for successful innovation. Edison's attention to such details helps to explain the extraordinary number of patents (1,093) issued to him during his career. Only a few were for the revolutionary inventions that made his reputation; most were for minor improvements that made these inventions more commercially viable. Indeed, much of Edison's career as a telegraph inventor was devoted to just such improvements of his own and others' basic inventions. What set him apart from most other inventors was the range of different technologies that he tackled and the fertility with which he conceived alternative designs.

Edison's work for Gold and Stock exemplifies this aspect of his work as an inventor-manufacturer. His most important contributions to printing telegraphy were the typewheel-shifting mechanism he had developed for the cotton instrument and a screw-thread unison he devised in May 1871. Because all of the market-reporting printers on a line were operated by a single transmitter at the exchange, synchronizing them so that they printed the same information created a special technical problem. Printers frequently fell behind the transmitter by one or more letters, making the message useless to the customer. As a result, exchange companies had to send employees to the office where the printer was running out of "unison" to reset it. This led to the development of automatic mechanical means to solve the problem. One of the most effective and longest used devices was Edison's screw-thread unison. In this design, Edison seated a peg in a screw-thread on the typewheel shaft. The peg moved to one side when the typewheel turned, and when the printing magnet was charged the peg was lifted and returned to its starting point by a spring. When the printing magnet was not charged, the peg continued moving until the arm holding it hit a stop on the typewheel, which arrested the rotation of the shaft. In this way, the transmitting operator could bring all the printers on a line into unison by sending sufficient impulses to turn the shaft of each machine until the peg hit the stop, and then by charging the printing magnet to bring their typewheels into unison.[10]

Edison continued to make other improvements of this kind for Gold and Stock printers. For example, on January 8, 1872, he wrote in his Gold and Stock notebook, "I am requested by General Lefferts to invent a peculiar unison for what is known as the Callahan 3 wire instrument."[11] His unison designs involved various combinations of escapements, sliding bars, and other mechanical elements. Other improvements described in these notebooks also relied heavily on his understanding of mechanical elements. For example, in an entry dated January 13 he described

a dead motion in a Star or wedge acting escapement for the purpose of giving the printing lever time to get away from The type wheel before it starts & not blurring the letter. I believing myself the first one who discovered or used this method,

Edison's Universal stock printer incorporated his new unison (at left) and typewheel-shifting mechanism (at right). From the Collections of Henry Ford Museum & Greenfield Village (Neg. B99251).

other parties (Phelps and Grey & Barton) using devices for throwing their printing levers to the type wheel & then quickly back they [the other inventors] not knowing they [these devices] are wholly unnecessary providing there is a slight dead motion in their Escapement which there generally is.[12]

Edison also continued to devise new printers for the company. The most important of these was the Universal stock printer he was in the process of developing when he signed his five-year contract with Gold and Stock. This machine was a greatly modified version of his cotton instrument. Commercial use of the earlier printer had suggested several modifications, some of which Edison incorporated. However, he also decided to design a new machine whose prototype he delivered to Gold and Stock at the beginning of June 1871. The new design included an improvement in his typewheel-shifting mechanism that reduced friction and that combined with a new paper-feed mechanism to greatly reduce the power required to charge the printing lever magnet.

As a result, battery life was greatly increased on circuits incorporating these instruments. As he worked on the new printer Edison made further refinements in the screw-thread unison and redesigned the printer magnets and shaft mountings to make them adjustable. These adjustable mountings meant that parts could be made interchangeable, and the company warned its service personnel not to "attempt to file, bend or tinker with the different parts of the instrument, as they are interchangeable and accurately made, and if any part should in time get defective, supply it with a new one which will be furnished from the New York Office." By the end of the year, Edison delivered 600 Universal stock printers. In 1872 he produced another 600 and by late 1874, he had manufactured nearly 3,600 of the printers, which had become a fixture on Gold and Stock lines.[13]

Over the course of its manufacturing history, the Universal stock printer continued to undergo modification as practical experience led Edison to make further improvements in its design. One of the most important improvements was the transmitter he designed for circuits using the printer. Initially, a hand-cranked breakwheel had been used, but in December 1871 Edison produced a new transmitter. Instead of indicating letters by turning a dial, an operator pressed the letters on a keyboard, a feature Edison had grown increasingly familiar with in his designs for automatic perforators and private-line printers. The transmitter was run by an electric motor controlled by a governor he had designed initially for automatic telegraphy. Edison was not alone in developing a keyboard transmitter. Patrick Kenny, Gold and Stock's superintendent of manufacturing, and George Scott, who became the company's general superintendent in 1872, also designed them. Kenny's transmitter looked like a dial telegraph, with the individual keys arranged in a circle, and Scott's keyboard looked very much like that of a piano. Edison's more elegant design had two rows of keys placed in a semi-circle around the electric motor.[14]

Edison's Gold and Stock notebook from the second half of 1871 and the first two months of 1872 was filled with other proposed design changes for the Universal stock-ticker. Many of these found their way into patent applications during the first half of 1872. Indeed, the first six months of that year marked one of the most productive patenting periods of his career, with twenty-eight successful applications, two-thirds of them for printing telegraphs. Most of these related to his Universal stock printer, which he also used as the printing portion of a new Universal private-line printer he developed during the spring. His notebook entries also show that Edison believed that a number of his improvements in the Universal stock and private-line printers could be adapted to other printers as well.

One aspect of his work for Gold and Stock that Edison could legally reserve was foreign rights for his patents. However, some of the men connected with Gold and Stock had ambitions to introduce stock printers overseas, and they organized the Exchange Telegraph Company in London in March 1872 to provide service from the London Stock Exchange. Elisha Andrews had begun negotiations toward this end in 1870, and with George Field and Marshall Lefferts he had begun to organize a stock reporting service in June 1871. At that time Field and Andrews, acting as importers of the instrument, also applied for a British patent on Edison's cotton printer. When they organized Exchange Telegraph they also applied for a British patent on his new Universal private-line printer. Once the company began operating in June 1872, they equipped its lines with Edison's Universal stock printers. Edison manufactured these instruments and also worked to develop a transmitter for the Exchange Telegraph system.[15]

Although his printing telegraph inventions were controlled by Gold and Stock and its officers, Edison apparently arranged with the company to use one of his printers, possibly the Universal stock printer, to start his own telegraphic news service in Newark, New Jersey. Known as the News Reporting Telegraph Company, the business was started by Edison and his manufacturing partner William Unger to provide "general news of the world—financial, commercial, domestic and foreign—the moment such news is received in the main Telegraph Office in New York, and several hours in advance of all newspapers."[16] Little is known of the company's operations, but Edison probably arranged with Gold and Stock to transmit commercial news to the News Reporting office located in the *Daily Advertiser* building in Newark, which also housed a Western Union office.

This venture, which operated only from mid-October to the end of December 1871, was short-lived, but it proved very significant in Edison's life. One of the company's employees was a sixteen-year-old Newark girl named Mary Stilwell, whom Edison married on Christmas Day 1871. An account of their brief courtship appeared many years later:

One day, when standing behind the chair of one of his female *employees*, Miss Ma[r]y Stilwell, that young lady suddenly turned round and exclaimed, "Mr. Edison, I can always tell when you are behind or near me." "How do you account for that?" mechanically asked Mr. Edison, still absorbed in his work. "I don't know, I am sure," she answered; "but I seem to feel when you are near me." "Miss Stilwell," said Mr. Edison, turning round now in his turn and looking the lady in the face, "I've been thinking considerably of you of late, and if you are willing to have me I'd like to marry you." "You astonish me," exclaimed Miss Stilwell. "I—I never—" "I know you never thought I would be your wooer," interrupted Mr. Edison, "but think over my proposal, Miss Stilwell, and talk it over with your mother." Then he added, in the same off-hand, business-like way, as though he might be experimenting upon a new mode of courtship, "Let me know as early as possible, as if you consent to marry me, and your mother is willing we can be married by next Tuesday." This was the extent of Mr. Edison's courtship. The lady laid the abrupt proposal before her mother, and next day informed her lover of the maternal consent. "That's all right," said Mr. Edison, in reply. "We will be married a week from to-day." And so they were. The two were married a week and a day from the beginning of Mr. Edison's novel and precipitate courtship.[17]

Edison's first wife, Mary Stilwell
Edison, at age 16.

Mary was the daughter of a Newark sawyer and inventor named Nicholas
Stilwell and his second wife, Margaret Crane Stilwell. Little is known of the
Stilwell family, but it would not have been unusual for a sixteen-year-old
working-class girl to have found employment to supplement the family's income. Like other daughters of the working class, Mary may well have considered telegraphy to be one of the more desirable occupations open to her.[18] By
catching the boss's eye, however, it became possible for her to quit working,
which was the expectation for many women in Victorian society. The twenty-
four-year-old Edison's rising status as an inventor and manufacturer not only
made him an attractive husband, but also offered her the possibility of advancement into the middle class.

After a brief honeymoon in Boston, where he no doubt introduced his
bride to old friends, Thomas and Mary established housekeeping in the home
Edison had purchased for $5,500 on November 21. Located at 53 Wright Street

in Newark, it was one of a series of row houses located in a nice residential neighborhood near the trolley line. With his newfound wealth, Thomas was able to spend around $2,000 to furnish the house, including a piano, to hire servants, and to buy Mary a wardrobe.

Although Mary could manipulate the telegraph instruments used in Edison's news reporting business, he was soon disappointed to find that she showed little aptitude for understanding his work as an inventor. His disappointment was expressed in a notebook entry of February 1, 1872, where he noted that "Mrs Mary Edison My wife Dearly Beloved Cannot invent worth a Damn!" Two weeks later, on Valentine's Day, he again commented, *"My Wife Popsy Wopsy Can't Invent."*[19] Edison's critique of Mary's ability as an inventor most likely concerned her lack of interest in his work rather than any expectation on his part that she would actually be involved in it. For her part, Mary was doubtless dissatisfied with Edison's tendency to work at night and to spend long hours away from home in his shop or laboratory. Although little is known of their intimate relations, this disparity of interests doubtless created some tension during their marriage.

The establishment of the news reporting business in October 1871 was not the only evidence of Edison's streak of independence. At the end of the month Edison left the American Telegraph Works, taking many of the workmen and some of the machinery with him to the Edison & Unger shop on Ward Street. The cause of Edison's split with Harrington is unclear, but appears likely to have been caused by a challenge to his authority over work in the shop when Harrington appointed S. M. Clark as superintendent of American Telegraph Works in place of N. W. Towne, whom Edison had placed in charge of the shop in May. Harrington had become disenchanted with Towne's constant promises to "have one of the large perforators done 'next week'" and questioned what he was doing with twenty or so workmen and $400 to $500 per week.[20] The fault was probably Edison's rather than Towne's. Throughout his career Edison frequently continued to refine his designs even as they were in the process of manufacture, thus delaying commercial production. Although both Harrington and Craig kept urging him to complete a model for manufacturing the fifty perforators they had ordered in March, Edison continued to modify the design to overcome continuing alignment and reliability problems. Maybe Harrington recognized that Edison rather than Towne was the problem and wanted his own superintendent who was not responsible to the inventor.

Daniel Craig also found himself increasingly frustrated by Edison's interminable inventing. Throughout the winter and spring of 1871 Craig had vigorously supported Edison's efforts to develop perforators and printers for the automatic system and also encouraged him to develop his "Domestic" telegraph, a central station signaling system intended to compete with James Ashley's new American Burglar Alarm Company. On February 13 Craig had even written Edison that "if you should tell me you could *make babies by machinery,* I should'nt

The Edison & Unger employees with Edison's Universal stock printer and private-line printer. Charles Batchelor sits next to the private-line printer (at left).

doubt it."[21] Nevertheless, Craig, too, found it necessary to complain about the slow pace of manufacturing. In April he expressed dismay at the prospect of an additional three-month delay and by June was becoming so exasperated that he implored the inventor to tell him "when are you going to have something to *show* in the way of the new Perforator & Printer."[22]

Edison had his own frustrations with the conflicting demands of manufacturing and inventing at American Telegraph Works. As the partner charged with the day-to-day running of the shop he found himself concerned with routine business affairs and complained to Harrington in July that "I cannot stand this worrying much longer about Bills—Pay roll etc= it engrosses my attention to the detriment of the machinery *You cannot expect a man to invent & work night and day, and then be worried to a point of exasperation about how to obtain money for bills.*"[23] Edison later claimed that "I kept no books. I had two hooks, all the bills and accounts I owed I jabbed on one hook and memorandum of all I owed to myself I put on the other."[24] In fact, he did keep careful accounting records. Furthermore, although records of accounts payable, accounts receivable, and weekly wages were typically all that most shop proprietors kept at the time, Edison also developed a system of accounts for the most important cost associated with his inventive work—the labor of his skilled machinists. Keeping such accounts was important for charging his experimental costs to the appropriate company, although he was always willing to use resources provided by one company to work on inventions for another. These labor cost accounts also allowed him to evaluate how effectively he was using his resources on a particular project.

A few months after complaining to Harrington about his worries over bills Edison left their manufacturing partnership. Although Harrington was upset by this and believed that Edison had used his money to furnish the Ward Street shop, their mutual self-interests in the fate of automatic telegraphy caused him to continue a largely cordial business relationship with Edison, and he later helped Edison expand his manufacturing operations at Ward Street. After leaving American Telegraph Works Edison devoted his manufacturing activities to the large orders given to Edison & Unger by Gold and Stock. Probably to help with overflow work from these orders, Edison joined with former American Telegraph Works machinist Joseph Murray, who also assisted Edison with his experiments, to establish Murray & Co in February 1872. Six months later, Edison decided to consolidate his two shops. At the beginning of July he took out a $10,000 mortgage and bought out Unger by giving him notes worth $7,100. He and Murray then moved the operations of Murray's shop to Ward Street and established Edison & Murray. Although the buyout of Unger created some financial pressures for the new firm, causing them to delay the payment of bills and give notes to creditors, they were able to expand their manufacturing operations at the beginning of 1873 by arranging with Harrington to acquire the business and machinery of the American Telegraph Works, which had continued to make instruments for Automatic Telegraph.[25]

As Edison sought greater independence as a manufacturer, his inventive work in automatic telegraphy also took on a more independent aspect than either Harrington or Craig had anticipated. Initially hired by them to develop a practical perforator and printer, by the summer of 1871 he increasingly devoted his energies to exploring ideas for new systems of automatic telegraphy. By October, as delays continued to plague the production of the promised perforator and printer, Craig found it necessary to write Edison and urge him not to

hold the wire a moment beyond what is necessary for you to test your Perforator & Printer. We have absolutely perfect Transmitting & Recording devices, and at the present moment it will make serious trouble with Little, if he sees an effort being made to supplant him in what he justly regards as a discovery of the means of very rapid & correct Telegraphing. We cannot afford to have any wrangling. By and by it will be in order to make improvements in the Little System—but we are now in too much haste for *practical work*, to afford even one hour for any unnecessary tests. Give us perforations & plain Print. There is glory enough in that for a lifetime.[26]

By the following May Craig became even more concerned because Edison's efforts on behalf of Gold and Stock seemed both to be taking precedence over his work for Automatic Telegraph, and to draw him into closer association with Western Union. He appealed to Lefferts to "get Edison into such a position that he will work to promote our interests rather than the interests of our opponents, actual or possible, and I should esteem the situation *very much safer* if you could so manage him as to get his interests where you could fix their account and keep him faithful to our side in any & every contingency."[27] Craig's concerns over Edison's loyalty to the Automatic Telegraph interests were not without foundation. Although Lefferts retained a stake in automatic telegraphy and may have felt some interest in aligning Edison's work for Gold and Stock with his work for Automatic Telegraph, his primary concern remained the business of Gold and Stock. And Edison's own ambitions and inventive interests were much broader than those envisioned by Craig.

Within a few months of Craig's letter to Lefferts Edison had begun again to turn his attention to duplex telegraphy. His renewed interest in this technology was spurred by Western Union's adoption earlier in the year of Joseph Stearns's improved duplex system. Western Union had adopted the invention after several months of experiments that radically improved the system's effectiveness through the addition of a condenser to overcome the effects of "static return discharge." The condenser, which accumulated and stored an electric charge, was placed in an artificial line that matched the electrostatic capacity of the main line to counteract the effect of the static discharge and prevent the receiving relay from responding to outgoing signals. The Stearns duplex allowed Western Union to nearly double the capacity of the wires on which it was used. This substantially reduced the need for new wires, thus saving both construction and maintenance costs. Even more important, in the opinion of president William Orton, the duplex also allowed the company to temporarily increase the capacity of a line when wires failed or when particularly heavy traffic taxed the capacity of a line being worked in one direction only. Duplexing also allowed the company to better serve tourist resorts, which needed extensive communications facilities only during certain seasons. Orton soon came to view the Stearns duplex as the most important improvement in telegraphy since Morse's original invention.[28]

During the fall of 1872, as Edison began to conduct experiments on duplex telegraphy with his assistant James Brown, he approached Orton about the possibility of gaining support from the company for his research. Already familiar with Edison's ability to devise ingenious variations on existing technology for Gold and Stock, the Western Union president encouraged him to pursue these efforts but made no promises of support. Orton was kept abreast of Edison's work by Norman Miller, the secretary and treasurer of Gold and Stock, who had become friends with Edison and now acted as their intermediary. By the end of January 1873 Edison's experiments had produced sufficient enough results for him to write Miller, "I have struck a new vein in duplex telegraph; 'no balance' works well enough in shop to order set made. Think t'will be success." He also told Miller, "My shop is so full of non-paying [i.e. experimental] work that I should like to saddle this on W.U. shop, where they are used to it." Orton responded positively on February 6, telling Miller "that I am ready to treat for [Edison's] duplex, and that he may set it up in our office at any time."[29]

This decision resulted in a series of meetings between the Western Union president and the inventor that led to an informal agreement of support for Edison's duplex experiments. As Edison had suggested to Miller, Orton agreed to let the Western Union shop run by George Phelps make his experimental duplexes, and he also allowed him to test his instruments over the company's wires by providing a loop circuit between New York and Boston. Edison in return gave the company the right to purchase any of his patented duplex designs. Because this arrangement was never formalized into a written contract, it ultimately depended on the personal understanding between Edison and Orton. Orton would come to regret his failure to secure Edison's services with a formal written contract.

The Western Union president initially hired Edison to, in the inventor's words, invent duplexes "as an insurance against other parties using them—other lines."[30] Orton later explained to Joseph Stearns that

> I became apprehensive that processes for working Duplex would be devised which would successfully evade your patents, and also that your [Stearns's] attorneys had not done their work in shutting out competitors, as might have been done. I therefore, sent for Edison, and after several conferences and much discussion with him, I employed him to invent as many processes as possible for doing all or any part of the work covered by your patents. The object was to anticipate other inventors in new modes and also to patent as many combinations as possible.[31]

Nonetheless, when Edison asked the Western Union president whether "he should avoid any infringement of the Stearns' patent," Orton replied that it "would be just as valuable, in my opinion, if he could make improvements upon the Stearns' which could be successfully used . . . to make independent inventions."[32]

Edison took a significantly different approach from the one most commonly employed by those working on duplex telegraphy. Most other inventors sought to balance the relay electrically at the transmitting station to prevent it from responding to incoming signals. Edison instead used a neutral relay at one end to respond to variations in current strength and the familiar polarized relay at the other end to respond to changes in the polarity of the current. In developing designs that would not interfere with Stearns's patents, Edison also tried using extra resistance and additional electromagnets in place of condensers to overcome the effects of static discharge.

During their negotiations, Edison had boasted, as Orton remembered it, that "the business of making a duplex [w]as a very trifling affair; he said he could make a dozen, and I think he said he could make me a bushel, and that they were of no sort of account particularly."[33] He was able to back up this boast; by mid-February he had devised seventeen different designs for both duplexes (sending two signals in opposite directions) and diplexes (sending them in the same direction). One of these included his first ideas for combining a duplex and diplex to send four messages at once, two in each direction. A month later Edison reported that he had tried "with make-shift instruments, seven duplex, between New York and Boston. Six of them worked charmingly. The seventh was a satisfactory failure. I have fifteen more to try."[34] In fact, by the beginning of April he had "tried twenty-three duplex systems; nine were failures, four partial success, and ten were all right; one or two worked rather bad, but the principle is good, and if they were to be used could be improved in detail; eight were good, one of which requires no special instruments. . . . Ten models for different duplex have been delivered to Munn & Co., patent solicitors."[35]

It is not known why Edison had his duplex patent applications prepared by Munn & Company, the patent solicitors connected with *Scientific American*. It may be that Serrell's connection with the Automatic Telegraph interests made Edison wary of using him for the Western Union work. However, he found Munn & Company ill prepared to handle sophisticated electrical patents. The applications prepared by the firm were so poorly drawn up that neither Edison nor the patent examiner could understand them. The Patent Office initially rejected all of these applications, and one particularly crucial application was granted only after significant amendments. Edison's subsequent work for Western Union would be handled by Serrell, who had special knowledge of electrical patents.[36]

While Edison sought to keep his work for Automatic Telegraph separate from that for Western Union, he and Orton did discuss the relative merits of duplex and automatic telegraphy. According to Orton, Edison "was strongly inclined to put the automatic process very much ahead of the duplex; and from his point of view, he thought duplex could be ground out with great rapidity."[37] The Western Union president, however, was strongly opposed to automatic telegraphy. His primary objection went to the heart of automatic's greatest potential advantage—its much higher transmission speed. Orton felt this could be an advantage only when transmitting long messages such as news stories or by combining several short business messages together. However, he particularly objected to delaying business messages until a sufficient number had accumulated to send them by automatic. He felt that the shorter time needed to prepare and transcribe an ordinary, individual message transmitted by the Morse system made it more advantageous for common messages.[38] Furthermore, unlike Craig and other promoters of automatic telegraphy, who believed the automatic could advantageously employ cheap, unskilled labor, Orton argued that "the telegraph will never run itself. Human intervention will always be necessary to some extent. The errors which, it seems to me, dreamers upon these subjects fall into, result from the attempt to treat ideas, and the intangible processes of their transmission to a distant point, as physical things to be disposed of in bulk by the application of mechanism and power."[39] In Orton's view even automatic telegraphy required skilled operators to prevent errors during message preparation and translation. Finally, from his perspective as Western Union president, he believed that automatic telegraphy would require extensive investment in complicated and expensive instruments, whereas duplex telegraphy allowed the company to continue using inexpensive Morse instruments with little additional cost. The diametrically opposed views held by the Western Union president and those connected with Automatic Telegraph probably explains why neither side felt it necessary to prevent Edison's work on improvements that might benefit the other. Each believed that the technical superiority of their system would drive the other from the field.

Automatic Telegraph finally began to compete with Western Union on December 14, 1872, when it opened its line between New York and Washington. As Orton presumed, the company used skilled operators, who proved essential to the proper working of the automatic system during the entire period of its commercial use. Up to the point of commercial introduction, Edison's most significant contribution to the automatic system had been his perforator, which incorporated an arrangement, first suggested by Craig, in which a dash signal was generated by the combination of a long hole punched next to and overlapping two small holes. Automatic Telegraph may also have adopted one of Edison's printer designs, and it is likely that he also altered the company's transmitters and receivers to allow them to work better with his perforator. By the time Automatic Telegraph general superintendent Edward Johnson began preparing the line for commercial operation during the fall of 1872, Edison had also begun to turn his attention to the persistent electrical problems that still plagued transmission over long lines—most notably tailing.[40]

Transmission difficulties in automatic telegraphy presented some of the same issues as those involved in multiple telegraphy, and Edison's experiments in duplex and automatic overlapped to some extent. In both systems he employed a variety of electromagnets, induction coils, rheostats, batteries, and condensers in shunt circuits. During the winter and spring some of the arrangements developed for his duplex experiments began to find their way into his automatic circuit designs, and he even designed a duplex automatic. Of particular significance was a system of line balancing that he patented in which an artificial line at the receiving end had a resistance equal to that of the transmission line. By empirically adjusting a rheostat in the artificial line, he was able to place the receiver at a neutral point or "center of resistance" between the two lines.[41]

Edison's experiments in automatic telegraphy required new funding, and on November 5, 1872, Josiah Reiff, who had become the secretary of Automatic Telegraph, agreed that he would personally provide Edison with an annual salary of $2,000 "in Consideration of the special attention now being given & to be Continued in the interests of automatic telegraphy" by the inventor. This agreement was an addition to the Edison-Harrington partnership agreement of October 1870, which had established the American Telegraph

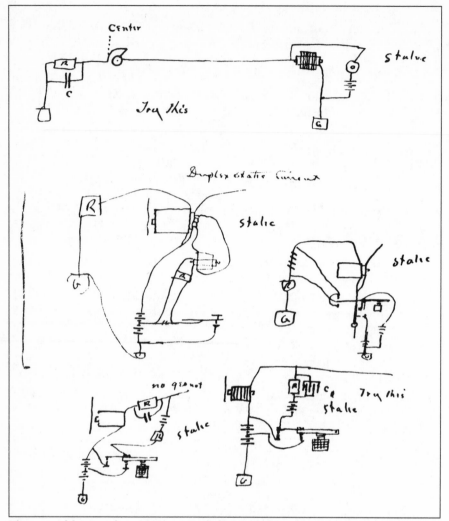

This page of drawings from 1873 contains Edison's plan for placing his automatic telegraph receiver at a neutral point or "center of resistance." It also shows several duplex designs, all of which are intended to reduce static discharge and induction currents on the line.

Works. Although their manufacturing partnership had ended, Harrington continued to retain his interest in Edison's patents, and this agreement now made Reiff an equal partner in the patents on the condition that he would "secure the best market & most advantageous terms" for the sale of both American and foreign patent rights, with Edison guaranteed a minimum of $10,000 for each.[42]

Like others who provided support for Edison, Reiff too developed great faith in the inventor's abilities. Little is known about Reiff prior to his involvement in Automatic Telegraph other than the fact that he was associated with William Palmer in the Kansas Pacific Railroad and other joint ventures during the 1860s. Reiff apparently had considerable wealth of his own, and he became the principal financial backer of Automatic Telegraph, investing some $175,000. A significant portion of this money funded Edison's experiments in automatic telegraphy over the next several years and paid him the $2,000 annual salary. Reiff provided additional support for Edison as well. He loaned Edison $3,100 in February 1872, which allowed the inventor to provide necessary funds for his brother Pitt's street railway ventures in Port Huron and Sarnia, Ontario. Edison had acquired a substantial stake in these railroads the previous July. In March 1873 Reiff agreed with Harrington to support Edison's experiments to develop a new roman letter system of automatic telegraphy. Later he loaned Edison money for the Edison & Murray shop. The two men remained friends throughout their lives. Many years later, after their financial positions had become reversed, it was the inventor who helped his friend out of financial difficulties.[43]

Edison's work on both duplex and automatic telegraphy culminated in a flurry of patent applications in April 1873. These were prepared in anticipation of his impending trip to England for Automatic Telegraph. For three years, Craig had been lobbying the British Post Office Telegraph Department to test the Little automatic as an improvement over Charles Wheatstone's slower ink-recording system. The Post Office engineers had resisted these efforts, skeptical not only of Craig's claims that the system could successfully transmit 1,000 to 1,500 words per minute in commercial operation, but also of the advantages of increased speed when they were not even using the Wheatstone automatic at its full capacity.

Although Little was British and would have been the logical choice for this trip, the fact that Edison went instead suggests that the company now considered him the primary figure in the technical development of the system. The Post Office engineers certainly felt this to be the case as they began to refer to the system as Edison's rather than Little's after his arrival. Edison left New York on April 23, accompanied by Jack Wright, an experienced operator with Automatic Telegraph, who was to assist with the tests.[44]

After a rough voyage on the aptly named *Jumping Java*, Edison arrived in London in early May. Although this was his first trip abroad, both contemporary documents and his reminiscences suggest that he paid little attention to anything other than the tests of his system. The official Post Office tests took place on a line between London and Liverpool. Originally scheduled for May 10–12, these tests did not take place until May 23, 26, and 27. Several circumstances caused delay: the instruments Wright took to Liverpool were damaged in transport, they ran out of chemical paper after using more than anticipated during trials, and most significantly, Edison experienced an unforeseen technical problem. He had to ask that the instruments be moved to the outskirts of the two cities so they could be connected directly to overhead wires after trials showed that the underground wires used at the ends of the line seriously distorted the signals. Required to transmit eight messages of 1,000 words each day at an average rate of 500 words per minute, during the three days of tests Edison successfully sent six, eight, and nine transmissions at this average speed with a low of 437 and a high of 572 words per minute.[45]

Although largely successful, these tests did not lead to adoption of Edison's automatic by the British Post Office. Although they were impressed with the experimental speeds shown by the system, telegraph officials remained skeptical of its practical value in daily commercial service. Furthermore, they saw Edison's failure to work his system with underground wires, which were commonly used at the urban termini of the Post Offices main lines, as a serious drawback. Although Edison claimed that he could overcome this difficulty by using a more powerful battery, Post Office telegraph engineers objected that such a battery would destroy the insulation used on these wires. They also pointed to other problems with Edison's system, such as the impermanence of the recorded message and the large work force its use required. Nonetheless, it is clear that the engineers felt that these technical drawbacks could eventually be solved. Indeed, after his return Edison spent much of the next six months working to improve the system and make it acceptable to British officials. Ultimately, however, the most important argument made by the Post Office engineers to their superiors was that Edison's system was only the old Bain automatic with an improved method of compensating for inductive effects. They argued that they could devise their own improvements in the older system as a way of getting around Edison's patents. By mid-1874 negotiations between the Post Office and Edison's backers came to an end as the British engineers decided that chemical recording offered no advantages over the Wheatstone automatic.[46]

However, Edison's tests on the British Post Office lines attracted the attention of leading figures in the British cable telegraph industry, who thought that his system could greatly increase message density and thus reduce the need to lay costly new wires under the ocean. Following the Post Office tests, Edison remained in London for another two weeks to conduct experimental cable tests of his automatic. These tests were done using a coiled 2,200-mile cable stored at the Greenwich works of the Telegraph Construction and Maintenance Company, which manufactured and laid most of the world's undersea cables. Unaware that the coiled cable greatly increased the distortion normally experienced on a long undersea cable, Edison was shocked when the first dot he sent recorded a twenty-seven-foot mark on his chemical paper. After two weeks of experiments he was unable to transmit more than two words per minute. Although these experiments were unsuccessful, several cable investors, including John Pender and James Anderson of Eastern Telegraph Company, a leading British cable enterprise, decided to acquire the foreign rights to Edison's automatic system. For several months they conducted tests of it on their lines and lobbied the Post Office department to adopt it. However, Edison's automatic was never used commercially by either the cable companies or the British government.[47]

Although ultimately unsuccessful from a commercial standpoint, Edison's trip to England proved extremely important to his career as an inventor. His encounter with the sophisticated British electrical community and with new problems of electrical transmission would lead Edison to a growing appreciation of how much he did not know about the electrical and chemical phenomena involved in cable and automatic telegraphy. As he set about developing an experimental program to investigate these problems, Edison began to equip a full electrical and chemical laboratory at his Newark shop and to alter his approach to invention.

CHAPTER 6

From Shop to Laboratory

The twenty-six-year-old Edison returned from Great Britain bursting with ideas for experiments and with a new appreciation for how much he did not know about the complex issues of electrical transmission. Even before leaving England he had begun to fill his notebooks with plans for investigating problems he had experienced during experiments with his automatic telegraph system on British underground and cable lines. These included investigating inductive effects on electrical transmission and electrochemical research on batteries and automatic recorders. Following his return home, Edison focused his experiments on electrical and electrochemical phenomena rather than on the electromechanical designs that had made his early reputation. To do so he established a small laboratory in his Ward Street machine shop. Within six months he could boast that it contained "every conceivable variety of Electrical Apparatus, and any quantity of Chemicals for experimentation."[1] As Edison refined his experimental approach the laboratory would continue to grow in size and importance until it absorbed the machine shop.

Edison was joined in his laboratory by a new experimental assistant. Charles Batchelor was a British-born textile mechanic who had come to the United States in 1870 to install equipment at the Clark thread mills in Newark. Later that year he went to work for Edison at the American Telegraph Works. Although Batchelor had no prior experience with electrical technology, his skills as an experimental machinist and draftsman soon made him an important partner in Edison's work. When Edison left American Telegraph in 1871, Batchelor joined him in the Ward Street shop. Edison valued Batchelor's great skill at conducting delicate and precise operations, and it is probably for this reason that Batchelor became Edison's chief experimental assistant in the summer of 1873, soon after Edison's return from England. Affectionately known as "Batch," he worked closely with Edison for the next twenty years, becoming the inventor's friend as well as his right-hand man.[2]

Batchelor joined Edison at a propitious time for expanding his understanding of electricity. Even though Edison's primary concern remained the production of practical technology, many of the experiments they conducted were designed to produce a more general understanding of the electrical or chemical action of the devices with which they worked. At times this research even verged into the scientific as they explored little understood phenomena and even proposed more general theories to account for their results. Although the competing interests of Western Union and Automatic Telegraph continued to provide the primary impetus and support for Edison's experiments, patentable technology was only one of his goals. Indeed, for nearly a year following his return from England Edison's experiments produced few patents. Instead they provided him with a deeper understanding of electrical technology that helped bring him to the top of his profession.

Even before his British trip Edison's work on multiple and automatic telegraphy had begun to present him with inductive effects hitherto encountered by few American inventors or telegraph engineers. By contrast, British telegraphers had been making induction a subject of serious study since the 1850s, when the first submarine telegraph cables were laid. Indeed, William Preece, a British Post Office telegraph engineer, believed that attention to induction had produced a profound difference between American and British practice. He asserted that the

> absence of Submarine Cables, underground wires and complicated apparatus, and the climate [in the United States], require less attention to the more abstruse laws of Electricity than has been the case in England. At home the intricate laws of induction have not only called forth the closest attention and study of the Telegraph Engineer, but the operations and researches of the Engineer have materially advanced our knowledge of the Science itself. Many new laws and striking facts have emanated from the practical telegraphist. Hence the English Telegraph Engineer has become essentially a scientific man.[3]

Preece might also have pointed out that submarine telegraphy not only introduced incentives for scientific study into British telegraph practice, but had also attracted the attention of several prominent scientists, who helped to give British telegraphy its scientific character. The leading telegraph engineer in Britain was Glasgow University professor of natural philosophy William Thomson (later Lord Kelvin), who was also the country's leading scientific figure. Thomson had been among those most responsible for the success of cable telegraphy by designing instruments and developing the first mathematical theory of cable transmission. Thomson was also a major figure in the establishment of standard electrical units, and with his consulting partner, telegraph engineer William Varley, he played an important role in developing testing instruments and procedures. Varley later introduced some of these procedures into the United States when he was hired by William Orton to investigate the condition of Western Union's lines in 1867. Another important figure in submarine telegraphy and instrumentation was Charles Wheatstone, the professor of experimental physics at King's College. Wheatstone, whose electrical "bridge" was an important test apparatus and also a major element in some circuit designs, had helped devise both the country's first commercial telegraph system and the ink-recording automatic system used by the British Post Office.[4]

Edison had acquired a smattering of knowledge about submarine telegraphy from reading in British telegraph manuals and even claimed that his line balancing method could be used for cables as well as automatic telegraphs, but his experiments at Greenwich had made apparent his relative ignorance of this subject. Willoughby Smith, electrician of the Telegraph Construction and Maintenance Company, later wrote that after the failure of his experiments with the cable in Greenwich, Edison "admitted that he was not prepared for this 'darned induction,' and that he 'would go back to think about it.'" Smith, who thought Edison's candor to be quite unusual for an inventor, commented, "It was really not only interesting but instructive to see with what dexterity he worked his instrument and manipulated his connections; in fact he was thoroughly acquainted with the subject in hand, quickly realised the cause of the defeat, and what is all-important, freely admitted it."[5]

To think about the subject of cable telegraphy, Edison talked with a number of British telegraphers he met in England, including Smith and T. E. Weatherall, also of Telegraph Construction and Maintenance; David Lumsden, the cable superintendent for the British Post Office who was one of the engineers responsible for supervising Edison's automatic tests; and Richard Culley, chief engineer of the British Post Office and former chief engineer for Eastern Telegraph. Edison also met and talked with Josiah Latimer Clark, a co-founder of the British Society of Telegraph Engineers, who was another of the central figures in the study of electrical phenomenon connected with submarine telegraphy and in the establishment of standard units of electrical measurement. After returning to the United States, Edison would continue to consult Clark about cable questions. During his experiments at Greenwich, Edison also began to develop designs for artificial cables that he could use in laboratory experiments both to further his knowledge of submarine telegraphy and to adapt his automatic telegraph for use on cable lines.[6]

During 1874 extensive experiments were made in England with Edison's automatic on the cable lines of the Eastern Telegraph Company. James Brown and Jack Wright, who had remained behind to conduct further (and ultimately unsuccessful) tests for the British Post Office, conducted these experiments with the assistance of Latimer Clark. Even with his long experience in submarine telegraphy Clark, who acted as a consultant for Pender and Anderson, was unable to help adapt Edison's automatic system for use with cables. In a letter of April 28, 1874, in which Wright summarized five weeks of cable experiments, he informed Edison that "I dont think [Clark] knows any more than I do, and thats not much. Your questions to him are 'pearls before swine' I'm afraid." Even before receiving this letter, however, Edison had confided to Clark that his own knowledge of "cable phenomenon could be put in a very small book."[7] Within a few weeks, Edison virtually ended his cable experiments, even as Reiff and Harrington urged him to return to Britain to solve the remaining technical problems and reassure their British investors.

Although Edison's cable experiments produced no practical improvements in submarine telegraphy, they provided him with new insights and techniques that he applied to his other research in automatic telegraphy. In his attempts to overcome inductive effects on cables he employed a variety of circuit arrangements and electrical devices, including electromagnets, rheostats, condensers, batteries, and Wheatstone bridges, that were also applicable to automatic telegraphy. Edison designed many of the devices he used in these circuits. He experimented with the size and materials in the cores of electromagnets, tried different materials in condensers and storage batteries, and created adjustable rheostats. Although he had used some of these in automatic experiments prior to his British trip, he now undertook more systematic investigations, such as a series of experiments designed "to ascertain whether the discharge from a magnet is lengthened by an increase in the resistance of the circuit in which it discharges."[8]

Edison also began to introduce techniques used in cable and automatic telegraphy into his multiple telegraph experiments. Among the devices he began to employ were secondary batteries, which he first encountered during his Greenwich cable experiments. At that time he discovered that they "act like a Condenser but have the advantage that they send a long back charge & low resistance."[9] Upon his return to the United States, he made several storage batteries and began to use them on main lines and in shunt circuits of his cable and automatic telegraphs; within a short time he also began to experiment with them in duplex circuits. His magnet experiments produced another duplex design in which he replaced the condenser of the Stearns duplex with a new electromagnet he had designed with a ten-foot-long core. He also experimented with a duplex that worked by induction currents and considered ways to duplex a cable.

Another device that Edison introduced into his experiments at this time was a galvanometer, which was used extensively in British telegraphy both for measuring electric currents and as a receiving instrument on cables. His experience of British telegraph practice had created a new appreciation for such fine test instruments and precise measurement in conducting electrical experiments. At the Greenwich cable works and in telegraph offices and instrument-maker's shops he had seen a variety of measuring instruments and other electrical apparatus that far surpassed those available in the United States. Impressed by the quality of British electrical apparatus, Edison prepared a list of almost fifty items that he hoped to obtain for his new laboratory, including several different types of galvanometers as well as other electrical measuring instruments, condensers, rheostats, batteries, and even standard laboratory teaching apparatus such as static electricity generators. Although he was unable to afford all of this expensive equipment, he did purchase some items from Elliott Bros.,

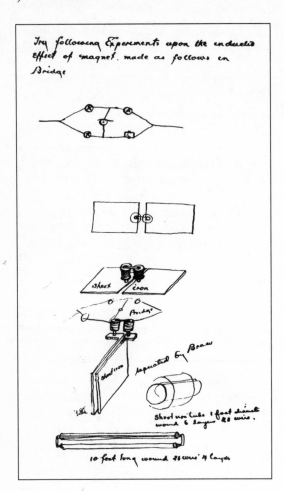

Edison's plan for experiments on electromagnets, including his design for a long magnet.

the well-known London firm that had built many of the instruments used for testing and working the first cable telegraphs. Edison even began to devise his own galvanometers and other test instruments. It was during this period that he also began to use variations in the marks made by his chemical recorder to measure the strength and duration of electrical signals.[10]

As Edison acquired more sophisticated electrical apparatus, he found it useful to study treatises written by British telegraphers to better understand their use. His reading of these works also provided insights into mathematical laws and techniques related to electricity. For example, he and Batchelor used Robert Sabine's *Electric Telegraph*, one of the books Edison had listed in his 1867 Cincinnati notebook, to study formulas and techniques such as those used in measuring and comparing electromotive force with a galvanometer.

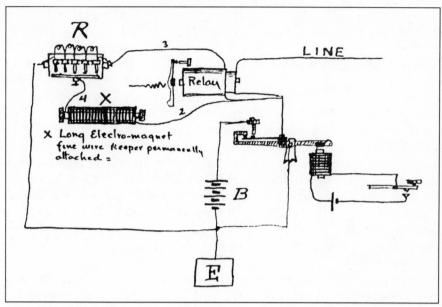

Edison placed his long magnet in a duplex circuit to neutralize the static discharge on the receiving instrument at the transmitting station.

Another book to which they devoted attention was Sabine's and Latimer Clark's *Electrical Tables and Formulae for the Use of Telegraph Inspectors and Operators*. Although Edison had obtained this book in April 1872, he appears not to have begun to use it seriously until after his return to the United States. Several pages of his copy of this book contain marginal notes that seem related to experiments he carried out after his trip. Furthermore, a notebook entry of February 22, 1874, contains the note "Galvanometer tests o[n] Page 84 Electrical Tables & Formulas. Work this & thoroughly understand it." On page 84 of Edison's copy can be found his marginal "OK" next to a section entitled "To measure the resistance of a galvanometer when no second galvanometer is to be obtained."[11] Not surprisingly, Clark and Sabine, who had both been involved in the establishment of standard electrical units, also provided an excellent summary of these units as well as the basic electrical laws developed by Ohm, Joule, Kirchoff, and others.

Although American telegraphers generally avoided higher mathematics, quantitative analysis of electrical circuits was an important element of telegraph practice. It was often crucial for understanding the operation of a particular instrument or system. Edison's own writings in the *Telegrapher* are typical in their presentation of such analysis. His first published article, for example, discussed the electrical relationships between the helices of the electromagnets, the adjustable resistances or rheostats, and the line used with his double transmitter: "The resistance at X is made equal to that of the main line L, added to that of the helix N' and the resistance R'. Similarly X' is made equal to [L + N + R]."[12] Later in the article he provided numerical values for these electrical components to illustrate how the system operated. Similar quantitative discussions of electrical relationships are found in his other articles and in his notebooks, along with occasional sophisticated arithmetic calculations. Edison is often depicted as showing little interest in or respect for formal mathematics, but he was comfortable with basic quantitative relationships and calculations. He was also willing to hire mathematically competent physicists and engineers such as Francis Upton, who later assisted with electric light experiments and thought Edison had an intuitive mathematical ability that allowed him to "guess better than a good many men can figure, and so far as my experience goes, I have found that he is almost invariably correct. His guess is more than a mere starting point, and often turns out to be the final solution of a problem."[13]

As Edison's British experiments led him to closer study of electrical laws, measurements, and instruments, they also drew his attention toward more intensive chemical studies. His tests for the British Post Office and his experiments with the Greenwich cable had pointed to several potential problems with chemical recording. British engineers particularly objected to the fact that the chemically treated paper tore easily and that the messages frequently transferred to other portions of the paper roll. They were concerned as well by the rapid fading of the recorded message. Batteries presented another obstacle as the Post Office engineers objected to the use of the Grove battery, even though it significantly improved the reception of automatic signals, because they feared that its higher voltage would destroy the gutta-percha coating used on their wires. Edison's notebooks also indicate that he began to consider how different chemical solutions, as well as paper thicknesses, might change the resistance of the recording circuit and affect the electrical condition of the line.

Although chemistry had been a subject of much interest to Edison as a boy, he had done little experimenting since. After returning from England, however, he took it up again in earnest. Edison's notebook from the summer of 1873 indicates that he began his studies with a relatively simple text, John Pepper's *Cyclopedia of Science Simplified*. He used information from Pepper's discussion of chemistry and electrochemistry to design experiments related to chemical recording. For example, finding "it stated by Pepper that oxygen is magnetic," he decided to "Try if the freed oxygen from a chemical recording pen can be attracted away from the pen and a decomposition partially prevented by a powerful local magnet with pointed poles The object being to attract the oxygen away from the iron pen after the current ceases to prevent an elongation of the mark upon the chemical paper."[14] Other notes based on his reading of Pepper concern possible alternative solutions and papers that he could use for chemical recording.

By the fall of 1874 Edison had expanded his chemical study with Pepper's *Playbook of Metals*, which provided basic information on the chemistry of the metals, as well as more sophisticated chemical works, including *Select Methods of Chemical Analysis (Chiefly Inorganic)* by the prominent British chemist William Crookes and *Laboratory Teaching* by Charles Bloxam, the professor of practical chemistry at King's College, London. He also began to subscribe to Crookes's journal *Chemical News*, to the *Boston Journal of Chemistry*, and to the *Druggist's Circular and Chemical Gazette*.[15]

Edison's reading in the chemical literature helped to make his experiments more systematic. For example, drawing particularly on Crookes, he began to test different combinations of metal recording styli and receiving solutions to find the best combination for his automatic system. These experiments led to his discovery in early April that electrochemical reactions could reduce friction and cause his recording pen to move freely over the chemical paper; in some instances he also found that these reactions increased friction. Edison considered the effect of "chem[ical] Decomp[osition] moving a Lever" to be a "new force," which he later termed the "electromotograph."[16] Over the next several years he would experiment on and off with the electromotograph, using it for such things as telegraph relays and telephone receivers.

Edison's work on recording solutions was guided by a theoretical framework that he developed sometime during the winter. His basic concept was nicely summarized by reporter Edwin Fox in an article about Edison's automatic that appeared several years later in *Scribner's:* "Mr. Edison found the law, by means of which he was enabled to make many hundreds of working solutions. In all cases it is the proto-salt of the metal which is formed, that is the salt with the least oxygen in its composition. Knowing this, one has only to moisten the paper with a chemical that gives a coloration with this oxide, and called its re-agent."[17] Edison's own discussion of his experiments can be found in an essay that he drafted during the winter of 1874 but never published. He indicated in this essay that "to obtain the best results the reagent for that oxide must be used which with an iron point is not [the] ferrocyanide but the Ferridcyanide of potassium."[18] Thus, his standard recording solution consisted of one ounce of potassium ferridcyanide, one pound of sodium chloride, and a gallon of water. Nonetheless, he continued to experiment with alternative solutions and patented several. His continuing electromotograph experiments also periodically returned his attention to recording solutions. Edison's experiments with recording solutions, pens, and paper were influenced by both electrical and chemical considerations. Thus, he came to favor tellurium for recording pens because he found that it "has the property of cutting the signals off very sharply. This serves as another device for overcoming the static discharge of the line." And his experiments with papers eventually led him to adopt "thick, well-washed bibulous cotton-paper, moistened with water, in which a little salt had been dissolved" to improve its electrical conductivity, because it gave "the clearest and sharpest signals."[19]

Edison's chemical experiments from the fall and winter also included extensive battery experiments intended not only to develop batteries suitable for his automatic system but also to increase his knowledge. Soon after his return he began "experimenting on a patent battery the object of which is to transmit 100 words per minute [by automatic] over the Atlantic Cable."[20] These experiments involved Edison in two important aspects of battery design—polarization and diffusion.

Polarization was caused by the accumulation on the negative electrode of the hydrogen gas released by chemical reaction in the electrolyte. This decreased the battery's current by increasing its internal resistance and setting up a counter electromotive force. To overcome this problem, improve the constancy, and extend the life of batteries he studied depolarizing methods. One common method was to employ a chemical substance—often zinc sulphate—near the negative pole that would absorb the hydrogen gas. In the gravity batteries with which Edison was experimenting the zinc was kept separate from the copper sulphate by the difference in their specific gravities, but over time a phenomenon known as diffusion occurred as the copper solution rose and deposited on the zinc. Although the zinc could be raised higher in the battery cup to delay this effect, the battery's internal resistance increased as a result. After "experimenting upon a large number of gravity batteries arranged in innumerable forms" Edison found that he could prevent diffusion by placing the copper sulphate solution "*under the Copper plate* instead as heretofore [above] it." The electrolytic action of the battery kept the solutions separate so that even when the battery was disconnected for a short time and the copper sulphate began to rise and mix with the zinc, "it immediately went back under the copper when the poles were connected." After extensive tests he found this battery design to be "perfectly constant the galvanometer needle not varying a degree for months." These positive results prompted him to submit the idea to Latimer Clark in the hope that "it may add as my mite to the Society of Telegraph Engineers." He also considered sending a description of his method for the "prevention of the diffusion of Liquids by electrolytic action" to the noted British physicist James Clerk Maxwell, who had published an article discussing his own experiments with diffusion in a September 1873 issue of *Nature*.[21]

Edison's growing confidence in his abilities as an experimenter seems to have increased his self-assurance that he was someone whose ideas warranted consideration by the electrical community. Besides sharing his method for preventing diffusion with Clark and others in Britain, he also considered asking Clark to propose him as a foreign member of the Society of Telegraph Engineers, although his membership application was not advanced until several months later.[22]

It was during the winter of 1874 that he also worked in earnest on the telegraph book he had begun making notes for a year earlier. According to his draft preface, Edison did not want "to merely reproduce on its pages that which has already been published on this subject nor to describe elementary laws [of] electricity." Instead he planned to present "a series of experiments as performed by him. Having been for a number of years actively engaged in experimenting in telegraphy and electricity in general." He also proposed to "explain numerous observed phenomena in electricity they having been noticed by him and which is generally not known."[23] Edison's draft table of contents suggests that he planned to discuss a combination of practical devices and more general phenomena. He planned to devote two chapters to automatic and chemical telegraphs, with separate chapters for duplex, printing, and miscellaneous telegraphs, and include a chapter on contact points and breakwheels that would also include many of the electromechanical devices used in printing telegraphy. He intended to discuss a wide range of electrical circuits and relays in two chapters and describe a variety of repeater designs in another. Edison expected to devote the remaining chapters to those subjects he had been investigating since his return from England: batteries, electromagnets, secondary voltaic action, static charge, induction, testing, and electrical measurement. His partial draft of the chapter on electromagnets suggests the kind of phenomena he hoped to explicate and provides insights into his motivation:

> One of the laws of electro magnets is that charge and discharge is in proportion to the length of the iron core. The why and wherefore of this the cause etc I have been unable to glean from any investigations heretofore published that have come to my notice.
>
> I was led from this want of data to undertake a series of investigations with the view of learning if possible the causes of some of the phenomena noticed by different investigations and described in works upon electricity and magnetism.[24]

Although Edison soon gave up his work on this manuscript, in the summer of 1874 he began to publish parts of it as a series of articles he wrote as the science editor of the *Operator*, a new telegraph journal launched the previous March.

Many of Edison's experiments were guided by his reading of scientific and technical literature, but he was first and foremost an adept empirical experimenter. This has led many to characterize him as a cut-and-try inventor who disdained theory, a view that has been reinforced by the statement of his official biographers, Frank Dyer and T. C. Martin, that "trusting nothing to theory, he acquires absolute knowledge" through his experiments.[25] This statement, however, should be understood within the context of nineteenth-century Anglo-American scientific and technical practice, which can be illustrated by the example of two premier scientific figures—William Thomson and Michael Faraday. Each of these men created an impressive body of theoretical work but each also believed in theory derived from direct knowledge through experimental practice. In the words of Thomson's biographers, "The general point seems to be that tactile and visual experience are of a different kind from, and more efficient and more trustworthy than, mental constructions." Prominent in Thomson's scientific style was the construction of models, "which allow us to know a thing by literally making it ourselves," whereas accurate experimental measurement and calculations, "which give a knowledge of the relative and varying magnitudes of things," were the basis upon which to build theory.[26]

Faraday, whom Edison called the "Master Experimenter" and took as one of his principal models, explained his own use of experimental knowledge in a statement that echoes Dyer and Martin's analysis of its role in Edison's work: "I was never able to make a fact my own without seeing it, and the description of the best works altogether failed to convey to my mind, such a knowledge of things as to allow myself to form a judgment upon them."[27] Unlike Thomson, Faraday was not comfortable with mathematical analysis. One scholar has argued that Faraday employed a method of quantitative analysis he terms dynamical geometry," in which pictorial, spatial, and kinetic models are used to analyze physical forces. This method of analysis produced "generative and heuristic" understanding rather than the kind of "quantitative precision" valued by Thomson. Edison, who praised the absence of mathematics in Faraday's *Experimental Researches in Electricity*, seems to have taken a similar approach in his own study of quantitative relationships.[28]

Edison followed Faraday's example in other respects as well. Like the British scientist, he had what his official biographers called an uncanny "ability to detect errors quickly in a series of experiments."[29] Both were attuned to the potential value of unexpected experimental results, and neither considered failed experiments to be anything other than a source of potentially useful knowledge. Edison's notebooks show him frequently interrupting more practical work to explore unexplained phenomena. Although he was always quick to seize on any possibilities for application, his primary interest was in gaining experimental knowledge and even producing an explanatory hypothesis.

Although primarily concerned with experimental knowledge that he could apply to practical inventions rather than to theory building, Edison did occasionally propose hypotheses of his own on electricity and other subjects in the course of making experimental notes. His battery experiments, for example, led him to suggest that

> It is probable that a single [battery] cell generates its electricity in waves following each other with great rapidity, and that in consequence of static induction even upon bodies at great distance from the cell or even the cell itself the time between the waves is bridged over by the static charge. Although we are unable as yet to isolate as far from all bodies & determine by instrumen[ta]tion the existence of these waves an obvious inference of their existence can be drawn from the fact that waves intermitted by a telegh key when transmitted through a long conduction close to surrounding bodies that these waves are continuous when made rapidly.[30]

Another note regarding inductive effects on a cable also makes use of his ideas about the wave transmission of electricity: "The transmission of waves of electricity are instantaneous no matter what the length of the cable. The retardation noticed by electricians in cables is not properly retardation but the leyden charge sending its current against the charging current. The same as an electromagnet placed in an electric current. The first part impulse will be weakened by the counter charge against the magnetizing current."[31] Such hypotheses occasionally provided an underlying framework for Edison's design of telegraph circuits and devices. In some cases they even directly influenced his designs, as in the case of a chemical receiver that relied, according to Edison's patent attorney, on "his idea that every atom of matter has a positive or negative polarity."[32]

More typically, Edison's understanding of the electrical or chemical properties of particular devices, rather than the theoretical foundation for those properties, provided the means for turning his experimental knowledge to practical use in designing new inventions. His successful 1874 design for a practical quadruplex telegraph (transmitting two messages simultaneously in each direction over a single wire) provides an excellent example. Like other inventors, Edison knew that such a system was feasible if he could design a practical diplex to send two messages in the same direction and then combine it with a duplex. He had first considered doing this in a February 1873 letter to his patent attorney Lemuel Serrell, which described seventeen duplex designs, including a diplex arrangement alongside of which he wrote "Four-plex Why not."[33] Edison's approach to the problem differed somewhat from that of his contemporaries. The common approach to diplex was the use of weak and strong batteries to produce signals of different strengths with relays at the receiving end designed to respond to one or the other signal. However, it proved difficult in practice to prevent the sensitive weak-signal relay from responding to the stronger signal current. Edison tried a different approach that used a common element in many of his designs—the polarized relay. He continued to use one receiver with a common, or neutral, relay that responded only to changes in current strength, but employed a second receiver with a polarized relay to respond to changes in the polarity of the current. By combining this diplex with a standard duplex that prevented receivers at each end of the line from responding to outgoing signals, Edison could transmit four signals over a single wire—two in each direction.

Although quadruplex signaling was practical in theory, in practice it proved to be very difficult to achieve. The use of current reversals created a momentary drop in current strength and caused the common relay to lose its magnetism just as it was supposed to act, thus mutilating the signal and causing false breaks. It was while he was in England that Edison first came up with a possible solution to this problem. Rather than trying to prevent the moment of no magnetism he decided to isolate its effect electromechanically so that it would not interfere with the signal. He did this by means of what he called a "bug trap." Instead of preventing the neutral relay from releasing when the current fell to zero during the moment of reversal, he used it to work a local relay interposed between it and the sounder relay. This local relay was adjusted so that it responded sluggishly to the signal and thus failed to act before the neutral relay regained its magnetism and acted on the sounder relay. In essence, Edison used a cascade of electromagnets to bridge over the time during which the reversed current regenerated the magnetic field in the main relay magnet. This solution represented an important approach that Edison often took when confronted by particularly intractable problems: rather than completely eliminating a defect he found a way to use its own effects to obviate the problem it caused.

Edison included his first bug trap designs in a patent caveat he drew up in early August, but he experimented only intermittently with diplex and duplex circuits for several months. His primary focus remained on automatic and cable telegraphy as he sought to adapt his automatic to British lines. As it became clear that this effort would not succeed Edison decided to renew his efforts in multiple telegraphy and again approached Western Union for support. Having failed the previous spring to get authorization from William Orton to test his duplex designs on the company's wires, Edison now turned to Western Union electrician George Prescott. In exchange for his personal help and the use of Western Union facilities, Edison offered to name Prescott as co-inventor and divide any profits equally between them. At the urging of William Orton, Prescott agreed to this arrangement, and by early June 1874, Edison was conducting experiments at Western Union's headquarters with instruments made for him by the company's factory.[34]

With renewed support from Western Union, Edison began a period of intensive development of quadruplex telegraphy. Over the next several months, he conducted extensive experiments in his laboratory and over working lines, altered the design of electromagnets and other elements in his relays, rearranged the contact levers on his transmitting keys, and devised a variety of bug traps. As he tested his instruments on longer circuits, he discovered that it was also necessary to employ arrangements of electromagnets, resistances, and condensers to compensate for the moment of zero magnetism.

The first public notice of the quadruplex appeared in a *New York Times* article on July 10 that described a successful test over a 200-mile loop circuit between New York and Philadelphia. Although the *Times* described the new system as "the result of the joint labors of Messrs. George Prescott and Thomas A. Edison," the new system was entirely Edison's.[35] Prescott's role had, in fact, been limited to supporting Edison's work by arranging to have instruments made in Western Union's New York shop and allowing tests over the company's wires. As a result, when Edison named Prescott as joint inventor on the series of duplex and quadruplex patent applications he submitted to Serrell in mid-August, his attorney argued that this would invalidate the patents. Serrell recognized that most of the designs shown in the applications had been developed by Edison prior to his May offer to make Prescott joint inventor. They therefore decided instead to list Edison as sole inventor and to draw up a new partnership agreement giving Prescott half ownership in the patents.

By the end of September Edison had the new system working successfully from New York to Boston, and within a few days Western Union placed it into

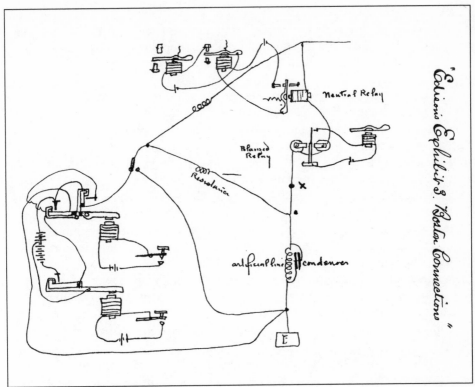

Edison's drawing of the connections used during September experiments with his quadruplex telegraph between New York and Boston. It shows the neutral relay (top), polarized relay (center) and the condenser (bottom). At X, Edison made changes before the Chicago trials in November.

commercial service on that line. On October 14, Orton told the Western Union stockholders that the quadruplex was "an invention more wonderful than the Duplex" and that negotiations were pending to acquire the patents. He noted, however, that "the terms will not be settled until after the character and extent of its capacity for work have been more fully ascertained."[36] When he successfully placed a quadruplex circuit in operation between New York and Chicago in early December, thus satisfying the conditions set by Orton, Edison anticipated that they would soon reach agreement on terms for the purchase of the system.

Edison desperately needed this money. Like many other small businessmen, Edison was feeling the effects of the general economic depression caused by the Panic of 1873. As financial markets contracted and business activity declined, Edison and Murray received fewer orders from Gold and Stock and Automatic Telegraph. To make up for these, they undertook several contract jobs for other firms so as not to lose their skilled workers. Equipment and experimental costs in the new laboratory also increased Edison's expenses, though these also were a potential source of new revenue. Having trouble meeting his payrolls and in danger of losing his shop, Edison had to give up his house and move his family into a small apartment over a drugstore in downtown Newark.[37]

Edison had developed several new products during the first half of the year that provided some of the needed additional income. His experiments with induction coils had led to the inductorium, a medical electric-shock device. Several instruments of this type were being marketed as cure-alls for a variety of diseases and to rejuvenate the nervous system. Edison advertised his at one-third the price of competitors and as a "specific cure for rheumatism." Perhaps recalling the practical joke he had played in Cincinnati by attaching an induction coil to the washstand at the telegraph office and watching as other operators received shocks, he also thought it could serve as "an inexhaustible fount of amusement."[38] After putting it on the market in May, Edison had sold more than one hundred inductoriums by July. A less successful product he had developed during the spring was a practice instrument for apprentice telegraphers that allowed them to improve their Morse code signaling by examining a recorded copy of their messages. Unfortunately, he sold very few of these. Edison had initially conceived the "shocking machine" and the student telegraph as products for a proposed "Scientific Toy Company."[39] Other merchandise would have included scientific apparatus, electric locomotives, steam engines, and sewing machines. Edison's idea for a Scientific Toy Company also provides the first evidence of his thinking on the subject of childhood education. He would later suggest in a 1911 *Century Magazine* interview that "there are great possibilities in starting the mind right with toys. Give them problems to work out that will make them think for themselves . . . a kind of scientific kindergarten."[40] Nonetheless, he ended up selling the inductorium and student telegraph as practical instruments for adults.

A potentially more significant source of income was another telegraph system that Edison had developed during the winter and spring of 1874. He designed a full-scale district signaling system to compete with one marketed by American District Telegraph Company, which used instruments designed by Gold and Stock inventor Edward Calahan. In 1872 Edison had sold rights to this company for his patent caveat on electromechanical signaling instruments. In district telegraphy, these types of instruments were placed in businesses and private homes to allow subscribers to call for messengers and other services from a central office by simply pushing a lever and sending an automatic signal. Many district telegraphs also offered private fire and police alarms. During the first months of 1874 Edison designed two devices to get around American District's patents, a fire alarm and an automatic, chemical recorder to record the signals at the central station. At the end of March he also formed the Domestic Telegraph Company with his manufacturing partner Joseph Murray and Jarvis B. Edson, an inventor and engineer best known for his automatic steam gauge. By June the company had begun to promote its system, competing unsuccessfully for the contract to provide fire-alarm service in Utica, New York. It was not until the end of the year that Domestic Telegraph was actually able to establish its first systems, setting up lines in New York, Newark, and Canada with instruments made by Edison and Murray. Although the orders for these instruments provided needed income for their shop, Edison and Murray had to pay much of their material and labor costs before they received payment for the finished instruments.[41]

Like many other small businessmen, Edison often struggled to pay his bills. He followed a common practice of delaying payments or paying only part of what he owed; Edison's own customers did the same thing. Throughout much of 1874, his financial condition was made even more precarious by obligations arising from the dissolution of his partnership with William Unger two years earlier. On July 3 Edison was scheduled to pay Unger $10,000; failure to pay would mean forfeiture of the shop. While the Automatic Telegraph investors got Unger to delay for a few days so that one of them could raise the money, Edison turned to Western Union. Although Edison hoped Orton would arrange a loan, the Western Union president provided only a $3,000 advance on Edison's Gold and Stock account and may have done so because of the partnership agreement between Edison and Prescott. When Harrington returned to New York on July 9 and heard that Edison had just that day signed the partnership agreement, he begged him to "see *me* before you sign any more papers, take any more money or go to any other place."[42] One of the Automatic investors, William Seyfert, was able to raise $6,600 by selling some land bonds and in return for this money, which he used to cancel Unger's lien on the shop, Edison gave Harrington some promissory notes, which would later cause him a great deal of difficulty.

By early December, when the first of the Harrington notes became due, Edison was facing the prospect of additional financial difficulties. He would soon have another mouth to feed—Mary was nearing the end of her pregnancy with their first son, Thomas Alva Jr., who was born on January 10. The financially pressed inventor again turned to Orton. Writing at the end of the first week of December, he told Orton of the successful Chicago quadruplex test and informed him, "I need 10, 9, 8, 7, 6, 5, 4, 3, or 2,000 dollars—any one you would like to advance."[43] A few days later Orton gave Edison a $5,000 advance payment on the quadruplex, and Edison and Prescott then presented him with a proposition for the sale of their patent rights. They continued to negotiate, and at the end of the month, just before Orton left on a trip to Chicago, Edison gave him a memo outlining two propositions for terms of the sale. Orton later claimed he told Edison he would make an offer similar to these upon his return, but Edison felt he had received no assurances, and in his straitened financial condition he decided to listen to a new offer from the notorious financier Jay Gould.

The strategic importance of the telegraph to the movement of railroad traffic and to American business in general had prompted Gould to form a telegraph empire as an adjunct to his railroad empire, and in 1874 he acquired control of the small Atlantic and Pacific Telegraph Company and combined it with the telegraph lines on his railroad network. This presented a new challenge to Gould's longtime rival, railroad baron Cornelius Vanderbilt, who was also Western Union's principal investor. To expand his telegraph system to compete more effectively with Western Union, Gould had begun to negotiate with Reiff and Harrington, who were planning to organize a new company that would combine Automatic Telegraph with several railroad telegraph lines. Also involved in these negotiations was Thomas Eckert, superintendent of Western Union's eastern district, who had grown restive under Orton. On December 30 Gould and Reiff reached an agreement under which Atlantic and Pacific would purchase Automatic Telegraph and Gould would enter the negotiations with the railroad companies. At the same time they agreed to make Eckert president of Atlantic and Pacific and to appoint Edison as the company's electrician.[44]

Late that night Gould, Eckert, and Eckert's lieutenant Albert Chandler came over to Edison's shop to see the automatic. Edison also demonstrated the quadruplex, and a few days later Eckert took Edison to Gould's house to negotiate secretly for the invention. Edison recalled that they met at the Windsor Hotel, and then they "went down [a] cellar and along an alley way into Mr. Gould's office."[45] Gould offered and Edison agreed to accept $30,000 for his rights in the quadruplex, with part of it to be paid in cash and the rest in Union Pacific Sinking Fund bonds. By the time Orton returned in the second week of January and accepted Edison's offer of $25,000 plus a royalty of $233 per quadruplex circuit per year, Edison had signed his agreement with Gould. Edison was anything but a passive figure in this intrigue. In a note to Gould he even suggested how the publicity regarding the merger of Automatic Telegraph and the appointment of Eckert as president of Atlantic and Pacific should be handled, concluding that they should "keep the thing boiling all the papers." Although Gould wrote "All right—go ahead" on Edison's note, the publicity campaign proposed by Edison did not take place. However, on Friday January 15 the Gould-controlled *New York Tribune* did publish an article about Eckert in which it also noted that "Thomas Edison of Newark, N.J. will probably be chosen electrician" and announced that the company would begin using his automatic system on its Washington to Boston line the following Monday.[46]

The first thing Edison did with his newfound wealth was to buy several hundred dollars worth of books and scientific equipment for his laboratory, including a microscope, a spectroscope, a thermopile, and an air pump. He then visited Port Huron and spent nearly $10,000 to settle accounts for his brother Pitt's street railway and pay off a loan for his father. On his return home he paid off old bills and loans, including one of the notes due Unger, and he gave money to his wife and members of her family. Mary spent part of this money to give a masquerade party for his birthday. By the beginning of spring Edison was able to move his family into a rented house in a pleasant residential area about a mile west of the shop. By this time, the household also included Edison's father and Pitt's son Charley, who were assisting in the shop and laboratory. The shop itself was placed on a firmer financial foundation so Edison was able to provide funds to tide it over while waiting payment from Atlantic and Pacific for an order of instruments.[47]

During the first months of 1875 Edison spent much of his time working as an Atlantic and Pacific electrician. During the last week of January he visited each of the company's offices in New York, Connecticut, and Massachusetts to determine the state of their operation and to supervise the installation of automatic instruments. His inventive work also focused on Atlantic and Pacific's needs, as he sought to solve problems in the operation of the automatic system and renewed his work on a system of roman letter automatic. Edison had first conceived this system, which sent and recorded messages in plain English, in 1871; he had worked on it intermittently since March 1873, when he signed an agreement with Reiff and Harrington for its development. After his return from England he had built a roman letter perforator, and during 1874 he had begun experimenting with receivers. Gould agreed to provide additional funding for these experiments, which had the potential to save on labor costs because the message did not have to be translated from Morse code. Edison found it extremely difficult to develop a practical system that used as few as two wires, but he also complained to Gould that Eckert was failing to provide sufficient resources for his experiments.[48]

Edison's relations with Eckert deteriorated rather quickly after he began working for Atlantic and Pacific, but he and Gould got along very well, and he even felt comfortable offering the financier advice on the telegraph business and on the operations of the company. Edison, who recalled that he saw a great deal of Gould during this time and that they often discussed business, found that "Gould had no sense of humor. I tried several times to get off a funny story, but he failed to see any humor in them." Edison did admire Gould's attention to the details of his business and the long hours that he worked, but thought that his "conscience appeared to be atrophied, but that may be due to the fact that he was contending with men that were worse." Edison himself was accused of a similar lack of conscience in his own business dealings. Given his work for competing interests in the telegraph industry, it is perhaps not surprising that conflicts arose. How he dealt with these suggests something of his personal values. His reminiscences of Gould indicate one of the ways in which he distinguished the greater purity of his own motives. Gould, he thought, "took no pride in building up an enterprise, he was after money and money only." By contrast, Edison claimed that "as long as my part was successful money with me was a secondary consideration."[49] Edison does seem to have valued money primarily as a means for acquiring the resources for his experiments, but he also appreciated the ways in which it made his and his family's life easier.

Whatever his motives, the sale of the quadruplex to Gould damaged his relations with Prescott and others at Western Union and fueled more attacks on his character in the pages of James Ashley's *Telegrapher*. Yet Edison was not alone in placing his personal interests above the corporate interests of Western Union—he was merely following the example set by Marshall Lefferts and Thomas Eckert. Unlike Pope and Ashley, who could resort only to personal attacks when they felt they had been unfairly sold out by Edison, Western Union could engage Atlantic and Pacific in a furious legal battle for control of his quadruplex. Prominent lawyers and political figures were mustered on each side, but only a merger between the two companies in 1877 resolved the complex legal issues caused by Western Union's failure to directly secure Edison's services as an inventor.[50]

The fate of the automatic interests was even less happy. In mid-April Gould purchased through Harrington the Automatic Telegraph rights for Edison's automatic patents; Gould, for his part, never assigned the patents to Atlantic and Pacific. However, instead of the shares in Atlantic and Pacific stock agreed to on December 30, Gould gave Harrington the value of those shares in cash and bonds. Harrington, who had been ill for some time, then left for England where he spent the remainder of his life. This angered the other Automatic investors, who insisted on stock and refused to take the cash settlement instead. They decided to set up a new company, American Automatic Telegraph, which they hoped to use to challenge Gould's right to Edison's automatic.[51]

Edison's active employment at Atlantic and Pacific had virtually ended by early June. At that time, perhaps in an effort to induce him to remain with the company, Albert Chandler, the company's vice-president, wrote Edison a formal letter of appointment as the company's engineer. Chandler told Edison that he would "in that capacity have charge of the transmission of business entrusted to us: meaning the arrangement of circuits and the batteries and apparatus necessary to secure the most prompt and efficient transmission possible."[52] Edison had begun to drift away from Atlantic and Pacific because he found it difficult to obtain support for his automatic telegraph experiments from Eckert. He also was more interested in undertaking other new experiments than in working on day-to-day engineering problems. As a result, he decided to return to full-time invention.

By the beginning of May Edison had already begun to spend most of his time in the laboratory. In the middle of the month he and Joseph Murray had agreed to dissolve their partnership (they signed formal papers two months later), and Edison took the "top room and Half next floor and $1/4$ cellar" of the four-story shop for his laboratory and Murray established his own manufacturing business in the rest of the building.[53] Edison also retained some of the machinery as well as the services of experimental machinists Charles Wurth and John Kruesi for his laboratory. By making his experimental machine shop entirely independent of manufacturing and incorporating it into the research laboratory, Edison completed the process he had started nearly two years earlier following his return from England.

CHAPTER 7

New Directions

A t the same time he was setting up his laboratory Edison was also asserting his independence from his corporate sponsors. The first thing he did was to sit down with Charles Batchelor and draw up a list of possible products they could develop to support the shop. They had been experimenting for years on some of these, such as improved batteries and electromagnets. Others, for example a system for sending six messages simultaneously, grew naturally out of Edison's ongoing telegraph work. However, most of these were new projects unrelated to his prior work. Some of them Edison experimented with only briefly, if at all, whereas others continued to occupy his attention for a considerable time, in some cases for years afterward. Included on the list of projects were improving methods of making and working cast iron, developing a new plastic as a substitute for celluloid, designing a kerosene lamp that did not require a chimney, inventing a process for extracting low-grade ores, and devising "a copying press that will take 100 copies & system."[1] The last item became the first subject of experimentation at the laboratory and its first product.

Along with Batchelor and machinists Charles Wurth and John Kruesi, Edison was joined in his new laboratory by a new experimenter, James Adams. Little is known of Adams's background, but later Edison recalled that he was an ex-sailor who first appeared at the Newark shop sometime during the spring of 1874 when he became an agent for the inductorium. At the time he was also working as an agent for the Walters Burglar Alarm Company. By the summer Adams was occasionally assisting Edison with experiments, and he had become a full-time member of the experimental team by the time Edison set up his new laboratory. Although Edison would occasionally be assisted by his old associates Edward Johnson and Ezra Gilliland and by his nephew Charley Edison, Batchelor and Adams were his principal experimental assistants, and he rewarded them with shares in the royalties from his inventions.[2]

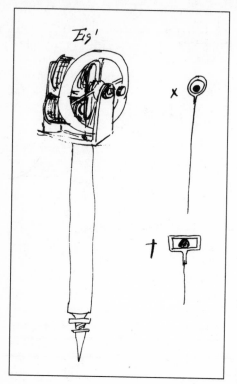

Charles Batchelor's drawing of the first
design for the electric pen.

Edison, Batchelor, and Adams had experimented briefly with a copying
system at the end of April, but in the new laboratory they began working on it
in earnest. Their first idea was to find an ink that would allow them to transfer
copies from one piece of paper to another under pressure. Although Edison
later developed and marketed a copying ink, he and his assistants turned their
attention instead to the idea of creating a stencil by using a pen with a sharp
reciprocating point. The copy was made by squeezing ink through the holes in
the stencil onto another piece of paper. By mid-July they had a pen that ran by
clockwork. However, it did not work very well, and they decided to replace the
clockwork with a small electric motor. At the same time, they began to design
a cabinet for their copying press. "We propose," Batchelor wrote on July 20, "to
make ou[r] press etc consist of a cabinet with iron frame attached, to paste the
letter to, the cabinet to have a cloth top."[3] By the beginning of September they
were ready to manufacture the electric pen and copying press.

To manufacture his new invention Edison turned to his old friend Ezra
Gilliland, who had joined him in Newark and was assisting with some of the

laboratory experiments. Prior to joining Edison in the spring of 1875, Gilliland had been manufacturing telegraph apparatus in Cincinnati. After arriving on the east coast he had set up a shop in New York under the name Gilliland & Company to sell products manufactured by Edison & Murray. During the summer Gilliland & Company moved to Ward Street, where Edison provided the funding and tools for manufacturing his new copying system. Although the experimental shop in his laboratory had no manufacturing responsibilities, Edison still needed manufacturing facilities to bring his inventions to market. Because Joseph Murray was busy manufacturing telegraph equipment, Edison turned to Gilliland.[4]

Once manufacturing was under way Edison needed a way to bring the copying system to market, and in September he began to establish agencies for the sale of "Edison's Autographic Press & Electric Pen." Edison initially sold it "for $30 giving our agents 33$^1/_3$ per cent that is about the price of a copying press here." He had high hopes of finding a ready market among merchants, lawyers, insurance companies, and other firms that "seem to have a great deal of reduplication."[5] However, even though the New York agent, an ex-telegraph operator named Mullarkey, found the pen and press "highly praised everywhere," he told Edison that "it would be harder to sell than you anticipate." Mullarkey found that "Bankers and Insurance people do not seem to want to take hold of it until it is established" and that "the chief objection comes from clerks who do not want to use it." Some had "such trifling objections as noise," and Mullarkey, who had to carry the outfit from office to office, found the "box is infernally heavy and nearly drags my arms off to carry it," but the primary problems with the new system were mechanical defects in the pen and the difficulty of taking care of the battery that powered it.[6]

The difficulties with the pen proved relatively easy to resolve. By the middle of October Edison and Batchelor had identified fifteen mechanical refinements that not only improved the pen but also made it cheaper to manufacture. The battery, however, continued to be a problem. Electrical apparatus was not yet a common feature of business machinery, and when such apparatus was used service companies commonly made an effort to prevent customers from having to deal with messy acid batteries. Thus, in printing or district telegraphs main-line rather than local batteries were usually used. When local batteries were required experienced telegraphers were often employed to take care of them. For the pen to be successful, Edison had to find a way of making batteries acceptable to the clerks who would be in charge of the apparatus. Edison and his coworkers found, however, that the battery they planned to use "was easily tipped over and the rod which serves to raise and lower the zinc [electrode] in the liquid become stuck in its holder by oxidation and by crystalization of the salts." After extensive experiments, they redesigned the battery compartment so that it was "easily cleaned & comes all apart, it cannot tipp over."[7] They also made it easy to lift up the carbon and zinc electrodes to prevent the battery from draining power when not in use.

While the battery continued to prevent some sales, the electric pen and autographic press proved to be a successful product, and Edison quickly established an office in New York. He soon had a dozen agents operating along the east and west coasts and in parts of the Midwest and Canada. As the new business grew, Edison asked his friend Norman Miller to take charge of it and also offered William Orton an interest. Orton was impressed with the new invention and told one prospective agent that the "Edison Autographic Pen is an apparatus that excites much interest wherever exhibited, and with a little practice can be, I think, made to serve a useful purpose in many cases. The apparatus has met with a ready sale here. Indeed, it has been difficult to supply the demand. I incline to think you would do well to secure the agency for Pittsburgh and vicinity."[8] Miller ran the business for only three months before resigning in mid-January. Edison then placed Batchelor, who along with Adams shared in all of Edison's pen royalties, in charge of the operation. Batchelor proved to be a more energetic manager than Miller and quickly increased pen sales in New York from two every five days to six per day. To improve the financial condition of the business, Edison sold an interest in the invention to Gilliland's father and even planned a stock offering for the Edison Pen and Press Company.[9]

While the electric pen and press looked to be a successful invention, Edison could not rely on it alone to support his laboratory and his staff of skilled machinists and experimenters. Concerned about his expenses, Edison decided that he needed a regular source of income for the laboratory. Not surprisingly, he again turned to the telegraph industry he knew so well. In July he and Orton began discussing the possibility of Edison's working on acoustic telegraphy for Western Union. At the time Orton was concerned that Elisha Gray's new system, in which a number of tuning forks or reeds were used to transmit several different frequencies over a single wire, might provide an effective alternative to Western Union's duplex and quadruplex systems. To stimulate Edison's thinking on this subject Orton sent him a description of Philip Reis's 1861 "telephone," which transmitted a sound when a contact point pressed against a vibrating membrane. To protect his company, Orton also negotiated with Gray. After Gray demonstrated his system between the Western Union headquarters in New York and its main office in Boston in late August, Orton agreed to provide him with financial support and access to Western Union facilities. Orton also continued his discussions with Edison, but the uncertain status of the inventor's relationship with Atlantic and Pacific may have prevented them from reaching an immediate agreement.[10]

Although Edison conducted some experiments on an electromotograph repeater for automatic telegraphy during the summer, he was otherwise little involved in technical work for Atlantic and Pacific. He did attempt to develop an independent scheme for sending night letters over Atlantic and Pacific wires, but nothing came of this. Then, when Jay Gould began merger negotiations with Western Union in August, Edison wrote him a proposal for settling the disputed claims of the Automatic Telegraph interests. Edison suggested a number of "Plans for paying much from nothing" to Gould that included the sale of the automatic system to Western Union or the possibility of using it in negotiations for a merger of the two companies. After these merger negotiations broke down in September Edison had nothing further to do with Atlantic and Pacific, although he did suggest to Gould the following February that the company sell its disputed quadruplex rights to Western Union.[11] By November, when he heard a rumor that Atlantic and Pacific officials were planning "to lay claim to my services after Octo 1/75, without compensation," Edison agreed to help Reiff and the other Automatic investors with their new American Automatic Telegraph Company.[12] Both Edison and Harrington reassigned their rights in his patents to this company. These reassignments then became the basis for a legal challenge that began the following spring when Reiff filed suit on behalf of Edison and Harrington against Gould and Atlantic and Pacific. Although the case was finally decided in their favor in 1906, Edison and Reiff (Harrington had died years earlier) were awarded only a dollar, but in 1911, the same year that Reiff died, the decision was annulled and their subsequent appeal to the U.S. Supreme Court was dismissed.

The contested financial arrangement between Gould and Automatic Telegraph haunted Edison in other ways as well. The promissory note to Harrington, which he had renewed in December 1874, had been given to William Seyfert. Seyfert was supposed to return it upon receiving his allotted share of Atlantic and Pacific stock. When no stock was forthcoming Seyfert kept the note, and his wife later made claims against Edison based on it.[13] Even with these legal and financial difficulties Edison never held a personal grudge against Gould. The financier had, after all, provided money when he badly needed it and had also been willing to support his development work on automatic telegraphy. Edison blamed Eckert rather than Gould for the failure of the automatic on Atlantic and Pacific lines and for his own departure from the company.[14]

Although Edison did not formally resign as Atlantic and Pacific electrician for another two years, his involvement in the company had effectively ended by the fall of 1875. In mid-November, Edison began conducting acoustic telegraph experiments for Western Union. To prevent the kind of legal complications that surrounded Edison's work on the quadruplex, Orton had him sign a series of agreements on December 14 aimed at clarifying his relationship to the company. Among other things, Edison agreed that he would "not make, invent or operate any system or apparatus for telegraphy for any Company opposed to or competing with the Western Union Company." He also agreed to give Grosvenor Lowrey, the company's general counsel, his power of attorney in connection with all patent matters, with the company paying legal costs. He and the company also agreed to a mutual release from any claims arising out of the quadruplex patent dispute. In return for Edison's work Western Union agreed to provide him with $200 per week in experimental expenses, although any disbursements had to be approved by Orton. The company also guaranteed him a minimum of $6,000 plus royalties if he succeeded in developing an acoustic system capable of sending five or more messages simultaneously.[15]

Even before Edison had entered into discussion with Orton on the subject of acoustic telegraphy he had read about Gray's work, which prompted him to begin "to read upon the subject of acoustics, as I was interested in not having my Quadruplex replaced by another method."[16] Edison soon obtained a translation of Frenchman J. Baille's *The Wonders of Electricity*, which discussed methods of acoustic telegraphy. As he began his investigations into this new technology Edison felt the need to further his knowledge of acoustics, and he engaged Robert Spice, a Brooklyn High School professor of chemistry and natural philosophy. Spice had provided Edison with private instruction in chemistry the previous fall and now acted as his expert on sound. Besides furnishing information on the science of acoustics Spice spent most of his evenings between December 1875 and February 1876 assisting with the experiments at Edison's laboratory.

To supplement Spice's expertise, Edison also read some of the standard writings on the subject, notably German physicist Hermann von Helmholtz's *Sensations of Tone*. Edison had recently acquired the 1875 edition of this authoritative work, and his marginal notes indicate his careful reading. One of these notes also suggests the differences between the acoustical scientist and the telegraph inventor. In an appendix to his book, Helmholtz describes an electromagnetic tuning fork design intended to replicate vowel sounds for acoustic study. Edison found this design "no good for telg[rap]hy on wire" and suggested an alteration that would make it serve as a telegraph instrument.[17] Edison also attempted to turn other Helmholtz apparatus to practical work in telegraphy.

Edison's early experiments were greatly influenced by Gray's system, which he had probably seen in New York during the August demonstration. Edison considered his first acoustic experiment on November 16 to be an improvement on Gray's, and in the caveat he executed six days later he claimed to be able to "transmit a greater number of messages over a single circuit at once than is possible with the devices of Gray."[18] However, he had not yet experimented over a working telegraph line. The November 22 caveat, in fact, marked the end of Edison's acoustic telegraph work for nearly three weeks as he and his staff explored a curious phenomenon they had noticed during their experiments.

Edison had been using a vibrator magnet in his acoustic telegraph experiments. This was a form of automatic circuit-breaker that was capable of producing continuous vibrations of "almost inconceivable rapidity."[19] In this device the charging of the electromagnet by a battery attracted a pivoted metal lever that was horizontal to the magnet cores and rested on a contact point. As the lever was attracted by the magnet it moved off the contact, breaking the circuit and discharging the magnet. This released the lever, which reestablished the circuit and started the cycle again. While experimenting with the vibrator the laboratory staff noticed a spark passing between the cores of the magnet and the lever that was similar to sparks they had frequently seen "in relays, in Stock printers when there were a little iron filings between the armature & core & more often in our new electric pen." They had always attributed this to induction, "but when we noticed it on this vibrator it seemed so strong that it struck us forcibly there might be something more than induction." They soon found that they could get the spark by touching the vibrator with a piece of iron and that the "larger the body of iron touched to the vibrator the larger the spark." They then connected the apparatus to gas pipes in the laboratory and found they could draw sparks from the pipes anywhere in the room. They could even draw sparks by placing a piece of metal as much as three inches from the end of the lever. After discovering that it failed to register on a galvanometer and did not have any taste, Edison concluded that "the cause of the spark is a *true unknown force.*"[20]

This seems a surprisingly bold deduction for Edison to have made from a few simple experiments. After all, the sparking phenomenon had been observed for years by Edison and others and his first experiments seem more suggestive of future research than evidence for such a profound conclusion. As it turns out, Edison thought he had found a new force for the simple reason that he was searching for one. The first evidence of Edison's interest in new forces had occurred in April 1874 when he noticed the electromotograph phenomenon. The following November, having decided that the electromotograph was an interesting and potentially useful phenomenon but not a new force, he conducted a series of experiments specifically designed to find such a force. These experiments were apparently prompted by his reading a discussion of the "odic" force of German chemist Karl Reichenbach. In the 1860s, Reichenbach claimed he had discovered a heretofore unknown force that explained various spiritualist or occult phenomenon. Although Reichenbach's results were not generally accepted by the scientific community, the subject of spiritualist phenomena did interest several prominent British scientists, some of whom also thought that unknown forces might provide an answer. William Crookes, in particular, conducted experiments along this line in the hope of discovering a psychic force.[21]

Edison too believed that unknown natural forces might provide the explanation for phenomena that might otherwise be considered supernatural. Edison's interest in such problems led to his brief flirtation with theosophy in 1878. Although little interested in the ideas from ancient Egyptian and Asian religions that the movement's founder, Helena Blavatsky, had incorporated into her theology, he was attracted by her attempts to explicate occult science. Henry Olcott, who cofounded the American Theosophical Society, recalled Edison describing his own experiments on occult forces (which appear to be those he conducted in November 1874). According to Olcott, Edison had connected a pendulum to various kinds of conductors, "wire of various metals, simple and compound, and tubes containing different fluids," and then placed the other end of the conductor against his forehead in an attempt to move the pendulum by "will-force."[22]

Even though he was intrigued by the idea that new forces might provide a scientific explanation of spiritualism, Edison was more interested in their potential practical applications. His May 31, 1875, list of experimental projects had included a "New force for Telegraphic communication," and he had tried some experiments in this direction on May 2 and 3.[23] A month later he and his staff spent three nights on another series of experiments that also proved unsuccessful. When he noticed the sparking phenomenon on November 22 Edison was prepared to believe that he had finally found his elusive new force. To protect his claim to this scientific discovery, Edison had Batchelor keep detailed records of their work in the new "Experimental Researches" notebook they had begun using at the laboratory in mid-October. Batchelor also kept a second account of their experiments in his personal notebook.

Their first experiments were designed to determine whether the phenomenon was, in fact, the manifestation of a new force. Edison and his assistants conducted tests to see if the effect was inductive and whether it registered any electrical charge. The negative results of these experiments only reinforced their belief that they had truly discovered a new force, which they termed "etheric." They proceeded to explore the strength of the effect by placing various resistances and insulators in the circuit and tested twenty-eight different metals as vibrator levers to see which one produced the strongest effect. To detect the spark more easily they also devised an ingenious dark box with an eyepiece aimed over a spark gap, which they called an "etheroscope." Not surprisingly, they also tried transmitting the new force over a telegraph line to New Brunswick, New Jersey. As a result of this experiment, Edison concluded that his etheric force would make it possible to cheapen telegraph communication by allowing Atlantic cables to be laid without insulation and by transmitting on land through railroad tracks or with uninsulated wire laid in the earth, thus saving the cost of poles and insulation.[24]

Convinced that he had made a fundamental scientific discovery, Edison demonstrated his etheric force to a number of people, including the chief electrical examiner of the U.S. Patent Office, and then announced his discovery to the press. These reports, which began to appear in the Newark papers on November 29 and in the New York papers the following day, provided a summary of his experiments, sometimes quoting directly from his notebooks, and repeated his claims that the new force could revolutionize telegraphy. A particularly positive and extensive article in the December 2 *New York Herald* contained Edison's theoretical explanation of the phenomenon:

> Under certain conditions heat energy can be transmitted into electric energy, and that again, under certain conditions, into magnetic energy, this back again into electric energy, all forms of energy being interchangeable with each other. It follows that if electric energy under certain conditions is transformed into that of

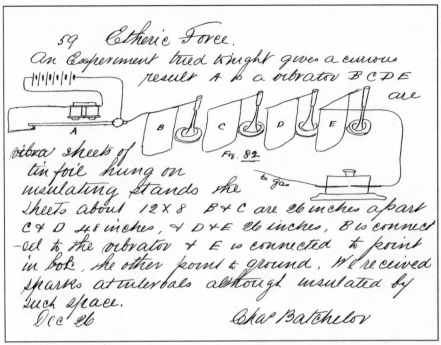

59 Etheric Force.

An Experiment tried to night gives a curious result A b a vibrator B C D E are

Fig. 82.

to gas

vibra sheets of tin foil hung on insulating stands the sheets about 12 X 8 B & C are 26 inches apart C & D 48 inches, & D & E 26 inches, B is connected to the vibrator & E is connected to point in box, the other point to ground. We received sparks at intervals although insulated by such space.

Dec 26   Chas Batchelor

Charles Batchelor's drawing of the last etheric force experiment, which was conducted the day after Christmas in 1875.

magnetism under other conditions it might be transformed into an entirely un-known force, subject to laws different from those of heat, light, electricity or mag-netism. There is every reason to suppose that etheric energy is this new form.[25]

Several newspapers also reported his belief that Reichenbach's odic force was in fact his etheric force.

Although initial press reports were generally approving and accepting of Edison's claims, skeptical commentary soon appeared. The *New York Times* ridiculed Edison's discovery and its connection with Reichenbach's discredited odic force. James Ashley at the *Telegrapher* was, of course, quick to mock "Edi-son's New Moonshine" and his claims that it would revolutionize telegraphy. A more measured, though still dubious, reaction appeared in the *New York Evening Post*, which thought Edison's observations remarkably similar to the "weak sparks" reported in 1875 by German physicist Petrus Riess. The *Post* did wonder, however, at the timing of Edison's announcement, which appeared just after Riess's work had been discussed in an American publication. Al-though reporting that Western Union's electricians had frequently noticed these sparks but never considered them evidence of a new force, the *Post*'s edi-torialist was nonetheless willing to state that "it is possible that it may develop into something of importance," although he cautioned the telegraph company to wait "until more definite results are reached" before giving up its insulators.[26]

The scientific and technical communities also entered the debate. Edison found an ally in Dr. George M. Beard, a pioneer researcher in neurology whose work focused on electrotherapeutics. Edison had first attracted Beard's attention with his inductorium, and the New York physician now became his collaborator and public champion. Beard provided Edison with a galvanic frog and helped him conduct etheric force experiments that Edison reported in a letter to the *Scientific American*. Beard also conducted his own experiments, including some at Charles Chester's shop in New York, where he worked with telegraph inventor John E. Smith. Smith had witnessed some of Edison's experiments, but like many in the telegraph community he considered the effect to be caused by induction. Beard published an extensive account of his experiments in a letter to the *New York Daily Tribune* in which he offered his own theory that the etheric force was a new and different form of electricity and suggested that it be called "apolic" because of its lack of polarity. Beard also attempted to deflect criticisms by disassociating the etheric force from Reichenbach's odic force and Riess's weak sparks. Another of Beard's objects in writing his letter was to encourage scientific research, which he thought might have been discouraged by the unfortunate "manner in which it was introduced to the public." Newspaper reporters, he felt, were ill prepared to produce accurate accounts of scientific research.[27] Beard's most extensive discussion of the experiments he and Edison performed came during a public lecture before the Polytechnic Institute at the Cooper Union. A detailed report of this lecture and the accompanying demonstration by Edison appeared in the *New York Tribune*, but ultimately Edison lost the scientific contest over his alleged discovery because neither he nor Beard published a carefully argued account in a scientific journal.

Edison's most significant opponents in the scientific controversy surrounding his discovery were Elihu Thomson and Edwin Houston. Houston was a science teacher with whom Thomson had studied at Philadelphia's Central High School. They had conducted scientific and technical experiments together for several years, and both were active members of the Franklin Institute and the American Philosophical Society, two of the most important American scientific institutions of the day. In 1871 Thomson had made observations similar to Edison's, but he had concluded that they were caused by induction. Following the first published reports of Edison's discovery, Thomson and Houston conducted a series of careful experiments that they argued proved that the effect was inductive. Disdaining the popular press, they wrote for the scientific community and reported their results in the *Journal of the Franklin Institute*. Their article was widely reprinted in the scientific and technical press, appearing in the January 29 issue of *Scientific American Supplement*, where Edison saw it. His reply, in a letter to *Scientific American*, prompted further experiments by Thomson and Houston that proved decisive. Their careful account in the April 1876 *Journal of the Franklin Institute* demonstrated to the satisfaction of most scientific researchers that the spark was caused by opposite induced currents, which was also the reason that it did not exhibit polarity. These results were confirmed by physicist Silvanus P. Thompson in two papers published in British scientific journals.[28]

It turns out, however, that Edison had in fact made an important observation, one that was not understood until years later. What Edison termed etheric force was really high-frequency electromagnetic waves. Even though James Clerk Maxwell had developed a mathematical theory to explain how such waves could travel through space, no one at the time recognized that this is what Edison had generated and observed. It was not until after Heinrich Hertz experimentally validated Maxwell's theory in 1889 that researchers understood the significance of Edison's experiments as well as the possibility of using such waves for radio telegraphy. It is not surprising then that Edison had failed to press his claims over a decade earlier. Although he conducted an extensive series of experiments in July 1876 to examine Thomson's and Houston's tests and conclusions critically, Edison never made his results public and withdrew from the contest.[29]

Perhaps more surprising than his inability to press his claims adequately before the scientific community was Edison's failure to develop his ideas about the use of the etheric force in telegraphy. During his experiments, Edison had developed experimental apparatus with which he might have sent and received radio signals. Furthermore, he had suggested the potential cost savings from a system of etheric telegraphy. Yet, other than writing out a draft caveat that apparently he never completed, Edison did not attempt to develop a telegraph system using etheric force until many years later. He turned away from his etheric experiments because of pressure from Western Union. On December 10 Norman Miller sent him a letter discussing the impending contract with the company and commenting that the "papers are so full of 'new force' that I want you to show that it has not taken up too much of your time."[30] Taking the hint, Edison dropped his etheric force investigations and quickly returned to acoustic telegraphy. Although the potential of using uninsulated wires and even railroad tracks to send signals might have attracted Western Union support, the company still would have needed to lay new lines and replace wires that corroded and broke. On the other hand, acoustic systems presented another way of lowering costs by further increasing the number of signals that could be transmitted over a single wire. However, turning this theoretical possibility into a commercially viable system proved extremely difficult for Edison and other inventors.

The basic problem in acoustic telegraphy was to find a suitable method of separating the different signal frequencies. Edison's basic designs used tuned reeds or tuning forks, vibrating at a set frequency that were brought in and out of the circuit by a standard Morse key. At the other end, the electrical impulse would register on similarly tuned reeds or forks that activated a telegraph sounder and made the Morse dots and dashes audible. Edison also experimented with resonating tubes in which vibrating iron diaphragms reproduced the signaled sound. Among his other transmitter designs was a "harmonic engine" in which a revolving double breakwheel with alternating contacts sent rapid pulses, and his alternative receivers included automatic ink and chemical recorders incorporating vibrating reeds. To deal with electrical effects during transmission Edison employed various arrangements of artificial lines, induction coils, batteries, and resistances similar to those he had used in automatic and quadruplex circuits.[31]

Although the careful record keeping that marked the first six months of work in the new laboratory came to an end with the flurry of work on acoustic telegraphy, the records that remain provide insight into the interaction between the machine shop and laboratory research. During November Edison had his machinists build several receiving tubes. Each had a different diameter that allowed it to respond to a particular frequency and acted as a sounder when its iron diaphragm was attracted to an electromagnet with the tube reinforcing the sound for the operator. While experimenting with these, however, Edison became dissatisfied with the poor response of the iron diaphragm to the incoming signal. At some point, he tried replacing the diaphragm with a strip of metal vibrated by a polarized relay. Although this design also failed to work satisfactorily, Edison included it in both a caveat and a patent application.[32]

A more significant modification took place on December 20, when Edison sketched a new receiver in which a rectangular metal strip replaced the circular iron diaphragm. In this design, he also used a flexible rubber listening tube that could slide in and out of the stationary metal tube to which the diaphragm was attached to tune the receiver. Edison gave the sketch to Batchelor, who instructed Kruesi to "start on this right away with Jim [Adams]. If you want brass there is an order you can fill on my desk." Kruesi apparently had trouble obtaining the kind of brass needed for the instrument, and Edison told him "Tin will do if you cant get right brass."[33] Within twenty-four hours Kruesi had made three of these instruments, using iron coated with tin for the rectangular diaphragm.

Even though Edison later claimed that this new design proved "capable of rendering audible any sounds whatever, transmitted telegraphically," he continued to experiment with alternative receivers.[34] In an important laboratory test of December 26, during which he successfully transmitted three messages in the same direction, Edison used "a reed with a resonator to pick out the sound better & tube to put in the ear."[35] During these experiments, Edison also made a major modification in his transmitter circuit by using a separate battery for each transmitter that prevented fluctuations in current strength when they vibrated in and out of the circuit.

It is not clear which receiver design Edison was using when he wrote Orton on December 29, "I struck the right principle for the transmission of vibra-

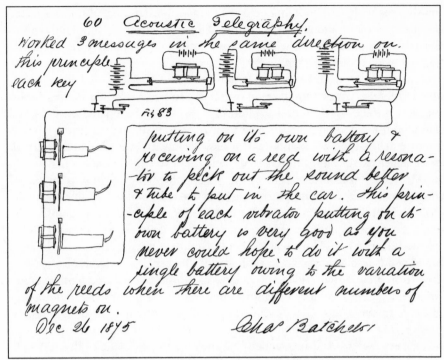

In Charles Batchelor's drawing of a December 1875 acoustic telegraph test the three receivers at left are of different sizes with the smallest receiver resonating at the highest frequency and the largest at the lowest frequency.

tions last night, and received two different messages on my adjustable resonators without interferance. Tonight I am trying to transmit three. I have only one resonator and it hasnt enough range to pick the third message out, but will have some tubeing tomorrow for new ones."[36] However, when he brought his instruments into New York for tests on Western Union lines in early January, he was using reeds in his receivers.

As Edison and his staff conducted tests in the laboratory and at Western Union headquarters he made many changes to his instruments. On January 10 Edison gave Batchelor a sketch with the note "have [transmitting] reeds altered for tonight this way," and Batchelor instructed Kruesi to *attend to this.* The same day Edison developed a new transmitter circuit but found he had to alter the reeds so "as not to produce a node [dead spot] in them in vibrating."[37] Edison made further alterations in his transmitter design on the 15th, with Charles Wurth making the modifications in what he now designated the "New Style Vibrator." Ten days later, Edison decided to use a rigid point in his transmitter instead of a spring vibrating point, and he also had his staff design the transmitters with higher frequencies to reduce interference. When he tested this arrangement on January 25, Edison, Batchelor, and Ezra Gilliland worked the receiving instruments while Adams, Robert Spice, and Edison's father Samuel worked the transmitters.[38]

Even before this test Edison was sufficiently confident in his system that he asked Orton for permission to test it over a line to Boston. While waiting for his machinists to complete the instruments for this test, he prepared a caveat that included his new modifications, and he made still further changes during tests in early February. Most notable was a new arrangement for holding the reeds in his receivers and transmitters that made them less rigid. Edison had Wurth modify several instruments in this way, and after further experiments instructed him to make further alterations intended to make them more easily adjustable. Unfortunately, it is just at this point that the record of Edison's acoustic telegraph experiments ends except for a tantalizing note to Orton in mid-February in which he declared "I have at last got the animal tamed a seance will be held monday or tuesday whereat the professor of 'Acousticity' will exhibit the latest theft from the German Telegraph books."[39] (Edison was making light of James Ashley's frequent references to him as the "professor of duplicity and quadruplicity" and his claim that Edison had stolen his duplex and diplex designs from earlier German telegraph experimenters, even though their published plans had never worked in practice.)[40] Whatever the outcome of this test, Edison put his experimental work into hiatus as he prepared to move his family and his laboratory to Menlo Park, New Jersey.

Edison later claimed that he decided to abandon Newark because of a lawsuit brought by Thomas Slaight, the padlock manufacturer who owned the building where he had established a small shop with Joseph Murray in February 1872. According to Edison, a Newark law "made a monthly renter liable for a year" and this "seemed so unjust that I determined to get out of place that permitted such injustice."[41] Most likely, Edison simply wanted to build the kind of laboratory that he had begun working toward ever since his return from England and he found Newark too costly. In December 1875 he had sent his father to investigate possible sites, and at the end of the month he purchased two tracts of land and a house in Menlo Park. A mere whistlestop located twelve miles south of Newark on the railroad line to Philadelphia, Menlo Park had been part of a failed real estate development and Edison was able to purchase this property for $5,200. As the new year opened, he set his father to work erecting the new laboratory, which cost over $2,500 and was completed by March 25. A few days later, Edison moved into the new laboratory where he would not only produce some of his most famous inventions, but also create a new model for invention that became the cornerstone of modern industrial research.

CHAPTER 8

The Invention Factory

E dison's Menlo Park laboratory has long been recognized by historians as providing a new model that helped transform American invention, and Edison himself has been described as a transitional figure standing between the lone inventor of the nineteenth century and the industrial researcher of the twentieth.[1] Working in a tradition of cooperative shop invention, neither Edison nor most of his contemporaries were *lone* inventors, although they were generally *independent* inventors. The creation of the laboratory itself, however, was made possible by the growing interest of large-scale, technology-based companies such as Western Union in acquiring greater control over the inventive process by supporting the work of these inventors. Although constrained by nineteenth-century beliefs in the unpredictability of inventive genius, Western Union president William Orton clearly perceived the Menlo Park laboratory as an extension of the inventor himself. But he also recognized that the laboratory enabled Edison to make invention a more regular and predictable process and was thus willing to provide direct support for it. The support Edison received for his laboratory from Western Union and later from the Edison Electric Light Company helped to demonstrate the value of invention to industry and showed that invention itself could become an industrial process.

The Menlo Park laboratory did not mark a sharp break away from the shop tradition of invention. Instead it represented Edison's continuing efforts to elaborate on rather than replace that tradition. At Menlo Park the machine shop continued to be a key element in Edison's inventive style. Now, however, the skilled workmen were able to devote themselves to invention, and the tools that had been used in the Newark telegraph shops were adapted solely for inventive work. This allowed Edison to rapidly construct, test, and alter experimental devices, significantly increasing the rate at which he could develop new

The original Menlo Park machine shop was located on the bottom floor of the original building and contained precision tools from Edison's telegraph shops.

inventions. The Menlo Park laboratory was designed to be an "invention factory" where Edison planned to produce "a minor invention every ten days and a big thing every six months or so."[2]

Nonetheless, Menlo Park also looked forward to a new model of research as Edison continued to merge the shop tradition with the increasingly sophisticated style of laboratory research that he had been developing since his return from England in 1873. Edison was not alone in these efforts. Electrical—and to a more limited extent chemical—laboratories could be found in a number of American telegraph shops. Edison had seen Moses Farmer's small laboratory above Charles Williams's shop in Boston with its "immense quantity of valuable electrical and experimental apparatus."[3] After arriving in New Jersey, he had experimented in Dr. Leverett Bradley's telegraph shop in Jersey City, where he found a fine electrical laboratory used by Bradley in designing and manufacturing the first American-made galvanometer. Western Electric Manufacturing Company, where rival inventor Elisha Gray conducted his experiments, had a laboratory with "ample accommodations for electrical, chemical, and other scientific investigations."[4] What set Edison's effort apart from those of his contemporaries was its scale and scope. The laboratory he built in Menlo Park was the largest private laboratory in the United States and certainly the largest devoted to invention.

Some of the scientific and chemical instruments on the second floor of the Menlo Park
laboratory that made it the best-equipped private laboratory in the United States.

The laboratory building was a rather unassuming white, two-story frame
structure, surrounded by a white picket fence and located on the crest of a hill
about 200 yards from the railroad station. Reporters described it as "looking, for
all the world, like a country meeting-house, minus the steeple, and with the addition of a porch" and as "a country school-house pulled out three times its
length."[5] G. M. Shaw provided one of the best descriptions of the laboratory's
interior in an 1878 issue of *Popular Science Monthly*:

> On the ground floor, as you enter, is a little front-office, from which a small library
> is partitioned off. Next is a large square room with glass cases filled with models of
> his inventions. In the rear of this is the machine shop, completely equipped, and
> run with a ten-horse-power engine. The upper story occupies the length and
> breadth of the building, 100 x 25 feet, is lighted by windows on every side, and is
> occupied as a laboratory. The walls are covered with shelves full of bottles contain-
> ing all sorts of chemicals. Scattered through the rooms are tables covered with
> electrical instruments . . . microscopes, spectroscopes, etc. In the centre of the
> room is a rack full of galvanic batteries.[6]

As unpretentious as the laboratory's exterior appeared on first encounter,
the village of Menlo Park itself seemed even less auspicious to visitors. One
journalist characterized it as "the merest hamlet—half a dozen houses in

shades of yellow ochre and chocolate, and of the usual suburban type."[7] The suburban character of Menlo Park may have been part of its attraction for Edison. By the 1870s the detached suburban home and yard on a sizeable tract of land had become the ideal for those of the upper and more prosperous middle classes who could afford the price of commuting by train into the city as they sought healthful, secure environments for their families. The nation's growing cities were increasingly perceived as crowded, unhealthful, and dangerous places. Newark in particular was becoming a very unhealthy city, with poor sanitation and outbreaks of epidemic diseases resulting from its rapid growth. Its very success as a manufacturing center, which had been an attraction for Edison when he initially settled there, was making Newark a place where he did not want to raise his family. The more expensive northern suburbs of Newark did not provide the cheap land he needed for his laboratory, and Menlo Park may have seemed an excellent alternative. Although it was a failed development, Menlo Park exhibited some of the features of a more finished suburb with its position on the railroad line twelve miles from Newark, its broad, laid-out streets, and its community park. Menlo Park also had a semi-rural character that hinted at memories of Edison's boyhood home in Port Huron. Menlo Park's advantages over the city were nicely captured by a reporter for the *Newark Daily Advertiser*:

> Mr. Edison has probably made a very wise selection for his field of operations. He is not hampered by the noise and confusion of a large city, while near enough to reach one in a short time. It is singular that Menlo Park has attracted so little attention: as a building site it has not equal between Newark and Philadelphia. It is so high as to command a view of New York and Brooklyn, with a rolling surface, good soil and water, and an atmosphere pure and invigorating. Perhaps its falling into the hands of land speculators a few years ago may have injured its prospects, as it has at present but nine dwelling houses.[8]

The Edison house in Menlo Park, described by one reporter as "one of the best, — comfortable, but without a trace of ostentation," appears in photographs as a substantial three-story house, with a spacious front porch, sitting on a large plot surrounded by a white picket fence.[9] The household furnishings, insured for $3,000, included Mary's antiques and curios, described by the insurance company as "Bronzes and Articles of Virtu" [antiques and curios], a "Piano-Forte," and "Household furniture useful and ornamental beds bedding linen pictures printed books and family wearing apparel."[10] Living in the house with Thomas and Mary were their children, four-year-old daughter Marion and three-month-old son Thomas Alva Jr. (nicknamed Dot and Dash by their father), Mary's sister Alice, and three black servants; in October 1878 the Edisons had their third child, William Leslie. Edison's father Samuel returned to Port Huron, but at some point Mary's fifteen-year-old brother Charles moved to Menlo Park to work in the laboratory and probably lived with the family. When Edison's nephew Charley joined his uncle in the laboratory he probably lived with the family as well. Edison's closest associate, Charles Batchelor, bought a home in Menlo Park for his wife Rosanna and his two daughters, two-year-old Emma and two-month-old Rosa; they apparently shared this house with John Kruesi and his wife. Nothing is known of the living quarters for the rest of the laboratory staff, which included James Adams and Charles Wurth.[11]

Edison seems to have been quite happy in his new home, inviting a friend to come strawberrying in "the prettiest spot in New Jersey."[12] Charles Batchelor, too, considered Menlo Park to be "a beautiful country place where . . . we all feel considerable benefit from the change." Nevertheless, to calm his wife, he kept "one big Newfoundland dog and two smaller ones and a seven shooter under my pillow nights."[13] Mary Edison also found the isolation of Menlo Park menacing, especially as her husband continued to work nights, and daughter Marion remembered that her mother also "slept with a revolver under her pillow" because her father frequently did not come home "until early morning or not at all."[14] Edison's tendency to neglect Mary for his work made her isolation even worse and she frequently visited her family in Newark. Thomas, who seems not to have appreciated Mary's feelings of isolation, had little to do with his wife's social life and would not attend the many parties she gave for her Newark friends.

Mary's sense of isolation in Menlo Park was no doubt exacerbated by its predominantly male environment. Aside from a few wives such as Rosanna Batchelor, the community was made up entirely of laboratory and factory workmen. Initially the small laboratory staff was supplemented by a larger group of men who worked in Ezra Gilliland's electric pen factory, which Edison had moved from Newark into a building located near the Menlo Park railroad station in late April. To accommodate the growing number of single men working at the laboratory by October 1878, and perhaps to provide more female companionship for his wife, Edison invited the recently widowed Sarah Jordan and her thirteen-year-old daughter Ida to Menlo Park. "Aunt Sally" (Mary's father's stepdaughter from his first marriage) set up a boardinghouse for the single men who worked at the laboratory. The domestic space of the boardinghouse, along with the nicely furnished homes of Edison and Batchelor, provided a distinct contrast to the laboratory and factory. The laboratory, as a place of work, was sparsely furnished except for chairs and workbenches; instead of domestic bric-a-brac on the walls there were bottles of chemicals, and the tables held laboratory instruments rather than candlesticks and fine china. The distinction between female and male environments was preserved within the boardinghouse, where Sarah and Ida's more elaborately furnished parlor and living quarters were off limits to the workmen who lived in spare bedrooms.[15]

Edison clearly reveled in the environment of the laboratory, with its manly comradery. At the laboratory he could tell jokes and pull pranks, as he had enjoyed doing during his days as a telegrapher. The rough and tumble character of the laboratory was enhanced by a young black bear that they kept as a pet until he got loose and had to be killed, as well as by the brass band organized by the laboratory and factory employees. Although the laboratory was only a short block from his home, Edison usually did not go home for meals; when she was old enough his daughter would bring him something, or he would order in late-night snacks and beer from the local tavern. On days off he might go fishing (his favorite recreation) with the laboratory staff rather than spend time at home. Although Mary was no doubt glad when Edison did come home, he often was too tired to spend time with her. One of these occasions, which was witnessed by some of the laboratory employees, highlights the contrast between the domestic environment of the home and the gritty workplace. An exhausted Edison fell asleep in the spare bedroom where Mary found him "rolled right over on the bed in all his dirt and grease on my nice white counterpanes and pillow shams." Although she claimed that "I don't care as long as he gets his rest and sleep," such behavior clearly exasperated her.[16]

The move to Menlo Park occurred at the end of March 1876. Edison and his small group of co-workers then spent the next five weeks preparing the new laboratory for work. When experiments resumed during the second week of May, Adams acted as Edison's principle assistant while Batchelor commuted into New York City to oversee the electric pen business. The first experiments in the new laboratory centered on the effort to develop an acoustic system of multiple telegraphy using paired tuning forks or acoustic reeds. To conduct line tests, Western Union provided Edison with a connection to its main East Coast line, which allowed him to experiment on loops to Philadelphia, located about 60 miles south of Menlo Park, and to Washington, another 140 miles past Philadelphia. By the end of May, Edison had executed five patents on his acoustic system. He had also begun to experiment on yet another new system of telegraphy.[17]

Edison called his new system acoustic transfer telegraphy. Instead of using pairs of electrically vibrated tuning forks or reeds to send particular frequencies over a line, he used them as electrical switches to allow several sets of Morse instruments to time-share the same transmission line. Each set was connected to one of several contacts on the vibrating fork or reed at each end, which switched them on and off the line so rapidly that the signal was transmitted and received as if the instruments were continuously on line. The system depended on complete synchronization between each set of transmitters and receivers so that they were on line at the same time. Edison's system, arising as it did out of his work on acoustic telegraphy, differed from those of other inventors who employed rapidly revolving disks or breakwheels to switch sets of instruments on and off line.

As Edison continued his efforts to develop a new telegraph system, his earlier inventions were being exhibited at the U.S. Centennial Exhibition, which opened in Philadelphia on May 10. Edison's large display in conjunction with Western Union, which was not ready when the fairgrounds opened, included all of his inventions, except for his automatic telegraph and his electric pen. His automatic telegraph was used by the Atlantic and Pacific Telegraph Company, which ran the fair's public telegraph office, and it received a prize from the awards committee headed by British physicist Sir William Thomson, who called it "a very important step in land-telegraphy." Thomson, who visited Edison at Menlo Park in July, also praised the electric pen, for which the committee gave another prize, as an invention of "exquisite ingenuity and . . . usefulness." The electric pen exhibit was in the main building, where Batchelor had four men demonstrating the copying system.[18]

The market for the electric pen soon expanded as Edison sold the British rights and appointed agents in Cuba and South America. Edison had been attempting to sell European rights since the beginning of the year with the assistance of Marshall Lefferts; when Lefferts died unexpectedly on July 3 while on his way to the Centennial, Edison turned to Frederic Ireland, who was in New York negotiating on behalf of British businessmen John Breckon and Thomas Clare. Breckon and Clare, who had learned of the pen from Edison's Canadian agent John Gloyn, acquired the British rights and soon formed the Electric Writing Company to market the invention in Britain. They placed Ireland, who was also acting as Edison's agent for continental rights, in charge of the business.

Edison's efforts to negotiate foreign rights to his electric pen show his relative inexperience. His discussions of the matter with three different parties left the legal status of these rights somewhat confused. In February he had been approached by John Gloyn, the electric pen agent in Ontario, Canada, about British rights. Edison had given Gloyn an option for sixty days following the filing of the British patent specification. Then, in early March, Edison had signed an agreement with Lily Yeaton of New York for the sale of foreign rights to be negotiated by her husband Charles Yeaton, who was involved in the effort to form a stock company for the electric pen. A month later Amasa Mason, a London-based acquaintance of Lefferts, had approached Lefferts regarding foreign rights to Edison's pen and Lefferts had sent him a pen outfit for use in attracting foreign investors. When it became apparent that the Yeatons would be unable to carry out their contract, Marshall Lefferts had agreed to help Edison negotiate foreign rights. But Edison then discovered that Gloyn's option had not, as he thought, expired, because although Edison had filed the provisional British patent specification in October he had not filed the full specification until April. Thus, Edison and Lefferts found themselves bound by Edison's option to Gloyn. Following Lefferts's death, Edison negotiated the final sale to Gloyn and his associates. The complicated negotiations for Edison's foreign rights on the electric pen taught the inventor a valuable lesson. The previous efforts to promote his inventions overseas, notably the Universal stock printer and his automatic telegraph system, had been undertaken by his backers in America. If the Gold and Stock president had lived, Edison may well have decided to rely on him not only for the electric pen but perhaps also for other inventions. Lefferts, after all, had been involved in setting up Exchange Telegraph in Britain with Edison's Universal stock printer, and Edison was glad to rely on his judgment and experience in negotiations regarding the electric pen. Now, however, Edison learned that he had to rely on his own judgment of potential investors and promoters. In the future he would pick men with whom he forged personal bonds and long-term relationships that gave him the trust and confidence he had found in his personal relationship with Lefferts.[19]

Although Edison's new British agents actively promoted his invention—Clare, for example, demonstrated it before the Royal Society—the new business met with only modest success. According to Ireland, "the British public—with its usual stupidity—did not take kindly to the apparatus as it *was* and it has had to be practically revolutionized."[20] To meet objections they had redesigned the handle of the pen and substituted a closed battery. They also pressed Edison to develop a fast rotary press. Although Edison and Batchelor spent much of January and February 1877 working on such a press, which other pen agents also thought necessary, they failed to develop a commercial model. One customer at least expressed satisfaction. Oxford mathematician Charles Dodgson (better known as Lewis Carroll) thought the electric pen "quite the best thing yet invented for taking a number of copies of MS, drawings, and maps." Nonetheless, sales lagged because "the management of the outfit requires more care than office officials are disposed to bestow."[21]

Sales in the United States, unlike those in Britain, increased rapidly during 1876, and Edison decided to place the entire business in the hands of the Western Electric Manufacturing Company. Besides his belief that Western Electric had better manufacturing facilities for the growing business, Edison also wanted Batchelor to return to the laboratory. In November 1876 Edison signed a contract with Western Electric stipulating that he and his partners were to receive a $5 royalty on each set of duplicating apparatus with a minimum guarantee of $250 each month. Western Electric also agreed to pay $1,500 for the special tools that had been developed for its manufacture. The company's president, Anson Stager, who was also Western Union's central division superintendent, placed former telegraph operator and manufacturer George Bliss in charge of marketing, and by April Batchelor had turned the entire foreign and domestic pen business over to him. Over the next three years Bliss worked hard to make the electric pen a success in America and Europe, and Edison received regular royalty payments. However, by 1880, according to Edward Johnson, the pen business was in serious decline because it could no longer compete "against a field borne of its own seed."[22] One of the electric pen's offsprings was the mimeograph developed by A. B. Dick in the mid-1880s. Dick not only acquired rights to Edison's copying patents but also his assistance in marketing the system as the Edison Mimeograph.

Throughout 1876 Edison's primary research remained multiple telegraphy, particularly his new acoustic transfer system. By the beginning of August he had developed it into an "octruplex" capable of sending eight simultaneous messages, and in mid-September he successfully tested it over the loop circuit to Philadelphia and also demonstrated it to Western Union officials. Although

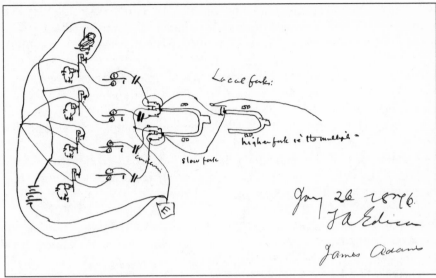

In Edison's acoustic transfer system the tuning forks acted as electrical switches to allow several sets of Morse instruments to time-share the same transmission line. This design used polarized relays (immediately to the left of the fork at center).

the acoustic transfer worked satisfactorily on artificial lines and between New York and Philadelphia, Edison informed William Orton at the end of December that "on longer line the phenomenon of the Static Charge causes mutilation of the signals and I have been unable up to the present time to devise a compensation sufficiently powerful to counteract this effect beyond a distance of 100 miles." However, he reassured the Western Union president that "it is only a question of time when the system will be perfected as the principle I am sure is correct, but you will readily allow that it is a very complicated subject and requires some elaborate contortions of the brain to manipulate these signals and eradicate the defects and thence the experimental labor is exceedingly tedious."[23]

As was often the case, even when concentrating his energies on one line of research Edison allowed himself to be distracted by others. For example, while focusing on his acoustic transfer system he briefly considered it as a way of working his roman letter automatic with fewer wires. In another case, experiments that used his electromotograph as an automatic telegraph repeater led him to think about the device as an alternative to an electromagnet for activating the tuning forks of his acoustic telegraph system.[24] This kind of serendipitous exploration was a crucial aspect of his creativity, and he frequently drew on elements of one technology to improve another or used experiments in one direction to suggest ideas for other lines of research. Sometimes he did no more than note ideas that emerged from such explorations in his notebooks or patent caveats, but at other times they became the basis for a new research project. For example, during the summer of 1876 Edison experimented with large tuning forks in his acoustic transfer system. At that time he conceived "the idea that the greatest amount of power can be got out of a magnet by the aid of a tuning fork" and devised an electromagnetically driven tuning fork motor for printing telegraphs. He also set Batchelor to work adapting it for sewing machines. By December, after three months of work, Batchelor had "not met with very much success" and concluded that the "power derived from an electromagnet is the most deceptive thing possible."[25] These experiments were soon discontinued, but the idea that prompted them was not forgotten and re-emerged during Edison's early work on electric generators.

Other examples of the way in which research could produce unexpected offspring can be found in Edison's experiments with a shipment of fine electrical apparatus that he received from London at the end of July. The most expensive item in the July shipment was a set of resistance coils, and Edison became interested in the possibility of making inexpensive resistances out of carbonized paper. As he later recalled, "Strips of cardboard or Bristol board, about a quarter of an inch wide and five inches long were placed in gas tubes and carbonized by placing the same in a furnace and heating the tube to a white heat. The strips were packed in the tube one upon the other and the interstices were filled with charcoal powder." Edison's experiments with carbonized paper soon became "quite extensive" as he experimented with different thicknesses and weights of paper for other items such as battery carbons and chemical crucibles.[26] He planned to market these products through the American Novelty Company, which he formed with Edward Johnson in November 1876. However, the only products actually marketed by the company were a duplicating ink developed by Edison and Batchelor and Johnson's ribbon mucilage. Edison was also dissatisfied with the expensive galvanometers he had acquired, and he attempted to design his own by using his electromotograph as a sensitive indicator of electrical charge. This effort led him to briefly renew his efforts to develop a fast and sensitive electromotograph repeater for automatic telegraphy, but even more significantly, experiments with the electromotograph soon led Edison to an idea for a new system of high-speed Morse telegraphy.[27]

On September 7 Edison began to develop his "New system based on the Electromotograph" by designing a combination recorder-repeater for regular Morse telegraphy.[28] He conceived one part of the instrument as an automatic-style puncher operated by an electromotograph capable of responding to very rapid impulses. This high-speed transmission would be accomplished by the instrument's automatic paper-tape transmitter. To prepare the original tape for transmission, the puncher would be connected to a Morse key. When used as a receiver, the instrument would allow a Morse operator to read the message in

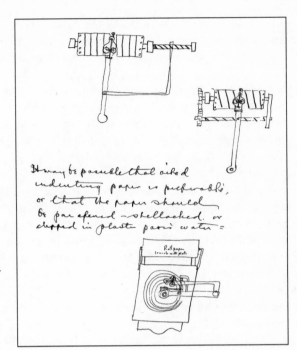

It may be possible that oiled indenting paper is preferable, or that the paper should be paraffined —shellacked. or dipped in plaster paris water=

Roll paper l-nnuh with platn

Edison's combination recorder-repeater recorded on discs but he also experimented with cylinders. These designs influenced Edison's early phonograph experiments.

the ordinary manner by playing it back at a slower speed and copying from a sounder. The basic idea was similar to the Morse register practice instrument that Edison had developed as a telegraph operator. This device had the potential to be particularly valuable for such things as press copy that required high-speed transmission to a number of offices.

After experimenting for several weeks and applying for a patent, Edison abandoned both the electromotograph and the punched paper tape. Instead, he developed a recorder-repeater that embossed the message on a paper disk. In early December he asked for George Prescott's help in introducing the new device, which he claimed would "allow *one* man to work one end of a Quadruplex:= no change in present system= all morse."[29] After further development work Edison demonstrated the instrument at Western Union headquarters in March 1877. Orton was sufficiently impressed to ask Edison to make several instruments to conduct further tests of the system.

Although Edison's contract with Western Union specified work on standard acoustic telegraphy, Orton was clearly interested in his experiments on acoustic transfer and on the Morse recorder-repeater. He was thus receptive when Edison suggested expanding the agreement to encompass "every invention that I can make . . . which is applicable to commercial telegraphy in the US & the Co[mpany']s system." Edison broached this idea because he was dissatisfied with the financial arrangements of his Western Union contract. Although confident of his work, he told Orton that when "the experimenting has not been satisfactory to myself, I find it impossible to screw up my courage to the point of asking for the $200" per week due under the contract. Instead, he suggested changing the terms so that he could regularly receive $100 per week without obtaining prior approval from Orton. In making his case to Orton, Edison described the advantages of his new laboratory, which "with machinery & apparatus cost about $40,000." Noting that this provided him with "unusual facilities" for "perfecting any kind of Telegraphic invention," Edison proposed that Western Union pay the "running expenses of my [machine] shop," which "including coal kerosene & labor is about 15 per day or 100 per week." No doubt believing that Orton understood the significance of a machine shop for inventive work, Edison stated that he would "be compelled to close it unless I am able to provide funds for continuing the same and keep my skilled workmen the loss of which would seriously cripple me." Orton agreed to Edison's proposal, and on March 22 they signed a new agreement that included much of Edison's language justifying the company's support for his laboratory. But Orton also widened the scope of the agreement to include all of Edison's "inventions and improvements *capable of being used on land lines of telegraph or upon cables.*" This wording was designed not only to prevent a duplication of the quadruplex controversy but also to secure Edison's research in the new field of telephony.[30]

The most striking telegraph exhibit at the Centennial Exhibition had been Alexander Graham Bell's newly invented telephone. A teacher of the deaf in Boston, Bell had been inspired by the success of Joseph Stearns's duplex to develop a multiple telegraph with which he might secure his fortune. Like Edison, he had drawn on Helmholtz's work; like Edison, he found a congenial environment for experimentation at Charles Williams's shop on Court Street (where he was supplied with a skilled mechanic named Thomas Watson as an assistant). Bell also found a ready backer in Gardiner Hubbard, the father of one of his students (and Bell's future wife), who had a strong interest in telegraphy and was a fierce opponent of Western Union. Although both Edison and Elisha Gray had also experimented with devices for acoustic telegraphy that were capable of transmitting voices, Bell was the first to be successful.[31]

The ability of Bell, the amateur, to prevail over two very experienced and successful telegraph inventors in creating the telephone was in part a consequence of his status as an outsider in the telegraph industry. Both Gray and Edison came very close to their goal. Gray had certainly thought about the possibility of transmitting speech and included a device for this purpose in the caveat he filed on February 14, 1876, the same day that Bell filed his first telephone patent application. Edison, too, filed a caveat, in January 1876, that contained a device he later called the "First Telephone on Record" and that he said he had designed and tested the previous November. Edison, however, made no claim at the time regarding the transmission of speech. Only after

Bell demonstrated his telephone did either Gray or Edison see any commercial possibility in such an instrument, and during 1876 they both continued to focus their efforts on acoustic telegraphy. Western Union, which was backing their efforts, was interested in multiple telegraph technology. The "verdict of practical telegraph men," as Gray told his patent attorney in November 1876, was that the "talking telegraph is a beautiful thing from a scientific point of view. . . . But if you look at it in a business light it is of no importance. We can do more . . . with a wire now than with that method."[32] Even Gardiner Hubbard, who backed Bell's efforts, had attempted to push his future son-in-law to put aside the telephone and go forward with his work on acoustic telegraphy.

Bell was also the first to arrive at the telephone because of the particular circumstances of his background and his other scientific and technological interests. His father Alexander Melville Bell had developed a method known as Visible Speech for teaching the deaf to speak, and Bell continued his father's efforts to place the system on a scientific basis while working as a teacher of the deaf. This had prompted his experiments with Helmholtz's acoustical system of tuning forks and electromagnets for studying speech. These experiments led in turn to his work on acoustic telegraphy for Hubbard. His scientific research on speech led him to build an electromechanical ear called the phonautograph to allow the deaf to see speech patterns. This device gave Bell key insights into the reproduction of speech and provided him with a crucial mechanical analogy to the nature of hearing that helped him to develop the telephone.[33]

Edison became aware of Bell's work after the Boston inventor astounded visitors to the Centennial by speaking a short distance over his telephone to William Thomson and Dom Pedro, the emperor of Brazil, when they visited his exhibit on June 25. Among those who witnessed this demonstration were Josiah Reiff and Edward Johnson. After hearing their accounts Edison began to conduct his own telephone experiments in early July. This was not the first time that Edison had contemplated the possibility of transmitting speech. He had briefly considered it a year earlier while reviewing the article Orton had sent him on Philip Reis's telephone. At the time, Edison recognized that the make-and-break circuit of Reis's telephone could transmit only the pitch of a sound. While thinking about how "to turn the Reiss transmitter into an articulating instrument" Edison conceived a key element of telephony.[34] He proposed to transmit changes in volume and tone by varying the strength of the current and sketched a number of ways for doing this by varying the resistance of the circuit. Primarily interested at the time in the problem of acoustic telegraphy, Edison did not experiment with his ideas on telephony.

Even after hearing reports of Bell's telephone, Edison remained focused on multiple telegraph technology and experimented only briefly with the new technology during July and early August. Assisted by Adams and Gilliland, he was able to "get a good many words Plain such as How do you do" in some of his first experiments and tried a variety of plans and apparatus over the next month.[35] Only occasionally did Edison return to the problem by having Adams conduct a few desultory experiments. Edison's indifferent approach to telephony suggests that he agreed with others in the telegraph community who thought telephones to be "very wonderful and interesting" things that might eventually be made useful for telegraphy, "but at present, of course, are merely scientific toys."[36]

By the time he signed his agreement with Western Union in March 1877 Edison had become more serious about telephone research. The weak point in Bell's telephone system was its transmitter, and Edison focused his efforts on improving this component. In Bell's transmitter sound waves vibrated a permanent magnet that in turn set up an induced current in the instrument's electromagnet. Instead of telegraphy's make-and-break signal, the telephone used a continuous variable current (termed undulatory) that could be turned back into sound waves by the receiver after it was transmitted through the line. However, the weak current set up by Bell's transmitter limited the distance over which it could be used. Edison decided instead to employ a battery current on the line and to use the sound waves to vary the current's strength. His telephone research focused on the idea he had first sketched in relation to the Reis telephone—varying the resistance of the current. Edison would later explain that "Bell got ahead of me by striking a *principle of easy application* whereas I have been plodding along in the correct principle but harder of application."[37]

Edison's approach was recorded by Batchelor in a February 12, 1877, notebook entry that also marked the beginning of their sustained effort to develop an improved telephone: "Edison thought that the *speaking telegraph* of Bell was very imperfect, seeing that it could be used on very short lines, and he maintained that if we could by any means get the resistance of the circuit increased and decreased by the raising or lowering of your voice, it could be used on long lines."[38]

In his July 1875 designs Edison had varied the current resistence by the movement of a diaphragm pushing a contact in and out of a liquid. When he undertook his first experiments a year later, he tried shunting resistance coils and batteries in and out of the circuit. In October 1876 Edison began his first experiments using carbon as a resistance medium. His interest in carbon may have been stimulated by his recent research with carbonized paper resistances, but the experiments he asked Adams to conduct used an idea that dated back to his artificial cable experiments from the fall of 1873. At the time he had tried to make "resistance coils of Kansas stone & plumbago graphite."[39] For the telephone experiments, Edison had Adams attach a stick of Arkansas oilstone coated with plumbago, which was black lead (also called graphite), to the center of the diaphragm so that as the diaphragm vibrated it moved the stick in and out of a cup of water where it acted as a battery electrode in combination with an immersed plate.

Although this first carbon telephone transmitter was unsuccessful, it helped jog Edison's memory of a phenomenon he had noticed during his 1873 experiments with artificial cables. Edison had designed a carbon rheostat in which

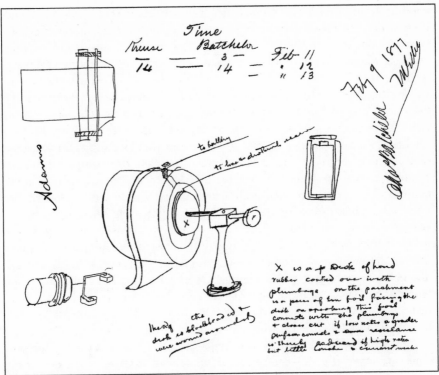

Edison's February 1877 drawing of a telephone design uses the resonating tubes from his acoustic telegraph experiments but replaces the vibrating reed or tuning fork with a diaphragm of parchment and tinfoil and a disk of rubber coated with plumbago.

several glass tubes were filled with powdered graphite, but he had had to abandon the device after discovering "that the resistance of carbon varied with every noise, jar or sound, and were too unreliable where a definite resistance was required."[40] Now, however, he was searching for a way to obtain just this kind of variable resistance.

During February and March Edison experimented almost equally with carbon and noncarbon devices. In many of the latter designs he used a series of projecting pins or vibrating reeds, each connected to a different resistance or battery. As the diaphragm vibrated it touched more or fewer of these pins or reeds, thus bringing more or less battery or resistance into the circuit and varying the current. Edison's first telephone patent application was based on a carbon transmitter experiment of February 9. In that experiment, he and his staff put a tinfoil facing on a parchment diaphragm that pressed against a disk of hard rubber coated with plumbago and completed the circuit. This instrument responded differently to high and low notes—low notes caused more of the foil to touch the plumbago, thereby reducing the resistance, whereas high notes touched the plumbago less and increased the resistance. Carbon also gave promising results during experiments recorded by Batchelor on February 12. Although this notebook entry includes a noncarbon instrument, carbon was the main subject of research. In his first design Edison used a vibrating diaphragm that moved two rollers over a stone coated by carbon in the form of a lead pencil mark. As the rollers came into greater or lesser contact with the mark, the resistance varied. This device did not work well, but Batchelor was delighted by their next transmitter, in which they placed a disk of black lead in front of a diaphragm so that as it "vibrates it touches in more places and reduces the resistance. With this apparatus we have already been able to distinguish clearly (known) sentences well between New York and Menlo Park."[41]

The telephone experiments mark Edison's increasing reliance on his experimental assistants Charles Batchelor and James Adams. "I am so deaf," he wrote, "that I am debarred from hearing all the finer articulations & have to depend on the judgement of others."[42] He also resorted to such tricks as testing a transmitter by sending its signal through a telegraph relay that he held between his teeth. Nonetheless, Edison claimed that his limited hearing was an advantage as he had to improve the transmitter so that he could hear it.

Edison depended not only on the better hearing of his assistants but also on their ideas. The laboratory notebooks detailing the work on telephony sometimes make it very difficult to tell whose ideas are represented. Edison, Batchelor, and Adams all wrote down ideas and experimental results. Sometimes these were designated as Edison's ideas or designs, but at other times they were designated as "our's." Furthermore, Batchelor sometimes described his work on particular instruments in ways that make it difficult to know whether a design was his or Edison's. Nonetheless, it was Edison who produced page after page of possible approaches to the problem and who decided which were worth pursuing.

Certainly, the basic approach of both varying the current strength and using carbon to accomplish this was Edison's idea. During the first two months of intensive experimentation, he and his staff had tried a variety of ways to vary the current by bringing resistances, batteries, or condensers into the circuit and using carbon, but by the beginning of April the latter approach was producing the most promising results. On March 18 they had tried "a transmitter in which the diaphragm struck against two *discs* of *Plumbago* fastened to springs," which "seemed a little better." A week later they used this arrangement in a multiple-diaphragm transmitter over a line to New York and found that it gave "very fair speaking."[43] Then on April 4 Edison discovered during experiments with other forms of carbon, such as black oxide of manganese and coal, that these "only give a moderate resistance somewhat higher than plumbago and that enormous difference of resistance is obtained by Varying the pressure for instance Anthracite Coal having a resistance with light pressure of 1700 ohms is reduced to 300 ohms by pressure, Manganese Oxide, from 1500 to 600."[44]

He quickly began listing other substances that varied their resistance under pressure and that he might be able to use as "imperfect contact points" for his transmitter. Although he experimented with these other substances, plumbago remained the most promising material, and by the end of May he had settled on it for his telephone transmitter. He even designed a new telegraph relay on the "principle of the difference of Plumbago when under pressure."[45]

Edison's telephone experiments were producing promising results, but they were not the only line of research he was conducting for Western Union. Edison's new contract with the company had been prompted by his work in multiple telegraphy. His December letter to Orton initiating discussions for the contract had described the potential advantages of the acoustic transfer system and also indicated that more regular payments by the company would enable him to move ahead with his acoustic telegraph experiments. However, by the time he actually signed the agreement, Edison was instead developing his high-speed recorder-repeater and experimenting on yet another system of multiple telegraphy.

In 1875 Edison had first considered and briefly experimented with the idea of developing a "sextuplex" telegraph to transmit three messages in each direction simultaneously. His first idea was to combine his quadruplex with an electromotograph for the third set of signals. By the time he renewed his experiments in March 1877 Edison had replaced the electromotograph with acoustic instruments. Over the next three months he experimented extensively with sextuplex telegraphy. Although he tried out electromotograph relays and acoustic transfer circuits as well as acoustic instruments such as a "reed worked by induction," his efforts soon focused on the design of multiple-contact relays that responded to signals of different strength.[46] As he worked on the sextuplex, Edison used some of the same techniques, such as compensating circuits and bug traps, that he had employed in his quadruplex experiments. Although Edison had high hopes for the system, he virtually abandoned it following unsuccessful tests between New York and Boston on June 8 and 9.

Even as he gave up on the sextuplex, Edison renewed his work on the recorder-repeater. In late June, as Murray was finishing the six instruments that Orton had ordered in March, Edison and Batchelor began testing the instruments; on July 3 they took them to Western Union headquarters and demonstrated them to Orton, Prescott, and other company officials, as well as to British electricians William Preece and Henry Fischer, who were in the United States to study the country's telegraph systems. Unfortunately, they discovered during this demonstration "considerable bugs amongst which the connections were wrong." To overcome these difficulties Batchelor spent part of his time during the next two months working on the instruments at Western Union. By August 31, however, Edison had little doubt what Orton's answer would be when he wrote to ask "which shall it be= more Telephone, or the Embosser!"[47]

The telephone had undergone extensive development during the spring and early summer. Having settled on plumbago as the best substance for his imperfect contact points at the end of May, Edison set his laboratory staff to work investigating different compounds he could use in making plumbago cakes for the telephone transmitter. Over the next three weeks they tested plumbago in combination with a variety of substances and chemical compounds, including resins, gelatins, isinglass, plaster of paris, and even sugar, salt, and flour. Before they were through they tried over 150 different compounds, and rubber proved the most promising substance. The staff studied changes in resistance by pressing these compounds under different weights and by testing them in transmitters to determine which provided the best articulation and were most durable in actual use. They also investigated the best shape for the plumbago compound to ensure good contact with the diaphragm.[48]

Although he considered the transmitter to be the weakest element in Bell's telephone system, Edison also experimented with alternative receiver designs. In an important series of experiments on March 18 he discovered that "the best way to receive and hear the words is on the Electromotograph principle." However, the electromotograph receivers Edison and his staff built over the next month worked well enough to receive speech in laboratory tests, but they proved inadequate for transmitting articulate speech over a line. Edison discovered that they received music transmitted over a line remarkably well and in late April he exhibited his apparatus at the Newark Opera House as his "musical telephone." During a week of demonstrations the instrument received wind instruments, singing, and a high-pitched laugh.[49]

The Newark demonstrations attracted press attention as well as an invitation to exhibit the musical telephone before a local scientific society. Edison arranged to have this demonstration made by his nephew Charley Edison and George Caldwell, who had headed the Centennial electric pen exhibit. He also gave them an exclusive right to exhibit the musical telephone "in every town where there is a possibility of our receiving a pecuniary benefit for our venture." They agreed to show it "six nights every week if possible" with Edison receiving a royalty of $25 per show.[50]

The attention Bell himself had received for his public lectures on the telephone probably provided the incentive for this arrangement. At the time he made the proposal to Edison, Charley was anticipating a lecture by Bell at Chickering Hall in New York City. This lecture provided the occasion for Batchelor, who accompanied Charley, to compare Edison's telephones with Bell's. Taking the "opportunity to speak over the wire to New Brunswick," Batchelor found that although others "got it very well I could not." He also thought that "the singing was not so good as ours."[51] Although Edison's musical telephone produced better singing, Charley and Caldwell soon discovered that the lecture business did not pay and soon gave it up. Within a short time, Edward Johnson would take up the instrument and prove to be a much more capable showman.

As Edison abandoned his experiments with the electromotograph receiver for speech, relying instead on modified Bell receivers, his carbon transmitter was beginning to show great promise. In early June Batchelor wrote that "our speaking telephone as now improved is far plainer and better than Bell's," although they found it difficult to get "such sounds as are accompanied by the *stress of air* such as P, B. Sh, Th, etc."[52] In fact, the transmission of sibilants proved a difficult problem for all of the early telephone inventors. William Thomson, for example, had experienced difficulty hearing such sounds during the Centennial demonstration of Bell's telephone. Edison felt that the ability to transmit sibilants was "absolutely essential to perfect the speaking Telegraph" and experimented with a variety of approaches. Two techniques in particular seemed to offer the best results and became the focus of his experiments. In one scheme he used two sets of speaking tubes and diaphragms, one to transmit vowel sounds and the other for sibilants. In the other he used a "hissing Consonant vibrator" consisting of a reed or a piece of stretched material such as rubber or parchment that he attached to the transmitter tube in a variety of ways that enabled it to respond to and reinforce sibilant vibrations.[53]

During experiments with a vibrating reed on July 17 Edison thought he had solved the problem and wrote in his notebook, "Glorious= Telephone perfected this morning 5 AM= articulation perfect got ¼ column newspaper every word. had ricketty transmitter at that we are making it solid."[54] Nonetheless, on July 31 they found that "our apparatus for getting the Sh, Th, and S, is not perfect." Finding "that these sounds will vibrate a diaphragm when spoken across a tube same as speaking across the mouth of a bottle," they again tried using a second tube and diaphragm to reinforce the "ishing" sounds. This also led them to try new experiments with diaphragm materials and shapes, including an effort to prevent harmonics (overtones). These diaphragm experiments produced a new and more successful approach to the problem of sibilants. Instead of using a second tube or a vibrator, they cut "a slot in the mouth piece so that these sounds strike on the edge the stress of air passing down and out but causing a vibration that makes the diaphragm" respond to the hissing sounds.[55]

The end of July also brought a new direction in their plumbago experiments. They found that the slight pressure of the vibrating diaphragm on "solid plumbago compositions" was insufficient to produce the amount of variation they required. Instead they tried rubbing plumbago on fine wool and then pressing it into a cake. After placing this cake between a spring on the diaphragm and a platina-faced adjusting screw, they found "the talking is absolutely perfect." Although Edison claimed that "my speaking Telegraph is now *absolutely perfect*," the plumbago "fluff" continued to present a problem, as it was "a little liable to shake out and consequently to deteriorate."[56] They soon found that silk worked much better, although the form of the fluff continued to be a subject for experiment, as did the best way to hold it in the telephone transmitter.

By the end of August, when he asked Orton whether he should continue to work on the telegraph recorder-repeater or focus his efforts on the telephone, Edison had already demonstrated his carbon-fluff transmitter and Orton gave him permission to conduct experiments on Gold and Stock lines in New York. By September 3 Edison was able write to William Preece that comparative tests between his improved transmitter and Bell's "proved 1st that the articulation of mine was far better,= 2nd that it was 4 times louder. 3rd that there was no noises, 4th that it worked on every wire tried and but few wires were found that Bells could be worked on owing to cross leakage; on a majority of wires the leakage sounds overpowered the talking."[57] Following another test two weeks later, during which Orton "expressed himself decidedly in favor of [Edison's] and said there was no comparison between the two," the Western Union president ordered 150 sets of instruments to be made at Joseph Murray's shop in Newark.[58]

Even though his transmitters compared well to Bell's, Edison remained dissatisfied. While Murray was manufacturing them for Western Union, he and Batchelor continued to modify their design based on the results of their tests on working lines. Besides the data he gained from his New York experiments, Edison also received valuable feedback on his instruments from T. B. A. David, who was testing both Edison's and Bell's telephones for the Central District and Printing Telegraph Company of Pittsburgh, and Franklin Badger, who acquired rights for Edison's telephone for Canada. They agreed that Edison's telephone overcame line induction that made Bell's unusable, but complained about its inconsistent articulation; David, in fact, felt that Bell's was generally superior on this point. To improve articulation, Edison experimented with the material used in his fluff and with the means by which he adjusted the pressure exerted on it by the diaphragm. He also experimented with a variety of mouthpiece designs and diaphragms. By early October he had made several significant alterations in his design. First, he used a "small sharp edged hole" in the mouthpiece to improve the transmission of sibilants.[59] Second, he adopted a rubber-backed mica diaphragm that damped high-frequency vibrations and reduced harmonics. Third, he devised a new fluff holder and mounted it against a spring. And finally, he placed a small rubber tube between the diaphragm and the fluff. These last two alterations provided significantly better adjustment of the pressure on the fluff, as well as increased dampening of diaphragm harmonics.

Edison told Orton that with these improvements "in the way of constancy and hence articulation . . . Murrays machines will I think work well & give satisfaction." Nonetheless, his enthusiasm for the new design was tempered by his "experience in articulating telephones [which] have learned me better."[60] Indeed, he soon found it necessary to make other alterations. The first concerned the form of carbon he used in his transmitter. After finding that silk saturated with plumbago would shake loose after extensive use, he had begun to cover the silk with a thick paste of plumbago and dextrin, which he then cut into thin disks and placed together in a fluff holder. Though the plumbago did not come loose in this arrangement, the disks tended to become flat so that it was difficult to achieve good contact with the diaphragm. As a result of these experiments,

Edison came to the conclusion that better contact produced by increased pressure rather than the pressure itself was responsible for the changing resistance of the plumbago. He therefore decided to try hard disks of plumbago mixed with other materials. In early November, Edison settled on lampblack mixed with rubber, and by the end of the year he had discovered that pure lampblack produced even better results.[61]

The shift to lampblack coincided with another crucial change. Edison had begun to use an induction coil to amplify the line signal. He had experimented briefly in this direction in September. At that time he had hoped that small changes in the resistance of his carbon semiconductors could be augmented by the primary circuit of the induction coil that would then induce a much larger line current. However, the resistance of the semiconductors he was then using proved too high for the induction circuit to work well. In November, as he experimented with lampblack, Edison again tried using what he referred to as a "polarizing circuit" and found that "the resistance of the [lampblack] disc could be varied from 300 ohms to the fractional part of a single ohm by pressure alone." This allowed him to work his telephone inductively. He also discovered that "with plenty of pressure it is not so liable to alter and get out [of adjustment]." Edison now believed that he had a telephone "that is Constant."[62]

As Edison brought his telephone toward a state of commercial introduction, Western Union made plans to begin competing with the Bell Telephone Company. On November 17 Western Union established the American Speaking Telephone Company by combining its interest in Edison's telephone patents with those of Elisha Gray, which were controlled by the Harmonic Telegraph Company. As part of the merger, Gold and Stock was given exclusive rights to manufacture, sell, and lease telephone instruments protected by the Gray and Edison patents.[63]

Western Union also set its resident inventor George Phelps to work on telephones. Much to Edison's chagrin, William Orton and the Western Union electricians described Phelps's new magneto telephone as "simply perfect" during a comparative test with Edison's in early January. In a letter to Uriah Painter, a journalist and Republican political insider associated with Gardiner Hubbard, Edward Johnson described Edison's annoyance over their claims that its "articulation was distinct and you get all the modulations of the human voice even when whispering." Edison became even more upset after he and Johnson, who drew on his experience exhibiting Edison's musical and speaking telephones in public lectures, explained that Edison had designed his transmitter for "practical work on lines" and that it was necessary to trade off some articulation to get "plenty of sound from *low talking*." Their explanations, Johnson told Painter, were "*met in silence* no one *assenting* or *dissenting*" and "not a single remark, from Prescott, Phelps, Barton [of Western Electric], Walker (V. P. Gold & Stock) or any of the lesser lights present, to show that Edisons aim to produce a *practical* Instrument was appreciated." When Edison went home that night, Johnson wrote, he was "aggravated beyond anything I have yet seen" and felt that "the whole movement was one of Blackmail."[64] Both Edison and Johnson believed that the favorable view of Phelps's instrument and the downplaying of Edison's was a consequence of bad feelings left over from Prescott's role in the quadruplex. Edison decided to complain privately to Orton, who recognized the importance of unbiased tests to Edison's relations with the company. Edison felt he had "received so little encouragement . . . except from Mr. O[rton] and so much opposition from the *Scientific* (sic) dept that it got my mind in a condition not active in matters Telephoniqué."[65] This changed after Orton asked Henry Bentley, whose Philadelphia Local Telegraph Company was affiliated with Western Union, to make careful tests of Edison's telephone. These tests would not only soothe Edison's hurt feelings, but also prove crucial to the refinement of his design.

These tests took place over the course of the next three months, and with encouragement and assistance from Bentley Edison was able to produce important improvements that led Western Union to adopt his transmitter for commercial use. Initially, Edison tried to improve the articulation of his telephone by devising better induction coils and circuit arrangements. Although these produced significant improvement, the most important change came in early March when Edison began to experiment with methods of improving the "constancy of adjustment" of the carbon transmitter.[66] Finding that the rubber tube pressing on the carbon button became flat and required frequent adjustment to produce the proper pressure, he decided to try using metal springs instead. Further experiments led to a crucial discovery on March 12. Finding that the metal spring

> gave out a musical tone which interfered somewhat with the effects produced by the voice; but, in the hope of overcoming the defect, I kept on substituting spiral springs of thicker wire, and as I did so I found that the articulation became both clearer and louder. At last I substituted a solid substance for the springs that had gradually been made more and more inelastic, and then I obtained very marked improvements in the results. It then occurred to me that the whole question was one of pressure only, and that it was not necessary that the diaphragm should vibrate at all. I consequently put in a heavy diaphragm, one and three quarters inches in diameter and one sixteenth inch thick, and fastened the carbon disk and plate tightly together so that the latter showed no vibration with the loudest tones. Upon testing it I found my surmises verified; the articulation was perfect and the volume of sound so great that conversation carried on in a whisper three feet from the telephone was clearly heard and understood at the other end of the line.[67]

The new design worked so well that Bentley "told Phelps to throw away his magneto Telephone it was no where . . . the Carbon Telephone was the telephone of the future." Apprised of this, Edward Johnson gloated that the "Electricians Dept. have got their tails between their legs."[68] After seeing the new design demonstrated, Orton immediately opened negotiations to determine an appropriate royalty for Edison's invention. Although Orton quickly agreed to

Edison's request for $6,000 per year, a formal agreement was delayed while he sought approval from the Board of Directors and from William Vanderbilt, the company's principal stockholder. In the meantime, the Bell Telephone Company became interested after their own tests showed that the new carbon transmitter was a significant improvement. Gardiner Hubbard began negotiations with Edison in case those with Western Union broke down. At the end of May, however, Western Union finalized its arrangement with Edison and Gold and Stock began commercial use of his telephones on its lines in New York.

The carbon transmitter made the telephone a commercial technology and added further luster to Edison's growing international reputation as an electrical inventor. He had been praised by William Thomson and Joseph Henry, two of the most renowned electrical scientists in Britain and the United States. After seeing a demonstration of Edison's telephones in November 1877 Henry had called him "the most ingenious inventor in this country . . . or in any other."[69] Just thirty years of age, certainly Edison had an impressive list of accomplishments. Yet, he might have remained little known outside of the scientific and technical communities engaged in electrical research except for an unexpected invention that emerged during his 1877 telephone research.

CHAPTER 9

The Wizard of Menlo Park

The invention of the phonograph was the most important of Edison's career. It made his reputation as the "Inventor of the Age."[1] Prior to 1877 Edison's name had made only an occasional appearance outside of the technical press. Although his automatic telegraph had received some attention from the local Newark newspapers, the announcement of the quadruplex in the *New York Times* barely mentioned his name. The etheric force discovery had created a minor stir in the New York papers in late 1875, as did the court battle between Western Union and Atlantic and Pacific for control of his quadruplex patents during the spring of 1877. That year newspapers in New York and other northeastern cities also reported on exhibitions of Edison's telephone. Nonetheless, in the public mind Edison remained a minor figure associated with Alexander Graham Bell's famous invention. In 1878, however, he became celebrated in his own right when he astonished the world with his talking machine.

The phonograph was a marvel that amazed both the scientific and technical community and the public because of its utter simplicity. Acoustics was a subject of much scientific interest during the nineteenth century. Scientists working to duplicate the variety of tones and overtones necessary to reproduce human speech had devised complex mechanisms for this purpose. Furthermore, they recognized the ear as one of the most complicated parts of the human anatomy. As a result, the simple mechanism and operation of the phonograph seemed astounding and prompted some initial skepticism. Edison even received a letter from one professor, who called the "idea of a talking machine ridiculous" and advised Edison protect his "good reputation as an inventor among scientific men" by denying an account of the phonograph that appeared in the *New York Sun* and that he believed could only have been "calculated to injure you."[2] But most of the scientific and technical community soon came to agree with Alfred Mayer, professor of physics at the Stevens Institute,

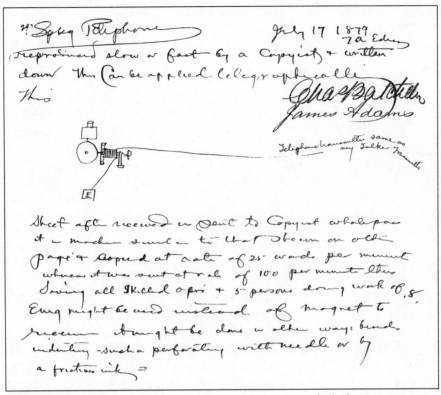

Edison's first conception of the phonograph was as a way to record telephone messages so they could be played back and transcribed at a slower speed in a manner similar to his Morse recorder practice instrument.

who wrote Edison after witnessing a demonstration of the phonograph in mid-January:

> Ever since my return home your marvelous invention has so occupied my brain that I can hardly collect my thoughts to carry on my work. The results are far reaching (in science), its *capabilities* are *immense*. I cannot express my admiration of your genius better than by frankly saying that I would rather be the discoverer of your talking machine than to have made the first best discovery of any one who has worked in Acoustics.[3]

Like the telephone that gave rise to it, Edison's invention of the phonograph again demonstrates that the experiences of an inventor and the context in which he works make possible the conceptualization of a new technology. Alexander Graham Bell considered it

> a most astonishing thing to me that I could possibly have let this invention slip through my fingers when I consider how my thoughts have been directed to this

subject for so many years past. So nearly did I come to the idea that I had stated again & again in my public lectures the fundamental principles of the Phono- graph. In showing to an audience the tracings produced by the Phonautograph I had said if the motions indicated by the curves could be produced mechanically in any way the sounds would be audible.[4]

In this case, however, Bell failed to grasp the phonograph because he was an outsider in the telegraph industry. On July 17, 1877, Edison had been thinking about the possibility of recording telephone messages. Thinking of the tele- phone as a form of telegraph, he and others in the industry thought that it would be necessary to produce a written record. He therefore envisioned using a recorder similar to the embossing recorder-repeater he was then developing for Western Union. Still reflecting on this idea the following day, he experi- mented "with a diaphragm having an embossing point & held against paraffin paper moving rapidly." Finding that the sound "vibrations are indented nicely" he concluded "theres no doubt that I shall be able to store up & reproduce automatically at any future time the human voice perfectly."[5]

Although Edison put aside this extraordinary idea to push ahead on his telephone, he returned to it periodically during the next six months. In early August during one of his telephone exhibitions Edward Johnson astounded his audience by describing what Edison "proposed to do in the way of recording speech." A week later Edison labeled the speech recorder he had drawn in his notebook, which looked very much like an automatic telegraph recorder, the "Phonograph." A few days later he discussed methods of recording on paper with "my apparatus for recording & reproducing the human voice."[6] He also described how it would work as a telephone recorder. Although he drafted a kind of press release to announce the new invention on September 7 Edison felt that the phonograph was not yet at the point where he could bring it before the public, and he decided not to publish it.

The telephone took all of Edison's time during the rest of September and October, and he did not return to the phonograph until the beginning of No- vember. The phonograph he sketched on November 1 still looked very much like an automatic telegraph and still recorded on paper tape. Whether Edison had a working machine or not, he was finally willing to publish the text of his September press release as a letter from Edward Johnson to the editor of *Scien- tific American*. Nonetheless, Edison was clearly not satisfied with the paper tape recorder and was beginning to develop a different design that drew on an alternative embossing recorder-repeater he had experimented with the previous summer. On November 10 Edison sketched a drawing of a lathelike device with a handcrank that turned a large, grooved cylinder mounted on a long shaft with a screw pitch of ten threads per inch. Instead of paraffined paper, Edison also planned to use a piece of tinfoil wrapped around the cylinder as a record- ing surface. By the end of the month Edison was satisfied with this design and set machinist John Kruesi to work making the instrument. The phonograph

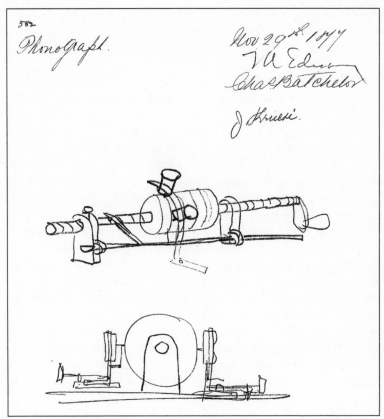

Edison's November 29, 1877, drawing for the first phonograph, which his machinists finished making a few days later.

that Kruesi built during the first six days of December 1877 astounded Edison and his associates by working the first time they tried it.[7]

The day after it was finished Edison, accompanied by Batchelor and Johnson, took the new cylinder phonograph to the New York offices of *Scientific American*. There he amazed the staff by placing the little machine on the editor's desk and turning the handle to reproduce a recording he had already made. According to the journal's editor, "the machine inquired as to our health, asked how we liked the phonograph, informed us that *it* was very well, and bid us a cordial good night. These remarks were not only perfectly audible to ourselves, but to a dozen or more persons gathered around, and they were produced by the aid of no other mechanism than the simple little contrivance explained and illustrated below."[8] By the New Year Edison had an improved

phonograph that he exhibited at Western Union headquarters, where it attracted the attention of the New York newspapers.

These first public demonstrations produced a trickle of articles that soon
turned into a steady stream and by the end of March had become a veritable
flood. Initially the news reports contained little more than descriptions of the
phonograph and how it worked or accounts of demonstrations of the new invention. News editors soon became interested in the instrument's inventor as
well and began to publish more personal accounts. They sent their reporters to
the laboratory to interview Edison, printed anecdotes about him and the phonograph, and provided biographical sketches, including some by those who
had known him during his days as a telegrapher.[9] Most of the interviews were
conducted by reporters connected to the New York papers and journals, although occasionally newspapers in other large cities sent reporters to visit him
at the laboratory. Papers in small cities and towns had to be content to reprint
accounts from the large city papers, especially those in New York.[10]

New York was the media capital of the United States, and its papers led in
the development of new journalistic techniques that helped bring Edison to
the notice of a wider public. Influenced by Charles A. Dana's New York Sun, the
city's newspapers had begun to combine information with entertainment, presenting stories on a wide range of topics with human interest. Interviews were
an important feature of this approach, and Edison proved to be a good interview. Furthermore, as an inventor Edison was seen as a source of novelty who
could almost be guaranteed to have something new to talk about. The Sun,
which sent its main reporter and managing editor Amos Cummings to Menlo
Park, found Edison to be a favorite subject, presenting interviews with him
nearly every month, as well as printing frequent stories describing his activities
and inventions.[11]

The Sun's major competitor, James Gordon Bennett Jr.'s New York Herald
also was soon featuring frequent Edison interviews and articles. The Herald's
interest was influenced by reporter Edwin Fox, who had known Edison as a
telegrapher. Fox not only kept Edison's name in the paper, but also gave the inventor advice about his public image. Speaking of an article that appeared in
the Sun, he told Edison that it was

> of the character that does you harm. It makes you do too much talking. My
> friendly advice to you is not to be fair to any more reporters. Let them write all they
> please about your inventions, let them if they desire confab with every employee in
> the laboratory, but keep yourself aloof and reserved. Your works speak for them-
> selves. In all that I have written about you I have sought to keep you on a high
> pedestal. Holding you out to the world as a chewer of tobacco and all such trash as
> does the Sun in the interview published is really too bad.[12]

Although Edison no doubt appreciated Fox's concern about his reputation, the
Sun's style was part of its human interest approach to the news, and its charac-
terization of Edison helped to make him look like a man of the people.

The seemingly intimate portrait of the inventor that these interviews provided was supplemented by drawings of Edison and his inventions that began to appear in illustrated papers and journals such as the *New York Daily Graphic, Frank Leslie's Illustrated Newspaper,* and *Harper's Weekly.* In March and April the *Graphic* provided readers with many drawings of the inventor, his phonograph, and his laboratory, including an impressive set of full-page illustrations, one of them a portrait of Edison, that appeared on April 10 in an article that dubbed him "The Wizard of Menlo Park." This became his most famous nickname. The *Graphic's* reporter, W. A. Croffut, became friendly with Edison and began to vie with Fox, Cummings, and other reporters for exclusive accounts of his new inventions. Croffut made his own unique contribution to the publicity about Edison with an April Fool's Day article in which he claimed that Edison had invented a "machine that will feed the human race." Edison, who was always willing to give a reporter a good story and was not adverse to stretching the truth to provide one, was amused by Croffut's article.[13]

Edison was quite willing to accommodate the press and to use it in promoting himself and his inventions. As a former press-wire operator he was familiar with newspaper practices and made friends easily with reporters and editors. Some of these men, such as Edwin Fox and Thomas Maguire, a reporter for the *Boston Globe,* were former operators whom Edison had known during his itinerant years, and others, Croffut and Cummings in particular, became friends as a result of their reporting of his activities.[14] Edison's continuing efforts to improve the phonograph and his development of additional acoustic instruments provided them with plenty of copy.

Even though the phonograph had worked unexpectedly well the first time it was tried, Edison found that turning it into a commercial product was a particularly difficult task. During the year following its invention, the basic tinfoil phonograph underwent significant modification. The machine demonstrated at Western Union headquarters at the beginning of January was already quite different from the original phonograph built by Kruesi a month earlier. The cylinder was longer, it had a single mouthpiece, diaphragm, and needle arrangement for recording and playback instead of separate ones for each, and it used a cone-shaped funnel to concentrate the sound on playback. Soon after exhibiting this machine at Western Union, Edison added a heavy flywheel to allow steadier rotation of the handcrank. Though these modifications improved the sound quality, the phonograph remained little more than an exhibition curiosity.[15]

Edison had grander designs for his invention. As he told Croffut in one interview, "this is my baby and I expect it to grow up to be a big feller and support me in my old age."[16] He envisioned a number of uses for the phonograph. In an article published in the June issue of *North American Review* he described a host of potential business and personal uses: sending dictation cylinders that did not have to be transcribed, preserving the voices of family members and famous people, reading books aloud, teaching elocution and music, advertising, speaking toys and clocks, and, of course, a telephone recorder.

Edison's efforts to realize the commercial potential of the phonograph were supported by three different groups of investors. His main support came from the Bell telephone interests, led by Gardiner Hubbard, with whom he entered into negotiations at the end of December. In late January the Bell interests agreed to provide Edison with $10,000 for his experiments and formed the Edison Speaking Phonograph Company to market the invention. As part of the arrangement Edison was to receive royalties from sales and exhibitions of the phonograph.[17]

Earlier in January Edison had also made two separate arrangements to develop phonographs for use in clocks and in toys. The first of these was undertaken with the Ansonia Clock Company, and although Edison conducted some initial experiments, the company did most of the ultimately unsuccessful development work on phonograph clocks. The toy contract was made with two New York entrepreneurs and was equally unsuccessful, even though they brought in other investors and even paid John Ott, one of Edison's former Newark machinists, to conduct experiments at Menlo Park. Ott remained at the laboratory after conducting this research and became one of Edison's most trusted assistants.[18]

As he had done with all of his inventions, Edison reserved foreign rights for himself. The primary market for such inventions was, of course, the industrialized countries of Europe, and Edison entrusted both his telephone and his phonograph there to Theodore Puskas. Puskas was a Hungarian-born entrepreneur who had come to the United States seeking telephones for use in central exchange telegraph systems. He met Edison in mid-December 1877, just after the successful demonstration of the phonograph, and immediately began negotiating for the rights to it and to the carbon telephone. Edison immediately took a liking to Puskas, who seemed to have both the money and the technical background to promote his inventions. Puskas agreed to pay the costs for all Edison's patents on the Continent of Europe and to act as his agent for the sale of those patent rights in return for a portion of the proceeds from any sale. At Edison's urging, he also agreed to give George Bliss, whom Edison had earlier agreed to let act as his agent, a small percentage of any proceeds.[19]

Puskas actually began his efforts in London, where he and William Preece exhibited the phonograph to the Society of Telegraph Engineers. Other successful demonstrations followed, and Puskas arranged with George Nottage, Alderman and Sheriff of London, to market the phonograph through his London Stereoscopic and Photographic Company. This company, according to Puskas, did a large retail business and had its principal store on Regent Street where they "have the best customers of London."[20] Nottage bought the patent rights for £1,500 (over $7,000), and Puskas placed the monies received for negotiating the sale on account with Lemuel Serrell to pay for Edison's patent applications in Britain. Puskas then went on to Paris, where he set up his headquarters to promote the phonograph and take out patents on the Continent.

Edison's British interests were soon being looked after by George Gouraud, who had been involved in the promotion of the automatic telegraph in Britain in 1873. Gouraud was an American who had settled in London to promote the railway and land businesses of William Palmer. When Palmer and his associates took an interest in Edison's automatic telegraph, so too did Gouraud. Now, with Edison's emergence as a major inventor, Gouraud traveled to New York to meet with him and discuss the possibility of acting as his agent in Britain. Edison subsequently agreed to give him control of his telephone inventions there, and Gouraud also tried to negotiate with Puskas for an interest in the British rights for the phonograph. Edison established close personal relations with both Gouraud and Puskas, and they continued to act as his agents in Britain and Europe respectively for many years.[21]

By relying on Puskas and Gouraud, Edison hoped to limit the costs involved in promoting his inventions overseas. They found the money to pay for foreign patent applications, which were much more expensive than in the United States. Edison also relied on their extensive business connections to find investors who would purchase the patent rights and market the inventions. Although Edison hoped that the companies marketing his inventions would be successful, he knew that the royalty payments and stock dividends he was to receive from them were only the promise of future success. His immediate return came from payments for his patent rights. Edison subsequently made similar arrangements for his telephone and phonograph in Latin America, Australia, and Asia, with individuals experienced in marketing American products who agreed to pay patent costs and find local investors.[22]

According to the phonograph company's general manager, Charles Cheever, Edison had received "a large number of applications from professors of various colleges and other people who wish to buy them just as a novelty." This led him to conceive the idea of a small, inexpensive machine to illustrate the principle of the phonograph and to pique public interest without compromising the sales of the proposed standard phonograph. Edison explained to Cheever that "a good deal of money could be made in selling these small traps as a novelty, explaining to the customer that it was merely as an example of what the machine would do and not a finished working machine."[23] He had Batchelor build a couple of prototypes. These machines, capable of recording about 50 words, had a short cylinder with a relatively massive rim that served as its own flywheel to help maintain a fairly even rotation. At first, the volume of these small instruments was about half that of the large cylinder machines and their articulation was "no better than the ordinary run of telephones [which was still poor], owing to the impossibility of rotating the cylinder evenly by hand," but by early March, when Edison began to loan them out for lectures, he was able to get them "speaking as clear as the large ones."[24]

Edison expected that Puskas would be able to sell hundreds of these small phonographs during the Universal Exposition in Paris, due to open on May 1, and that the Edison Speaking Phonograph Company could sell large numbers in North America as well. In March Edward Johnson, who had become general manager of Edison Speaking Phonograph, arranged to have Sigmund Bergmann, a former Edison machinist, make twenty-five of the small demonstration phonographs at his New York shop, S. Bergmann & Co. The phonograph company advertised these small machines, which were to be sold for $30, as suitable for "private use and instruction, being very portable."[25] Although the models made at the Menlo Park laboratory had been used for public lectures at Chickering Hall in New York and at the Franklin Institute in Philadelphia, the ones manufactured by Bergmann proved inadequate for commercial use and the company sold only five. Batchelor complained to Bergmann about the poor workmanship in these phonographs and noted that they "cannot be worked by inexperienced hands and I had the greatest difficulty to make it work myself."[26] Thomas Watson, superintendent of the Bell Telephone Co., who obtained one of these machines, also reported that "after some alterations I have made it work indifferently well, as received it would not work at all. If it had gone to any one who was not a mechanic and had no tools it would have done the Phonograph Co great injury."[27] (This machine was probably later used at Bell's Volta laboratory in Washington, D.C., to develop wax recording, which revived the commercial prospects of the phonograph.)

To turn the phonograph into a commercial instrument, Edison planned to produce a spring-powered disk phonograph that would serve as a "standard" machine for dictation and other business purposes. He built working prototypes of a disk phonograph but ultimately failed in his efforts to produce a commercial machine. Edison also experienced great difficulty in producing a clockwork-driven cylinder phonograph as an alternative. His experimental machines demonstrated the value of using a power drive because they produced better and more consistent articulation than did the hand-cranked versions. However, Edison and his staff found "it is easy to make a good clockwork but difficult to make one without extra vibrations."[28] In England and France, where machinists had greater experience with clockworks, some commercial clockwork-cylinder machines were actually manufactured, but in the United States all commercial cylinder phonographs were hand-cranked.

Frustrated in his efforts to develop a commercial disk or clockwork cylinder phonograph, Edison turned instead to the challenge of developing an improved machine for the Edison Speaking Phonograph Company's new exhibition business. The company's managers had decided to establish exhibition agencies rather than sell phonographs outright in the belief that once they had Edison's promised standard, existing machines would be "a detriment to us rather than a benefit if in the hands of the public and we therefor prefer to call them in and smash them up."[29] In early May they hired James Redpath, a former journalist who had established the Redpath Lyceum Bureau in Boston in 1868, to manage their exhibition business. By mid-May the company was training eighty men who each paid $100 for the right to exhibit the phonograph.

These exhibitors were to charge a 25¢ admission for each exhibition, and the company was to receive 25 percent of the gross receipts. Edison received royalties on the sale of the machines and 20 percent of the net receipts, after the deduction of Redpath's salary, from the exhibitions, which continued through October 1. By the end of the year he netted over $4,000, a quarter of which came from exhibition receipts.

The difficulty of operating the exhibition phonograph made it necessary to train exhibitors. As Redpath informed one prospective exhibitor, "Written instructions wont help you, because although you might be able to run it imperfectly, you could not obtain the best results without some personal instruction. If the needle got out of adjustment, you would be quite helpless. . . . We do not want to take your money and place you in a position where you will not only have no returns, but find yourself with a sort of white elephant on your hands."[30] This problem prompted Edison to begin work on an improved model, and by early June he had developed a new design and built a prototype. The most significant improvement, a still larger and heavier flywheel that allowed operators to turn the cylinder at a more uniform speed, was the first of several modifications incorporated into the existing exhibition machines.

By the end of August Edison, Batchelor, and Johnson had developed a new cylinder design that became the standard. This new design was based on the large flywheel phonograph developed by Edison and Batchelor during June, with modifications made by Batchelor after the Newark manufacturer Pool & Co. delivered ten of these instruments in mid-August. The design also incorporated changes made by Johnson to the old exhibition machines during July and August. At the beginning of September Johnson began to exhibit one of the new phonographs in New York. This standard demonstration machine came in two models. The first was an "exhibition instrument" made entirely of iron except for the brass cylinder "grooved with twenty-four threads per inch." The second was a fine "drawing room instrument" with a cylinder that had forty threads per inch, which gave it "nearly double the recording surface on a cylinder of the same size." The company claimed that this also "adds a trifle to the distinctness of the articulation, and approximates more nearly the quality of the voice." The drawing-room instrument was made entirely of "brass, hand-filed and beautifully finished throughout. The fly-wheel, base, etc. being of brass, the instrument is given a rich appearance. It is mounted upon a handsome rosewood and inlaid box, with drawer for tools." The iron machine was mounted on a "neat white wood box" that also had a tool drawer. Besides tools and materials for repair and adjustment, each machine came with a set of instructions, six styli, five pounds of tinfoil, and "a funnel for increasing the volume of sound in reproduction." All of these phonographs were manufactured by Bergmann's shop, which also supplied the tinfoil. The first fine brass machines became available in mid-October, but the company only sold a few of these, and its sales of the less expensive exhibition machine rapidly declined by the end of the year, although Johnson continued to sell a few during 1879, along with an inexpensive $10 phonograph he developed himself and that became known as "Edison's Speaking Parlor Phonograph."[31]

Neither Edison nor Johnson were able to turn the tinfoil phonograph from a curiosity suitable for exhibitions and lectures into a consumer product. Although the development of a suitable power-drive might have made it more acceptable for commercial purposes, the phonograph's real drawback was not the mechanical design on which they focused their efforts but the tinfoil recording surface. Compared to the later wax recording surfaces developed in the 1880s, tinfoil recordings had very poor fidelity and also deteriorated rapidly after a single playback. To overcome this, Edison attempted to develop a method of producing copies, either by electro- or stereotyping, that could be played many times, but he never succeeded. He also experimented with other metals and materials as recording surfaces, but he continued to favor tinfoil. As a result, for the next decade the phonograph remained little more than a scientific curiosity, albeit one that continued to attract interest and attention.

Edison's extensive experiments with sound recording led him to develop a variety of other acoustic devices during the first months of 1878, and these, too, were commercial failures. They included the aerophone, which used compressed air to loudly reproduce a recording for fog horns, advertising, and other purposes; the phonomotor, which was little more than a toy for turning sound vibrations into rotary motion, although Edison hoped it actually would be powerful enough to bore a hole through a board; and the megaphone, also called the telephonescope, which allowed sound to be heard over long distances. The one that attracted the greatest public attention, however, was his projected hearing aid—the aurophone. Edison hoped to adapt his megaphone for this purpose by finding a way of telescopically collapsing its large listening tubes to make them portable.[32]

The other acoustic instruments had grown directly out of Edison's research, but the aurophone was a result of his growing fame. In March Edison had begun to receive letters from sufferers of hearing problems asking him to invent a device to aid them. They were prompted to write because reporters represented the phonograph as the greatest acoustic invention of the age, and they believed that someone who could invent such a marvel could also solve the problem of deafness. They thought as well that Edison's own hearing problems would make him receptive to their pleas.

Edison received a few letters of this sort as news of the phonograph spread, but the real impetus was his mention in an April 19 interview in the *Washington Evening Star*, where he described an "apparatus to enable me to hear theatrical plays." Although he told those who inquired that this apparatus "would be generally impracticable owing to cumbersomeness," Edison also informed them that he had decided he was "going to work soon on an apparatus to accomplish the object in a practical manner." Two weeks later he replied to *Chicago Tribune* editor Joseph Medill, whose own hearing problems had prompted him to write to Edison about this subject, to tell him that "the many

letters that I have received on the subject of an apparatus for the deaf has convinced me that the demand would be enormous. So I have put two of my most
skillful assistants at work testing my ideas." After Medill published this letter,
which included Edison's prediction that he would "produce a practical apparatus within six months," the demand for the promised invention became so great
that he had to send a form letter as a reply to the many inquiries. By the end of
1878 Edison had received over 600 letters on the subject, and although he continued to receive many new requests and follow-up letters over the next few
years, he never succeeded in making a practical hearing aid. Instead, he began
to recommend the audiophone of N. R. Rhoads, to whom he had been introduced by Croffut.[33]

Newspaper reporters often noted the irony that two of the great acoustic
inventions—the phonograph and the carbon-button telephone—had been the
product of an inventor who was partially deaf. Reporters were amazed that his
hearing seemed not to be a serious obstacle in his acoustic researches, although Edison did acknowledge that it caused him some difficulty during the
telephone research when he had to depend on the more acute hearing of his
assistants. The state of Edison's hearing at this time is suggested by his book-
keeper and part-time secretary William Carman, who told one inquirer about
the hearing aid that "I have to holler to him." Although some medical doctors
suggested that they might be able to cure Edison (one even offered to do so in
exchange for a phonograph), he declined. Edison's reluctance arose in part
from a previous attempt to cure the problem, which he claimed "increased the
deafness."[34] But he also found it convenient to use his hearing loss as an excuse
for not attending social events, and he claimed that it allowed him to concentrate better by reducing distractions.

The many letters Edison received from those afflicted by hearing loss were
part of the larger phenomenon described nicely by George Bliss in an April 13
letter: "The Mania has broken out this way— School girls write compositions
on Edison. The funny papers publish squibs on Edison. The religious papers
write editorials on Edison. The daily papers write up his life. The Rev. Woodbury is writing a magazine article on Edison &c &c. When shall we get a rest."
He concluded by asking, "Why dont the Graphic fill up exclusively with Edison and [be] done with [it]?"[35]

The next week Edison garnered more publicity, as well as increased public
stature, when he traveled to Washington, D.C., to exhibit his phonograph before the National Academy of Sciences. He had been invited to do so by the
Academy's president Joseph Henry, who already considered Edison to be "the
most ingenious inventor in this country . . . or in any other."[36] The phonograph
secured this reputation. While in Washington Edison also demonstrated the
phonograph to members of Congress and to President Rutherford B. Hayes,
who invited him to the White House. Edison commemorated his trip to Washington by sitting for what became a portrait with his phonograph in the studio
operated by famed photographer Matthew Brady. Such a sitting was regarded

This photograph of Edison and Charles Batchelor with the first flywheel phonograph was taken at Matthew Brady's studio in Washington, D.C. Another photograph with Edison alone became one of the most famous pictures of the inventor.

as "a rite of passage for the rich and famous, a sign of having arrived," and this widely circulated photograph became one of the best known images of Edison.[37]

Edison's reputation had also spread throughout Europe. The earliest foreign accounts of his phonograph appeared in Britain. Charles Batchelor provided a description to the *English Mechanic* in December, and the first news report, which appeared in the *London Times* on January 17, was reprinted in other British papers. The *Times* claimed that "Mr. Edison is well known in the States, and scarcely less so in England, for several valuable practical applications of electrical science, among Mr. Edison's other inventions being an exceedingly well-arranged telephone."[38] However, although the scientific and technical communities were already aware of Edison's work, it is unlikely that his name was very familiar to the general public. As in the United States, it was the phonograph that brought him to larger public notice. When the first phonograph arrived in London in late February and was exhibited by Preece and Puskas, Edison began to receive additional favorable publicity.

Elsewhere in Europe the phonograph initially came to public notice through reprints of accounts from American papers and journals. The real breakthrough occurred in March when Puskas arrived in Paris with the machine. Puskas's promotion soon had "every Parisian paper [printing] long articles about it," and Puskas considered putting a "stop [to] exhibiting until he [had] several hundred ready for market." After his demonstration before the members of the French Academy of Sciences "there was great excitement and a storm of applause." And when the Universal Exposition opened in Paris that summer Edison's reputation had grown to the point that he was awarded the Grand Prize "not on any particular invention but as the Inventor of the age in which we live."[39]

Edison's stature as the "inventor of the age" prompted many would-be and less successful inventors to write to him for advice or to ask his help in developing their ideas. A few even wrote to suggest ideas for Edison's own inventions. Although many began their letters by praising Edison's accomplishments, most were surprisingly direct, perhaps agreeing with a German writer who began by stating "You do not need my compliments about your inventions. So I go in for a question." They sought his advice about their inventions because they believed that his opinion "would be of importance" or because they thought that his skill and knowledge could help them perfect their inventions. They also turned to Edison because they had neither time nor money for their experiments and hoped that he would take up their ideas in exchange for a percentage of any profits. Edison answered many of these letters, often merely indicating that he had no time to take up anyone else's work, but sometimes by agreeing to examine their plans, allowing them to come to the laboratory, or even conducting an experiment or two. He was careful, however, to advise them to "write out your plan in detail accompanied with illustrations and have the same witnessed by several of your neighbors. Then you can safely write me & explain your idea & I will give you my opinion on it."[40] These inventors saw Edison as one of their own number who had succeeded beyond their dreams. However, apart from being self-taught, Edison and his more successful inventive colleagues were quite different from Edison's correspondents, who more clearly fit the stereotype of the lone inventor. Working in an industrial setting with connections to leading companies and entrepreneurs, Edison and his colleagues had access to much greater financial resources for their work and they could more easily employ skilled assistants and machinists.

Besides the many individuals who wrote Edison requesting advice on inventions, there were numerous others who sought charity, autographs and photographs, or to act as agents for Edison's inventions. They felt comfortable writing to him because they had, as one letter writer told him, "become well acquainted with you through the medium of the newspapers."[41] Although frequently referred to as a genius and a wizard whose feats defied analysis, he also was presented as a common American. The depiction of Edison as a wizard has been emphasized by cultural historians, who see in it an uncertainty over the rapid changes wrought by technology, but what stands out in newspaper and magazine articles and seemed most to capture the public imagination was the representation of Edison as a man of the people. The contrasting nature of the Edison image was captured by a reporter for the *New York World*, who wrote that "Mr. Edison is in many respects an odd man and in every way peculiarly American." Part of Edison's common-man image arose from physical descriptions that depicted him wearing clothes dirty from his labors in the laboratory with his face streaked (and sometimes in need of a shave) and his hair disheveled. In the words of a *New York Sun* reporter, "the picture was not that of an alchemist; it was more like a plodding apprentice to a machinist." He also seemed to possess an "affability and playful boyishness," and both reporters and the American public took to him for the same reason: "A man of common sense would feel at home with him in a minute; but a nob or prig would be sadly out of place."[42]

To handle the influx of mail Edison hired friend and former telegrapher Stockton L. Griffin as a full-time secretary. Handling the influx of visitors to Menlo Park, however, was a more difficult problem. Many of them were prominent people, others were members of the press, and still others common citizens. Although Edison showed great forbearance at these constant interruptions he clearly found them distracting, as evidenced by his reference to sixty prominent people who visited the laboratory as "all big bugs."[43] Such large groups were not an everyday occurrence, but there seemed to be a constant stream of visitors to the laboratory. Another large group that appeared at the beginning of May consisted of Newark citizens who came to express their pride in the city's former resident. The *Newark Daily Advertiser* reporter who covered the trip captured both the attraction of Menlo Park and the distractions facing Edison: "Menlo Park is the electrical Mecca. Thitherward will the pilgrims of science turn their expectant eye, and Mr. Thomas A. Edison, the high priest of the temple, will have little time for future inventions without he limits his visitors to one day in the week or encloses his laboratory in a brick wall and shuts them out entirely."[44]

Other papers also commented on the many visitors to the laboratory, many of whom were uninvited. In one newspaper report "an excursion party of a dozen or more made a raid on the laboratory, whereupon the great inventor fled." And according to the reporter, Edison determined to devise "some means to protect himself from these disastrous invasions of the ever-increasing army of bores." Another reporter called it "the duty of the press, especially of this State [New Jersey] to discourage such overwhelming visitations to Menlo Park." By mid-June, according to a local newspaper, Edison had become

so much annoyed by the curiosity-seekers that he has been obliged to give public notice that he can no longer entertain them at his laboratory at Menlo Park, and therefore he will hereafter only receive those who have important business to transact with him. He is in receipt of an average of from eighty to a hundred letters per day, most of them of no importance to him, and he begs people to hold up and give him a chance to attend to his business.[45]

Edison clearly reveled in his newfound fame and used it to his advantage, but he found all the attention exhausting. By the end of the spring he had begun to wear down both physically and emotionally.

Contributing to his low spirits was the unexpected death of William Orton on April 22 at the age of fifty-two. Edison described his feelings to a reporter from the *New York World*: "If I get to love a man he dies right away. Lefferts went first, and now Orton's gone, too."[46] Even though he doubtless had been troubled by Edison's actions with the quadruplex, like Lefferts Orton had acted as a friend and mentor to the inventor. Western Union attorney Grosvenor P. Lowrey, who was one of the last to see Orton alive, told Edison, "his last words to me were of you— I am sure it will gratify you to know that they were words of more than esteem—of affection. Even in the times when we were differing he had always a warm place in his heart for you, among those few who were admitted to that inner place."[47]

Beyond his personal affections for Edison, Orton's death also removed from the head of Western Union one of the few corporate officials in America who took a strong interest in the technical needs of his company. Besides developing close relationships with inventors such as Edison, Orton had a much greater appreciation for the inventive process than most managers. Edison's increasingly lucrative contracts with Western Union had been a direct result of Orton's interest. Following Orton's death telegraph invention at Western Union languished and Edison himself had little to do with the company. Orton's successor Norvin Green not only began negotiating with Bell Telephone to combine the two companies' telephone interests, but also took a more passive approach to telegraph invention in the belief that the industry was technologically mature. He did not develop the same kind of close relationship with Edison as had Orton. Indeed, Orton was seen by those close to Edison as his "only friend" at Western Union.[48]

Another source of disquiet in Edison's life was the vehement public controversy that erupted in early June over claims to the invention of the microphone. Edison first became aware of British inventor David Hughes's research regarding the amplification of sound after reading the May 2 issue of *Nature* that discussed Hughes's claim that semiconducting substances vary their resistance under pressure. This prompted Edison to write William Preece, "Evidently Mr H dont read the papers that is nothing but my carbon telephone."[49] The controversy really began, however, when detailed accounts of Hughes's work appeared in *Engineering*. An article titled "The Hughes Telephone" in the May 10 issue described Hughes's experiments and claims, based on his paper read the previous day at a meeting of the Royal Society of London. This article not only confirmed Edison's belief that Hughes had done nothing more than rediscover the principle of his carbon telephone, but also no doubt angered him with its claims that "of all the marvels connected with telephonic electricity we have no hesitation in saying that Professor Hughes's discovery . . . is the most marvelous of all." Besides giving Hughes credit for a fundamental discovery, *Engineering* also described his instrument as "a transmitting telephone surpassing in sensitiveness the beautiful instrument of Professor Bell" by "transmitting louder and clearer articulation."[50]

Edison became even more incensed when the May 17 issue of *Engineering* reprinted Hughes's Royal Society paper. This made it clear that Hughes believed he was both the first to discard the diaphragm and to use the change in pressure produced by sound waves to directly vary the resistance of a carbon semiconductor in a telephone and the originator of the microphone for amplifying sound. Edison had made these modifications in his carbon transmitter in March, and he had immediately communicated them to Preece. He was therefore furious when he came to the end of Hughes's paper and read: "My warmest thanks are due to Mr. W. H. Preece, electrician to the Post Office, for his appreciation of the importance of the facts I have stated, and for his kind counsel and aid in the preparation of this paper."[51] Edison felt aggrieved that Preece had not pointed out to Hughes that his telephone and microphone were nothing more than Edison's carbon transmitter. Edison was hardly mollified by Preece's May 22 letter explaining that "Hughes's doings border so closely upon yours that it is difficult to distinguish between what you have done and what he has done. You were on the very threshold of a great discovery, in fact, had it not been for the phonograph distracting your attention you must have anticipated what Hughes has done."[52] By the time Edison received this letter at the beginning of June, he had also seen the May 17 issue of the *Engineer*, which credited another discovery to Hughes—the use of the carbon principle for measuring heat. Edison had just communicated this idea to Preece and angrily cabled him June 4, "I regard Hughes heat measurer & Direct Impact telephone as abuse confidence. I sent you & others papers describing it. . . . if you do not set this thing right I shall with details." He also sent a telegram to William Thomson charging Preece with "great abuse confidence [on] his part in the Hughes matter."[53]

Two days later Edison set out his case in response to an editorial in the *New York Daily Tribune* that argued that by metalizing the carbon in his microphone and by not using a diaphragm, Hughes had made a distinct and different invention. Edison argued that his well-publicized discovery that the electrical resistance of plumbago varied enormously under pressure was the basis for Hughes's work and that the key features, such as the removal of the diaphragm, which were supposed to differentiate the microphone from his carbon telephone were, in fact, included in publications about his transmitter. Turning to Preece, Edison contended that his conduct was "a gross infringement of the confidence obtained under the guise of friendship." He told of how he had shown Preece the carbon telephone and pressure relay at the Menlo Park Laboratory in 1877 and "made him my agent for the presentation of this telephone, and subsequently of the phonograph, in England, and kept him informed, by copies of publications and by private letters, of my leading experiments, as he always manifested a great desire to be the means of presenting my discoveries to the British public." He also implied that Preece had alerted Hughes to the use of the carbon principle for measuring heat. Later in the year in a private letter Edison wrote of Preece: "When I said abused my confidence I did not imply that he gave to Hughes any ideas. But that he had abused the confidence I placed in his promise that he would bring my Carbon telephone before the authorities & societies there, a result which I had hoped for and [for] which I sent him one of my assistants with telephones."[54]

A further indication of Edison's anger over Hughes's "piracy" is found in Charles Batchelor's June 6 letter to James Adams, who was conducting tests of Edison's telephone in London and Paris. "This is the *damnedest* steal in the country and Preece knew it all the time," Batchelor told Adams, urging him to "defend it well and denounce Hughes' arrangement as an imposition." He then declared, "We intend to go for them bad. . . . We have got magnificent proofs and records on it and we will make Preece so *damned* sick he will wish he had never been born. We will spend $5000 if necessary to expose it even if we lose our telephone there."[55] Edison and Batchelor were soon busy compiling a list of leading figures in the British scientific and technical communities as well as other European luminaries, such as Hermann von Helmholtz and Werner Siemens in Germany and Count du Moncel in France. They sent copies of Edison's letter to the *Tribune*, published descriptions of the carbon telephone, and other proofs, including an 1877 *Journal of the Telegraph* article on his pressure relay, to the people on the list.

Because most participants in the dispute were either British or American, it became as much a question of national pride as of scientific claims. Not surprisingly, newspapers in both countries framed the debate in nationalistic terms, but even the more temperate technical and scientific journals seem to have been affected by such considerations.[56] In one of the most egregious examples, the London journal *Engineering* actually left out two important paragraphs when it reprinted sections from George Prescott's book on the telephone that Edison sent to support his claims of priority to the microphone. These concerned Edison's discovery that his principle could work without a diaphragm and that finely divided metals or metalized carbon could be used as well as plumbago. Although differences of opinion regarding Edison's and Hughes's specific claims were a legitimate point of debate, Edison was quite justified in arguing that *Engineering* had given credit to Hughes "for exactly what has been suppressed from the proofs sent."[57]

It is perhaps ironic that Edison's primary motivation stemmed from his desire for the respect of the British scientific and technical community. As Edison told his London friend Henry Edmunds in a letter of May 26, he felt particularly aggrieved to have his discovery "stolen without comment, especially in England where I want to stand well."[58] The controversy, however, served only to diminish his personal reputation in that country. William Thomson, who earlier in the year had called Edison "the very first Electrician of the Age," took him to task for the acrimonious nature of the dispute. Arguing that Edison should have tried to settle the controversy either in private or through a dispassionate discussion of his claims, Thomson criticized him for "his violent attack in the public journals on Mr. Preece and Mr. Hughes," which "has rendered it for the time impossible for either them or others to give any consideration whatever to his claims."[59]

Thomson's letter illustrates how the personal nature of this conflict affected the views of participants. He noted that the "physical principle" used in both the telephone and the microphone was the same as that used many years earlier by M. Clérac of the French telegraph service. Clérac had used variable resistance carbon tubes (similar to those Edison used in 1873) in the 1860s, and he had given a set of these tubes to Hughes and others in 1866. Furthermore, Thomson noted, Count Du Moncel had previously pointed out that increasing the pressure between two conductors in contact reduced the electric resistance between them. By bringing in Clérac and Du Moncel, Thomson showed how much his own views had been altered by the debate. After receiving Edison's June 4 telegram he had written Preece that "[Edison] does I think deserve the *first place* in respect to credit for the microphone on account of what you told us at Plymouth of what he had done which involved the essentials and some of the details of the affair very clearly I think. I should think Hughes has worked out what he had done quite independently."[60] Thomson was probably correct that Hughes arrived at his microphone through independent research, but this research was doubtless influenced more by Hughes's experiments with the new telephone technology than by any prior experiments with Clérac's tubes. Neither Edison nor Hughes, each of whom not only failed to cite Clérac's work as a precedent for his own research but also claimed the discovery as entirely his own, seems to have drawn any inspiration from Clérac's device. Perhaps if Edison had not launched a personal attack against Preece, Thomson and others in the British community might have been more willing to see his side and to concede him a share of the credit.

In the midst of the battle over the microphone Edison also found himself embroiled in another dispute with Elihu Thomson and Edwin Houston, who claimed that they were the first to use the microphone as a telephone relay. Like the microphone controversy itself, their dispute took the shape of letters to the editors of various technical journals. Responding to their claim, Edison pointed out that he had described the use of his pressure relay as a telephone repeater a year earlier. Recognizing that the pressure relay was one of Edison's principal arguments for his priority in the microphone dispute, Thomson and Houston replied that he would first have to make good his claim to priority of that invention. Rather speciously they argued that Edison had applied his pressure relay only to his "Speaking Telegraph," which they contended was "*not an articulating Telegraph,* but a species of harmonic telegraph." Edison concluded this exchange of letters with a comment that summarized his general feelings about the controversies regarding the microphone: "Change of form and name appears to be an easy and favourite method now-a-days of making discoveries and inventions."[61]

These priority disputes combined with the stress of constant public attention to awaken Edison's desire for a vacation, something he had not allowed himself since his honeymoon in 1871. He therefore gladly accepted an invitation from Henry Draper to accompany him and George Barker to Rawlins, Wyoming, where a party of prominent astronomers would be observing the eclipse of the sun on July 29. Also accompanying Edison was Edwin Fox, who planned to telegraph his report on the eclipse back to the *Herald*. Another reporter, who saw Edison off at the Pennsylvania Railroad station, described him as "as glad as a school boy" and "so filled with anticipation that he could hardly stand still." Edison told the reporter, "I can hardly wait until I get there. This is the first vacation I have had in a long time, and I mean to enjoy it. I have never seen the country. For the present I am in the hands of my friends, and I think they intend to go directly through. After we have made the observations, however, I am going further West, to take in the Yosemite, San Francisco and a portion of the coast."[62]

Draper invited Edison not only out of friendship, but also because of their mutual interest in astronomy. They had met a year earlier when Draper, a medical doctor and professor of natural philosophy at the City University of New York (now New York University), had accompanied Barker to Menlo Park. At the time they discussed Draper's discovery of oxygen in the sun, a topic that led to an exchange of correspondence regarding spectroscopic analysis in astronomy. Draper also wanted Edison to use his tasimeter (the heat measurer of the microphone controversy) to measure the heat of the sun's corona during the eclipse.

Edison had invented the tasimeter in response to astronomer Samuel Langley's suggestion in October 1877 that he try to devise a more sensitive thermopile for use in measuring small fluctuations in temperature. Edison designed the tasimeter with a hard rubber rod that expanded as it absorbed heat and pressed against a carbon button, like one of those used in his telephone. This altered the button's electrical resistance, which was measured by passing the small current through a Wheatstone bridge and registering it with a Thomson mirror galvanometer. Langley, who planned to observe the eclipse from Pike's Peak, requested that Edison send him one for his observations but never received it.

The professional astronomers who chose Rawlins as the site for their observations had arrived some time before Edison to set up their instruments. After he arrived Edison set up his tasimeter in a henhouse and tested it by measuring the heat of the star Arcturus. When the day of the eclipse finally arrived, a strong wind made observing conditions particularly difficult for Edison. While the makeshift observatories of the astronomers were little affected, Edison had to prop his up with boards from a nearby lumberyard, but the wind continued to give him trouble as the vibrations it caused threw the tasimeter out of adjustment. According to Fox, "Edison's difficulty seemed to increase as the precious moment of total eclipse drew near." But finally, about a minute from total eclipse, "he succeeded in concentrating the light from the corona upon the small opening of the instrument. Instantly the fire ray of light on his graduating scale swept along to the right, clearing its boundaries. Edison was overjoyed. The experiment had shown the existence of about fifteen times more heat in the corona than that obtained from the star Arcturus the previous night."[63] Edison's more sober account, presented at the August meeting of the American Association for the Advancement of Science (AAAS) in St. Louis, indicated that the scale of the galvanometer was inadequate to measure the coronal radiance accurately. Nonetheless, he told reporters that he was satisfied with the success of his observations and hoped to use the tasimeter to measure stars that were not visible through a telescope.

Edison's observations and his instrument proved of little use to the astronomical community. During the eclipse he had been able to show only the existence of heat radiation from the corona, which was of little significance. Charles Young of Princeton, who tested the tasimeter prior to the eclipse and found it impractical for use with a spectroscope, had already shown the corona to be solar in origin. George Barker claimed for Edison the credit of making the first attempt to measure the heat from the sun during an eclipse, and this was quickly taken up by the press as another triumph for the inventor. The astronomical community, however, knew that such measurements had been made with a thermopile as early as 1842. The tasimeter itself proved as insignificant as Edison's measurements with it. Edison sought to make it available to the scientific community through the British instrumentmaker John Browning and American telegraph manufacturers Partrick & Carter, who were to manufacture and sell the instrument without paying Edison any royalties. Although there was some initial interest among scientists few tasimeters were sold, and those who inspected the instrument found that it was too difficult to use and did not respond quickly enough or give sufficiently accurate measurements for scientific use.[64]

The real purpose of Edison's trip west was a vacation, and he thoroughly enjoyed himself in the weeks following the eclipse. Accompanied by Barker, he traveled west with free passes given to him by the railroad companies. Edison later recounted how Jay Gould, who controlled the Union Pacific,

gave me a letter to the various superintendents requesting that I be permitted to ride on the cow catcher of the locomotive at my own risk—In those days the schedule time was very slow, being only 20 miles per hour. The different engineers gave me a small cushion every day I rode in this manner from Omaha to the Sacramento Valley, except through the snow shed on the summit of the Sierra, without dust or anything to obstruct the view—only once was I in danger when the locomotive struck an animal about the size of a small cub bear, which I think was a badger. This animal struck the front of the locomotive just under the headlight with great violence and was then thrown off by the rebound. I was sitting to one side grasping the angle brace so no harm was done.[65]

After arriving in California Edison spent three days in San Francisco, where he was offered the hospitality of the Union Club. He then rode to the top of Glacier Point in Yosemite and stayed at the Mariposa Big Tree Hotel on the other side of the mountain. Next he traveled to Virginia City, Nevada, where he was the guest of the Washoe Club. While in Nevada he visited the Consolidated Virginia mine in the Comstock lode, where he suggested that it would be possible to detect ores electrically. On his return through the Rocky Mountains Edison went on a fishing trip in the wilderness, during which he pondered the possibility of transmitting electricity from the Platte River to provide power for a mine located miles away in the mountains. Edison had bought fishing gear and a Winchester rifle in Laramie City, Wyoming, and at some point he also went hunting with "Professor Barker, professor of physics of the University of Pennsylvania, Major Thornburg, several soldiers and a number of railroad officials . . . about a hundred miles south of the railroad in the Ute Indian country."[66] At each stop he met the local telegraph operators, some of whom he had known during his operating days. Edison apparently enjoyed the vacation and the outdoor life; reporters who visited him at Menlo Park after his return commented on how well rested and tanned he looked.[67]

While Thomas enjoyed himself Mary remained at home. She was expecting their third child, William Leslie, who would be born in October. Whether the pregnancy was difficult or because of other reasons, she seems to have suffered from nervous exhaustion while Thomas was gone. On August 5 Stockton Griffin wrote Edison to tell him that

> Mrs E's health is not of the best. She is extremely nervous and frets a great deal about you and about everything. I take it to be nervous prostration. She was so frightened yesterday for fear the children would get on the track that she fainted. This morning I telegraphed Dr Ward who came at noon. She is better now, but I have advised her to make her proposed trip among her friends at Whitestone L.I. as soon as possible and she will start Thursday next. She needs a change and right away as the cars keep her awake at night and this causes her to lose strength. Of course theres nothing serious in this, but I thought it might be of interest to you. If she should grow worse I would Teleg you.[68]

Mary's trip to Long Island proved no tonic, and on her return she became so ill that Griffin telegraphed Edison on August 20 "to return at once."[69] Edison, however, decided to go on to St. Louis to attend the AAAS meeting and wired back that he would return on the 23rd. Edison seems to have considered his wife to be something of a hypochondriac, unnaturally high-strung and nervous. This is suggested not just by the tone of Griffin's August 5 letter and Edison's response to her illness, but also by a page of doodles from several years earlier on which he wrote his wife's maiden name several times, eventually turning Stilwell into "Stillsick."[70]

Apparently untroubled by word of his wife's ill health, Edison was still in St. Louis on the morning of August 23 when he was formally presented to the Association as a new member by George Barker, who remarked "that the time has come when the scientist is no longer the only discoverer; the practical man has found science too slow, and has stepped in and discovered for himself." This statement echoed one he had made at the National Academy meeting in April, when he called Edison "the discoverer of the principle upon which the telephone operates and not simply an inventor."[71] In the afternoon Edison was scheduled to present four papers: "On the Use of the Tasimeter for Measuring the Heat of the Stars and the Sun's Corona," "On the Application of the Carbon Button as the Principle Involved in the Microphone," "The Carbon Telephone," and "A New Voltameter." However, he "could only be induced to read one of his papers—the first one mentioned. Prof. Barker read the other three for him, and a good deal of discussion followed all of them."[72] The paper on the carbon button included his claim to be "the first one to use finely divided conducting material for the purpose of translating sonorous vibrations into electric waves."[73] The following day he finally left for Menlo Park, wiring Griffin that he would be home on the 26th. In the meantime Mary again required the services of her doctor.

Whatever the impact of his trip on Mary, Thomas returned with renewed energy and with growing interest in exploring a rapidly developing new technology. Edison's enthusiasm was captured by Charles Batchelor in later reminiscences.

> When he came back from this trip he told me of many projects he worked up for future inventions, amongst them one for using the power of the falls for electricity & utilizing it in the mines for drills etc. He said he had talked a great deal with Prof. Barker [who] told him of some experiments he had seen at William Wallace's place at Ansonia, Ct. & wanted him to up there & see them.[74]

William Wallace, whose firm Wallace & Sons was the foremost brass and copper foundry in the country, had been working on an electric arc light system with electrical inventor Moses Farmer for several years. A friend of Barker's and Draper's, he had joined them when they visited Edison's laboratory in July 1877. At the time Edison was beginning to consider his own electric lighting experiments. His attention was drawn to this subject by reports of the successful demonstration in Paris of Russian military engineer Paul Jablochkoff's newly devised carbon arc lighting system. The Jablochkoff candle, as it was known, cast a less intense light than other contemporary arc lamps and was regulated by a mechanism that allowed several to be placed in a single circuit, thus making possible for the first time large-scale electric illumination for outdoor and large indoor spaces. The Jablochkoff system provided a new impetus to the field of electric lighting.[75]

Edison had briefly experimented with arc lights in September 1877 but focused his attention on incandescent lights. One of Edison's first experiments was with carbonized paper, a common substance around the laboratory that he had used for electrical resistances in the summer of 1876. Later he proposed selling the resistances along with other articles made from paper through the American Novelty Company. Edison's first carbonized paper lamp was made by Batchelor from a device that had been in the laboratory since 1875 and had been used to study electric discharges in rarefied gases. According to Batchelor "it was a difficult and tedious process to put the carbon" in the lamp, which they then exhausted with an ordinary hand-operated air pump. According to Edison, "We did not succeed in getting a higher vacuum than $2^1/2$ millimeters on the mercury gauge, and we could not make the carbons burn more than a few minutes at a time. Some of the carbons were brought up to brilliant incandescence, and probably gave thirty or forty candles of light. The carbons were brought up to various degrees of incandescence."[76] Most of their experiments used boron or silicon rather than carbon as incandescing elements. Describing the desultory electric light experiments he conducted in 1877 Edison later explained that

> we were trying to subdivide the electric light into a small number of burners, where the circuit was closed by solid conductors, and the reason why experiments were conducted with boron and silicon was because they were not subject to oxidation like carbon, which we had previously tried, and which did not last as long at a white incandescence as pieces of graphitoidal silicon. The results of the carbon experiments, and also of the boron and silicon experiments, were not considered sufficiently satisfactory, when looked at in the commercial sense, to continue them at that time, and they were laid aside.[77]

Although unsuccessful, Edison's electric light experiments did provide him with insights that proved useful when he took up the subject in earnest in September 1878.

Edison had conducted his early experiments with batteries, but he realized that a practical system would require electromagnetic generators. In his visit to Wallace's shop on September 8 he had a chance to see one of the most powerful electrical generators then in existence, the "telemachon" (from the Greek word for distance) that Wallace and Moses Farmer had developed a few months before and with which they were able to light eight lamps at once. Upon seeing the machine in operation Edison instantly recognized its potential for transmitting power from a distance, the very thing he had been thinking about in connection with mines. According to the *New York Sun* reporter who accompanied him,

> Edison was enraptured. He fairly gloated over it. . . . He ran from the instruments to the lights and from the lights back to the instrument. He sprawled over a table with the SIMPLICITY OF A CHILD, and made all kinds of calculations. He estimated the power of the instrument and of the lights, the probable loss of power in transmission, the amount of coal the instrument would save in a day, a week, a month, a year, and the result of such saving on manufacturing.[78]

Wallace had already experimented with using the power of the Naugatuck River a quarter of a mile away to power the machine, and Edison suggested that he could help improve the machine's ability to transmit power over a distance.

When he returned to Menlo Park the next day Edison began to work in earnest on the problem of electric lighting. However, he focused his attention on the light rather than the generator in the belief that Wallace had basically solved the problem of transmission. As he told the *Sun* reporter a month later, "[In Wallace's shop] I saw for the first time everything in practical operation. It was all before me. I saw the thing had not go so far but that I had a chance. I saw that what had been done had never been made practically useful. The intense light had not been subdivided so that it could be brought into private houses."[79]

It was this complex problem of subdividing the light that Edison rather naively set out to solve.

CHAPTER 10

Inventing a System

The incandescent electric light bulb has become a familiar symbol for that flash of inspired genius traditionally associated with invention. In part the light bulb's symbolic value comes from its obvious role as a visual metaphor of the "bright idea." But this symbolism also arises from its association with Thomas Edison—the electric light perceived as the greatest invention of the world's greatest inventor.[1] But the electric light was not a single invention emanating from an inspired genius. Instead it was a complex network of inventions produced by one of the first institutions of organized corporate research. As he invented a system of electric lighting, Edison was simultaneously reinventing the system of invention.

In September 1878, when he began working on the problem of electric lighting, Edison remained in many respects a traditional though highly ingenious inventor, working with two or three close assistants and a few skilled experimental machinists. Over the course of the next year, Edison added several new staff members with special skills, including chemists, glassblowers, and even a mathematician with graduate training in physics, to help with experiments on electric lighting. By the beginning of 1880, as he turned from basic research to the development of a commercial system and added even more new staff members, Edison had begun to resemble the modern director of research and development. His extremely creative and imaginative mind continued to provide intellectual direction for the enterprise, but increasingly others contributed essential ideas and skills. And like the modern research director, Edison depended on the support of corporate capital. While Edison the individual is celebrated as the inventor of the electric light, it was the less visible corporate organization of laboratory and business enterprise that enabled him to succeed.

Edison's team research approach to invention and the resources of his Menlo Park laboratory proved crucial to his eventual success, allowing him to experiment more rapidly and on a broader front than his rivals and thus to quickly outpace them. Nonetheless, his personal creativity in organizing the research and providing its intellectual direction cannot be ignored. His success relied to a large degree on what scholars interested in creativity might call his cognitive style. The origins of this style are not as easily analyzed as his style of laboratory research or the knowledge of electricity and chemistry that he and his staff drew on, but they are clearly visible in the way he worked. Those interested in creativity have noted that the "ability to construct fruitful analogies between fields" is an important mode of creative thinking.[2] From early in his career Edison used analogies with familiar devices, electrical actions, or chemical effects to deal with unfamiliar technologies or to move into a new path of research. This is the aspect of Edison's inventive style that historian Thomas Hughes describes when he says that Edison possessed an "ability to find metaphors that allowed him to draw on what he knew to suggest order in what he did not know."[3] A second and perhaps less common attribute of his creative mode of thinking, was a remarkable ability to conceive countless design variations, which Western Union attorney Edward Dickerson likened to the "turning of a kaleidoscope producing new permutations."[4]

It was these qualities of Edison's mind that seemed to set him apart from his contemporaries and to attract the support of investors. Just as his experience and proven record as an inventor helped him to raise the funds needed to conduct his experiments, they also provided him with the tools and confidence necessary to move into the new field of electric light research. His earlier work in telegraphy, for example, had given him the critical insights and crucial analogies he used to approach the new problem. It also enabled him to quickly produce what he believed to be a solution to the problem of subdividing the electric light.

On September 8, 1878, the same day that he visited William Wallace, Edison sketched out his first tentative idea for a lamp with a thermal regulator. Two days later Charles Batchelor recorded their first experiments, and by September 13 Edison had drawn up his first electric light patent caveat and wired Wallace to "Hurry up the [dynamo] machine. I have struck a big bonanza."[5] Convinced he had solved the problem, Edison publicly announced his success in a *New York Sun* article of September 16. "I have it now!" he told the *Sun* reporter. "With the process I have just discovered, I can produce a thousand— aye, ten thousand—[lamps] from one machine. Indeed, the number may be said to be infinite." He claimed that he had accomplished this goal by "an entirely different process than that from which scientific men have ever sought to secure it. They have all been working in the same groove, and when it is known how I have accomplished my object, everybody will wonder why they have never thought of it, it is so simple."[6] In this article, Edison also described his plans for a complete electric lighting system to replace gaslight in lower Manhattan. He would generate electricity using fifteen or twenty Wallace dynamos run by a 500-horsepower engine and distribute it through underground

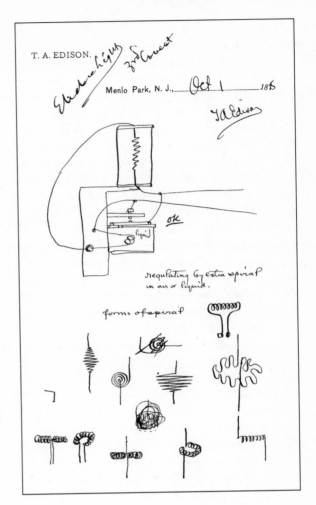

One of several drawings
made by Edison in October
1878 for one of his electric
light caveats shows the
telegraph-style relay he used
to divert the current from
the platinum spiral burner
before it melted, and also
several alternative forms for
the spiral burner.

mains similar to those carrying gas. In fact, he planned to have his entire system replicate the familiar gas lighting system. He would use existing gas pipes
to carry his electric wires through buildings and place his lamps in converted
gas fixtures. Customers would be charged by a meter similar to those employed
by gas companies. The analogy with gas lighting helped determine more than
a marketplace, it affected the very technical design of the system as Edison
sought to make it resemble the older system even to the extent of using gas fixtures to make the transition easier.

Although Edison did not provide the details of his "big bonanza" to the
Sun reporter or to others outside the laboratory, his early notes and patent
caveats indicate that he believed the solution to the problem of "subdividing
the light" lay in developing a thermal regulator to prevent the incandescing

element of his lamp from melting. Edison reached this conclusion by thinking of electric lights as analogous to telegraph instruments and treating the lamp regulator as a form of electromechanical switch similar to those he used in multiple telegraph designs. Having arrived at this solution, Edison began designing lamp regulators in the same fecund manner that he had previously varied the relays and circuits of his telegraph designs. His first electric light caveat describes "devices whereby the heat arising from the passage of [the] current is utilized to regulate the temperature of the incandescent metal which serves to give the light so that it is never allowed to reach its melting point no matter how strong a current attempts to pass through."[7] Most of his designs used either a shunt circuit with a metal that heated and expanded at some appropriate ratio to the incandescing element or the heat expansion of the element itself to move a lever or other circuit breaker. As the shunt or element cooled, it contracted and again allowed the completion of the circuit through the lamp. During the period when the lamp was not in circuit the incandescing element would continue to glow enough to provide light. Edison devised many alternatives to these basic designs and also came up with a pneumatic regulator in which he used the expansion and contraction of air heated by his incandescing element to affect the lever of a circuit breaker. In typical Edisonian fashion he also considered using extra resistances, induction coils, and storage batteries to regulate the current going to the lamps.

The lamp regulator appears to have been Edison's "big bonanza," but another key to his early confidence was his insight regarding the relationship between high-resistance lamps and parallel circuits. Because the regulator temporarily removed the lamp from the circuit, he had to place the lamps in parallel circuits so that each individual lamp could be turned on and off without affecting any others in the circuit. This was also desirable for customers used to independently operated gas lamps. As early as November 1877, Edison had determined that high-resistance lamps were best suited for parallel circuits. When he realized that this arrangement provided the best economy is unclear, but the cost benefits were certainly well understood in the laboratory by the following November when Charles Batchelor wrote of a competing design that it "would want enormous large conductors owing to [the] small resistance" in each lamp.[8]

Edison's ideas regarding lamp resistance were at least in part a product of his understanding of Ohm's and Joule's laws regarding electric circuits. From Joule's law he knew that to reduce energy lost to excess heat in his distribution system he had to increase the cross section of his copper conductors but that this would raise their cost and make the system uneconomical. However, he also recognized that the electrical relationships embodied in Ohm's law provided another method of reducing the size of the conductors by increasing the voltage proportionately to the current. This in turn would require him to use high-resistance lamps. Although he tended to disdain formal mathematical analysis Edison understood the quantitative relationships of the electric circuit, and this provided him with a key insight that made subdivision possible.[9]

Edison certainly believed that he had solved the basic problems of incandescent electric lighting when he made his announcement in the *New York Sun*, but this announcement was more dramatic than his experiments warranted. As he later explained, "It is very difficult to make a practical system and introduce it. A few experiments in the laboratory would prove the practicability of a system long before it could be brought into general use." Edison understood, however, that reporters were looking for the bold statement that would produce an eye-catching headline. This, of course, meant that he had to periodically explain why it was taking him so long to bring his light into public use. Almost immediately after his announcement he began to explain that "there are the usual little details that must be attended to before it goes to the public." Of course, he took advantage of this fact to keep his work in the public eye and to answer his critics. As he explained to one reporter in late October, "No machine . . . has ever been got up that did not require years for improvement. I ought to be allowed at least two years to improve mine. Now, old man, get out and let me go to work."[10]

Edison had lots of work to do. His initial optimism over his conceptual breakthrough had been replaced by the frustration of reducing these ideas to practice. As quick success eluded him, Edison's laboratory research grew more sophisticated as he and Charles Batchelor began to investigate the characteristics of his lamps. One of the key problems lay in the materials used as incandescing elements. To select the best material Edison drew on his already extensive knowledge of chemicals and metals growing out of his work in telegraphy between 1874 and 1876 and his telephone experiments of 1877. As in those previous efforts he supplemented his experimental knowledge by reading chemical literature. In particular he drew on Henry Watts's 1875 *Dictionary of Chemistry and the Allied Branches of Other Sciences,* which had become a standard source of information for the laboratory staff.[11] From Watts's *Dictionary* he determined that the platinum group of metals with their relatively high melting point and resistance to oxidation made them the most likely materials for incandescent lamps. He had already determined from his 1877 electric light experiments that carbon, the other common material used by experimenters for incandescent lamps and one with which he had great familiarity, was easily oxidized and difficult to protect with existing vacuum technology. Edison was not unique in focusing his electric light investigations on platinum or in experimenting with carbon in a vacuum. A list of twenty known incandescent light experimenters who preceded Edison shows that all of them chose either platinum or iridium heated in air or carbon heated in a vacuum. A few experimenters also tried the metals in a vacuum or the carbon in nitrogen gas; one tried hydrocarbon gas.[12]

Watts's and other chemical works helped Edison to focus on those materials that seemed most promising, but he often experimented with other materials that existing literature suggested would not work well. It was characteristic of his chemical research to confirm existing knowledge experimentally, particularly when applying materials under new conditions as he did during the course of the electric light work. Thus, he experimented briefly with sticks of carbon because they would be less easily susceptible to oxidation than carbonized paper but found that "when brought up to give the same light as platina it melts very easily."[13] Even though it was often empirical, Edison's chemical research was usually informed by existing chemical knowledge, and perhaps even more significantly by theoretical parameters he established for the research based on his understanding of the problem at hand. In the search for a lamp material these were the combination of characteristics best suited for heating to incandescence and for obtaining high resistance, but economic factors also weighed heavily. Platinum was extremely expensive and from the first he experimented with other, cheaper metals, such as iron and steel, that existing literature suggested would not work as well. He also investigated the use of alloys that might reduce the amount of platinum needed or increase its melting point.

Besides investigating materials, Edison also began to experiment with the proper form for his incandescing element. He tried thin wire filaments, thin pieces of metal foil, and even pencil-size sticks or buttons of metal, carbon, and other materials. The most important set of experiments took place in mid-October, as he sought to determine the relationship between radiating surfaces, temperatures, and light emission of his incandescing elements. By November 15 he had established a new "Electric Light Law" that stated that the "amount of heat lost by a body is in proportion to the radiating surface of that body." He argued that "if the radiating power or time of a substance is decreased, the gain in light is directly to the decrease, for instance if I could with platina coils obtain 4 burners of 15 C[andle]. P[ower]. each per H[orse]. P[ower]. then by reducing the radiating power 50 per cent I would obtain 8 burners."[14] Because he understood that energy consumption was proportional to the radiating surface of the lamp and not a result of its resistance, Edison realized that high-resistance lamps would not require more energy to operate than low-resistance lamps. This key insight confounded most of the experts in the field.

To reduce radiating surface and increase resistance Edison used very thin filaments of wire wound in tight spirals. To prevent the spirals from touching and short circuiting, Edison turned again to nonconducting coatings, with which he had first experimented in late September as a means of reducing the amount of current and heat required to bring the element to incandescence. Coating experiments became even more important the following spring as Edison worked out the ratio between wire length, diameter, and resistance, leading to the use of extremely long and thin platinum wires. As before he relied on Watts's *Dictionary* as a primary source of information about the best substances to use, and he focused his coating experiments primarily on oxides of the alkaline earths.

As Edison began to expand the scope of his lamp experiments, he also completed negotiations that would provide him with the resources necessary for further research. His first public pronouncements generated considerable interest on the part of several people connected with Western Union who already held him in high regard as an inventor. On September 19 Tracy Edson, one of the principal stockholders of the Gold and Stock Telegraph Company, asked to see Edison "at your earliest convenience. I have something to say to you of so much importance to you and myself, that I wish you would appoint an early day, say Saturday next at 11 o'clk to meet me as above. As you will readily imagine, it is in relation to your new discovery, of which you spoke to me on Monday last."[15] Other Western Union financial figures, including Hamilton McKay Twombly, who represented the interests of his father-in-law William H. Vanderbilt, the principal shareholder in Western Union and a heavy investor in gas utilities, soon joined with Edson in negotiating for Edison's light. Edison was represented in these negotiations by Grosvenor Lowrey, the Western Union attorney who had been acting as Edison's patent attorney on behalf of the company since December 1875. Because the electric light inventions were independent of any corporate interest by Western Union, Lowrey told Edison "that it will be most for your interest and mine, in dealing with them, that I should act with and for you, entirely; and I shall therefore decline to be interested, and will approach the whole matter from your side of the business." As negotiations drew to a close during the first days of October, Edison wrote "Friend Lowrey" to tell him to "Go ahead. I shall agree to nothing promise nothing and say nothing to any person leaving the whole matter to you. All I want at present is to be provided with funds to push the light rapidly."[16]

Delighted by the final arrangements, Edison wired the details to his European representative Theodore Puskas on October 5:

The electric light is going to be a great success. I have something *entirely new.* Wm. H. Vanderbilt and friends have taken it in this country and on Monday next advance $50,000 to conduct experiments.

I retain $1/2$ of the capital stock of the Co. they are to form and also receive a royalty of $30,000 yearly if it proves more economical than gas, which *I am certain it will do.* Vanderbilt is the largest gas stock owner in America.[17]

When the Edison Electric Light Company incorporated in New York City on October 16 the incorporators included, besides Edson and Twombly, Western Union president Norvin Green, who became the company president; James H. Banker, a leading Western Union stockholder; financier Robert L. Cutting Jr.; three of Lowrey's law partners; and Egisto Fabbri, a member of Drexel Morgan and Company, the leading American investment bankers, who had extensive international interests.[18]

At the end of October Lowrey, whose law offices were in the Drexel Morgan building at the corner of Broad and Wall streets, began to negotiate foreign patent rights with the banking firm. On October 30 an enthusiastic J. Pierpont

Morgan, who sat on Western Union's board of directors, wrote about these negotiations to his brother-in-law Walter Burns in Paris:

> I have been very much engaged for several days past on a matter which is likely to prove most important to us all not only as regards its importance to the world at large but to us in particular in a pecuniary point of view. Secrecy at the moment is so essential that I do not dare put it on paper. Subject is Edison's Electric light— importance can be realized from the editorials in London Times & other papers & the effect upon gas stocks which have declined from 25-50% since rumours [of] Edison's success. It is not unlikely that I may cable for you to come to London . . . this matter needs careful handling if anything comes of it. It is not entirely certain. I shall do nothing until it is—but when that time comes . . . we must be prepared to strike. I fear father will think I am imagining but I am sure he will change his mind.[19]

Morgan's interest in Edison's light experiments was certainly stirred by Lowrey, but he was also reacting to the power of Edison's reputation as the inventor of the age, which was powerful enough to produce a panic that caused the price of gas company shares to drop in New York and London.

By the end of December Drexel Morgan had agreed to take the entire rights to Edison's British electric light patents and to become his agent for all of Europe except in Italy. Italy was to be controlled by Fabbri through his firm Fabbri and Chauncey, a major shipping and commercial firm that did a great deal of business in South America, where they also took an interest in Edison's light patents. The international standing of these firms conformed with Lowrey's desire that "the dignity, & importance of the invention to the world, demand that it shall be introduced by men possessing a comparative strength & power in the financial world." The banking partners, Lowrey assured Edison in January 1879, were "not to be very easily frightened away from a thing they once made up their mind to."[20] Drexel Morgan and its houses in London and Paris also acted as bankers for the Edison Electric Light Company and other foreign Edison companies, and they acted as Edison's personal bankers as well.

When he began negotiating the British rights Lowrey expressed the hope that these would provide Edison with

> money enough not only to set you up forever but to enable you at once if you desire to build and formally endow a working laboratory such as the world needs and has never seen. I should like immensely to see your name given to a place of that sort which while conducted as nearly as possible on self supporting principles would give a fair opportunity for indigent but ingenious men to have their ideas exploited or exploded as the case might be.[21]

Edison was little interested in a laboratory to serve others, but he did have plans to expand his own laboratory facilities as he began contemplating the necessity for developing other components of the electric lighting system.

Edison had initially focused his work on the lamp because he saw it as the critical problem and was convinced that the Wallace dynamo could easily

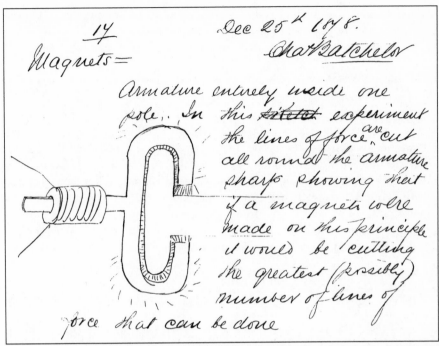

14

Magnets =

Dec 25ᵗʰ 1878.

Chas Batchelor

Armature entirely inside one pole,. In this ~~title~~ experiment the lines of force are cut all round the armature sharp showing that if a magnets were made on this principle it would be cutting the greatest (possibly) number of lines of force that can be done

This December 1878 drawing by Charles Batchelor describes an experiment to determine the best relationship between the armature and field magnets of a generator and is one experiment that he, Edison, and Francis Upton conducted in an effort to learn the principles behind the electromagnetic generation of current.

meet the requirements of an incandescent lighting system. However, after a month of experimentation with the Wallace dynamo Edison had begun to doubt its suitability for his purposes. With the expectation of new funds from the Edison Electric Light Company he had begun to shop around for other machines, ordering a larger dynamo from Wallace on October 4 and one of Edward Weston's electroplating dynamos six days later. He also made inquiries about the Gramme dynamo, the Arnoux and Hochhausen dynamo, and Charles Brush's arc light generator. After the Wallace and Weston machines arrived, Edison set one of the new assistants he had hired to work making comparison tests.

Edison had begun to consider his own dynamo design as well. His first design, which he mentioned in his September 13 caveat draft and experimented with during October, was unlike any other previously devised. It also did not work. As with Edison's lamps, his telegraph experience provides an explanation for the peculiar design of this dynamo. While conducting experiments on multiple telegraphs, Edison had developed the idea that the vibration of a magnetized tuning fork in combination with the electromagnets of a motor would increase the amount of available electric current. He and Batchelor had built motors based on this idea, and the similarity of motor and dynamo design made this an obvious first step for Edison to take. Edison again used an analogy to his telegraph experience, but in this case it quickly became apparent that this analogy provided an inadequate solution.[22]

The inadequacy of his tuning fork dynamo and his dissatisfaction with the Wallace and Weston dynamos combined to convince Edison that he needed to know more about generator design. As he informed the *Sun* in mid-December, "I am all right on my lamp. I don't care anything more about it. Every bit of heat is utilized to producing light as far as art will allow. The theoretical and practical results are pretty satisfactory. My point now is the generator."[23] Although his lamp was, in fact, far from satisfactory, his experiments had brought him to the point where the generator now appeared as the critical problem standing in the way of his success. Much to Wallace's chagrin, Edison also told the *Sun* reporter that the Wallace generator was not suited to his purposes and that he would now work to "find the machine that will give the greatest amount of electricity per horse power." Wallace responded to Edison's criticism by telling him "I was very sorry to see [the article] and cannot but feel that you do me a great injustice (not intentionally on your part I cannot believe) still the effect is the same greatly injuring the sale of my machine. . . . The machine you have was intended for the electric arc and is too intense. If you would say just what you desire I could build one better suited to your purpose."[24] Edison had already decided to design his own generator and thus began a careful study of existing designs as a basis. There was, however, only a small literature on generators. Furthermore, Edison found that the patents could be an unreliable source of information; he later recalled that "Upton, Batch, & myself worked three days & nights on Siemens' patent to figure out how the devil he connected up his armature & we never succeeded in doing it from the patent."[25] Edison instead found it much more useful to study the machines themselves and soon acquired a Gramme dynamo, then considered the most advanced design, to go along with the Wallace and Weston dynamos he already owned.

While experimenting with generators, Edison again relied on his experience with telegraph technology to provide a useful analogy that guided the laboratory research. He and his staff treated the magnetic lines of force in a generator as analogous to the internal currents of a battery and compared the flow of current in an armature with that in a battery. In one of the laboratory notebooks, Batchelor noted of the Gramme dynamo armature that "the top half has a current running in one direction and bottom half in the other direction . . . and the product is the same as two batteries for quantity."[26] Drawings by Upton show armatures as a series of alternating zinc and carbon battery elements. The generator experiments also included extensive experiments with electromagnets intended to produce a fuller understanding of the principles of electromagnetic generation of current. By the beginning of January, after what Batchelor described as "a few weeks hard study on magneto electric principles," they had advanced their understanding of generators sufficiently that Edison set the machine shop to work building a new design under Batchelor's direction.[27]

Edison's ability to experiment with generators was greatly enhanced by his new financial resources. As he wrote Puskas on November 13, "I am now erecting a brick building 135 feet long by 25 feet wide with two powerful engines & boilers, in short all the means to set up & test most deliberately every point of the Electric Light." This new building and a brick office and library he was also having built for the laboratory represented Edison's growing recognition of the enormity of the task before him. "I have the right principle and am on the right track," he told Puskas,

> but time, hard work, & some good luck are necessary, too.
>
> It has been just so in all my inventions. The first step is an intuition and comes in a burst. Then difficulties arise. This thing gives out then that. "Bugs" as such little faults and difficulties are called, show themselves. Months of intense watching study & labor are required before commercial success—or failure—is certainly reached.

Ever confident of his abilities, Edison assured Puskas, "Before I have done with it I mean to succeed."[28]

With the new facilities, machinery, and assistants made possible by his financial backers, Edison could pursue research on a broad front. Other electric light inventors had focused their energies on the lamp, which was not only seen as the critical problem for incandescent lighting, but was also the easiest problem to tackle with limited resources. Edison, on the other hand, could now experiment on other components and begin to address the requirements for an entire lighting system. He could also take full advantage of his own propensity to approach problems from several different directions at once.

The cost of Edison's new facilities and the growing costs of the research effort did, however, cause some concern among the Light Company directors. While willing to risk large sums of money on his experiments, the investors required Edison to demonstrate his progress and required more than his personal assurances that he had "the only correct principle" and that it was just a matter of time before he would be ready to publicly demonstrate the light. Edison had been privately exhibiting the light to reporters, and Lowrey pressed him to exhibit to the investors as well, arguing that this would provide the means for the inventor to educate his backers about the complexity of the task he had undertaken. As he prepared for these visits, Lowrey told Edison, "It is all the better that they should see the rubbish and rejected devices of one sort and another. Their appreciation thereby becomes more intelligent." After the last of these visits in early December, Lowrey informed Edison that they had accomplished their purpose:

> Our friends had their imaginations somewhat tempered, but their judgements are instructed, and we now have to deal with an intelligent comprehension of things as

they are, which makes both your part and mine much easier. They realize now that you are doing a man's work upon a great problem and they think you have got the jug by the handle with a reasonable probability of carrying it safely to the well and bringing it back full.[29]

The investors were no doubt encouraged not only by seeing lamps and other apparatus in operation but by encountering the full force of Edison's charismatic optimism.

Nonetheless, the speed with which Edison spent their money continued to cause them some concern. After visiting Menlo Park in late December, Edson and Banker told Lowrey that "the cost of buildings was much greater than they had been led to suppose was necessary," although agreeing that "it was allright, of course, if it was actually necessary." Lowrey was able to get them to have "a very good natured laugh over their disappointment at their visit," where they found "that the general dilapidation, ruin and havoc of moving, caused the electric light to look very small," but he also offered assurances that Edison would in the future carefully maintain his experimental accounts.[30]

The electric light investors also sought assurances that Edison was indeed working along original lines. Soon after forming the Edison Electric Light Company, they had been approached by inventor William Sawyer and his partner Albon Man, who claimed both a practical incandescent lamp and controlling patents. This led the Light Company's board of directors to hire Edward Dickerson, one of Western Union's attorneys in the quadruplex case, and give him "authority to employ such experts as he may elect, to examine the state of the art &c &c." According to Stockton Griffin, upon being informed of this Edison became

visibly agitated and said it was the old story— i.e. lack of confidence. The same experience which he had had with the telephone, and in fact with all of his *successful* inventions was being re-enacted. . . . [He] remarked that if he had a voice in the matter the Electric light should not be so treated—no combinations, no consolidations for him. . . . He said it was to be expected that everyone who had been working in this direction, or had any knowledge of the subject, would immediately set up their claims upon ascertaining that his system was likely to be perfect. All this he anticipated but had no fears of the result knowing that the line he was developing was entirely original and out of the rut.[31]

Lowrey moved quickly to reassure the inventor that

my confidence in you as an infallible, certain man of science is absolutely complete: and whatever it may be necessary to say in talking with businessmen, who of course are liable to be misled, but who on the whole generally come right and do not make mistakes, you may be sure that the party which has been made up has put in their money in absolute confidence in you and nobody else.[32]

Somewhat mollified and certain that any examination into the state of the art would confirm his claims, Edison asked his patent attorney Lemuel Serrell for a list of all U.S. patents on electric lighting and suggested that Howard Butler of the Gold and Stock Telegraph Company be hired as the expert. When Banker and Edson proved reluctant to let him take time from Gold and Stock, Butler recommended Francis Upton, a young man who had just entered his office. Upton was the son of a New England manufacturing family who had received the first master's of science degree awarded by Princeton and had just returned from a year of postgraduate study in Berlin with Hermann von Helmholtz. Edison agreed, and Upton was hired in early November. He soon filled two notebooks with an exhaustive search of all the American and British patents as well as scientific and technical articles on the subject of electric lighting. Edison no doubt felt vindicated when Upton reported as he neared the end of this work, "I feel sure that the total you have is new, no matter if parts have been before used."[33] Although his search had turned up numerous regulators for keeping carbon arcs at the correct distance from each other, these were very different from Edison's unique designs for incandescent lighting. Edison was also alone in appreciating the importance of high resistance.

Impressed by Upton's literature search, Edison decided to hire him to assist with the electric light research. Besides appreciating his knowledge of the state of the art, Edison could also make use of Upton's background in electrical science and his mathematical abilities. In fact, one of the first tasks Edison gave his new assistant after he arrived at Menlo Park in mid-December was to make the necessary calculations to confirm his ideas regarding the use of high-resistance lamps in parallel circuit. In making these calculations, Upton referred to the formulas for Joule's and Ohm's laws in Edison's copy of Sabine and Clark's *Electrical Tables and Formulae*. Besides confirming Edison's ideas about the electric distribution system, these calculations helped to refine its parameters. Edison also put Upton to work assisting with experiments, and he soon came to play a key role in the development of the dynamo.[34]

Before further experiments on dynamos could take place the laboratory staff had to wait for the machine shop to finish building Edison's new design. While Batchelor supervised the construction of this machine, Edison turned his attention to acquiring knowledge about what was going on in the lamp in the same careful way he and Batchelor had investigated the fundamentals of dynamo design. Instead of constructing numerous prototypes as before, Edison now began observing the behavior of platinum and other metals under the conditions required for incandescence. On January 19 he began a series of careful "Experiments with Platina & Platinum-Iridium alloys 20 per cent Ir—at the incandescent point with galvanic battery to determine any changes that may take place." Edison soon turned to studying the effects of incandescence on other compositions of these metals and in comparison with other metals, including piano wire, as he sought a cheaper material for his lamps. He carefully observed these metals under different heating conditions and in different forms, using various gauges of wire and thicknesses of foil from different manufacturers. He noted all differences, including structural changes such as the cracks and air bubbles that he found when examining the materials under the laboratory microscope. Edison studied chemical as well as physical changes in the metals by carefully weighing them and conducting flame tests. Edison even experimented by using an arc light connected to the Gramme generator to heat some of his metals, but soon discontinued this practice because the bright arc light caused his eyes to "suffer the pains of hell."[35]

After a few days of experimenting, Edison thought he might have achieved "a great discovery for the electric light—in the way of economy" when he found that nickel "becomes brilliantly incandescent *without fusing*" and appeared to be "nearly if not equal to platinum."[36] Hearing reports of this discovery from visitors to Menlo Park, and concerned that a major change in the lamp might undermine investor confidence, Lowrey cautioned Edison to "be sure you are right about nickel and everything else before having anybody know it."[37] These cautionary words proved prophetic when further experiments on January 24 showed nickel to be highly susceptible to oxidation.

Nearly two weeks of experiments satisfied Edison that although platinum or a platinum alloy was best suited as a lamp element, heating did cause structural weaknesses leading to cracking and disintegration of the metal. However, his discovery that the metal seemed to absorb gases during heating suggested that at least part of the problem was caused by heating the metal in air. Although Edison had turned to platinum in part to get around the oxidation problems of carbon, it was now apparent that the atmosphere was a problem for the metal as well. This marked a significant shift in Edison's conception of the lamp problem as he realized that merely protecting the platinum from melting through electromechanical regulators was no longer sufficient. He now saw the necessity of using a vacuum to protect it from the effects of oxidation. Further experiments led him to develop a vacuum treatment process that annealed the platinum by driving out the air through gradual heating of the metal as the lamp was evacuated.

In turning to a vacuum pump, Edison was following the lead of other electric light experimenters. What was new and significant was his theoretical framework for doing so. With the resources at his command he could also afford to devote considerable attention to developing better vacuum technology. The laboratory staff did have some familiarity with vacuum pumps. They had used a mechanical hand pump in some of the early lamp experiments and turned to it again for the new experiments. However, such pumps provided an inadequate vacuum and the staff began to investigate the state of the art of vacuum technology by searching through scientific and technical journals. The best pumps of the time were Sprengel and Geissler mercury pumps. After an unsuccessful effort to acquire a Sprengel pump from nearby universities, Edison had a Geissler pump made by the New York glassblowing firm of Reinmann & Baetz. He obtained another from Cyrus Brackett, Upton's former professor at Princeton. William Baetz also came to Menlo Park periodically for the next several months to help to develop vacuum pumps for the laboratory. By mid-August he had assembled several different arrangements of Geissler and

Sprengel pumps, including combinations of the two; a McLeod gauge was also added to the Menlo Park pump design later in the year. The advantage of combining the two designs was that the Geissler pump produced a vacuum more quickly while the Sprengel pump provided a higher vacuum. When Baetz turned down Edison's offer to join the laboratory staff, Edison hired Ludwig Boehm, a young glassblower who had worked with Geissler in Germany before immigrating to the United States.

As he experimented with vacuums, Edison came to the conclusion "that the melting point is determined greatly by the amount of gas within the pores of the metal which by expansion disrupts the metal and makes it fuse easier."[38] He therefore developed a process for treating the wire by heating it gradually in a vacuum to expel the gases contained in the metal. This hardened the wire and increased its melting point.[39] The problem of fusibility was not entirely resolved by the use of the vacuum, and Edison continued to rely on regulators. In part, the continued design of regulators represented Edison's long-standing tendency to find electromechanical solutions to problems. It also pointed to the still-undeveloped state of vacuum pump technology.

By the end of March Batchelor was so confident in the ultimate success of the lamp that he wrote Adams, "The light is the biggest success we've ever had." A few days before, Edison had demonstrated it to his investors and "subdivided the light into 20 burners each burner being equal to 16 candles, or one gas jet. . . . That any electric lamp may be turned up or down the same as gas. I have demonstrated that for every horse power taken from the engine that six electric jets are obtained each equal to a gas jet which brings the cost to $^1/_3$ that of gas. That there is not as much waste of energy by leakage or otherwise as in gas."[40] Furthermore, Edison felt certain that he could produce lamps with a resistance as high as 750 ohms, and thus significantly reduce the cost of copper conductors. What remained to be accomplished, he told Puskas in an April 8 letter, was "1st The proper generator both in regard to economy in construction and amount of electricity generated per horse power applied, its reliability and adaptability to my system. 2d A standard lamp free from all mechanical objections, and of the most extreme simplicity that is attainable." A month later he felt confident that he had "completed the standard generator which exceeds in simplicity and economy all generators previously devised by any one; the size being less and from 88 to 90 per cent of the horse power applied is thrown into the form of current" and that "nothing more remains but the construction of the standard lamp, and the working up of the mechanical details for a large central station."[41]

During February and March, Edison, Batchelor, and Upton had conducted extensive generator experiments that led to a major breakthrough in the design of dynamos for incandescent electric lighting. Although it is unclear whether these experiments were informed by the important experimental work on generators published by Philadelphia electricians Elihu Thomson and Edwin Houston in late 1878 and early 1879, Edison and his staff reached the same conclusion—generators with equal internal and external resistance generated maximum current, but those with a small internal resistance produced more efficient power output.[42] Edison clearly considered the economic efficiency of his system to be related to the number of lamps per horsepower (a concern he had already shown in lamp experiments). He and his staff measured the work output of their generators by employing an electrodynamometer to convert the electrical energy obtained from their generators into foot pounds. (Thomson and Houston had made similar measurements.) Upton seems to have taken the lead in these experiments, and his calculations provided the basis for determining that they could design a more efficient dynamo by making the internal resistance much smaller than the external load, rather than having equal internal and external resistance as was standard in other generators of the time. In reducing the amount of wire used in his armature winding, Edison also drew on other experiments, some dating back to December, regarding energy loss due to friction. He turned these design insights into a "law" that treated the relationship between the external resistance of a generator and its internal resistance in proportion to loss of energy due to friction and other factors.[43]

The other key feature of the Edison dynamo was its large bipolar magnets, which gave the generator its nickname, the "long-legged Mary-Ann" (a somewhat rude joke among the all-male laboratory staff). In arriving at this design Edison probably drew in part on Michael Faraday's half-century-old work about the electromagnetic generation of current by a conductor (the armature) moving through the magnetic lines of force generated by a field magnet. Understanding that the more lines of force crossed in the most direct manner, the more productive the generator, Edison probably conceived his large magnets as a concentrated source of Faraday's lines of magnetic force. But Edison's understanding of the relationship between lines of force and magnet length was also influenced by his continuing use of the battery analogy as applied to generators. In a March 1882 letter discussing the British patent for his generator design, Edison drew on Ampère's work and his own experiments to argue that a permanent magnet could be considered analogous to a series of copper and zinc battery plates. Thus,

> the longer the battery, i.e. the greater the number of plates in series the greater will be its capacity for overcoming resistance such as the air space forming an arc, or the metallic resistance. It is just the same with the long magnet. The diameter has to do with the resistance of the magnet that is the number of lines of force it can furnish but not with the length or space through which the lines of force are propagated. This fact seems never to have been brought out by any person in connection with Dynamo machines but it is of the greatest importance. It explains the reason of my employing long magnets.

Edison further explained that it was "better to invest in iron and copper up to a certain point than suffer from a loss of power."[44] By the beginning of July 1879 Upton felt confident that "We have now the best generator of electricity ever

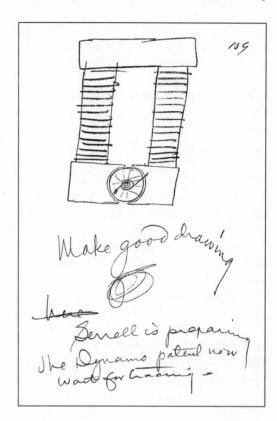

Edison's drawing of what became his basic generator design for a British provisional that he filed in the spring of 1879.

made and this in itself will make a business."[45] From this point on the basic design of the dynamo underwent little change, although much attention was paid to details such as the arrangement of commutator brushes and the design of armature windings.

Having solved the basic generator problem, the work of the laboratory now focused on the continuing difficulties of lamp design. The most significant design improvement occurred as the laboratory staff developed vacuum pumps that far surpassed any others yet devised. With Boehm's assistance, they designed a combined Sprengel-Geissler pump that, although difficult to keep in working order, was probably the most efficient then in existence. As a result, the staff produced ever-better lamps. At the end of August, when Edison attended the American Association for the Advancement of Science meeting at Saratoga, New York (this time accompanied by his wife), to read a paper on his observations about occluded gases in metals, he noted that his vacuum treatment process had "increased [the] capacity of platinum to withstand high temperatures" and now enabled him "to employ small radiating surfaces and thus reduce the energy required per candle light."[46] By summer's end even better

vacuums were making possible the production of platinum lamps without regulators, although the problem of a satisfactory coating remained.

Even though Edison's research on metals and the development of high-
vacuum pumps had increased the prospects for the platinum lamp, the use of
this rare metal presented Edison with what appeared to be an intractable problem. Platinum's high price would make his system uneconomical for central
stations, although it might still be used for isolated lighting plants for the
wealthy and for manufacturing plants, such as cotton mills, where there was
great danger of fire from gas. Edison approached this difficulty in a way that became characteristic when he was faced with questions about the commercial
availability of a substance that he believed would solve a technical problem —
he conducted an exhaustive search for plentiful supplies of the material. Beginning in the late spring Edison had begun to send circular letters to mining
districts in the United States and wrote personally to American ambassadors
and others in countries with platinum mines. He also studied geological reports
and other literature about sources of platinum and developed a process for separating platinum from the black sand residue of gold mines. Edison spent considerable time during the summer reading and answering the voluminous correspondence that arrived in response from the mining communities of the west
and assaying the ores that they sent. He also employed two chemists to help
with the assays: Alfred Haid, a Ph.D. chemist hired specially to assist in this
work, and John Lawson, who had joined the staff in January as chemical assistant.[47] Although Edison relied on existing metallurgical literature, his search
was guided by an underlying worldview that associated the bounty of nature
with human technological and social progress.

Edison's platinum search did not yield a cheap and plentiful source of this
rare metal, but fortunately the improved vacuum achieved by his laboratory
staff not only allowed him to get rid of his regulator, but also enabled him to
experiment again with a much cheaper substance — carbon. He now had the
means to protect it from oxidation. Furthermore, from his long experience with
this substance he knew that it possessed high resistance. But the shift to carbon
may not have taken place (or at least may not have taken place when it did) if
not for Edison's propensity for working on several projects at once.

Throughout his experiments on electric lighting Edison had continued to
make improvements to his telephone and sought to improve his electromotograph receiver sufficiently for it to compete with Bell's. In the fall and winter of
1878–1879, during the first intensive period of electric light research, Edison's
nephew Charles Edison was kept busy experimenting with the electromotograph receiver. By the end of February the receiver had progressed sufficiently
for Edison to send Charley and six of the instruments to England, where Gouraud's efforts to form an Edison telephone company were being impeded by
fear that Bell Telephone Company would bring an infringement suit over the
use of an electromagnetic receiver. On May 10, however, a successful demonstration before the British Royal Society that was attended by the Prince and

Princess of Wales and several members of Parliament soon led to the formation of the Edison Telephone Company of London. Edison received an advance payment of $5,000, which he promptly used to order about 500 books for his library and to take care of his payroll. He also gave $1,000 to his wife.[48]

The formal organization of the company did not end the effort to improve the receiver. If anything, this became even more necessary as the receivers sent to England proved extremely troublesome in daily operation. Edison also had to provide a new technical expert for the London company. James Adams, who had been ill for some time, died in Paris just prior to the May 10 exhibition, and Charley, on his own for the first time, traveled to Paris against the company's wishes and was promptly fired. Although ordered home by his uncle, Charley remained in Paris, where he had become involved in what may have been a homoerotic relationship with American artist and photographer O. Murray. A few months later he died in Paris of peritonitis, ending what had been a promising inventive career. Edison once again turned to his friend Edward Johnson, who finally agreed to go to England in July. Edison set up a small "school" of telephone engineering at Menlo Park to train several men whom he sent to London to assist Johnson.[49]

Edison and Batchelor spent much of their time during the summer and early fall on telephone experiments. Edison's primary attention was directed at the electromotograph receiver during this period, but his most crucial contribution to telephone technology remained the carbon-button transmitter. The carbon buttons for the transmitters were still being made at the laboratory even though the rest of the instrument as well as the receivers and switchboards were manufactured at Sigmund Bergmann's and other outside shops. The buttons were made from lampblack scraped off the glass chimneys of a series of kerosene lanterns that were kept burning day and night in a little shed next to the laboratory. It was the ready availability of this material that led Edison to a fortuitous analogy that prompted him to try carbon in his lamp again.

Almost from the beginning of the light research, Edison had determined that the most efficient form for his incandescing element would be the thin wire spiral that would allow him to decrease radiating surface and increase resistance. It was his realization that the lampblack could be rolled like a platinum wire and then coiled into a spiral that led Edison to try carbon again as a filament material. The first newspaper account of his successful carbon lamp describes his eureka moment and suggests the analogy that came to his mind:

> Sitting one night in his laboratory reflecting on some of the unfinished details, Edison began abstractedly rolling between his fingers a piece of compressed lampblack until it had become a slender thread. Happening to glance at it the idea occurred to him that it might give good results as a burner if made incandescent. A few minutes later the experiment was tried, and to the inventor's gratification, satisfactory, although not surprising results were obtained. Further experiments were made, with altered forms and composition of the substance, each experiment demonstrating that the inventor was upon the right track.[50]

Once again Edison used his powers of analogy to find a useful starting point that directed him onto a new track. But it was the months of hard work to develop a vacuum capable of protecting carbon from oxidation that enabled him to draw this analogy in the first place. The importance Edison attached to his spiral design is evident in his first carbon-filament lamp patent (U.S. Patent 223,898), which he executed on November 1. By that date Edison had, in fact, given up the attempt to make carbon spirals following two weeks of futile effort by Batchelor to form them out of lampblack. Instead, they began to consider alternative ways to make carbon burners for the lamp by using other substances. On the morning of October 22 they began what Charles Batchelor called

> some very interesting experiments on straight carbons made from cotton thread so. We took a piece of 6 cord thread No 24 which is about 13 thousandths in thickness and after fastening to Pt wires we carbonized it in a closed chamber. We put bulb in vacuo and it gave a light equal to about $^1/_2$ candle 18 cells carbon [battery], it had resistance of 113 ohms at starting and & afterwards went up to 140—probably due to vibration.[51]

After the lamp had been left burning for $13^1/_2$ hours, they added enough battery cells to increase its light to the equivalent of three gas jets (at least 30 candles). Although this caused the bulb to overheat and crack after another hour, the laboratory staff had for the first time produced a lamp that showed true commercial promise.

In the weeks following the first carbon thread lamp experiments, the laboratory staff tried nearly every carbon substance readily available in the laboratory. A list of twenty items carbonized by Batchelor on October 27 suggests the range of materials they investigated—a variety of woods and papers, vulcanized fiber, celluloid, cotton lampwick, flax, cork, coconut hair and shell, and fishing line.[52] The optimism produced by the carbon breakthrough was apparent in Francis Upton's letter home on November 2:

> The electric light is coming up. We have had a fine burner made of a piece of carbonized thread which gave a light of two or three gas jets. Mr. Edison now proposes to give an exhibition of some lamps in actual operation. There is some talk if he can show a number of lamps of organizing a large company with three or five millions capital to push the matter through. I have been offered $1,000 for five shares of my stock. . . . Edison says the stock is worth a thousand dollars a share or more, yet he is always sanguine and his valuations are on his hopes more than his realities.[53]

Although the carbonized thread showed promise, the difficulties of producing a commercial carbon lamp were becoming apparent and Upton confessed the following week, "The Electric Light seems to be a continual trouble for as yet we cannot make what we want and see the untold millions roll upon Menlo Park that my hopes want to see."[54] By November 16, however, they had "the first lamp that answers the purpose we have wished. It is—cheap much more so than we even hoped to have":

The lamp is obtained from a piece of charred paper which is bent thus [into a horseshoe shape]. The burner is made from common card board and cut to about the size shown [1″ high]. This is then sealed in a glass bulb and the air exhausted and then a current of electricity passed through it which heats it to a brilliant whiteness so that it will give a light equal to that from a good sized gas burner.[55]

Edison's belief that the natural world would provide the means for human technological progress was reinforced by this success and he told a reporter, "I think the Almighty made carbon especially for the electric light."[56]

Edison quickly moved forward with his plans to exhibit the light. Using linemen provided by Western Union, he wired the laboratory complex, houses, and other buildings at Menlo Park. The wires were carried on poles with lamps to light the streets and connected with the generator located in the machine shop. He began to show the system privately to the electric light stockholders and made plans for a New Year's Eve demonstration to the public. Although Edison resisted his natural inclination to bring in news reporters, he did let his friend Edwin Fox take detailed notes that he would use to write a long article that would appear after the demonstration. As word of the preparations leaked out, however, news reports appearing in other papers prompted the *New York Herald* to run Fox's story on December 21. Edison was "very much provoked" by this premature publication out of concern over his foreign patent applications, which he wired his European agents to push through.[57] On the other hand, the ever-cautious Light Company directors now had little choice but to allow public demonstrations to go forward.

Following reports of a successful demonstration for the Electric Light Company investors on December 27, crowds of curiosity seekers mingled with the capitalists and scientists who were invited to see the new system. On December 30, according to the *New York Herald*, "Menlo Park [was] thronged with visitors coming from all directions to see the 'wonderful' electric light. Nearly every train that stopped brought delegations of sightseers until the depot was overrun and the narrow plank road leading to the laboratory became alive with people. In the laboratory the throngs practically took possession of everything in their eager curiosity to learn about the great invention." Somehow amidst all the confusion final preparations were finished for the public demonstration the following day. The *Herald* described another enthusiastic crowd for the New Year's Eve demonstration:

Extra trains were run from east and west, and notwithstanding the stormy weather, hundreds of persons availed themselves of the privilege. The laboratory was brilliantly illuminated with twenty-five lamps, the office and counting room with eight, and twenty others were distributed in the street leading to the depot and in some of the adjoining houses. The entire system was explained in detail by Edison and his assistants, and the light was subjected to a variety of tests.

On New Year's Day large crowds again came to the laboratory where they "went pellmell through the places previously kept sacredly private." By the end of the day, the *Herald* reported, Edison felt compelled to order the laboratory closed to the general public, "directing, however, that the private dwelling in Menlo Park, as well as the street lamps, be kept burning nightly, so that those who come will not be disappointed."[58]

Edison closed the laboratory to visitors to continue work on the lighting system. He understood better than anyone that he had only demonstrated that it worked on a small, experimental scale. Bringing the system into commercial operation would require an intensive effort to refine each part of the system to make it reliable for public use. Perhaps even more important, he recognized that he would succeed only if he could compete economically with gaslight.

It was Edison's appreciation for the requirements of a commercially practical system that most set him apart from his competitors. This becomes readily apparent when he is compared to William Sawyer, his foremost American rival. Edison clearly had some very practical advantages over Sawyer. He had been a full-time inventor for ten years when he began to work on electric lighting, while Sawyer had invented intermittently on telegraph apparatus while working as a journalist (he very likely had worked previously as a telegraph operator). Like most inventors of the era, Sawyer relied on a local capitalist with limited financial resources. In his case New York lawyer Albon Man provided him with funds to set up a well-equipped but small experimental shop in New York City and proved to be a willing experimental partner with an interest in electrical science. The Electro-Dynamic Light Company, which Man formed with some friends, provided no more than $4,000 for Sawyer's shop and experimental expenses between March and June 1878. The company also paid the expenses for another small shop they occupied beginning in September 1878. In sharp contrast, Edison had built what was the finest private laboratory of its time with support from Western Union, one of the country's largest corporations, and had substantial income from royalties that he put toward his inventive work. His electric light research was paid for by the Edison Electric Light Company, which provided nearly $130,000 by the time Edison moved into New York in March 1881 to begin commercial introduction of his system. Sawyer never worked with more than two or three full-time assistants and a couple of part-time assistants, including a graduate in chemistry from the Columbia University School of Mines. Although Edison began his research assisted primarily by Charles Batchelor and a couple of general laboratory assistants, he also had several full-time machinists to produce devices for experimentation and soon hired additional experimenters and laboratory assistants, including Francis Upton, and he was able to expand his machine shop and its staff. By October 1879 Edison had over thirty employees. Edison had achieved the kind of resources and financial support akin to those of modern corporate research and development, whereas Sawyer worked with the more limited resources of the independent inventor.

Even with his limited resources, Sawyer did some very creative experimental work with carbon lamps. He might even have eventually developed a lamp comparable to Edison's if he had not suffered from alcoholism, which seriously impeded his work by March 1879. In addition, Sawyer did not have Edison's grasp of the requirements for a system or the wherewithal to develop the full lighting system that would make the incandescent lamp a commercial product. His failure to grasp the system requirements was evident in his lack of understanding of the need for high-resistance lamps. When Sawyer testified during an 1881 patent interference with Edison, he noted that although at one time he thought that "the most perfect electric lamp would be one in which the incandescent conductor had the highest resistance" he later came to believe that one with the lowest possible resistance would be best and "began to reduce the resistance to as low as one ohm; at present I make them as low as one-quarter ohm."[59] The lack of importance Sawyer attached to resistance is further emphasized by his testimony that he and Man had not even bothered to measure the resistance in some of the higher-ohm lamps they made. They also failed to agree on a desirable resistance for their lamps by the time they began commercial production.

The design of other system components received even less attention from Sawyer and Man. They paid most attention to the generator, but even here their experiments seem unfocused and desultory. Like Edison they tried several generators, experimenting with a Weston electroplating dynamo and a Farmer-Wallace machine that they acquired by loan, and with two or three electroplating dynamos manufactured by Arnoux and Hochhausen, in whose building they had their experimental shop. Arnoux and Hochhausen expressed some interest in entering the field of incandescent lighting and even made one specially wound machine, but there is no evidence to suggest the kind of systematic research undertaken by Edison. Sawyer and Man also made no effort to develop a generator to be used specifically with their incandescent lamps. They spent even less time considering other components.

Historian Thomas Hughes has persuasively argued that it was the systems approach that was central to Edison's inventive method. It certainly distinguished his work from others' in the field of electric lighting. Edison, however, used a more haphazard approach to systems than the one Hughes describes in his writings on Edison's lighting inventions. During his work on electric lighting, Edison only slowly realized what features were necessary for the system and only through experimentation did he develop the necessary understanding of how to design each element. He was, however, always conscious that his inventions ultimately would be part of a larger system. Edison nicely summarized his method in a February 1879 letter to the lawyer and politician Benjamin Butler concerning proposed changes in the patent law:

> My own practice for many years—a practice not adopted as the result of any plan or purpose, but arising from the natural habit of my mind, has been to study a subject for a time, and then taking out patents for such parts of a general system I may succeed in making. . . . As completed they are a *system* based on *different* inventions or discoveries, some of which have been made years before the others, and as I went along, finding my way from day to day and year to year.[60]

Not only did Sawyer and Man fail to recognize that the system itself presented a crucial problem, but they also differed from Edison in failing to understand the point at which commercialization became possible. Thus, Sawyer and Man gave up their first shop in June 1878, according to Man's later testimony, because "we had got our lamp and other inventions perfected and did not desire to go further until we secured our patents, and desired to avoid expense, while we did not need a workshop or laboratory."[61] In fact, the lamp was far from perfected. They found it necessary to continue their experiments the following September after moving into the shop where they planned to manufacture (or more properly assemble) lamps. Lacking experience as an inventor and as a manufacturer, Sawyer failed to recognize that an invention that worked well experimentally must be refined and tested before it can be successfully commercialized. In contrast with Sawyer, Edison recognized that the successful demonstration of his system proved only that electric lighting was technically feasible. Instead of moving immediately to manufacture the lamp, he began a new period of development research designed to make his system economically competitive with gaslight.

CHAPTER 11

From Research to Development

The shift from research to development during the first weeks of 1880 turned the Menlo Park laboratory into a true invention factory. During the research phase almost all work at the laboratory had relied on Edison's guiding hand. As Edison recalled, "Suggestions generally came from me. If any change was to be made, my assistants would speak to me about it, and if I thought best the change was made."[1] This mode of operation was described by the New York Herald of January 17, 1879:

> Edison himself flits about, first to one bench, then to another, examining here, instructing there; at one place drawing out new fancied designs, at another earnestly watching the progress of some experiment. Sometimes he hastily leaves the busy throng of workmen and for an hour or more is seen by no one. Where he is the general body of assistants do not know or ask, but his few principal men are aware that in a quiet corner upstairs in the old workshop, with a single light to dispel the darkness around, sits the inventor, with pencils and paper, drawing, figuring, pondering. In these moments he is rarely disturbed. If any important question of construction arises on which his advice is necessary the workmen wait. Sometimes they wait for hours in idleness, but at the laboratory such idleness is considered far more profitable than any interference with the inventor while he is in the throes of invention.[2]

Francis Upton also remarked upon Edison's central role in a letter to his father in April 1879: "One thing is quite noticeable here that the work is only a few days behind Mr. Edison, for when he was sick the shop was shut evenings as the work was wanting to keep the men busy."[3]

By the next year, with the push to commercial development and an even larger work force, which had grown to over sixty employees, Edison could no longer afford the time or expense of keeping his staff idle while they waited for his directions. He learned to subdivide the work, assigning each detail of the system to a particular staff member or a team of researchers and machinists. Although Edison provided initial guidance and suggestions on how to approach each problem, the experimenters were often allowed, and indeed encouraged, to find their own way to a solution: "I generally instructed them on the general idea of what I wanted carried out, and when I came across an assistant who was in any way ingenious, I sometimes refused to help him out in his experiments, telling him to see if he could not work it out himself, so as to encourage him."[4] The experience of Wilson Howell, whom Edison assigned the task of devising insulation for the underground cables, was typical:

> Mr. Edison sent me to his library and instructed me to read up on the subject of insulation, offering me the services of Dr. [Otto] Moses to translate any French or German authorities which I wished to consult. After two weeks search, I came out of the library with a list of materials which we might try. I was given carte blanche to order these materials . . . and, within ten days, I had Dr. Moses' laboratory entirely taken up with small kettles in which I boiled up a variety of insulating compounds. . . . Of course there were many failures, the partial successes pointing the direction for better trials.[5]

Howell typified not only the new pattern of research at Menlo Park, but also the laboratory assistants who joined the staff in 1880. Although a few experimenters, such as Charles Clarke and Julius Hornig, were hired because of their formal training as engineers, most were young men attracted by the aura surrounding Edison and his laboratory. Howell, for example, was one of a group of young people whom Upton had invited to the laboratory in December 1879 to see the new light. Howell was so impressed that he returned the following day to seek a place at the laboratory and agreed to work without compensation to get a chance to learn about electric lighting. William Hammer, George Crosby, and Albert Herrick were other young men who were willing to work initially for little or no pay in exchange for a chance to learn. Samuel Mott, a trained draftsman who received a weekly wage, said that he would have been willing to pay Edison for the privilege of working. As they gained experience and Edison's trust in their abilities, these men were given greater responsibilities and wages. Many of them subsequently became pioneers in the Edison lighting businesses.

The young men found Menlo Park an exciting place to work. Edison led by example, dressing and acting as one of the boys, but working harder than any of them. The normal sixty-hour workweek typically stretched to eighty hours. As Charles Clarke recalled,

> Laboratory life with Edison was a strenuous but joyous life for all, physically, mentally and emotionally. We worked long night hours during the week, frequently to the limit of human endurance; and then we had time off from Saturday to late

The Menlo Park laboratory complex in 1880 included the large machine shop (rear), the original building (center), the library-office (front), and the electric railroad (right).

Sunday afternoon for rest and recreation. . . . Here breathed a little community of kindred spirits, all in young manhood, enthusiastic about their work, expectant of great results; moreover often loudly emphatic in joke and vigorous in action.[6]

Practical jokes among the "boys" were common and usually carried out in a spirit of fun, but there was one exception. Because of his mannerisms and what many at the laboratory perceived as too high an opinion of his own abilities, Ludwig Boehm was constantly teased and became the butt of many pranks. By the time he left the laboratory in October, because of a dispute over his role in the lamp factory glassblowing operations, Boehm's life at Menlo Park had become increasingly unpleasant. Unlike the other foreign-born laboratory employees, Boehm never fit comfortably into the shop culture of the laboratory.

Although the laboratory was a product of industrial and corporate culture, it retained the informal preindustrial patterns of craft traditions that were part of shop culture. Practical jokes, such tests of strength as a competition over who could produce the highest voltage with a hand-cranked generator, late-night meals and beer, playing the laboratory pipe organ (which Edison had been given for his phonograph experiments), and telling jokes and singing silly or bawdy songs all provided relief from the pressures of work. The staff relieved the tedium of long nights spent testing lamps by betting on how long the lamps would last before they burned out. Edison also occasionally provided recreation by

Edison, seated in the middle and wearing a scarf around his neck, with some of his laboratory assistants in February 1880.

taking his staff fishing in nearby Raritan Bay or by letting them use the experimental electric railway that he built in 1880 as transportation to a nearby fishing hole. And workers who lived nearby were free to come and go at the laboratory as long as the work was done.

Edison maintained the informal work patterns of shop culture in his laboratory, but the demands of corporate organization required more up-to-date methods of recordkeeping. Edison required careful records of each experiment to take advantage of what Andre Millard refers to as "the economies of scale of a large work force and well-equipped laboratory, as well as the economies of scope that emerged when a result generated in one experiment proved useful in the successful conclusion of another."[7] In his Newark shops technical "drawings were made on all sorts of scraps of paper and thrown in a drawer," but after establishing his laboratory at Menlo Park he "commenced the practice of placing note books all over my laboratory, with order to my assistants to draw out and sign every experiment."[8] As he subdivided the work in 1880 notebooks would be assigned to a particular project or test series rather than used at random as had been Edison's previous practice. As the scale and scope of the work expanded, Edison also found it useful to have a member of his office staff (which now numbered six) keep a daily record of work in the laboratory so he could more readily follow the progress of each project. To better allocate resources among the many projects in the laboratory, Edison required his bookkeepers to maintain careful records of the labor, material, and other experimental costs incurred by each project. This also allowed him to charge these costs to the Edison Electric Light Company, Western Union, or other financial backers.

Having come to learn from the master inventor, his assistants were content to defer to Edison and understood that they were working on his ideas. This was evident to Edward Acheson, who joined the staff in August 1880. When Edison responded to Acheson's suggestion regarding electrochemical meters by saying "I do not pay you to make suggestions to me; how do you know but I already have that idea, and now if I use it you will think I took it from you," Acheson assured him that "I considered anything I could produce while in his employ and pertaining to his interests, belonged to him; that my thinking on those lines was due to my being in his laboratory and cognizant of his needs and lines of work." Similar views were expressed by other assistants, who later recalled Edison as the "sole directing mind."[9]

Regardless of how his assistants perceived their role, as Edison evolved from an inventor experimenting intensively with a few close associates to a director of a large-scale research and development laboratory, it becomes ever more difficult to represent him as *the* inventor. This had become problematic even before Edison moved to Menlo Park as he collaborated with skilled machinists and laboratory assistants. Charles Batchelor, in particular, is closely identified with Edison's most important inventions. Edison himself recognized Batchelor's role by arranging to give him 10 percent of all royalties and profits from his inventions. He also had given James Adams a royalty percentage for his role in developing the electric pen, the carbon telephone, and the phonograph. He now gave Francis Upton a 5 percent interest in the electric light.

Instead of assigning royalties to his assistants Edison could have named them as co-inventors in his patents, but he did not do so, in part because any joint patents were open to challenge under the existing patent law. The notebook evidence as well as the testimony and later reminiscences of Edison's assistants suggest that his were the key insights that produced these inventions. Such insights, rather than the mechanical skills used to help turn the insight into a tangible product, were judged to be the true mark of inventive genius. Invention was still considered an individual act, not yet a product of collaborative research in laboratories. Furthermore, according to standard legal texts, it was a "settled rule of law" under the U.S. patent system that when an employer conceived the principle of an invention, any "suggestions from an employee, not amounting to a new method or arrangement which in itself is a complete invention" would be regarded as the property of the employer and properly part of the employer's patent.[10] This may explain why Edison had so few jointly patented inventions, and evaluating the relative contributions of his assistants remains a problem for the historian.

The electric light work helps to highlight the tension between individual and organization that characterized Edison's career. Ideas are the product of an individual mind, but these ideas can be stimulated and influenced by others. It is difficult, if not impossible, to know how Edison was affected by his collaborative style of invention. Furthermore, ideas also emerged during the process of experimentation, and here his assistants clearly played an important role. Edison certainly displayed inventive genius in his ability to imagine an almost endless stream of ideas for an invention, but whether he was always the one to produce the crucial insight is less clear. Perhaps most important, Edison possessed a real genius for organizing invention that enabled him to rapidly explore his own ideas and to use the ideas and skills of others to greatest advantage.

The lamp remained the most important subject of research during 1880 as Edison sought a commercial device capable of hundreds of hours of use. The research focused on each part of the lamp, from the filament to the electrical connections to the glass bulb. The research was guided by careful testing as Edison had his staff make electrical and photometric measurements of each lamp and record how long it burned and why it failed. An experienced manufacturer, Edison considered the problems of lamp manufacture as well. He had his experimenters and machinists design special tools for making filaments, clamps, and bulbs. The most important work focused on improved vacuum pump designs intended to reduce the time required to evacuate a lamp. By late spring Edison began to convert the old electric pen factory into a lamp factory. Although technical problems remained, Edison wanted to work out some of the manufacturing difficulties and to make large test runs of experimental lamps.

The most critical problem in the lamp that had to be solved before commercial production could begin remained the filament. The cardboard horseshoes had proved sufficient for demonstration purposes, but showed serious deficiencies for use in a commercial lamp. One of his assistants recalled how Edison discovered that "Paper is no good. Under the microscope it appears like a lot of sticks thrown together. There are places where the fibres are packed and other places where there are few fibres, dense spots and great open holes." If carbon was the solution, he still needed to find the best form of it. In typical Edisonian fashion he told his staff, "Now I believe that somewhere in God Almighty's workshop there is a vegetable growth with geometrically parallel fibres suitable to our use. Look for it. Paper is man made and not good for filaments."[11] Edison assigned one of his chemists, Dr. Otto Moses, to make a systematic study of the literature on carbon substances that helped to guide the research. Experiments soon focused on certain kinds of wood and bast fibers. When the latter proved more stable after carbonization, the research turned to other grasses and canes, such as hemp, palmetto, and bamboo, which had long, uniform fibers that would make sturdy, long-lasting filaments. By summer, bast and bamboo had become the primary foci of attention, and bamboo soon demonstrated its superiority as a filament. To assure himself that there was no better fiber available, Edison launched a search that rivaled his effort to find platinum, sending one man to Cuba, another to Brazil, and a third to China and Japan. This search not only confirmed the superiority of bamboo, but also disclosed the source of a superior form of the plant that Edison used in his commercial lamps.

During the spring Edison also began installing a full-scale model of his underground system at Menlo Park. This system would allow him to test each component and also provide more exact cost information. Economy was an important factor in the work. For example, Charles Mott indicated in his journal entry of May 31 that Francis Upton was conducting experiments "to determine some of the laws governing the construction of electric generators, and to study the economical proportioning of the same."[12] Edison himself designed a new dynamo for central stations that he believed would "do away with a very considerable loss of power, and at the same time the outlay for machinery is very much reduced."[13] To reduce the energy lost in the linkage between generator and engine, Edison proposed to couple a large 100-horsepower generator with a steam engine rather than run several smaller dynamos with belts and pulleys. He developed this design with steam engine maker Charles T. Porter, who designed a special high-speed engine. Charles Clarke, a mechanical engineer who had been Upton's classmate at Bowdoin College, was given the job of supervising the construction and testing of this dynamo. Clarke was one of two mechanical engineers whom Edison hired to assist with the task of designing commercial central stations. Edison also employed Julius Hornig as a draftsman to help "make building plans, arranging steam machinery to drive his dynamo machines in central station plants."[14]

The installation of the Menlo Park underground system provided the impetus for work on many of the components that would be used in a commercial system. Edison had put aside this work while focusing on the dynamo and lamp. For example, he had conceived an electrochemical meter for measuring current use as early as December 1878. With the expansion of the laboratory staff in 1880 he could now assign these minor though important components to his assistants to develop. The underground system itself presented new problems, as Edison discovered that he needed better insulation for the wires, and he placed Howell in charge of devising an insulating compound. Another spur to the development of components occurred when Edison agreed to the first demonstration of his system outside of Menlo Park. Henry Villard, head of the Oregon Railway and Navigation Company and an electric light stockholder, asked Edison to install lights on his new steamship *Columbia*, which was being outfitted in New York during March and April 1880. Besides demonstrating potential uses for his light, Edison was no doubt attracted by the publicity that the first shipboard lighting system would generate. As they outfitted the ship, Edison and his staff developed the first lamp socket, key switch, and safety catch (or fuse) to prevent wires from overheating and causing a fire.

The *Columbia* installation indicated some of the possibilities for small isolated stations for ships, factories, and other purposes, but Edison's attention remained focused on central stations. The economy of a central station system still depended on the cost of conductors. Although overhead wires were less costly and had worked well for the 1879 demonstration, two factors led Edison to insist on putting his lines underground. The first was his continuing use of the gaslight analogy that provided the basic model for his main and feeder system of distribution. The other was his experience with overhead wires for telegraphy. He knew that overhead lines were subject to damage from weather and vandalism. Perhaps even more important, he was aware of the political problems created by the jumble of overhead wires in the already crowded streets of major cities. As telephone and electric lines began to compete for space with the already existing maze of telegraph lines, local governments were beginning to pass laws requiring companies to place them underground.[15] As he planned his underground system, Edison assigned Charles Clarke the task of compiling a table of conductor dimensions for central stations based on Upton's guidelines about resistance and energy loss.

As he studied the economics of electrical distribution, Edison also considered the important issue of load balancing. Knowing that lights would primarily be used at night, and so his expensive plant would be left underused during the day, Edison experimented with electric motors that could be used to run hoists, elevators, sewing machines, and other equipment that did run during the day. Another potential use of electric motors was for electric railways. Edison placed Hornig in charge of building a one-half-mile-long track at Menlo Park and designing both passenger and freight cars. They also estimated the cost for converting the Manhattan Railway to electricity. Although Edison experimented on the Menlo Park railroad for several years and produced some crucial patents in the field, he failed to develop a commercial system of electric street railways. Surprisingly, one reason was his failure to see passenger streetcars as the primary electric railway market. Instead he thought that electric railways could be built more cheaply than steam railways for freight traffic in wheat-growing states, such as Iowa, where he thought they "would be of great value for drawing grain to the main lines of railroad and thus extend the radius of economical grain operation."[16] Edison was able to continue these expensive experiments through 1882 with substantial financial assistance from Henry Villard, who had significant investments in railroad stocks.

The electric railway was only one of several technologies that Edison was able to explore, even in the midst of the intense effort to develop his lighting system. He was able to do this because he had begun to make the transition from experimenting intensively with a few close associates to directing a large-scale research and development program. He could assign members of his expanded staff to experiment on a variety of other projects, ranging from improvements on telephone and telegraph instruments to preserving food in a vacuum. Another project, the separation of gold ores, grew out of the effort to obtain platinum from black sands and led Edison to develop a method for electromagnetically separating iron ore, which he then attempted unsuccessfully to commercialize over the next two years and to which he would return at the decade's end.

As Edison moved toward commercialization of his lighting system in the winter of 1881 he shifted his base of operations from Menlo Park into New York City. He also began to transfer the research, which had been centered in the Menlo Park laboratory, to the new electric light manufacturing shops. Edison established these shops as partnerships with some of his closest laboratory associates, and he continued to reward them by providing them with an interest in his inventions. Charles Batchelor, whose arrangement with Edison allowed him 10 percent from all inventions, received the same interest in the manufacturing companies. Francis Upton received the same 5 percent interest in the Lamp Company shops that he had in the lighting companies. John Kruesi was a partner in the Machine Works and managed the Electric Tube Works, in which he and Charles Clarke both had shares. Charles Dean, whom Edison appointed general manager of the Edison Machine Works, was not a partner, but Edison did allow him 7 percent profit on certain types of work undertaken by the shop. And Sigmund Bergmann and Edward Johnson, who also received a 5 percent interest in the Edison Lamp Company, formed Bergmann & Company to manufacture light fixtures with Edison as their silent partner.[17]

Edison continued to be directly involved in planning and directing experiments as they were dispersed among his shops and laboratories, but as he had begun to do at Menlo Park, he gave his researchers a certain amount of freedom to use their own experience and insights as they carried out their tasks. John Ott described in testimony how Edison directed his work on an automatic voltage regulator in the spring of 1882. According to Ott, Edison provided sketches showing alternative designs and "gave me an explanation how to go to work and make them; also the results that might be noticed, and instructed me to guard against these results and give him a copy of the notes." He explained that "guarding against results" meant to look for unexpected results that "might lead to an invention."[18] These experiments took place at the Menlo Park laboratory, and Edison frequently came out from New York, where he now spent most of his time, to examine Ott's work, offer additional ideas, and sometimes participate in the experiments.

Ott's testimony about these experiments took place during a patent interference in which the opposing lawyers attempted to show that Ott rather than Edison was the actual inventor, thus making Edison's oath of invention and the resulting patent invalid. Both Ott and another assistant, Martin Force, testified that Edison should be considered the inventor of the voltage regulator "because it was Mr. Ott's business to work for Mr. Edison and put Mr. Edison's inventions into mechanical shape."[19] The testimony about Ott's role fit the prevailing conceptions and laws of the day, but his contributions were certainly judged important by Edison himself. He allowed Ott to apply for and receive

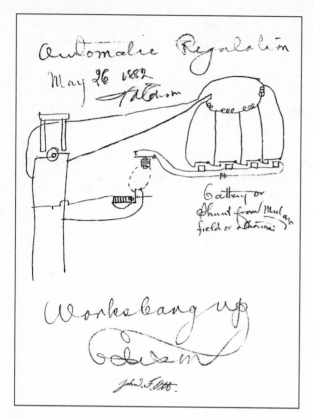

One of the many automatic voltage regulators experimented with by Edison and John Ott included this design using a telegraph relay and shunt circuit that Edison thought "works bang up."

three patents covering specific details and applications of automatic voltage regulators. However, Edison reserved the broad claims on regulators for his own patents. This was consistent with a new policy Edison evolved during the course of the development work on electric lighting. When their contributions warranted it, he allowed his assistants to apply for patents on details while leaving the basic patent with broader claims for himself. This policy had the additional advantage of letting Edison and the Edison Electric Light Company limit the royalties that had to be paid for secondary patents.

Although Edison continued to operate his laboratory at Menlo Park after 1880, he spent relatively little time there. He usually relied on Ott and Thomas Logan, who oversaw the machine shop, to conduct experiments at the laboratory. Charles Hughes, who was in charge of the electric railway work at Menlo Park, conducted the experiments on preserving fruit in a vacuum that were being funded by George Gouraud. The laboratory also served as a lamp testing facility, and the lamp factory was located in the old electric pen factory at

Menlo Park. When the factory moved to larger quarters in East Newark (later Harrison), New Jersey, in the spring of 1882, the testing department went with it. The last hurrah for the Menlo Park laboratory was during the spring and summer of 1882, when Edison briefly made it his headquarters again. By the end of September, however, Edison decided to close the laboratory permanently and establish a new one on the third floor of the building recently purchased for Bergmann & Company at Avenue B and 17th Street in New York City.[20]

The Menlo Park laboratory had already ceased to be the center of experimental work on the electric lighting system by the spring of 1881, after Edison and his family moved into New York City. Edison established his headquarters at the offices of the Edison Electric Light Company on 65 Fifth Avenue, and most of the experimental work took place in the manufacturing shops. The lamp factory was responsible for the experiments on lamp design and manufacture while the Edison Machine Works staff experimented on dynamos and meters. These experiments took place in its testing room, where the staff also conducted tests and experiments on conductors and insulators used by the Electric Tube Works, on junction boxes and joints designed by Kruesi and Edison, and on lighting accessories such as lamp sockets and safety fuses developed by Bergmann & Company. Edison himself made periodic visits to the shops to review the manufacturing processes to improve them, to make suggestions for research and examine experimental results, and to conduct experiments himself. He also sent his experimenters written instructions from his Fifth Avenue offices. The company collected reports on the operation of the system from its agents and customers in the United States and abroad; this information helped Edison determine which technical problems to focus on.

The shift of experiments from the laboratory to the shops dispersed responsibility for recordkeeping, and most of Edison's instructions and the detailed notes kept by experimenters in the shops no longer exist. Those that do, along with brief summaries of the work found in letters and occasional formal reports, provide a general sense of what experiments were undertaken but little in the way of specific details. Additional insights can be gleaned from later reminiscences and accounts written by participants, along with a careful reading of Edison's notes to his patent attorneys and the patents issued to him and his experimenters. With these records it is possible at least to characterize the experimental program undertaken in Edison's manufacturing shops and to give some idea of his role.[21]

Just as the lamp had been the most difficult feature of the system to invent, its manufacture also required constant experimental efforts. Upton noted in the spring of 1884 that a total of 2,774 lamp experiments had been conducted at a cost of over $70,000.[22] And experiments continued to cost more than $1,000 a month. These experiments covered all the aspects of lamp design and manufacture necessary to produce long-lived lamps at low cost in a variety of candlepowers, though most attention was paid to the standard 16 candlepower lamp.

Manufacturing concerns drove many of the experiments at the factory as Edison and Upton sought to improve each step of the production process. One of the most troublesome areas was the carbonizing process. Edison and his experimenters at the lamp factory conducted experiments to prevent the filaments from developing weaknesses caused by uneven heating, fiber shrinkage, or absorption of air during heating. To accomplish this they carbonized the filaments under pressure to increase heat, used weights and moveable blocks to place the filaments under stress, and found ways to exclude air from the carbonizing process. Another problem they found was the tendency of the nickel molds to melt under the high heat of carbonization, thus ruining the fibers. In the attempts to find a better mold material, cheaper manufacture was also considered, and Edison had the lamp factory experiment with plumbago carbonizing molds to replace the more expensive nickel molds. In August 1882 Edison described the improvements to Batchelor so that they could be adopted at the lamp factory that Batchelor had recently established in Paris. "We are using carbon forms & weights for holding fibres instead of nickel and are getting even better carbons. . . . [you] will never have any more trouble about melting forms etc. We have run over 50 heats with them and they actually improve."[23]

Once the filaments were carbonized, they had to be attached to the lead-in wires in the lamps. The tiny screw clamps originally used were difficult to manufacture and clamp properly, however, and Edison proposed electroplating the filament to the wire. John Lawson conducted an extensive series of experiments on this process in the first months of 1881, trying "all the experiments [Edison] mentioned with extreme care so as to be sure of the results," and soon he developed a successful method of copperplating the carbons to the wire.[24] Even after the process was adopted, experiments continued to improve it.

One of the trickiest parts of lamp manufacture was the vacuum process. Constant experiments were undertaken to reduce the time required to evacuate the bulbs and to improve the quality of the vacuum. A particularly significant problem was caused by the production of water vapor in the bulb during evacuation. Although heating the filaments during evacuation drove off much of the moisture in the bulbs, Edison ordered a series of experiments at the lamp factory to find a drying agent that would eliminate the remainder, eventually adopting phosphoric anhydride. To maintain the vacuum more securely, other experiments were designed to improve methods of sealing the lamps. Even with these improvements the vacuum process remained a problem, as indicated by a careful analysis made by Batchelor at the Paris lamp factory in 1883. After studying the problems that caused bad lamps to be produced during the vacuum process he concluded that although some of these could be attributed to the poor quality of the French glass used in the pumps and lamps, others were a product of the vacuum process itself.[25]

Although Edison lamps continued to be made with bamboo filaments, Edison constantly experimented with other materials. In part, these experiments were driven by his failure to find alternative sources of natural fiber. The bamboo that was used, Madake, grew only in one region of Japan. Concerned with having to rely on this single source, and worried about the cost of the filaments, Edison and Upton wanted to find a way to make them from inexpensive materials such as paper. As Upton noted in a May 1881 letter to Edison that discussed some of the first experiments along these lines, the difference in cost had to be substantial to replace the quality of the bamboo "as the life of a lamp depends entirely on the carbon [and] if the bamboo is 10% better we have saved the 2 cts [difference in cost]. Bamboo is far more than 10% better than paper."[26] Nonetheless, Edison continued to experiment, using such materials as tissue paper, pulp, cellulose, and flour paste. One potential advantage of these materials was that it was easier to form them into filaments. In 1882, for example, he proposed making filaments from cellulose or flour paste, which could be formed into a solid mass and forced through dies into the proper shape. Another idea was for a hollow core filament, which could be made by wrapping a piece of metal with tissue paper or coating it with pulp or cellulose and then removing the wire or eating it away with acid. While these could be "bent in shape & carbonized in the regular manner," Edison also indicated that they could be made "square oval or any shape."[27]

From the first paper filaments made by Alfred Haid in 1881, attempts to use these artificial materials often included coating them with hydrocarbon gases to make them more uniform. Such experiments also were tried with the standard bamboo filaments. Some of these experiments were driven by competition, with Edison seeking an alternative to the patented Sawyer and Man process for coating filaments, which reduced voltage fluctuations in the lamp. But many of the experiments with hydrocarbon coatings took place for other reasons as well. In July 1882, for example, Edison asked Upton to "please have Lawson dip several carbons in kerosene for $1/2$ hour then plate the ends if OK. . . . I think this will prevent carbons from absorbing water & oxidizing & do no harm as the kerosene will evaporate in the vacuum." He also patented the use of hydrocarbon gases used to increase the atmospheric pressure during carbonization, having found that this raised the temperature and made the filament "more compact and homogenous."[28]

Many of the experiments at the lamp factory were initially carried out by chemists John Lawson and Alfred Haid, who had been with Edison since 1879. Another important experimenter was John Howell, a recent graduate of the Stevens Institute, who was placed in charge of the lamp factory test room in July 1881. Although these and other experimenters made important contributions, their experiments at the lamp factory, as at the laboratory, were seen primarily as carrying out Edison's ideas, and they applied for few patents. Most of the patents for improved lamp designs and manufacturing techniques during these years were granted to Edison. One important exception, however, was a patent issued to William Holzer, superintendent of the lamp factory, who designed a flat seal for the lead-in wires. This seal, according to a history of lamp manufacturing, greatly "simplified the production of this part, permitting the use of less skilled labor."[29] Another exception was the improved standard screw socket patented by Sigmund Bergmann, who received several patents for lamp fixtures sold by Bergmann & Company.

Lamp manufacture proved to be a troublesome business. Although Upton tried to keep Edison informed by writing him about "all the trials I have, for scarcely a day passes without a new 'bug' showing itself," Edison became convinced in November 1881 that "Upton had got way off his base and was trying to get back without informing me." Lamp life had diminished from an average of 600 to 400 hours, and Edison spent a week at the factory, working on what he claimed was "just 13 hours sleep," to get production back up to standard. As a result of this experience, Edison vowed to "pay a visit to the Lamp Factory once a week if not twice a week." His visits to the factory continued to improve production, and at the end of the year he wrote Charles Batchelor that he hoped within "the course of six or seven weeks to materially reduce the cost of the lamps so that we can make some profit on them."[30] However, when the factory moved to East Newark in the spring electrical arcing in the lamp caused a new problem, and Edison again spent considerable time at the factory, as well as at the Menlo Park laboratory, in an effort to solve it.

Lamp life was affected not only by lamp design and manufacture but also by the generators that powered the lights. Because isolated plants usually were run by steam engineers and others with little knowledge of electricity, Edison had to devise a method to regulate generators automatically to prevent lamps from being run at the wrong voltage, which severely reduced their life. In November 1881, as the Edison Company for Isolated Lighting was being organized, he wrote Edward Johnson

> I have got the nicest thing for the Isolated Business you ever saw for notifying them when the lights go beyond eight or sixteen candles as the case may be. I have been fishing for it for a long time & have always felt uneasy not to have had it. It was a far more difficult thing to get than I at first supposed. It is now working "bang up" downstairs here [at 65 Fifth Avenue]. . . . I congratulate myself that this is a pretty good thing for Isolated business as without it we should constantly be at variance with purchasers as to the life of our lamps.[31]

It would be another year, however, before Edison "at last got what I consider a really reliable Automatic Regulator."[32] This was the design on which John Ott spent much of his time during the spring and summer of 1882 and that temporarily brought Edison back to Menlo Park.

As he worked on voltage regulators and other problems related to dynamo design, Edison spent considerable time at the Edison Machine Works on Goerck Street in New York City, usually supervising tests and experiments being carried out in the testing room. In particular he took charge of experiments with the central station steam dynamos. One of these impressive machines (each with its own directly connected steam engine) was appropriately nicknamed "Jumbo" when it was shipped to Paris for the Electrical Exhibition aboard the same ship that had recently brought P. T. Barnum's famous elephant, also called Jumbo, to America. Working out bugs in their design proved a larger task than Edison originally had anticipated. Thus, during July 1881 he spent nearly all his time at Goerck Street conducting experiments and tests on the generator. One set of experiments from this month required "working 55 men days and 60 nights for 8 days and nights."[33] By the time Edison was satisfied with the new dynamo he had spent over $6,000 on experiments. After they were installed in the station on Pearl Street, he found it necessary to develop a governor so they could be operated in unison. He soon found that this problem was caused by the steam engine and decided to replace both the Porter-Allen steam engines and the governor with a new steam engine designed by the firm of Armington and Sims.

The design of new dynamos to meet the particular needs of customers was largely an engineering problem. Charles Clarke, one of the few Edison employees at Menlo Park with formal engineering education (albeit in civil and mechanical engineering), played a large role in the design of the Pearl Street dynamos. He also took much of the responsibility for designing the various generators used in isolated plants and other central stations. Edison consulted him on other elements of the system as well and appointed him chief engineer of Edison Electric. In that position, Clarke was careful to "consult [Edison] on all points pertaining to your system and never take or have taken the initiative without your assent."[34] To ensure the quality and reliability of each piece of equipment for the station, Clarke spent some time nearly every day at Goerck Street "to make his inspections, to give advice, and to lay out plans for investigations as, for example, standardizing the alloy from which the wire of our safety fuses were made."[35] He also took instructions from Edison for experiments to be carried out in the shop's testing room.

Francis Jehl, who had charge of the room, conducted experiments and tests on several components. Among the most important were those connected with the electric meter for central stations. Edison asked Jehl to "Keep me posted by letter every day what you are doing and give results of every kind"[36] about that meter. Clarke, too, kept a careful watch on the meter experiments and reported back to Edison. Edison used this information to make meter improvements, such as the thermal regulator he designed based on Jehl's experiments about the effect of temperature changes on the meter. Jehl and his testing room staff also did work for the other shops, such as testing insulation and wire for the Electric Tube Works and fuses and other electrical appliances for Bergmann & Company. When Jehl was sent to Europe to introduce the Edison meter at the end of February 1882, William Andrews took his place at the testing room and was responsible for much of the experimental work at the Machine Works. George Grower, another assistant in the testing room who continued Jehl's experiments with meters, later moved to Edison's laboratory at Bergmann & Company.

Because Edison's hopes for electric light central stations rested on the success of the New York station, he spent much of his own time during 1881 and 1882 overseeing its installation. Even before starting the installation, he had devoted considerable attention to the details of the station. To demonstrate the new system, generate favorable publicity, and interest new investors, Edison and Lowrey had decided to light the downtown area that included Wall Street and the offices of the city's newspapers. Edison sent canvassers door to door to ascertain how much gas light was used at night and how much power was consumed in operating hoists and other machinery during the day to determine the load requirements for the first lighting district. He hired Hermann Claudius, an experienced electrical engineer formerly associated with the Austrian Imperial Telegraph Department, to take this information and construct a small-scale working model of the underground network from which they determined the requirements for the installation. Edison carefully calculated the station's installation and operating costs, worked out a system of bookkeeping, and even drew up careful lists detailing the necessary preparations to be made for the installation. While Edison prepared plans for the station, Grosvenor Lowrey guided legislation through the Board of Aldermen that would allow Edison's people to place the conductors underground. Lowrey also convinced several of the larger Edison Electric stockholders, led by Drexel Morgan, to organize the Edison Illuminating Company of New York to fund and operate the station.

The most costly and time-consuming part of the installation involved laying the underground conductors. Edison placed John Kruesi in charge of this work, which took from the spring of 1881 to the summer of 1882. Kruesi supervised the manufacture of the conductors at the Electric Tube Company factory by day and oversaw their installation at night, and he was frequently joined by Edison. Francis Jehl later recalled how the two men would sometimes rest on cots in the station building and discuss the progress of the work. When work was completed, the nearly 100,000 feet of conductors (Edison had anticipated using 80,000 feet) cost over $180,000; the entire station installation cost around $300,000.[37]

By early July the first dynamo was installed and tested, and over the next two months careful tests were made of the entire system. Finally, at three o'clock in the afternoon of September 4, station engineer John Lieb threw the switch and started the station as Edison turned on the lights in J. Pierpont Morgan's offices, where the Edison Electric Light Company directors had gathered. The following day the *New York Herald* reported:

> The lighting, which this time was less an experiment than the regular inauguration of work, was eminently satisfactory. Albeit there had been doubters at home and abroad who showed a disposition to scoff at the work of the Wizard of Menlo Park and insinuate that the practical application of his invention would fall short of what was expected of it, the test was fairly stood and the luminous horseshoes did their work well.

To the *New York Sun*, Edison stated simply, "I have accomplished all I promised."[38]

In the process, he had also redefined invention by developing the first full-scale research and development laboratory. As an institution, however, it was still the product of an individual inventor rather than a corporate organization. And Edison's very success led to his laboratory's demise as his own energies were devoted to developing the new business arising from the research and development effort. The memory of the old Menlo Park laboratory remained, however, as a source of inspiration to others. Alexander Graham Bell was influenced by what he called Edison's "celebrated laboratory at Menlo Park" when he set up his own Volta Laboratory in Washington, D.C., in 1881.[39] The Bell Telephone Company likewise drew on the example of Edison's laboratory when it established an experimental shop in 1883 that company officials placed under the direction of Edison's friend Ezra Gilliland. Other electrical inventors, such as Edward Weston, also were inspired by Edison's example as they set up laboratories of their own. The influence of the laboratory even extended to the scientific community. In 1880 mathematician and astronomer Simon Newcomb of the U.S. Naval Observatory and physicist Albert Michelson of the U.S. Naval Academy were planning new measurements of the speed of light, one of the key physical problems of the nineteenth century, when Edison invited them to conduct their experiments at his laboratory. Michelson objected to the lack of hotel facilities at Menlo Park, "otherwise," Newcomb wrote, "I should like very much to accept your kind offer, as I think the advantages of your laboratory would be very great."[40] Newcomb was one of many American scientists who found Edison's laboratory better equipped than their own. The most lasting influence of the Menlo Park laboratory was on American industry. By showing how invention itself could be an industrial process and that corporate support for it could produce large benefits, Edison helped lay the groundwork for modern industrial research and development.

CHAPTER 12

Inventing an Industry

When Edison had first come to New York City in 1869, he was just beginning to make himself into a professional inventor. For more than a decade this had been his primary occupation. As a manufacturer of telegraph equipment he had usually relied on his partners to take charge while he experimented. His inventions were always marketed by others; even the electric pen business had been supervised by Charles Batchelor while Edison remained in the laboratory. When Edison moved back to New York in February 1881, however, he found himself less and less able to focus on laboratory research and the practice of invention. Faced with the complex task of introducing electric lighting on a large scale, he could no longer be a full-time inventor.

Edison did not give up inventing, but his time was more and more consumed by the demands of the new industry he had helped to create. However, he never stopped thinking like an inventor. In fact, the years 1881 to 1883 were in some ways his most prolific; he executed an astounding 259 successful patent applications and many other unsuccessful ones, almost all related to electric light and power. This continued a trend that had begun in 1880, when he shifted his Menlo Park laboratory from research to the development and commercialization of the new electric lighting technology. That year he produced 59 successful patent applications (all but 4 of them related to the new system).[1] As in 1880, Edison assigned many of the experimental projects to his assistants, but now the manufacturing shops joined the laboratory as a site of inventive activity. Experiments in the shops and Edison's own periodic sojourns in the laboratory were designed primarily to solve specific problems encountered in the production and operation of electric lighting apparatus rather than to produce the innovative new technologies with which the name Edison had become associated. The continuing stream of patents and improvements produced by this diversified research organization helped to maintain Edison's reputation as a premier inventor, but they were just part of his struggle to create a new industry.

Edison could not rely on a well-established business organization, such as Western Union, to adapt his new lighting technology to its existing business or to open new markets for it. Instead he had to help establish and guide new organizations to market the technology. Because Edison had been the one whose vision had driven the enterprise during the period of research and development, his corporate backers continued to turn to him for advice in establishing company policy as they moved into the commercialization phase. Nonetheless, unlike the research and development phases, when technological issues dominated, commercialization involved business issues with which corporate officers were more familiar and that caused them to be more willing to challenge Edison's ideas and vision for the new industry.

Edison did possess a certain business acumen and understood the importance of economic factors and commercial requirements in developing new technology. However, his business strategies reflected his years of experience as an inventor and manufacturer. He consistently sought technological solutions to business problems. At the core of his strategy was an abiding faith that he could produce technology superior to any competitor's and thus beat anyone in the long run. This was particularly evident in his views on patent infringement suits; he consistently argued against bringing such suits as they "would require me to give my personal attention to the matter & take me off other far more important work, besides involving us in a great deal of expense & giving our opponents a notoriety which it is hardly desirable they should gain at our expense. . . . When they affect our business then we shall have reason to sue them but so long as their work is conducive to their own ruin I see no reason for attacking them." Furthermore, his experience as an inventor made him confident that "If we are proved infringers on any point, I can probably take care of that myself."[2] Not until 1884, when it became apparent that competitors were beginning to make inroads, particularly in the isolated lighting station business, did Edison finally concede the need to press forward with infringement suits.

More significantly, Edison saw continued innovation as the best means of defeating competition. Thus, he told the Edison Electric Light Company Ltd. of London "The patents I am now taking are more valuable than those already taken. Those already taken were to secure if possible the science of the thing. Those I am now taking are commercial." It was these "commercial" patents that Edison believed would "secure the system that replaces gas with great *profit*" and give him a decided advantage over competitors. As he explained to the managers of the British Edison Electric Light Company that had been established by Drexel Morgan:

> Do not fail to remember the fact that there are 8 or 9 things in our system of general distribution, any one of which if maintained will give us the commercial monopoly of the general distribution business and the patents which are now coming

out and which will come out in the course of the next year will be just as important in maintaining the monopoly as the patents which have been already issued.[3]

Because of his technological orientation, Edison was also more willing than his corporate backers to spend money on new experimental work. The financiers who created Edison Electric certainly had confidence in Edison's inventive ability and understood the necessity for continued experimentation. To provide funds for these experiments, they even agreed to increase the company's capital stock at the beginning of 1881. Nonetheless, as experimental costs continued to mount, the company's new president, Sherbourne Eaton, sought to exert control over Edison's rather free-spending ways. Eaton established a policy that either he or the corporate secretary, Calvin Goddard, had to approve all requisitions for labor or materials. Although Edison appears to have acquiesced in this policy, he found that "the rendering of [experimental] accounts of this character is usually a matter of great irritation."[4] Conflict also arose over who should pay for experimental costs incurred by the manufacturing shops.

As an experienced inventor-manufacturer, Edison understood that manufacturing his own inventions would provide important insights that he could use to improve the products and make them more cheaply. However, he found himself unable to convince the light company financiers of this fact. As he recalled, "we sought in a most determined way to induce our friends in the parent company, as well as others to join us in the undertaking. In this we signally failed. We thereupon determined upon taking all the risks and carrying the burden ourselves to the best of our ability—more with an object to make the Edison electric light a success than to make money by manufacturing." By 1883 "it [was] admitted by all" that if Edison had not undertaken the manufacturing the Edison lighting business would have been seriously impaired.[5] Their growing recognition that the manufacturing businesses were not only becoming profitable but also were important to the Edison lighting business would lead to efforts by the financiers to consolidate the shops into a reorganized and larger corporate structure.

The reorganization efforts, which Edison resisted, highlight the tension that existed between his dependence on corporate capital to support his inventive efforts and his more traditional approach to business organization. In a letter to Edison Electric director Henry Villard, Edison and his manufacturing partners argued for a traditional business philosophy that held that "the personal supervision and self interests of the present owners of the several factories is far more likely to secure economy of production than would result from corporative control and management."[6] The traditional business organization usually was organized as a partnership or a closely held corporation (the style Edison would later pursue as his enterprises grew). Decision making in such firms rested with the owner-managers and their personal representatives, and there was usually no bureaucratic structure such as that represented by the Committee on Manufactures and Organization chaired by Villard for Edison Electric. Edison's preferred style of ownership and management is typical of entrepreneurial firms, and it is generally considered more conducive to innovation; it is not surprising that as an inventor interested in the introduction of new technologies, Edison chose to organize and run his businesses in this fashion. Although he often depended on corporate capital, Edison remained more comfortable operating as a traditional proprietary capitalist. In his relations with Edison Electric he tried to replicate his role in the telegraph industry as an independent small businessman supplying inventions and manufactured goods under contract to a large corporation.

Personal relationships were the basis on which traditional business firms were organized, and in establishing his manufacturing shops Edison chose as partners some of his closest laboratory associates. This also furthered his efforts to reward those who had assisted his inventive efforts by providing them with an interest in his inventions. To establish these businesses, Edison invested much of his personal wealth. His private secretary Samuel Insull later described how on his first day of work "Mr. Edison started out by drawing from his desk a checkbook and stating how much money he had in the bank. He wanted to know what European telephone securities were most salable, as he wished to raise the necessary funds to put on their feet the Incandescent Lamp factory, the Electric Tube works, and the necessary shops to build Dynamos."[7] Besides selling telephone stock, Edison also took out loans from Drexel Morgan & Company using his stock in the Edison Electric Light Company and the Edison Illuminating Company of New York as collateral, and sold off some shares of his stock in the Edison Electric Light Company and the Edison Electric Light Company of Europe to raise additional funds. His partners in these ventures—Charles Batchelor, Francis Upton, John Kruesi, Edward Johnson, and Sigmund Bergmann—also risked money they had received from Edison as shares of stock in the Edison electric lighting companies.

As he had at Newark, Edison left the day-to-day operations of the shops to his partners and managers. The lamp factory, however, did require his periodic attention. Unlike other parts of the system, advancements in lamp technology relied to a significant extent on improvements in manufacturing techniques. Manufacturing techniques were much less significant for improved dynamos, underground tubes, or lamp fixtures and meters than they were for lamps. The other shops could also draw readily on existing methods of machine and instrument building, but the lamp factory required entirely new manufacturing techniques. For these reasons Edison spent considerable time at the lamp works in fall and winter 1881–1882, and the Edison Lamp Company's experimental costs remained very high.

Even with continued improvements in manufacturing practice, profit eluded the lamp factory for some time. Meeting bills was a constant struggle for Upton, whose letters to Edison and Insull constantly refer to financial difficulties and the need for additional sources of revenue, plans to raise money through bank loans, assessments on the partners, and the problem of getting prompt payment from other Edison companies. On the other hand, by the end of 1882 large orders for isolated plants in the United States and Europe and the opening of the first New York central station generated renewed optimism about the future, as well as the potential for steady sources of income.

Large orders allowed the factory to produce lamps at a much lower cost. The 54,000 lamps made during March 1883 reduced the cost per lamp to 29.3 cents, but when only 14,282 lamps were made in July the cost per lamp jumped to 45.5 cents. The key in Upton's opinion was to run the lamp factory like the textile mills of his native New England—"make one article in large quantities, by subdivision of labor."[8] By the beginning of 1884, although it was not yet doing the large business per month that Upton wanted, the company was in much better financial condition. "The business is in such shape," he told Edison, "that we can hold our own and earn interest on our capital, on the sales of lamps in this country alone, at present prices and in the same amounts as last year. During the coming year I am anticipating an increased demand for lamps and hope by Jan. 2, 1885 to bring our indebtedness down to running bills."[9] Upton's optimism was well deserved. The company had increased its sales from a mere $13,175 in 1881 to $91,230 ($54,644 of which was foreign sales) in 1882 to $139,755 ($62,790 foreign) in 1883. With new central station and isolated plants continuing to be built the demand could only increase. However, to secure profits, Upton also urged Edison to renegotiate his manufacturing license with the Edison Electric Light Company to increase the price he could charge for lamps from 35 to 40 cents per lamp.

The lamp contract exemplified the tension between Edison's entrepreneurial interests and the more conservative corporate interests of Edison Electric. As Eaton noted in his 1883 report to stockholders, "the policy of the Company thus far has been merely to perform the duties of owner of the Edison patents, and to derive income from licenses and royalties thereunder."[10] To set up as a manufacturer, Edison actually had to license his patents from the company. However, when he suggested a five-cent-per-lamp profit for manufacturing, the company's directors, seeking to secure a more immediate return on their already large investments, objected and reduced it to three cents. They also insisted that the contract be made with Edison alone and not with his partners in the Edison Lamp Company. By controlling Edison's manufacturing profits, the company hoped to increase its own, as well as to make the price of equipment more favorable to potential customers.

A similar divergence of interests occurred over the role of the company in promoting the lighting system. Whereas Edison was committed to central stations as the basis of the electric light industry and as the primary customers for his shops, Eaton found that it was difficult to establish local illuminating companies "because people will not go into them until our big central station on Pearl St. is a success, and because they take so much capital." He also explained to Edison that "our Board of Directors have been unwilling to fix the price for a license, except in rare instances."[11] The price they did establish was considered by some to be too high. Furthermore, the principal Edison Electric stockholders had established the Edison Illuminating Company of New York primarily as a promotional scheme to demonstrate the value of the system. By the time the first station opened they expected the central station business to grow without much effort on their part, as the isolated lighting business had. However, while the installation of a costly central station depended on local business interests pooling their resources, an individual firm could consider the purchase of a relatively inexpensive isolated plant in the same way it did other types of capital equipment. Isolated plants had shown that they could produce immediate profits, whereas Edison's vision of the central station remained a costly experiment. Edison Electric thus promoted the rapidly growing isolated business while allowing the central station business to lag until Edison decided to promote it himself.

In developing his system, Edison had given little thought to isolated lighting. As he told one prospective isolated customer in January 1881:

> You perhaps know that all my efforts have been and all my appliances are devised especially for the general distribution of electricity throughout a city to be sold by meter, and not for the lighting up of a single building hence I am at present moment at a slight disadvantage when asked to light up a single building. I could very much easier light up a square mile with 1500 to 2000 houses than I could a single building although that may seem a paradox to you.

However, the success of the *Columbia* installation and numerous requests for plants had convinced Edison and the light company financiers of the potential value of this new market, and he now expected "very soon to accommodate my system for isolated lighting."[12]

Just what Edison required to "accommodate" his isolated lighting system is suggested by the first annual report of the Edison Company for Isolated Lighting, which had been formed by some of the leading stockholders of Edison Electric Light Company in response to the growing demand for this business:

> When the company was formed a year ago [November 1881], the business of isolated lighting was entirely undeveloped, and no data existed whereby the future development of the business could be foretold. At that time Mr. Edison, was making but one size of isolated dynamo, namely the Z dynamo [based on the original bipolar design of 1879]; we had no reliable steam engine; the innumerable details relating to installations, such as fixtures, safety catches and other appliances, were still either unperfected or were not manufactured on any considerable scale.[13]

As a consequence of these developments, the growth of the electric lighting industry, so essential to the success of Edison's shops, was initially led by the isolated business. The effect of the new isolated business on the manufacturing plants was most marked at the Machine Works. In the fall of 1881 Edison had nearly 90 dynamos readied in anticipation of the new business. These expectations proved well founded. By April 1882 all but 18 of 264 sixty-light dynamos had been sold, and Insull informed Batchelor that the Works had "been running with little [financial] support from T.A.E. all this year. Their debts are not even $30,000. My only fear is that Edison may order things in advance of requirements & if so will put him in the same hole financially as he has just got out of as in such a case the machine works will draw on him heavily."[14] This fear proved unfounded, and in September 1882, when the Machine Works had a backlog of over 130 dynamos worth nearly $140,000, Insull was pleased to tell Batchelor that "instead of losing money here now as heretofore there is some slight amount being made. Edison has taken out of the business $38,000 and you have been credited on my books with $3800 being 10% of same." They anticipated an additional dividend of $40,000 once all the machines in stock were sold.[15]

During 1882 the Machine Works began manufacturing a full range of dynamos for different size plants. With the help of Charles Clarke, Edison designed 150-, 250-, and 500-light machines to supply a growing isolated business for large factories. Many of these were for textile mills, where gaslight posed a serious fire risk. As one mill owner remarked, "I expect the difference in insurance rates will pay the whole expense inside of two years."[16] The safety fuse designed for the *Columbia* proved to be an important feature of the Edison system and was effectively used by the Edison companies to compete with gaslight. In August 1882 the Isolated Company had to establish a New England department to handle the growing textile mill business. By the beginning of 1883 there were more than 150 isolated plants in the United States and Canada, over 100 in Europe, and a dozen or so in Chile and Cuba. Most of these were in mills and factories, but many hotels, stores, theaters, railway stations, steamships, and shipyards had the new lighting plants, as did the residences of several wealthy individuals, including J. P. Morgan.

The growth of the European isolated business was a direct result of Edison's successful exhibit at the International Electrical Exhibition in Paris during the summer of 1881. Edison's exhibit had been managed by Charles Batchelor, who remained in Paris to direct Edison's European operations. The superiority of Edison's system was readily apparent even to those who had been most critical of him. William Preece's glowing praise was not only typical of many of their comments, but also particularly gratifying to Edison:

> The completeness of Mr. Edison's exhibit was certainly the most noteworthy object in the exhibition. Nothing seems to have been forgotten, no detail missed. . . . Mr. Edison's system has been worked out in detail, with a thoroughness and mastery of the subject that can extract nothing but eulogy from his bitterest opponents. Many unkind things have been said of Mr. Edison and his promises; perhaps no one has been severer in this direction than myself. It is some gratification for me to be able to announce my belief that he has at last solved the problem that he set himself to solve.[17]

Edison's exhibit had been paid for by the Edison Electric Light Company of Europe, which had been formed in January 1880 through the efforts of James Banker after he acquired an interest in the European rights from Edison and his European agents, Theodore Puskas and Joshua Bailey, who subsequently became the company's agents as well. Having seen his European telephone companies forced into consolidations with those of other inventors, Edison urged Banker and others to form a large syndicate for Europe that could capitalize a company to manufacture and operate his light on the Continent. Edison wanted the manufacturing company run by his own men so "there would be no doubt about the technical success of the enterprise and if the technical success is assured the commercial success would naturally follow and the whole thing would be a success while most inventions sent over there have been just the opposite."[18]

Through the efforts of Puskas and Bailey in association with Grosvenor Lowrey, who was in Paris for the Exhibition, the Edison interests attracted the support of Paris financiers Charles Porges and Elie Léon, who organized a large syndicate of European banking houses and established the Compagnie Continentale in February 1882. This company assumed control of the European business and began to license companies in other European countries after acquiring patent rights from the European Edison Company, which retained the right to veto all contracts. The Paris syndicate also formed the Société Electrique to market isolated plants and the Société Industrielle to manufacture the system. To satisfy Edison's desire for control of the manufacturing operations, Charles Batchelor was placed in charge of the Paris factory. He also became engineer of the other two companies and supervised the European isolated business. Indeed, as Batchelor himself noted, "My job here is no fool of a job what with *lamps*, dynamos, chandeliers, and all the extras, I am just in up to my neck; then I have so much outside work of such a responsible nature and involving so much money, that I *wear a hat about three sizes larger* than when I left New York."[19]

Batchelor's importance to the enterprise was indicated by a remark he made to Edison in a March 1883 letter: "Everything goes well as long as I continually boost it but if I should leave here before we have a Central Station working [in] Paris I really believe it would go to the devil."[20] Indeed, after he returned to New York in spring 1884 the Paris station was abandoned. Up to that time the Compagnie Continentale had had some success establishing agencies in many of the leading European cities. The company also signed contracts that led to the establishment of the German firm Deutsche Edison Gesselschaft, which was organized by Emil Rathenau and associated with the major German electrical manufacturer Siemens & Halske. Within a few years this would become the most important of the European Edison companies.

While Batchelor was successfully installing isolated stations throughout Europe, the European central station business moved much more slowly. The first was started in Milan, Italy, in 1883, and other stations soon followed in

Rotterdam and St. Petersburg. Plans also went forward for a Berlin station, but delays in establishing a Paris station frustrated Batchelor, as did growing differences with Porges over the management of the European business. Before Batchelor left, however, he found a new manager for the Société Industrielle and most important, he found a new financier to take over the management of the Paris companies, which were consolidated in a reorganized Compagnie Continentale.

In establishing his foreign enterprises Edison tended to rely on trusted agents in those countries, and the companies they formed had only limited connections to his U.S.-based operations. Neither Edison nor his business associates seem to have considered bringing the European enterprises together into a single multinational business, although Drexel Morgan's interest in Edison's foreign patents and their international banking connections might have logically led to such an enterprise. Edison, in fact, had hoped that Drexel Morgan would "endeavor to get the control of the European Co. when they see the first district is going to be a success."[21] However, even though the firm's Paris branch, Drexel Harjes & Company, was involved in the Compagnie Continentale, Drexel Morgan was satisfied to focus its efforts in Britain and the United Kingdom.

To promote the Edison light in Great Britain, Drexel Morgan had funded an exhibit at the London Crystal Palace Exhibition in the spring of 1882. Edison again sent Johnson, who had previously spent a year and a half in London promoting the Edison telephone, to London to organize the exhibit. Working with him was William Hammer, one of the many young men who had joined the Menlo Park staff in late 1879 and one of the first people to perceive the potential of electric lighting as commercial display. Johnson's success can be judged by the reaction of the *London Daily News*: "Mr. Edison is far and away in advance of all rivals. . . . His exhibition is the wonder of the show, and his representative is certainly the prince of all showmen. There is but one Edison and Johnson is his prophet."[22] As Batchelor promoted and protected Edison's interests in Paris, Edward Johnson performed the same task in London.

Johnson also was in charge of another impressive exhibit of Edison's system. During the first weeks of 1882 he installed a central station on the Holborn Viaduct in London. This location had been chosen in part because of its proximity to the city's financial and newspaper centers and to the General Post Office. The main reason, however, was the difficulty the company found obtaining permission to lay wires underground. By choosing the viaduct they could hang the wires underneath. This also greatly reduced the time needed for the installation. The viaduct became a testing ground for the several elements of the New York station, including the steam dynamos, safety fuses, and regulating devices. Although Holborn was the first commercial central station in the world, it was intended to be only a temporary demonstration station that would be superseded by more permanent installations in the city.

   The opening of the Holborn Viaduct station and the Crystal Palace display spurred the formation of the London company that Morgan partner Egisto Fabbri had begun negotiations for in 1881. Johnson became chief engineer of the Edison Electric Light Company Ltd. after it was formed in March. The Edison company was one of nearly twenty companies formed during the spring as investor enthusiasm created a great deal of speculation in light company stocks. By summer, however, the bubble had burst and it became difficult for light companies to get financing. At the same time, Parliament passed legislation that favored municipal ownership of electrical lighting companies, and the price of gas in London was low. These conditions combined to slow the development of the new industry in Britain for several years. The Edison company was also plagued by conflict between Johnson and company secretary Andrew White, who managed the firm. White felt that the great competition between lighting companies for isolated plants had proved ruinous, and according to Johnson he let many contracts fall to competitors. Johnson felt that this contributed to the company's poor financial condition, which prevented it from moving more quickly to develop the central station business. Although Johnson effected a change in management during the first half of 1883, the London financiers forced a merger with the Swan United Electric Light Company Ltd. out of concern over what they perceived as British inventor Joseph Swan's strong patent position in regard to the lamp.[23]

   Joseph Swan was a successful manufacturer and chemist who had first experimented with incandescent lamps in 1848, when Edison was only one year old. He experimented sporadically on electric lights until 1877, when he began a full-time investigation in partnership with Charles Stearn. Although his earlier experiments had included attempts to use charred paper in vacuum, his experiments between 1877 and 1879 focused on slender carbon rods in vacuum. He successfully demonstrated a lamp of this type before the Newcastle Library and Philosophical Society in February 1873. An account of Swan's work was also published in the July 12, 1879 issue of *Scientific American*. Because Edison turned to carbon in October 1879, soon after the article appeared, a cause-and-effect relationship has long been assumed. However, the undated notebook in which Edison made note of the *Scientific American* article is one of several that he began using in January 1881. Furthermore, Edison was most interested in fact that Swan used *"Cylinder* carbon." His subsequent investigations of Swan's work, including reading the original *Journal of the Chemical Society of Newcastle* article, convinced Edison that Swan "knew nothing about the value of high resistance or a flexible filament of carbon." Swan himself believed that he had anticipated Edison in regard to the carbon lamp, but appreciated "that Edison is entitled to more than I . . . he has seen further into this subject, vastly than I, and foreseen and provided for details that I did not comprehend until I saw his system."[24] From the standpoint of the Edison Electric Light Company Ltd., an even more significant patent dispute concerned the two inventors' patents for vacuum treatment of the filament. Edison's failure to include his process in his original British carbon lamp patent had allowed Swan to receive a patent on this prior to Edison; the company's lawyers feared that this "might prevent us from Manufacturing Lamps in which this process is employed." Questions about whether Edison's patents would be sustained only confirmed Edison's views that the British "have a beautiful system of patent law invented I think by King Canute or some other ancient ruler who understood the needs of our times," in which the "only advantage gained by taking out Patents at all is that you have the privilege of paying heavy fees to the British Government."[25]

There were, however, other good reasons to consider a merger between the two companies. Swan was an experienced chemist and manufacturer who produced a process for making filaments from squirted cellulose that created a more uniform fiber structure than occurred naturally in the bamboo used by Edison. Improvements in squirted cellulose filaments would make them superior for lamps, but in 1883 Upton reported unfavorably on Swan's lamps following tests by the Edison Lamp Company. The Swan company was also the British Edison company's most important competitor. Finally, Swan himself had the respect of the British financial and technical communities, and the Edison company, which desperately needed new funds, found that "the moneyed class won't give us £100 much less £250,000 while we are at loggerheads with Swan."[26] After a concerted effort, the London company finally convinced Edison, who reluctantly agreed to the merger. It took place in October 1883.

Several months before this merger Edison had already determined "that our London friends think they can get on better without us. If so the best thing is to let them do so and to give our attention to the 'Western Empire' alone." He therefore told Johnson to "do the best you can to get through by the end of this month [March 1883] and then come right back here as there is plenty to do and few to do it." At the time Edison was preparing to actively push the central station business in the United States. He wanted Johnson to "hurry back as we want your assistance. We *know* there is plenty of money to be made in our business in this country and that here we can get things done just as we say, and I therefore think it is best to concentrate our efforts on an *American certainty* rather than an English possibility."[27]

At the time that Edison wrote to Johnson the New York station had been in operation for six months, and Edison was growing impatient with Edison Electric's failure to promote the central station business. During 1882, while the New York station was still being finished but after Johnson had successfully started the Holborn Viaduct station, Edison had urged Eaton to appoint an agent "to visit the different cities & work up the local companies."[28] While Eaton negotiated with local interests from other cities who approached the company, he did not make a special effort to work up the business. Edison therefore decided in March 1883 "that if the business is to be made a success it must be by our personal efforts and not by depending upon the officials of our companies." He announced that he was "going to be simply a business man for a year. I am now a regular contractor for electric light plants, and I am going to take a long vacation in the matter of inventions. I won't go near a laboratory." That same month, when he wrote Johnson to urge him to return from England to help with the new business, Edison explained that "we are doing all we can to rush the Village business. There is immediate money and plenty of it in the business and I propose getting up some big Syndicates in order to boom the business, and by this means provide work for our shops."[29]

The village system had emerged during the work on the Pearl Street station, when it became apparent that the expense and time consumed in the underground system would severely inhibit its use in any but the largest cities. Because the houses in most towns and villages were scattered over a wide area, Edison felt that distributing the current by underground conductors would be too expensive. Therefore, to reduce the cost of conductors, Edison designed a village system in which the wires were strung on poles rather than being placed underground. He also used 330 volts in the system rather than the 110 employed at Pearl Street, and he grouped three lamps together in a series circuit rather than placing them individually in parallel circuits, although this meant that a single lamp could not be turned on and off by itself. The first central station based on this design opened in Roselle, New Jersey, on January 19, 1883.[30]

Although he considered this system adequate for a small town such as Roselle, Edison felt that it would prove inadequate for a large manufacturing town such as Lawrence, Massachusetts, where a group of leading citizens had recently organized an illuminating company and was negotiating with Eaton for a central station. Edison therefore developed an alternative plan that soon became the standard for central station design. Two months after the Pearl Street station opened for business, Edison executed a patent for what became known as the three-wire distribution system "in which currents of high tension can be used, while at the same time each lamp is entirely independent of all the others."[31] In the simplest design, two generators were arranged in series to provide 220 volts in the outside wires and a neutral wire in between the generators acted as a compensating conductor. The distributing wire carried positive currents from one side of the generators and the return wire on the other side carried negative currents. The middle wire carried either positive or negative currents depending on which side of the circuit had fewer lamps in use. In effect this design enabled Edison to arrange his lamps in series of two while still allowing them to be used independently of each other. This design was arrived at almost simultaneously by Edison, by the British engineer John Hopkinson, who worked as a consultant for the London Edison company, and by the Anglo-German electrical inventor William Siemens. Although Hopkinson's British patent of July 1882 was the first for this design, Edison was confident that he would be upheld as the original inventor in the United States as "I can go away behind Hopkinsons first English date so there is not fear of his beating me on interference if one should at any time be desired."[32]

Having decided that he would have to market these village and small-city systems himself, Edison established the Thomas A. Edison Construction Department. On March 13, 1883, he had corresponded with banker George W. Ballou regarding "the matter of lighting small cities and towns by electricity" in an apparent effort to find outside capital for the business, but he ended up financing the venture himself as an unincorporated company. Edison had planned on Edward Johnson's help in running the business, but the latter decided to remain in London to "put [a finish] on this last transatlantic job of mine." Edison turned instead to another close and trusted assistant, his private secretary Samuel Insull, to whom he gave the power "to sign contracts for the erection of Edison Electric Light Installations to receive payments and give receipts for same to make settlements and transact any other business whatsoever appertaining to my Central Station Construction Department."[33] Insull handled most of the business affairs of the company while Edison concentrated on its technical operations.

Although only twenty one years old when he joined Edison in March 1881, Insull had quickly become one of the inventor's most trusted assistants. He had come from London upon the recommendation of Johnson, who was impressed by the way the young man served as George Gouraud's private secretary. Edison, too, was impressed by the boyish looking Insull, who recalled that Edison soon gave him considerable authority over his affairs, "from buying his clothes to financing his business."[34] Like Edison's former secretary Stockton Griffin, Insull took care of Edison's voluminous correspondence. However, he also redefined the position of private secretary to the great inventor. Insull was soon handling all of Edison's personal financial affairs, and by 1883 he had primary responsibility for the shops' finances and was consulted on even minor financial matters. To ensure Edison's interests, he was also placed on the board of directors or made secretary of the other Edison electric light companies.

Alfred Tate, who worked under Insull in the Construction Department and later replaced him as Edison's private secretary, provides one of the most insightful characterizations:

> His devotion to business almost constituted a religion. He permitted nothing to interfere with his duties towards the interests he was handling. . . . He loved power and gloried in the exercise of authority. He was highly appreciative of the aid rendered him by his subordinates but never praised them to their faces. Commendation of this nature he might express to a third person, but in his direct relationship he seemed to think that sustained criticism was the most effective spur towards efficiency.[35]

Another early associate said of him, "Yes he was able, but too confident in his ability to do most anything and in the correctness of his judgment, when he ought to have consulted others to get their opinion."[36] These traits did not always endear him to others in the Edison businesses, but Insull was absolutely loyal to his employer and constantly sought to further his interests.

Insull's loyalty and willingness for hard work led him to adapt readily to Edison's irregular and demanding schedule:

I used to more often get at him at night than in the day time, as it left my days free for me to transact his affairs and enabled me probably at a midnight luncheon to get a few minutes of his time to look over his correspondence and get his directions as to what I should do in some particular negotiation of finance. This arrangement might result in my visiting him at Menlo Park or at Goerck street or in Bergmann's shop, or wherever the necessities of the moment compelled him to give attention to experimental work. I think it rather grew to be a habit for me to transact my business with him at night time. If for any particular reason he was spending his time regularly at the office at 65 Fifth avenue during the day he made a practice, and consequently so did I, of spending the evening there as well.[37]

Their "midnight luncheons" usually took place at Edison's favorite restaurant, Delmonico's, which was conveniently located on the corner of Fourteenth Street and Fifth Avenue near the Edison Electric Light Company headquarters at 65 Fifth Avenue. Insull shared Edison's office at 65 Fifth Avenue and also slept in one of the bedrooms provided on the third floor for some of the "boys" who had moved from Menlo Park into the city.

Edison established the Construction Department as an independent company to promote and install central stations using the Edison system. But he operated out of 65 Fifth Avenue and coordinated its efforts with those of the Edison Electric Light Company and the Isolated Company. Although Edison and Insull were principally responsible for negotiations with the local illuminating companies, Sherbourne Eaton also played an important role. In his capacity as president of Edison Electric, Eaton could license companies in cities with gas systems; as president of the Isolated Company, he was responsible for stations built in towns without gas service. Eaton also kept a watchful eye on the installation and operation of these stations. In exchange for its license the local illuminating companies paid the parent company 20 percent of their total capital stock as shares and 5 percent in cash. The local illuminating companies had to sign a separate contract with Edison to have his Construction Department install the plant and operate it for thirty days; Edison supplied all materials and equipment at 12 percent over cost. The local companies agreed to pay Edison 25 percent of the installation price at the time the agreement was signed, 50 percent when the station was completed, and the final 25 percent thirty days after the station was started. Because so much of his own money was invested in the construction business Edison preferred these payments in cash rather than stock, although he sometimes had to accept the latter.[38]

To "form local companies for us and influence local capital to go into our business in competition with their local gas companies" Edison and Insull relied on local agents, including several Isolated Company agents who were already knowledgeable about conditions in their regions, to contract new work and to provide information about competitors.[39] Spencer Borden, who headed the Isolated Company's New England division, and P. B. Shaw, who became the agent for Pennsylvania and parts of Ohio, were particularly effective as agents for the Construction Department. Ohio also was marketed by Archibald B. Stuart, who established the Ohio Edison Electric Installation Company. Although not paid salaries, the agents were rewarded with "a liberal share [usually 10%] of such stock and cash as our parent company receives for the license they give the local company."[40]

To help promote his system and find markets for his stations, Edison sent canvassers to survey towns and collect data that could be used in estimating the cost of a station. The canvassers had to find a one-mile square district, preferably a mix of residences and businesses, that would make the station profitable. They then did a street-by-street canvass similar to those done for the Pearl Street district to provide Edison with information about each potential customer. Because most of these towns would use overhead wires, he also had them record information about trees and telephone and telegraph lines that might interfere with his own lines. The canvassers recorded this information in log books and also transferred the data to street maps that were then sent to the Construction Department offices for use in preparing plans and estimates for the station.

The data from the canvass reports were used by the Construction Department mappers to determine the circuit arrangements for the proposed lighting district and then prepare maps of the system. Originally the determinations were made by Hermann Claudius and a small staff located at the Menlo Park laboratory. As he had done for Pearl Street, Claudius made his determinations by constructing small-scale models of the distribution system. However, by the end of 1883 Edison had dismissed Claudius and placed Frank Sprague in charge of these determinations after Sprague, according to a later account, showed him "how to calculate the drop in feeders without laying out a whole city in miniature, determining in a few hours what had previously required weeks of experimental work and a considerable financial outlay."[41]

Sprague was one of the new breed of mathematically trained engineers who contributed so extensively to the development of electric light and power in the United States. Educated at the U.S. Naval Academy in Annapolis, Sprague had been secretary to the Crystal Palace jury and was in charge of its dynamo tests. He then worked for Edward Johnson as a consultant on electric lighting matters in London, and provided an analysis of Hopkinson's three-wire system that may well have influenced Edison's own patent on this system.[42] Johnson recommended Sprague to Edison as an expert on electric railways, but Edison hired him instead as an electrical expert for the new Construction Department. Along with his work making electrical determinations, Sprague also helped with the engineering design of central stations and developed improvements in elements such as switches. He was one of the men Edison relied on to take charge of the actual installation of the central stations. Sprague was involved with two of the most important three-wire stations built by the Construction Department, assisting Edison with the first overhead system at Sunbury, Pennsylvania, and taking charge of the installation of the first underground system at Brockton, Massachusetts.

Another key figure in the Construction Department was William Andrews, who had joined the Menlo Park staff in December 1879 and later succeeded Francis Jehl as head of the Machine Works testing department. At the testing room Andrews had been in charge of the first tests of a small-scale version of Edison's three-wire system. By the time Edison started the Construction Department he had come to rely on Andrews's advice and ideas about system components and in November 1883 appointed him chief engineer. Andrews also assisted Edison with the Sunbury station, which was the first station built by the Construction Department as well as the first one to use the overhead three-wire system, and he supervised the construction of several others.

Edison himself supervised all the technical work and approved all decisions dealing with station design. Nonetheless, with the Construction Department Edison was for the first time actually running a business, and he had to rely on others to tackle many of the technical problems that he would have previously reserved for himself. Edison also relied on his engineers to take charge of station installations (except the Sunbury station, which he personally supervised because of its experimental status as the first three-wire station). He did examine the work at all these stations during installation and was available to help out with any special problems. Although Edison had great confidence in Andrews, Sprague, and W. D. Rich, who was in charge of station construction, he found it more difficult to rely on the engineers employed by the local illuminating companies to operate the stations once they opened for business.

The inexperience of these local engineers was not the only source of difficulty at these stations. Inexperienced workers were also used to do the wiring inside of buildings. Initially, Bergmann & Company had set up a wiring department for this purpose, but by September 1883 wiring was being placed in the hands of local contractors, often plumbers, who were instructed by Construction Department employees. In contrast, the more crucial outside wiring was entirely under the control of Edison employees, and all underground work was supervised by John Kruesi and the Electric Tube Company. Edison's employees, under the direction of H. Ward Leonard, also installed the meters and trained employees of the local companies on how to take exact measurements with them.

The lack of trained electrical engineers threatened to seriously hamper the development of the new industry and led Edison to take steps to remedy the situation. He had discussed the establishment of an electrical engineering program at Columbia University and offered school officials his electric lighting plant from the Paris Exhibition, but they also wanted him to provide the rest of the money required to establish the program. Other colleges also asked Edison's assistance in establishing electrical engineering education, but no programs were established before he set up his Construction Department. As

Edison set out to build up the central station business he found his work "seriously retarded by my inability to obtain competent engineers" and turned the Goerck Street testing room into a school complete with examinations.[43] Edison, with assistance from others in the Construction Department, took charge of developing a set of instructions and test questions for local station engineers while Charles Clarke set up a school at 65 Fifth Avenue for other employees of the Edison companies and prepared a small textbook for them. Such schools were typical of the early electric light industry.

While Edison handled the technical operations of the Construction Department, Samuel Insull brought the work of its employees under his tight control. Ever reluctant to delegate authority, he ordered "that all correspondence of the Construction Department is to be conducted through my office."[44] His office also handled all orders for supplies and equipment for the central station installations. Insull was never reluctant to criticize those who failed to follow his orders, and he criticized even the engineers when he felt they overstepped their bounds. Thus, he sent Frank Sprague a letter under Edison's name that chided him for making suggestions directly to the president of the Brockton illuminating company and ordered him to make any future suggestions through his office only. Sprague, recognizing that the letter was written by Insull, complained to Edison about its "unnecessary sarcasm and criticism" and told Edison that he recognized "but one head to the Edison system, and that head is the originator."[45] Sprague was not the only one who felt Insull had too much influence over Edison's affairs. Francis Upton, for example, found himself exasperated by Insull's control over Edison's financial interests and the constant juggling of money due the manufacturing companies from Edison's central station business. Although he demanded "that definite instructions be given regarding the responsibility in the financial concerns of the Lamp Co, as regards meeting various obligations as they become due," Edison made no change in Insull's authority over financial matters.[46] Edison's trust in Insull was evident when he left him entirely in charge of the Construction Department business during February and March 1884 while he went to Florida with his family for a vacation.

Soon after Edison returned from Florida it became apparent that the Construction Department was too much of a financial drain on him, and he began negotiations with Edison Electric to reorganize the business. While on vacation Edison asked Insull to see what Eaton was doing about "putting agents all over the country to get these towns started."[47] And Insull himself worked diligently to increase the number of estimates in hopes of getting more contracts. However, by the time Edison returned the number of signed contracts was insufficient for him to continue to carry the business by himself. Even with additional contracts it is unclear whether he could have continued on his own; too much money had to be expended by the Construction Department before it received any return. Even before any contracts were signed, canvasses and estimates had to be undertaken. An account from November 1883 showed that the

Construction Department spent about $10,400 canvassing and estimating for eighty cities and towns but had contracted for only twelve stations. Although Edison appears to have been reimbursed by Edison Electric and the Isolated Company for some of these expenses, they were nonetheless substantial. Edison also had to pay much of the construction cost of the stations before receiving reimbursement from the local illuminating companies, and he found it difficult to collect final payment from many of them once they began operating the stations themselves.[48]

By the end of April Edison found himself in "a very bad hole" and asked William Andrews to try to collect the payment for the Piqua, Ohio, station as soon as he started operation there. Although he supposed that Andrews would say there was "nothing new" in these financial difficulties, Edison had already decided he could no longer afford to continue the Construction Department.[49] On April 24, he wrote Eaton:

> Owing to the fact that I am rapidly finishing up the outstanding work in connection with the Construction Department and that the agents of the Light Company are not forming any new Companies and that in consequence I am not getting new contracts I find myself in the position of being obligated to immediately disband my organization as the expenses in connection with it are too large to allow of my continuing it unless I have work in hand.
>
> I very much regret being compelled to take this course, and in as much as it has been suggested that the Isolated Company should take in hand the work now being performed by the Construction Dept. I would suggest that the matter be considered and an immediate decision arrived at.[50]

Eaton called together Edison, Insull, Edward Johnson, and Francis Upton to work out the details of the takeover of central station business by the Isolated Company. As Edison began trimming his work force, Eaton also agreed to have Edison Electric pay the salaries of those members of the Construction Department engineering staff whom Edison considered "indispensable to the business" so as not to lose their training and experience.[51] At the beginning of September the Isolated Company took over the entire central station business, including those plants built within gas territory, and Edward Johnson became company president.

The change in the central station business was only part of a larger reorganization of the Edison lighting companies that took place during 1884. The driving force behind the reorganization effort was Sherbourne Eaton, who had been urging Edison Electric's directors to consolidate the business and take over the manufacturing shops since his 1882 annual report. He renewed this effort in January 1884 with a letter to the company's directors calling for "proper economy, and a wiping out of all interests that, in the nature of things are antagonistic to the best welfare of the several companies."[52] He wanted to form a large new company that would merge Edison Electric, the New York Illuminating Company, and the Isolated Company. He argued that the Edison lighting business required coordination to beat its competitors in the market and to challenge their use of Edison's patents in the courts. He also renewed his efforts to bring the manufacturing shops into this new company. In doing so he pointed to what he considered the natural antagonism between the interests of the shops and those of Edison Electric. Edison and his partners, however, believed that these interests coincided and that any antagonism was the result of Edison Electric's failure to appreciate the contribution the shops had made to the business. As Eaton pushed forward with his efforts at reorganization, deep-seated differences with Edison and his partners soon precipitated a battle for control of the Edison lighting business.

The antagonism between Edison Electric and the manufacturing shops had been growing from the moment the company had declined to take an interest in establishing the factories. Although Eaton had come to appreciate that manufacturing represented both a business of "great importance" to the future of Edison Electric and a source of "great profit," Edison and his partners could hardly have been pleased when his 1882 annual report urged the company's directors to consider taking over the shops.[53] The directors seriously considered Eaton's proposal, but Edison and his partners merely wanted "to obtain a more satisfactory definition of our relations as manufacturers."[54] The subsequent negotiations over manufacturing licenses brought to the surface the antagonistic interests to which Eaton would refer the following year. Eaton refused to consider granting exclusive manufacturing licenses to the shops, and Upton considered the proposed Lamp Company agreement to be "poor as protecting the Lamp Co. from the Light Co. breaking the contract." In fact, he did not believe Eaton and Lowrey "intend to give us any contract but one that they can drive through in the future . . . they never intend to tie the Light Co's hands to any one place to get lamps." He considered Edison Electric to be a "soulless corporation" that wanted to reap all the profits after the shops had taken all the risk.[55]

When negotiations broke off at the beginning of February 1883 similar sentiments were expressed by Edison and his partners in a letter to Eaton. They complained that the negotiations seemed "to breed nothing but hostility and suspicion on the part of those gentlemen who represent the [Company], they apparently being wholly unable to see anything in our actions but an ulterior design upon them." Furthermore, they felt that the sentiment expressed by the directors that "'they should like to feel that Mr. Edison's interests were identical with theirs and not antagonistic,' does not only him, but the rest of us a great injustice." The directors failed to appreciate that Edison and his partners had not only taken all the risk after the company declined to be involved in manufacturing, but also "invested more money in our various factories than has yet been put into the business of developing the system in other directions." Believing that further negotiations would only "foster the suspicions which are already too apparent," they told Eaton that they would withdraw from the negotiations and "allow matters to remain as they are."[56]

When Eaton renewed his effort to consolidate the shops the following year, Edison and his partners made it clear that they would resist any such effort. A series of negotiations between Lowrey and Charles Coster (a Drexel Morgan partner) on behalf of Edison Electric and Edison and his associates eventually produced a reorganization plan that left the shops as independent organizations, allowed them to incorporate to better protect the interests of the partners, and provided exclusive manufacturing licenses. The manufacturing agreements, signed at the beginning of September, did allow Edison Electric to license other manufacturers under certain conditions and limited the profit that the shops could make. Edison Electric also received the right of first purchase to any company stock that was sold and to all patents obtained by the shops. Under the rest of the reorganization plan, also carried out in September, Edward Johnson was placed in control of the Isolated Company, which also took over the central station business. Sherbourne Eaton was to remain as president of Edison Electric, but he would "put his energies entirely into prosecuting suits etc," leaving Johnson in charge of sales and promotion of the Edison system.[57]

Although the reorganization was to a large extent very favorable to Edison and his manufacturing partners, they decided to wage a proxy fight at the stockholders' meeting in October and acquire control of Edison Electric. They probably acted in part to ensure the security of the new contractual relationship between their shops and the company. Grosvenor Lowrey, one of the company's directors who was replaced at the meeting, suggested as much in a letter to Edison in which he complained "that after all this wrangling the other members of the board would [not] have passed those contracts if they had known or suspected that their complicated provisions were to be interpreted by a new board controlled by the interests on the other side of the contract."[58] That Edison did not trust the existing management of the company is apparent in a letter from Insull to Tate in which he noted that Johnson would "have full control of business" while a figurehead would be put in as company president, which "will certainly put Mr. Edison in a much better humor, and enable him to go ahead on other things."[59]

Another cause of the takeover appears to have been the growing distrust of Eaton and some of the Edison Electric directors by the manufacturing partners. What Eaton called the naturally antagonistic self-interests of corporate officers and manufacturing partners had developed into personal antagonisms, particularly on the part of Samuel Insull. Insull's role as the manager of Edison's business affairs had brought him into conflict with Sherbourne Eaton as the latter sought to coordinate the business of the Edison lighting companies. Ironically, Insull's dislike of Eaton stemmed in part from the Edison Electric president's criticisms of the way in which Insull provided him with information from Edison's office and his management of the Construction Department, complaints that Insull himself frequently made of his own subordinates (although Insull probably did not consider himself to be Eaton's subordinate).

When it became clear that Eaton would be replaced, Insull gloated to Alfred Tate,

> The renowned and illustrious S. B. Eaton retires on this Tuesday next. . . . The controversy has been compromised by the Light Co. cutting out all their objectionable men and electing the men nominated on Mr. Edison's ticket. . . . Thus you see I am at last getting even. I have often told you that I would, and that the great "Mogul" in the back room would have to clear out. . . . Eaton disappears from the business entirely. . . . You can imagine my feelings. There is no one more anxious after wealth than Samuel Insull, but there are times when revenge is sweeter than money, and I have got mine at last.[60]

Although Edison clashed with Eaton over his experimental accounts and may have seen criticisms of Insull's management of the Construction Department as indirect criticism of himself, he did not develop the same personal animosity toward him as did Insull. Eaton remained connected with Edison Electric as general counsel, continued to act as president of the Edison Electric Light Company of Europe, and became Edison's personal attorney four years later.

Whatever personal reasons drove the contest for control of Edison Electric, real differences existed regarding the effort to promote the Edison system. Edison clearly thought that lawyers Eaton and Lowrey were too cautious in their approach to the business. As he told a reporter, "we want a Board with less law and more business." The telegraph investors who had formed Edison Electric had substantial experience with the use of new inventions to modify an existing system of technology but not with the type of innovation required to introduce an entirely new system. The Drexel Morgan partners, too, had no experience with innovation, and in fact were much more interested in promoting industrial consolidation as a way of making the new industry a safe investment. Edison's goal was to make the company more innovative. "I have worked eighteen and twenty hours a day for five years," he told a reporter, "and I don't want to see my work killed for want of proper pushing."[61] Edison's approach to remaking the company, which drew on his long experience as a proprietary manager and relied on close personal relationships, was in many ways similar to that of a modern entrepreneurial firm where personal management plays a more important role than bureaucratic organization.

To gain control of the company, Edison and his partners had to challenge the stockholder interests associated with Drexel Morgan. Although these stockholders were powerful enough to contest Edison's effort to gain control of the company, Drexel Morgan came "to the conclusion that the most graceful thing to do is to give Edison what he wants."[62] They understood his importance to the company as inventor and manufacturer and feared that a challenge would alienate him and undermine the Edison lighting business. Furthermore, the leadership he had shown in establishing the manufacturing shops and promoting the central station business to the benefit of the Edison interests made it much easier for them to allow him to try his hand at running the entire business.

Edison himself was confident that Pierpont Morgan considered him a man with "ideas of business" capable of "conduct[ing] several large manufacturing establishments besides superintending the installation of the Light here, having no small say in the policy of the various companies & conducting experiments on half a dozen widely different subjects all at the same time."[63] Nonetheless, he and Morgan held very different views regarding business strategy. Edison trusted self-interested management by personal associates and free market competition whereas Morgan was a leading proponent of industrial consolidation and centralized corporate management to limit competition and provide a safe environment for investors. Their differing views on the nature of business organization and competition eventually would challenge the leadership of Edison and his managers.

Now that his close associates were in charge of the Edison lighting business, Edison was able to turn his attention to matters closer to his heart. His withdrawal from business gave him time to attend to family matters following the unexpected death of his wife in August 1884. Indeed, her death may have been one of the factors that led him to engage in the proxy fight for control of Edison Electric. With Edward Johnson running the Edison lighting business, his former laboratory assistants in charge of the manufacturing shops, and Samuel Insull representing him on the Board of Directors of the Edison companies as well as handling all his personal business affairs, Edison could spend time with his children and go through the process of grieving for his loss. At the same time, he could return to his first love—the laboratory—which doubtless proved a source of refuge from grief over his wife's death.

CHAPTER 13

Family Matters

E dison certainly felt a sense of loss from his wife's death. His daughter Marion recalled finding her father "shaking with grief, weeping and sobbing so he could hardly tell me that Mother had died in the night." He may also have felt a sense of guilt for the long, hard hours he had worked at the expense of his family. During 1881 and 1882 Edison had spent most of his time working on the problems associated with his new lighting system and the installation of the Pearl Street central station. He spent not only his days but also many of his nights working on technical problems. He barely found time to discuss business matters and answer his correspondence during midnight lunches with Samuel Insull, let alone spend time with his wife and children. Edison's frantic pace hardly let up during the year he operated the Construction Department. Besides continuing efforts to improve the technical operations of his system, Edison also traveled to meet with officers and investors in the local lighting companies and to inspect and consult on the installation of their stations. Although he did compromise with Mary by devoting certain periods of the year to family vacations, Edison spent relatively little time with his family on a daily basis. Marion recalled that "seeing my Father on Sunday was not enough for Mother."[1]

Although New York was a bustling city, it may at first have seemed even more isolating for Mary than Menlo Park, which had begun to become a community of families as well as workmen. When Edison first opened his famous laboratory only the Edison, Batchelor, and Kruesi families lived in Menlo Park. Over the years, however, they had seen Sarah Jordan and her daughter Ida move to Menlo Park, along with the families of several of Edison's assistants and machinists, including Francis Upton and Charles Dean. All of the wives, except for Lucy Upton, probably came from the same working- and lower-middle-class background as Mary. With the move to New York City, however, she found herself in a very different social circle.

Mary had no home to call her own in the city. After moving to New York City in February 1881 the Edisons first occupied rooms in the Lennox, a small family hotel across from the office at 65 Fifth Avenue. A few months later they moved to a fashionable brownstone annex to the Clarendon Hotel on Union Square, which was then the city's shopping and theater district. Marion recalled seeing some of the famous actresses of the day at the Clarendon. Edison and Mary had occasionally gone into New York City to see performances when they lived in Menlo Park, and Edison no doubt took advantage of this location to take his wife to the theater. They did not go as often as Edison might have liked because his deafness made "it hard for me to hear what the actors say."[2] However, when he could get a front-row seat so that he had no trouble hearing the music he was able to enjoy light opera such as Gilbert and Sullivan or opera *bouffe*. The occasional evening out, however, could not make up for the lack of time Edison spent with his wife and children.

Although Mary seems to have enjoyed the bustle of city life, she grew increasingly unhappy over her husband's constant attention to business and neglect of his family. In January 1882 she suffered another breakdown in her health, and family doctor Leslie Ward advised Edison that

> My experience in treating your wife has convinced me that her uterine troubles yield much more readily to treatment when her nervous system is in a fair condition. I have noticed during the past few weeks that she seems very nervous and despondent and thinks that she will never recover &c. I believe that an entire change would be of benefit and if you will take or send her to Europe for a few months she might return improved in health and be better pleased with her surroundings here. She seems so changed physically and mentally of late that something ought to be done and I can suggest nothing better than the above.[3]

Although Edison did not send Mary to Europe, he did take a break from his work to spend time with her in Florida during February and March. They liked to spend time in Palatka and in the health resort of St. Augustine. Although this region had a healthful environment, they found that it could be cool in the winter, and they also spent time in the warmer climes of Sanford, located farther south at the head of the navigable portion of the St. Johns River. Here Edison was able to enjoy hunting and fishing. These trips to Florida became an annual event, and according to Marion, "Mother was never happier than when we went to Florida, for then Father belonged entirely to her."[4] Edison also began taking his family on vacations to the seashore each summer. Even on vacation, however, he kept abreast of work in his laboratory and business affairs through letters and telegrams with Insull and his laboratory assistants.

After their St. Augustine vacation during the winter of 1882, the family returned to their home in Menlo Park and Edison spent much of the spring and summer experimenting at his laboratory. He also installed Insull and his patent attorney Richard Dyer in the office there. During the summer, however, Edison began to spend much of his time in the city, attending to the completion of the Pearl Street central station, and after the station opened he moved his family and office back to New York City. Life at Menlo Park had not been the same. The work of the laboratory had largely been transferred to the shops and the lamp factory had been moved to East Newark. The rural New Jersey village must have seemed even more lonely and isolated to Mary and probably held few attractions for her husband either. In September Edison took a two-year lease on a house at 25 Gramercy Lane, where he moved his family as well as the library from his Menlo Park office. He also decided to move his personal laboratory from Menlo Park to the top (fifth) floor of Bergmann & Company's new building at the corner of Seventeenth Street and Avenue B, leading Insull to write Batchelor, "Do you not think this looks very much as if he will never go back to Menlo Park again?" Although Edison told Insull that the move "was in consequence of the necessity of his being close to the central station. In the next breath he said he would never come near the city if it was not for the women constantly bothering him to do so. Johnson and myself are of the opinion that he wants to come in just as much as the women do."[5]

The Edison family's return to New York City was made more pleasant by the prospect of moving into a real home. Their new house was in a quiet and fashionable neighborhood of red brick and brownstone townhouses surrounding small and private Gramercy Park, whose high iron gates could be opened only by the wealthy residents who lived there. Located a few blocks uptown from Union Square, the exclusive Gramercy Park residence cost Edison $400 per month. His personal wealth was sufficient to pay such high rent, but Edison's ready cash was often tied up in his businesses. Insull was constantly struggling to balance Edison's finances and often delayed paying the rent on time, forcing landlord James Pryor to plead with him constantly for more prompt payment.[6]

The Edisons lived at Gramercy Park for only a year before Mary became so ill that the doctor ordered her to give up housekeeping. They again moved into the Clarendon Hotel and sublet the house to Baron Huppmann Valbella for $250 per month (leaving Edison to pay the rest of the rent and forcing Insull to ask the Clarendon to reduce the family's rent during their annual Florida vacation). By the time the family took its annual winter vacation in Florida Mary's health was much improved, but soon after their return her father became quite ill. On April 9 Edison had to send for a "trained man nurse who is not afraid of person out of mind" to come to their Menlo Park home to take care of his father-in-law.[7] Two days later Nicholas Stilwell was dead, and Edison canceled his appointments to spend the next few days consoling his wife. At the end of April they decided to move from the Clarendon Hotel back to the house on Gramercy Park. Apart from a brief illness at the end of April, when Mary complained that "my head is nearly splitting and my throat is very sore," she seems to have been in good health during the spring. However, sometime during the summer she again became ill and they returned to the house in Menlo Park where she died unexpectedly on August 9th. The actual cause of Mary's death is unknown, but her doctor attributed it to "congestion of the brain," and not typhoid fever as her daughter Marion later recalled.[8]

His wife's death left Edison a widower with three children. Mary's recently widowed mother Margaret, known to the children as "Grammach," eased the burden by keeping house for the family. Edison also assisted his wife's family financially and paid for the schooling of her youngest sister, Eugenia, as well. For a variety of reasons, the Edisons remained in Menlo Park only a short time after Mary's death before moving back to New York City, where they lived in a large flat at 39 East 18th Street with the very affordable rent of $1,300 per year. The Menlo Park house had been very much Mary's home and Edison's decision to leave Menlo Park was due in large measure to her death. There were, however, very practical reasons for moving as well. Edison's laboratory as well as his business operations were all in New York City. Most important, perhaps, the Menlo Park property was entangled in legal complications.[9]

The note that Edison had given Harrington in December 1874 had subsequently ended up in the hands of William Seyfert's wife, who sued Edison for payment. Edison refused to settle because he believed that the investors in Automatic Telegraph had not intended to hold him personally responsible for the note. To avoid having his Menlo Park property sold to the sheriff, he had placed it in Mary's name, but her death had upset those plans. He tried to claim that the laboratory was actually the property of the Edison Electric Light Company. He may also have tried to escape the clutches of New Jersey justice by moving to New York City. However, all of his efforts proved unsuccessful and the property was sold at a sheriff's auction, where it was bought by Charles Batchelor.[10]

Because her grandmother relieved Marion from taking on the role of female head of household, with responsibilities for the younger children and the housekeeping, Edison's daughter was able to become her father's almost constant companion. Marion recalled that during this period

> Father and I were inseparable. For the rest of the summer, once a week at least, I would drive him through the beautiful countryside. I felt instinctively that he did not want to talk and had more important things to think about. It seems wonderful now, if not at the time, that Father had so much time for me. He was interested in my clothes, diary, the novel I was going to write. He even had time to take me to the dentist. . . . I accompanied Father on all his trips, bought his cigars for him; being economy minded, even then, I saw no reason for buying Havana Cigars when he enjoyed five cent ones. I also took money to the banks and cashed checks for him, which made me feel very important as I was only twelve years old.[11]

Marion also accompanied her father to the International Electrical Exhibition in Philadelphia during the middle of September. The previous July Edison had experimented with an apparatus meant to produce electricity directly from anthracite coal, and he had hoped to display it at the exhibition, but he found it to be "extremely 'nasty' and dangerous." In these experiments he constructed a large vessel in which he placed anthracite carbon and a metal, which he heated to incandescence. He then injected thin vapors of gas that when heated would ionize and set up an electric current as the positive and negative ions were attracted to their respective electrodes. According to the *Operator*, although Edison "obtained a very strong current in this way . . . all the windows were blown out of his laboratory in the process," probably because a combination of gases proved explosive.[12] These experiments, designed to produce a new and economical electric generator that Edison called a pyromagnetic generator, were part of a much larger program to investigate the convertibility of the natural forces—electricity, magnetism, heat, light, and gravity—and possibly to discover a new force. In undertaking this research Edison followed in the footsteps of his hero Michael Faraday, who had demonstrated many of the relationships between forces and whose famous Christmas lectures in 1859–1860 "On the Various Forces of Nature" had concluded with a discussion of "The Correlation of the Physical Forces" and "their mutual conversion one into another."[13]

Whether because he needed to make repairs to the laboratory after the pyromagnetic generator accident or to cope with grief following his wife's death, Edison did not return to his laboratory above Bergmann's shop until the second week of October. When he did return, his daughter again accompanied him. She probably joined him in the late afternoon after attending Madam Mears's school on Madison Avenue; he was generally at his laboratory in the afternoon and evenings. Edison seems to have taken some time from his experiments to help Marion with her homework; one notebook from this period contains a map of Europe drawn by Edison as well as some of her school notes. The emotional support Marion's presence provided him at this time is suggested by Edison's doodles in a telephone notebook entry dated October 10: "Dot Edison angel Miss Marion Edison Sweetest of all." As Marion assisted in the laboratory, Edison began to refer to her as "George." Among the tasks she undertook was writing out notes on some of the telephone experiments her father and John Ott were performing.[14]

Edison's return to the laboratory had been spurred by a discussion with his longtime friend Ezra Gilliland at the Philadelphia electrical exhibition. Gilliland was in charge of experimental work as head of American Bell Telephone Company's mechanical department, and he later recalled that with his electric light completed and "practically off of his hands," Edison was looking for other subjects to investigate.

I suggested taking up the phonograph, and reducing it to a practical instrument. I also suggested a patent train signal that I own, and the Smith induction car telegraph, in which I own a half interest, and a long-distance telephone transmitter on which I was at that time at work for the Bell Telephone Company. The telephone transmitter seemed to strike him as the best thing to turn his attention to at that time.[15]

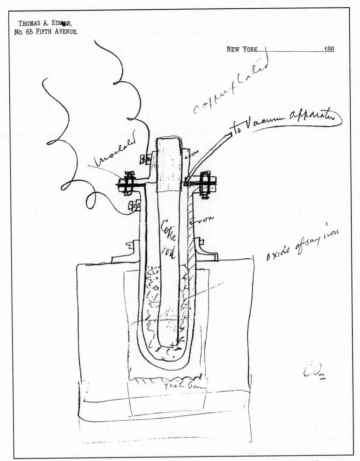

In his first pyromagnetic generator Edison placed anthracite carbon and a metal in a large vessel, heated them to incandescence, and then injected thin vapors of gas, which became ionized and set up an electric current when the positive and negative ions were attracted to their respective electrodes.

Although Edison and American Bell general manager Theodore Vail quickly reached agreement over the terms under which he would work for the company, negotiations dragged on because of his prior contract with Western Union regarding work on telephony. For several months Edison conducted his experiments without a contract and Vail agreed to advance him monies in expectation that an accommodation soon would be reached. By May, however, as both opposition within the company to retaining Edison's services and negotiations with Western Union delayed the signing of a contract, Vail decided to suspend further payments. By November Edison had become so fed up with the delays that he dropped the negotiations and Insull concluded it was unlikely that he "will resume them or that he is likely to experiment on Telephone."[16] However, two months later Edison applied for a patent on an improved carbon transmitter that caused American Bell to resume negotiations and finally sign a contract on February 16. Edison's application covered a multicontact transmitter using granules of roasted anthracite carbon that proved harder, more uniform, and more durable than the fragile carbon button of his original design. It also had better electrical properties. The importance of this invention to the Bell company is apparent from the fact that this form of carbon continued to be used for telephone transmitters into the 1970s.[17]

Edison had begun experimenting with anthracite carbon in October 1884. These experiments were probably influenced by his attempts the previous July to produce electricity directly from carbon. One plan for his pyromagnetic generator used a batterylike arrangement in which anthracite carbon was put under pressure; this might have suggested to Edison the possibility of using the anthracite carbon in place of the carbon button in his transmitter. If nothing else, his extensive experiments with anthracite carbon had made him familiar with this material by the time he began working on telephones again. Edison had begun his long-distance transmitter experiments with the idea that he could make a "loud telephone" by "the most powerful utilization of the whole voice to produce the maximum change of resistance."[18] To do this he planned to have the diaphragm make contact with the entire carbon electrode rather than just at a single point of the button as in his standard design. He tried several methods of making carbon electrodes and in typical Edisonian fashion drew on work with one technology to develop another. Characteristically the use of anthracite carbon grew out not only of his pyromagnetic generator experiments, but also his extensive experience in carbonizing substances for lamp filaments—Edison even tried using a series of carbon filaments as an electrode.

After one of his visits to Edison's laboratory during December, Gilliland described the work in a letter to Vail:

> I have carefully looked over the experiments and tested the apparatus and am pleased to report that he is making great progress in the direction of improving our long-distance telephone transmitter, and has also produced a very satisfactory telephone repeater. He has also produced an individual bell, working upon an entirely new principle, and in a laboratory test it works admirably, being simple in its construction and working quickly. Any of ten subscribers placed upon one circuit can be selected and rung up, within five seconds.[19]

Gilliland recommended that tests be made over a working line, and Edison came up to Boston just before Christmas to conduct some experiments. Further tests were made after the new year and Edison was also given permission to use one of the company's cables stored in Jersey City for his experiments.

By mid-January Edison had executed nine telephone patent applications, including two with Gilliland. Although they submitted these to the company in the expectation that it would speed up negotiations, Vail told Edison in early

May that after a "careful examination . . . we do not find anything in the same, which it would be to our advantage to purchase." At the same time Vail informed the American Bell executive committee that corporate counsel Chauncey Smith thought there would also be no advantage to the company "retaining, or making any arrangement to retain, the services of Mr. Edison, either as expert, advisor, or experimenter."[20] Theodore Vail soon resigned because of policy differences with the board of directors, and negotiations lagged until the following winter.

Although American Bell was ambivalent about Edison's telephone inventions, Gilliland had no such concerns and worked closely with him. Furthermore, this work led to a renewal of their personal as well as professional friendship. In February and March Edison and Gilliland traveled together to the World Industrial and Cotton Centennial Exposition in New Orleans, where the Bell Telephone exhibit included Edison's telephone inventions. Before going to New Orleans they stopped first at Gilliland's father's home in Adrian, Michigan, and then in Cincinnati to see friends from their days as telegraphers. After the exhibition they went on to Florida for a vacation. Accompanied by Marion and Gilliland's wife Lillian, they stopped first in Jacksonville, then went on to St. Augustine, and finally crossed over to the west coast where they sailed down to Punta Rassa, terminus of the cable telegraph to Cuba, where they hunted and fished. While there Edison acquired an option to buy thirteen acres of land that included four hundred feet of riverfront in Fort Myers, a cattle town of some two hundred residents located just up the Caloosahatchee River from Punta Rassa. In September he purchased the land for $3,000. He and Gilliland built identical winter homes on the property, and Edison also put up a small laboratory.[21]

During their travels, Edison and Gilliland discussed ideas for new inventions, including a system of induction telegraphy for communicating with moving railway cars. This would enable every train to send "reports to the fixed stations all the time; so that even if the car in which the instrument was overturned, it would not matter. The operators and train dispatchers would at once suspect an accident and telegraph accordingly."[22] Gilliland owned a half interest in a system devised by William Wiley Smith, whom Edison probably knew from his days as an operator in Indianapolis and Cincinnati. Edison and Gilliland had first talked over their ideas for improving Smith's system the previous December, and just before leaving on their trip they formed the Railway Telegraph & Telephone Company to exploit the system. The banking firm of J. W. Seligman & Company became a major stockholder in the company and provided much of the money for experiments. Edison and Gilliland continued to discuss their ideas about railway telegraphy during the train ride to Adrian, and after arriving Edison wrote to his patent attorney Richard Dyer to prepare a patent application for Gilliland. Once they reached New Orleans, Edison sent instructions to John Ott for a set of experiments and asked Ott to send him the results at St. Augustine. During Edison's stay in Florida, he received

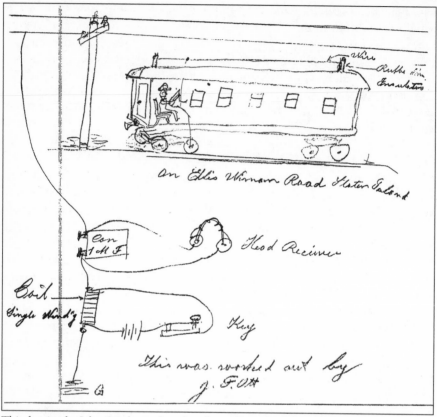

This drawing by John Ott shows alterations he made to the Edison-Gilliland railway telegraph system while experimenting with it on the Staten Island Railroad during 1885–1886. (Courtesy of Charley Hummel)

experimental notes from Ott and sent back additional instructions. After Edison and Gilliland returned to New York City on March 23 they conducted further experiments at the laboratory. On March 27 they executed their first joint patent applications on the system after Dyer advised them that Edison's contribution was too significant for the patents to be taken only in Gilliland's name.[23]

Smith's original system had employed telephone transmitters and receivers for voice communication with moving railway cars, but Edison and Gilliland focused on developing a telegraph system instead. In their design the signal was transmitted as a musical tone created by a metallic reed vibrating five hundred times a second. The opening and closing of a regular Morse key broke up the continuous tone into dots and dashes that could be understood by an operator who received the message by listening to a telephone receiver with a headphone set. The signal was transmitted by induction between the metal roof of a train car and the ordinary telegraph wires along the railroad track. As Edison described it,

> the roof acts as one side of a condenser, and the usual telegraph wires stretched on poles along the edge of the road-bed form the other side of the condenser. The current from the car battery and the roof of the car is of such a nature that the wave of electricity sent from the apparatus in the car lasts only about one 500,000th of a second. During this short period the air seems to conduct electricity; but if the current were allowed to remain any longer the air would enter into such a state as to oppose any further transmission. If now an interval of time is allowed to elapse the air regains its normal condition and another wave can be transmitted.[24]

Edison's work on this system drew on his experiments a decade earlier to develop acoustic telegraphy with similar transmitters, which had also led to his etheric force investigations during the fall of 1875 when he sent signals through the air for distances of twenty to thirty feet. At that time Edison had considered the possibility of using this phenomenon for telegraphy, and he had drafted but did not file a patent application for an "etheric telegraph." After returning from Florida he and Gilliland conducted experiments at Menlo Park "to determine the distance over which the audible signals could be made to jump." These tests "showed that we were enabled to pass audible signals from a telegraph wire to a strip of metal representing a car, and vice versa, over a distance of more than five hundred feet."[25] During these experiments they transmitted signals between elevated balloon kites and Edison soon conceived a system using towers or captive balloons as a means of overcoming the blockage of signals due to the curvature of the earth and interference from buildings, hills, or other obstructions. Edison thought such a system might prove particularly useful for ship-to-ship or ship-to-shore communication. Although his assistant Martin Force conducted further experiments with this system and Edison received a patent for it, he never developed it commercially.[26]

Edison had only slightly better luck with the railway telegraph. Having gotten their system to work in the laboratory, he and Gilliland received permission from Erastus Wiman, president of the Staten Island Railroad, to test it on the company's lines. Edison and Wiman were friends—they had met in 1882 during Edison's electric railway experiments—and Wiman subsequently became a stockholder in Railway Telegraph & Telephone. Edison's assistants John Ott and W. T. King began placing instruments on the line in late May, and they experimented for several months to get the system, now known as the "grasshopper" telegraph, to work properly. The main problem was that the road's iron rails did not make sufficient ground contact, but they also found considerable interference from quadruplex lines and experienced electrical problems caused by the fact that the island's telegraph and telephone lines tied into cables at each end. They finally got the system working well enough for public exhibitions at the beginning of February 1886, and the following month the Milwaukee and St. Paul Railroad began to test the system on its line between Milwaukee and Chicago.[27]

The tests on the Milwaukee line were conducted by the railroad's telegraph superintendent C. H. Rudd and Edison's assistant S. K. Dingle between March and June of 1886. By the end of April continuing difficulties in the operation of the system led the Board of Trustees of Railway Telegraph & Telephone to ask Edison "to proceed to the scene of action, and expedite by his effectual presence the business in hand."[28] Edison and Gilliland confined their experiments to the laboratory instead and relied on regular reports from Rudd and Dingle about the Milwaukee tests. In mid-May, Edison told Rudd about some tests he was making on another telegraph system, the phonoplex. Edison suggested that an arrangement of small condensers he had just developed for the phonoplex might be adapted for the grasshopper telegraph. Edison also assured Rudd "I am trying a great number of experiments to help you out, and I certainly believe that between the two of us we will bring the invention to perfection." Dingle soon reported that they had added the condensers to the circuit and the "improvement is so marked that [Rudd] thinks we are going to come out all right."[29] In the middle of the month Rudd and Dingle successfully demonstrated the system to the Association of Railway Telegraph Superintendents meeting in Minneapolis, but it continued to be plagued by problems in day-to-day operation.

The final outcome of the experiments on the Milwaukee road is unclear, but the railroad company appears not to have adopted the system. Gilliland continued to conduct experiments at Edison's laboratory, and a company to exploit the invention overseas was formed in the fall, but the system was not brought into commercial use. By early 1887 Railway Telegraph & Telephone had opened merger negotiations with the Phelps Induction Telegraph Company, which used a competing system developed by inventor Lucius Phelps. This system required a special wire placed in a covered box on the tracks, and it probably would have been more expensive than the Edison-Gilliland system. The merger between the two companies was apparently prompted by a Patent Office interference between their patents (it was finally decided in Phelps's favor in 1888). The Consolidated Railway Telegraph Company, organized in April, began exhibiting a railway telegraph that was described by *Scientific American* as "a simplification in some respects of the Edison system," on the Lehigh Valley Railroad line in September; five years later Lehigh Valley was the only railroad company still using the system. Little is known about Consolidated Railway Telegraph or its system, but from the time of the merger Edison had little to do with the company.[30]

Edison's lack of involvement in Consolidated Railway Telegraph, or in Railway Telegraph & Telephone prior to the merger, was due in part to a new system he was developing for ordinary railroad telegraphing. During the spring of 1885, while experimenting with Gilliland on their grasshopper telegraph, Edison began to consider how to allow intermediate offices to send messages to each other without interfering with main-line transmissions and to duplex these local way-wires as well. Edison's first conception for this design, which he called a way duplex, dated back to 1878. The new system was similar to the railway telegraph that he and Gilliland had been working on in that it used induced currents for signaling and the same basic apparatus of induction coil, vibrating transmitter, and telephone receiver (initially Edison used his electromotograph receiver), but Edison also placed a condenser shunt around the Morse signaling apparatus to prevent interference.[31]

Two weeks after devising his new system Edison wrote to Erastus Wiman of the Staten Island Railroad, who was also president of the Great Northwestern Telegraph Company of Canada, that he was "ready to take any way wire through or local or Railroad with 2 or 20 offices and make two absolutely independent wires of them telegraphically. The second circuit being as independent of the regular circuit as if it never existed. There is no drawbacks as in Quadruplex & duplex where it is necessary to adjust the balance from time to time."[32] Wiman encouraged Edison to test his new system on the lines of his Canadian telegraph and also became involved in negotiating with Western Union on Edison's behalf about the way duplex. At the end of the summer Edison arranged with Wiman to send Alfred Tate, whose contract as a Canadian agent for Edison Isolated had just expired, to make tests of the way duplex on the Great Northwestern Telegraph lines. By this time Edison was calling his new system the phonoplex.

Tate worked closely with the company's general manager, H. P. Dwight, and after some difficulty in getting the equipment through customs, they finally installed it along the 333-mile-long Grand Trunk railroad line between Toronto and Montreal during the second week of October. Tate sent detailed reports of his tests to Edison, keeping him informed of each difficulty and of his attempts to overcome it. Problems were numerous and ranged from bad chalk and noise in the electromotograph receiver to interference from other circuits. Once, after discovering interference from a line plugged into the switchboard next to his, which he solved by placing a condenser shunt around it, Tate told Insull "the further I go in this electrical business the less I seem to know—wonder if electricity *absorbs* man's brain!"[33] Tate kept Edison informed of his work through detailed letters, and Edison in return sent him instructions and suggestions.

Edison continued his own experiments on the system. After making plans to go up to Canada and assist with the tests there in November, he instead went to Boston to conduct some experiments with Gilliland on one of the American Bell Telephone lines. During these experiments he had great success with a weighted-diaphragm receiver that he promptly sent to Tate to replace the electromotograph receiver. The same technical problems that had plagued the motograph for telephone service also made it unsuitable for daily use on the phonoplex; it was difficult to keep the equipment in adjustment because the fragile chalk cylinder had to be kept constantly wet and rotated steadily. The new receiver, on the other hand, could be adjusted easily by changing the distance between the magnet and the diaphragm with a screw located at the base

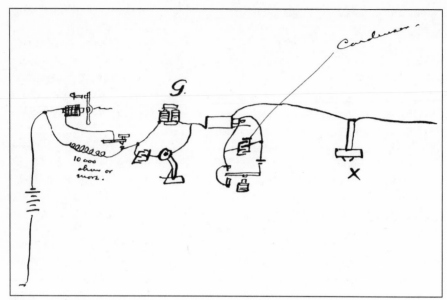

Edison made this drawing for his patent attorney in October 1886 to show a new arrangement of his phonoplex system with a magneto telephone at X (right), an additional condenser (center), and a high resistance placed around the telegraph key and relay (left).

and by using different weights to compensate for different electrical conditions. "When the phone current is very weak a very light weight is used," Edison informed Tate, "where it is strong heavier weight can be used." Edison also reported that he had successfully tested the new receiver "four nights between New York and Boston on a copper wire grounded at each end with induction so strong that they are unable to work it (the line) with telephone for talking when grounded but have to use metallic circuit to enable them to talk."[34] These tests convinced him that the phonoplex should be worked on lines no longer than 100 to 125 miles.

Tate promptly installed the new receiver on part of the line and found that it greatly improved the working of the phonoplex.

> In regard to induction this new receiver enables one to at once locate the line which interferes because any wire which is loud enough to disturb the phone comes out *distinctly* in it so the writing can be *read*. There is no "frying pan" induction or "morse hash" to drown the writing of the phone key and the adjustment is so simple, the apparatus so easily taken care of, that it can be used in many offices where the motograph would have been nothing more than a dead letter.[35]

After successfully demonstrating the new apparatus on December 11 to Dwight, who promptly telegraphed Wiman the result, Tate proceeded to equip the entire Toronto-Montreal line, which was divided into three circuits of about 100 miles each.

The success of the phonoplex was in marked contrast to the grasshopper. While Rudd and Dingle were trying to get the grasshopper to work properly over the Chicago-Milwaukee line in March, Tate was already successfully working one phonoplex circuit for the Baltimore & Ohio Railroad and the company's superintendent ordered a second circuit. Other railroads were also asking about the new system and plans went ahead for installing it on the lines of Western Union's chief competitor Postal Telegraph Company. The contrast between the two systems was apparent to Samuel Insull, who wrote Edison on March 29, "My strong belief is that Railway Telegraph will not amount to a great deal in a long time. I do not think Railway Co's will adopt it with much of a 'rush.'" Although Eugene Crowell, who had become president of Railway Telegraph & Telephone, was "painting glowing pictures of the business," Insull suggested to Edison that he sell some of his stock.[36] By July the phonoplex was a full-scale business being run by Insull and Tate, while the railway telegraph remained an experiment. Over the next few years the phonoplex was widely adopted by railroad lines, and Western Union and Postal Telegraph both installed phonoplex circuits as well. The system continued to be used into the first decade of the new century.

The indifference shown by American Bell to his work on telephony had spurred Edison's interest in other technologies. Gilliland, too, may have begun to question the company's commitment to him after its patent expert, Thomas Lockwood, declared that a receiver he had designed was not patentable even though Edison called it the "best receiver I ever saw" and instructed his own patent attorney, Richard Dyer, to work up the application for Gilliland.[37] Ignored by American Bell, Edison and Gilliland decided to develop a telephone system that would get around the Bell patents. What Edison planned to do was to "bust the undulatory theory" of Alexander Graham Bell's telephone. During his telephone experiments in 1877 Edison had explored the possibility of using a telephone transmitter that would make and break the circuit rather than cause the current to fluctuate (that is to create an undulatory current) to get around the Bell patents. Later he discussed this idea with Sigmund Bergmann and Edward Johnson, and in 1883 he and Bergmann had filed a patent application. Bergmann and Johnson continued to work together on this idea, and in July 1885, after experimenting for some time with one of Johnson's designs, Edison felt that he was "pretty certain to sell that telephone but will have to put in 4 or 5 months on it myself to get it stable and commercial & a good receiver."[38]

Edison, representing Bergmann and Johnson, attempted to negotiate an agreement with attorney J. H. Howe, who represented Zalmon G. Simmons, president of the First National Bank of Kenosha, Wisconsin. Simmons and Howe probably were introduced to Edison by Jim Gilliland, Ezra's brother. They agreed that Simmons would provide $5,000 for experiments and

$100,000 if the system was successfully developed, but the negotiations faltered over Edison's role. Whereas Simmons wanted Edison to provide "his own best personal services, to do whatever is necessary to fully perfect, develope, and complete the said several inventions & devices," Edison wanted to confine his own experiments to developing apparatus that would demonstrate "that the present theory of the electrical transmission of articulate speech by undulatory currents is incorrect," although what he meant by this is unclear.[39] He planned to have Ezra Gilliland come to work in his New York City laboratory and conduct the experiments necessary to make the system commercially practical. Although Simmons decided not to support Gilliland's experiments in Edison's laboratory, Gilliland, who had sided with Vail in his dispute with management at American Bell, decided to give up his position in the company and join Edison in New York City. Although American Bell showed no interest in this new system, even as a hedge against infringers, Gilliland and Edison did not approach its competitors, and they subsequently sold their own improved carbon transmitters to the company.

While Gilliland was still working in Boston, Edison had made several trips up there to conduct experiments and to negotiate with American Bell. Some of these visits were social occasions rather than business trips. During one of his visits with the Gillilands, Edison renewed his acquaintance with a young woman he had met during their trip to New Orleans a few months earlier. Nineteen-year-old Mina Miller, recently returned from Europe, had accompanied her father Lewis Miller to the World Industrial and Cotton Centennial Exposition, where his firm Aultman, Miller & Company had an extensive exhibition of their agricultural machinery. Lewis Miller was an inventor in his own right, with several important reaper and mower improvements to his credit. He was even more noted for his work with Reverend John Heyl Vincent in founding the Sunday School teachers institute in 1874 during a Methodist camp meeting at Chautauqua Lake in New York State. This initiative soon grew into the famous Chautauqua Institution, where Protestant nondenominational adult education was mixed with cultural and recreational activities.

Miller was a strong proponent of education for girls as well as boys, and he advocated college education for women. All of his daughters attended college preparatory schools, and two of them went on to attend Wellesley. Mina attended a women's seminary in Boston, where she became well acquainted with the Gillilands. This seminary, like most at the time, was a finishing school designed to prepare students for marriage as well as possible higher education. Mina studied music at school, and this was one of the things that attracted Edison to her. He also found himself captivated by the "handsome brunette" with her "great dazzling eyes," she became for him "a sort of yardstick for measuring perfection."[40] His friendship deepened into "admiration as I began to appreciate her gentleness and grace of manner and her beauty and strength of mind." Although there were "lots [of] pretty girls" at the Gilliland's during the summer of 1885, Edison found himself thinking constantly about the "Maid of Chau-

Mina Miller Edison, about
the time of her marriage to
Edison.

tauqua." On one occasion he went into Boston and upon seeing a woman who
looked like her "Got thinking about Mina and came near being run over by a
street car."[41]

While Mina joined her parents at Chautauqua for the summer, Edison
and Marion spent July at Woodside Villa, the Gilliland's summer home on the
north shore of Boston Bay, living a life of middle-class domesticity. It is perhaps
a sign of how infatuated he was with Mina, as well as with the presence of other
educated and cultured young women at the Gilliland's, that the inventor who
so loved the rough, masculine environment of the shop and laboratory found
himself playing parlor games, reading literature, and engaging in other middle-
class cultural activities. Although Edison was quite capable of fitting into high
society, as shown by his relations with prominent capitalists, he had always
sought to escape from his wife's parties and disliked dressing up. During this
summer he seemed to relish these pursuits and even dressed in new starched
shirts and for the first time in his life "bought a pair of premeditatedly tight
shoes" because they were "small and look nice." Edison's reading encompassed
such works as Goethe's *Sorrows of Young Werther*, Rousseau's *The New Heloise*

and *Emile*, and Hawthorne's *English Notebooks*. Finding the latter an uninteresting description of "old churches and graveyards and coroners," he wondered whether he was "a literary barbarian and . . . not yet educated up to the point of appreciating fine writing." More interesting to him was a collection of short biographies of Thomas Macaulay, Charles Dickens, Charlotte Brontë, and Sidney Smith, whose "flashes of wit" he particularly enjoyed, and he even read aloud from the *Memoirs and Correspondence of Madame Récamier*. The company also kept diaries. Edison found Gilliland's quite witty, and he too joined in this passion for about two weeks.[42]

Besides these domestic activities they went out on the bay in Gilliland's yacht and Edison briefly contemplated buying one of his own but decided that "the expense is too great when you get the proper yacht."[43] Besides sailing around the bay, they fished rather unsuccessfully. After enjoying the fine fishing in Florida Edison found the fish "rather conservative around this bay. One seldom catches enough to form the fundamental basis for a lie."[44] The household also went out occasionally in the evening to eat ice cream or attend a cultural event such as a band concert in the local park or a performance by Lillian Russell and other musicians in Boston. Gilliland and Edison, who had taken to referring to each other as Damon and Pythias respectively, also spent part of their evenings discussing plans for their winter homes in Fort Myers.

As pleasant and relaxing as he found the summer activities, Edison missed having Mina around. He pined for her in his diary, mentally triangulating the moon by using a baseline of the earth with its endpoints at Woodside Villa and at her family home in Akron, Ohio, and writing despondently, "this celestial mud ball has made another revolution and no photograph yet from the Chataquain Paragon of Perfection. How much longer will Hope dance on my intellect."[45] A few weeks later he and Marion accompanied the Gillilands to Chautauqua. Edison had been invited in 1878 by John Vincent to lecture the assembly on electricity, but the trip to Rawlins to view the solar eclipse had caused him to forego the lecture, which he doubtless found an intimidating prospect. Now he went to see Mina and enjoy the pleasant surroundings of the tent camp. Although intending to stay only about four days, he spent a week. Also at the camp was Vincent's son George, who was also Mina's suitor and the one both families expected she would marry. Unlike her father, even though he had become less strict in his Methodism as he gained worldly success, Mina may well have considered the Vincents too stern. She apparently did "not like them well enough to be one of them" and found Edison to be more a man of the world like her father.[46]

Edison and Lewis Miller not only respected but also genuinely liked each other. Edison, who felt his conscience to be "oblivious of Sunday" and "incrusted with a sort of irreligious tartar," got on well with Mina's devout father.[47] While not one for formal religion, Edison clearly believed in a creator, though not one concerned with human affairs. A nice summing up of his views can be found in the last of his diary entries: "What a wonderfully small idea mankind has of the almighty! My impression is that he has made unchangeable laws to govern this and billions of other worlds, and that he has forgotten even the existence of this little mote of ours ages ago. Why can't man follow up and practice the teachings of his own conscience, mind his own business, and not obtrude his purposely created finite mind in affairs that will be attended to without any volunteer advice."[48] Miller's God was more personal, but both he and Edison shared a belief in the Golden Rule as the basis for moral action. Perhaps more important, they shared an interest in manufacturing and invention and both saw money making as an activity that provided the means for them to carry out their life work. Edison, who made money to invent, later wrote of Miller: "He was one of the kindest and most loveable men I ever knew, and spent his life trying to make it possible for all mankind to reach the higher planes of living. To me, he seemed to be eternally making money in his factory in order to enable him to better carry on his schemes in education."[49] He also found Miller to be "better versed on more subjects than any man I know." Miller on his part found himself impressed by Edison's "greatness and genuine good heart." He also enjoyed Edison's "witticisms and stories." He always found him "ready with some witty remark no matter what was up. And always in such nice language as compared with . . . others. Nothing of low order came from his lips. Sometimes he would tell some story that if any one else but him would have told it would have been put in such language as would have been low of cast but not once did he let himself down."[50] Others in the family also appreciated Edison's talents as storyteller. Even Mina's mother, a very devout and serious woman, joined the rest of the family in "wishing we could tell every thing as he can . . . our folkes try to tell storys when they gett along a little ways they will stop and say O if Mr Edison was hear he could tell it."[51]

While at Chautauqua, Edison invited Mina to join his party for a trip to Alexandria Bay on the St. Lawrence River in upper New York State and then to the White Mountains of New Hampshire. To carry on their courtship in private while in the company of others, Edison taught Mina the Morse code. "Nobody knew anything about many of our conversations on a long drive in the White Mountains," he later remarked. "We could use pet names without the least embarrassment, although there were three other people in the carriage." During the trip he gathered the courage to propose marriage by tapping it out in Morse code and was delighted when Mina signaled back "Yes."[52]

After returning to New York City, Edison, possibly with Insull's help, composed a letter asking Lewis Miller for his daughter's hand in marriage. Relying on his reputation, which "is so far made that I recognize I must be judged by it for good or ill," Edison assured his future father-in-law "that the step I have taken in asking your daughter to intrust her happiness into my keeping has been the result of mature deliberation, and with the full appreciations of the responsibility and the duty I have undertaken to fulfill." But he also remarked that Miller's answer "will seriously affect my happiness, and I trust my suit may meet with your approval."[53] Miller invited Edison to Oak Place, the Miller home in Akron, and gave his approval to the match between the thirty-eight-year-old Edison and his twenty-year-old daughter. Plans were set to hold the wedding at Oak Place on February 24, 1886.

The reaction by Mina's mother, Mary Valinda, and older sister Jane (known as Jennie), to the proposed marriage was not initially enthusiastic. Both women seem to have been a little intimidated by Edison. Even after the wedding Mina's mother seems to have felt unworthy in his eyes. Jennie (and one suspects Mary Valinda as well) believed that Mina had been influenced in her decision by Lillian Gilliland. Jennie even encouraged her to put off the wedding, arguing that February was too soon and that Edison should be willing to "wait for a year or six months at least." Jennie seems to have come around to the marriage after Mina assured her that she had chosen Edison over George Vincent for her own reasons. By the time of the wedding she felt that he was so "kind and loving" that Mina "could never have gotten a better husband."[54] Mary Valinda, however, continued to have doubts about the match. Mina's sister Mary recalled how during the ceremony their mother's "face expressed all the love and anxiety she felt at the great step you were taking. She was not quite so sure as Father that the future would be mostly roses—but she did not stand in [y]our way."[55] Although Mary Valinda liked Edison and soon accepted him as part of the family, she remained troubled by the fact that he was not a churchgoer. Although she accepted his claim that he did not like to attend church because of his deafness, for "it is hard and not plesent to go any place and not hear what is said," Mary Valinda nonetheless believed that "church is a grate help and comfort and a privilege we should not miss" and urged Mina to have Edison "go so as the others would go." In this way he would be "doing all he could for his family."[56]

While the Miller women had their doubts, Edison easily won over the younger Miller boys John and Theodore. He seems to have got on well with younger children, although he would have trouble with his own children as adolescents. They were probably thrilled to have the famous man in their house, even if Edison hoped that the next time he visited they would "not watch me and Mina so closely."[57] He taught them something about electricity and for Christmas sent them an induction coil and battery, instructing them in its use, as well as a telegraph set and a telescope. Although nothing is known of the reaction of the older Miller boys, as men of the world involved in manufacturing they too were probably impressed that the famous inventor was wooing their sister.

Mina and her sister came to New York City before the wedding so she could spend time with her future husband discussing their plans. When he offered her a choice of a townhouse on Riverside Drive in New York City or a house in the country, she chose the latter because neither of them was fond of the city. Edison found her a large mansion in Llewellyn Park. Located in Orange (later West Orange), New Jersey, a few miles from Newark and near a train line to New York City, Llewellyn Park was the nation's first exclusive

Glenmont, Edison's home.

suburban enclave. One of the largest homes in the park was Glenmont, which had been built by Henry Pedder with funds he embezzled from Arnold Constable & Company, a fashionable New York City department store. Designed by noted architect Henry Hudson Holly in the Queen Anne style, the twenty-three-room red-timbered house contained grand rooms with stained glass windows, carved wood paneling, and frescoed ceilings. The extensive grounds included greenhouses, stables, and other outbuildings. Together with its furnishings the estate had cost about $400,000; Edison was offered the property for around $235,000 because of Pedder's legal problems. He and his family had already moved out of their apartment, taking up residence in the Normandie Hotel across from the Metropolitan Opera House at the end of September. After deciding to buy Glenmont, Edison agreed to let his lawyers finally settle the Seyfert suit to protect the estate from legal entanglements. Edison also contemplated building a laboratory at Llewellyn Park and sketched out plans for the building, but after returning from his honeymoon he decided not to build it.[58]

On the Saturday before the wedding, Edison's friends threw him a bachelor party at Delmonico's, although Charles Batchelor noted in his diary that Francis Upton and John Kruesi "had somehow been overlooked."[59] They did, however, join the rest of "the boys" in a special railroad car hired for the trip to Akron for the wedding. On the afternoon of February 24, they were among more than eighty guests, including Edison's father Samuel, his sister Marion, and his brother Pitt, who gathered for the wedding ceremony at the Miller home. At three o'clock in the afternoon, to the strains of the wedding march from *Lohengrin*, Edison entered the parlor in his Prince Albert coat. He was accompanied by his best man Frank Tappan, a naval officer and a friend of Edison's and Gilliland's who apparently began handling investments for Edison and his companies about this time. Edison was followed by Mina's mother, brothers, and sisters, who formed an aisle for Mina and her father. The ceremony was performed by Reverend Dr. E. K. Young of the Akron First Methodist Episcopal Church while Edison and Mina knelt before him on a velvet cushion. At the conclusion of the ceremony, the party adjourned to the library accompanied by the music of Mendelssohn's wedding march. There they were received by the newlyweds who stood under a canopy of roses with E-M spelled out in pink carnations. They then enjoyed a dinner catered by Kinsley's of Chicago, complete with a giant wedding cake.[60]

That night the newlyweds, joined by Marion, traveled by train to Cincinnati, where Edison had a chance to show off his new bride to old friends. The next day they traveled on to Atlanta. During the train ride through the South Edison conceived an idea for a cotton-picker that he sketched out and described to reporters at their hotel. They then spent time in Jacksonville, Florida, while Gilliland rushed to complete work on one of the new homes in Fort Myers. Although the buildings had been prefabricated in Maine and then shipped to Fort Myers, they were not ready by the time of the wedding, and Edison and Gilliland had decided to finish one in which their two families would live together until the other was complete. To allow time for the work to be completed, Edison, Mina, and Marion did not arrive in Fort Myers until March 17. Gilliland, who complained to Insull that "there is not even a jews harp down here and we need music badly," tried to make the new house seem more like a home by ordering an organ from New York.[61]

As always, Edison could not leave work entirely behind. He wrote Insull and asked him to have John Ott and Gilliland's brother Jim, who was working with them in the laboratory, keep him "posted every two or 3 days what progress they are making—also Tate [on the phonoplex]."[62] Edward Johnson also wrote Edison about his ideas about improvements in the Edison municipal outdoor lighting system, which prompted Edison to compose an eight-page letter of plans for experiments by Ott and Hamilton. The day after arriving in Fort Myers, Edison began to keep a notebook of ideas and plans for experiments. Fortunately for Mina the laboratory her husband and Gilliland had planned for Fort Myers was not yet built, and rather than spend his days experimenting he shared his ideas with her. She witnessed all the entries in this notebook and another that he kept during their stay, and she even recorded several of his ideas herself. Unlike Mary, who couldn't "invent worth a damn," Mina seems to have been able to appreciate his work. Not only did he share his work with her on their honeymoon, but after their return that summer she joined him in the lamp factory laboratory and helped to record the results of filament experiments. She would also help out with filament experiments in May of 1887.[63]

The several notebooks Edison filled with ideas at Fort Myers included plans for his ongoing work in telegraphy and telephony. Among these were the railway telegraph, balloon telegraph, phonoplex, and quadruplex. He also sketched out notes and drawings for other technologies that he was considering, including the cotton-picker and a plan for separating cream that had been prompted by correspondence with David Hamlin Burrell, a manufacturer of dairy equipment in Little Falls, N.Y. In other entries he returned to old projects, such as the phonograph, hearing aids, and artificial silk. He also recorded ideas related to the ongoing electric light work, including dynamos and electric railway designs, for Batchelor to make at the Machine Works and filament experiments for the lamp factory.

The most interesting entries, however, were those related to his ongoing pursuit of unknown natural forces. The experiments with induction telegraphy had reawakened his interest in this subject, and on December 8, 1885, he had begun a notebook for "ideas as to the discovery of a new mode of motion or energy and also to the conversion of heat directly into electricity."[64] The notebook contained his ideas for generating and detecting this new force, which he called the "XYZ force." Edison had been thinking about such a force since at least July 1885, when a newspaper reported that "he does not pretend to know what it is. But he says that there are many phenomena which are not explained by any force yet recognized, and it is these which he is going to investigate."[65] This notebook, however, details Edison's first concerted effort to investigate the XYZ force, which he continued to experiment on well into the twentieth century. At Fort Myers, as he pondered this problem he also considered the relationship between the known forces of gravitation, heat, light, electricity, and magnetism. He saw gravity as an electromagnetic phenomenon and conceived the "Theory that gravitation is due to the circulation of an electric current around the earth due to the rotation of the earth on its axis cutting the lines of force thrown out into open space by the sun which is a magnet whose polar center is parallel with that of our earth." He also considered the possibility that "our solar system is rotating as a whole and the sun rotating cuts its own L[ines] of F[orce] & thus the heat is accounted for."[66] These speculations led Edison to try to determine the relative strength of the lines of force of the planets in the solar system. Upon returning home he began to read works on astronomy, which led him to further speculations regarding whether sunspots were caused by electric arcs forming across "faults in the molten surface of the sun" and whether the tails of comets were "due to breaking of arcs from repellent action as they approach the sun."[67]

Edison's ideas about the action of forces in the solar system were informed by his understanding of the nature of matter. Arguing that each atom had a

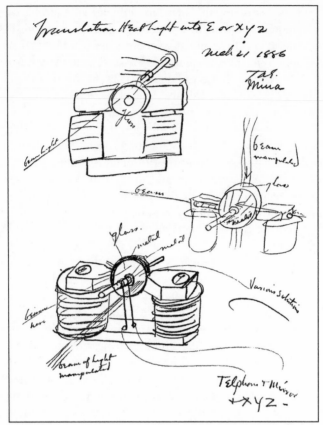

During his honeymoon Edison drew these ideas for apparatus to use in his experiments on the conversion of heat into light or electricity and in his efforts to discover a new force he called XYZ.

north and south polarity, he explained gravity as "the mutual electrical attraction of all atoms." Furthermore, he argued by analogy from chemistry that the "substances we call elements are composed of molecules of diferent atoms [and] all atoms are primal hence matter is composed primarily of one substance, the primal molecule. Our solar system is a *Cosmic Molecule*."[68] As with his ideas about the XYZ force, Edison proposed several experiments to test his ideas on the electromagnetic origins of gravitation. Many of his entries about these and the XYZ experiments he labeled "fundamental."

Not all of the notebook entries concerned serious work. Edison and Mina tried to "shock an oyster [to] see if it wont paralize his shell muscle & make the shell fly open," but this proved to be a "Dead failure."[69] They also spent time planning the landscaping of the estate, considering its layout and plantings.

One notebook also contains what appear to be writing lessons done by Edison's daughter Marion. She appears to have copied these from her father's newspapers and letters, although one may have been a story her father told or that she found in a book. This story, concerning a contest of wills between a mother and her young daughter, may have been particularly meaningful to Marion, who never became entirely reconciled to her new stepmother. Mina after all was only six and a half years older than Marion and had usurped her position as her father's companion. Marion would later call the years following the marriage "the most unhappy of my life."[70]

Although her relationship with Marion would become increasingly difficult, immediately after her honeymoon Mina expressed joy in her new home and family and in the husband whom she loved "more and more." Nonetheless, she did have doubts about her ability to carry out her new family responsibilities, and her sister Jennie found it necessary to assure her that "you are deserving of everything that Mr. Edison has given you and I haven't any fear but what you are going to manage everything all right."[71] Both Jennie and her mother also offered Mina advice on servants and the care of her husband and children. Running the huge mansion that was Glenmont proved no small task.

After spending so much time together for several months, Mina no doubt found it difficult to adjust to the normal busy schedule of her husband, who plunged back into his work. Immediately upon his return from their honeymoon, Edison faced a new crisis in his business affairs. On May 1, while he and Mina were visiting her family in Akron before leaving for their new home, a committee representing the workers at the Edison Machine Works presented Charles Batchelor with a demand that the shop be unionized and that management agree to a set of rules concerning pay and hours. Batchelor agreed to institute the rules temporarily until he could discuss the matter with Edison and the other company directors, but he did not agree to recognize the union. Although the directors were willing to give ten hours' pay for nine hours' labor and extra pay for overtime, they refused the demands for a union shop, the end of piecework, and the requirement that there be a man hired for each machine. Complaining that too many machines were run by one or two men and that the piecework system reduced pay by as much as 25 percent compared to other electrical works, the workers decided to strike on May 19. The labor dispute prompted the directors to begin looking for a new shop in another city. The company clearly needed larger facilities—it recently had set up its casting operation in Brooklyn. When the directors learned that the McQueen Locomotive Works in upstate Schenectady, New York, had gone out of business, leaving its shops available for a low price, they decided to move. In the meantime, some of the men returned and on May 26 the Machine Works began operating again. Five days later, the rest of the workers capitulated.[72]

Batchelor, who had taken the lead in negotiating with the workers, had not given in to any of their additional demands and got them to return under the condition that the shop was "to be run just as the managers decide & no interference whatever to be tolerated." He had fought to retain the traditional management style that had worked in the Newark shops, where piecework rewarded "the better class of mechanics" who operated as independent contractors. In an era of small machine shops such "inside" contracts were a way for a machinist to retain his independence and possibly gain the means to establish his own shop. By the mid-1880s, however, workers were increasingly employed in larger factories, where they ran more than one machine and where piecework was a way for management to pay less for their labor. However, the entrepreneurial aspect of piecework also provided a kind of shop discipline. Thus, speaking to reporters, Batchelor argued that "When a man is making the same thing over and over again, we make a contract with him and he goes on his own hook. If he loafs or gets drunk he loses his own time, not ours, and the men make from 25 to 75 per cent more than they would on weekly wages." Although he was not directly involved in the strike, Edison supported Batchelor's negotiating position and felt no qualms about moving the works to Schenectady. He later said that he wanted "to get away from the embarrassment of the strikes and the communists to a place where our men are settled in their own homes."[73]

Edison also took a limited role in other business matters. He left the affairs of the Edison Electric Light Company to Edward Johnson, but he did send Francis Upton to Europe to help Henry Villard reorganize the Edison lighting interests there; he also worked on the plans for a new lighting district in New York City. He agreed to have the manufacturing shops that formed the Edison United Manufacturing Company take over the central station construction business from the Isolated Company, and he discussed plans to consolidate their management. Edison spent most of his time at the laboratory of the Edison Lamp Works. After his marriage he had moved his personal experiments to this laboratory in East Newark, which was closer to his home in Glenmont. While he continued to work on a variety of projects, most of his experiments were concerned with improvements in the Edison lamps.

In early June Edison again found it necessary to "take charge of the manufacturing to get it back on to a solid basis" because Upton had failed to deal with complaints of bad lamps, although Edison admitted that a deterioration in manufacturing could take place "without anyone knowing the 'why or wherefore.'"[74] Nonetheless, he had criticized Upton earlier for his lack of attention to the technical side of the business and suggested that he "personally learn the Lamp business ie the Carbonization. Your are a scientific man like myself Batch etc. It seems to me if I was running the Lamp factory that there wouldnt occur any such thing as losing the art, as the financing is rather easy I suggest you do like the rest of us learn the business thoroughly & not be dependent on others= you are degenerating into a mere business man— Money isn't the only thing in this mud ball of ours."[75]

Assisted by John Ott, Edison conducted extensive experiments to increase lamp life and improve its manufacture. He discovered that heating the filament during lamp evacuation to drive off the occluded gases was unnecessary because the amount of gas was inconsequential. It turned out that most of the gas drawn off from the lamp came from the inner surface of the glass globe. Instead of heating the filament, Edison decided to heat the globe from outside to drive off its gases, which were then withdrawn from the lamp as it was evacuated. In one set of experiments, Edison used a spectroscope to examine the lamps and found that "vapor of mercury condensed on the inside of the lamp when cold & apparently there was a very high vacuum, but heat turned it into vapor again & caused the vacuum to become exceedingly low so that there was a good medium for the carrying action."[76] To overcome this he tried putting a water jacket around the tube leading to the lamp and freezing it so that the mercury would be deposited on the side of the tube. He also used separate tubes containing iodine, chlorine, or bromide to absorb the mercury vapors or phosphoric anhydride or other moisture absorbents for water vapors. By the end of July, Edison had applied for three patents based on this research.

As August began a new assistant joined Edison and Ott in the lamp factory laboratory as they began a new set of experiments to increase the life of electric lamps. Over the next two months a series of eighty bulbs were evacuated with different pump arrangements and absorbents while hydrocarbon and other gases were used to coat the filaments and glass globes as a way of preventing electrical carrying. The careful notebook record of these experiments and of the time these lamps burned was kept by Mina Edison. It may be that the masculine pet name he used for her—"Billy"—dates from this time period in much the way that "George" became his nickname for Marion when she had joined him in the laboratory two years earlier.[77]

What led Edison to bring his wife to the laboratory is unknown. Perhaps it was a result of the interest she had shown in his work during their honeymoon and the fact that his children were with her parents for the summer. It also may have been influenced by Edison's ideas about women's role in society. Even though he certainly was not a feminist, and in fact felt that "direct thought is not at present an attribute of feminism," he nonetheless thought this situation a misfortune caused by man using his physical strength to gain dominance over woman. By treating woman as chattel he had "delayed her growth." The result was that women had been occupied by "petty tasks which, while holding her attention closely, had not given her brain exercise." Edison argued that man's selfishness and "lust for ownership" had prevented him from making "woman [an] equal partner in his various activities, and so he held her back from an ability to fill an equal partnership." Edison believed that modern technology would release women from mundane everyday tasks and allow them to develop their brains properly. He thought that the result would be "real sex independence" and allow humankind to "begin to reach its ultimate." Edison expressed these sentiments in a 1912 interview, but how much they represented his ideas twenty-six years earlier cannot be known, particularly as Mina soon disappeared from the laboratory and into the role of wife and mother, especially once she became pregnant in 1887 with their first child, their daughter Madeleine, who was born the following May. Nonetheless, it is striking that she was ever there.[78]

There also is the very real possibility that Mina helped to mold his views during their years of married life together. Her mother was a pious woman who felt that a woman's highest purpose was her husband's happiness, but Mina had been encouraged by her father to gain an education and have grander ideas. At the New Year, Mary Valinda Miller cautioned her daughter "not to look to grateness and nobility in things far beyond your reach . . . grateness is in being ready and willing to make little things grate and useful."[79] Even the role of housewife had a grander dimension for Mina, who saw herself as a home executive, or in the words of her husband's 1912 interview, "a domestic engineer." In later years Mina also became quite active in civic affairs. Nonetheless, she echoed her mother's ideas when she told *Collier's* in 1925 that her "job has been always to take care of Mr. Edison—to take care that his home contributed as much as possible to his doing the work that he had to do to the best advantage." Being the wife of a man who was as wedded to his work as to her, Mina had learned to "always put his work first."[80]

The diminishing of Mina's role in the laboratory occurred as Edison began to turn his attention to other experimental projects. At the end of August Ezra Gilliland, who had been ill for some time following his return from Fort Myers, finally joined Edison at the laboratory and set to work on these projects. They included new experiments with anthracite coal for the carbon transmitter, tests of Edison's new arrangement for the railway telegraph, and the redesign of the village electrical system. Many of Edison's own experiments continued to focus on lamps, particularly on John Ott's effort to develop more uniform filaments, but he and Gilliland also began to discuss new projects, most notably an improved phonograph for use as a dictating machine. By the beginning of December Edison was so "anxious about his experiments" that he asked Batchelor to resign from the management of the Machine Works and join him in the laboratory.[81] Although Batchelor, in the midst of supervising the transfer of the Machine Works to Schenectady, declined, Edison nonetheless began to focus his energies on new inventions.

With her husband fully engaged in planning and carrying out experiments, Mina seems to have experienced the full effect of Edison's devotion to work for the first time. This may have contributed to the discouragement she felt during the fall. Responding to her daughter's mood, Mary told her that many women found "the first year after being Mareid every thing was so different and so many things to learn and to do but after a little they would learn the easere they took things and not worre the better all around both for self and famaly and friendes in every way now be happy and contented." Mina faced particular difficulty with her stepchildren, especially Marion, and Mary advised her to "take the little folkes with you and talk with them tell them everything that will pleas them and win them to you try and get them to think and feel towards you as there was no other person like you try and love them and they will love you and Mr Edison will be perfectly happy." She suggested that Mina make "small talk with Dot all you can ask her how she likes thing and if she wants any thing." However, Mary also sympathized with Mina "in having one around the house that I do not like." The resentment that Marion felt toward her new stepmother was clearly having its affect on Mina, leading her father to caution her that "Dott will be very much influenced by you. No doubt she sees your feeling about her and you must win her or else it will not be just what all hope and de- sire."[82]

Mina's difficulties with Marion were exacerbated when her husband be- came very sick with either pleurisy or pneumonia at the end of the year. By mid-January he began to improve, and the doctors made plans to send him to Florida, but according to Batchelor he remained a very sick man. At the end of the month he was well enough to sit up during the day and attend to some business affairs, and by the second week of February he was well enough to travel to Fort Myers with his family and the Gillilands. Although Edison still was not fully recovered, Mina wrote her mother at the end of February that she was "more happy this last 25th of Feberary than a year ago." However, she told her father, who had joined them in Fort Myers, that she felt she "did not have his full affections." He, however, reassured her that "He seems to me just as he did a year ago. Kind and affectionate in all his ways" and "true to you and true to what he appears to be."[83]

After they had been in Fort Myers for a month, Batchelor joined them to help Edison set up his new laboratory there and to assist with experiments on Edison's new motor design. They also discussed plans for a new laboratory that Edison wanted to build near his home; a few days after his return Batchelor be- gan to design it. During the time Batchelor was in Fort Myers, Edison devel- oped an abscess below his ear that required an operation; he had another oc- currence in early April that caused the doctors to fear erysipelas, an acute bacterial infection accompanied by fever and skin inflammation. He soon re- covered, however, and Mina and Marion left for home while Lewis Miller and Ezra Gilliland remained behind with him.[84]

This gave Lewis Miller "a better opportunity to get acquainted" with Edi- son as they spent much time together fishing, hunting, talking, and reading. This only served to increase his estimation of Edison, whom he thought so- cially superior "to most any one I know." It also gave him a chance to get a bet- ter sense of his character so he could assure Mina of her husband's feelings to- wards her. He had discovered, he told her, that "the many remarks he makes which are seemingly some kind of assinations or critizisms are genuine inno- cent wit," and he reassured her that Edison made such remarks only to those "with whom he is well acquainted." He cautioned her that "he is so in the habit of those witty remarks to his men in the works that he cannot & I think ought not try to suppress them when he comes home. You must try and meet him with wit." He also explained that the large amount of money Edison had spent on Glenmont had "made him a little cautious which was right enough but made it quite hard for you." However, Edison was very pleased with Mina's sense of economy and also open to her "great desire to make the home the place for entertainments instead of running about." Her father's letter no doubt heartened Mina, who was despondent that Edison had not answered any of the four letters she had written him since her return, prompting Marion to tell her father to write Mina "very often if you dont intend having a cyclone soon."[85]

Edison seems to have reassured his wife in other ways. First, they decided to start a new family. This prompted Jennie to suggest that Mina tell Marion all about it as "she cannot help but love a little one of yours and I think if you sort of confide in her about it she will feel better."[86] Although Marion never spoke ill of her half-siblings, it is unlikely that she was overjoyed by this news. Her parents also decided to send her away to school before the child arrived. After the move to Glenmont Marion had been tutored at home by a Miss McWilliams, but in the fall they sent her to the Bradford Academy in Bradford, Massachusetts. This was one of the older female academies in the country, founded in 1802, and one of the better private schools for girls. Marion seems to have enjoyed her first year at the school, earning good marks in history, composition, music, geography, arithmetic, and Bible study.[87]

Bradford was also known for its science classes, but this was not true of the school her brothers attended two years later. At first, the boys had gone to the Dearborn-Morgan School in West Orange, a coeducational institution that prepared its students for both college and business. But Mina sent Tom and William to St. Paul's in Concord, New Hampshire, one of the elite private preparatory schools in the country, even though Edison was sharply critical of the type of traditional classical education that it offered. The decision to send them there was clearly Mina's—this was the school her younger brothers attended. She expected her stepsons to follow her brothers at Yale, which also provided a classical education. This, too, was quite opposite their father's feelings about college. His own preference was for engineering schools such as MIT or Cornell. However, like many of his contemporaries, Edison left matters regarding the upbringing of his children, including their education, to his wife.[88]

Edison's remarriage had created an abrupt shift in the class position and expectations of his children that went beyond their father's rising fortune. Their own mother had grown up in a working-class family, and at Menlo Park they had experienced an artisanal middle-class upbringing. Their experiences living in the Gramercy Park neighborhood of New York City brought them into contact with upper-middle-class society, and Marion had attended fine private schools in New York, but Edison certainly had not prepared the two boys for entry into elite culture. Mina's family characterized the Edison boys as somewhat wild but believed they would settle down under her influence. Thomas and William could only have felt great confusion when they were sent off to a private school with a classical curriculum of the type their father criticized and into whose social life they did not easily fit. He had certainly done little to indicate that he believed formal education of this type was important to their future. The changes in their family and social circumstances, as well as their father's frequent absences, probably made it even more difficult for Edison's children to find their way in the world. But as 1887 drew to a close the troubles that would plague Edison's relationship with his children still lay in the future. The stability of his family life seemed to renew his enthusiasm for invention, and he looked forward to opening his new laboratory near their home in Orange, New Jersey.

CHAPTER 14

A New Laboratory

In August 1887, as his new laboratory was rising from its foundations, Edison drafted a revealing letter describing the new complex and his aspirations for it. "I will have the best equipped & largest Laboratory extant, and the facilities incomparably superior to any other for rapid & cheap development of an invention, & working it up into commercial shape with models patterns special machinery—In fact there is no similar institution in existence." The new laboratory was to be even larger than the one at Menlo Park, whose superior resources of men, machines, and resources had enabled him not only to beat other inventors to the electric light but also to develop the other components of the system required to make electric lighting a commercial enterprise. The new laboratory would have a machine shop "sufficiently large to employ 50 men," and 30 others could be engaged in experiments "in the other parts of the work." Edison planned to "carry stock of almost every conceivable material of every size and with the latest machinery"; he expected that "a man will produce 10 times as much" as he could in the smaller, less well-equipped laboratories of his rivals.[1]

Edison anticipated that his new laboratory would enable him to maintain his reputation as America's foremost inventor. Although this reputation remained unmatched, it was not without serious challenge. Since leaving Menlo Park, Edison had seen others stake their claims to having the best private laboratory. Only the year before, electrical inventor and manufacturer Edward Weston of nearby Newark, New Jersey, had built what was then considered to be "the most complete private lab in the country." Weston, who was being hailed by reporters as "the new competitor of the great Edison," had been a bitter rival of Edison's since their heated debate about dynamo designs in the pages of *Scientific American* in 1879. Weston's biographer later described the laboratory

Weston had built behind his home in Newark as "a remodeled wooden build-ing with a good-sized brick addition, and a small boiler room between." It con-tained a well-equipped machine shop, a chemical laboratory, and a physical laboratory as well as an office and a library with 10,000 volumes. Weston's lab-oratory with its staff of five men resembled Edison's early Menlo Park labora-tory and was superior to the facilities that Edison had had at his disposal for sev-eral years. No doubt Weston's laboratory provided Edison, who believed that enemies were a crucial spur to success, with an incentive to "have the best equipped & largest Laboratory extant."[2]

Edison's concern with his status as a public figure is evident in his early plan for the laboratory. Even before Weston had completed his laboratory, Edi-son sketched his first ideas for a grand three-story building with a tower, court-yard, and mansard roof that gave "the invention factory the dignity of a public building."[3] When Edison had made these sketches in early 1886, as he pre-pared for his wedding to Mina, he probably conceived this grandiose design as appropriate to his public standing and as a means of consolidating his status among the nation's elite. By 1887, when he bought fourteen acres of land at the bottom of the hill leading up to Llewellyn Park and asked Batchelor to oversee the design of the new laboratory, Edison had become more concerned with its utility. Under Batchelor's guidance, Hudson Holly, the Glenmont ar-chitect, designed a structure that looked more like a handsome factory than a civic building.[4]

The new laboratory retained elements of Edison's original conception, most notably a large and imposing library and private experimental rooms for the inventor. Rather than being housed in a separate wing, however, the labo-ratory's machine shops were intimately connected to the experimental rooms. Downstairs was a heavy machine shop that would have dwarfed the large one at Menlo Park, while a precision machine shop was placed upstairs near the experimenters. With these facilities Edison felt that he could "build anything from a lady's watch to a Locomotive."[5]

The central position of the machine shops reinforced the shop-culture tra-dition out of which Edison had developed his earlier laboratories in Newark and Menlo Park. But Edison had achieved his great success at Menlo Park by combining the tradition of shop invention with unmatched chemical and elec-trical research facilities. As his new laboratory building took shape, Edison real-ized that it did not provide the necessary space for these research activities. During the summer he decided to add four smaller one-story buildings that would each be 25 x 100 feet, about the same size as one floor of the original two-story Menlo Park laboratory building. The first of these new buildings was a physical laboratory, which became known as the galvanometer room. At the center of the building were "8 stone foundations for galvanometers & acurate experiments."[6] The structure itself was made out of nonferrous materials (cop-per was used for nails and pipes and the roof was of granite) so that it would not

In this photograph the main building of the West Orange laboratory complex is at the right (the large curved windows in front are those of the library); in order from front to back at the left are the physical lab, the chemistry lab, the building housing the chemical store-room and patternmaking shop, and the metallurgical lab.

affect the delicate electromagnetic instruments used for precise electrical experiments and tests. The galvanometer room was also separated by a courtyard from the three other new buildings.

Directly across the courtyard was the chemical laboratory. In his 1886 design Edison had placed the chemical laboratory in the wing opposite the main experimental rooms. As he began to plan the location of the chemical laboratory and other experimental rooms in the new laboratory, however, he realized that it took up nearly a third of the total space available for experimental work on the second floor. Faced with the prospect of either reducing the scale of his chemical laboratory or restricting his options for the other experimental rooms, Edison decided instead to devote an entire building to chemical work. He also provided additional space for this purpose by using the front half of the third building as a storehouse for dangerous chemicals; other chemicals were stored in the stockroom of the main building. In the rear he placed a shop for patternmaking and other carpentry work. Edison designated the last of the new buildings as a metallurgical laboratory where he could carry out assays and other research related to ore-milling technology.

The inside of the physical laboratory, known as the "galvanometer room."

Edison entrusted the plans for these secondary buildings to a new architect, Joseph Taft, whom he had hired at the end of July. Although Holly was a respected architect, Edison had become dissatisfied with the contractors he had hired and employed his own man, Jeff Waldron, to supervise their work; Edison also spent much of his own time checking up on the building's progress. Waldron found that the contractors were doing substandard work and also came to the conclusion that they were trying to cheat Edison and that "the architect & contractors are *all in* together."[7] Edison became increasingly incensed over what he considered slipshod work and at the end of July he replaced Holly with Taft.

As Edison expanded the size of his laboratory he needed additional funds to pay for it. Samuel Insull, who remained responsible for Edison's financial affairs even after moving to Schenectady to run the Edison Machine Works, complained to Alfred Tate that Edison

wants a great deal more money than he at first anticipated, but this is simply a repetition of what has occurred so frequently before. The trouble is, that Mr. Edison does not have anyone with him who urges him to curtail his expenses on his new laboratory. Exactly how I am going to carry out his wishes and give him what he requires, I don't know. Heretofore, when I have had to provide money, I have always had something to say about how much should be spent. My position now is somewhat different and I propose to wait and see how the experiment turns out.[8]

Insull was also concerned about Edison's purchases of machinery and supplies. Edison expected to spend $180,000 to build and equip his new laboratory, and he had spent about $140,000 by the end of 1887.

Besides ordering the best machinery available for his machine shops, Edison purchased over $6,000 of pure chemicals and planned to order "a quantity of every known substance on the face of the globe . . . all kinds of ores, metals, fabrics, gums, resins, and samples of every imaginable material," including all kinds of vegetable substances as well as animal skins, horns, teeth, shells, and feathers. This would enable him "to have on hand, at the time of the opening of the laboratory for work, materials of all kinds now known, in sufficient quantity to last for five years' experimentation."[9] These items were stored in the drawers of the laboratory's stockroom, which was located downstairs between the library and the large machine shop. In April 1889 *Cosmopolitan Magazine* noted that "the whole of nature seems to have been laid under contributions to stock these long, deep drawers." Through long hours of research, Edison had become highly skilled at material analysis. Experience had taught him that "an experimenter never knows 5 minutes ahead what he does want," and he intended to avoid delays and loss of momentum by having as complete a storehouse as possible.[10]

The stockroom also housed all the materials necessary to prevent delays in the construction of experimental devices. According to *Cosmopolitan*, there were "rolls of woven stuffs, sheet metals, and all sorts of papers, gums, and linings . . . bits of machinery, bolts, screws, nuts, angle-irons; tools such as hammers, vises, drills . . . everything one can think of, from a packet of needles or a tooth-pick, to a sledge-hammer or a sewing machine, can be found here."[11] With these materials at their disposal, Edison's machinists could rapidly turn rough sketches into experimental models, alter apparatus, and build full-scale versions of new inventions. *Scientific American* described how "rough sketches will be submitted to model makers, who will secure from the vast supplies of material blanks for the necessary parts, or possibly completed pieces of apparatus, and as many work men as can be employed to advantage will be at once detailed for the work, and thus the working model will be brought out in a very short time."[12]

The stockroom represented the empirical, shop-based style of research that often predominated at the Edison laboratory, especially when the problem was one of materials. Nonetheless, this was never the kind of blind empiricism that both contemporaries and later commentators have sometimes characterized as the hallmark of the Edisonian method. Existing knowledge always provided the basis for research. For instance, the periodic testing of a wide range of materials for such inventions as lamp filaments, phonograph recording cylinders, and

The laboratory library, with three stacks of books, also served as Edison's office; his desk is in the foreground.

battery elements always started with research in the laboratory's well-stocked scientific and technical library. As research progressed, Edison and his researchers might return to the library to search for further information that would allow them to refine their investigations. The laboratory library was maintained for the staff; Edison also had an extensive personal library at his home. Edison and his researchers could find almost any important scientific or technical reference, including copies of patents, necessary to obtain state-of-the-art knowledge about any project. If the library's holdings proved inadequate, Edison would quickly order the required literature. The library later contained an extensive study collection of minerals that Edison acquired from George Kunz, a noted mineralogist associated with Tiffany & Company.[13]

The library also was Edison's office, and it was the one room that signified his status. It was paneled in dark-varnished yellow pine with arched windows open to the main street. At one end stood a large fireplace, and a large carved wooden clock given to Edison by his staff in 1889 hung above it. Bookcases lined the alcoves of the main floor and the two open tiers of galleries above. Some of the bookcases were enclosed by glass fronts and displayed Edison's inventions. Although the room itself was something of a showcase for the inventor, Edison gave little thought to its furnishings beyond those necessary to conduct business. One of his employees recalled that it was initially "a comparatively gaunt and cheerless abode, depending solely on its literary treasure-troves and scientific models for adornment." In 1889, however, the laboratory staff surprised Edison for his birthday by redecorating the library with the clock, rugs, pictures, plants, tables, and, as described by William Dickson in his 1892 biography of Edison, "eighteen handsomely carved chairs, in oak and leather, embellished with the monogram—T.A.E." Later that year Edison returned from the 1889 Paris Exposition with the marble statue "Genius of Light"—a winged figure standing on a broken gas lamp and holding up an incandescent lamp. Over the years, Edison continued to add to the library's decoration with mementoes of his career.[14]

Edison probably spent little time in the library beyond that required to look over his mail and conduct his business affairs. His real place of business was his private experimental room on the second floor. Located at the top of the stairs that came up from the library, this room overlooked the central courtyard and the smaller buildings that flanked it. Across the hall from Edison was a room occupied by his personal experimental machinist, Fred Ott. Down the hall could be found other experimental rooms divided by wooden partitions that could be rearranged to fit the needs of various projects. Here, too, were rooms devoted to glassblowing and vacuum pumping for experimental lamps. At the end of the hall was the precision room, the machine shop headed by Fred Ott's brother John, who oversaw a staff of skilled experimental machinists. On the third floor was space for additional experimental rooms that could also be rearranged as needed, a lamp test room, and a large room that served as a lecture hall and sound recording studio.

Even before his impressive research facility was completed, Edison was growing concerned about the cost of operating it. "The Lord only knows," he told Edward Johnson in July 1887, "where I am to get the shekels—Laboratory is going to be an awful pull on me."[15] Although he expected some of the cost to be borne by the Edison lighting companies, Edison's ambitions for his new laboratory were much grander than a corporate research facility. In August he approached both Drexel, Morgan & Company and the Boston investment banker William Lloyd Garrison Jr. about his plans for other experimental work in the hope that they would provide additional support for the laboratory. In letters to Garrison and J. Hood Wright, a Morgan partner who sat on the board of the Edison Electric Light Company, Edison described his ambition "to build up a gradually and surely a great Industrial Works in the Orange Valley" with the "Laboratory supplying the perfected invention models pattern[s] & fitting up necessary special machinery in the factory for each invention. My plan contemplates to working of only that class of inventions which require but small investments for each and of a highly profitable nature & also of that character that the articles are sold to Jobbers, Dealers etc—No cumbersome inventions like the Electric Light." Edison wanted the investment bankers to help him

Edison at work in the back room of the chemical laboratory c. 1890.

form a company that would provide up to $25,000 a year for experiments on these inventions and to set up factories to manufacture them. Instead of earning a royalty, Edison proposed that he receive half the profits on each manufactured invention once earnings reached 10 percent. Although Edison expressed optimism in early September that Drexel Morgan would accept his proposal, they declined involvement, as did Garrison, who told Edison that even though "the amount of capital asked is modest, too modest in my opinion . . . owing to the peculiar state of the money market, it is not easy to interest capital in new enterprises."[16]

To attract capital for this proposal, Edison drew up a prospectus for what he called the Edison Industrial Company that largely followed the plan he had outlined in his August letters to Garrison and Wright. He also drafted a contract that set out the terms of his relationship to the company. Edison planned to provide the company with a variety of new inventions other than those for electric light and power, telegraphs and telephones, phonographs, and ore milling that he was developing under existing contracts (or in the case of telegraphs for which he hoped to make separate arrangements). The company would set up the factories and manufacture and sell the inventions.[17]

Edison soon found a prospective backer in Henry Villard, who had funded his electric railroad experiments at Menlo Park. Edison drew up several lists during his negotiations with Villard that indicate he was hoping to develop over twenty such inventions; other lists of experiments to be carried out at the new laboratory suggest that he had several other ideas in mind as well. These lists resemble those he had drawn up for his first independent laboratory in May 1875, and a few projects, such as a method of making malleable cast iron, had even appeared on those lists. Other subjects of long interest to Edison included a hearing aid, ink for the blind, and artificial silk and ivory. Some of the ideas were inventions he had experimented with over the previous two or three years, including artificial mother of pearl, railroad signals, and a method of producing electricity directly from coal. Edison initiated other projects after receiving correspondence that suggested a significant market for them. For example, although he first conceived the idea of developing a cotton-picker while on his honeymoon, he only began to actively develop a machine after James Richardson, the owner of a large cotton plantation, wrote asking him to do so in December 1887. Similar requests from the Parrot Copper and Silver Company to devise a process for electrically refining copper and from manufacturers of butter-making machines to take up the process of producing butter directly from milk also influenced his list of projects. Edison hoped to improve, among other things, the machinery for drawing brass wire and methods for making bolting cloth and sheet glass. He also conceived a process of electrotyping in a vacuum that had grown out of his lamp experiments. He even thought about designing a machine for compacting snow to clear city streets. In several instances, Edison investigated the annual sales of existing products and the potential savings that his proposed improvements in manufacturing processes might bring.[18]

During their negotiations in the early part of 1888 Villard and Edison began to discuss the possibility of Villard paying for all laboratory expenses not covered by Edison's existing contracts for experimental work. This marked a significant shift in the negotiations and a departure from Edison's original proposals to Drexel Morgan and Garrison. Edison originally had been willing to advance all experimental funds himself and to be reimbursed only for those inventions that were subsequently manufactured. Now, faced with the large expenses involved in actually running his laboratory, Edison needed money in advance to pay for his experiments. During their negotiations, Villard suggested a five-year partnership agreement in which he would pay all experimental expenses (except for projects Edison was developing under other arrangements) in return for a half interest in each invention. Responding to this proposal in a letter of January 19, Edison estimated that his laboratory would cost $60,000 to operate for a year, and that $27,000 of that sum was covered under existing arrangements.[19] By the time they drafted a contract, however, Edison realized that he had seriously underestimated the actual amount and cost of research at the laboratory. His new figures showed annual laboratory expenses of $90,100, with $52,000 covered by existing contracts. Edison wanted Villard to invest up to $42,100 per year for all his other experiments, including $4,000 to cover the cost of materials. Edison's ambitions apparently exceeded Villard's pocketbook, and Villard decided not to become involved in this venture. Edison therefore had to cover the costs of those experiments he had already begun, and he decided not to resume others that he had experimented with prior to the opening of the new laboratory. Most were abandoned by April, and at the end of the year the projects he had hoped to develop for the Edison Industrial Company were listed as "Dead" experiments. Edison also never developed the few inventions, such as artificial pearls, the manufacture of malleable wrought iron, and methods of drawing wire and making plate glass, on which he had applied for patents.[20]

Just as his negotiations with Villard turned to direct support for his laboratory expenses, Edison sought similar support for his experimental costs related to electric light and power. At the end of January he asked the Edison Machine Works, the Edison Lamp Company, Bergmann & Company, and the Edison Electric Light Company each to make "a weekly advance to cover the cost of experiments which I shall conduct in the interests of each of the four concerns," requesting weekly amounts of $350 each from the Machine Works and the Lamp Company and $150 each from Bergmann and the Light Company.[21] Although only the Lamp Company agreed to the full amount, Edison was able to acquire significant direct support for the laboratory from the light companies.

Edison had to provide the funds himself for other experimental expenses, although he expected to be reimbursed for two major projects he had under way at the laboratory. In October 1887, as the laboratory neared completion, Edison had organized the Edison Phonograph Company and reorganized the Edison Ore Milling Company to obtain support for his work on these subjects. In both cases he agreed to fund experiments himself with the expectation that if he was successful he would be reimbursed by these companies. Edison also carried out contract research for other firms with which he was associated. Negotiations with Western Union about new telegraph inventions proved unfruitful, but the Bell Telephone Company finally agreed to pay for Edison's telephone experiments, and the A. B. Dick Novelty Company funded his experiments on a typewriter, ink, and improved stencils for the device that Dick sold as the Edison Mimeograph. Edison also briefly experimented with a motor for the Sims-Edison Electric Torpedo Company.[22]

Edison did not entirely forego work on the kind of inventions that he had hoped Villard or someone else might fund. For example, tobacco merchant

S. P. Carr asked Edison to experiment on methods of bleaching tobacco to the rich yellow color that brought high prices for wrappers. Carr offered to give Edison a substantial share of the profits if he succeeded. Edison would also be allowed to keep the process secret by sending his own man to take charge of the manufacturing. This proposition no doubt appealed to Edison, who was an inveterate smoker of cigars and chewer of tobacco, and he kept two men at work on the project during the spring and summer of 1888. Although they succeeded in bleaching the tobacco every process they tried ruined the flavor, and Edison abandoned the experiments by the fall. Other projects of this type periodically intrigued Edison, but he invariably limited the expense of the experiments carried out on speculation.[23]

Throughout his career Edison had been keenly aware of the value of knowing his experimental costs, and he further refined his system of recordkeeping and cost accounting at the West Orange laboratory. In a letter to Tate Edison sketched out his plans for the laboratory cost accounting:

> I want a better time sheet used for the Experimenters. Something which describes nature experiment, time consumed & Roughness of amount material used so in charging up we know somewhere the amount material used—
>
> Also we must apportion the rent of diferent parts of Laboratory, say Laboratory costs complete without supplies or tools, $80,000. Eliminate the Library & Store Room—then take the sqr feet in the balance; & divide it in the $80,000 this will capitalize each room—charge $2^1/2$ pct for taxes, 1 pct for insurance, 10 pct for interest, 3 percent for depreciation. The proportionate cost of heating & Lighting & this will be the rental of rooms— In the shops charge all supplies at a profit of 30 percent as I have to carry so much deadstock, & 65 cents an hour for each workman, and 50 cents an hour for each experimenter, & an extra General Expense of 45 percent— You must attend to getting that Store bookeeping started right off— Lots of material is going out every day & nothing should go out without we know what to charge it to, and also to know what we have left so as to keep our stock intact at least every 6 months.[24]

He also assigned each project a number that could be used to track its costs through the labor records, material and equipment vouchers, and account books. With these careful records, Edison could not only satisfy the needs of the companies that paid for experimental work but also evaluate the resources he allocated to each project. And he and his staff could use the records to estimate manufacturing costs.

As the laboratory was being finished Edison drew up a plan for staffing it. He planned to bring four experimenters from the laboratory of the Edison Lamp Works—Arthur Payne, H. De Coursey Hamilton, Patrick Kenny, and William Kennedy Laurie Dickson—and to hire "six smart young fellows as assistants, couple from College who understand physical measurement" to join them. He also wanted "One person familiar [with] scientific matters to translate must understand English French German & Italian, a good operative chemist, organic & inorganic, [a] good practical mathematician, and a person thoroughly

Edison (seated center) surrounded by his experimenters.

familiar with optics & optical." The machine shops were to be staffed by Fred
Ott and A. K. Keller, both of whom had worked at the Lamp Works laboratory,
a foreman, a "Machinist who understands buffing & polishing," and "15 good
workmen." To round out the staff he planned to have a blacksmith, a photographer, and "a general cleaner & sweeper."[25] It is not clear how many men
were working at the laboratory when it opened in December, but by the beginning of January there were about seventy-five men, including some who were
still finishing work on the buildings. By February, the payroll for the laboratory
staff alone included over eighty men, and during its first two years of operation the labor force would fluctuate between eighty and one hundred depending on Edison's needs and finances. Like the laboratory itself, the staff that
worked there was on a scale that far exceeded that found in other research
institutions.

The main experimental staff consisted of twenty-five to thirty experimenters and experimental assistants, including young men who came as ap-
prentices hoping to learn from the master inventor, and thirty to forty machinists. They were supported by an additional labor force of thirty to forty men and
boys that included three to five pattern makers, three or four draftsmen, an

engineer and a fireman for both day and night shifts, a blacksmith and a steam fitter, each with an assistant, a few carpenters and several laborers, a clerk and an assistant each for the stockroom in the main building and for the chemical storeroom, a couple of errand boys, a boy to operate the elevator that carried material between the machine shops, two office clerks to assist Alfred Tate, and nightwatchman James Walrond. There was considerable turnover among the rest of the staff during these two years, but a faithful nucleus of about twenty to twenty-five experimenters and machinists remained at the heart of the laboratory.

Contrary to the common belief that Edison disdained theoretical knowledge and formal education, Alfred Tate noted that most of the "young men employed in the Laboratory are usually graduates of the various technical schools, who have some knowledge of electrical matters, and who come here to extend their knowledge."[26] Edison's staff chemists, too, were largely college graduates, and several of them had advanced training in German universities. Nonetheless, a college education was no guarantee of advancement at the laboratory. Edison was always willing to hire ambitious young men who had practical experience, including several who had worked for the Lamp Company and Machine Works, and he often favored those with practical experience when choosing someone to take charge of an important experimental campaign. In fact, most of the key group of experimenters at the laboratory were men whose experience was primarily practical.

Edison's chief electrical assistant for six years was Arthur Kennelly, a self-educated British telegraph engineer with great proficiency at mathematical analysis. Although Edison often is depicted as denigrating abstract mathematical analysis, in fact Kennelly's mathematical abilities commended him to Edison. Like Upton and Sprague before him, Kennelly provided the kind of formal mathematical analysis that Edison often felt uncomfortable making himself. Furthermore, Edison had admired the exacting quality of British telegraph engineering since his 1873 trip to England. As a result, he hired the twenty-six-year-old Kennelly without meeting him, although he apparently examined some of his published work. Edison placed Kennelly in charge of the electrical experimenters in the galvanometer room and also gave him the responsibility of equipping it. Kennelly found the laboratory to be "just heaven. It is certainly one of the finest in the world, and the finest in the States."[27] Edison allowed Kennelly to take advantage of these facilities to conduct his own research, and Kennelly made important contributions to electrical engineering theory.

The chemical department was headed by Dr. Erwin von Wilmowsky, but the most important chemical experiments were often entrusted to members of the staff whose training was largely practical. The man who became Edison's chief chemical experimenter was Jonas Walter Aylsworth, who had joined Edison at the Lamp Works laboratory in 1887 after a year at Purdue University. Aylsworth remained connected with Edison for most of his career and played an important role in several technologies developed at the West Orange laboratory. During this time he made important contributions to the development of plastics with his work on phenol resins.[28]

The career of another key chemical experimenter during the early years of the laboratory suggests the value Edison placed on practical experience. At the time he came to work for Edison, Reginald Fessenden had no experience as a chemist. He had attended college, where he studied mathematics and languages, and he taught mathematics for a time, but his technical experience was limited to that gained from private study and his work as a tester of underground wires in New York for the Edison Machine Works. Edison probably decided to hire Fessenden because of his combination of practical experience and mathematical abilities, as well as by his earnest statement that "I am not at all afraid of work, no matter how rough or dirty," always a prerequisite for Edison's assistants.[29] When Fessenden arrived at the laboratory Edison was not yet ready to conduct electrical experiments and assigned him instead to the effort to develop a fireproof insulation for electrical wires. As a result, Fessenden ended up doing chemical rather than electrical experiments, and by October 1888 Edison felt that he would "soon make a first class chemist."[30] In early 1890 Edison decided to discharge Wilmowsky and another German chemist, Henry Wurtz, who was working on the insulation project, because even though they were fine chemists he felt that they didn't get results. He then installed Fessenden, with little over a year's experience as a chemist, in place of Wilmowsky as head of the laboratory's chemical department.

Beside favoring those with practical experience, Edison liked his assistants to be generalists rather than specialists, willing to tackle any problem he might assign them. William Dickson, whom Edison placed in charge of ore-milling experiments in the metallurgical laboratory, exemplifies this kind of multifaceted but practical experimenter. Dickson's classical education at Cambridge may have worked against him when he initially applied for a position at Menlo Park in 1879, but his strong interest in electrical invention led him to persevere and eventually obtain a position with Edison in 1883, when he went to work in the testing room of the Edison Machine Works. By the next year Dickson had become superintendent of this department. Edison became familiar with Dickson's work, as many of the tests and experiments he carried out were done under Edison's direction. Thus, when the Machine Works moved to Schenectady, Edison made Dickson an experimenter in the laboratory at the Lamp Works. By the time Edison moved into his new laboratory in West Orange, Dickson had become the lead experimenter on magnetic ore separation and was put in charge of research in the metallurgy laboratory. Dickson also turned an interest in photography into a position as Edison's official photographer and spent part of his time in a photographic studio in the main building. He thus became the logical choice to head Edison's efforts to develop motion picture technology, a project that he carried on part-time while continuing to head the ore milling research.[31]

Such versatility and individual initiative were hallmarks of the shop-based invention that characterized all of Edison's laboratories. In the culture of the machine shop, skilled machinists were expected to be able to make any device; the most skilled and ambitious were also given the best pay and the most interesting work, often of an experimental nature. Over the years, several of Edison's experimental machinists had become experimenters in their own right and shared in the financial rewards of his successful inventions, a practice that continued at the West Orange laboratory. The laboratory's machinists could also add to their earnings through inside contracting in which they bid on work within the shop for the construction of experimental apparatus, demonstration or manufacturing models, and special tools for manufacturing them. Taking on such a contract required initiative that might lead to other responsibilities and possibly a supervisory role in Edison's factories. Failure, however, could mean dismissal. Edison paid his machinists "as high wages as any factory"—often better than the pay his experimenters received. And Edison rewarded machinists as well as researchers who made crucial contributions with a share of royalties or an interest in or a significant position with the companies that manufactured or marketed his inventions. As he told a reporter for the *Cincinnati Enquirer*, the young men who experimented for him "know that if I am successful that I don't keep it all for myself."[32]

The possibility of sharing in Edison's success was one of the ways he encouraged his experimenters to show initiative. Another was to give them higher pay or more responsibility. Thus, when Charles Deshler, who conducted lamp and vacuum tests at the laboratory for the Lamp Company, complained to Francis Upton about his pay, Edison observed that "The position Labor etc of Mr Deshler is not worth any more than he is getting. He can readily see himself that the position will not warrant a greater salary. Had he any ambition he would assist in experimenting & initiate things himself and not always be told to do this & that— If he would make himself more useful which he can easily do I would be agreeable [to an increase in wages] but not now."[33] Edison did, however, suggest that Upton show Deshler this response as a way to motivate him to show more initiative. Deshler apparently took Edison's advice to heart; he eventually had charge of lamp experiments at the laboratory and was one of Edison's more highly paid experimenters.

Edison also encouraged his staff to use the resources of the laboratory as a forum for self-improvement. His employees could take advantage of a weekly lecture series on scientific and technical subjects that he provided exclusively for his staff. They also had access to one of the finest scientific and technical libraries in the world. Reginald Fessenden recalled that he and Arthur Kennelly used to study mathematics together during lunch and that he often spent an hour or so studying theoretical physics or chemistry at the end of the day. Both of their names appear frequently in the notebooks used to record library books checked out by the staff. Herbert Read was another employee who took advantage of these opportunities by reading many of the elementary and standard works on electricity and chemistry in the library. This course of self-study helped him to advance from storeroom boy to lamp-test room assistant to full-fledged lamp experimenter.[34]

Edison usually organized his staff into experimental teams devoted to a particular line of research. As he later explained to Sigmund Bergmann, "The way to do it is to organize a gang of one good experimenter and two or three assistants, appropriate a definite sum yearly to keep it going . . . have every patent sent to them and let them experiment continuously."[35] As special equipment or experimental models were needed, the head experimenter would order them from John Ott, who was the superintendent of experimenters. Ott would make the necessary drawings, order materials, and assign the work to one of the experimental machinists whose time would be divided as necessary among the various projects at the laboratory.

Research usually began with written instructions from Edison. Chemist David Marshall, a Rutgers University graduate, recalled that on his first day of work Edison handed him a notebook in which were "orders to 'make' or 'do' enough different things to keep me busy for a long time."[36] Edison's notes may have provided the starting point for a set of experiments, but according to Fessenden, those men in whose abilities Edison had developed confidence and who "had been 'indoctrinated' in his methods" were given "a very considerable opportunity of developing their individuality in the working out of problems." He recalled that after working under close instructions from Edison "I finally got to understand his methods pretty well and seldom needed to bother him about details."[37] Nonetheless, the men working for Edison understood that their individual initiative was to solve the problems he set before them.

Fessenden's use of the term indoctrination is telling, for Edison often hired young men whom he could shape as experimenters, just as he had at Menlo Park. This contributed to the intense loyalty they gave Edison. It also may help to explain their common belief that they merely carried out Edison's instructions and that he was the true inventor regardless of their own very real contributions. After achieving his own considerable success as an inventor after leaving Edison's employ, Fessenden wrote, "The inventions are always Edison's; the particular assistant who does the work is not material . . . while much credit should be given to his assistants, the results are his." Fessenden also credited his later success to his apprenticeship at the West Orange laboratory, where he claimed Edison "taught me the right way to experiment."[38] Fessenden's statements echo those of his predecessors at Menlo Park.

Edison oversaw the work of his experimenters by making daily rounds to see how research was progressing. Fessenden, who sometimes accompanied Edison on these morning rounds, recalled that Edison was "most considerate, and never found fault with the work, merely, when things were going wrong, explaining what should be done to make them go right," and sometimes "apparently casually, shift[ing] the development to an entirely new, and generally better, line."[39] A slightly different impression is given by Marshall who remembered that Edison liked to challenge the statements of his researchers "to see if one were in earnest, or sure of one's position." Marshall also noted that Edison was not above "biting sarcasm or ridicul[ing] one into extinction" and would on occasion "get mad and make the sparks fly." Nonetheless, he recalled, "we were a happy family at the Laboratory."[40]

As he had at Menlo Park, Edison used the traditions of shop culture to create a sense of community in his new laboratory that spurred his assistants to hard work and long hours. Like the master machinist, Edison worked alongside his men, often putting in longer hours, and taking a leading role in the practical jokes and horseplay that helped to ease the tension of an intense experimental campaign. His own efforts inspired those of his men, who always called him Mr. Edison to his face and referred to the forty-year-old inventor as the "Old Man" amongst themselves. Edison also used the informal work routine of the shop to advantage. The intensity of work at the laboratory waxed and waned as research dictated and when necessary might go on all night and day, followed by time off to recover from the effort. Marshall recalled that "on several occasions when enthusiasm on insulation ran high, I had worked all night."[41] Edison himself often worked for several days at a time, taking little cat-naps on a folding bed located off his experimental room. Other members of the staff also kept their own hours. In his memoirs, Fessenden described a typical day as starting at nine in the morning and continuing until midnight or later. He and Arthur Kennelly usually took a break in the afternoon to exercise at the YMCA gymnasium in Orange, followed by a leisurely walk and supper. At eight in the evening they returned to the laboratory where Fessenden would work until midnight; then he and his assistant John Dorr liked to stop for coffee and biscuits. Fessenden would then work for another half an hour, followed by an hour's study of theoretical physics or chemistry before he went to bed. Fessenden's routine, however, was frequently broken during those frequent periods "when we worked all day and night." He estimated that this occurred about twenty-five percent of the time, "because there were always problems coming up which had to be solved very quickly if there were not to be large financial losses."[42]

During its first ten years, Edison focused research at the laboratory in three major fields—electric light and power, the entertainment technologies of phonographs and motion pictures, and ore milling. Edison's role in these inventive campaigns varied widely during the course of research and development. He had to be both a corporate manager of innovation and a creative inventor and researcher. His ideas still remained the starting point for inventive activity at the new laboratory in West Orange. While the resources of the laboratory allowed him to carry on simultaneous research on these major projects as well as other miscellaneous subjects, Edison's central role meant that work tended to ebb and flow as his personal involvement changed. This was evident during the first months of work at the new laboratory as Edison devoted most of his own time to the effort to develop a commercial dictating phonograph.

CHAPTER 15

Inventing Entertainment

O ver the course of the next decade, the new phonograph that Edison developed during the first months of work at his new laboratory led him into the entertainment industry. Although he had always envisioned entertainment uses for the phonograph, Edison designed his improved wax-record phonograph, the first new product of the West Orange laboratory, as a business machine rather than as an entertainment device. Edison and the other major figures in the early phonograph industry shared a background in telecommunications; they were ill prepared to imagine and create an entertainment industry. When Edison began work on motion pictures at the end of 1888, with his phonograph as a model, he had an even less clear understanding of the potential new entertainment market for films. He later remarked that "[we] knew we had an interesting and novel apparatus, [but] we generally regarded it more or less as a curiosity with no very large practicable possibilities."[1] Inventing the technologies of entertainment, as it turned out, was not the same as inventing their commercial use.

Edison and others who pioneered these technologies had to negotiate unfamiliar territory. They had to use their experience with older forms of entertainment to help define the place of these new technologies even as they created new possibilities. In doing so they were both responding to and helping to create a growing leisure-time entertainment industry that was spurred in part by the same technological and business innovations that Edison had used to reach the top of his profession. Taking advantage of the national telegraph and railroad networks that had emerged by the 1870s, businesses increasingly were able to manufacture and distribute their goods nationwide. Business leaders found that they could best coordinate these activities by developing the same kinds of corporate organizations that had served the telegraph and railroad industries. As the number of corporations grew, so too did new classes of workers who flocked to the nation's cities to staff corporate offices. Male middle managers and female secretaries with higher incomes and more leisure time than harried small business owners or fatigued factory workers led the search for new forms of recreation. But even factory workers were beginning to experience a growth in real wages and a drop in working hours that would allow them greater access to leisure activities. This was evident during the 1886 strike at the Edison Machine Works, although the gains made by workers were undercut by the company's move to Schenectady. Although they were unwilling to give up their growing authority over the pace of work, the Machine Works managers were willing to give ten hours' pay for only nine hours' work. By the turn of the century such outcomes increased workers' ability to participate in leisure consumption, but it came at the expense of real power in the workplace.[2]

The growth of leisure time and in the consumption that came with it helped to shift the manufacturing economy from producer to consumer goods. As Edison's experience shows, the transition could be difficult. His prior experience was with producer technologies. His telegraph, telephone, and electric lighting systems, his electric pen, and his early phonographs were all developed and sold primarily for business use. By the end of the 1890s his two most successful businesses would be his phonograph and motion picture companies, which catered to consumers rather than businesspeople. Yet, in the 1890s Edison continued to devote most of his own time to electric lighting and to his process for extracting low-grade iron ore in iron and steel mills. In the 1900s, drawing on the income from these consumer goods, he continued to focus his own efforts on producer markets, developing improved methods for making the cement used in buildings and a storage battery for automobiles. Edison's personal involvement in his new consumer entertainment businesses remained quite limited until the 1910s, and when he finally did take a larger hand in their operations, his participation was of dubious benefit to his companies.

Edison's development work on phonographs and motion pictures was also a product of his very different understanding of their potential markets. Edison expected his phonograph to fit into an expanding market for business machines such as typewriters and telephones. He therefore put the full resources of his new laboratory to work on the problem of an improved dictating phonograph. At the same time he devoted some of these resources to development work on sound recording and record duplication for entertainment purposes. In contrast, the work on motion pictures remained a minor project at the laboratory with a small staff of researchers who worked on it part-time. Edison planned a large factory and sales campaign for the phonograph, but his manufacturing and marketing plans for motion pictures were relatively haphazard.

Edison had begun to plan the development of a new dictating phonograph with his inventive partner, Ezra Gilliland, in October 1886. Unlike his earlier phonograph designs, the new machine would be designed for use by a single

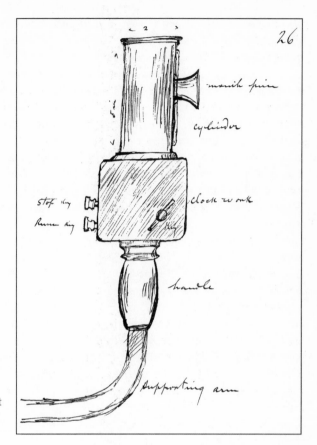

Ezra Gilliland's October 1886 drawing of the proposed dictating phonograph shows the recording cylinder and mouthpiece at top and a clockwork drive at center.

person working in the quiet of an office. Thus, the recording would be made by a person speaking into a flexible tube rather than shouting into a mouthpiece, and the recorded sound would be heard when a listener would hold the tube up to his or her ear. It would not be amplified and broadcast into the room by a funnel. Edison and Gilliland hoped that this would reproduce the human voice "about as loud and clear as a good telephone on a short circuit." In his notebook, Gilliland described the new phonograph as "a small compact instrument suitable for office use" that would be run by a small electric motor. He also proposed recording on a polished glass or metal cylinder covered with "shellac, gum or wax or something of that nature which can be applied by a brush." By turning to such recording surfaces, Gilliland and Edison were clearly influenced by a new competitor to Edison's tinfoil phonograph.[3]

This was the graphophone developed by Charles Sumner Tainter at Alexander Graham Bell's Volta Laboratory in Washington, D.C. Tainter, a skilled machinist who at one time had worked for Charles Williams in Boston, had been working with Alexander and his cousin Chichester Bell to improve the phonograph since 1881. They had begun by experimenting with a small 1878 Edison tinfoil phonograph, but Tainter soon suggested that wax would be a good recording surface, and an experiment in which they filled the phonograph cylinder's grooves with wax showed promise. Although the Volta associates experimented with a wide variety of recording methods and surfaces, wax became the focus of their experiments. Because the phonograph was just one of many inventions under development at the laboratory, it was not until 1885 that Tainter finally devised a wax-cylinder phonograph that showed commercial promise. This machine used a wax-covered paper cylinder and listening tubes for hearing the recording, which was made by speaking into a funnel. Unlike Edison's and Gilliland's proposed design, it was hand-cranked like the original tinfoil phonograph. In naming their new machine the graphophone, the Volta associates paid homage to Edison's phonograph by reversing the letters in its name.[4]

In the summer of 1885, as they progressed to the point where they began to consider commercial development, the Volta associates decided to approach Edison. Bell's father-in-law, Gardiner Hubbard, contacted Edward Johnson and Uriah Painter, his associates in the Edison Speaking Phonograph Company, and proposed joining the Bell-Tainter phonograph interests with those of Edison and the company on a fifty-fifty basis. However, after three months of discussions, Edward Johnson, who was negotiating on Edison's behalf, remained uncertain whether to recommend joining forces "for an invention that might or might not prove ultimately of real practical value."[5] Although Tainter's demonstration of a new machine during the first week of October produced better results than ever before, Johnson advised waiting for further developments. By the end of the year the Bell-Tainter group decided to move ahead on their own and formed the Volta Graphophone Company. As the graphophone proceeded toward commercial introduction, Edison decided that it was time to return to the phonograph. Although he never acknowledged it publicly, the graphophone was clearly the source of inspiration for this renewed effort and provided an initial model for the new phonograph design.

Neither Edison nor Gilliland did much work on the new phonograph until after Edison had begun to make plans for his new laboratory. It was an exhibition of a Bell-Tainter graphophone at the St. James Hotel in New York City in early May 1887 that spurred their renewed interest in developing this machine. The influence of the graphophone is evident from Charles Batchelor's description of Edison's new plan for "making a phonograph that will be able to lift out cylinder as well as stop and start at will etc."[6] The graphophone on exhibit recorded on a removable paper cylinder coated with a $1/8$-inch layer of ozokerite wax, and it had a stop motion that enabled an operator to start and stop it while continuing to supply power to the drive mechanism with a foot treadle. Several other features were designed to improve the quality of recording and playback: the foot treadle had a governor that provided uniform rotation speed to the cylinder; a funnel concentrated sound waves onto the diaphragm and needle that cut the recording into the wax surface; the record was reproduced by a second diaphragm whose needle was attached by a thread to reduce pressure and wear-and-tear on the wax; and a listening tube made it possible to hear dictation quite clearly.

Aware that the soft ozokerite wax of the graphophone cylinder tended to dull and clog the recording stylus and wear down under the pressure of the reproducing stylus, Edison initially focused his research on finding a better recording wax surface and developing a reproducer that would not wear down the recording. With Gilliland unable to assist him because of an illness that kept him away from the laboratory for several weeks, Edison relied on Batchelor, whom he set to work "making cylinders of plumbago, mixtures, and steatite" so that "the dust falls away leaving in shaving etc." Within a short time they discovered that waxes, particularly paraffin mixed with resin, did indeed provide a better recording surface, and they focused their research in this direction.[7]

In the meantime Edison also began to design sensitive reproducers. One of his first ideas is particularly interesting as it embodied a form of magnetic pickup—"the receiving needle never touches the surface of the record but is itself electrified and is attracted to the surface more or less as the record is indented more or less." Edison did not follow up on the possibilities of electrical recording. Instead he and Batchelor experimented with a variety of substances, such as camel's hair, sealskin hair, chamois skin, silk thread, and fish cord, which could be made into very thin points to reproduce a talking voice, yet were soft enough so that they produced little or no scratching noise. As their experiments continued into June, Edison and Batchelor also altered the diaphragm and the manner of attaching the needle to it. One particularly promising design was a rounded diaphragm that Edison modeled on the ear. During the last week of June they again turned their attention to recording cylinders, and Batchelor spent several days trying "to get a suitable & cheap material to make the phonograph 'sleeve'" by combining resin with substances such as kaolin, starch, plumbago, paraffin, and wood pine tar and molding these onto tinfoil, paper, and papier-mâché.[8]

Other than these May and June experiments, little is known of the work on the phonograph prior to the opening of the West Orange laboratory in the fall. Although Edison wrote George Gouraud on July 21 that he already had "a much better apparatus" than the graphophone and was "building the factory to manufacture" it, there is little evidence to support these claims or his optimism that "in the course of a couple of months I will be prepared to put this improved instrument upon the market."[9] Electric lighting and the construction of the new laboratory rather than the phonograph occupied most of Edison's time for the remainder of the summer. By the beginning of October, however, he had made sufficient progress to offer Gouraud all foreign rights for his new phonograph and to place Gilliland in charge of manufacturing it.

To market the improved phonograph, Edison decided to set up a new company rather than revive the old Edison Speaking Phonograph Company. He was led to this decision in part because the Bell interests with whom he was now competing retained a stake in the old company. Indeed, when Chichester Bell and Gardiner Hubbard learned of the new company, they again approached Edison about combining their interests, but as Uriah Painter told Edward Johnson in a letter of October 9, 1887, "he declined saying he thought two were better & let the best one win." Edison's decision to form a new phonograph company was also influenced by his belief that the old one had not lived up to its end of the bargain, although this last criticism could as easily have been lodged against Edison, and, in fact, was by Uriah Painter. When Edison offered a one-third interest in the new Edison Phonograph Company to Painter and other stockholders in the old company they declined, complaining that the terms offered were not only inadequate but dishonorable. Painter also doubted Edison's claim that "his machine was as good a commercial machine" as Tainter's and declared that Edison "was a man whose talk was always loudest when he had the least to back it up."[10]

Edison in turn argued that "I am doing fair by the old stockholders" and that his proposition "based on actual biz is better than if the old contract was alive, but of course in a stock speculation view it is not, but this is not going to be a stock speculating Company, like the Graphophone, if I can prevent it."[11] As negotiations broke down, he also raised a new issue, arguing that the failure to file the basic U.S. phonograph patent prior to the foreign ones meant that with the expiration of the British patent the field was wide open. Although he blamed the company for this, in fact Edison and his patent solicitor were probably the ones at fault. Even with the unfortunate lack of patent protection, Edison asserted that "with my experience & facilities I should have an advantage in competition sufficient to pay a good dividend notwithstanding and I have made the offer to P[ainter] & others so they should realize in part at least what they originally expected= their rejection of the same put it out of the pale of friendship & honor & places it on a business basis."[12] Within a few months Edison had broken completely with Painter, and his relations with Edward Johnson, who sought to mediate their differences, became considerably strained.

Painter's skepticism regarding Edison's claims seem to have had some basis in fact. Although Edison told a *New York Post* reporter in October that he had two prototypes ready and hoped to have 500 manufactured for sale by the end of January, he did not actually deliver a production model to the factory in Bloomfield, New Jersey, until early November. And Gilliland, who was in charge of manufacturing the instruments, felt that they had serious design flaws, telling Edison in mid-December that the machines "would not compare favorably in any respect with the Graphophone." Gilliland was disappointed, however, that Edison seemed not only uninterested in but critical of his efforts at improving the phonograph. The rather unfinished appearance of the machine depicted in the December 31 issue of *Scientific American* suggests that Gilliland had good grounds for complaint. Besides providing a more finished appearance, Gilliland indicated that his own design was "worked out for manufacturing to advantage." Gilliland's effort to adapt the machine so that it could be "run by any form or Motor" or be worked by hand also suggests that problems remained with the small motor, which Edison claimed ran "at a perfectly regular rate of speed, is noiseless, and starts or stops at the touch of a spring."[13]

If Edison had made any significant improvement over the graphophone, it was the spectacle-shaped frame he had devised for the recorder and reproducer. This device facilitated changing between the two operations and allowed the recording and reproducing diaphragm and needles to be removed for repair, adjustment, or replacement. Nonetheless, this device had a thumbscrew adjustment that required considerable trial and error to set properly and that Gilliland attempted to improve by adding a spring adjustment. After Sigmund Bergmann saw the machine during the first week of January, he wrote Painter, "Unless you have money to throw away I would advise you to wait a while as they admitted to me that they were not yet finished experimenting."[14]

Although reluctant to admit it publicly, Edison realized that his new phonograph required considerable improvement. With the resources available in his new laboratory, he would be able to duplicate the kind of research and development effort that he had undertaken eight years earlier at Menlo Park when he turned his electric lighting system from an experimental into a commercial product. As he had done with the electric light system, Edison subdivided the work of improving the phonograph and its recording cylinders among his experimenters. Arthur Kennelly and the galvanometer room staff were in charge of experiments on motors and batteries; Jonas W. Aylsworth was given the task of developing better waxes for the recording cylinder; Theo Wangemann, an experimenter and also an accomplished pianist, was assigned the task of making experimental recordings of both voices and music; and Dr. Franz Schulze-Berge, a German Ph.D. who had worked for a decade in Hermann von Helmholtz's physical laboratory before joining Edison, experimented on processes for duplicating records. Before moving to the third floor of the main building to take charge of the research on electroplating and duplicating phonograph cylinders, Schulze-Berge had conducted electrical experiments in the galvanometer room under Kennelly.[15] Edison focused his own efforts on the phonograph itself, although he kept a watchful eye on all phases of the research and frequently offered suggestions and conducted experiments.

Edison's description of the effort to develop the record duplicating process provides insight into his team research approach. He described his own efforts on this project as "kind of a fishing sort of an experiment; trying to get a general result—quick result—and drawing conclusions therefrom and starting fresh experiments, they were sort of preliminary experiments." To Schulze-Berge he assigned the "accurate experiments . . . all the drudgery . . . of determining temperatures over long periods and carrying out the exact methods of the process."

The very process of carrying out series after series of chemical experiments, however, allowed Edison's experimenters to gain insights and knowledge that led them to make significant contributions. As Edison himself noted, the properties of simple substances might be well understood, but the compound substances used for phonograph cylinders "have different properties [and] are accompanied by different phenomena . . . it is a very long, tedious problem, in experimenting with these materials, to obtain what is desired."[16] Thus, the young chemist Jonas Aylsworth, who conducted many long series of experiments on wax cylinder compounds, became Edison's expert on this technology and was responsible for most of the improvements in waxes and manufacturing processes for the recording cylinders used with Edison phonographs over the next several decades.

When Aylsworth began experimenting on cylinder compounds in January 1888, Edison was using a wax composition of carnauba wax and ceresin. He also had come to the conclusion that it was better to mold a cylinder of a single compound of wax or a waxlike substance rather than placing the wax over a backing material. In this way the cylinder was less susceptible to cracking and peeling. For the first five months, Aylsworth worked with carnauba and other natural waxes as well as gums and resins, trying over 700 experimental compounds.[17] At the end of May he conducted an experiment using oleic acid mixed with carnauba wax, and he found the result "very encouraging as it gives an opening to a new and promising field." Oleic acid was a form of soap derived from the metallic salts of fatty acids, and Aylsworth now focused on soaps of this type to produce "artificial wax-like materials." By late July the results were so encouraging that Edison moved Aylsworth from the chemical laboratory to Room 14 in the main laboratory building so that he could "get more familiar with the operations of molding" being experimented with by Arthur Payne.[18] As usual, Edison took out the basic patents for wax cylinders made with metallic soaps, but the standard formula that Aylsworth developed in the fall remained a trade secret. Indeed, during a January 5 interview concerning the phonograph patent situation, Edison declared, "I am so thoroughly convinced of the uselessness of patents that one of my objects in building my present laboratory is to search for trade secrets [particularly chemical processes] that require no patents, and may be sources of profit until some one else discovers them."[19]

While the efforts to develop wax compounds, molding, and duplicating processes involved tedious experimentation that Edison was happy to leave to his assistants, the redesign of the phonograph involved the kind of mechanical challenge that Edison enjoyed and at which he and his machinists were so well practiced. It was also the type of work for which they left few of the written detailed records like those made by the chemists during the research on record materials. Nonetheless, improvements in the phonograph were the type Edison considered essential to protect with patents, and his applications as well as other evidence suggest how much had been reworked by the summer of 1888.[20]

Edison and some members of the laboratory staff with George Gouraud and the "perfected" wax-recording phonograph. From left to right (standing) W. K. L. Dickson, Charles Batchelor, A. Theodore Wangemann, John Ott, Charles Brown, (seated) Fred Ott, Edison, and Gouraud.

The recording and playback mechanisms, although similar in design to the 1887 model, were substantially improved by Edison as he worked to find the combination of diaphragm and needle arrangement best suited for good articulation. Characteristically, he tested a variety of materials for use as diaphragms and recording and reproducing styli. His experiments were also influenced by simultaneous research he was conducting on telephones, where he discovered "that the loudness of sound produced in a telephone-receiver . . . is dependent upon the sharpness of the impulse rather than upon its strength." When his microscopic examinations of recorded cylinders showed that the hissing consonants or sibilants that had given him so much trouble in all his phonograph designs "appear longer and of less depth, and hence more gradual in their rise and fall, than those for vowel sounds," he concluded that these sounds did "not move the reproducing-diaphragm with sufficient abruptness to reproduce the sound-waves with clearness."[21] By redesigning the linkage between diaphragm and stylus and by altering the angle at which the stylus cut into the cylinder, he found that he could greatly improve articulation.

The rest of the phonograph also underwent radical change. The battery-powered motor was completely redesigned to provide the constant low speed needed by the phonograph. It was now connected to the drive-shaft of the phonograph by a belt that also served to isolate the recording and playback mechanism from the vibrations of the motor. To better suit the needs of dictation, the phonograph now included a start-stop mechanism and an auto-return device that made it easier to pause or return to a particular part of the recording. It also had an improved cutting tool to shave a used cylinder so that it could be rerecorded. Finally, the new design was housed in a handsome wooden cabinet better suited to an office.

The "perfected" phonograph, as Edison termed it, was designed with manufacturing in mind. Ten years earlier Edison had suggested that "a practical, marketable machine . . . can only be built on the American principle of interchangeability of parts like a gun or a sewing machine." At the time he thought that such a machine would have to "be simple and easily made and one that will be hard to improve, otherwise we will be changing and improving all the time, which lessens profits."[22] Now, however, he saw interchangeability as a way of allowing him to make continual improvements in the phonograph. By using special-purpose machine tools operated by semi-skilled workers who carefully gauged each part as it was manufactured, Edison felt that he could ensure that "any new designs will be adapted to instruments already sent out, requiring only the removal of the part intended to be replaced—nothing else will be interfered with." Edison believed that his manufacturing system would allow him to beat the Graphophone Company, which had started a factory in Bridgeport, Connecticut, because "Tainter [was] not practical man: don't know how to make cheap."[23]

To establish phonograph manufacturing using the American system of interchangeable parts, Edison and Batchelor organized the Edison Phonograph Works at the beginning of May and began to build a factory next to the laboratory. Whereas the small-scale hand operations of Edison's Bloomfield factory were capable of producing only twenty-five to thirty-five phonographs per day, Edison expected the new factory to produce two hundred per day. Because so much of his own money was tied up in the electrical manufacturing shops, Edison tried to interest Henry Villard in the enterprise as part of his general effort to have Villard become the primary backer of all his enterprises. When that effort fell through, Edison himself had to become the primary financier for the factory, which cost nearly $250,000 to build and equip, including special tools and machinery, before manufacturing began in earnest in the fall.[24]

Production of phonographs had continued at the Bloomfield factory during the winter, and by mid-March Gilliland informed Edison that "we are within two weeks or less, of having machines ready for market." However, as the general agent for the Edison Phonograph Company, Gilliland also expressed his concern that there was "not one contract closed with any agent and no printing or advertising matter of any kind," and he told Edison that "the commercial end of the Phonograph business needs my personal attention badly and I think from this time forward I shall give it all of my time." Having learned from Edison's complaints about his independent efforts to improve the phonograph, Gilliland also decided that it would be essential for him to get Edison's approval for "every step I take."[25] By the end of March Edison arrived at the basic form of the "Standard Phonograph," and although the commercial machine would be delayed for several months as he continued to make improvements, it was clear to both men that the new design was vastly superior and they agreed to begin promoting it and securing sales agents.

As they contemplated putting the new phonograph on the market, Edison and Gilliland used the sewing machine and typewriter businesses as a model. As Gilliland explained, "the salesman and canvassers obtain the order, the machine is delivered in our wagon and an inspector, who will also be an instructor will follow and set up the machine and instruct the purchaser in the use of it."[26] Although they differed over how such instructors would be trained, they agreed that instructors were particularly important in introducing new technologies to the general public. This was quite apparent in May 1889, when George Gouraud wrote about his difficulties marketing the phonograph in England and complained about the expert knowledge required to operate it. Edison replied that "I have never yet seen a piece of special mechanism designed for ultimate use by the general public, that could be placed directly in their hands without employing experts to teach and instruct them." To emphasize his point, Edison noted that

> even so simple an instrument as an improved flat-iron involves a certain amount of explanation by an "expert" before it can be intelligently introduced into domestic use. Probably ninety per cent of all the sewing machines employed are operated by women and the Companies employ paid agents or "experts" to educate these, which takes from three to four weeks time. Every new device which from time to time is brought out by sewing machine people has to be explained by an expert, and compared with this instrument, the phonograph is a marvel of simplicity. It takes us just about two hours to thoroughly instruct a person with no previous knowledge in the operation of the phonograph, but the instructor must be thoroughly competent and familiar with the machine, or his instructions would serve only to confuse and add to the ignorance of the pupil.

He suggested that this was the very cause of Gouraud's trouble as he had "no one who is master of the new instrument" and capable of training others to act as expert instructors to purchasers. As a result, Edison maintained, "the phonograph is blamed for faults which exist only in those who handle it." Nonetheless, Edison did recognize that the public resisted new technology that seemed too complex and suggested hopefully that as "the term 'experts' conveys the idea of intricacy," if they called these men "'Phonograph Operators' seventy-five per cent of the visionary difficulties of the instrument would disappear."[27]

Edison and Gilliland both believed that the phonograph's most important market would be businessmen who would use it for dictation. Yet, contrary to what has generally been written about his phonograph business, Edison did not fail to recognize the potential for an entertainment market nor did he actively oppose such use. Certainly, the articles published under his name in *North American Review* about his original phonograph of 1878 and his "perfected" phonograph of 1888, both pointed out such uses. Indeed, in 1888 he claimed that

> through the facility with which it stores up and reproduces music of all sorts, or whistling and recitations, it can be employed to furnish constant amusement to invalids, or to social assemblies, at receptions, dinners, etc. Any one sitting in his room alone may order an assorted supply of wax cylinders, inscribed with songs, poems, piano or violin music, short stories, anecdotes, or dialect pieces, and by putting them on his phonograph, he can listen to them as originally sung or recited by authors, vocalists and actors, or elocutionists. The variety of entertainment he thus commands, at trifling expense and without moving from his chair, is practically unlimited.[28]

Edison not only suggested that his phonograph be used for entertainment, he actually became involved in two efforts to develop them for this purpose. The first of these was a talking doll that he set Batchelor to work on in February 1888. Edison had originally proposed the use of the phonograph for toys in 1877 and an unsuccessful effort had been made in this direction in 1878. In the mid-1880s William Jacques, a Bell Telephone researcher, and his partner Lowell Briggs developed a talking doll after learning of the improvements in the Bell-Tainter graphophone, and in October 1887 they approached Edison about the manufacture and sale of this device. Edison agreed to the formation of the Edison Phonograph Toy Manufacturing Company, and Batchelor began trying to improve the mechanism and records for the doll. Unhappy with Jacques's management of the toy company, Edison placed his own man in charge, and in 1889 he began manufacturing the dolls at the Phonograph Works. Although he planned to have a large shipment of dolls ready for Christmas 1889, the talking doll continued to have serious technical shortcomings, particularly because of the fragility of its small record, and production did not begin in earnest until the following January. Although more than 3,000 were made and tested by the end of March 1890, Edison withdrew them from sale the following month because of complaints over the reliability of the phonograph mechanism. He entirely suspended manufacturing in October and refused to commit any of his own resources to it, especially after the toy company became embroiled in legal disputes.[29]

Another, even less successful effort at exploiting the entertainment possibilities of the phonograph was the attempt to establish an "Amusement Phonograph Co."[30] Among those who hoped to join Edison in this projected company were journalist George Parsons Lathrop and Erastus Wiman, who had helped Edison develop his railway and phonoplex telegraph inventions. Laboratory experiments on a record duplicating process were clearly designed for use with an amusement phonograph as were those concerned with recording musical instruments such as a piano. Even after events led to the exclusive promotion of the phonograph as a business instrument, Edison would continue these experiments and support efforts to use his instrument as an amusement device. Nonetheless, it is clear that Edison's primary efforts at improving the phonograph were designed to make it a better dictating machine and not to enhance its use for entertainment.

As Gilliland began to focus on the commercial end of the phonograph in March 1888, a new promoter entered the talking machine business. Jesse H. Lippincott, who had made a considerable fortune in the glass industry, arranged with the Graphophone Company for an exclusive license to market its machine. Soon afterward, Gilliland showed him the new phonograph; concerned that it could affect his graphophone business, Lippincott determined to gain control of Edison's machine. He commenced negotiations with Gilliland, offering to purchase the Edison Phonograph Company for $500,000. Gilliland broached the idea to Edison through Edison's attorney John Tomlinson. At the end of June, after extensive negotiations, Edison finally agreed to the sale. The course of the negotiations and the agreement itself indicate that Edison retained his producer-goods frame of reference. While willing to give up control of the marketing of his phonograph Edison was adamant about retaining exclusive manufacturing rights. This had been characteristic of his early years as an inventor-manufacturer in the telegraph industry, and his experience in electric lighting suggested that manufacturing would be the most lucrative business in a new industry.[31]

Unknown to Edison, the negotiations also involved a private deal between Lippincott, Gilliland, and Tomlinson. Lippincott agreed to purchase Gilliland's agency contract in exchange for $250,000 of stock in a new company he was forming to exploit the two talking machines. Tomlinson received part of this settlement, ostensibly because he had an interest in Gilliland's contract but possibly also for his role in arranging the deal. Fifty thousand was to be paid upfront with an option to buy the additional $200,000 within four months of Edison's signing his agreement with Lippincott. Edison finally learned about the cash settlement with Gilliland and Tomlinson in September when Lippincott had difficulty making his required payment to the inventor. Edison became enraged upon learning about it, contending that the other men had been looking out for their own interests and not his when they got him to agree to the sale. By the time Edison learned about their secret arrangement Gilliland and Tomlinson were in Europe, where Gilliland was exhibiting the phonograph. Edison immediately cabled Gilliland: "I just learn you have made a certain trade with Lippincott of a nature unknown to me. As you did not have permission to sell from Company I have this day abrogated your contract and notified Mr Lippincott of the fact and that he pay any further sum at his own risk. Since you have been so underhanded I shall demand refunding all money paid you & stoppage of further payments and I do not desire you to exhibit phonograph in Europe." Protesting his innocence, Gilliland replied

"You certainly are acting without knowledge of facts and are doing me great in-justice have in this and at all other times worked faithfully in your interests Shall return at once."[32] Edison, however, refused to see him and permanently severed connections with the man who was his oldest and closest friend. He also removed Tomlinson as both his personal lawyer and counsel for his com-panies. The fallout with Gilliland and Edison's strained relations with Johnson, which were exacerbated by conflicts over the electric lighting business between several of Edison's close associates, had arisen in part because Edison contin-ued to treat them as inferiors rather than equals, even when they played crucial roles in his inventive or business enterprises.[33]

Edison's deal with Lippincott ended the effort to market a phonograph for entertainment purposes. According to Lathrop, their negotiations with Lippin-cott had caused Gilliland and Tomlinson to "suddenly put down the brakes on the incorporation of the Amusement Phono Co., & [they] could not even be induced to consult any further about it." Although Lathrop's contract "for the use of the 'amusement phonograph' was what [Edison] called 'the best kind of contract,' viz. 'his mouth,'" the inventor no longer controlled the business of marketing his invention.[34] Jesse Lippincott clearly had no interest in the enter-tainment market, and Edison made no effort to push him in that direction, al-though he did continue his experiments with musical recording and cylinder duplication and provided musical cylinders to Gaston & Marsh, who had ear-lier arranged with Gilliland to market the phonograph in Michigan. Nonethe-less, Edison agreed with Lippincott that the business market was primary.

Lippincott's plan for marketing the phonograph was one with which Edi-son was quite familiar and of which he seems to have approved. Rather than sell phonographs as the sewing machines or typewriters were sold, Lippincott drew on the model of the Bell Telephone Company by proposing to rent in-struments through exclusive state territories. It may be that this plan was influ-enced by the Bell Telephone interests connected with the Graphophone Com-pany, who also clearly saw the graphophone as a business machine. Edison, with his experience in the telephone industry and earlier in the telegraph mar-ket-reporting industry, which also leased instruments, would have found this a plausible scheme, especially as businessmen would be familiar with it and might feel more comfortable if the phonograph company was responsible for maintaining the instruments. To carry out his scheme, Lippincott organized the North American Phonograph Company and immediately began organizing some thirty local subsidiary companies that would be assigned territories within which they would market the instruments to customers who would be given a choice between the phonograph and the graphophone.[35]

Almost from the beginning, the phonograph was considered the better of the two machines because of its superior recording and reproducing capabili-ties. Unlike the phonograph, the graphophone, according to North American vice president Thomas Lombard, failed to reproduce sibilants and "required a man to talk in a very loud tone of voice, very often, in order to make any record at all."[36] Furthermore, the graphophone was poorly constructed—Edison had been right about his advantage in manufacturing—and used a recording cylinder that deteriorated too easily. The thin cylinder that Tainter had designed for the graphophone did, however, provide it with one distinct advantage over Edison's phonograph—the recording and reproducing mechanisms required little if any adjustment. In contrast, the thick wax cylinder that Edison designed to be shaved down and reused required a new adjustment with each thickness, and it was also more fragile. Businessmen found that when they changed one cylinder for another, the thicknesses differed, and they objected to constantly readjusting the instrument. Edison devoted considerable effort to developing an automatic adjustment to meet this criticism and introduced a much better design in November 1889.

The simpler design of the graphophone presented another problem for the phonograph, according to Lombard, when a customer chose the graphophone "because of its apparent simplicity. After using it and becoming disgusted, he refused frequently to consider the phonograph, fearing the same trouble."[37] This led Edison to develop a treadle machine for those who objected to the batteries of the electric phonograph. He also developed an electric phonograph for use with electric light circuits. Nevertheless, Edison's battery phonograph remained the standard, particularly after he improved the batteries.

Edison's superior research facilities enabled him to respond to complaints from local companies and to make improvements to the phonograph that virtually drove the graphophone from the market. But the market itself remained very limited. In June 1891, at the second convention of local phonograph companies, they reported renting only a little over three thousand machines. Just one out of fifty of these instruments was a graphophone. By the end of the year, all but a few graphophones would be replaced by Edison's improved phonograph. However, many businessmen still considered the machine too complex for themselves and for their clerks.[38]

Even as the business market stagnated, the local companies were finding profit by using their phonographs for entertainment purposes. Beginning in May 1889, North American Phonograph Company had begun to offer recordings made at the Edison laboratory and duplicated by the Phonograph Works, and a few of the local companies had begun using musical recordings to promote the phonograph. By the 1891 convention, the companies were using one out of every three phonographs in a coin-in-slot amusement device. Many agreed with the editor of the *Phonogram*, who complained in January 1891 that this diminished their ability to sell them to businessmen: "Those companies who fail to take advantage of every opportunity of pushing the legitimate side of the business, relying only on the profits derived from the 'coin-in-the-slot,' will find too late that they have made a fatal mistake . . . as it has the appearance of being nothing more than a mere toy, and no one would comprehend its value or appreciate its utility as an aid to businessmen and others for dictation purposes when seeing it only in that form."[39] Edison, however, thought that the business of making duplicate records would become "a trade that will net us ten thousand dollars a year" and sought to control it, although he was satisfied to leave the making of original recordings to the local companies.[40]

The record business had been stimulated by local companies that placed particular emphasis on using the phonograph for amusement purposes. Officials of two local companies particularly promoted this market. Louis Glass, general manager of the Pacific Phonograph Company in San Francisco, reported to the first convention of local companies in 1890 that his company drew all of its profits from coin-in-slot phonographs placed in public houses, such as saloons. He had even patented a coin-in-slot device for this purpose. Felix Gottschalk, secretary of the Metropolitan Phonograph Company in New York, had gone even further and organized the Automatic Phonograph Exhibition Company. During the first months of 1890 he attempted to corner the market for coin-in-slot phonograph devices by acquiring Glass's patent and securing the cooperation of both North American and Thomas Edison, who set John Ott to work developing what he hoped would be a standard machine for the company. Following the 1890 convention other companies began to convert their phonographs into exhibition machines.[41]

The coin-in-slot phonograph business gave Edison his first real experience with a consumer market for entertainment technologies and provided him with a model he was to use in developing a new one—moving pictures. On October 8, 1888, while working to improve his phonograph, Edison sat down to draw up a patent caveat for a device he called the kinetoscope. In this caveat he stated that he was "experimenting upon an instrument which does for the Eye what the phonograph does for the Ear, which is the recording and reproduction of things in motion, and in such a form as to be both cheap, practical, and convenient." Like so many of Edison's first ideas about new inventions he was using an analogy with a familiar technology to think about a new one. In his caveat, Edison proposed photographing a series of pictures at intervals of eight seconds or more "in a continuous spiral on a cylinder or plate in the same manner as sound is recorded on the phonograph." The pictures would then be viewed with a microscope. To produce the intermittent motion necessary to give the illusion of motion to a series of pictures, Edison suggested a variety of mechanical movements like those he had used in his telegraph instruments, including tuning forks.[42]

Although the phonograph provided Edison with a mechanical analogy, his thinking about the problem had been stimulated by a visit from photographer Eadweard Muybridge, who was famous for his stop-action photographs. On February 25, 1888, Muybridge lectured before the New England Society in Orange, New Jersey, and demonstrated his zoopraxiscope. This device projected drawings, based on his photographs of animals, which were painted on a revolving glass disc and produced the illusion of motion. Two days later Muybridge came to the West Orange laboratory and discussed with Edison a plan for combining the phonograph with a series of photographs of a speaker to pro-

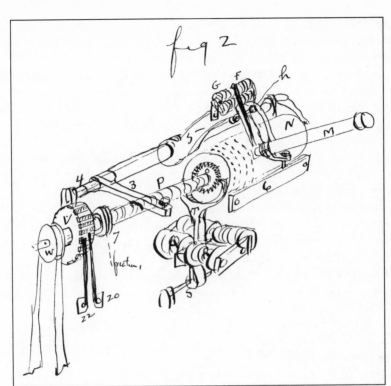

In Edison's first conception of a motion picture device from October 1888 the pictures were to be photographed "in a continuous spiral on a cylinder or plate in the same manner as sound is recorded on the phonograph" and viewed with a microscope.

duce talking motion pictures. According to a reporter for the *New York World,* "This scheme met with the approval of Mr. Edison and he intended to perfect it at his leisure."[43] When Edison finally received a set of Muybridge's photographs that fall, he began to seriously consider the problem of moving pictures. And he included in his October caveat Muybridge's idea of producing talking pictures, which Edison proposed to do by connecting the phonograph and kinetoscope cylinders.

Having conceptualized the problem, Edison set about developing a practical technology. Edison had no clear vision of a market for his proposed kinetoscope, as he had for the phonograph, and he was unwilling to devote many resources to the research. Instead he set up a small research team, like those he later recommended to Sigmund Bergmann, made up of an experimenter and one or two assistants. The experimenter he chose was William Kennedy Laurie Dickson, who besides being a trusted experimenter was also a photographer. The iron-ore-milling project remained Dickson's primary research, however, and he and his assistant, machinist Charles A. Brown, experimented on moving pictures only as they found time.

Edison assigned Dickson the photographic and optical research while he took personal responsibility for the electromechanical design. Besides Dickson's experience in these matters, of course, the experiments with photographic emulsions involved the kind of routine chemical research that Edison liked to delegate to his assistants. But this division of labor also played to Edison's great strength. He had after all been producing electromechanical designs since his early years as a telegraph inventor, and he no doubt expected that his recent experience designing the improved phonograph would prove useful in developing a practical kinetoscope.

During the first months of 1889 Dickson developed an arrangement of lenses and microscope objectives that enabled him to take microphotographs, and he experimented with a variety of photographic emulsions applied directly to metal and glass drums. Eventually he found that wrapping sheets of photosensitive celluloid on an aluminum cylinder produced the best images. In the meantime Edison was working on better electromechanical arrangements. They also experimented with methods of providing the bright light necessary to illuminate the images for viewing. By the time Edison left for Europe at the beginning of August, the kinetoscope, though still in a rudimentary stage of development, showed promise.

It was while he was in Paris to attend the Universal Exhibition of 1889 that Edison learned of the work of the physiologist Étienne-Jules Marey, which would prove crucial to his development of motion picture technology. Marey, who was among the notable French engineers and scientists who Edison saw in Paris, had been making photographs of animal motion. He used a camera of his own design that was capable of producing sixty frames per second on a roll of paper-based photographic film. Marey discussed his photographic techniques with Edison and also presented him a copy of his book, *Physiologie du mouvement: vol des oiseaux*, which described them in detail. After his return to West Orange, Edison drew up a new caveat describing a kinetoscope in which "the sensitive film is in the form of a long band passing from one reel to another." With this design Edison turned to an even older conceptual model than the phonograph—telegraphy. Not only did the photosensitive film on reels resemble the electrochemical paper used in his automatic telegraph, but he planned to use sprocketed film "into which double toothed wheels pass [as] in the Wheatstone Automatic telegh instrument." And to produce the intermittent motion necessary to take and view photographs at a rate of ten per second he planned to use an escapement mechanism controlled by a favorite device from his telegraph years—the polarized relay.[44]

While Edison was away Dickson had constructed a special building for kinetograph experiments, but otherwise he had made little progress. Now, however, as Edison began to consider the use of filmstrips, Dickson began to

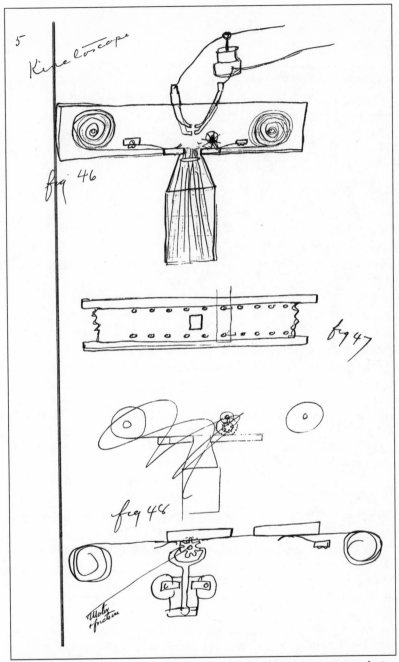

Following his return from Paris in 1889, Edison altered his motion picture device to use roll film that would be sprocketed like the paper used in a Wheatstone automatic transmitter. In order to produce the intermittent motion necessary for giving the illusion of motion he planned to use a polarized relay (bottom).

approach the problem from a different direction. The American photographic community had recently become interested in German inventor Ottomar Anschütz's tachyoscope, and Dickson had one built in December. This device used a metal disc with a glass periphery on which were mounted a series of pictures. As the disc rotated rapidly, each picture was illuminated by the bright light of a Geissler tube and projected on a screen, giving the illusion of motion. By March, Dickson had connected the tachyoscope to a phonograph and demonstrated the first talking picture to Edison. Dickson himself was the subject of this first film, in which he raised his hat while saying "Good morning, Mr. Edison, glad to see you back, I hope you are satisfied with the kinetophonograph."[45] The film concluded with Dickson counting to ten on his fingers to show the synchronization of sound and motion. Dickson apparently gave a press demonstration of his tachyoscope in April, but Edison seems to have decided that future experiments should focus on the use of filmstrips. His growing interest in the coin-in-slot phonograph also convinced him that a similar arrangement should be used for motion pictures, and no further projection experiments were conducted at the laboratory.

Motion picture work did not actually resume until the fall of 1890, as Edison and Dickson focused their attention on the ore-milling project and spent most of the summer at the mine in Ogden. When Dickson returned to the project, he had a much larger staff of assistants. William Heise and the Ott brothers, John and Frederick, all of whom had worked on telegraph instruments in Edison's Newark shops, and Charles Kayser, another experienced machinist, all spent time on motion picture apparatus. This now included a camera that became known as the kinetograph as well as the peephole kinetoscope for viewing. By the spring of 1891 both instruments were well advanced, and on May 20 they were shown publicly for the first time. The audience was composed of delegates to the convention of the National Federation of Women's Clubs, who were given an elaborate lunch at Glenmont by Mina Edison and then invited to the laboratory by her husband. It was clear from newspaper accounts that although Edison believed that he had the "base principle right," he did "not yet have a perfected machine at work." Although Edison optimistically told a reporter that he considered it "only a question of time and a matter of details about completing the machine," he would not have a commercially acceptable design for two more years.[46]

Nonetheless, work had proceeded to the point where Edison felt confident enough to apply for basic patents on the kinetograph and kinetoscope. In the fall Dickson filed his own application, which was never granted, and John Ott, who had been working on a coin-in-slot device for the phonograph, applied for a similar device to operate the kinetoscope. Dickson also continued to work on the camera and adopted wider film stock obtained from the Eastman Dry Plate and Film Company. It would be another year, however, before Dickson developed the camera and film technology to the point where Edison felt that motion pictures were ready for commercial introduction.[47]

By this time, because of Jesse Lippincott's health and financial problems (he died in 1891), Edison had gained virtual control of the North American Phonograph Company. His private secretary, Alfred Tate, was acting as vice-president of the company and running it with Lippincott's old associate Thomas Lombard. As they were preparing the company's exhibit for the World's Columbian Exposition in 1893, they also arranged with Edison to market the kineto-scope there and received permission from the Exposition to exhibit 150 of the motion-picture viewers. Although the first prototype was ready by May 1892 and Dickson had completed the construction of a movie studio and began to make films in anticipation of the demand, the first twenty-five kinetoscopes were not completed until the following March. Edison was anxious to have one of his kinetoscopes on exhibition at the Columbia Exposition, but he had done little to ensure that this would happen. It would be another year after the first machines were finished before he seriously began the business of marketing the new invention.

Edison organized his motion picture business in April 1894 as the Kineto-scope Department of the Edison Manufacturing Company. He had established this company in 1889 to manufacture and market the Edison-Lalande battery used with his phonographs and for telegraph and telephone systems, including the phonoplex. Its manufacturing plant, located on forty-seven acres in nearby Silver Lake, New Jersey, was a scaled-down version of the grand industrial works scheme he had proposed to Villard. Edison Manufacturing was under the direction of William Gilmore, formerly connected with the Edison Ma-chine Works, whom Edison also put in charge of the Phonograph Works in 1894. Two years later, after reacquiring control of the phonograph business by forcing North American Phonograph into bankruptcy and buying its assets, Edison formed the National Phonograph Company, which Gilmore ran as well.

By this time Edison was clearly enthusiastic about the future of the amuse-ment phonograph. Writing to the managers of his English phonograph com-pany in 1893, he said that "Our experience here shows that a very large num-ber of machines go into private houses for amusement purposes—that such persons do not attempt to record nor desire it for that purpose they simply want to reproduce. It has always been my idea that one of the greatest fields for the phonograph was in the household for reproducing all that is best in oratory & music but I have never got any one to believe it until lately."[48] Nonetheless, Edison still expected the manufacture and sale of phonographs and duplicated records, not the production of original recordings, to be the primary business of his phonograph company.

When Edison began his effort to regain control of the phonograph busi-ness in 1894, he had been planning to market a new electric phonograph with a large cylinder capable of recording "1/2 hour for music & 1 hour for talking that records and reproduces music with as near absolute perfection as can be."[49] By the time he finally succeeded in reorganizing the business, however, he found that the market had shifted because of the introduction of cheap spring-driven machines better suited to a mass market for home entertainment than his expensive and cumbersome electric phonograph. Edison's experiments with spring motors for the tinfoil and early wax-recording phonographs had led him to conclude that they could not produce the even and constant cylinder rotation required for quality recording and playback. He thus chose to use electric motors that overcame the problem, but also significantly raised the cost of the phonograph and required users to deal with the expense and difficulty of maintaining the chemical solutions of primary batteries. In the mid-1890s several local phonograph companies, facing declining income from their phonograph parlors and in the market for business machines, began to adapt spring motors to the Edison phonograph to offer cheap instruments suitable for home entertainment.

In 1895 Frank Capps, an employee of United States Phonograph Company in nearby Newark, had designed a triple-spring motor for the standard Edison electric phonograph, and Edison agreed to let the company sell machines using the motor while he developed his own design. The sturdy Capps motor had the advantage of being easier to use than the electric motor, but it sold for about the same price, $100. To compete with the cheaper machines being marketed by the Columbia Phonograph Company, Edison decided to develop a spring-motor phonograph to sell "for about $40.00, thus placing the instrument within the reach of everybody as a formidable rival to the limited music box."[50]

Columbia, which incorporated in January 1896, gained control of the American Graphophone Company and sued to prevent Edison from using graphophone patents in his machines. However, Columbia's own machines relied extensively on Edison's patented improvements and the two companies agreed to license each other's patents in December 1896. By then Edison had introduced his new "clockwork" phonograph with a motor designed by a Connecticut clock company. This two-spring motor was designed to play two two-minute cylinders without rewinding, but like other early attempts to adapt clock motors to phonographs it proved inadequate. After Edison redesigned the motor to operate with a single spring and patented a much better speed regulator for it, National Phonograph began selling machines using it as the "Home" phonograph, a name much better suited to the consumer market.

Soon after the Home phonograph made its appearance, however, Columbia Phonograph presented a new challenge by offering even cheaper machines, which Edison and his staff met by designing other models. National Phonograph soon introduced a $20 "New Standard" phonograph to compete with the $10 Columbia phonograph, which cost as much as $22 if the customer purchased a case and a speaker for recording. National Phonograph also dropped the price of the Home to $30 to compete with Columbia's $25 machine. At the same time, it reduced the price of the electric phonograph to $75, and after taking over United States Phonograph in 1897 it began selling the spring-motor phonograph made by that company (which later became known as the Edison "Triumph" phonograph) for the same price. Recognizing that the tendency was toward low-priced phonographs, Edison designed an even cheaper machine, known as the "Gem," which National Phonograph began selling in early 1899 for $10. Although the phonograph market was driven by low-cost phonographs—the Gem, Standard, and Home models dominated sales—Columbia also introduced an expensive large-cylinder machine for an upscale market willing to pay for increased volume and sound quality, and Edison soon matched this with his "Concert" phonograph.[51]

Spring-motor phonographs revitalized the phonograph business, and by the fall of 1897 the Phonograph Works had trouble keeping up with orders. After manufacturing a total of only 774 spring-motor and 465 electric phonographs by February 1897, National Phonograph began to see a dramatic increase in sales. During the next year the Phonograph Works produced 4,905 spring-motor machines, but only 260 electric. In the summer of 1898 an elated Edison wrote to Mina at Chautauqua that "the phonograph business is booming—we have over $40,000 of orders now being made at the Phonograph Works."[52] Production of spring-motor phonographs for that year totaled nearly 14,000, and even the number of electric phonographs increased slightly to 422 (although their production declined precipitously in the following years). However, the real boom in phonograph sales occurred in 1899 when production exceeded 45,000.

Phonograph model design during this period relied primarily on engineering refinements rather than new inventions in sound recording technology. As we have seen, throughout his career, dating back to his days as a telegraph manufacturer, Edison had been concerned with just this kind of product improvement, and his experience helped to ensure that Edison phonographs remained the industry standard. To compete with his competitors' cheap models, Edison had to develop special tools and machinery to reduce the cost of production. This was evident as early as February 1898, when an agent for Edison's British phonograph company reported that "Edison has a new Automatic machine, which does the work of a number of men, and makes a number of parts in one operation, and I do not believe that anyone will be able to manufacture Phonographs as cheap or as good as Edison."[53] To maintain the growing market for entertainment phonographs, however, Edison also needed to improve the reproduction quality of both records and machines. During the next few years he devoted considerable effort to refining the technical quality of sound recording. As a result, even though his machines tended to be somewhat more expensive than those of his competitors, during the early years of the phonograph boom their technical superiority combined with the name Edison often made them more desirable to consumers. But as the novelty of hearing recorded music wore off and consumers began to pay more attention to the artists and their music, Edison began to face considerable competition because he failed to recognize that musical recordings involved art as well as technology.

In the early years of the motion picture business, as in the early years of the phonograph business, the subjects of the films were initially secondary to their novelty, and once again Edison focused his attention and that of his company on the technology. As with the phonograph, Edison expected the manufacture of kinetoscopes rather than the production of motion pictures to be his primary source of income. This influenced his decision to place the motion picture business under the direction of the Edison Manufacturing Company. Dickson and his assistant Heise remained the primary filmmakers for Edison, and most of their subjects were best suited to the interests of men such as their associates in the laboratory—prize fights, vaudeville performers, and workplace scenes. During the first year, the sale of kinetoscopes certainly matched Edison's expectations, totaling nearly $150,000, while film sales just exceeded $25,800. However, during the next year, kinetoscope sales fell under $25,000 while film sales were a negligible $2,800. The kinetoscope was in danger of becoming little more than a novelty. Edison initially sought to solve this problem by again trying to combine the kinetoscope with the phonograph. Even if he had been successful, it is unlikely that this could have sustained the business much beyond its novelty character.

As kinetoscope sales fell in 1895 and film production declined, Norman Raff and Frank Gammon, as sales agents for the Kinetoscope Company, tried a new approach to filmmaking. Together with Alfred Clark, who was responsible for film production and sales for the Kinetoscope Company, they sought to "reorient and broaden the Edison Manufacturing Company's approach to [film] production."[54] Under Clark's direction, Edison Manufacturing made several films of famous historical scenes that suggested the possibility of film narrative rather than the acts of popular performers. These innovative films failed to increase sales and Raff and Gammon, who were seriously contemplating ending their film business, decided to try projecting films to an audience in a last effort to revitalize their enterprise. Although Edison agreed to develop a projection system, because his own interest was tied to kinetoscope sales he worked only halfheartedly to produce one. According to Gammon, "his firm had been endeavoring for months to have Mr. Edison produce for them a successful machine for this work," but he "had not been able to produce such a machine, and . . . did not believe anyone else could."[55] Only as sales continued to fall would Edison come to accept the need for projection. By then, Raff and Gammon had turned elsewhere.

Motion pictures, like phonographs and sound recordings, were being defined by the way in which they were exhibited as well as by their inventors.[56] From their beginning, motion pictures had been influenced by contemporary projection techniques such as those developed by Muybridge and Anschütz. And as motion pictures moved into commercial use, exhibitors drew on a tradition of screen practices developed by lecturers using illustrated slides and stereoscopic pictures. With these visual aids, lecturers created narrative programs. Film exhibitors were working out of these traditions, and it is not surprising that they influenced the evolution of the motion picture business as projection replaced the peephole kinetoscope.

Inventors in Europe and the United States had been working on projection throughout 1895, and by the end of the year the Lumière brothers had introduced a commercial system in Paris. William Dickson, who had grown increasingly frustrated by his secondary role in the motion picture business, left Edison in the spring of 1895 to develop a projector with Woodville Latham and his sons, who had organized the Kinetoscope Exhibiting Company to show prize fights with an oversized kinetoscope and had become convinced that projection would enhance their business. Among others working on projection were C. Francis Jenkins and Thomas Armat, who exhibited their phantoscope at the Cotton States Exposition in October 1895. The Lathams also exhibited their eidoloscope projector while Frank Harrison, representing Raff and Gammon, was exhibiting the kinetoscope. Harrison told Armat that "Raff and Gammon were exceedingly anxious to secure such an apparatus."[57] In December Gammon came to see Armat, who by that time had split with Jenkins, and succeeded in acquiring rights to his projector. After acquiring these rights Raff and Gammon approached Edison. Although he had belittled the Latham projector earlier in the year, the precipitous decline of the kinetoscope business as well as the appearance of new competitors such as Latham made Edison willing to adopt an invention produced outside of his laboratory. On January 15 he and Gilmore agreed that the Edison Manufacturing Company would manufacture the projectors and supply films for them.

By the time a new projection system was introduced commercially, Edison's name rather than Armat's was associated with it. The reason for this was explained by Raff and Gammon, who told Armat in March:

> No matter how good a machine should be invented by another and no matter how satisfactory or superior the results of such a machine invented by another might be, yet we find the great majority of the parties who are interested and who desire to invest in such a machine have been waiting for the Edison machine and would never be satisfied with anything else, but will hold off until they found what Edison could accomplish. . . . evidently believing that Edison would in due time perfect and put out a machine which would cast the others in the shade.[58]

This, of course, was part of the Edison image that had been evolving since the original invention of the phonograph first placed his name before the public as the "Inventor of the Age" and the "Wizard of Menlo Park." The accommodating Edison had proven to be a good subject for reporters, and he in turn recognized the value of keeping his name before the public. Although many of his claims were hyperbolic and he often claimed success before actually achieving it, his public image was based on real accomplishment and a real commitment to producing technologically superior products. The Edison name had come to serve as a form of assurance for untried new technologies. Many of those involved in the early motion picture industry knew what had happened in the phonograph industry. Edison's phonograph had won the day over the graphophone because he had the resources to continually improve its performance and outstrip the graphophone. They were not prepared to bet against Edison. Raff and Gammon therefore argued that it was necessary to associate Edison's name with Armat's projector "in order to secure the largest profit in the shortest time."[59]

Edison's name could produce short-term profits, but his early experience with both phonographs and motion pictures suggest some of the problems that would continue to confront him and his companies as new competitors entered the field. With his background in producer goods, Edison felt most comfortable as a manufacturer selling to businesspeople. He knew how to respond to complaints about technical problems. He was less certain about the aesthetic issues associated with the consumer market. The early projection systems were not necessarily technologically superior to the peephole kinetoscope, but they produced a more satisfactory aesthetic product for viewers. Once he had adopted projection, Edison was well prepared to make important technical improvements. But because his efforts to dominate the market focused on technology and patents, his companies would struggle as the ground shifted to the aesthetics of film subject and presentation after the turn of the century.

Edison always had a much clearer vision of the consumer market for phonographs than he did for motion pictures. For this reason, his phonograph business was much more successful. Nonetheless, here too he had to learn hard lessons. As early as May 1892 Tate had suggested that the Phonograph Works seek to gain control from North American Phonograph of the recording of original musical records as well as their duplication to ensure quality. "Perfect knowledge of the Phono.," he argued, "is necessary to take such records and with good material must come the change from curiosity to satisfaction, from Phonograph as plaything 'to use.'" Furthermore, the men who ran the Phonograph Works not only possessed the necessary knowledge but also had "the name of Edison at heart."[60] With the organization of the National Phonograph Company, Edison took on the task of developing improved recording technology and producing original recordings. In doing so he faced the new challenge of keeping up with shifts in consumer demand. As was the case with motion pictures, Edison would continually struggle between his tendency to focus on technology and the necessity of meeting the tastes of consumers. When technological issues regarding the design of phonographs or the quality of sound recordings dominated consumers' concerns, Edison was well prepared to satisfy them, but he and his companies often struggled when these concerns turned to aesthetic issues. Nonetheless, the ability of Edison, his laboratory, and his shops to produce technologically superior machines continued to provide important competitive advantages for the Edison phonograph and motion picture businesses.

CHAPTER 16

Industrial Research

Although Edison's phonograph and motion picture businesses would become his most important enterprises by the late 1890s, they remained largely a sideline during his first decade in West Orange. He had high hopes that research at his West Orange laboratory would enable him to establish new manufacturing enterprises such as these, but during its early years the laboratory primarily served as the center of innovation for the Edison lighting companies. Nonetheless, Edison strove to keep the laboratory as independent from these companies as possible so that he could set the agenda for the lighting research himself and continue to tackle other technologies that interested him. His desire for independence had been an important reason for moving his research from the Lamp Works to West Orange.

Edison also expected the managers of the electrical companies to defer to him on all questions relating to research and development. Not surprisingly, this gave rise to some conflict between them, particularly as the lighting business grew increasingly competitive, creating a need for better coordination between the Edison lighting companies and for increased capital to expand their production and marketing operations. The clashing interests of Edison and the managers of his light companies first became apparent during the winter of 1888 when he asked them to provide direct support for his laboratory. Only Francis Upton agreed immediately to this request, largely because Edison had already moved most of the lamp experiments from the Lamp Works to the West Orange laboratory. Nonetheless, Upton asked that one of the Edison Lamp Company employees conducting experiments at the laboratory sign all bills related to lamp experiments. Asserting the right to run his laboratory as he saw fit, Edison objected that "we have a Superintendent of experimenters [John Ott], who authorizes all orders issued for material used by those under him, and it will complicate matters very much to carry out your suggestion." Upton agreed instead that the laboratory would render bills *"in a thoroughly comprehensive manner which can easily be verified by your records."*[1]

Edison had much more difficulty obtaining payments from the other companies. Writing on behalf of the Edison Electric Light Company, Edward Johnson told Edison that he would "be in favor of making you a reasonable allowance on account of these expenses," but wanted assurances that Edison would offer any improvements "without payment of royalty or consideration other than such proportion of expenses as we may agree to assume." This incensed Edison, who responded that although this had been his intention "to make it mandatory . . . puts it in a business light & it would be manifestly unfair that I should give my time & expense to devising apparatus without consideration other than being a $^1/_{16}$th owner of the Co. The $^{15}/_{16}$ of my partners would benefit."[2] As only one of the principal stockholders in Edison Electric but the majority owner of the shops, Edison apparently decided it was in his best interest to withdraw his request that Edison Electric contribute toward the expense of the laboratory.

He also found it necessary to reduce his demands on the Edison Machine Works and Bergmann & Company. Insull argued that the amount requested by Edison actually meant a significant increase in the Machine Works's experimental costs. In reply Edison explained that

it was my intention to furnish you from here with all the models for new machinery which I may get up and relieve you entirely of your experimental expense account at Schenectady. . . . Of course I could, on the other hand, send you working drawings and stop there my work in connection with your experiments, which would bring the amount of your remittances down to, say, $250 per week. What I want to settle now is, a basis on which we can start. We can tell in the course of a month or two whether the same is too large or too small and adjust it accordingly.[3]

Insull agreed to this suggestion, but also told Edison that "You cannot possibl[y] wipe out entirely our experimental account here. There are lots of *little* things which it would be absurd for us to send to Orange to be tried, because we have all the parts here which are available again for regular Machines, and can do such work here much more economical than it would be possible for you to do at Orange, because we would either have to send you these parts or else you would have to have them made."[4] Bergmann also got Edison to reduce his weekly assessment to $100 by arguing that his shop would need to continue some experimental work on electric light apparatus beyond that done by the West Orange laboratory.

The weekly payments were only an advance on experimental expenses for each of the companies; Edison also billed them for additional monies needed to conduct experiments on their behalf. Edison, of course, took it upon himself to determine what other experimental work should be done, although some of these experiments were requested by the companies. Insull, in particular, complained about his lack of control over experimental work and asked to have "a full understanding as to what experiments are conducted for our account. . . . You must remember that we are running this business to show profit, that experimental expenses like other expenses have to come out of our profits." Insull also objected to the lax manner in which the laboratory rendered its bills as well as Edison's methods of charging for labor and material and concluded, "It will take more than the profits of an ordinary business to meet the charges received from Orange for experimental expenses."[5]

Even with these disagreements, Edison and his managers were basically in accord regarding the direction of research. Their primary concerns were to reduce manufacturing costs and increase the operating efficiencies of electric light apparatus. One of the key means for accomplishing these goals was to standardize the equipment used in the Edison system, and in December 1887 they decided to revive the Standardizing Bureau, a group of technical experts within the company that determined standards for equipment. According to its new director W. J. Jenks, the Standardizing Bureau was to "fully weigh the practical opinions of the experimenter, the manufacturer and the practitioner as to secure their combined wisdom, and avoid the friction that would otherwise be inevitable in making any necessary changes in standards."[6] Jenks, who had been appointed by Edward Johnson with Edison's approval, had previously managed the Edison central station in Brockton, Massachusetts, the Edison Company for Isolated Lighting, and the Municipal Department. The other Bureau members were Edison, Batchelor, and representatives of the shops and the Light Company.

Edison gave the Standardizing Bureau the use of a room in the main laboratory building, but most of its testing and experimental work took place in the galvanometer room, which was the primary site for electrical research at the laboratory. Electrical research also relied on the laboratory's electric light station, which provided electricity throughout the laboratory complex as well as to Glenmont and other houses in Llewellyn Park. The power station, located in a structure attached to the main building, was the place for experimenting with and testing commercial Edison dynamos and new designs and became known as the dynamo room. Switches, meters, regulators, and other central station equipment also were installed in the basement of the main building to be tested on the system.[7]

One of the first important research efforts authorized by the Standardizing Bureau involved the meter for the three-wire system. In a letter to Jenks, Charles Wirt, who was employed by the Bureau to assist with its work at the laboratory, described the tests he was conducting with Arthur Kennelly to determine whether changes could be made "in the electrical constant of the meter, which if found practical will largely decrease the expense of meter work." They studied the effect on the meter of changes in temperature, voltage, and other conditions of operation as well as "the comparative accuracy of pure and commercial zinc" and other materials used in the meter.[8] The laboratory, in fact, soon became the supplier of chemically pure zinc solutions for the electrolytic meters used throughout the Edison system. The tests made by Kennelly and Wirt resulted in a thirty-five-page report that described methods of reducing errors in measurements from the meters as well as a variety of potential improvements to increase their efficiency; this report also became the basis for a new pamphlet on the meters. Other work performed by Kennelly and Wirt for the Standardizing Bureau, such as tests on the carrying capacity of conductors, were made available to the operating companies through papers delivered at the annual meeting of the Association of Edison Illuminating Companies, which Jenks encouraged Kennelly to attend.

Most of the electrical research undertaken by Kennelly and the galvanometer room staff involved dynamo and motor design for the Edison Machine Works, including the continuation of work that had been previously undertaken at Schenectady, and some of which had been under way for more than a year. This research included the development of alternating current technology; the design of motors for street railways, sewing machines, elevators, and other uses; and the devising of more efficient dynamos that would be less costly to manufacture. Prior to the opening of his new laboratory, Edison had entrusted much of this research to Charles Batchelor, who worked with his assistant Henry Walter at the Edison Machine Works. Edison wanted Batchelor to supervise a variety of projects at the new laboratory, and he turned over most of the electrical research to Kennelly, whom he found he could rely on to work out his ideas for new dynamo and motor designs just as Batchelor had for years. Kennelly played a crucial role in the effort to standardize components such as armature and field-magnet windings by working out design equations that would guide the Machine Works in building machinery. This experimental work resulted primarily in better engineering efficiency rather than in the development of patentable improvements. Edison, in fact, took out few patents on generators and motors during the late 1880s and 1890s. Those he did take were largely concerned with very specific engineering problems, such as the heating of armatures and pole-pieces or the sparking of commutators, or with reducing the cost of manufacturing by laminating pole-pieces to use less iron, providing a cheaper way to wind ring armatures, and redesigning field-magnet windings so the pole-pieces could be made from a single casting.[9]

The experimental work done by Kennelly and the galvanometer room staff in the effort to improve dynamo efficiency also involved fundamental research on aspects of electricity and magnetism. The use of such research is one of the little-appreciated aspects of Edison's work on electric light and power. As historian Ronald Kline has noted, "research of a more fundamental nature in the realm of engineering knowledge, that is, determining the operation of machines and the properties of materials," played an important role in engineering design in the late nineteenth century.[10] However, Edison and his laboratories have not been generally associated with such work. Edison, of course, contributed to this assessment of his work by statements to newspaper reporters that "I am not a scientific man. . . . I am an inventor." He continued:

There is a difference between them, although it may never have struck you. A scientific man busies himself with the theory. He is absolutely impractical. An inventor is essentially practical. They are of such different casts of mind that you rarely find the two together. I do not think they can very well co-exist in the one man. As soon as I find that something I am investigating does not lead to practical results, I drop it. I do not pursue it as a theory. The scientific man would be content to go on, and study it up purely as a theory. I do not care for that.[11]

Although it is true that unlike Kennelly and others in the forefront of electrical engineering science, Edison did not work to develop engineering, let alone scientific, theory, he was interested in and undertook experiments to investigate the phenomenon these theories were designed to explain. What he lacked were the mathematical inclinations and abilities that might have allowed him to contribute to the analytical literature of electrical engineering science. But it was precisely because he lacked such abilities himself that he had hired Kennelly.

Many of the experiments Kennelly conducted at the West Orange laboratory for Edison and the Edison companies involved basic research that became the basis for Kennelly's own contributions to electrical engineering theory. For example, Kennelly conducted several series of experiments on such subjects as magnetic permeability, inductance, and reluctance, from which he sought to derive mathematical theories and about which he published papers in the leading electrical engineering journals. The extensive nature of these experiments indicates that Edison clearly supported such work. Unfortunately, most of Edison's notes to Kennelly about experiments to be carried out are no longer extant. However, a set of instructions from 1888 for experiments to "determine if Magnetic stress is greater or less through different Diamagnetic material" show that Edison was quite involved, at least at that stage, not only in determining what experiments should be done but also in how they were to be carried out. Other notes from the early months of the laboratory include Edison's instructions on investigating whether "there may be such a thing as polarization at the ends of magnets" and experiments "to ascertain if there is any substance which retards lines of magnetic force." In another 1887 notebook Edison described experiments to magnetize insulated iron wire wound with copper wire to investigate the way "magnetization decreases conductivity of iron" so as to provide data for a table "to get value of this phenomenon for practical application."[12] Edison had long been interested in collecting data on electromagnetic phenomena that might prove useful in developing commercial devices, and many of Kennelly's experiments continued research that Edison had been conducting on and off for many years regarding the fundamentals of electromagnet design principles.

Although Edison's own experimental approach did not involve mathematical analysis or mathematical theory, he was interested in the practical information that such fundamental engineering research could provide. Commercial potential, however, was not the only reason for these experiments. Regardless

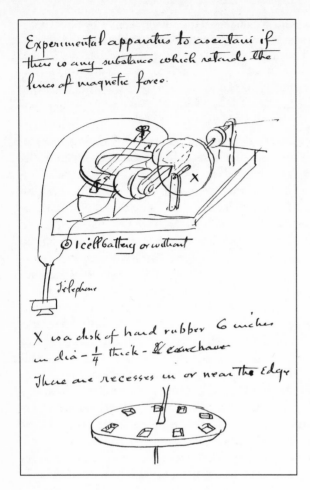

Edison designed this experimental apparatus in the fall of 1887 in order to find another "substance which retards lines of magnetic force," perhaps for use in his efforts to design a pyromagnetic generator.

of his public statements, Edison was interested in understanding electricity and magnetism at a deeper level and was willing to conduct experiments to further his knowledge of these phenomena even if they did not lead directly to practical applications. During the 1880s and 1890s investigations by the British scientific community into the relationship between electromagnetic theory and theories of the ether stimulated Edison's own research. In early 1892 he read through much of this literature and had Kennelly conduct a few experiments on Maxwell's earlier effort to explain Faraday's lines of magnetic force and other electromagnetic phenomena as characteristics of a universal fluid ether. Edison also recorded his own ideas on the subject in several extensive notebook entries, including one in which he offered a descriptive alternative to Maxwell's rigorous mathematical theory. Such speculations and experiments seem to have served Edison as a way of visualizing the unseen forces of electromagnetism relevant to his own practical work. Thus, his 1892 notebook entries focused on the ways in which copper and iron—the two metals most extensively used in electrical equipment—acted under conditions of magnetic stress by condensing or displacing the ether; he was trying to understand why only iron was magnetic even though both metals conducted electricity. Edison's 1892 speculations are similar in character to those from 1873–1874 in which he discussed the wave theory of electricity to explain inductive effects; he updated his wave theory during 1901 experiments on storage batteries by incorporating the ether into it.[13]

There is no evidence that Edison actually used such theories as a basis for his inventions. He did, however, frequently seek to find ways of applying phenomena he had either read about or observed in his own experiments. Perhaps the most well-known example of Edison's application of scientific phenomena is his work on X-rays following their discovery by Wilhelm Röntgen in December 1895. By this time Edison had largely abandoned electrical research, and Kennelly had formed a partnership with Edwin Houston as a consulting electrical engineer. Yet three weeks after Röntgen's discovery was first announced in America, Edison wired to Kennelly in Philadelphia: "How would you like to come over and experiment on Rotgons new radiations. I have glassblower and Pumps running and all Photographic apparatus. We could do a lot before others get their second wind."[14] Like other leading electrical inventors, engineers, and scientists, Edison was fascinated by the reports of Röntgen's discovery, sought to replicate his experiments, and even speculated on theoretical explanations for the phenomenon. But his primary aim was to work "on the scientific end to perfect the apparatus."[15]

With the extraordinary resources he had available to him, Edison and his staff were able to experiment with 150 different vacuum tube designs in only two months. They tested different materials and shapes for the tube and electrode, varied the electrode arrangements and electrical connections, and changed the amount of vacuum. They also tested several power sources and spark generators, different exposure times of photograph plates, and how readily the rays penetrated different materials. These experiments enabled Edison to reduce the cost of tubes considerably below that of the standard Crookes tube used in experimenting with the ray, and he gave away many of his improved tubes to other researchers. Kennelly and Houston, reporting on Edison's results in the March 18 issue of the *Electrical Engineer*, commented that his insights into the design of tubes and other apparatus "cannot fail to be valuable to many practical workers with Röntgen rays."[16] By this time, Edison and his staff had also conducted experiments with nearly 1,300 compounds in an effort to find the best fluorescing salt for the X-ray photographic plates and screens that were beginning to be used in medical work. On March 13 he cabled to an associate in England, "Please inform Lord Kelvin [Sir William Thomson] that have just found calcium tungstate properly crystallized give splendid fluorescence with Roentgen ray far exceeding platinocyanide rendering photographs unnecessary."[17] He also published his research on these salts in the *Electrical Engineer*. Edison saw his research as contributing to science and refused to patent the calcium-tungstate screen, which he termed the fluoroscope. He also arranged for it to be manufactured and sold at a modest price for medical uses. Edison believed that the fluoroscope's ability "to do in one minute what the photograph required an hour to do" was a great improvement, but the permanent record of the X-ray photograph was preferred by doctors and researchers and his device soon fell into disuse, although calcium tungstate continued to be used for certain X-ray purposes.[18] Edison may have been less interested in the theoretical underpinnings of the new ray than other researchers, particularly physicists, but he was nonetheless considered by them to be part of the same research community. Physicists, electrical inventors, and engineers had been exploring electromagnetic phenomena associated with technical systems for several decades, and Edison's research had long interested university physicists, who established many of the first electrical engineering programs. Even though his theoretical speculations about X-rays were rejected, Edison was respected as someone who contributed better apparatus and experimental knowledge that could be used to further theoretical understanding.

Edison used both well-known scientific principles and new discoveries in his inventive work. This was apparent in his continuing effort to produce electricity directly from coal, a problem that he claimed had "occupied the closest attention of the ablest inventors for many years." Like other researchers Edison hoped that a successful device would produce tremendous cost savings. He had been working on the problem since 1883, and in 1887 he conceived a new approach based on a well-known "principle that the capacity of iron for magnetism diminishes as its temperature is raised and that at a bright-red heat it become practically diamagnetic." During his experiments on this idea Edison discovered that when "iron is powerfully magnetized say nearly to saturation that its magnetization is extremely sensitive to heat, a slight increase of temperature producing a powerful diminution of magnetism so that a great portion of the energy of the heat is transformed into actual motion for various uses."[19] He applied this idea first in the design of a motor, but he also patented an alternating-current generator based on it.

Although he liked to call himself an inventor and not a scientist, Edison nonetheless considered himself part of the scientific community. Thus, he presented a paper on his new pyromagnetic motor and generator at the August 1887 meeting of the American Association for the Advancement of Science. Edison had a generator built just prior to the AAAS meeting and began to experiment with it after his return. By the end of the year he had conceived a new design based on his discovery "that the resistance of air to magnetic lines of force is about 1200 times that of soft iron."[20] In his new generator design Edison used two short, stout magnets that were divided in half and had their faces ground so that they fit snugly together. He then covered half of each magnetic circuit with wire. By using the expansion of a heated metal rod he could open a small gap and interpose the air resistance, which produced a powerful induction current. His experimental program to find another "substance which retards lines of magnetic force" was apparently undertaken to improve this design.[21] Although Edison continued to be intrigued by the possibility of developing a method to economically convert coal directly into electricity, he had largely abandoned the effort by the end of 1888. The development of more efficient designs for standard generators offered a more immediate payoff and more certain support for experiments from the Machine Works.

Besides the work on dynamos and motors conducted by the galvanometer room staff, the Machine Works also funded another line of research that Edison assigned to his chemists. In the summer of 1887 Insull and John Kruesi had discussed with Edison the need for a flexible, waterproof, and fireproof insulation for house wires, which they expected would become a major business for the Machine Works. Edison immediately began experiments at the Lamp Works laboratory, but assured them that this difficult problem would be solved at his new laboratory, which would have the facilities "to settle anything in a short time."[22] In fact, the insulation research lasted over two years and involved considerable effort and expense.

The experiments at the Lamp Works probably followed the line suggested by a patent application Edison filed in September 1887 in which he described "a mixture of rubber with an infusible material in the form of a powder."[23] When he transferred this research to the new laboratory he instructed his staff "to start by mixing some of every chemical in alphabetical order . . . with linseed oil, and record in our note books how it stood a Bunsen burner." Reginald Fessenden, one of the primary insulation researchers, discovered while experimenting in this fashion that antimony trichloride did not burn and went to the library to "read up on combustion and oils and organic chemistry." This research led him to conclude that the antimony trichloride formed a substitution compound in which the hydrogen atom was replaced by chlorine, which had little affinity with oxygen. He explained his substitution theory to Edison, who told him to try it out but also to continue with the original experiments. According to Fessenden, Edison "would never be led away from any line he had laid out, because of apparent success in a side line, until he had followed the original line to the end."[24]

One reason why Edison continued the original line of experiment was to learn about these various compounds. His own notebooks are filled with discussions of material properties based on his reading and experiments. Furthermore, he realized that information gained from one line of research, such as insulation, might provide a new direction for research in another line, such as lamp filaments or phonograph cylinders. Indeed, one of Edison's own notebooks on the results of insulation experiments contains notations about using particular compounds for filaments. During research on any of these three technologies, but particularly on filaments and phonograph cylinders, Edison and his staff were always careful to examine the properties of each compound to see whether it could be applied to one of the others. He also read the chemical literature with an eye toward determining how the same materials might be used for a variety of technologies. For instance, one day, while looking through Watts's *Dictionary of Chemistry*, he noted of one compound that it "might be a good solvent for insulation as its alkaline & a good gelatanizer & useful for many purposes." On the very next page his notes from Watts on stearic acid end with a comment to "work up stearic a[cid] comb[inatio]ns for both Insul[ation] & phono."[25] Similarly, Fessenden's idea about chlorine substitution compounds seems to have found its way into Edison's filament research and possibly into battery experiments as well. Finally, as Edison later noted, much of industrial chemistry was "colloidal in its nature. . . . Hard rubber, celluloid, glass, soap, paper, and lots of others, all have to deal with amorphous substances, as to which comparatively little has been really settled."[26] Thus, Fessenden found that because substitution compounds had been little investigated up to that time, his work with them had to be "entirely experimental and largely at first empirical."[27]

By May 1888 Insull was pressing Edison to send the promised insulation so that the Machine Works could test it in its wire-covering machinery. He emphasized again to Edison the importance of going "into this house wire trade right away. We have spent so much money on experimental work on insulation that we ought to be getting some results out of it. Unless we bring a wire out within the next week or so we shall lose the whole of this seasons trade, and might just as well wait until this time next year, as the greater part of this business is done during the Spring and Summer months."[28] Edison assigned Batchelor to the task of getting the insulation in shape for the Machine Works, but when Kruesi tested it at the laboratory in June the insulation proved neither fire- nor moistureproof. Insull felt that the laboratory's lack of facilities "to make up the wire in the manner that we would be compelled to make it for commercial purposes" had prevented the research staff from adequately testing it.[29] Thereafter, Edison had his staff send each promising compound to Schenectady for testing, but he also had machinery made for the laboratory staff to use in its own tests.

Batchelor's notes from the summer of 1888 indicate that the manufacturing process presented a major obstacle to the development of a good insulating compound. In mid-July he noted that they had "tried many mixtures but as yet have not arrived at what we want for hardness just after putting in a wire so that it can be put on & covered at the same operation. . . . What we want at present is some mixture . . . that will enable it to come out of the 'Squirter' hard enough to go right into the cotton coverer."[30] The laboratory staff had a difficult task in developing a compound that would be sufficiently hard yet liquefy satisfactorily when heated to penetrate the cotton thread.

In the fall Batchelor stopped experimenting with insulation to devote his time to other work, and David Marshall, who with Fessenden was one of the primary experimenters on insulation, became the laboratory's liaison with the Machine Works. By December Insull had become exasperated with the failure of the insulation compounds to meet the company's commercial requirements and complained that Edison must not be "aware of the kind of stuff that those fellows who are experimenting on compound sent us. We have got to do something in order to get a good house wire. Unless we go ahead within the next month or so we shall lose next season's trade. There is upwards of 1,300,000 yards of this class of wire used a month, and we are practically getting nothing of the trade." In reply to these complaints, Marshall noted that he had sent several new compounds (out of a total that now numbered over 325) since the one Insull complained of and told him "you have been a long while letting us know" that it was "worthless."[31] The insulation project was made more difficult by poor coordination and communication between the laboratory and the Machine Works as a result of their geographic separation, a problem that sometimes plagued other research and manufacturing efforts for the company. By early January 1889 several promising solutions had been developed, and by June over 580 different compounds had been tested; each, however, proved inadequate in one or another aspect. Some compounds needed to be more inflammable or more waterproof, others to have a higher melting point, others to liquefy better, and still others proved too brittle. In some cases, the insulation also destroyed the cotton or the wire itself.

Although the Machine Works Wiring Department did manufacture and sell insulated house wire, it is unclear whether the laboratory ever developed a single insulation that met the requirements of being flexible, inflammable, waterproof, and reasonably cheap. Fessenden and Marshall, who both wrote reminiscences many years later, disagreed about the final result of this experimental effort. Fessenden stated that they had succeeded, whereas Marshall recalled that he never tested an insulation that proved entirely fireproof. In fact, whatever insulation they produced ultimately proved inadequate, and Edison had Jonas Aylsworth conduct further experiments in the fall of 1890. Aylsworth produced some promising compounds, including one in December 1891 that he thought was "as cheap a moisture-proof and non-inflammable compound as it is possible to make by chemical treatment of organic compounds." By the following February, however, Edison claimed that he had "lost all hope of ever getting anything satisfactory in these insulating substances."[32]

Edison's role in the insulation research remains as unclear as its results. Apart from developing or approving approaches to the problem and making some experiments himself early on, he seems to have been little involved except for checking on the research during his daily rounds. Yet he was the one who filed the basic patent in May 1889 on the chlorine substitution method. Fessenden believed that the results of research at the laboratory were always Edison's and that who did the research was "not material," but in this case the idea embodied in the patent seems to have been Fessenden's rather than Edison's. In the corporate research laboratories of the twentieth century such ideas would be clearly credited to an individual researcher such as Fessenden, even though the patent would be owned by the company. In the more fluid and less bureaucratic environment of Edison's laboratory, where he was involved in each project to some extent, it was often difficult to assign clear credit for an invention or a specific line of development. This was especially true because so much of the experimental work was based on research programs laid out by Edison and carried out with resources he provided. Thus, he continued to reserve for himself those patents, such as the insulation patent, that he considered basic, and to confine members of his staff to ancillary patents.[33]

If evaluating Edison's role in the insulation research remains problematic, this is not true of the experimental work on electric lamps. Of all the electric light research undertaken at the laboratory, lamp technology was the one subject in which Edison was most involved personally as an experimenter. Whereas his role in much of the electric light research could be considered that of a research director, setting the agenda but not taking part in much of the research, he was clearly the chief experimenter and team leader in the lamp research. Edison's team of lamp researchers included a group of men who had come with him from the Lamp Works: glassblower Joe Force, lamp tester Charles Deshler, and experimenters Arthur Payne and John Marshall. Martin Force continued to assist with experiments at the Lamp Works, where he was joined by Joseph and William Ward. John Ott, who was Edison's principal assistant in much of the lamp research at the Lamp Works laboratory and was now responsible for coordinating the work of all the experimenters and machinists, played only an indirect role in lamp research at the West Orange laboratory. The staff that came from the Lamp Factory was joined by other experimenters. Charles A. Brown and Dr. Johannes Braun (whose entire stay at the laboratory lasted only six months), conducted experiments on plant fibers. Stockroom boy Herbert Read began to assist Deshler with lamp tests soon after joining the West Orange staff and later helped Deshler with experiments as well. Many of the chemical experimenters at West Orange also participated in the lamp research from time to time, particularly David Marshall. Others included Jonas Aylsworth, who conducted research on carbon filaments for a short time before becoming the primary researcher on phonograph cylinder waxes (in 1891 he returned to this research when he took charge of the Lamp Works plant for making filaments), Erwin von Wilmowsky, Reginald Fessenden, and James Gladstone.[34]

Most of the lamp research at West Orange continued work that Edison had begun after moving his laboratory to the Lamp Works in the summer of 1886. Many of Edison's experiments were aimed at producing carbon lamps with more uniform fibers to increase lamp life. As usual, Edison chose to attack this problem in part by ransacking nature's warehouse. Repeating the effort of 1880 and 1881, when he had determined that madake bamboo from Japan made the best filaments, in November 1886 Edison began sending agents to all parts of the globe looking for better plant materials. By August 1888 the Lamp Com-

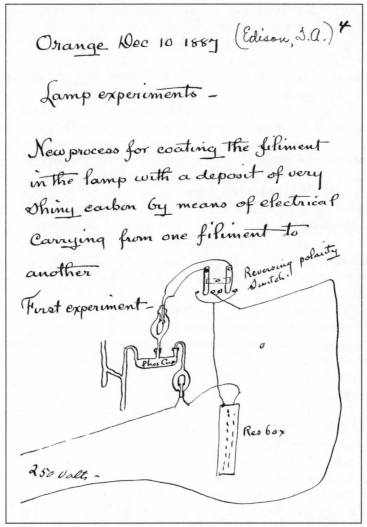

The first page of a December 1887 notebook containing Edison's plans for a series of lamp experiments shows his idea for coating filaments by using the effect of electrical carrying, which caused blackening of the lamps and which he was also experimenting to prevent.

pany had spent $11,000 for this purpose, and Upton feared that additional expenses would amount to another $5,000. Estimating that the sample fibers cost $150 each, he told Edison that the Lamp Company would require "a million and a half Fibres at one cent a piece to pay for this expense."[35] Sobered by these figures, Edison agreed that these expeditions had produced enormous expense but little result and brought them to an end.

Experiments with plant fibers sent back by his agents were only a small part of the laboratory work related to lamps. Beginning in the summer of 1886, Edison had begun trying to coat the bamboo filaments to make them more uniform. Initially he tried various oxides. After one set of experiments in which he attempted to "lock the oxides together" by dipping them first in coal tar or licorice solutions, he decided to experiment with soaking the filaments in syrupy solutions of these and other carbonizable materials such as sugar and molasses both before and during carbonization. By November 1886 Edison felt that this soaking process was promising enough to apply for a patent on it. In his application he claimed that by filling the pores of the bamboo he could produce a filament with "a dense and homogenous carbon structure" that heated evenly when brought to incandescence.[36] It is unclear if this method of treating the bamboo was actually adopted by the Lamp Company, but by 1888 he had developed a method of treating the filaments with a thin coating of asphalt that somewhat improved the lamps' efficiency. To improve efficiency, Edison continued to experiment on a variety of methods for treating filaments with oxides or carbon substances, particularly asphalt and other bituminous materials.

Edison was not the only inventor developing ways to treat carbon filaments to make them more uniform and longer-lived. His patent on the soaking process, though applied for in late 1886, was issued only in January 1893, after he and his patent attorneys finally satisfied the examiner that his method of treatment differed from those described in patents already issued to other inventors. A particularly important process developed by William Sawyer and Albon Man was used by several competitors of the Edison Lamp Company. In the Sawyer-Man process, known as flashing, the filament was heated together with hydrocarbon vapor, usually gasoline, at a high temperature that decomposed the vapor and deposited additional carbon on the filament. With this process manufacturers were better able to control the amount of carbon deposited and more accurately regulate the resistance of the lamp itself. To get around the Sawyer-Man patent, Edison experimented on and off with both hydrocarbon flashing and similar methods of treating the carbon by using residual gases derived from compounds other than carbon. For a brief period in the early 1880s the Lamp Company had used a flashing process, but the strong patent position of Sawyer-Man forced Edison to give this up. Explaining his failure to employ the widely used flashing process, Edison remarked that his company had "never stolen or infringed a patent yet, and never will if I can prevent it, and notwithstanding that the competitor who owns the patent in question has infringed more than 50 of ours, we have not used what is his in retaliation."[37] It also was unclear from tests whether flashing produced sufficient improvements in the bamboo filament lamps to take the risk of using the process. Only after the patent situation changed in 1893 did the Lamp Works begin treating filaments by flashing them. In the meantime, Edison looked for other ways to improve his lamps.

Many of Edison's efforts were devoted to another approach that was also taken by several other experimenters. This was the effort to develop filaments composed of artificial rather than natural fibers. Much of this research was carried out in Europe, particularly in England. Joseph Swan had developed the first commercial lamps of this type by treating cotton with nitric acid to produce nitrocellulose, which could be dissolved in acetic acid. He subsequently devised a method to reconstitute the nitrocellulose by squirting this solution through a small nozzle into alcohol, which acted as a coagulant. This squirting process produced a finer and more uniform filament. Because nitrocellulose, also known as gun cotton, had to be denitrated before it could be safely carbonized, John Powell, another Englishman, developed a safer process for producing artificial cellulose filaments by dissolving cotton in zinc chloride, which was then put through a squirting process. Edison conducted some experiments with cellulose, but probably because of patents he focused his efforts on artificial squirted filaments made from bituminous substances, such as asphaltene and coal tar, or resins such as linseed oil. These experiments began in earnest in 1888 at the West Orange laboratory, and Edison received a patent for filaments of this type in 1891. However, the Lamp Works never made lamps with these filaments and only began making squirted cellulose filaments in 1893 after the patent situation had changed.[38]

Squirted cellulose lamps were made in England by the Edison and Swan United Electric Light Company, which Edison had agreed to form in 1883 to avoid an expensive legal battle with Swan over their respective lamp patents. In the United States Edison felt his patent position to be much stronger and he resisted all efforts to combine with competitors there. Nonetheless, it was only in 1892 that his basic carbon filament patent was finally upheld by the U.S. Circuit Court of Appeals; for a while it had even been judged invalid on the basis that Edison's description was inadequate and that incandescent carbon lamps had been anticipated by other inventors. The long contest over the lamp patent was one of many suits and countersuits between the Edison lighting interests and its major competitors, particularly the Thomson-Houston and the Westinghouse Electric Companies. Edison felt that he held the fundamental patents on direct current lighting systems, and even argued that the "principal reason why there are so many advocates of alternating *may perhaps* be found in the fact that we have the principal & *broad patent on Direct* If our patents were public property you wouldnt find an alternating man in the US." He thus supported the litigation effort and even suggested additional suits that might be brought on "small detail patents."[39]

Although issues raised in patent litigation influenced the general direction of some of Edison's electrical research, such as his efforts to develop alternative filament treatment processes, he also found it necessary to react directly to court decisions. For example, he had to develop a new cutout for his municipal lamp when the courts upheld a Thomson-Houston patent over his own. Fessenden recalled that when the courts initially ruled Edison's basic incandescent lamp patent invalid, he was spurred to intensify his work on squirted filaments. Like-wise, Edison's competitors worked to evade his patents. When Edison's lamp patent was upheld in 1892, Westinghouse used a noninfringing lamp as a tem-porary measure until the patent expired two years later. Although inferior to the Edison lamp in life and efficiency, this lamp gave adequate service at a lower price and allowed Westinghouse to successfully compete in the interim.[40]

Edison felt certain that his basic electric light patents would be upheld in the courts, but his disgust over the constant litigation proved to be a major fac-tor in his repudiation of the American patent system. Edison felt that patent law favored infringers by giving them the benefit of the inevitable delays involved in litigation.

> After a thing is perfected and commercially introduced so as to show there is money in it half a dozen parties start to infringe it. The theory upon which the[y] act is, that it will be several years before I can get a final decision, and in the mean-time they make money, and when I do get a decision it is probable that no dam-ages can be collected as they have covered their tracks by organizing an irresponsi-ble corporation. . . . There is bound to be a delay; why not give the benefit of this delay to the man who has the patent and has worked the thing up to a practical success and not to the infringer who comes after and has no patent. In other words give the man with the patent the preliminary justice until the Court has time to de-cide the case. Madam Justice has got this thing reversed it seems to me.[41]

In 1890 Edison even suggested an amendment to the patent law on this point that he had his attorneys submit to Congress. However, the House Committee on Patents failed to act on it out of concern that this would "pre-cipitate a discussion on the whole patent law, and might endanger important amendments now in hand and well advanced" because of the "strong feeling in Congress, particularly on the part of Western and Southern members, against patents."[42] Frustrated in his effort to reform the system, Edison suggested that the Edison company sue at once on about one hundred of his patents and urged his lawyers to push pending patent applications to sue on them as well.

Besides his outrage at the failure of the courts to protect inventors, Edison also complained about other aspects of the patent system. By 1888 he had "be-come extremely skeptical as to the value of any patent, and so long as our patent law remains in its present iniquitous shape, I shall try to do without patents."[43] Thus, his plan to develop many of his inventions as trade secrets. He particularly objected to the fact that U.S. patents became inoperative before the end of their seventeen-year term if a foreign patent expired first—he had particularly strong feelings on this issue because it cost him his basic patents on the phonograph and almost claimed his basic lamp patent as well. Edison also felt that the Patent Office had become biased against him. Even after his patent attorneys tried to reassure him that this was not the case, he remained steadfast in his belief "that where the issue is one of any *Value* I get beaten." At one point he even considered "the system of declaring interferences the chief weak-ness of our present patent system" and suggested that the "first man in the office should have the patent."[44] To protect poor inventors he also advocated that applications should consist of only a brief description in the inventor's handwriting, without the need for expensive detailed drawings, and a one dollar filing fee. He apparently thought better of this idea, which would have added to another major problem identified by Edison. This was the granting of impractical patents that were "brought forward for purpose very similar to black mail" after an inventor had disclosed a practical means of accomplishing something.[45]

Although Edison periodically received correspondence from others seeking reform or offering their own ideas for changes, he grew increasingly cynical about the possibilities of reforming the patent system. Answering an 1888 request for his assistance in pushing Congress to act on patent reform he told Tate to "Write & say I have lost all faith in patents Judges & everything relative to patents & dont care if the whole system is squelched." By June 1893 he really had given up on the system. Asserting that he was "through with patents," he told one patent solicitor that "my Patent Office business hereafter wouldn't pay your office boy's expenses."[46] True to his word, between May 1893 and January 1897 he applied for only five patents (including two in December 1893). Although this was in part a consequence of his efforts to develop his iron ore concentrating plant during the 1890s (see Chapter 18), it is notable that Edison did not take out the extensive range of machinery and process patents for that project that he did for his cement works after 1900, even though his cement technology was largely derived from the earlier ore-milling venture. Regardless of his distaste for the patent system, Edison still found his time much occupied with patent litigation, particularly in his phonograph and motion picture businesses.

The uncertainty of litigation and the ability of inventors to get around patents made efforts to increase the economy and efficiency of lighting systems more important than patent suits in the competition over electric lighting systems. Consequently, an important aspect of lamp research at the West Orange laboratory focused on reducing the cost of lamps. In July 1891, for example, Edison described several improvements in a letter to Insull. These included "(1) Machines for sealing in lamps (2) Use of straight inside part (3) New Platina seal (4) Dipping of vacuum pump tubes in collodion (saving Labor and glass)."[47] The next year Tate noted that the books of the Lamp Company showed a credit of $23,000 in savings due to Edison's lamp improvements. Although he did not describe these improvements, they probably related to 1891 changes that reduced the amount of platinum in the lead-in wires. An earlier cost savings had resulted from the substitution of inexpensive carbon paste for copper clamps to attach the filaments to the lead-in wires. Edison also sought to lower cost by improving manufacturing techniques to reduce the number of waste lamps. However, as often happened with changes in lamp manufacturing resulting from improvements developed at the laboratory, Edison found in March 1891 that "the Lamp factory is off again the lamps being very poor and

I am now hunting the bug." To ensure that his improvements were properly adopted, he installed Charles Brown, one of his lamp experimenters, to act as his inspector at the lamp works "to simply report to me if the scientific methods are carried out according to my instructions."[48]

The most intractable lamp problem facing Edison was also the most important from a competitive standpoint. This was the diminishing candlepower of a lamp over the course of its life. From the earliest days of lamp manufacturing Edison had had to contend with the "electrical carrying" of carbon that coated and blackened the glass, thus reducing the lamp's candlepower. This was a major problem for all lamp manufacturers and Edison spent much time and effort trying to solve it. During his experiments he discovered that reduced candlepower also occurred when a lamp changed resistance during use. Although Edison believed that this change in resistance *"is not a loss to the station or to the customer,"* unlike "blackening which is a *real loss to* both," customers complained about any loss in the amount of light.[49] Furthermore, even though Edison lamps often lasted longer than those of competitors, their continued loss of candlepower reduced this advantage. As a result, by 1889 the Lamp Company increasingly found many Edison isolated and illuminating stations replacing their Edison lamps with those of Sawyer-Man. Although Edison was able to obtain a 10 percent reduction in the loss of candlepower by heating the filament to a red heat after it was sealed in the evacuated bulb, the Edison lamp continued to lose market share, part of a more general loss of market share for the Edison lighting system.

By the late 1880s Thomson-Houston and Westinghouse were challenging Edison's dominance in electric lighting by using alternating current systems to extend the central station business beyond the limits of Edison's direct current system. The challenge of alternating current spurred Edison's work at the laboratory and a publicity campaign challenging the safety of the new system, as well as Edison's push for a renewed effort at patent litigation. Patent litigation would ultimately prove costly and time-consuming and of only limited value in the competition between the three firms. However, it did encourage efforts at cooperation in the form of cross-licensing of patents and helped to influence a drive toward consolidation that was already under way as each company sought to better coordinate and finance its central station business.

CHAPTER 17

Competition and Consolidation

Although he declined to finance Edison's new laboratories, Henry Villard was primarily responsible for pushing the reorganization of the Edison lighting companies in the United States. Following his successful effort to consolidate the Edison lighting interests on the European continent, Villard had attempted to arrange manufacturing rights for Siemens & Halske's armored cables with Edison Electric. Growing frustrated with the need to placate the variety of interests in the American companies, he decided that it would be best to combine the manufacturing companies controlled by Edison with Edison Electric, and he arranged with a syndicate of German investors to provide funds for this purpose. The syndicate included the Deutsche Bank, for whom Villard was an investment adviser, the banking house of Jacob Stern, Siemens & Halske, and the German Edison Company, which had been reorganized in 1887 as the General Electric Company.[1]

Edison agreed to go ahead with this plan in the expectation that it would free him from the burden of providing working capital to the manufacturing shops. In return for their interests in the shops, Edison and his partners received an equivalent amount in stock shares of a new company, Edison General Electric, which also took over the business of the Edison Electric Light Company and the Edison Isolated Lighting Company; stockholders in these companies, including Edison, also received shares in Edison General. Edison may have received some additional compensation as well. As he later told Villard, "when I sold out, one of the greatest inducements was the sum of cash received, which I thought I could always have on hand, so as to free my mind from financial stress, and thus enable me to go ahead in the technical field."[2]

He was doubtless pleased that Drexel Morgan, which had a controlling interest in Edison Electric, had finally recognized its mistake in not funding the shops originally. But Edison wanted assurances from Villard that Drexel Morgan would not have a controlling interest in the new combined company, "his experience being that when money was required for the business it was next to impossible to get it so long as Drexel Morgan & Co controlled the business, or if obtainable at all the money could only be got at ruinous rates." He felt that if they were "able to exercise control the value of his property would be very seriously affected as he considered them incapable of exercising proper judgement in relation to such business matters as the Company would have to deal with and moreover that he would on no account want to place himself in a position where Drexel Morgan & Co could squeeze any interest that he owned." Villard told Edison that he had never felt a need previously to call on Drexel Morgan for funds. Furthermore, because Drexel Morgan was investing only $250,000, a one-seventh interest, while his syndicate of German investors was investing $1.75 million, "control rested with [Villard] and his friends and Mr. Edison, that in the management of the new Company he relied upon working with Mr. Edison."[3] In fact, Villard worked closely with Edison in drawing up plans for the organization and operations of the new company.

Negotiations began in earnest in August 1888, and although Edison got his partners in the manufacturing concerns to go along, there were some differences of opinion that strained relations between them. As Edison himself commented, "we have peculiar relations with each other in re[gard to the] shops & from long friendship & ass[ociatio]n."[4] However, these friendships nearly did not survive the merger. Edward Johnson, whose relationship with Edison was already under stress because of the phonograph business, was an example. Johnson and Sprague had established the Sprague Electric Railway and Motor Company in 1884 to exploit Sprague's inventions. The company's manufacturing was done by the Edison Machine Works and had become so important by 1889 (two-thirds of the Machine Works orders were for Sprague motors and electric railway equipment) that Johnson wanted to bring the Sprague company into the consolidation. Sprague's rather caustic personality grated on Edison, Insull, and others in the Edison companies, and when Edison heard that Johnson had accused the inventor of "knifing" him during an interview with Villard, Edison fired off a bitter letter to his longtime associate accusing him of first failing to do justice to Edison's electric railway inventions as president of the Electric Railway Company and then joining forces with Sprague. "You know," he told Johnson, "that your bringing Mr Sprague in the family has been a galling thorn in the side of all the boys but they kept still because you were their friend, and as I told you two years ago in Tomlinson's office that it was only a matter of time when it would break up old associations which it has about done."[5]

Edison's relations with Sigmund Bergmann also became strained at this time. Bergmann, who had manufactured Edison's original phonograph, felt he should have been given manufacturing rights to the new one, but Edison was greatly distressed by Bergmann's negotiations with Lippincott regarding the manufacturing of the graphophone. Bergmann also resented Insull's role in the accounting necessary for the consolidation and thought that certain manufacturing rights should go to his company rather than the Machine Works. In addition, he felt hurt that Edison seemed to believe that Bergmann had become wealthy only through his association with the inventor. In reply to Bergmann's own long, bitter letter Edison replied:

> I have always done everything to help every one of the boys; I have always been glad they were getting wealthy; the more they made the better it pleased me; I am glad you are well fixed; would not do anything to prevent you making money; all the money you have you made yourself through your ability; that you had a chance to exercise that ability was due to me; you have been worked up to a state of dam foolishness by your enemies, of which you have a very choice and extensive collection.[6]

Edison felt great resentment that his "plan of division dont seem to work with some of my friends" and told Johnson he had "about concluded to fall into the regular routine and do just as other men do, which conclusion they generally reach when they are 40 to 45 yrs of age."[7] However, in the winter of 1889 Edison, his manufacturing partners, Drexel Morgan, and Villard's investors finally agreed on the organization of Edison General Electric, which was incorporated on April 24. Edward Johnson resigned as president of Edison Electric and devoted his energies to running the Sprague Company, which was acquired by Edison General. While he and Edison remained friends, they were never as close again, although Edison did continue to help Johnson out of financial difficulties throughout his life. Edison and Bergmann had never been as close friends, but they were able to patch up their differences and remained good friends even after Bergmann resigned as head of his shop in 1891 and left for Germany to found a new manufacturing company.

The new company was run by Villard, who became the president of Edison General, and Samuel Insull, who served as vice-president and manager of the shops. Although Edison had no official role in the company apart from his positions as a member of the board of directors and as a contract inventor, his name and reputation, as well as his continuing technical contributions, remained crucial to the company. Villard and Insull therefore not only consulted him on major policy decisions but frequently found it politic to defer to him.

While the various parties involved discussed the best plan for organizing Edison General, extensive negotiations also were taking place with Thomson-Houston, which had previously aligned itself with Westinghouse. In 1887 the Edison company's two rivals had agreed to a cross-licensing arrangement to avoid litigation over alternating current transformer patents. At the time Westinghouse also gained the rights to sell Thomson-Houston arc-lighting systems and to use the Sawyer-Man lamp patents. The following year, to finance an expansion of its arc and central station lighting businesses, Thomson-Houston sold both the patent rights and its own lamp company to Westinghouse in exchange for a patent license. However, when a Westinghouse suit on a transformer patent proved unsuccessful in August 1888 the arrangements between them regarding arc and alternating current systems fell apart. At that point Thomson-Houston approached the Edison interests.

The negotiations between the Edison and Thomson-Houston companies included a proposal for Thomson-Houston to take over the small-town central station business and be given access to all patents controlled by the Edison company, except those related to electric railways and power. In exchange Thomson-Houston would acknowledge the validity of Edison's three-wire system patent, which was then being litigated, and turn over its lamp replacement business. Edison himself wanted Thomson-Houston "to turn over their incandescent business to us who know it and own it, and keep their arc light to themselves, and work together; but they do not want this; they keep everything and propose a working arrangement which would give them everything and us a sum precarious in reception and entirely inadequate to reimburse us for loss of business prestige and other things." Furthermore, Edison felt that there was "a law in commercial things as in nature. If one attempts to obtain more profit than general average he is immediately punished by competition." He was therefore "a believer in *Insuring the permanency of an investment* by keeping prices so low that there is no inducement to others to come in an[d] ruin it." As a result, he argued that

ruinous competition may be correct in their point of view, but I assure you that prices are too high now . . . to do a great business in this country, prices must be got down 50 to 75 per cent lower than now. And the moment the leaden collar of the Light Company is removed, it will be done, and we will make a great profit at prices that would show our competitors what good, brainy, aggressive competition means. But to do this, the new Company must stand alone, unencumbered by any alliances or contacts. The money we will have will be sufficient if you find it difficult to raise any more. If you make the coalition, my usefulness as an inventor is gone. My services wouldn't be worth a penny. I can only invent under powerful incentive. No competition means no invention. It's the same with the men I have around me. It's not the money they want, but a chance for their ambition to work.

Edison decided that it would be best to "wait a couple of years & decide the litigation, then we can talk about licensing. . . . Remember if we win in litigation we will get *paid* for all the plants they sell & if we fail they wont pay thereafter= so our money is assured any way."[8]

Although the three-wire system devised by Edison in 1883 had made it possible to extend his lighting system economically beyond a one-mile radius from a central station, the Edison system still remained uneconomical outside of cities and large towns with dense concentrations of buildings. To extend the use of electrical systems in these areas, electrical engineers had begun to develop high-voltage, alternating current systems that had the potential to pro-

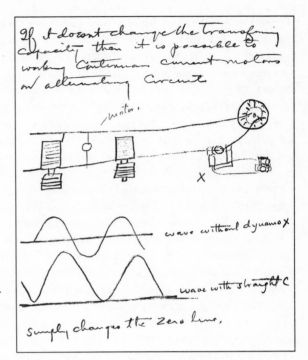

Edison asked Arthur Kennelly to make the necessary calculations for this November 1887 plan of using direct ("continuous") current motors with alternating current.

duce much larger savings in copper costs by using much thinner conductors. To employ high voltages to transmit electricity long distances they had to convert the current to lower voltages before it was used by customers. Beginning in 1886 Westinghouse began to market an alternating current system to electrify sparsely populated districts located on the edge of large cities or in small cities and towns where the Edison direct current system would require prohibitively large and expensive copper conductors.[9]

Edison and others connected with his lighting companies had been following alternating current developments in Europe for some time, but only in the fall of 1886, under pressure from Westinghouse competition, did Edison fully examine the pros and cons of alternating current. By November Edison had concluded that it was inefficient, uneconomical, unreliable, and dangerous, an opinion confirmed by a report from Siemen & Halske, which manufactured Edison lighting equipment in Germany. This report provided a detailed comparison of alternating current systems used in Europe with the Edison-Siemens direct current system. These early alternating current systems had operating inefficiencies, particularly with regard to power losses in the transformer used to convert from high to low voltage. Both Edison and Siemens & Halske argued that the costs of conversion would obviate any savings from lower copper costs.

They also believed that high-voltage alternating current was less economical than low-voltage direct current for isolated plants and for central station operations that did not require long-distance distribution and that the use of transformers made it more difficult to maintain a constant voltage, an important requirement for long lamp life. Furthermore, alternating current systems lacked two important technical features—a meter for measuring current use and a motor, the growing use of which was becoming an increasingly significant factor in balancing the load factor of central stations during daytime hours.[10]

By themselves these technical and economic factors might not have prevented Edison from adopting alternating current. In 1886 and 1887 he even made some preliminary efforts to move into alternating current work. Edison Electric also acquired rights to one of the leading European systems while Edison applied for patents to regulate the voltage of alternating current systems and to reduce the energy loss from the transformers used with them. He also worked on transforming alternating into direct current to drive electric motors for street railways. Nevertheless, Edison finally refused to adopt alternating current because of his concerns about its safety.[11]

Edison had been concerned about the issue of safety from the beginning of the electric light industry. One of the arguments he used in competing with gas lighting was the greater safety afforded by electric lights, and he sought to ensure that safety by developing a safety fuse to prevent fires. Edison was also able to claim that "there is no danger to life, health, or person, in the current generated by any of the Edison dynamos" and that "the wires at any part of the system, and even the poles of the generator itself, may be grasped by the naked hand without the slightest effect."[12] In response, the gas industry pointed to the accidental deaths of linemen and occasional innocent bystanders caused by arc light systems. These, however, employed alternating currents at higher voltages than those of his direct current system. It is therefore not surprising that Edison feared that "just as certain as death Westinghouse will kill a customer within 6 months after he puts in a system of any size. He has got a new thing, and it will require a great deal of experimenting to get it working practically. It will never be free from danger."[13]

Even though he feared the dangers of high-voltage alternating current, Edison nonetheless believed that he could safely use high-voltage direct current, and he proposed to Johnson a system using his 1,200-volt municipal dynamo (isolated and central station dynamos were 110 to 140 volts) in combination with a three-wire distribution network and inexpensive and efficient transformers to compete in the growing market for long-distance distribution systems. In describing this idea to Johnson, Edison explained that "there would be very little danger to our men in repairing a 2000 volt const[ant]-high pressure main, for even if they did get it, it would not produce death, but I cannot for the life of me see how alternate current high pressure mains—which in large cities can never stop, could be repaired."[14] He immediately applied for a patent on this high-voltage direct-current system, but it apparently did not work well enough for commercial use. By the following September he had modified it into a five-wire system by substituting subfeeders for the transformers. Edison Electric engineers objected to the complexity of this system, and it, too, never came into commercial use, although the company did pay to have an experimental five-wire plant put up at the West Orange laboratory.

It is unclear if the failure to adopt a high-voltage direct current system was the result of technical difficulties or concerns about safety. Although Edison believed that high-voltage direct current was safer, he nonetheless was aware that it could produce a fatal accident that might turn the public against his system. The 1887 rules issued by Edison Electric for its municipal system declared that "as a matter of protection to the reputation of the business, it is necessary that an expert be furnished to superintend the construction of the first plant installed by a new contractor" and sternly warned about the need for extreme caution to protect the public from the higher voltages (1,200 volts) of direct current used in the system.[15] At a time when city and state lawmakers were becoming increasingly concerned about the safety of electric wires, Edison may have decided to focus his efforts on improving the efficiency of his low-voltage system.

When he proposed his high-voltage direct current system to Johnson in November 1886, Edison declared "that even the gains due to our system is nothing as compared to a lamp that is 50% more economical . . . it is in the lamps that I hope to make it positively impossible for [competitors] to exist in Central station work to say nothing of Isolated."[16] This may in part explain Edison's extraordinary personal attention to lamp experiments. His efforts to improve the lamp included a higher resistance lamp that he introduced in late 1886 and that provided the company with significant savings in the amount of copper used in its three-wire system. This same lamp, however, also faced criticism from managers of local companies, who complained that it had a shorter life and blackened more quickly than the old lamps. In 1891 Edison experimented on a 200-volt lamp that he expected would reduce copper use "by 75% theoretically, and perhaps 70% practically" and enable his system to cover sixteen square miles.[17] Edison's efforts to develop higher resistance lamps to reduce the amount of copper in the distribution system resembled his original approach to that problem in 1878, but this ultimately proved inadequate for long-distance transmission.

Just as Westinghouse began to make inroads in the growing market for small-town stations, Edison was presented with an opportunity to dramatize his concerns over the dangers of alternating current. In the fall of 1887 Dr. Alfred Southwick, a Buffalo dentist who had been appointed in 1886 to a New York State commission charged with finding a more humane form of execution than hanging, requested Edison's support for the use of "electricity as an agent to supplant the gallows." Having witnessed an accidental electrocution, Southwick became an advocate for the position that it produced a quicker and less painful death than hanging and he even conducted some experiments on electrocuting animals with this idea in mind. "Civilization, Science and humanity demand a change" in the manner of execution, he told Edison, and "the reputation you have as an Electrician will help as much with the Legislature as lawmakers in changing the code."[18] Edison replied that he would prefer "an effort to totally abolish capital punishment," but agreed to aid Southwick in the belief that "while the system is recognized by the State, it is the duty of the latter to adopt the most humane method available for the purpose of disposing of criminals." He agreed that electricity would provide this method and urged the use of alternating current generators "manufactured principally in this country by Geo. Westinghouse." He also noted that "practical evidence" of the ability of alternating current to produce "instantaneous death" could be supplied by the authorities in New Orleans, where during the past six months "two men have been killed and others injured by this quality of current."[19] In January the commission recommended electrocution, and in June a bill providing for this form of execution was signed by the governor of New York. At the same time this bill was being debated, Edison was approached by Henry Bergh of the American Society for the Prevention of Cruelty to Animals regarding the substitution of electrocution for drowning as a more humane method of killing stray animals. Edison responded by suggesting the use of "the ordinary Brush [alternating] current on the street [arc] lighting circuits."[20]

Edison's involvement in the public debate over the efficacy of alternating current as a humane agent of death for both humans and animals might have gone no further if another person had not called on him for assistance. In early July a little-known consulting electrician named Harold P. Brown approached Edison after being vehemently attacked by advocates of alternating current for a letter he had written to the New York Post. In this letter Brown termed alternating current "damnable" and urged the New York Board of Electrical Control to follow the example of Chicago in banning its use. After pointing out that the low-voltage direct-current Edison system was safe, Brown claimed that the "only excuse for the use of the fatal 'alternating' current is that it saves the company operating it from spending a larger sum of money for the heavier copper wires. . . . That is, the public must submit to *constant danger from sudden death* in order that a corporation may pay a *little larger dividend*."[21] Given Brown's inflammatory rhetoric it is not surprising that some responses sent to the Board of Control included personal attacks against him.

There were several reasons why Edison responded positively to Brown's request that he be allowed to conduct experiments at the Orange laboratory. Holding similar beliefs about alternating current himself he was only too happy to help Brown prove his case. Furthermore, Edison's past involvement in similar public battles over etheric force and the microphone probably inclined him toward defending Brown against charges of incompetence leveled against him because he was entirely self-taught in electricity. Edison, who always placed practical experience before formal education, appreciated that Brown's prejudice against alternating current had arisen from his personal experience of working five years for the Brush Arc Light Company. Finally, Brown had a personal connection to Edison through George Bliss, in whose electrical shops he had worked and with whom he had been associated selling Edison's electric pen, as well as in manufacturing telephones and electromedical apparatus at Western Electric. Edison was thus willing to provide Brown not only the use of his laboratory, but also the assistance of his chief electrician, Arthur Kennelly.

During July and August, Brown and Kennelly carried out experiments at Edison's laboratory, and Brown also conducted public demonstrations at Columbia University using equipment provided by Edison and with the assistance of Dr. Frederick Peterson, a member of the New York Medico-Legal Society, which had been given the responsibility for determining the best means of carrying out electrocutions. These experiments using high voltages of both alternating and direct current to electrocute dogs showed, as Kennelly wrote in a letter to the New York World, that "the rapidly alternating current is under otherwise similar conditions beyond all doubt more fatal than the continuous current."[22] Studies made in the 1970s showed that alternating current was more lethal by two and a half or three times, although these studies also demonstrated that electrocution is neither as instantaneous nor painless as the 1888 experiments appeared to indicate. Kennelly and Charles Batchelor, who assisted with some of the laboratory experiments with dogs, also personally experienced the differences between these types of current, which confirmed their more objective tests. During his experiments Batchelor electrocuted a dog with an Edison municipal dynamo that was used for street lighting near the laboratory and that had been adapted to produce alternating currents. Fortunately, this machine was running direct current when he accidentally received a painful, but nonfatal shock while fixing one of the lights on the circuit. Kennelly experienced a similar shock in December 1889 while preparing a municipal dynamo for experiments on a transformer for street railways.

The Brown and Kennelly experiments, combined with Edison's reputation as the nation's preeminent electrician, proved crucial to the adoption of electrocution by New York State. Indeed, historian Terry Reynolds and electrical engineer Theodore Bernstein have argued convincingly that "probably more than any other single man, Edison influenced the early evolution of electrocution as a mode of capital punishment," including the method of using alternating current with an electric chair.[23] His reputation proved crucial because it was so difficult for laymen to judge the expert testimony offered by Edison and others in legal proceedings and before official bodies. This was compounded by their failure to withhold opinions on points where their knowledge was weak. Edison, in particular, lacked any knowledge of the medical effects of electricity beyond the results of experiments with animals undertaken at his laboratory. Yet, he still offered firm opinions on the subject. Faced with contradictory testimony by Edison and other experts, public officials and the general public ultimately relied on Edison's personal reputation.

The electrocution experiments also changed the tenor of Edison Electric's campaign against Westinghouse and alternating current. Before the experiments the company had focused on questions of economy and efficiency. These questions and the charge that competitors were infringing Edison's basic patents on electric lighting were the primary focus of the red-covered pamphlet entitled "A Warning from the Edison Electric Light Company" that the company issued in early 1888. The issue of safety was raised as the final point against alternating current, and several pages of the appendix reprinted newspaper reports of accidental deaths caused by high-voltage arc and incandescent light systems, but it remained a secondary element in Edison Electric's public relations campaign. Likewise, the debate in the electrical journals focused on the comparative economy and efficiency of alternating and direct current systems; this included an article by H. Ward Leonard, a contractor for the Edison lighting system who had begun his career with the Edison Construction Department, that provided a detailed cost comparison between the two systems. In late 1887 and early 1888, Edison and his managers even discussed a plan to market an alternating current system that was identical to that of Westinghouse to demonstrate the superiority of the Edison direct current system for central stations.

Only after Brown began his campaign to demonstrate the dangers of alternating current did Edison Electric make safety concerns a key feature of its publicity. Company treasurer Frank Hastings seems to have taken the lead in developing a promotional campaign based on the issue of safety. He was the one who asked Edison to support Brown's public demonstration at Columbia and made arrangements for the company to provide equipment for it. Hastings also helped to arrange experiments on the electrocution of cows and horses at the West Orange laboratory for the Medico-Legal Society to determine if electrocution would work on animals larger than dogs, including humans. Although there is no clear evidence that the company provided funds for Brown's booklet *The Comparative Danger to Life of the Alternating and Continuous Current* or paid for his circular letter regarding the decision of the Medico-Legal Society to use alternating current for electrocution to be "sent to the Mayors, members of city Governments, Insurance men and principle buisness men in every city and town of over 5,000 inhabitants in the United States," these involved large expenses.[24] Brown denied any direct connection with Edison Electric, but it is probable that Hastings and the company did more than merely encourage his efforts.

Edison was content to let Brown take the lead in attacking George Westinghouse and his company, including a challenge in which Brown offered to take a charge of direct current if Westinghouse himself would take alternating. While encouraging Brown's attacks, Edison took the high road by playing the role of public spirited expert. Besides his testimony on the use of electricity for execution, Edison published an article in the November 1889 issue of the *North American Review* on "The Dangers of Electric Lighting." In this article, which did not mention any alternating current system by name, he argued for public regulation to limit the amount of voltage used in electric lighting systems. Such regulations would have effectively banned alternating current by making it uneconomical to use. Edison made his case for government regulation by pointing to a recent accident in New York City and "a record of nearly one hundred deaths, which furnishes an unanswerable argument" in support of the danger of high-voltage alternating current. "With the increase of electric lighting," he asserted, "and the multiplication of wires, these dangers which exist now in a thousand different parts of the city will be manifolded many times." "My personal desire," he wrote, "would be to prohibit entirely the use of alternating currents." Thus, he told his readers, although "the electric-lighting company with which I am connected" had rights to an alternating system, "up to the present time I have succeeded in inducing them not to offer this system to the public, nor will they ever do so with my consent."[25]

It is somewhat ironic that Edison's opposition to alternating current echoed the technically conservative approach that had characterized the critics of his own early work on direct current lighting systems. In 1878 many experienced electricians thought that the problem of subdividing light was insoluble. Now Edison, the inventor who had solved that problem and whom the general public thought capable of solving any technical problem, argued that the difficulties associated with alternating current were insurmountable. Edison may have had the best equipped laboratory in the country, but it was his competitors who conceived a concerted research and development effort to overcome the technological limitations of their systems. Inventors supported by Westinghouse and Thomson-Houston, the two principal companies using alternating current systems, soon improved the safety of these systems, increased their operating efficiencies, and developed meters and motors for use with them.

The contrast between the three companies is most apparent in their approach to the safety issue. It is unclear to what extent safety issues entered into Westinghouse's thinking about the commercial introduction of alternating current, but the experience of arc lighting systems suggested that if care was taken during installation the general public would be protected. After all, Edison Electric considered this adequate for its own high-voltage direct current municipal system. However, because Edison perceived a difference in the relative dangers of alternating and direct current, which was reinforced by the experiments in killing animals that took place at his laboratory, he decided that alternating current could not be made safe for the public. In contrast, Elihu Thomson focused on safety as a key issue in developing an alternating current system for Thomson-Houston. However, his company did not stress this advantage in marketing the system, and utility companies using it often cut costs by not installing safety devices. When the Edison interests began to raise the issue of public safety, Charles Coffin, who headed Thomson-Houston, sought to play up this aspect of the company's system, but Thomson refused to become involved in this campaign because of the failure of Thomson-Houston installations to take adequate safety precautions. Without the aid of its chief inventor, Coffin decided that it would be prudent for Thomson-Houston to keep out of the debate between Edison and Westinghouse while Thomson focused his efforts on promoting system safety to the electrical engineering community.[26]

Despite the heated rhetoric sparked by the issue of safety, alternating current was winning the battle of new installations. Because Edison's opposition to alternating current was primarily based on a real belief in its dangers, he consistently refused to adopt it even at the cost of lost sales. Although his system had advantages in densely populated cities and towns, Edison Electric agents found that "there is an enormous pressure everywhere for a system to cover distances." In small towns they found "that there is a small business centre and the wealthiest people live upon the out-skirts of town. The people you desire to interest always want the light in their residences. With the alternating current this is no trouble." While the Edison three-wire system made it "necessary to establish the entire system of distribution at the outstart," an alternating system could be started on a small scale and then extended as necessary to add new customers.[27] At the August 1889 convention of the Association of Edison Illuminating Companies, representatives of the newly formed Edison General Electric Company answered questions about this problem by describing efforts to develop 400- and 500-volt three-wire systems. After the meeting Edison had Kennelly investigate what additional savings in copper might be gained by adding additional neutral wires to create direct current systems of up to seven wires. They also noted that "the demand for an alternating system being recognized, it is now proposed to offer one of the most efficient types at its actual value, as being dangerous and inefficient at best, but procurable on demand."[28]

Edison General planned to develop "an alternating system which will follow as closely as possible the model of the Westinghouse system." But, rather than actually compete with Westinghouse, they planned to use it to demonstrate the inefficiencies and dangers of alternating current in promoting the Edison three-wire direct current system. As Edison noted in a letter to Edison General vice president J. H. Herrick, "we are, of course, agreed that the Edison Company has no desire, and no intention of actually selling alternating current electric lighting if they can possibly avoid it."[29] Although Edison had Kennelly conduct tests of a Westinghouse transformer in early 1890, there is little evidence that Edison took action to develop such a system. He also decided against using a high-voltage direct current system. As he explained in a May 14, 1890, memorandum,

> To meet competition with Westinghouse, there were great demands that we should make a system whereby the outlying parts of towns could be reached. It was necessary to use a continuous transformer. A great many experiments were tried in this connection. . . . Since, however, the great dangers in the distribution of high tension currents by means of induction have been shown, it was concluded that the Edison Company had better not risk even the use of a continuous current transformer, which is far less dangerous than an alternating.[30]

Nonetheless, it had become clear by the summer of 1890 that Edison General needed to do something about competition from alternating current. In July, with the annual meeting of the Association of Edison Illuminating Companies approaching, Insull told Edison, "It is of the utmost importance that we should be able to go ahead on alternating apparatus, so as to be ready for our next season's business." He therefore ordered the Machine Works to wind one of Edison's new multipolar dynamos to produce alternating current. This idea had emerged during Edison's and Kennelly's work on a direct current high-voltage transformer system for street railways. Insull requested that Edison provide information about transformers "to know definitely from you what I can promise to our District Managers throughout the country."[31]

The tone of Insull's letter to Edison suggests that he wanted a practical system to compete with Westinghouse rather than merely for use as a marketing ploy. Initially, however, Edison had Kennelly design a transformer based on the Westinghouse machine he had tested earlier in the year. By the time the new transformer was ready in the third week of August, Edison, under pressure from the company, had resigned himself to the necessity of developing a practical competing system. Realizing that both the transformer and the alternating multipolar dynamo needed to be redesigned, he sat down with Kennelly to plan a new system. By early October Kennelly was busy designing the first Edison alternating system. He planned to use a multipolar dynamo that would be capable of generating 60 kilowatts and lighting 600 lamps. Kennelly finally produced a working system the following June, after several months' hard work devising a better armature and improving the transformers. But he was also busy designing a host of small low-speed, direct current motors to provide an additional advantage for the Edison three-wire system by expanding the market for electric power.[32]

Edison played an important role in developing the design criteria for both the alternating system and the small motors, and he conducted experiments with them both at the West Orange laboratory and at the Machine Works in Schenectady. He devoted much of his personal attention, however, to improvements in electric railways. This included alterations in a Sprague motor, which Insull reported reduced complaints from customers, and the development of a new railway motor to compete with an improved Thomson-Houston design. Edison also attempted to develop a low-voltage electric railway system in which the current was supplied through the rails rather than by trolley wires, which were considered to be a nuisance in crowded urban areas where city governments were attempting to banish overhead wires entirely. By using low voltage Edison claimed that he could produce a safe system and at the same time significantly reduce energy loss. Kennelly assisted in the design and tests of Edison's electric railway inventions, including some that took place at Schenectady. Henry Villard funded most of Edison's electric railway experiments and the construction of a quarter-mile test track at the West Orange laboratory.[33]

In October 1890, after more than a year of negotiations, Edison General finally agreed to a new contract providing support for all of Edison's other electric light and power experiments. The five-year agreement provided Edison with an average payment of $1,200 per week for his laboratory (work done by the shops was not included in this amount) and gave him nearly $33,000 for the experiments he had already made during the previous year and a half. In return, Edison would devote half of his time and three-fourths of his laboratory force to experiments for the company. Edison would also receive one-fifth of all profits derived from his inventions.[34]

The long negotiations regarding this arrangement had proved frustrating to Edison, who had seen his income decline as a consequence of trading his majority interest in the manufacturing shops for shares in Edison General. In February 1890 he had complained to Villard that prior to the consolidation he had

an income of $250,000 per year, from which I paid easily my Laboratory expenses. This income by the consolidation was reduced to $85,000, which is insufficient to run the Laboratory. I do about $20,000 worth of work for the General and local Companies of such a nature that I can't charge for it, and devote about half my time to the same work. . . . The fact that I am placed in such a position that my active connection with the Lighting business costs half my time, which is 18 hours a day and $20,000 a year, with an income insufficient to pay my expenses, has produced absolute discouragement, and I feel that it is about time to retire from the light business and devote myself to things more pleasant, where the strain and worry is not so great.[35]

By April Edison's lack of funds required him to lay off most of his chemical staff, including Fessenden and David Marshall. In July he even approached Villard about a new Edison Industrial Works scheme like the one he had proposed in 1887. As Insull explained in a letter to Villard, "we could make an arrangement between Mr. Edison and the General Company by which anything manufactured by the Industrial Works and invented by Mr. Edison could be exploited by the General Company, upon some royalty basis, agreeable to Mr. Edison."[36] Although Villard failed to adopt this scheme, Edison soon had the money from his experimental contract with Edison General.

For the next year Edison lived up to his bargain with Edison General. Although he is usually depicted as having largely turned his attention to ore milling once the company decided to move forward with alternating current technology, laboratory records indicate that electric light and power remained the primary work of the West Orange laboratory as well as the subject of most of his personal experiments. However, his commitment to electric lighting had begun to wane. His growing disenchantment was evident by February 1890, when he wrote to Villard about the time and money he claimed to have spent on experiments without reimbursement from Edison General. In the same letter Edison also expressed his concern over Villard's request that he contribute 1,000 shares of his personal stock to allow the Vanderbilt interests to become investors in Edison General. After telling Villard "I am pretty well broken down with overwork and am going to down in the North Carolina Mountains to freshen up," Edison explained that "Your request has worried me so much that it is the principal reason for breaking me down in spirits. It disturbed all my plans for the future by bringing in an element of uncertainty about money if I did what you requested. The reason I delayed notifying you was because I wanted to comply with your request, and yet in another sense I did not." Edison's reluctance to accede to Villard's request was probably prompted by the close ties between the Vanderbilt interests and Drexel Morgan. His frustrations over his financial and contractual relations with Edison General prompted Edison to conclude his letter: "I think up to date I have performed every duty asked of me, made every concession, and I would now ask you not to oppose my gradual retirement from the lighting business, which will enable me to enter fresh and more congenial fields of work."[37] While he continued to devote much of his work and that of his laboratory to the needs of Edison General and signed the new experimental contract in October 1890, Edison had lost his enthusiasm for the industry he founded. Increasingly his interest was in new challenges, particularly the iron ore-milling operation he established in the mountains of northern New Jersey, where he began to spend much of his time during the second half of 1891.

In February 1890 Villard had revived negotiations with Charles Coffin of Thomson-Houston on cross licensing patents. Their discussions once again turned to the possibility of consolidation, but for the moment they settled on arranging a cooperative agreement on patents. Edison, however, felt that Edison General had much the stronger patent position and generally opposed an agreement without substantial consideration from Thomson-Houston. In the face of Edison's opposition, Villard briefly considered asking Thomson-Houston to give up their incandescent lighting business, and the negotiations soon broke down. The failure to reach a general agreement on patents spurred an extensive period of litigation in late 1890.[38]

Patent litigation was just one factor favoring cooperation and consolidation. As Villard noted in a March 1890 letter to Drexel Morgan, the growth of the business had "rendered the provision for working capital made upon the organization of the Company entirely inadequate. Instead of one million, several millions are imperatively wanted to meet the current demands of the several manufacturing departments."[39] The need for capital became acute for Edison General during the fall of 1890 when Villard's German bankers recalled their loans to him after the passage of the Sherman Silver Purchase Act and the failure of the London brokerage firm Baring Brothers created uncertainty in international monetary affairs. This in turn caused the failure of Villard's North American Company, which he had established to promote Edison lighting companies in the Midwest and to control Edison's electric railway patents. It also weakened Edison General, which had to obtain loans through Drexel Morgan. Westinghouse, too, faced financial difficulties at this time. Only Thomson-Houston, which had strong relations with the Boston banking house of Lee, Higginson & Company did better; however, Henry Higginson felt that consolidation of the leading electric companies was essential and pushed for a combination with either Edison General or Westinghouse. By early 1891 Villard and Coffin were again discussing the possibility of a merger, but the favorable decision on Edison's lamp patent in June prevented these discussions from progressing.

By the end of the year it had become apparent to Edison General's managers and investors that Thomson-Houston had a better organizational and marketing structure that allowed it to outperform its larger rival. During 1891 Thomson-Houston had earned $2.7 million on sales of $10 million and a return on investment of 26 percent, whereas Edison General earned only $1.4 million on sales of $11 million and a return of 11 percent. The Morgan and Vanderbilt interests took over the negotiations from Villard, whose precarious financial position had forced him to cede control of Edison General. By mid-February 1892, negotiators for the two companies had agreed on a merger, and in April they incorporated a new company, known as General Electric. This new firm was dominated by the more effective management team from Thomson-Houston. Insull was the only Edison manager invited to remain as an officer, but he decided to move to Chicago to become president of Commonwealth Edison. Edison remained on the board of directors, but he had no involvement in the management of the new company.

Edison's reaction to the merger and whether he agreed to it or was forced to accept it is not entirely clear. In a public statement he supported the merger and denied the rumors that "this is a game of 'freeze-out' . . . I expect the consolidation will result financially to my advantage." His statements about his relation to the lighting industry, however, were somewhat disingenuous: "I cannot waste my time over electric lighting matters, for they are old. I ceased to worry over those things ten years ago and I have a lot more new material on which to work. Electric lights are too old for me. I simply want to get as large dividends as possible from such stock as I hold. I am not business man enough to spend my time at that end of the concern. I think I was the first to urge the consolidation."[40] In his memoirs Edison's secretary Alfred Tate maintained that Edison had not even been aware of the merger until the day an agreement was reached. Samuel Insull later claimed that "Mr. Edison was not in real sympathy with the consolidation. He insisted on dropping the use of the name of Edison when the General Electric Company was formed." Contemporary news reports also alleged that Edison, Villard, and Insull had all been kept in the dark over the terms of the proposed merger and that Villard and Edison blamed Insull's mismanagement of Edison General for the state of affairs leading to the merger. In his own memoirs, Insull acknowledged that during the negotiations "I had the only misunderstanding with Mr. Edison of the entire period of my connection with him." Insull thought that the enemies he had made among Edison's associates had told the inventor that Insull had sold him out, but Insull argued that he favored the consolidation as being in the best interests of

Edison and his associates. Insull maintained that the "misunderstanding lasted but a very few weeks and our friendship was shortly resumed," but he acknowledged that the "spell had been broken" and he never again played an intimate role in Edison's career.[41]

Edison was probably ambivalent about the merger. He certainly could not have been happy that the Drexel Morgan and Thomson-Houston interests had gained the upper hand. Although he had no interest in having any role in the company's management, even as a member of the board of directors, he did develop friendly relations with Charles Coffin and other officers of General Electric. He seems to have been sufficiently impressed with their management of the company to offer to develop a new lamp that would make it possible to run twenty lights per horsepower with an average life of 600 hours. General Electric agreed in October 1895 to pay him a retainer of $15,000 per year to develop this lamp as well as to conduct other lamp experiments; after the first year they agreed that the limited time Edison was able to devote to GE work warranted a smaller figure.[42]

Between December 1895 and March 1898 Edison and his assistants, notably Charles Dally, conducted extensive experiments on a variety of filament compounds and also experimented on a fluorescent lamp that had emerged out of his work with X-rays in 1896. Edison also experimented with a high-resistance lamp made from carbon particles mixed with rare earth oxides and applied for a patent on it in March 1898. Edison's work with rare earths, such as zirconium, was part of a more general effort by lamp experimenters in both the United States and Europe to develop metal-filament lamps. This work had been spurred by the growing use of the Welsbach incandescent gaslamp mantle in the mid-1890s. German chemist Carl Welsbach had developed his mantle impregnated with rare metals in 1886, and Edison had briefly experimented with improving the Welsbach mantel in 1887–1888. Welsbach and another German chemist, Walther Nernst, both developed incandescent lamps using rare earths about 1897, which may have spurred Edison's experiments in this direction. While the Nernst and Welsbach incandescent lamps came into commercial use at the beginning of the new century, Edison failed to develop his lamp into a commercially practical design and General Electric never used it. It is unclear whether he succeeded in his original effort to develop a more efficient carbon lamp.[43]

Although Edison did not entirely divorce himself from electric lighting he was no longer constrained by the need to devote his own time and money to lighting research, and he took full advantage of the opportunity to turn to other experimental work. For the rest of the 1890s he would devote most of his time and energy, as well as a substantial portion of his income from patent royalties and the sale of his stock in the electric light companies, to an effort to revolutionize the iron ore industry.

CHAPTER 18

Innovation and
Enthusiasm

Through much of his career Edison had depended on corporate capital to bring his inventions to market. However, as he had discovered in the early years of the electrical industry, corporate capitalists could be conservative. When the capitalists who financed his research and development work on electric lighting had failed to push his vision of central station service and refused to take up manufacturing, Edison felt compelled to use his own resources to establish factories and to promote and install central stations. His later complaints about being shackled by the "leaden collar" of the Edison Electric Light Company, were directed at the conservative approach to innovation taken by the company's financiers. As he moved away from the electrical industry and into new fields, Edison decided to rely once again on his own resources and those of his close associates, as he had done in establishing the electrical manufacturing shops. In this way he hoped to avoid the conflicts that had sometimes frustrated his efforts to innovate.

Innovation entails a high degree of risk and is often made possible only by an innovator's faith in and commitment to a new product or process. This situation, however, can produce a difficult dilemma when the innovator has to decide whether the degree of risk has begun to outweigh the possible rewards. Edison faced such a dilemma at several points in his first major undertaking outside of electric lighting—a decade-long venture to develop a commercial process for milling low-grade iron ore for sale to the eastern iron and steel mills. Edison would eventually spend much of the personal fortune he had made in the electrical industry on this project, which would prove to be his greatest commercial failure. Faced with enormous obstacles and high costs, why did he continue to pursue what one historian has called "Edison's Folly?"[1]

Such an appellation indeed seems most appropriate, for it suggests obsession as well as the dictionary definition of "an excessively costly or unprofitable undertaking."[2] The reminiscences of two Edison associates from that time help to explain why his personal commitment to the enterprise seems to have bordered on obsession. Alfred Tate claimed that Edison was so deeply hurt by the merger that formed General Electric and removed his name from the company that he declared, "I'm going to do something now so different and so much bigger than anything I've ever done before people will forget that my name ever was connected with anything electrical."[3] The ore-milling project was that big thing. Tate's story suggests that pride and bitterness helped to fuel Edison's desire to make his ore-milling venture a success that would overshadow his efforts in electric lighting, but a reminiscence by an associate in the venture, Walter Mallory, suggests more positive reasons. Mallory recalled a conversation with Edison in which he told the inventor that his General Electric stock would be worth over $4 million if he had not sold it to provide funds for ore milling. Edison's response—"it's gone, but we had a hell of a time spending it,"—hints at the enthusiasm he had for the project and the joy it brought him.[4]

The ore-milling project certainly provided Edison with the sort of large technical challenge he relished, and it also allowed him to experience again the sort of male camaraderie that had characterized the telegraph fraternity and his early career as an inventor before domestic duties and fame made their demands on him. In an era when Teddy Roosevelt was preaching "the doctrine of the strenuous life" as a way to save American manhood from the corruption of bourgeois domesticity, Edison was "roughing it" at the mine.[5] Whether Edison subscribed to Roosevelt's ideas about manhood (he did support him politically), he certainly enjoyed the strenuous life of the mine. Nonetheless, it is Edison's technological enthusiasm for mining that seems to offer the best explanation for his long struggle to revolutionize the production of iron ore.

Edison had first become interested in the subject of mining technology in 1874 while searching for cheap and plentiful sources of tellurium in connection with his automatic telegraph. The following year he conducted his first experiments in this line, briefly working on a "Detector for Gold and Silver at a distance" and a "cheap process for the extraction of low grade ores." In 1877, when investors in a Lake Superior silver mine expressed interest in his detector, Edison responded by telling them "their ore is peculiar, and it would require a great labor in preliminary testing to establish an accurate method of testing lodes and deposits, but it can be done."[6] However, he did not pursue the subject any further. Further evidence of Edison's fascination with mining was evident during his trip west in 1878. While visiting the Consolidated Virginia mine in the Comstock lode of Nevada, he again proposed using electricity to detect ores and also described a method for reducing the amount of moisture in the shafts to lower the oppressive humidity and temperatures faced by the miners. On the same trip he traveled through mining districts in the Rocky Mountains and at one point pondered the possibility of transmitting electricity from the Platte River to provide power for a mine located several miles away.

Edison began a sustained involvement in mining during the spring of 1879 when he began searching for a cheap source of platinum for his electric lamp. Expecting to use large quantities of the rare metal, Edison needed to find a source of supply that would bring down its price. His study of mining literature convinced him that the metal occurred in sufficient quantities in gold tailings to make its recovery commercially feasible. He proceeded to launch a search of gold mining regions in North America and had prospectors send ores to the Menlo Park laboratory where they could be assayed by his chemists. Edison's interest in the subject is apparent in the extensive comments he wrote on the large number of letters he received in response to his queries. These notes describing the nature, location, and methods of extracting platinum ores also reveal something of the wide-ranging research he had undertaken in the literature of mining and geology. Edison delighted in the process of assaying ores and often joined his chemists at the task.

While studying the problem of extracting platinum, Edison came to the conclusion that he could recover large amounts of the fine gold found in the tailings. After he turned to carbon for his lamp filament, Edison focused his efforts on this precious metal and developed a process that he thought would be capable of extracting gold ore at an average cost of $5 per ton. In December 1879 James Banker and Robert Cutting, who had been among the incorporators of the Edison Electric Light Company, helped him to form the Edison Ore Milling Company to exploit his inventions in this field. Edison also made arrangements to test his process on tailings from a California mine. Throughout the spring and summer of 1880 he and several of his assistants, including chemists Alfred Haid and Otto Moses, conducted a variety of experiments on ore separation. One of the processes they experimented with was a magnetic separator for low-grade ores that Edison devised in March and patented in June. In this device, sand from tailings or crushed rock were poured through a hopper so that they fell in a thin, broad stream in front of an electromagnet that attracted magnetic particles, such as iron, into one receptacle while nonmagnetic particles, such as gold, fell straight through into another bin. This use of magnetic separators to concentrate low-grade ores would be the basis for Edison's subsequent efforts in ore milling.

By August 1880 Edison had made several improvements in his separator and had applied for four patents, although only one was granted, the design in which he used a series of magnets and hoppers "to insure thorough separation."[7] The following June he filed another successful application for adapting his magnetic separator to hydraulic mining. By this time, Edison had decided that "instead of throwing the magnetic portion away it [could] be worked up into the very best iron equal to Swedish bars at a cost which makes it far more valuable than working the gold tailings."[8] The Edison Ore Milling Company tested Edison's separator on iron sands at Quogue, Long Island, and then decided to establish a commercial operation at Quonocontang Beach, Rhode Island. By October they were separating and concentrating seven to eight tons a day at Quonocontang Beach, but had difficulty marketing the ore because few iron manufacturers had facilities for working the small particles, which required great heat and could not be smelted in ordinary iron furnaces. Their first customer, the Poughkeepsie Iron and Steel Company, had to cancel its order when its furnace burned out. After sending samples of the ore to iron and steel manufacturers throughout the country the Edison company finally received another order from Shimer & Company of Philadelphia, but this firm ultimately determined that they could not use the ore. Efforts to ship ore to another potential customer, the American Swedes Iron Company in Rockaway, New Jersey, were frustrated by the lack of adequate shipping facilities at Quonocontang Beach and by a dispute with the iron company over the quality of the ore. Unable to find other customers, Edison Ore Milling decided to shut down the operation in late 1882. The superintendent of the Rhode Island operation, M. R. Conley, would continue his own efforts to improve the process, forming the Ocean Magnetic Iron Company. This company made arrangements to use the Edison separators in 1885, but its operations were still in an experimental state two years later when Edison again focused his attention on ore separation.[9]

By March 1887 Edison had begun some promising new experiments on separating gold from magnetic iron sands, and in June he proposed reorganizing the Edison Ore Milling Company to provide further funding for his experiments. When the company was reorganized in October, however, Edison decided to take upon himself the risk of experimental development. While the company increased its capital stock from $350,000 to $2 million, it was committed to reimburse Edison only if he succeeded in developing a commercial process. Drawing on his experience with electric lighting, Edison seems to have decided that commercial success required his personal commitment to a sustained innovation effort. Edison Ore Milling became little more than a patent holding company that like the Edison Electric Light Company depended on Edison to be the innovator in promoting and establishing enterprises to introduce his ore-milling processes into commercial use.[10]

In June Edison had placed William Dickson in charge of the research and development work on gold ore separation. During the next six months Dickson was primarily occupied with this effort as he investigated all elements of the gold separator. He investigated the design of hoppers to ensure that the sand would be fine enough for separation and fall in a uniform stream at an appropriate speed in front of the magnet; the size, arrangement, and power of the magnets themselves; and the arrangements of the collecting bins. He experimented with ways of arranging a series of hoppers and magnets to further refine the ore and the use of a vacuum to separate very fine gold ores, several of which worked well as laboratory experiments but proved impractical for commercial use. Dickson also experimented with processes Edison had been working on intermittently since 1879 to magnetize the gold ore so it could be more readily separated. In one process he heated sulphide ores to drive out sulphur and reduce it to magnetic pyrite, and in another he separated gold from pulverized quartz ore by using an electrified plate to attract the lighter quartz particles.[11]

When Edison renewed his experiments on ore separation in 1887 he initially focused on gold ores, but by early October his attention was again directed to iron when Witherbees, Sherman & Company sent iron ore from their mine in Port Henry, New York, to the West Orange laboratory to see if Edison could find a way to reduce its phosphorus content, which made it too brittle for use by the commonly used Bessemer process. They arranged this experiment, which proved to be a catalyst for Edison's reentry into the iron ore industry, through Edison's secretary Alfred Tate, who spent part of his time at an office in the same Wall Street building where Witherbees Sherman had its offices. Dickson, whom Edison placed in charge of the Witherbees Sherman experiments, tried several methods of separating the iron from the phosphorus in the ore, including tumbling and blowing it to physically separate the two, and roasting it to increase the magnetic properties of the iron so it could be more effectively used with Edison's magnetic separators. After representatives of Witherbees Sherman visited the laboratory to see some of these experiments they became interested in the ore separator and Edison agreed to design one for them.[12]

At the time, Witherbees Sherman's consulting engineer was John Birkinbine, one of the country's leading iron mining engineers. After inspecting Edison's iron ore separator at the laboratory in late May, he was sufficiently impressed to offer his services as consulting engineer to Edison. When he met Edison Birkinbine was in the midst of preparing a paper on "Prominent Sources of Iron-Ore Supply" that discussed the great problem facing the eastern iron industry, the declining quality of its ore deposits. The mines and furnaces of New York, New Jersey, and eastern Pennsylvania found themselves facing increased competition from the Midwest, where large new deposits of high-grade iron ore had recently been discovered in the Lake Superior region. Birkinbine felt that Edison's invention had the potential to make this low-grade ore more competitive with Lake Superior ores. Birkinbine therefore offered his services to Edison for $2,500 per year and agreed to promote Edison's method on his visits to iron mines and through papers in the technical press and to engineering societies.[13]

Birkinbine worked industriously over the next few months, introducing Edison's ore separator to important people in the eastern iron industry and conducting tests of the separator with different ores. He also kept Edison abreast of other iron separation and concentration methods that were being introduced. Finally, he arranged for the United States Association of Charcoal Iron Workers and the American Institute of Mining Engineers (AIME) to visit the laboratory. Birkinbine presented a paper to the AIME, with Edison named as coauthor, on "The Concentration of Iron-Ore," and Edison demonstrated his separator to the members. This paper described Edison's method and placed it in the context of other efforts to use either magnetic separation or mechanical methods of concentrating low-grade iron ores. Birkinbine pointed out that "Edison's unipolar non-contact separator differs from the forms described in that it has no moving parts," and added that the "simplicity of the construction, which is the result of patient and thorough investigation of many designs and methods, will commend itself." He also noted two other advantages. The capacity of Edison's separator was larger and it could readily process "mugwump" (residue from the separation process that contained small particles of magnetite) by passing the waste through either the separator or a secondary series of magnets and hoppers. As a result, Edison claimed that he could "make a higher grade of iron with less loss in tailings, and hence work a very low grade ore with profits."[14] Birkinbine concluded the paper by discussing tests that had been made at Edison's laboratory using ores from several New York and Pennsylvania mines.

Other papers presented to the AIME over the next few years indicate the extensive interest shown by the eastern iron industry in the subject of concentrating low-grade ores in the hope that this would keep the region's iron industry competitive with that of the Midwest, which had the advantage of the relatively cheap and plentiful Lake Superior deposits. The continuing encouragement given Edison by those in the eastern iron industry, of whom Birkinbine was the first, also helps to explain Edison's commitment to the long and expensive effort to accomplish this. He was not alone in allowing his technological enthusiasm for a potential revolution in iron mining to blind him to the larger problems the industry faced in competing with iron and steel mills of the Midwest, which had the advantage of not only proximity to cheaper and richer ores, but also of newer and more technologically advanced plants. These advantages were not entirely obvious in the late 1880s. In fact, as late as 1897, when Edison was embarking on his final effort to revolutionize eastern iron ore milling, Birkinbine still believed that many of the eastern mines that had succumbed to competition had "resources of ore which may again be called for, if methods of extraction and [treatment] can be so cheapened as to permit of the mineral finding a profitable market." His faith in the resurgence of this industry was bolstered by the fact that many of the "older iron-producing districts of the United States" had "cheapened the exploitation, and in some instances improved the quality of local ores; so that it is not to be expected that the proportion which the Lake Superior ores bear to the total output will be greatly augmented in the immediate future."[15] Historians have argued that Edison's decision in 1890 to discontinue Birkinbine's services as consulting engineer meant that he lost access to a valuable expert who might have altered his perception of the industry and made him more cautious about his ore-milling enterprise. However, it is notable that during the time he was connected with Edison, Birkinbine, like other mining experts associated with Edison's enterprise, "only reinforced Edison's perception of the industry."[16] In his study of another eastern iron mining operation, historian Bruce Seely argues that the series of failures between 1830 and 1930 at an Adirondack mine "highlight the importance of a community of investors, businessmen, and experts, who shared a set of attitudes, assumptions, and beliefs."[17] These kind of shared values help to explain Edison's great failure.

One of the experts to whom Edison turned was Walter Mallory, a Chicago manufacturer of iron and steel goods such as boiler plates and sheet metal. Mallory, who had met Edison in 1885 through Mina's brother Ira Miller and had attended their wedding, would eventually become Edison's closest associate in the ore-milling venture. Mallory first became interested in Edison's ideas about ore milling during their first conversations at Chautauqua in 1885. When he learned that Edison was making improvements on his iron ore separator in 1888, Mallory proposed that they establish a company to exploit it in the mining regions of Michigan, Wisconsin, and Minnesota. During June and July of that year, he toured mines in Michigan and Wisconsin and arranged a preliminary agreement with the Edison Ore Milling Company to license Edison's inventions in exchange for a royalty of fifteen cents for each ton of saleable ore. When Mallory and Edison decided to establish a pilot plant at a mine in Humboldt, Michigan, they organized the Edison Iron Concentrating Company to fund it. This company was a family affair; the stockholders were Edison, his father-in-law Lewis Miller, his brother-in-law Ira Miller, and Walter Mallory and his father E. B. Mallory. In August Walter Mallory began drawing up plans for the concentrating works, which were ready for operation by the beginning of December. The ore separators and dynamos, however, were made at the Edison Machine Works, and did not arrive until the following month. Mallory began to test the plant early in the new year and had commenced operations by the time the AIME met at Edison's laboratory in mid-February.[18]

Several difficulties surfaced almost immediately at the new plant. First among them was the problem caused by dust from the finely crushed ore used by Edison's separator. Besides the difficulty the men operating the separator had working in an atmosphere with such fine dust, Mallory found that the blowers used to help separate the dust from the ore removed too much iron, and so he had to alter the arrangement of the blowers. While the separator itself generally worked well, Mallory found that there was "a great bother with the iron sticking to the magnet" and suggested that a smaller face on the magnet might be necessary.[19] He also had difficulty controlling the stream from the hopper, which had too large a capacity for the amount of ore they were able to work. To solve this problem he added a box with an adjustable slot. Although Mallory was able to solve many of the mechanical difficulties, he was unable to produce a concentrate of at least 65 percent iron. By the beginning of April he was "pretty badly stuck" and wrote the Millers to ask "whether he better not shut down the mill and discharge the men." Ira Miller requested that Edison send someone to Humboldt to "put our machine in shape there so that it will produce the result that we must have from it." Edison responded by wiring Mallory to "shut down for a month, so that we can experiment" and asking him to ship both crude and crushed ore to the laboratory.[20]

As was often the case, Edison was overly optimistic about the time required for troubleshooting. Although he was working on several ideas for improving the working of Mallory's fine talc ore by the end of May 1889, the Humboldt mill would not go back into operation until the following spring. In the meantime, Edison and Dickson were joined in their experiments by Charles Batchelor and F. P. Swarts, Mallory's superintendent. Arthur Kennelly also played an important role by testing and designing magnets for the separators and conducting experiments on the magnetic properties of ores. Little record remains of these experiments, aside from some Edison caveat and patent drawings and descriptions, a few entries by Batchelor in his journal, and Kennelly's notes on his own work. From these it appears that Edison adapted some of the approaches Dickson was using with gold ore to Mallory's fine iron ores. Edison's caveat drawings from April and May 1889 show him employing a chamber or tumbling barrel in which there was a magnet that held the iron particles while the dust was either blown out by air or washed away with water. In July Edison applied for a patent on his water separator, and by September they were making extensive tests of it. However, they experienced considerable trouble with this design, and at Swarts's request, Mallory "protested vigorously against the use of water, on account of the difficulty of using it in cold weather up in the Lake Superior region."[21] Edison agreed to develop a simpler design that they had discussed the previous spring. This is probably the machine designated as the contact separator in accounting records, but the exact nature of its design is unclear, although it may be related to drawings made by Batchelor in October.

Edison continued to experiment with water separators, including the use of a belt conveyor and a multiple magnet arrangement that he had also conceived in the spring. With separator designs using belt conveyors or other devices, such as long tubes, Edison found that he could concentrate progressively finer particles of iron as the crushed rock passed through a series of magnets. The belt separator was jointly patented by Edison and Dickson, and in late November experiments on the Mallory ore focused on a design of this type with a blower arrangement to remove the dust. By March, Edison had settled on a belt separator with thirteen magnets to work the Humboldt ore.[22]

By this time Edison had greatly expanded his ore-milling operations. In December 1888 he and Robert Cutting had formed the New Jersey and Pennsylvania Concentrating Works (NJPCW) with a capital stock of $30,000. Edison was determined after his experience in the electrical industry "to control absolutely such inventions as I make " without "being subjected to the mysteries

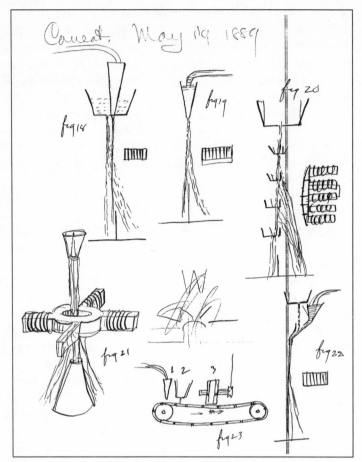

Edison's May 19, 1889, patent caveat contained a variety of methods for electromagnetically separating magnetic iron ore from rock and sand.

of Wall Street manipulation."[23] He therefore decided not to place NJPCW stock in the open market and instead approached potential investors whom he knew personally. Edison and Cutting each provided $10,000, with the remainder divided among Edison's associates Samuel Insull, Alfred Tate, Joseph Hutchinson, general manager of the Edison United Manufacturing Company since its formation in 1886, and Harry Livor, general manager of the Edison Shafting Manufacturing Company, which had been established in 1884 and had been made a department of the Edison Machine Works the following year. They used the $30,000 to establish a pilot plant at the Gilbert Mine in Bechtelsville, Pennsylvania. Livor became the NJPCW general manager and was placed in charge of setting up the mill, which he had ready for operation by the beginning of July. The initial results were promising. After Edison visited the mine during the second week of July, Insull reported to Tate, "The plant at Bechtelsville is a remarkable success. There is no doubt but that we are going to make a great deal of money in concentrating iron ores. Livor and Edison are practically intoxicated by the business." Insull, however, was somewhat more cautious and felt it necessary to "[discount] what they have to say and [estimate] that the cost of production will be twice as much as they really estimate," but nonetheless he felt "sure we have got an extremely [good] thing."[24] Edison and his associates in NJPCW quickly decided to expand the operation at Bechtelsville to recover the fine iron dust lost in the tailings and voted to increase their capital stock to $100,000.

Edison expected the Bechtelsville plant to be the first of many and told those inquiring about his process, "we do not sell our concentrating machinery as we have gone into the business of concentrating ourselves. We have two mills in operation and several others in course of construction. We only undertake to erect and concentrate for a fixed sum per ton, providing the supply of ore and available market furnish conditions for permanency." By this time Edison had decided that "if I could get possession of practically all the magnetic ore deposits in the center of the coal and iron district of Penn[sylvani]a I would have a monopoly of one of the most valuable sources of national wealth in the U.S." He and his assistants began extensive surveys of the iron mining districts of New Jersey, New York, and Pennsylvania (and even investigated mines as far north as Canada and as far south as North Carolina). In making these surveys they used an extremely accurate magnetic dipping needle devised by Arthur Kennelly that Edison claimed allowed the surveyors to detect unknown iron deposits, "tell where to sink shafts or run tunnels the extent width & length of the vein depth & give a close guess at the quality of the ore." Edison discovered large deposits of low-grade ore and eventually secured the rights to "97% of all the concentratable ore within freight areas to the Centers of ore consumption" in the three mid-Atlantic states.[25] One of the first properties for which Edison acquired mining rights was the Ogden Mine in northern New Jersey, near the town of Ogdensberg. In July 1889 the NJPCW stockholders agreed to set up a concentrating works there. It would become the centerpiece of Edison's ore-milling operations for the next decade. To build the new plant, they also decided to increase the company's capital stock to $150,000.

While the Ogden mill was being constructed, the Bechtelsville plant was running into difficulties. Almost from the beginning of operations there Livor had complained to the superintendent P. F. Gildea that the amount of iron concentrate was not adequate to meet their contracts, although he recognized that this was a consequence of the lean ore they were getting from the Gilbert mine. Tate reported in December 1889, "The concentrates are sold to local furnaces, which use 25% of these fine concentrates which are ground to 10 mesh, with 75% of regular large ore," but in late January, Livor informed Edison that "the Gilbert mine looked very bad" and was "about as mixed up a mess as it can possibly be." The ore they were getting was not worth putting through the mill and he felt that it would be necessary to go deeper in the mine. Unwilling to take "the responsibility of making any further large expenditures on the mine" without Edison's opinion, he asked the inventor to accompany him and inspect the situation.[26] Edison initially planned to take charge of the operation at Bechtelsville so that Livor could devote himself to setting up the Ogden plant. Edison thought that in this way he "could learn the business from actual experience," especially "in view of the extent to which I am going into mining." After visiting Bechtelsville, however, Edison decided that "the Gilbert mine business is a fizzle" and informed the mine's owner, H. K. Hartzell, that he had "ordered the mill to shut."[27]

In contrast to the Gilbert mine, the one in Humboldt, Michigan, was showing promise. The Mallorys and the Millers had decided to restart the mill with its existing capacity rather than invest in a larger plant, but after only two months of operation, they were satisfied that with "the Mill in good working order, and the business is in as good a shape as it can be for showing results," they wanted "to see the business pushed and a large plant put up which will be capable of turning out large products, and will bring us back large profits."[28] However, they lacked funds for such expansion and proposed finding outside capital. Edison wanted to avoid outside investors, although he had approached Henry Villard, who declined, about becoming an investor in his ore-milling enterprises. Edison therefore suggested to Mallory that they delay any plans for expansion until the larger Ogden mill had proved successful. In the meantime, the Humboldt mill provided useful information about the working of the belt separator. Just as the Humboldt mill was getting its best results in early December, however, it burned to the ground. Although they made plans to build a new mill and explored another nearby mine, the Humboldt operation was finally abandoned. Mallory, though, remained interested in Edison's ore-milling work, becoming a stockholder in NJPCW and then superintendent of the Ogden concentrating works.

The Ogden concentrating works was designed on a larger scale than at either Humboldt or Bechtelsville. These early works had been little more than demonstration plants scaled up from the experimental mill at the laboratory. The mill at the Ogden mine was designed to take full advantage of economies of scale. Everything there was done on a large scale. By 1893 Edison could write, "The Mill as it stands today is the largest Crushing plant in the world— It exceeds in capacity all the stamp mills of California— It has double the capacity of the great Crushing work of the Calumet and Hecla Copper Mines of Lake Superior. . . . The mill is modern—everything is new, both Machinery & method . . . Handling by machinery has been carried to the very Limit."[29] Edison believed that the large capacity of the Ogden concentrating works was essential for producing commercial iron, but the very size and scale of the operation also created a host of unanticipated problems that he had to solve before the works actually began commercial operation.

When it was completed in 1890 the Ogden iron ore-concentrating works was impressive. The steam engine plant, which provided power for the works, was designed to be the "best equipped" and "most economical" in the United States. The mining was done by open-cut quarrying to provide sufficient ore for the mill's large daily capacity. With four rows of crushing rolls Edison planned to process 1,200 tons of crude ore every twenty hours, using three separators to concentrate 530 tons each of the crude ore and three others capable of concentrating the tailings. After making the first tests of the new plant during the early summer, Edison realized that he needed to add a refining mill as well to produce Bessemer quality ore. With the existing works he could produce ore with an average iron content of only about 55 percent. Although this was higher than the average for New Jersey ores, it was insufficient for ore used with the Bessemer process. Although adding the refining mill would cost more than $50,000, Edison expected to be able to produce Bessemer ore of 69 to 70 units of iron, which he expected would produce an extra profit of $132,000 per year." To pay for the new mill, Edison and his associates, who just two months earlier had increased the capital stock of NJPCW to $250,000, voted in July to raise it an additional $100,000.[30]

Edison, who was too busy with electric lighting work to spend more than a few days at Ogden, entrusted Livor with the task of setting up the new mill and sent Dickson to help to test the concentrating and tailing separators. Once they had the first separation mill fully operational at the end of July, it became apparent that its capacity was greater than that of the proposed refining mill and Edison decided to add additional machinery. The construction of the refining mill was also delayed by the redesign of the belt separators. Tests at Ogden and Mallory's experience with them at Humboldt indicated that the separators needed to be set at a steeper incline for fine ores and required a feed regulator. Edison also made some changes to the belting arrangement and found it necessary to obtain better belting for the machines. The new separators were huge affairs weighing six tons.

Dickson's tests during the summer revealed other problems, most notably that "the peculiarity of various grades of ore & condition of same—'loomy' 'damp,' 'dead dry' 'rich' or 'lean'—etc etc" required different settings for the magnets.[31] He was particularly troubled by fine ores, which became damp in rainy weather, clogged the screens, and required higher voltages to separate. The wet ore also caused a short in the magnet coils, but Edison readily solved this problem by having the coils painted with shellac. The clogging of the screens was a more persistent and difficult problem. Dickson attempted to solve it by cleaning the screens on a regular basis, but this provided only temporary relief. Edison decided to install heaters to dry the ore and make it easier to work, but these were not ready until the following spring. By the time the new belt separators were ready in the fall, poor weather began to cause further delays, and the refining mill was not completed until the beginning of the new year. Continued bad weather throughout the winter further delayed Livor's efforts to get the concentrating works in running order, and it was not until mid-March that it made sense for Edison to come to Ogden to put things in final order for commercial production. To pay for the additional equipment, NJPCW once again increased its capital stock, this time to $500,000.

By the time Livor began full-scale operations at Ogden in April 1891 the plant was running smoothly. They soon shipped their first concentrates of low-grade ore, 100 tons each for testing, to the Bethlehem Iron Works and the Pennsylvania Steel Company; the Cambria Iron Works and the Lackawanna Iron & Steel Company expressed interest in the ore as well. William S. Perry, the NJPCW treasurer, also made arrangements with H. K. Hartzell and Arthur Howe, an iron commission merchant, to act as the company's agents in selling ore to other iron works in Pennsylvania and New Jersey. By the beginning of May John Fritz, general superintendent of Bethlehem Iron, one of the nation's leading producers of iron and steel, was sufficiently satisfied with the results of his tests to place an order for 100,000 tons. With this order in hand, Edison telegraphed Mallory, "The furnace men are taking kindly to ore and we are shipping."[32]

Although the Ogden plant was producing ore, all sorts of minor difficulties prevented the mills from running at full capacity. Furthermore, the ore that was being produced did not meet Edison's expectations. Too much iron was wasted in the tailings and Bethlehem Iron complained that the ore it received had too much phosphorus. Edison's concern was evident when he wired Livor on June 10 to "Be careful or we will be ordered to stop shipping." As he tried to solve the problems inherent in starting up such a large and complex operation, Livor found himself accused of mismanagement by the other officers of NJPCW. They also criticized what they saw as his extravagant expenses, particularly his large payroll. Upon hearing from Tate and Perry that Livor had sixty men employed in the two mills, Edison complained to him that this was "away beyond anything that you estimated. There seems to be a great necessity for a number of men who are apparently occupied in watching things that are breaking down continuously." Livor's position became increasingly untenable during June as he was stripped of authority over the placing of orders and over the office staff at Ogden. Edison also failed to heed Livor's pleas to come to Ogden, and he instead sent Dickson. When Edison finally decided to go to Ogden at the end of June "to take hold of the technical part of the concern," Livor resigned. Edison vowed to remain in Ogden "until he ha[d] fixed the Mill if it took him six months."[33] After arriving in Ogden Edison arranged for the establishment of a U.S. Post Office for the village of three hundred workers, which was renamed Edison, New Jersey.

After spending some time looking over the Ogden works, Edison came to believe that the main problem was "poor construction," and he decided to rebuild much of the plant. When Batchelor returned from a European vacation with his family in early November, he discovered that "a very large amount of material taken out by Edison after the Livor failure has been used for other things and although there is quite a good deal thrown away there is nothing like the amount we expected to lose."[34] Batchelor, who was by this time the largest stockholder in NJPCW after Edison and Cutting, expressed his continued confidence in Edison's effort by purchasing an additional nineteen shares and agreeing to a further increase in the company's capital stock to $750,000.

Following the failure of the first Ogden plant Edison concluded that "Magnetic Separators are the least part of the problem of crushing 2,000 tons of ore in twenty hours. The trouble is the Crushing plant and the training of men."[35] Much of the reconstruction work was intended to improve the mining and crushing operations. He installed a new cable system to deliver the ore from the mine to the mill, where a series of coarse and then fine crushers was installed to prepare the ore for the separators. When Batchelor joined Edison at the mine in November they began an extensive series of tests and experiments on the crushing operations. As they began to test the mills they made other alterations as well. They redesigned the dryers used for wet ore and finding that all of the screens in one mill were too small for the capacity of the plant they replaced them and made changes in their design. They also conducted "a number of experiments to determine the best conditions for working the magnets and their feeds."[36]

During the winter, while Edison returned to the laboratory to experiment on lamp problems, his new superintendent, Owen Conley, worked with Batchelor and the plant's first mechanical engineer, Edward Thomas, to get the works in running order. Conley had replaced F. P. Swarts, Mallory's former superintendent at Humboldt, in November after Edison found that "the many little difficulties to be overcome in straightening out things here were too much for him."[37] Thomas, an MIT graduate, had been assisting Edison with some of the experimental work at Ogden, and as one of the laboratory draftsmen he had drawn the plans for much of the equipment erected there. Once again poor weather, problems with wet ore, and excess phosphorus plagued the operation, but they were able to deliver a large shipment of ore to the North Branch Steel Works in February 1892. Batchelor's experiments showed that the phosphorus problem was largely a result of excess dust clinging to the ore when it was crushed fine while wet. By drying and washing the ore and using additional fine screens they began to reduce the phosphorus. Following the decision to consolidate Edison General and Thomson-Houston, Edison again focused his efforts on ore milling and again began to spend most of his time at Ogden. As he turned away from electric lighting, Edison also devoted his laboratory increasingly to the problems of ore milling. While Batchelor focused his efforts on improving the operation of the dryer, Edison designed a screening system for the belts and experimented with acid-washing the ore concentrate to further reduce its phosphorus content. The stockholders of NJPCW again found themselves increasing the company's stock—to $1 million—in order to pay for these changes and additional equipment.[38]

Perhaps the most important change made at Ogden was the addition of a bricking factory in April 1892. Edison had first experimented with compressing his ore into bricks as early as January 1888 after hearing complaints that the fine ore concentrates produced by his process would not work in smelting furnaces. Mallory had also encouraged Edison to investigate this point in July 1889 after he found the Chicago blast furnace operators to be "very much against the very fine ore." During his initial investigation of this subject Edison learned that the Swedish government had failed in its attempts to brick ore but had been able to employ up to 70 percent fine ore in ordinary blast furnaces. As a result, he had concluded that "the trouble of dealing with fine ore was an assumed one and had not any real foundation."[39] However, after running into similar objections during his first efforts to market the fine Ogden ore, he began to conduct experiments and filed his first caveats and a patent on the subject in the spring and summer of 1891. At the end of March 1892 Edison had developed a cheap resin that he thought would make bricking practical. The bricking plant produced its first experimental briquettes in May, but several months' hard work was required before the bricker and its automatic mixers worked properly and were able to turn out twenty tons of bricks per day. However, Edison found the bricking plant dryer to be inadequate and had to have another one built. In the meantime the works was delivering seventy tons of concentrate per day to the Bethlehem Iron Works, which remained its only regular customer.

Although Perry reported in October that the mills and bricker were "running smoothly," Edison was growing dissatisfied with the enormous expenses involved in operating the Ogden concentrating works. In November Edison conducted a detailed study to determine where breakdowns occurred and how often. He discovered that most of the problems occurred in the crushing operations and that labor and material for repairs were a substantial percentage of his operating costs. As a result, he concluded that he needed to make "some radical changes" and "decided it would be cheaper for us to shut down the Mill until all the improvements are made."[40]

Because his ore-milling scheme depended on processing low-grade ore on a sufficient scale to make it profitable, Edison decided to redesign the entire concentrating works on a much larger scale and to install a set of giant rolls to crush larger rocks and increase the amount of ore going into the mills. One of Edison's goals in redesigning the works was to replace human labor with automatic machinery to enable him to process "twenty thousand tons of ore a day with two shifts of men, five in a shift."[41] He estimated that the proposed changes would take four months and cost $100,000, and the NJPCW stockholders once again increased the capital stock, this time to $1.25 million.

Edison had been using Brennan jaw crushers and rolls at the Ogden plant, but these had a very small capacity. To determine if his plan for giant rolls would be feasible, he conducted a series of experiments using 24-inch-diameter Hoagland rolls. Mallory, who had joined Edison in New Jersey by this time, later recalled that they used "different types of corrugations to determine, as far as possible, the angle of bite . . . by placing the rolls at varying distances apart." In his past experimental work, Edison had usually found it "possible to work out on models the principles involved, and in a measure to pre-determine the probabilities of success or failure of the device, but in this case our preliminary tests on the 24 inch rolls gave no indication as to whether or not the larger rolls would be successful, so the only thing to do was to boldly start in on the experiment, realizing the fact that if it failed we would lose many thousands of dollars."[42]

As spring approached and brought with it better weather for construction, Edison completed his plans for the new equipment. But one of his chief advisers, Charles Batchelor, was in Europe with his family. Batchelor had played a key role in all of Edison's major inventions, and Edison had grown to depend on his abilities as an experimenter, engineer, and draftsman and greatly valued his opinions on plans for buildings, equipment, and machinery. Edison told William Perry that he "would need [Batchelor] more than at any other time . . . when all the plans are finished." This led Perry to write Batchelor that "he has taken your leaving very much to heart. He made the remark that it was the first time you had gone back on him."[43] However, after his return, Batchelor never resumed his role as Edison's chief assistant; in the ore-milling venture and the cement works that grew out of it, Edison relied more and more on Walter Mallory. Batchelor's gradual withdrawal from active work highlights one of the significant factors about Edison's career. As they both neared fifty, Batchelor increasingly made his family a priority and was no longer as willing to spend long days and nights away from them no matter how fascinating the technical problem. In contrast not only to Batchelor but to many of his contemporaries, Edison retained the focus and drive of a much younger man.

A crucial element of the redesigned plant was the modified bricker completed in March 1893, which Edison had designed to make "the bricks so that they will not absorb moisture and yet are still porous."[44] The bricks had to be waterproof because they were shipped in open cars exposed to snow and rain to obtain lower freight rates, but they also had to be porous to react with the reducing furnace gases and strong enough to withstand rough handling. Getting a satisfactory brick proved more difficult than Edison had imagined, and over the course of the next year he and his staff conducted extensive experiments on bricking while continuing to alter the bricker plant.

Edison assigned the bricking experiments to Joseph Harris, one of his chemical experimenters at the West Orange laboratory. As Harris's notebooks make clear, Edison played a large role in determining the course of the experiments and participated in many of them. During the spring and summer, they experimented with different materials and solutions for the binding agent they called muck and with the machinery for mixing the ore and the muck. (Edison took to calling his researchers muckers and his experimenters later formed a fraternal organization known as the Muckers of the Edison Laboratory.)[45]

Harris also recorded a set of experiments to "determine the most economical proportions between time and temperature at which the brix of iron must be baked."[46] In the fall they investigated the best design of the brick molds and continued to experiment with a variety of concentrates, tailings, and muck mixtures baked at different temperatures. In one entry Harris described Edison's empirical test to determine the best results—throwing them in the air and seeing how they held up when they landed on the floor of the chemical laboratory. By late winter Harris was attempting to reduce the power required for the mixing machine by adding various petroleum products to the ore before mixing it with the muck. In the spring he moved to Ogden, where he continued the bricking experiments and helped with alterations to the bricker plant.

In his efforts to improve the manufacture and quality of his briquettes Edison worked closely with dealers and furnaces through his intermediary William Pilling. Pilling, who had first become aware of Edison's work on ore milling in 1888 when he was general manager of the Crane Iron Works, was a partner in Pilling & Crane, one of the leading eastern ore dealers. Pilling became one of Edison's primary advisers on the iron industry, and his firm became the general sales agent for the Ogden ore. They began to promote the Ogden briquettes in late 1892, and provided Edison with both feedback from the furnaces and other crucial information about their own operations and about competing ore suppliers. All during 1893 and 1894 Pilling & Crane found significant interest on the part of iron companies, even though Edison was still working to produce a commercially acceptable briquette. The firm's discussions with Joseph Wharton of the Bethlehem Iron Company confirmed what they had heard at the Pennsylvania Steel Company and other major furnaces, that Edison's "mill will work an entire change in the Eastern iron trade" and give it "a new lease on life."[47]

The remodeling of the rest of the concentrating works progressed slowly and was not finished until April 1894. Because the changes had required more time and money than Edison had originally estimated, NJPCW had to increase its capital stock yet again, raising it to $1.5 million in November 1893; Edison personally contributed just under fifty percent of the total, much of which he raised by selling his General Electric stock. Unfortunately a financial panic in 1893 greatly reduced the price of GE stock and made it difficult to pay suppliers with notes. Like Insull and Tate before him, Perry had to juggle the company's creditors, although it was Edison's "policy not to go into debt," and at one point he even angered the workmen at Ogden by paying them with checks rather than cash.[48]

One of the issues affecting the supply of commercial credit was the congressional debate regarding the tariff. This was a subject Edison had addressed during the 1892 presidential campaign when he issued a statement in favor of President Benjamin Harrison and the protective tariff. Edison's statement contains the same kind of homespun humor and forceful statements that helped make him an attractive subject for reporters whether he was speaking out on a public issue such as the tariff or advancing his inventions and companies. After a general but informed discussion of the tariff question and a description of the low margin he had in mining low-grade iron ore, Edison humorously described the impact that a tariff reduction would have on his work.

> If the tariff is taken off, the beautiful scheme of making the highlands of Jersey along its 60 miles of length alive with industry will get a black eye about seven miles in diameter, and the habitants there will go back to planting beans with a shot gun, and I can turn the Works into a Sanitarium for liver complaint, as it is asserted by inhabitants around there that the mine-water is a sure cure for liver complaint, as one of the oldest miners when he died had to have his liver killed with a club.[49]

Edison's views did not help Harrison in his bid for reelection, and they had little impact on the tariff debate. But they did mark the beginning of his growing interest in public issues. It was about this time that Edison filled one of his notebooks with his views on government regulation of business, particularly regarding the impact of the Sherman Antitrust Act of 1890 on business practices and on the temporary monopoly that a patent granted to inventors.

Even with the uncertain financial situation, Edison was nevertheless able to convince his associates in NJPCW to fund another increase in the company's capital stock in July 1894. The increase to $1.75 million was necessary because of design problems with the giant rolls and the need for additional modifications to the bricker plant. Perhaps to save money, Edison had built the giant rolls on wooden foundations. After they were tested in March and April of 1894 it became apparent that this foundation was inadequate and caused the rolls to get out of line, making it difficult to start them from a state of rest. Mallory recalled that "as many as a dozen men on the end of a long lever" were unable to start the rolls.[50] Once the rolls did start, the cast iron became hot, expanding and losing the ability to move freely, and the drive pulleys and belts proved inadequate. Edison replaced the wood foundation with cast iron, substituted babbitted bearings, and put on new drive pulleys with wire-rope friction. When the redesigned crushing plant was finally ready for tests in the fall they experienced difficulties with the bucket elevators used to take the crushed ore from the giant rolls to intermediate rolls. The elevators had also been constructed of wood rather than iron, and they too had to be entirely redesigned and rebuilt.

Needing money to finish the reconstruction and make additional changes to the giant rolls, Edison again turned to his fellow stockholders in the spring of 1895. For the tenth time he asked them to increase the company's stock, but they were unwilling to subscribe for the proposed increase to $2 million. The company's second largest stockholder, Robert Cutting, had died in 1894, and his son Walter refused to make the new commitment. To save money on administrative costs Edison moved the NJPCW offices from New York City to the West Orange laboratory. William Perry also resigned as treasurer and was replaced by John Randolph, who had become Edison's secretary in 1893 after having worked for him as a clerk and bookkeeper since 1878. The growing depression of the mid-1890s prevented Edison from raising much outside capital, and he ended up personally providing most of the funding for the Ogden plant during the rest of the decade. Edison again approached potential investors whom he knew personally, but he was unable to find anyone willing to make more than a modest investment or to commit large amounts of money until after the plant was in commercial operation, Edison provided almost all of the rest of the funding for the Ogden plant. This amounted to nearly $1.5 million between 1893 and 1900, bringing his total investment to about $2.2 million of the $2.5 million total for the ore-milling venture.[51]

Edison's growing commitment to Ogden was more than financial. Between 1894 and 1897 he spent most of his time at the works, usually coming home only on Sundays, although occasionally he would spend an entire weekend and sometimes Monday in West Orange. Emil Herter, the chief draftsman at Ogden and one of Edison's principal assistants there during the last half of the decade, recalled that during this time "as soon as one 'bug' would develop, [Edison] would scheme out a way to remedy that and when another 'bug' developed, start scheming again. . . . We worked all the way from one day to 36 hours without sleeping. This was the greater part of the time we were up there." The crushing and the bricking plants continued to provide most of the problems, but Edison also shut down the entire operation in August 1895 because workers seeking an increase in wages for overtime work threatened to strike. "At that particular time," Mallory recalled, "we were commencing to have some trouble in money matters, and also as we did not want to establish the paying of any extra wages for night and Sunday work, we decided to anticipate the threatened strike by ceasing all operations." On August 22, before the machinists who were leading the workers could call a meeting to put the strike into effect, Edison notified them that "all work on this plant is hereby suspended." Most of the workers left after work was suspended, including those he considered "ringleaders of the trouble." Edison did retain about seventy of his longtime employees whom he set to work completing the bricker plant. He did not resume work on the crushing plant until October or November.[52]

Before the threatened strike, the crushing plant had run only intermittently. "It might be running for a day and then repairing for a day or two days and then starting up and testing it again, and then something else would break in the crushing plant and we would have to shut down and repair that."[53] When Edison and his assistants started the plant again in the fall, they discovered that linkages used for the elevators were inadequate and decided to rebuild them using wire rope. They also rebuilt the furnace for the bricking plant after discovering that it produced uneven distribution of heat. To increase the capacity of the bricking plant to 300 briquettes per day, Edison decided to install six more ovens as well.

This drawing from the November 1897 issue of *McClure's Magazine* shows the giant and intermediate rolls at the Ogden mine.

Lack of funds periodically delayed the work at Ogden over the course of the next year, but by December 1896 Edison and his staff had made significant improvements that seemed to promise commercial success. The most important proved to be the addition to the giant rolls of slugger plates with knobs about four inches high. Edison had discovered that by running the rolls at a higher speed he could store up sufficient kinetic energy to deliver a hard blow from the slugging knobs to break up much larger pieces of rock. Before adding the plates, the largest rock that passed readily through the rolls was a piece 12 x 15 x 18 inches, weighing about 100 to 125 pounds, and that could be readily loaded from the quarry by one man. Even pieces this size would occasionally cause the rolls to slow and sometimes even stop; larger pieces would ride on top and invariably stop the rolls. With the addition of the slugger plates the rolls could easily crush a 3-foot cube weighing a ton and a half and could handle rocks as heavy as four or five tons. The enlarged capacity of the giant rolls enabled Edison to save on his quarrying costs. Previously, much of the dynamite had been used to break large rocks into smaller pieces rather than to break the stone from the quarry ledges. Now, he substituted steam shovels to load larger rocks and save on both dynamite and labor, thus cutting his quarrying costs by about one quarter.[54]

Edison and his staff made other improvements to the crushing plant as well. To overcome the lateral movement of the mandrel and shaft of the rolls, which frequently caused their bearings to burn out, they added end thrust bearings. The lubrication of the roll bearings and of the elevator conveyors presented one of the more vexing problems, because of the dusty environment in which they operated. Edison finally solved this problem by resorting to a technique that had served him well in the past. Unable to eliminate the dust, he made it work for him. He designed a simple but efficient grease cup in which the oil (which Edison discovered worked better than grease) mixed with the dust to form a paste around the opening of the cup. This effectively created a dam that prevented the oil from escaping through the bearings and at the same time prevented more dust from entering.[55]

Edison spent about $200,000 developing the rolls, and according to Mallory

> throughout the whole period of testing the giant rolls . . . a large majority and in fact I might say practically all our men were very skeptical as to the ultimate success of the giant rolls. In fact there have been times when Mr. Edison was the only man connected with the work who believed that they could be made successful. This feeling of discouragement was a matter which caused us considerable trouble in our construction and erection work. I have several times heard some of our men say, when taken to task for doing poor work, that it did not make any difference as the machinery was very often torn down almost as soon as it had been erected and completed.

Mallory even remarked that "personally I had my doubts whether the rolls would ever be able to break large rock."[56] Edison's confidence in his ability to solve nearly any technical problem and his enthusiasm for and commitment to the ore-milling venture sustained him even in the face of skepticism from his closest associates.

The bricking plant proved to be at least as troublesome as the crushing plant. Edison and his staff developed new model brickers during 1896, and by the end of the year Edison reported that they were running "with great success." However, they soon experienced two problems: "first one of the plungers of the bricker machine gave some trouble when there happens to be a lack of ore, second, the ore stuck to the mould bottoms of the bricker machines." After successful tests of a modified bricking machine Edison designed to solve these problems, Mallory optimistically reported that "when we start up again we expect little or no trouble from that part of our plant."[57] In February they decided to install fifteen of the new bricking machines, which also reduced breakage and increased the diameter and thickness of the briquettes. They also added eight new furnaces to bring the bricking plant up to the full capacity of the crushing plant and mills.

During January the bricker plant produced about 1,100 tons of briquettes that Edison sent to the Crane Iron Works for testing. The initial reports were very encouraging. Leonard Peckitt, the iron company's president, reported that "the quality of the iron steadily improved in proportion to the quantity of briquettes used. The iron made from all briquettes showed unusual strength and was, in fact, the strongest and toughest foundry iron we have ever made. Considered chemically, the iron could not be better, as the purity of the briquettes enabled us to make an iron very low in phosphorous and sulphur. For Bessemer Pig, the ore is an ideal one, as a furnace would make a large product, and the iron would be of the very best Bessemer quality." Peckitt believed that the briquettes offered several other potential advantages. Because of "the regularity of briquettes both physically and chemically," he told Edison, "the furnace using them would be likely to work with more uniform regularity than is now customary." He also thought that "with a continuous run of briquettes in the furnace, we would effect a saving in smelting cost of not less than 75 cents per ton" and that "it is quite possible that Eastern furnaces in using them will be able to use a smaller proportion of coke and a corresponding increase in anthracite coal, and perhaps all anthracite," which would produce a further reduction in fuel costs as the price of anthracite was only about three-quarters that of coke. Finally, he felt that "one of the most important advantages to be gained by the use of briquettes is that the yield of the blast furnace will be materially increased" by as much as 35 to 50 percent. Peckitt was "anxious to have the ore" and reported that his fellow Eastern furnace owners, nearly all of whom had come to see the tests, had "expressed their satisfaction at the working of the ore, and the prospective addition of briquettes to their source of supply."[58]

During the spring of 1897 the price of iron ore reached its lowest point ever, but Edison and his associates believed that they could make as much as a dollar per ton profit "owing to [the] physical characteristics of our Briquettes." Furthermore, they felt that the low price would actually work to the disadvantage of Lake Superior and foreign suppliers because of the "geographical position to our market as compared with all competitors," which increased their shipping costs. With the Ogden works running at full capacity Edison would be able to deliver about 300,000 tons per year. Because this was a relatively small percentage of the total used in the eastern furnaces, he felt "assured of a market for our out put under almost any condition of business, no matter how depressed."[59]

Certain that his concentrating works was ready to begin commercial operation in the fall, Edison finally invited newspaper reporters and technical journalists up to Ogden. They were duly impressed by the size and scale of the works and particularly by the "amazing absence of human labor."[60] From the time the ore was blasted from the quarry to the time the ore briquettes were loaded on railroad cars it was untouched by human hands. Edison had succeeded in his goal of making the Ogden plant fully automatic. However, he still had to employ an extensive work force of nearly 250 men working two ten-hour shifts. The complexity of the machinery and the difficult conditions under which it operated continued to cause frequent breakdowns. Recognizing that he could not prevent this, Edison decided instead to "allow $170,000 per year for repairs, renewals, and depreciation" and $160,000 for labor.[61] He also established an administrative system that reduced delays caused by repairs. He divided the works into three divisions with a superintendent responsible for each and assigned men to each machine who were in constant wire communication with their superintendent. When something went wrong the superintendent would determine whether an adjustment or minor repair could be carried out quickly or whether a major repair was needed. He then called on teams of skilled machinists to make the repairs. Edison had the men in charge of a machine keep a complete record of each problem and the time needed to fix it so that he and his superintendents could determine ways to minimize breakdowns and repairs. Even with his high repair and labor costs, which combined with fuel costs and administrative expenses brought the total annual operating cost to $400,000, Edison expected the Ogden plant to earn between $300,000 and $500,000 per year.

Unfortunately, an old problem soon resurfaced. After completing construction work in the fall, Edison discovered that the crushing plant dryers were not adequately drying ore rock made wet by snow and ice. After three months of work he finally overcame the moisture problem, but then discovered that he needed to make additional changes in the crushing plant. He designed new slugger plates for the giant rolls to increase their life from 100,000 to 200,000 tons. He also made other changes in the giant rolls as well as in the intermediate rolls of the crushing plant. The completion of these changes was delayed because of the difficulty of getting materials due to the start of the Spanish-American War. The unsettled financial situation produced by the war further complicated Edison's ability to find the necessary funds to keep the concentrating works running at full capacity.[62]

In August 1897 Edison sold his stock in the Edison Electric Illuminating Company of New York, explaining to vice president Richard Bowker, "I sold the stock and transferred it, as I actually needed the money. My Wall street friends think I cannot make another success, and that I am a back number, hence I cannot raise even $1000 from them, but I am going to show them that they are very much mistaken. I am full of vinegar yet, although I have had to suffer from the neglect of an absent minded Providence in this scheme."[63] He and Bowker attempted to put together a syndicate to raise the funds, but they were unable to do so and Edison had to rely on his own resources. He used nearly all of the rather substantial income he was beginning to receive from the National Phonograph Company as well as from electrical appliance and motion picture products sold by the Edison Manufacturing Company to fund his concentrating works. Mallory remembered that he and Edison "would figure up the probable profits for the next few months and proceed to spend them and later go back to the manager of the Phonograph and other Company and tell him we had these debts, which had to be paid." William Gilmore, the general manager of these companies, frequently complained to Edison and Mallory "that we were drawing money from him which he needed to extend his business" and at times became so exasperated that he threatened to quit. They would then "figure over the money on hand and that which apparently was in sight, and then would decide upon a limit as to the amount of our expenditures, always fixing this amount so we would not get into financial trouble." When they reached this limit the work at Ogden would stop. For example, in April 1898, Mallory informed Pilling & Crane to stop coal shipments because the need to "keep our pay rolls within certain limits" was delaying the start of the bricking plant as they did not want to "take away the best men we have" from the alterations to the crushing plant.[64]

Edison had always planned, once he had Ogden operating commercially, to build more concentrating works on other properties for which he had obtained mineral leases in New Jersey, New York, and Pennsylvania. However, in December 1898 he was compelled to relinquish these leases because "I have been unable to raise capital to work the properties." That same month Edison found that as the "cold weather came on . . . I lost so many men from lack of houses, that I had to close down."[65] Edison planned to erect enough housing for one hundred workers so that he could start the works again. The following November he was still working to construct more houses and make alterations to the plant. Although he finally succeeded in operating the plant for about six months in 1900, by October of that year he once again shut it down because he was unable to sell the ore due to "the present depression in the iron business and the large stock of raw material on hand at the Eastern Blast Furnaces." Although Edison planned to rebuild the plant on "steel and masonry" foundations the following spring he finally dismantled it in 1901. Edison never entirely gave up his belief that he could compete against the rich Lake Superior ores because of his proximity to the Eastern furnaces, and he even talked about rebuilding the plant on better foundations in 1902. As late as 1910 Mallory testified that "if we had been able to have realized our expectations in the way of manufacturing cost and would have kept all parts of the plant at Edison, N.J. in continuous operation, we would have been able to have competed on account of our geographical position in relation to our market."[66] Nonetheless, he also acknowledged elsewhere that they could not compete with these rich ores.

Beginning in 1898 Edison started several other ventures using the same technology. A British syndicate acquired rights to the iron ore process and established the Dunderland Iron Ore Company in 1902 to work iron mines in Norway. The plant they established in Norway was set up by one of Edison's draftsmen, who apparently designed it without Edison's input. The company went into liquidation in 1909. Edison also set up an experimental mill in New Mexico in 1898 to work low-grade gold ore from dry placer deposits. Although this plant showed promise, the ore proved to be of too low a grade for commercial exploitation. Edison attempted to improve his process and sought to interest other mines in it, even sending his principal assistant to New Zealand to attempt to work deposits there, but he finally abandoned it in 1905. Somewhat more successfully, he sold the crushing technology developed at Ogden to other mines, notably the New Jersey Zinc Company in nearby Franklin, New Jersey, and he began to transfer the Ogden mining and crushing technology to cement production.[67]

Edison never entirely gave up on his belief that he could make his ore-milling venture commercially viable, but he recognized that he would be unwise to sink any more money into the Ogden mine. Instead, in 1898 he began to turn his energy to two new projects that along with the booming phonograph and motion picture businesses would became the heart of a new industrial empire. Remarkably, Edison's reputation as an inventive wizard had not been diminished by the failure of the Ogden works, and several financiers approached him about investing their money in his new enterprises. He had no trouble gaining a willing audience of newspaper reporters when he announced his plans to revolutionize the cement business and to produce the first practical battery for electric automobiles, either. Even during the years when he spent most of his time in the New Jersey mountains Edison's legend had continued to make him a subject of fascination for the reading public.

CHAPTER 19

A Modern Legend

In 1878 a little-known French writer named Villiers de l'Isle-Adam was inspired by the emergence of the Edison legend to conceive a story he called *L'Andréïde paradoxale d'Edison*. He subsequently expanded this into a novel entitled *L'Eve future*, which he succeeded in publishing only in 1886. In the novel Edison creates an android—the Eve of the title—that is not only indistinguishable from its human model but even considered a marked improvement upon it. Although the means by which the fictional Edison employs his phonograph, microphone, electric motors, and even the techniques of mesmerism to create the android, have little basis in technological fact, Villiers's invocation of the famous inventor and his inventions provides a sense of verisimilitude for the fantastic tale that he tells.

In the preface to his book Villiers explained how he came to choose Edison as his protagonist:

In America and in Europe a LEGEND has sprung up in the popular mind regarding this great citizen of the United States. He has become the recipient of thousands of nicknames, such as "The Magician of the Century," "The Sorcerer of Menlo Park," the "Papa of the Phonograph," and so forth and so on. A perfectly natural enthusiasm in his own country and elsewhere has conferred on him a kind of mystique, or something like it, in many minds.

Henceforth, doesn't the personage of this legend—even while the man is still alive who inspired it—belong to the world of literature? For example, if Doctor Johann Faust had been living in the age of Goethe and had given rise to his symbolic legend at that time, wouldn't the writing of *Faust*, even then, have been a perfectly legitimate undertaking?

Thus, the EDISON of the present work, his character, his dwelling, his language, and his theories, are and ought to be at least somewhat distinct from anything existing in reality.

> Let it be understood, then, that I interpret a modern legend to the best advantage of Art-metaphysics that I have conceived; and that, in a word, the hero of this book is above all "The Sorcerer of Menlo Park," and so forth—and not the engineer, Mr. Edison, our contemporary.[1]

Nonetheless, Villiers clearly drew on contemporary newspaper and magazine accounts of the famous inventor in creating his fictional Edison. Furthermore, the Edison of the popular press was already becoming a legend capable of producing any invention he set his mind to as well as the very embodiment of the forces of science and technology that were transforming the modern world.

Villiers's book was among a growing number in the literary genre that would become known as science fiction. Like his contemporary Jules Verne, perhaps the best known science fiction writer of the day, Villiers imagined the ways in which contemporary scientific and technological achievements might give rise to future possibilities. As his fictional Edison explained, "Science has multiplied her discoveries; metaphysical conceptions have been refined. The techniques of reproduction, of *identification* have been rendered more precise and perfect, so that the resources available to man for new ventures of this sort are now different" from those available to past makers of automata whose "mannequins are nothing but an outrageous caricature of our species." This passage would prove unwittingly prescient. In 1889, the year in which Villiers set his novel, Edison himself was working to reproduce life not by creating it artificially but by capturing living beings through the media of sound recordings and motion pictures. His goal, like that of his fictional counterpart, was to render these reproductions ever "more precise and perfect." He even exhibited the hubris of Villiers's protagonist when he boasted in 1913 that he would "put before the world a phonograph that would render whole operas better than the singers themselves could sing them in a theater" by recording them so they would "sound better than when heard in a theater."[2]

Villiers's Edison was a descendant of both Faust and Dr. Frankenstein, and like the subject of Mary Shelley's story, his creation of an artificial life form becomes the vehicle for Villiers to meditate on the nature of humanity and the application of technological solutions to human problems. Throughout the novel Villiers is critical of the values of modern science and technology. In the opening chapters he recounts (fictional) American newspaper reports of how Edison devised a plan to prevent two trains from colliding head-on and to protect the patent convinced railroad officials to conduct an immediate test with two trains full of passengers. When a failure of nerve on the part of the train engineers caused a disastrous wreck, Villiers's Edison is heard to remark "Clumsy idiots!" and to be "astonished only that the Americans shrink from a second trial, or as he sometimes, says, 'a third, if need be'—until, in fact, 'the procedure is successful.'"[3] The dangers of technological enthusiasm are apparent in the book's main story as well. Edison's android does provide a temporary technological solution for the unhappy love life of Lord Ewald, his close friend in the novel, but the book's tragic denouement suggests that technological solutions cannot ultimately solve human problems. Yet, although Villiers certainly questioned the values of technological progress that Edison symbolized, and particularly in his story of the railway crash criticizes the actions that arise from such values, he still produced a sympathetic portrait of the inventor, whose positive public image may have made it impossible for Villiers to see him as a villain.

Villiers was not alone in using Edison as a symbol of modern science and technology. He was already depicted as such in the newspaper and magazine reports that Villiers drew on for his fictional Edison. Always willing to accommodate journalists requesting interviews, Edison had become a ready source of expertise on issues of science and technology. As the approach of the *fin de siècle* produced a growing interest in speculations about the future, they also asked him to meditate on its technological possibilities. In 1890, for example, the editor of the *North American Review* requested that he contribute "a few hundred words" on the future of electricity. A year earlier, the editor of *The Forum*, after publishing a humorous account of the year 2889 by Jules Verne, thought it appropriate to call on the world's preeminent inventor to write a more "serious article, undertaking to show what invention may possibly produce in 1000 years."[4] Although Edison declined both of these invitations, many journalists agreed that the man most associated with the creation of new technology ought to speculate about the future.

In the United States such speculations were especially stimulated by the publication in 1888 of Edward Bellamy's *Looking Backward*, which imagined how technological developments by the year 2000 might make possible a society built on scientific principles that would alleviate the inequality and poverty of modern industrial society. Bellamy's book captured the imagination of Americans who were concerned by the growing industrial strife that was resolved by the future he imagined. A host of clubs devoted to the principles found in the book soon formed and even gave rise to a short-lived Nationalist political movement.

A year after Metcalf's request that Edison provide a more serious follow-up to Verne's story, writer and journalist George Parsons Lathrop, who had developed a friendship with Edison, approached the inventor with another proposal inspired by the success of *Looking Backward*. At the time, Lathrop was writing for Samuel McClure's literary syndicate and had recently published "Talks with Edison" in *Harper's Magazine*. In this article, which included one of the first published descriptions of Edison's imaginative ideas about the animate nature of atoms, Lathrop told his readers how Edison had spoken one day at dinner

> as if out of a great revery, saying what a great thing it would be if a man could have all the component atoms of himself under complete control, detachable and adjustable at will. "For instance," he explained, "then I could say to one particular atom in me—call it atom No. 4320—'Go and be part of a rose for a while.' All the atoms could be sent off to become parts of different minerals, plants, and other

substances. Then, if by just pressing a little button they could be called back to-gether again, they would bring back their experiences while they were parts of those different substances, and I should have the benefit of the knowledge."

Although Lathrop described this as "only a passing fancy, an imaginative way of expressing the constant desire that exists in the inventor's mind for a more inti-mate knowledge of the nature of things," Edison was serious about the possibil-ity of atoms having individual intelligence and in later years would elaborate on this idea. What struck Lathrop at the time, however, was the "imaginative aspect of [Edison's] mind," which "reminds me of men having creative musical or poetic or artistic genius."[5] Edison's imaginative musing inspired McClure to suggest a collaboration in which Edison would supply the ideas and Lathrop the literary form for a novel about the future "after the style of Bellamy's 'Look-ing Backward.'" Edison liked to say that invention drew on the same creative faculty that produced success in other endeavors and that he "read everything. . . . Not merely scientific works, but anything that helps the imagination." Intrigued by the idea of imagining the future, he not only agreed to the col-laboration but also offered to provide sketches to be used in illustrating the novel. Lathrop was well aware that Edison did not consider himself a writer, but agreed with reporters that he was "a most entertaining talker. He has a charm of narrative which is delightful, and to hear Edison tell a story is to en-joy a bit of comedy and to hear an anecdote that is of itself good and is well acted."[6] To take advantage of this talent Edison originally planned to talk his ideas into the phonograph, but after finding himself unable to dictate his ideas in this fashion, he instead wrote out nearly one hundred pages of rough notes for Lathrop.

Only thirty-three pages of Edison's notes survive, but they certainly suggest the strong connection that existed between imagination and invention in his own work. Invention, after all, is about imagining the future, and many of Edi-son's ideas for the novel had been the subject of his experiments, including sev-eral items that he had asked Henry Villard to fund in early 1888. One idea he described in some detail to Lathrop was a combination of several inventions on which he had experimented off and on for years. This was a bare-wire Atlantic cable employing etheric force to transmit high-speed messages that would be recorded photographically. Among other items that had been the subject of his experiments were methods for photographing objects in the dark, electroplat-ing in a high vacuum, and producing electricity directly from coal. He also elaborated for Lathrop several of his ideas for manufacturing artificial sub-stances, such as silk, diamonds, leather, wood, and mother of pearl, which he had also proposed to Villard. Inspired by the literary collaboration, he even suggested to Lathrop that the "dwellings of the rich" in their novel should have "their walls inlaid with mother of pearl which are now produced in sheets of every variety artificially." Edison's notes also included his speculations about scientific and technical breakthroughs that were being researched by others, in-

cluding aerial navigation, electric vehicles, high-speed trains, and a single vac-
cination to inoculate children against a variety of diseases.

Among Edison's most fully developed notes were several containing accounts of dramatic changes to the earth wrought by both man and nature that
he sketched out in the style of adventure science fiction books such as those of
Jules Verne. These included the discovery by aerial navigation of a "region of
gigantic volcanoes" in Antarctica that was "arable and covered with beautiful
vegetation and highly populated by a people of the Mongolian type and highly
civilized with a literature of their own but without science." He imagined the
impact of a huge meteor in the year 2226 that was felt all over the earth and destroyed the cities of the West Indies. Human beings also contributed their own
changes to the planet by cutting a canal to the Mediterranean that formed a
Saharan sea. He envisioned this massive change in water pressure displacing
the earth's crust to form a new mountain range, shifting the planet's temperate
zone 800 miles south, changing the rotation of its axis, and altering its magnetic poles. Edison proposed the possibility of changing the rainfall in tropical
lands by using crude petroleum to sterilize vast areas that could then be kept
clear of excess growth to allow the creation of vast coffee, gutta percha, and
rubber plantations. Finally, he conceived of an experimental station in the
Amazon (on the model of the agricultural experiment stations of his own day)
formed by an international Darwinian society that through evolutionary breeding over several generations would create a species of apes that walked upright,
had little hair, and could converse in English. He "calculated that the 80th
generation would equal in intelligence & personal beauty the Bushman Tribe
of Africa." Appropriately for a novel about the future, he also fantasized about
discoveries and inventions that would allow space travel, including methods of
antigravitation, suspended animation, and interplanetary telegraphy.[7]

Lathrop was delighted by Edison's imaginative ideas, but he found the inventor an undependable literary collaborator. After agreeing to their arrangement in May 1890 (although Edison declined Lathrop's offer to an equal split
of royalties and refused to sign a formal contract) Edison did not make time for
Lathrop until October. Then he provided his first set of notes for the novel,
which they had decided to call "Progress." These notes were sufficient for Lathrop to use in writing the first few chapters, but he needed Edison to elaborate
on them if he was to finish the book. Although Edison finally supplied some
additional notes in January, by the following August Lathrop had become so
exasperated that he fired off a seventeen-page letter to Edison complaining
about the rather one-sided nature of their collaboration. Edison's secretary Alfred Tate explained that Edison "has been spending all his time" at the Ogden
Works, "which was almost destroyed by bad management and Mr. Edison has
found it necessary to work night and day in order to get things in shape. During
all this time we have not been able to get at him to do any business—in fact, he
has practically been retired from the world." Lathrop not only expressed his distress over Edison's difficulties but even conceded that "the embarrassment in

which I am placed is little, compared with his."[8] Perhaps to mollify Lathrop, Edison allowed him to publish the first full account of the kinetograph and continued to promise his continued participation in the project. However, in October 1891, when a newspaper interview appeared in which Edison discussed his idea for revolutionizing electric railways, Lathrop had to plead with him to not "give away any more of these matters to the reporters, if you care anything for the success of the novel. The Kinetograph has already been 'given away'; & soon there will be no novelty left to describe in my story." Edison reassured Lathrop that he could "suggest numerous novelties for description in your story," but rather disingenuously claimed that he was unable to "prevent reporters from obtaining information."[9] Although Edison produced some more material for Lathrop in early 1892, his time and energy were clearly being devoted to Ogden and Lathrop soon gave up on the project. The difficulties at the Ogden Works doubtless prevented Edison from collaborating with Lathrop, but his commitment to the literary effort seems never to have been strong after his initial enthusiasm. And Edison was primarily interested in those imaginative musings he could turn into practical devices.

Edison may have decided to leave literary efforts to those better qualified than himself, but he did inspire two other science fiction writers during the 1890s. Both writers published in forms most appropriate to Edison. The first was a series of dime novels about Tom Edison Jr., "a distant relative of a great American inventor, whose identity the reader can easily guess."[10] An inveterate reader of dime novels as a boy, it is fitting that Edison himself would have inspired a story about a boy inventor. And these in turn may have influenced Edward Stratemeyer, the creator of the Tom Swift stories. In the 1890s Stratemeyer published one of the Tom Edison Jr. novels and also wrote his own story about *The Electric Air and Water Wizard*. Stratemeyer initially failed in his efforts to develop a boy inventor series, but one of his stories from this time, *The Wizard of the Deep*, appeared under the pen name Theodore Edison. Other boy inventor series of the era may also have owed some inspiration to the Wizard of Menlo Park.

One of the major New York newspapers, William Randolph Hearst's *Journal*, provided the other appropriate vehicle for a science fiction story starring Edison. Between December 15, 1897 and January 11, 1898, the *Journal*'s editor, Arthur Brisbane, serialized a version of H. G. Wells's story *War of the Worlds* that took place in the New York area rather than in England. Brisbane also arranged for Garrett P. Serviss to write a sequel to this story to be called "Edison Conquers Mars." Brisbane had wanted Edison to collaborate on the story, but he refused to do so. Edison told Serviss he was "willing to figure in the story as the hero," but on January 12, the day the story began appearing, Edison surprised him by publishing a letter in the *New York Sun* that protested "against the many articles appearing in the sensational papers of New York from time to time purporting to be interviews with me about wonderful inventions and discoveries made or to be made by myself. . . . I especially desire it to be known . . .

that I have nothing to do with an article advertised to appear in one of the papers about Mars." In a telegram to Brisbane, Edison explained that the *Journal's* announcement about the forthcoming story was "worked in such a way that it undoubtedly brings me in as a collaborator." Although the story as it appeared was clearly the work of Serviss, Edison may have felt self-conscious about any appearance of literary pretensions as a consequence of his aborted novel with Lathrop. Newspaper rumors about the novel that had appeared in the fall of 1891 had been highly skeptical of his literary pretensions. One reporter suggested that he write a book instead "based on his own experiences, illustrated with anecdotes of his life, as he has frequently told them to his friends." Edison seems to have agreed. In a separate letter to Serviss, he remarked that "I am not literary with a 200 Horsepower imagination like yourself so dont want a reputation for things I cant do." The anecdotal Edison remained well represented in the popular press, and his speculations about the future of science and technology, which became even more prominent in the new century, appeared in a form that best suited him—the newspaper and magazine interview.[11]

In the United States, where few questioned the values of technological progress, Edison, the uncommon common man, had become a revolutionary figure akin to the founding fathers. He did not just invent new and useful things but changed the way men and women lived. The *New York Evening Telegram* made this very point in an 1878 editorial celebrating "The American Mechanic." Writing about Edison's visit to Washington that year, the *Telegram* had argued that his appearance in the nation's capital

> illustrates very strikingly the difference between the fields in which American genius has achieved its greatest triumphs in this century and in the last one. The chief benefits which America conferred upon mankind in the eighteenth century were political. The statesmen of our revolutionary period were instructors of the world in the art of government. . . . Our national fame in the history of the nineteenth century will rest upon practical discoveries and inventions in natural science and the arts tending to promote the conveniences of life. The Capitol symbolizes American triumphs in the last century, the Patent Office in this.

Because the mechanic of the nineteenth century had displaced the statesman of the eighteenth century, it was therefore natural "to find a degree of public curiosity attaching to all the details of the manners and methods of his daily life such as in former ages was displayed only concerning potentates of the earth."[12]

The intense interest in Edison's activities led to a similar editorial comment a decade later as he prepared to visit another national capital. Writing about Edison's forthcoming visit to the Paris Exposition of 1889 the *New York Daily-Tribune* declared that

> America could have in Europe no worthier representative of the consummate flower of its National life and progress than this modest scientific investigator and industrious mechanic. Its chief contributions to the world's stock of civilization

have been the works of its inventors. In that beneficent field of human effort its sons are unrivalled for practical skill, habits of scientific investigation and triumphs of mind over material forces. While the European Continent to-day is a circle of camps swayed by the caprices of sovereigns whose inherited functions are their only title to fame, America has expended its energies in working out an industrial development that is the marvel of Christendom, and the real leaders of its pacific progress have been and are its inventive mechanics—men of the Edison stamp.[13]

While the *Tribune* writer may have believed that Edison's "genius commands the homage of Paris, London and Berlin," the inventor and his associates made sure that his was a triumphal visit. Like the fame that inspired it, Edison's trip was a consequence of the masterful use that he and those who worked for him had learned to make of the "public curiosity" noted by the *Telegram* during his first months of fame in 1878. Throughout his visit the Edison entourage engaged in a publicity campaign designed to promote the inventor (and the products of his companies). Even the manner of his departure was designed to pique the interest of reporters. It was reported in the *Brooklyn Citizen* that he and Mina, "surrounded by mystery," had "for some unaccountable reason" sailed under Samuel Insull's name.[14] In contrast to the secrecy surrounding his departure, the Edison entourage made sure that the inventor's arrival in Le Havre marked the beginning of a whirlwind of public activities that continued until his departure nearly two months later. His ship was met by a tender carrying a host of representatives from the European Edison companies, as well as Alfred Tate, who had traveled ahead of his boss to make the necessary arrangements for the visit. Accompanying them was a representative of the Paris journal *Figaro*, who was there not only to write about Edison but also to invite him to a *soirée* in his honor that would include the leading scientific figures in Paris. At the Rouen train station there was a second welcoming ceremony led by the U.S. consul general and another at the Saint-Lazare station in Paris. Upon arriving at their hotel, the Edisons found their room decorated with baskets of flowers and signed photographs from many of the noted men of the day. Francis Upton's wife Margaret reported that "the day he arrived the papers all had long articles calling him, His Majesty Edison—Edison the Great— Vive l'Edison." She also found that "everywhere Edison goes the public stand in groups to stare at him." The press of admirers was such that Mina complained to her mother that it was "impossible to go anywhere with Mr. Edison. We never get out as somebody is after him all the time." During his time in Paris, Edison was "wined and dined so much that he had to open a book to keep track of his engagements." As usual he declined to give speeches, and Chauncey Depew, the president of the New York Central Railroad, and Whitelaw Reid, the editor of the *New York Tribune* who was then serving as the U.S. minister to France, spoke in his stead.[15]

Edison spent part of his time in Paris visiting the Exposition, where he was most impressed by the Eiffel Tower. Edison found its creator, Alexander Gustave Eiffel, to be "the nicest fellow that I have met since I came to France, so simple and modest." He inscribed Eiffel's guest book to "the brave builder of so gigantic and original a specimen of modern engineering, from one who has the greatest respect and admiration for all engineers, including the Great Engineer, the *bon Dieu*" and gave him a phonograph for his private apartments at the top of the tower.[16] Edison's meeting with Eiffel is still commemorated in a plaque depicting the two men placed next to a reconstruction of Eiffel's office. Edison found the Exposition itself to be a grand thing, but he agreed with Depew that the American display in the industrial hall was most disappointing. The same could not be said for Edison's own exhibit, which was organized by William Hammer, who had assisted with nearly every international Edison exhibit during the decade. The Edison exhibit took up one-third of the floor space allotted to the United States and included all of Edison's inventions; the *Electrical World* required nine issues and nearly fourteen of its oversized pages to produce an illustrated series about his exhibit. This was also the first time that Edison's "perfected" phonograph was exhibited on the Continent, apart from a demonstration at the Paris Academy of Sciences, and it became the most notable and popular device at the exhibition—every day some 30,000 people heard twenty-five phonographs talking in dozens of languages.

Edison spent his last two weeks in Europe visiting Germany and England. He had been invited to Berlin by Werner Siemens, the German electrical engineer and inventor whose work was in many ways comparable to Edison's but who identified himself very differently in the public mind. German culture honored and promoted learned men and scientific research much more than did the commercially oriented Americans. It is therefore unsurprising to find Siemens declaring, "My love always belonged to science as such, while my work and accomplishments lay mostly in the field of technology." His close friends were scientists, not businessmen, and they agreed with physicist Gustav Mie that "Siemens would not have been able to become the creator of a new vast branch of technology, if he simultaneously had not been an excellent physicist." In contrast, American culture celebrated the practical man; Edison always identified himself as an inventor, and his closest friends were businessmen. In Europe he found "the scientific men . . . greatly surprised that I was not more of a scientist, in the higher sense of the phrase. They could not understand that I am between the scientific man and the public."[17] Nonetheless, Edison was lionized in Berlin as much as he had been in Paris. He toured the Siemens-Halske works, where a group of scientific men conducted experiments with the phonograph, and was treated to another grand dinner hosted by Siemens. Siemens also invited Edison to Heidelberg to attend the meeting of the German Association for the Advancement of Science, where he was again the guest of honor at a large banquet.

After stopping for a day in Brussels at the invitation of a group of Belgian engineers he had met in Berlin, Edison and Mina traveled on to England. They used their time there to rest and recuperate at the country home of Sir John Pender, a cable telegraph pioneer who had originally become associated with Edison during the effort to promote his automatic telegraph in Britain in the mid-1870s. Edison did spend one day in London with Pender inspecting the stations of the Metropolitan Electric Supply Company and having lunch with the Lord Mayor, but he eschewed any public events. Before setting sail for home he and Mina returned briefly to Paris, where the French government named Edison a Commander of the Legion of Honor (the highest rank given a foreigner) in recognition of "the exceptional services you have rendered to science by your marvelous inventions, so greatly admired by both French and foreign visitors" to the Exposition.[18] Unlike his "secret" departure, Edison's return to New York featured a round of cheers led by a yacht full of friends and employees who met his ship. It was widely reported in the press, as were his impressions of Europe.

Edison delighted in his international celebrity and the attention of reporters for whom he was always willing to provide interviews. As one reporter remarked, "Edison is the Aladdin's lamp of the newspaper man. The fellow who approaches him has only to think out what he wants to get before taking the lamp in his hand and he gets it." A charismatic figure who readily inspired both assistants and financial backers to believe in his creative abilities, Edison proved equally adept at convincing reporters of his genius. Even when he had nothing new to announce, they would leave his laboratory believing that he was on the verge of something new and revolutionary after seeing the range of different projects on which work was progressing. Furthermore, as a reporter for the *Brooklyn Citizen* reported, "He is fond of startling his hearers with extraordinary statements, but so equally extraordinary are the things he has done that one is wise not to venture too far in pronouncing between fact and fancy." Edison had long been aware that reporters often relied "upon their own imaginations for about 90 per cent of these so called 'interviews,'" but did little to discourage their speculations and sometimes, in his willingness to provide them with stories, even contributed to their misconceptions.[19]

Some misconceptions that found their way into press accounts were not accidental. Edison actively worked to advance his image as a modern-day Prometheus who had single-handedly transformed the world with his inventions. In interviews with reporters he did not distinguish between his major and minor inventions and often made claims that the historical record would find hard to justify. For example, he claimed to be "one-half inventor" of both district telegraphy and the stock printer.[20] Edward Calahan was, in fact, the originator of both these technologies, although Edison does have some claim to be considered one of the two major figures in the development of stock printer technology. He had indeed made crucial improvements and his Universal stock printer did become the industry standard. On the other hand, Edison played no important role in district telegraphy, although he did assign an early caveat to Calahan's American District Telegraph Company and developed a competing system that Jay Gould used in connection with his Atlantic and Pacific Telegraph Company. He certainly had no claim to coinvention.

Applying the same standards of credit that Edison claimed for himself in telegraphy would rob him of the sole credit he claimed for other inventions. The single most original invention credited to Edison, and the one that made his reputation—the phonograph—became a commercially viable instrument only after Charles Sumner Tainter produced a practical wax recording technology and Edison's own assistant Jonas Aylsworth developed better waxes for it. Even more striking was William Dickson's contribution to the invention of motion pictures. He clearly was coinventor with Edison. Yet once again Dickson, like so many of Edison's assistants, willingly accepted the prevailing ideology of both the patent system and the Edison laboratory that men working under Edison's employ were only developing his ideas and deserved no independent credit. Edison's unwillingness to assign any public credit to his laboratory staff is evident in his reaction to a small pamphlet that Dickson and his sister Antonia published in 1895 on the *History of the Kinetograph, Kinetoscope and Kinetophonograph*. Edison objected to the claims made in a biographical sketch of Dickson, written by editor W. E. Woodbury, that appeared at the end of the pamphlet. This accurately described Dickson as "chief of the electromining and kinetographic work at Edison's laboratory in Orange, having matured the magnetic separation of iron and other ores; is co-patentee with Edison of magnetic ore separators, and has completed for the inventor the kinetograph, kinetoscope, and phono-kinetoscope." In an angry letter to Norman Raff, one of the promoters of the kinetoscope, Edison maintained that the "part about Dickson being co-inventor in the Magnetic Separator, etc, is incorrect, as there is no co-invention in the Ogden business with Dickson or anybody else. I have given Dickson full credit for his labors in my manuscript letter [which appeared at the beginning of the pamphlet], and I object to bringing in outside things in a Kinetoscope book. Mr Dickson will get full credit for what he has done without trying to ram it down peoples throats." Edison, however, was rather parsimonious in acknowledging Dickson's contribution to motion pictures. In his letter endorsing the pamphlet, which gave Edison "full credit for this work," Edison himself merely stated that Dickson was well qualified as author both "from a literary standpoint and the exceptional opportunities which [he] has had in the fruition of the work."[21] By his own standards, Edison should have treated Dickson as "one-half inventor" of the kinetograph and kinetoscope. He also should have been more magnanimous in his statements concerning Dickson's role in the development of the magnetic separator. Although the Ogden operation had clearly evolved beyond a mere system of magnetic separation, Dickson had played an important role in maturing the design of the separators. Edison may have been willing to share royalties with his assistants, but he reserved for himself all credit and public acclaim for his inventive work. No matter how much independence Edison gave his assistants in conducting experiments, he could not imagine the work without his guiding hand.

Edison's tendency to aggrandize his role was exacerbated by an admiring press that accepted the commonly held view that technological achievements were the product of individual genius. This constantly proved troubling to Edison's competitors. It had been Edison's reputation that had convinced Thomas Armat to sell his rights to the phantoscope, the motion picture projector he had developed jointly with C. Francis Jenkins, and to allow Edison to put his name on it. When the projector made its debut in New York City in April 1896, "the 'Wizard of Menlo Park' stood ready to play the role of inventor."[22] The widely reprinted stories filed by representatives of the New York newspapers who reported on the first screening, which was attended by Edison, all credited him with the invention of the device. By merely referring to the projector as Edison's Vitascope the promotional literature that accompanied it around the country could name the device as a product of Edison's genius without ever having to explicitly claim that he was its inventor.

Perhaps no one had greater cause to complain about the aggrandizement of Edison at the expense of others than Frank Sprague. Sprague had left his position with the Edison Construction Department in 1884 because Edison had asked him to do work on the transmission of electric power, a subject that Sprague had been investigating on his own. In his letter of resignation he told Edison that "to take up the subject in obedience to your request would be simply to make over my own work without due consideration, and a due regard for my future makes it impossible for me to do this. You will surely understand when I say that I desire to identify myself with the successful solution of this problem, and when I also say that I am actuated by the same spirit with which you attacked the electric light, with the result of making yourself world famous."[23] After the formation of Edison General Electric in 1889 Sprague had remained as vice-president of the Sprague Company, but he resigned in June 1890 when it became apparent that the parent company would not provide his railway department with "a workshop or laboratory where experimental work may be continuously and uninterruptedly carried on by individuals whose sole duty is the creation of new, and the improvement of old, apparatus." He believed that this placed him in "an anomalous position . . . which will result in the sacrifice of my reputation or the limitation of activity in that branch of work for which I feel especial fitness. . . . I am too young in years, too jealous of professional reputation, too well trained by education, experience and a natural taste, and too capable of earnest work to become a nonentity, and to stand still while others advance to the front as active workers in electrical science."[24] The officers of Edison General recognized that Sprague's name was inseparably connected with electric railway work and implored him to continue his association with their company as a consulting engineer, which he agreed to do only after receiving assurance that Edison himself approved. By the end of the year, however, he had angrily resigned and severed all ties with the Edison interests.

Two related incidents precipitated the break. First, electric railway work, like all other experimental work connected with Edison General, had become the province of Edison and his laboratory in West Orange. Not only did this exclude Sprague from any significant role, but Villard and Edison also concluded that the ban on overhead electric wiring in many cities might prevent the use of trolley wires. They therefore decided to replace the Sprague system and focused the company's experimental work on Edison's proposed low-voltage system, which supplied current through the rails. More significant, even though the company continued to use his motors and railway apparatus, Sprague saw his name disappear in connection with them. Edison General's policy of designating these as "Edison Motors" and the "Edison System of Electric Railways" may primarily have been a way of associating them with the company, but in doing so it also sought to take advantage of the general public's fascination with Edison himself, whose association with the company's products was a more important marketing tool than Sprague's. Whatever the reason for the name change, it quickly became part of a more general effort to denigrate Sprague, whom many in the Edison company disliked. Sprague had plenty of reasons to believe that the company had "set out to do everything possible to wipe out the Sprague name and to give to Mr. Edison the reputation properly belonging to other men's work. No statement is too strong, no representation as to ability, attainments or work done so false but that it find ready promulgation. He finds most favor who is most abusive of all things Sprague, and he meets with a cool reception who does him smallest reverence. The Edison fetich must be upheld, the Sprague name must be abolished; that is the law."[25]

Sprague furnished several examples in his letter of resignation. At a meeting of railway presidents a statement was made that the Edison Company pioneered electric railways, although the Electric Railway Company that originally controlled Edison's patents never established a single railway while the designs used by Edison General Electric were those developed by Sprague, not Edison. Edison General's chief engineer even told one railway official inquiring about Sprague equipment that "Sprague motors are good for a scrap heap of copper and iron." Sprague also objected to "editorial notice of the 'New Edison Motor,'" which incorporated an armature designated as the Edison-Eickemeyer. This design, he noted, was developed by Rudolf Eickemeyer, not Edison, and Sprague himself had been instrumental in securing it for the Edison company. Furthermore, this led to the designation of the "Standard Sprague Stationary Motor" as the "Old Style Edison Motor," which a rival company described in one of its circulars as "the 'withdrawal' of the Sprague motor from the market." Sprague even reported rumors that publishers of certain journals discussing electric railway matters had been told to suppress his name or risk losing the patronage of the Edison company. If there was a campaign against Sprague it was most likely led by Samuel Insull, who did not like Sprague, but Edison himself also had strong feelings about his former assistant. Sprague certainly believed that "not only Mr. Edison's subordinates and those who bask in the sunshine of their smiles, but Mr. Edison himself, forgetful of his dignity and jealous of any man who finds in the whole realm of electric science a corner no matter how small not occupied by himself, loses no opportunity to attack and to attempt to belittle me." Concluding that he was a consulting engineer who was not consulted and whose "intimate connection" with Edison General Electric was "neither desired nor desirable," Sprague resigned at the beginning of December 1890.[26]

Not only did Sprague find himself temporarily estranged from the industry that he had founded, but throughout the remainder of his life he had to contend with exaggerated claims about Edison's role in the invention of the electric railway that overshadowed his own crucial contributions. Sprague subsequently made other important contributions to the design of electric street railways and subways, but his pioneering role often was overlooked in the popular press. At the same time Edison's experiments at Menlo Park were commonly treated as the beginning of modern electric railways. In 1928, as the fiftieth anniversary of Edison's invention of a practical electric light approached, a host of articles began to appear that, as one electrical engineer remarked to Sprague, led the public "to believe that Mr. Edison is responsible for practically everything that has been accomplished in the realm of electricity during the past fifty years." Sprague responded personally to a *New York Times Magazine* article entitled "The Magic Edison Made for the World," which credited Edison not only for the "first electric car of the new era," but also with creating the "trolley age." In his response, which appeared as "Electric Railway Not Creation of One Man," Sprague argued that Edison's "relatively unimportant experiments [at Menlo Park] which exhibited neither originality in ideas nor continuity of influence" entitled him to little claim to any significant role in electric railway development. (Even though he perhaps unfairly denigrated Edison's experimental work, Sprague was correct in asserting that it had little influence on the subsequent development of electric railway technology.) Sprague pointed out that Siemens and Halske had demonstrated an electric railway in 1879, a year before Edison, and then staked his own claims to crucial inventions in the field, particularly the motor and electric trolley as well as the first commercial installation. Over the next several years, Sprague campaigned vigorously to set the record straight, and after his death in 1934 his wife continued this campaign, which culminated in 1947 when she published *Frank J. Sprague and the Edison Myth.*[27]

Many of Edison's rivals in the electrical industry felt that he had received too much credit for too long and responded positively to the efforts of Sprague and his wife to set the record straight. Following the publication of Sprague's *New York Times* article Elihu Thomson wrote him, "Great as has been the work of Edison in various fields to which he has given attention, it seems to me that the attempt to spread his fame over fields in which he has done very little, and sometimes done the wrong thing, is to be sincerely deprecated." He noted that "Edison stood out solidly against any transmission at high voltages, and was not in favor of an increase above 220, whereas it is not unusual to find advertisements today stating that transmissions are carried on at 220,000 volts, accompanied by the comment, 'His dream realized,' meaning, of course, the dream of Edison."[28]

Thomson also recalled an episode in 1891 when Edison's effort to avoid high voltage led him to propose an impractical low-voltage street railway system. This episode is illustrative of the subtle ways in which the symbiotic relationship between Edison and the press worked to the advantage of his companies. Following the publication of Edison's claim that he had devised a new electric railway system that would supplant existing ones, Thomson told Charles Coffin, the president of the Thomson-Houston Electric Company, that "the whole matter is characteristic. . . .These statements of Mr. Edison will, with people not fully posted, have a restraining effect on the placing of orders with rival concerns, and even though nothing came of the proposed schemes the advantage would been secured for the Edison Co. that a certain time in which to perfect their equipment and put them on par, if possible, with those already existing, would have been obtained." To counter this effect he suggested that "it would pay . . . to get together the unverified predictions of Mr. Edison in some concrete form as an assistance in getting at the truth in these matters."[29]

Edison was not entirely untroubled by the publicity he received, although he failed to acknowledge his own culpability in the matter. In his letter to Norman Raff about Dickson's motion picture pamphlet, for example, Edison indicated that he didn't see a need for the inclusion of his photograph (though one appeared), arguing, "It looks too much like conceitedness and self glorification on my part, and the public never take kindly to a man who is always working his personality forward. Its the thing they want to know about and not the man for whom they do not care a D——."[30] This echoed the objection he had made six years earlier to a scheme suggested by George Gouraud for promoting Edison's "perfected phonograph" in Britain. Gouraud had asked Edison to send photographs of him and his friends talking into the phonograph that could "be copied in all the illustrated papers, and will give us many thousand dollars worth of free advertizing." These photographs were to be part of an extensive publicity campaign that would also include a highly illustrated book about the inventor entitled *Edison and His Works*. Edison asked Tate to "write Gouraud a strong letter about these advertising schemes— I dont propose to be Barnumized & I will furnish *no* data for his proposed book— I[f] he does anything in that line other than dignified biz way we shall at once get into a Row." Edison insisted that Gouraud "not shove my name forward so prominently . . . want him to talk phonogh & not Edison." Tate's letter on Edison's behalf made clear that although Edison understood "the value of the assistance which the press is capable of giving us" he considered advertising schemes that focused on the inventor rather than the invention "distasteful" and "undignified."[31]

Edison may have wanted to believe that the many newspaper articles based on reporters' interviews with him emphasized his inventions, but even a casual reader would conclude that he was their real subject. Edison, in fact, had few rivals during the last quarter of the nineteenth century as a self-promoter. As much as he sought to deny it, he was very much in the mold of his countryman

P. T. Barnum. Edison might have argued that his were real accomplishments made for the benefit of mankind whereas Barnum was a mere huckster promoting cheap amusements, but he was as capable as the "Prince of Humbugs" at garnering personal publicity. Like Barnum, Edison used the press to achieve an unparalleled reputation as the source of novelty in his own field of endeavor. And both men became legends in their own times whose work and character was much more complex than was acknowledged by the myths that grew up around them.[32]

CHAPTER 20

Fame in the Family

T he celebrity that attended Edison had enormous effects on his family. It was not easy being the wife or child of a modern legend. The legendary inventive campaigns that kept him away from home certainly had some relation to his reputation as the inventor of the age. Edison's letters to Mina during his years of struggle to bring his revolutionary ore-milling venture to fruition suggest how much this myth had become part of his identity. Thus, in one letter he excused his absence by telling Mina, "All depends on my self. To come [to Glenmont] now it would be necessary to shut down at a most critical time technically and financially. Had I an intelligent assistant I could have come but . . . I have to watch every move made here so that there shall be no mistake made and the mill will be a permanent success." The mythological great inventor was even more evident in another letter: "I have no-one to help—owing to the immense number of things (details) which must be attended to instantly night and day—every one requiring thought. I could not leave for a moment. It makes me blue to think you so little realize the greatness of this undertaking, the whole carried out by one man." As Neil Baldwin points out in his biography, "Edison's torrent of language defines a solitary protagonist, surrounded by machines that heed only *his* bidding." The Ogden venture itself increasingly embodied this characteristic of its inventor's imagination as Edison sought to make it like the ideal he had proposed to Lathrop for their novel, "Factories auto[matic] run by one man." The mill that Edison showed the press in 1897, in fact, seemed to them "a wonderful example of automatic action." The few workers who remained were "merely watchers to see that all goes well." "What Mr. Edison has done has been to subdue to his service three great natural forces—momentum, magnetism, and gravity. . . . The complete subjection and masterful control of great natural forces is one of the most impressive aspects of the whole enterprise."[1]

Mina may have expected her much older husband to begin to slow down in his middle age, but his compulsion for work, which his reputation only reinforced, made her feel after ten years of marriage that she was but a small part of his life. Although he reassured her "That is all nonsense. You & the children and the Laboratory is all my life I have nothing else," the laboratory (and the project of the moment) clearly continued to come first. This is not to say that Edison did not love his wife and children (besides their daughter Madeleine, he and Mina had two sons, Charles, born in 1890, and Theodore, born in 1898). In his letters to Mina from the mid-1890s, which contain heartfelt expressions of love for his family, she was his "Darling Billy" and he her "real unadulterated lover." And when she was away with the children at Chautauqua while he remained at work, he would "get that longing to see you that I always get when I am left alone." Nonetheless, work always came before family reunions at Chautauqua; he would go when he could take a break from work but sometimes his work caused him to cancel or postpone his visits there. Furthermore, throughout the 1890s he never cut short his work at Ogden to return home to Glenmont, and from 1894 on he spent more and more of his time at the mine.

In neither his first nor his second marriage was Edison entirely comfortable with the constraints of domestic middle-class life, and the challenge of the ore-milling project was enhanced by his distance from its conventions. In the mountains of New Jersey he could be Mina's "lover always the same (who sleeps with his boots on & smokes 28 cent cigars)." Edison seems never to have understood how different were the expectations and experiences he and Mina had of married life. Mina's loneliness frequently gave rise to self-doubts, which Edison tried to overcome with letters of reassurance: "If you only knew how much your lover adored you & how proud he was to have such a good darling wife & such babies you would never worry about such matters, please dismiss such things from your mind." But he also thought her "blues" were the product of "a disordered liver or some long sinuous intestine that blushes from inflammation" and referred to her as his "Constitutional Growler." Although Edison in one of his letters did "wonder if Billy Edison truly loves me," he seems to have suffered little from the doubts about their relationship that plagued his wife. When he did miss his family Edison could "fight the feeling off by working a little nights." Mina, on the other hand, might throw herself into church and charitable activities during the day, but her nights were long and lonely. Eventually, she would reconcile herself to his long hours, helped not only by his return full-time to the laboratory in West Orange in 1899, which meant that he was home more often, but also by conceiving of herself as a home executive responsible for running the extensive Glenmont staff and overseeing the upbringing of her children. In the home, however, Edison's needs always came first. "My job," Mina told reporters, "has been always to take care of Mr. Edison—to take care that his home contributed as much as possible to his doing the work that he had to do to the best advantage. We have always put his work first, all of us. And we have tried to organize our home and our home life to give results just as much as the laboratory."[2]

Edison's children from his first marriage also had to accommodate their needs to those of their father and to find their way in life largely without him. Their paths to adulthood were further complicated by the changed circumstances resulting from their father's remarriage and by their status as the children of one of the most famous men in the world. The difficulties they were to face first became evident when Edison, content to let Mina handle all the details of his children's schooling, acquiesced in her decision to send them to the kind of exclusive private boarding schools she and her siblings had attended but that offered just the kind of classical curriculums he found most objectionable.

Marion went to Bradford because it was a superior place for college preparation, but the friction that existed between her and her stepmother no doubt contributed to the decision to send Marion away to school. Mina, like her father, was a proponent of college education for women, but her expectations for Marion's education were very different from those she held for Tom and William. Mina believed that college education allowed women to acquire "standards of judgment" and personal contacts that would help them if they went into the professions, but she saw college education primarily as a way of better preparing a woman for her job as manager of the home by providing "knowledge of technicalities for her material problems" such as the family budget and by educating her "spiritual self" so that she could "call upon the legions of literature and art" to make her home "a place of peace and contentment." For Mina, an "intelligently run" home provided a place to "refresh oneself and catch one's breath" and where "the materialism of living would be enhanced by the abundance of spiritual gain."[3]

It is not entirely clear what expectations Marion herself had about Bradford, although her earlier attendance at Madame Mears's school and before that at another school for young ladies in New York City had better prepared her for the social and academic environment of an elite school than the coeducational and more practically oriented Dearborn-Morgan school did for her brothers. Marion's letters home indicate that initially she enjoyed her experience at Bradford, and being away from home may actually have improved her relationship with Mina to some extent. While there she worked hard at being a dutiful daughter and tried to follow the Miller family tradition of writing a letter home each Sunday, even criticizing Mina for sometimes failing to write regularly. Marion's experience of other families during her time at Bradford also made her appreciate that the difficulties in her relationship with Mina were not entirely the fault of her stepmother. As she told Mina after spending time with a schoolfriend's stepmother, "I saw a great deal between May and she that proved to me that if ever we have had a little trouble at home I have I fear been doubtless many time in the wrong." Marion even expressed the hope that she could repay Mina for her "kindness by being good and grow up into such womanhood as will show you that your good bringing up has not been wasted or undeserved." Marion's academic career came to an end, however, during the winter of 1890. She failed to enroll for a full load of classes and with little to do she fell "in with girls who think almost entirely of fun, they do not all enjoy innocent fun but are not contented until they forget that they are women and indulge in smoking and many other 'innocent' pleasures." The teachers and many of her fellow students believed that her light load was due to her being "trained up to be a society girl." Marion felt it would be best for her to come home and study with her former tutor Miss McWilliams, but Mina decided to send her to join her own younger sisters Mary and Grace, who were studying in Paris. Mina's older sister Jennie was to be Marion's chaperone. Upon learning that she would be allowed to spend two years studying in Europe, Marion assured her stepmother that "*I shall never* give you cause to regret letting me go and I shall try and study hard and be good. You can remember this promise Mama and remind me of it if I ever brake it but I do not think you will have cause for I intend keeping it." Jennie offered the more cautious hope that "coming to Europe will not spoil her."[4]

Marion found Paris liberating, and soon after her arrival she sought to establish her independence from Jennie, whom she found rather dour and unaccommodating. Jennie herself recognized that she was "not the most amiable person that ever was," and even her sister Mary remarked that Jennie easily found fault with others. Marion found it hard to get her aunt to go anywhere she had not been before, and Jennie complained that Marion was primarily interested in the "innocent pleasures" of shopping and driving in the park. Jennie noted that after only two months in Paris Marion had spent more than the money allotted for half the year, and that she was "very harsh and severe" whenever they disagreed. Marion certainly found it difficult to meet the expectations imposed on her by the Miller girls; she and Mary also came into conflict over her expenses and her attempts to assert her independence.[5]

Besides its personal elements, Marion's defiance may have stemmed in part from a mild rebellion against the restrictions Victorian society imposed on young upper-middle-class women. Even though she fretted over falling in with the wrong girls at Bradford, she seems at the same time to have been attracted by the fact that they did not always act like proper young women. And Marion's status as Edison's daughter affected her expectations toward her expenses; for example, she refused to travel second class because if it was "not good enough for Papa's servants it is not good enough for his daughter." Marion contrasted Jennie's (and Mina's) admonitions to act like a proper lady and practice economy with her memories of her own mother, whom she recalled giving parties and wearing extravagant dresses (perhaps helping to explain Marion's purchases of such clothing while in Paris). Edison himself had fostered her sense of independence by opening up a larger world for her before his remarriage when Marion accompanied him to public events and even to his laboratory; it is notable that she continued to use "George," his masculine pet name for her, in her letters to him from Bradford. Nonetheless, Marion was not entirely comfortable as a nonconformist. When her rebellion against Jennie made it necessary for her "to walk on the streets alone," she found that she "did not relish it very much and I am old enough to know that it is not the thing."[6]

Marion's European sojourn would have enormous consequences for her relationship with her parents. For a time, her relations with Mina actually improved as a result of their physical distance. She also looked more favorably on her stepmother after spending time with Jennie, even writing Mina that "I miss you very much and wish you were here I like you more and more every day and hope you like me better." Even after spending time together with Mina, when she and Edison attended the 1889 Paris Exposition, Marion continued to be on good terms with her stepmother. Her relations with her father, however, became strained during this visit. She later remarked that "ever since we were in Paris together I could not help but feel that he was very much changed towards me." Subsequently, she would blame Mina for her estrangement from her father. Little is known of the time she spent with her parents in Paris and Germany, but Edison was no doubt as ever too busy to spend time alone with her and probably expressed some disapproval of her tendency toward extravagance. Before leaving for America, he and Mina decided to give her a monthly allowance of only forty dollars instead of the eighty she was expecting. Although Marion agreed that the reasons for cutting her allowance were good ones and confessed that she was "*very* careless and extravagant," money matters would continue to create conflict between Marion and her parents during her stay in Europe.[7]

The most significant wedge between Marion and her parents arose out of their actions when she contracted smallpox while visiting Dresden at the beginning of 1890. The disease scarred her face, and that was a traumatic experience for a young woman about to turn seventeen, but even worse, her family failed to demonstrate much concern for her condition. In March, as she began her recovery on the Riviera following several weeks in a Dresden hospital, Marion was unable to contain her distress and bitterness in a letter thanking Mina for a gift:

> You surely do not blame me for feeling hurt that I only heard from home twice during those long dreary weeks spent in the hospital. It was quite the talk of the hospital and you can imagine my mortification. I do not blame you so much but Papa is my own father & I never thought that he would treat me with anything other than kindness. I know that he did not mean to add a pang to my sufferings but it was at a time when I needed every proof of affection and two short letters in seven weeks did not prove that there was much. I wonder if I had died if you or Papa would ever have regretted not sending a few words of sympathy for those awful hours.[8]

Similar sentiments were expressed by her new chaperone and tutor, Mrs. Bingham: "It was a great grief to her & a surprise to every one that you have not written to her during this the most awful trial that could have come into her life." Marion, she felt, even blamed herself for this, although "other people were not so charitable." While Mrs. Bingham felt that "a loving letter from her *Father* would have been comfort unspeakable to your poor afflicted child," Edison apparently considered it sufficient to send Samuel Insull to visit her.[9]

Edison did try make his daughter happy by sending Mrs. Elizabeth Earl to join her as a companion and tutor after she left the hospital. Jennie had first recommended Mrs. Earl to Mina as a governess for Marion in 1886, and both had hoped that she could take on the young woman after Jennie returned home from Europe at the end of 1889. Marion had similar hopes after meeting Mrs. Earl soon after her arrival in Paris, but at the time the older woman was engaged with another family. It was Mrs. Earl who recommended Mrs. Bingham in June 1889 when Marion needed a traveling companion—she had refused to accompany the Miller sisters to a German spa where Mary was to be treated for an illness. By the time Marion became ill Mrs. Earl had returned to the United States and was available to take charge of the young woman for whom she would become tutor, confidante, and perhaps something of a substitute mother as well.

Marion spent the next two years traveling and studying in Europe. During that time she almost never heard directly from her father—on one of the few occasions when she did receive a letter from him she took nearly two months to reply. Mina remained her primary family correspondent, but their relationship clearly had been damaged by the lack of attention the family paid Marion during her illness. Whenever her parents urged their daughter to come home she insisted that she could not do so because of her scarred face, which clearly troubled her; for many months after her illness she wore a veil in public. By the summer of 1891, however, Mina had become convinced that she was the real reason Marion stayed in Europe. In a letter describing their difficult relationship, Marion assured her that

> I am perfectly certain that we have so changed in the last three years that I would have nothing to fear in going home. I am sure that I would be most happy with you as I feel for the first time since your marriage that you would like to have me with you. I have always thought that you would much rather not have me at home and this alone was the basis upon which all my feelings toward you were founded. Your kind sentiments toward me made me feel very happy as showing that you are not as I supposed entirely indifferent to me. You must not think that I feel that you have ever been unkind to me for certainly you never have been so, what most hurt me was that I knew you were kind to me because you thought it your duty to be so and not because you wanted to. I do hope Mama that you will believe me when I say that I would certainly come home if it were not for my face and that I feel perfectly confident that if I were to come I should be very happy with you.[10]

Finally, after resisting all previous efforts by her parents to call her home, Marion agreed to return in February 1892.

Initially, following Marion's return, she and her parents seemed to get on well together. That summer Mina's mother was delighted to hear about her "lovely drives with Marion" and that they were having "such good times together" and that Marion "likes dear little Madeleine and little Charles so well."[11] However, Marion's feelings about home changed dramatically after spending a summer at Glenmont with her father while the rest of the family was away at Chautauqua. Once again she played the hostess for her father and found that he treated her much more affectionately when they were alone. Deciding that she could never be happy living at home with Mina she decided to move out of Glenmont. She also began to address her stepmother as Mina instead of referring to her as Mama. Once on her own, she began to spend time with Mrs. Earl and finally decided to return to Europe the following year, where she soon met and married a German army officer named Oscar Oeser. She would not return home again until after World War I, when she separated from her husband.

Although Marion remained cordial in her correspondence with Mina she would always hold her responsible for alienating her father's affections. She expressed her true feelings about her stepmother in a 1932 letter to Henry Ford: "I thought Mrs. Edison would stop her unjust treatment of us after the notoriety given her because of Father's Will but I suppose until the end she will seek fame as she did wealth in the past."[12] (Edison willed the majority of his estate to the sons of his second marriage.) Her brother Tom blamed Mrs. Earl for Marion's feelings toward Mina and for her decision to remain in Europe away from her family, but Edison himself seems to have been the one primarily responsible for Marion's estrangement. He did little to reassure Marion about his feelings toward her after his marriage, and through his actions he demonstrated to his daughter that as long as Mina was around their relationship could never again be as close as it had been in the year following her mother's death.

There is no doubt at all that Edison was responsible to a great extent for the difficult relationship he had with his two eldest sons. These difficulties began with the decision to send them to St. Paul's even though Edison was highly skeptical of both the traditional classical education his sons would receive there and the value of the kind of college education for which it would prepare them. Furthermore, neither Edison nor Mina did much to help either boy to settle into his new social and academic environment. In their letters home both boys frequently expressed their unhappiness, especially their feelings of homesickness, and they both suffered frequent illnesses that may have been symptomatic of their low spirits. Tom was protective of his younger brother and encouraged him in his studies when they first arrived at school, but it was Tom who left the school first. He refused to go back in January 1893, after telling his parents "I have a great many reasons why I am so discontent here so many it is very hard to tell them all. . . . I have tried over and over again to be popular with the boys and masters but have failed in every attempt."[13] Never much interested in scholarly pursuits or a college education, he decided to go to work for his father.

William was the more willing scholar, although he found his lessons "very hard" and was constantly promising Mina that she would see an improvement in his reports and that he "was studying hard to please you and father and all the rest." He did reasonably well in his other studies, but struggled with the classical languages that his father thought useless. Edison later criticized traditional schools for "tak[ing] up too much time teaching things that don't count. Latin and Greek—what good are they? They say they train the mind. But I don't think they train the mind half so much as working out practical problems." Yet he entirely ignored his own son's struggles to master these subjects. William found St. Paul's an increasingly oppressive place, particularly after his brother left. In one letter home he declared that he would "rather be in prison than up here" and in another that he "would give all I have got, money, clothes, house and every thing to get out of this place." His pleas to come home and attend "a public school or any school near home" were finally answered when his parents enrolled him in the Trinity Preparatory School on Staten Island.[14]

When Edison enrolled William at his new school he finally asserted some authority over his son's education by asking the headmaster, John M. Hawkins, to prepare William for a Cornell University program that did not require him to take Greek. However, although Edison clearly thought highly of Cornell's engineering school he did not make clear to Hawkins that he desired his son to enroll there, and Hawkins thought that he should prepare William for the College of Philosophy. William himself eventually decided to attend the Sheffield Scientific School at Yale. His decision seems to have been influenced by the fact that "a whole crowd" of boys that he knew were attending Yale, including Mina's younger brothers.[15]

William, however, showed a decided tendency to procrastinate in preparing for his college entrance examinations because they required hard work. Instead he spent his time on athletics and other amusements, including girls. William's experience at Trinity made it apparent that his difficulties with the masters at St. Paul's were in large part his own fault. He also rebelled against Hawkins, who found the same wildness in his pupil that Mina's mother had remarked upon a decade earlier. Although he appreciated William's "excellent qualities of mind and heart" Hawkins found them "obscured by certain defects. He is careless about his person, his clothes, and in the preparation of his work in school, such as his writing, the preparation of his exercises, the recitation of his lessons. He is boisterous and rude, and this sometimes approaches disrespect." William also demonstrated "a talent for spending money. Whatever amount he may have, he may be trusted to get rid of it instantly."[16] This was a trait shared by his siblings, and the efforts made by his parents to get William to take more responsibility for his expenses were no more successful than they had been with Marion. Although Edison continued to have little to do with the details of his son's education, leaving these to Mina, he did write occasional letters criticizing William's bad habits. In particular, his father admonished him for his free-spending ways. In reply to these critiques William acknowledged that "I have one very grate fault among others and that is that I never stop to consider if I am doing the right thing or not." However, despite promising to "be more careful in the future," he continued to spend money with little regard for the consequences.[17]

After struggling to pass the examinations necessary for admission to Yale, William finally enrolled there in 1897. He proved to be as lax in his studies at Yale as he had been at Trinity. His enthusiasm for sports led to injuries that prevented him from attending classes and doing his schoolwork. The *New Haven Record* reported that his decision to drop out during the spring semester was due to the fact that he "was troubled with an eye difficulty all fall."[18] There may be some truth to this as William did experience eye problems at St. Paul's, but his letters home suggest that he was more troubled by the hard work and his own lack of diligence.

Although the *Record* stated that he planned to return to school the following year, William seems to have determined that college was not for him. Instead he decided to become an agent for his father's products and made plans to go to Rochester, New York, to open a store to sell them. Edison was not entirely pleased by these plans and asked his business manager, William Gilmore, to delay William from going to Rochester. At just that moment the Spanish-American War broke out and William ended up enlisting in the Army instead. He was soon wounded, and after a six-week convalescence he was discharged. (Mina's youngest brother was killed in the fighting just before she gave birth to a son, who was named Theodore in his honor.) After his return to New York William began selling phonographs in a shop on 59th Street, where he and G. M. Rogers formed a company to sell "an automatic picture machine called the Photoscope," which provided twelve pictures for a nickel along with songs from a music box. Although he and Rogers hoped that Edison would agree to manufacture the machines, William and his father soon had a serious falling out.[19]

Their differences were caused by William's marriage in November 1899 to Blanche Travers, the daughter of a Baltimore farmer and produce wholesaler and the niece of United States Senator John Daniels of Virginia. William's parents disapproved of the marriage because they thought him too young and unsettled. William felt that he was "very ready to paddle my own canoe," aided by the settlement of his mother's estate, and he told his father, "I can get along without your assistance as I have done in the past few months." Declaring that he would not "darken the doors of your house again," William expressed the hope that "when we meet again in a few years I trust we will become better friends and understand each other better." Assuring Edison that "I bear you no ill will," he blamed Mina for their falling out. Recognizing that her class expectations had changed his life, he told his father, "I look upon her as the one who ruined our happiness and future and yet you cannot blame her too much." However, by February, following the death of Edison's sister Marion, William began making an effort to reconcile with his father. He asked him to meet

Blanche, certain that his "objections would be removed if only you would con-descend to see her and have a talk." "I may have been a disobedient son," he implored, "but hardly a bad or worthless one." It would be another three years before Edison finally reconciled himself to the marriage.[20]

Tom Jr., like his younger brother, also had broken with his father and had equal difficulty in meeting his family's expectations. Initially, Tom worshiped his father, which would prove to be an important element in their growing rift. After leaving St. Paul's Tom worked with his father in the laboratory and at the Ogden mine. Beginning in 1897, however, his relationship with his father be-came strained, and he grew increasingly closer to his stepmother. In January 1897 Tom wrote from the mine that "mother and her folks do not understand me. . . . Why is it they keep continually asking me to do things that to me are absurd and yet when I refuse they cannot understand it. Do you like to go out to 'dances' 'receptions' 'dinners' and many other like things? No—it is very easy to understand why you do not but it is certainly very evident they do not realize that I am your son."[21] Nonetheless, he soon began to feel increasing affection for his stepmother. This growing attachment is evident in his handwriting, which began to change from a close replica of his father's to a blend of both parents'. By September, after he agreed to meet her wishes and prepare for col-lege, his handwriting came to closely resemble her own, and his correspon-dence with her became extremely, perhaps overly, affectionate.

Tom's growing affection for his stepmother was matched by an increasing distance from his father that was due in part to the intimidation Tom always felt around his father. In January 1897 he had written, "I don't believe I would ever be able to talk to you the way I would like to because you are so far my superior in every way that when I am in your presence I am perfectly helpless." He also felt that he had never pleased his father "in anything I ever have done." By the summer Tom's deteriorating relationship with his father reached the point that he felt unable to join the family at Chautauqua, even though he was staying there with friends, and he refused to come home to Glenmont as well. In Oc-tober, preparing to strike out on his own, he wrote Mina, "If father thought that after I finish college he could give me a position some where I would of course much rather work for him and for his interests. But as this out of the question as he will never have anything for one who is considered by him and probably others in his employ as unintelligent, I have in consequence given up all hope in this direction. . . . I was told to paddle my own canoe and I am going to do it."[22]

Tom had dreams of being an inventor like his father, but he demonstrated little understanding of the hard work that had led to his father's success. His in-ability to talk with his father made it difficult for him to learn from his father's experiences and to ask for his advice. "I have many ideas of my own," he told Mina, "which sometimes—yes—I may say on all occasions I would like to ask him or tell him about but they never leave my mouth." Edison, who consid-ered his son to be "very impractical," made no effort to guide him, and never willing to waste time on paid assistants whom he felt to be impractical, he was probably quite hard on his son at the laboratory. Tom recognized his own impracticality and acknowledged that "it is a difficult matter to change ones nature in a short time and it may take a very long time before I get so that my methods and ideas are practical in the eyes of some but I shall go on trying just the same."[23]

One important source of Tom's impracticality was his terrific ignorance and naivete regarding business. Because of his "inability to cope with men of experience" he frequently allowed himself to be taken advantage of by those seeking to use the Edison name for their own purposes. His first venture, the "Edison Junior Improved" incandescent lamp, was typical. Investors in the business seem to have been more interested in access to the Edison name than in any improvements that Tom might offer them. Although the newspapers reported that the lamp was based on his invention, they also noted that he planned to keep it a trade secret rather than patent it because he had learned from his father that patents provided little protection and large expense. A revealing letter he wrote to Mina soon after becoming involved in promoting the lamp suggests his own confusion over whether it was an actual invention or his name that he had provided to the company. "I call it my light for the present as I am in full charge of it" he told her, but "I have several valuable things which are and will be a great thing for the people of the world. . . . I shall first make some money out of this lamp business and eventually start up these various things." He also assured Mina "as far as I am able to find out it won't injure [my father] in any way—which I wouldn't want to do for the world—but it is a case of dollars and cents." Nonetheless, Edison, with good reason, believed that his son had been taken advantage of for his name. Although Tom disclaimed the news reports about this venture in a letter to his stepmother, he was secretly delighted that the papers seemed to take his side when his father criticized him in a *New York Herald* interview, and he felt that his father's comments were prompted by jealousy. Significantly, as he began to see himself as his father's rival, Tom also began to mimic his handwriting again.[24]

The newspaper reports about Tom all indicated that he had learned the craft of invention by working in his father's laboratory. This background enabled him to gain entree into the New York electrical community and garnered him an appointment as head of the Committee on Decorative Effects of the 1898 Electrical Exhibition planned for Madison Square Garden. It also boosted his reputation as an inventor, although this may have produced delusions of grandeur in his mind; in June he told a friend that the U.S. government had asked him "to take charge of some experiments." Tom was, in fact, busy promoting his ideas for inventions that he believed would surpass the lamp business. In April a group of investors from California, including the state's attorney general, wanted to promote his scheme for utilizing the ocean tides to produce power. They offered to put up the money for patents and provide $25,000 to build a working model and to provide Tom with a "handsome salary." This scheme fell through, apparently because Tom became concerned that they "want to take advantage of my age so that they can do me up someway." A month later he was promoting another scheme "I have been working a long time on . . . a process by which steel can be turned into iron." Tom and what he considered a prominent group of investors formed the Edison Junior Steel and Iron Company. He received one-third of the company's stock and was appointed president, even though he felt unqualified for the position, because it suited his investors. By September, however, he had become sufficiently discouraged to tell Mina that he was prepared to give up these schemes and prepare for college and then "try to get a position somewhere" with a sufficient salary "to live on and be comfortable."[25]

By this time Edison had grown increasingly disgusted with what he saw as his son's practice of "using his name as a drawing card," and in December he threatened legal action if Tom did not stop it. "The old man," William wrote his brother, "says he is through with you and that you have disgraced him enough." In a letter of reply to his father, Tom asserted that "domestic attentions [were] foreign" to Edison, "who has no more right in this world to be a father than a youth of six." He also derided his father's business sense and asserted that "you should have been—'ask any body'—a millionaire ten times over if you knew how to handle your own achievements. What have you to-day—ask the financial world [which had recently rejected Edison's attempts to raise money for the Ogden mill]—they know." Declaring that "I shall go on just as I have been doing until the law *only* compels me to stop," Tom told his father, "Your name has been a detriment to me from the day I started out—and always will be—where would I get any credit? No where—whatever I get up and will get up in the future you are and will be the inventor."[26]

With this exchange Edison and his son broke with each other. Tom soon started on a downward slide that began when he married chorus girl Marie Louise Touhey against his parents' wishes in February 1899, just a few months before his brother William's marriage. Unlike William's wife Blanche, Marie proved to be little more than a gold digger. She was unfaithful to Tom and boasted that she was playing his family for "suckers."[27] The two were soon divorced, and Edison gave her a twenty-five dollar weekly allowance on the condition that she not use her married name as a stage name; she died shortly thereafter. After the breakup of the marriage Tom turned to drink, and his health, which had never been good (he frequently suffered from severe headaches and dizziness), grew so bad that he entered a sanitarium in 1903. His drinking and health problems were exacerbated by legal difficulties arising from dubious business ventures designed to take advantage of the Edison name.

After breaking with his father Tom had declared himself to be "his father's competitor," and he tried a number of ventures in his effort to outdo him.[28] The first, and the one that seems most clearly to have been based on his own ideas, was a process for hardening steel that he claimed would be better than the current armor-plating process because it reduced the weight of the plating while increasing its tensile strength. Tom developed this process in 1899 in association with his uncle William Holzer, a former Menlo Park employee who had married Mary Edison's sister, Alice Stilwell. Together they formed the Thomas A. Edison Jr. and Wm. Holzer Steel and Iron Process Company. Although initial tests of their process by the Bethlehem Steel Company showed some promise, it was never adopted, and the company became embroiled in litigation over a claim by one William McMahon that he was due a large amount of stock for services he claimed to have rendered the two men. At the same time, Tom was sued for passing a bad check, which he seems to have done with some frequency.[29]

The failure of his iron and steel venture and of his marriage combined to devastate Tom, who later told his father, "I know of no business deal that I have ever made that I was not taken advantage of—having often been forced to enter into agreements to save myself from absolute poverty—with a few exceptions." Among these was a scheme known as the International Bureau of Science and Invention, which advertised itself as "The Inventor's Confidential Friend," with Tom serving as consulting expert. However, Edison appears to have made sure that this scheme did not go forward. Tom then became involved with a group of shady characters who had formed the Edison Chemical Company to market the "Wizard's Ink Tablets" and other such merchandise. After his father prevented them from using the name Edison, they paid Tom $5,000 to use his name and a $25 monthly salary. They continued to market the tablets and also began selling a worthless medical device designed by Tom called the "Magno-Electric Vitalizer." Tom received a $2 royalty for each device that was sold. During this period Tom was living in Newark with his mother's brother, Charles Stilwell, to whom he sold rights to his own name as well as presumptive rights to Edison's name upon his father's death, which Stilwell planned to sell in turn to the Columbia Phonograph Company. Stilwell also acquired rights to the Edison Junior lamp, which he hoped to sell to another company. Tired of the conflict with his father, Thomas wrote him at the end of 1902 that he was willing "to sign any reasonable agreement with you in which you can dictate your own terms—which will satisfy you forever—an agreement which will deprive me of all future rights to the name of Edison for the purpose of obtaining money and any other matter that is reasonable for the protection of yourself and at the same time myself."[30]

The signing of this agreement in June 1903 marked the beginning of Edison's reconciliation with his eldest son, although their relationship continued to be rocky for the next few years. When Tom asked for a place with one of his father's businesses, Edison, who had resumed giving his son a weekly allowance, refused because of Tom's bad reputation and advised him to "go into some small business."[31] Soon after Tom's health worsened, and he ended up in the sanitarium. There followed a long period of recuperation under the ministrations of his nurse Beatrice Heyzer Willard, with whom he fell in love. She proved a good match for Tom, and they were subsequently married. In the meantime Tom was sued for mail fraud in connection with the Edison Jr. Chemical Company, which Edison and his lawyer, Frank Dyer, resolved for him. Dyer also befriended the young man and acted as an intermediary with his father. It was through Dyer's auspices that Edison agreed to increase Tom's weekly income and to purchase a farm in Burlington, New Jersey, for his son and Beatrice. In his effort to start anew Tom even took his wife's name and called himself Burton Willard; he had previously thought of changing his name in 1898, telling his father, "If my name was Smith I would be a rich man today."[32] After settling in and making a small success with the farm he would go back to being Thomas Edison Jr.

Although Tom had been the main culprit in using the family name improperly, William, too, ran afoul of the efforts by their father and his companies to protect the Edison name. Edison had always been concerned over the fraudulent use of his name, but in 1898 he had become even more vigilant and adopted a policy of taking aggressive legal action whenever his name was used without his sanction. This concern arose from Tom's dubious business ventures, which took advantage of his name, and the growing consumer market for Edison phonographs. To protect himself Edison registered both his name and his signature as trademarks. In his trademark application he noted that the "essential feature" was "the word 'Edison' formed in characteristic autographic script," which "has been continuously used in my business since December 15, 1897."[33]

After William and his father reconciled in 1903, Edison staked him to the money he needed to open an automobile garage in Washington, D.C. After opening the garage, William formed a partnership with David Joslin, who fooled him into believing that he had gained Edison's consent to let them call their company the Edison Automobile Company of Washington, D.C. The formation of this company enraged Edison, who wrote angrily "You have now done just what I told you not to do—by organizing this co you are now doing me a vast injury because every automobile Co will now believe that I am interested in manufacturing automobiles and will fight shy of batteries. You are being used for your name like Tom and as you seem to be a hopeless case I now notify you that hereafter you can go your own way and take care of yourself." William quickly took steps "to annul the company that I so foolishly allowed to come into existence" and Edison relented, as he told his son, in the "hope that you will learn from this experience but the hope is pretty weak." Edison was clearly concerned with protecting his hard-earned reputation, and his sons encountered the same difficulty faced by Edison's assistants and competitors— there was to be only one Edison in the public eye. Both Tom and William had occasion to believe that they would be better off with a name like Smith.[34]

Although his garage achieved a solid reputation, it did not provide William with a good steady income. Edison had provided much of the money necessary to start the garage and Blanche wanted her father-in-law to invest additional money rather than bring in a partner, as Edison preferred. However, when she complained that the weekly allowance of forty dollars that Edison gave them was inadequate for "the children of *The Greatest Man of the Century*' . . . to live as they should," he responded angrily:

> I see no reason whatever why I should support my son, he has done me no honor and has brought the blush of shame to my cheeks many times in fact he has at times hurt my feelings beyond measure. For more than fifteen years I supported my family on less than two thousand per year & we lived well. And after allowing you as much as I do monthly to have you talk in the way you do shows an utter lack of gratitude. Let your husband earn his money like I did. I will continue to send the monthly installment until such time as I think best but in no case will I loan any more money or increase the monthly amount.[35]

William, who decided not to show his wife this letter, replied that he would "try and do my best without any further assistance from you." But although he acknowledged that "I have not been an honor to you," he also called his father's "attention to the fact that I never had the business training that most fathers make their sons go through." William's lack of business ability soon led him to give up his garage and instead work for a salary, feeling that "it is better to be tied down than to go it on your own hook." He and Blanche spent the next several years struggling to make ends meet as they "moved around to the most God forsaken place[s] on earth."[36]

During this time William worked for a number of automobile companies as an agent and as a factory superintendent. But he was also attempting to develop the spark plug designs that he had devised in the small laboratory he had had at his Washington garage. In 1907, when he began to manufacture and sell them, it finally seemed that one of Edison's sons would actually achieve some success as an inventor. Frank Dyer, probably at Edison's behest, took an interest in William's business affairs, as he had done with Tom's, and helped William to set up the Edison Auto Accessories Company, but William once again proved a poor businessman. Dyer found him "a willful and headstrong boy, full of pride, conceit and vanity, and the easy mark of men who are mean and contemptible enough to prey upon those features of your character. . . . I have no doubt that if we turned $100,000 over to you it would be spent in idle foolishness within two months and that at the end of that time we would hear the same complaints and fault findings." William also displeased his father by advertising his plugs as having "the full approval of my father, Thomas A. Edison, and to the general public this approval is accepted as nothing short of the highest recommendation . . . where you see the name Edison attached to an article, if genuine, you may rest assured that it is an article that will command attention throughout the world." Edison objected to the statement that he approved of the plug, claiming that he had never even seen it, which led William to complain that "this only goes to prove what I have thought for years past and that is, that he not only takes no interest in anything that I may do but if I am not sadly mistaken, he simply despises me."[37]

Despite being willing to help his sons get "started in a useful honest business career," the self-made Edison did not feel compelled to do what other prominent men did—and his sons thought he should—and spend "a small fortune before their [sons'] business adventures were a success."[38] Although he provided a basic living allowance to them and on occasion provided seed money for a business venture, he did not provide the type of funding that he himself had required for success early in his career. Edison clearly believed that this was something they should gain on their own. He believed that his sons should follow the advice that he based on his own experience and gave others on how to succeed as an inventor; that is, to make connections with people in a particular field whose guidance and industry associations could help to make the invention a success. Throughout their lives, this was a lesson that his sons never really learned. William seems never to have made connections in the automobile industry that might have benefited him in promoting his spark plugs, and he always remained on its fringes. Later, when Tom used his father's friendship with Henry Ford to propose his own ideas for automobile improvements, he failed to follow up on a plan to move to Detroit where his ideas might have flourished. Both sons ultimately settled for smaller ambitions as their father helped them to establish farms; beginning in 1910, William raised pheasants and other game birds. Like Voltaire's Candide they had to be content cultivating their gardens.

None of Mary's children were prepared by their father for the changes wrought by his marriage to Mina, and he also failed to offer them much in the way of fatherly guidance or personal encouragement. He was always too ready to condemn his sons for their failures and faults and too stingy with his praise. Besides having little to do with their upbringing when his sons were young, Edison failed to provide much counsel and instruction that might have benefited them early in their careers. Edison's impatience with those who did not quickly demonstrate initiative and practicality, combined with Tom's timidity around his father, prevented Tom's experience working for his father from being a useful apprenticeship. Away at school, William had little contact with his father, and when Edison did choose to write an occasional letter to him he frequently used it as an opportunity to criticize his son for such faults as his failure to consult Mina, his disregard for the value of money, and his poor spelling. Edison's practice of writing letters of criticism rather than praise continued once his sons were out on their own. William's 1909 letter to Dyer, in which he complained about his father's incessant criticism, could easily have been written by either brother: "For ten years I have not received what might be called a fatherly letter but on the other hand each and every one contained the statement that I can either 'paddle my own canoe' 'I'm through with you' 'if you don't make this go your name is Mud' and other very encouraging statements."[39]

Perhaps Edison's greatest failing toward his sons was his failure to insist that they receive the kind of education he believed would best prepare them for life. He felt strongly that the specialized technical knowledge required by invention and the commercial sense required to make one's way in the business world were best acquired through practical working experience. Even though he noted the importance of "books and actual demonstration," he argued that "work is the best kind of school to train the mind." Nonetheless, he could not "speak too highly of the technical schools. There they teach not alone from books, but allow the pupils to work at the bench."[40] By the late 1890s college education was becoming an important requirement for both technical careers and advancement through the ranks of corporate managers. This was true even in the Edison laboratory and business enterprises, which had always prided themselves on their tradition of practical shop education and advancement. Although he never acknowledged the mistake he made in sending his eldest sons to St. Paul's and in failing to encourage their technical education, Edison made sure that Charles and Theodore, his sons from his second marriage, received what he considered proper schooling.

Charles and his sister Madeleine attended the Dearborn-Morgan School as youngsters. At the age of twelve Charles entered the newly established Carteret Academy in Orange before spending two years at the Hotchkiss School, a preparatory school in Lakeville, Connecticut. Hotchkiss offered both a traditional classical curriculum with Latin and Greek and a curriculum that included a scientific course, and during his time there Charles did not take the classical languages. Although he was an indifferent student, Charles went on to study at the Massachusetts Institute of Technology, a school of which Edison thought very highly and to which he sent his youngest son as well. Charles was an undistinguished student at MIT, and when it came time to declare an engineering specialty before his senior year, an executive with the Boston Edison Company encouraged him to get a practical business education: "Why waste the year? . . . we'll put you through all the departments and show you what makes a business tick." Edison was delighted and told his son "That's the thing to do." Mina was less pleased by his failure to become the first of her children to receive a coveted college degree. After his year at Boston Edison, Charles spent a year traveling in the West, determined to earn his way so as not to call on his father for money. After his return to Orange he entered his father's employ as an assistant "with general duties he didn't bother to define very much."[41] In effect, Edison provided Charles with an apprenticeship that earmarked him as the future head of the Edison businesses.

In contrast to Charles, who proved indifferent to his engineering and science courses and focused on the business side of things, Theodore showed great technical aptitude. He liked to experiment, and at the age of fourteen, in an episode reminiscent of his father's youth, he suffered a mild injury while "experimenting with explosives . . . in an effort to invent a bomb that would float about on the water and explode with tremendous effect whenever it happened to be touched by a hostile vessel."[42] After attending the nearby Montclair Academy, Theodore assisted his father with some military experiments during World War I before entering MIT in 1919. He excelled in his science and

Thomas A. Edison and his second family in 1907. Left to right: Madeleine, Mina, Theodore, Charles, and Thomas.

engineering classes and went on to do a year of postgraduate work at MIT before joining his father at the laboratory. He would eventually become technical director of the laboratory and a member of the executive committee of TAE Inc. But Theodore found himself frustrated by the routine work that prevented him from having "a chance to work on things I really enjoy and that I am best fitted to do." He also felt very "badly to have to dismiss men from the laboratory" and had great differences with his brother and father on personnel policies. As he explained in an April 1, 1931, letter to Charles in which he resigned as a company director and asked to be allowed to spend only half of his time as director of the laboratory: "An even more important consideration is the fact that I am so built that I cannot help bringing a great deal of humanity into my business decisions. Possibly this makes me entirely unfit to have an executive position but I feel very strongly that it can be demonstrated that successful business and humanity are not incompatible." To try out his ideas about "certain economic principles" and to engage in experimental work Theodore formed his own very successful research and development company, Calibron, of which he assured his father, "you need have no fear of any abuse of the name Edison."[43]

Madeleine also attended college—after graduating from Oak Place School in Akron, which was run by Mina's sister Grace, in 1906 she entered Bryn Mawr. However, she was more interested in society life than in a college education, and she left college after two years. In 1916 she followed in what had become something of an Edison family tradition by marrying against her parents' wishes—in her case, to John Sloane, who was Catholic. But her father and mother did reconcile themselves to the marriage two years later, following the birth of their first grandchild, Thomas Edison Sloane. Having been raised in the upper social circles, Madeleine sought to maintain a lifestyle befitting this status, even though her husband could not provide all of the comforts to which she had become accustomed. She and John constantly struggled to make ends meet. Although Edison never helped his son-in-law with his business ventures, he did loan his daughter and her husband the money to pay off the mortgage on their home in South Orange, New Jersey, after Madeleine demonstrated fiscal responsibility. His letter to her concerning this loan suggests the contrast he felt between Mary's and Mina's children as he told her "I think now I have 3 children who know the value of money."[44]

Mina's children had some important advantages over their older step-siblings. Brought up in the spotlight of their father's fame and sometimes themselves the subject of newspaper articles because they were the children of a famous man, the younger Edison children were better prepared by their mother, who had doubtless learned from her experiences with Marion, Tom, and William, to cope with the social expectations of wealth and fame. Mina also had learned how to cope with the foibles of her husband and his celebrity. Edison himself proved to be a more active father to his younger children. Although he was not around much during their early years, unlike what he had done with his older children, he became more prominent during their school years and took a larger role in determining the type of schooling that the boys in particular received. Charles and Theodore always had a clearer vision of the expectations held for them by their parents than Tom and William, and as a consequence they moved more smoothly into school and career. Timing was also important. Tom and William were raised and sent to school at a time when the importance of technical education was just beginning to become evident. Edison's own lack of education may have proved a drawback to them as they sought to follow his example of practical education. By the time Charles and Theodore were ready for school no such ambiguity existed either in the culture at large or, more significantly, in Edison's own mind about the value of college education, although he did feel that colleges were doing an inadequate job of preparing their graduates for work. When a public controversy erupted over the general test that Edison began to give to college-educated prospective employees in 1920, *Scientific American* noted that "college men, taken as a class . . . are so much better than the men who have not had any college that Mr. Edison has practically made the college education a prerequisite for positions of the sort to which these questionnaires lead," that is, for management positions.[45] The public perception that Edison was skeptical about the value of education is not born out by his actions in promoting technical education, hiring college-educated engineers and managers, or sending his younger sons to MIT. These advantages of schooling combined with their birth into the upper-middle-class world of their mother better prepared Edison's children from his second marriage for coping with his fame and fortune.

CHAPTER 21

The Business
of Innovation

A s Edison came to personify the ingenious Yankee inventor, he was busy
pioneering the modern industrial research laboratory that in the twentieth
century would help to make the individual inventor seem like a relic of the previous century. Nonetheless, Edison's laboratory remained outside of the mold
of the new corporate laboratories that were beginning to emerge during the
first decade of the twentieth century. In his study of the West Orange laboratory, Andre Millard argues that Edison's approach to research and development
differed in a significant way: "The laboratory initiated the work of the greater
organization rather than responded to its needs."[1] In fact, it was the work of the
laboratory that brought forth the larger organization. Edison remained an independent inventor-entrepreneur whose primary goal was the introduction of
new technology and the creation of new businesses based on that technology.
Only during the 1880s and early 1890s, when Edison and his laboratories
served as the research and development arm of the Edison lighting interests,
can we speak of his work in the context of a greater organization, and even then
he sought to maintain as much independence as possible. Edison remained an
inventor devoted first and foremost to the business of innovation.

During the mid-1890s, as Edison focused his energies on the Ogden mill,
the West Orange laboratory had been reduced to an ancillary role and staffed
with only a skeleton crew. Only when Edison was home waiting for new machinery to be put in place at Ogden would there be the occasional flurry of experiments on other projects reminiscent of the laboratory's early years. After
Edison abandoned the Ogden plant in 1898 and returned full-time to the laboratory it was once again abuzz with activity. With a growing staff of assistants

(111 men in 1899), Edison began work on three major new projects: a better method for duplicating phonograph recordings, an improved process for manufacturing Portland cement, and a new storage battery to power electric automobiles. In the midst of these massive research efforts, Edison as usual also turned his attention on occasion to other small projects such as a method of recording and retransmitting telephone messages for the railroads. He also conducted occasional experiments on subjects without immediate prospect of practical development—such as radium, in which he became interested following its isolation by Marie Curie in 1900, and the XYZ force that he had been investigating off and on since 1886.[2]

Realizing that the revival of his phonograph business depended not only on the development of home machines for entertainment but also on good-quality low-cost records, Edison had revived his experiments on a record duplicating process in 1897 when the National Phonograph Company began to manufacture records. At the time they were made by a mechanical dubbing process during which an original recording and a blank record turned on the same shaft while a smooth reproducing stylus, riding in the grooves of the master record, moved a linked recording stylus over the blank cylinder, which cut duplicate impressions in it. This laborious and expensive process produced generally inferior reproductions, and both Edison and his competitors worked to improve it while also seeking a process better suited to mass production.

Although Edison and his laboratory staff had been experimenting on a molding process since 1888, this work had gone on intermittently until the booming phonograph business produced a new urgency. Among the methods with which they had experimented and that Edison patented early on was vacuum-plating the original record to produce a metal mold. In this process the original record revolved in a vacuum so that it would receive an even coating of fine metallic dust from the vapor produced when an electric arc was formed by the passing of a current between two metal strips. Edison eventually settled on gold as the best metal to use in this process, which proved to be a useful feature of the advertising campaign when National Phonograph introduced records made from its "gold molds." The thin metal deposit acted as a conducting surface so that the record could be copper-plated by conventional electroplating methods. After the copper shell was smoothed on a lathe and placed in a brass shell, it was put in cold water so that the master record could be taken out, leaving a metal mold from which duplicates could be made. After resuming his experiments, Edison improved this process and filed a new patent application on it.[3]

Several problems occurred in duplicating from these molds, but perhaps the most crucial was the contraction of the molded duplicate during cooling so that it had a finer number of threads per inch than the original master recording made on a standard 100-thread screw phonograph. To solve this problem, Edison decided that the master should be recorded on a phonograph with fewer threads so that the duplicate would shrink to the standard pitch. Charles

Wurth, who had been experimenting for Edison making master molds since 1889, devoted much of his time to determining the best shrinkage ratio, and he devised a recoding machine that allowed him to easily adjust the number of threads. Over the years Wurth conducted hundreds of experiments, so that according to Edison the master molds could be made "cheaply in large quantities and so that the matrices would be very perfect and without flaw."[4]

While Wurth experimented with the master molds, Walter Miller, who was in charge of National Phonograph's mechanical duplicating plant but also conducted experiments on recording methods, and Jonas Aylsworth, Edison's wax expert, worked to improve the process for duplicating records from the molds. By 1900 these experiments produced a promising method known as the dipping process, on which Edison applied for the basic patent, but it was Miller and Aylsworth who took out the patents on crucial improvements that made it a commercial success. The new records, which played at a higher speed than the 100-thread standard, also used a new hard wax composition developed by Aylsworth. Although the publicity about the molded records ascribed their development to Edison's inventive genius, within the company the dipping method became known as the Miller and Aylsworth process.[5]

As the molded record process moved from experiment to commercial production, Edison placed Miller and Aylsworth in charge of a small manufacturing plant that began making about 500 molded records per day in February 1901 and soon reached a capacity of 2,000 per day. That fall they began operations in a larger plant, and by March 1902 they were turning out 10,000 records a day. The speed of manufacture was in marked contrast to the mechanical process, which produced about 30 records per day from a single master. When the large plant was at full capacity it could make up to 120 records per day from a single master and was capable of working with as many as 100 master molds, all of them with better sound quality than was possible with mechanical duplication. By the time National Phonograph began selling molded records in January 1902 there were over 122,000 ready for market. The new records were one of two improvements announced by the company in January 1902. Because the new records were of higher quality, Edison had improved the reproducers by developing a more sensitive mica diaphragm with a new form of sapphire needle. Sales of records and phonographs soon reached a new high. After holding steady at just over 41,000 in 1900 and 1901, phonograph production rose to nearly 80,000 in 1902 and over 112,000 the following year and the number of records produced increased from about 2 million a year between 1899 and 1901 to over 4 million in 1902 and 7.5 million in 1903.[6]

The growth of the phonograph business had been the result of a long period of innovation in the development of both a market and a technology suited for it. In the early years of the twentieth century, the phonograph and recordings remained sufficiently novel that National Phonograph could continue to lead the industry by relying on Edison's reputation for superior technology. To ensure this, Edison would devote some attention to developing better recording and reproducing technology made necessary by the improved quality of the records. Improvements in the machines themselves, however, were turned over to the laboratory staff, particularly Edward Aiken, Alexander Pierman, and Peter Weber, the general superintendent of the Phonograph Works, all of whom made important contributions to the engineering quality of Edison phonographs. Aylsworth also continued to work on improving record duplication and developing better wax compositions. The improved phonograph technology also enabled Edison to introduce a modified design for business use, but he turned over the subsequent development of this device to Charles Hibbard, who was hired specifically for this purpose. William Gilmore continued to run the National Phonograph Company, although Nelson Durand, a longtime Edison employee formerly associated with the Lamp Works, was placed in charge of the business phonograph. Edison's lead in the phonograph business would be challenged before the end of the decade, not by better technology but by consumer demands for more easily stored disc records and by a growing appreciation of sound recording as an art.

Edison had almost no involvement in his other major business, motion pictures, because they already had evolved into an art form and the important innovators were filmmakers, not the inventors of new technology. The most important figure in the Edison motion picture business was filmmaker Edwin Porter. Edison did, however, have an important role to play in defending his patents in the courts. A ferocious legal contest between Edison and his major competitor, the American Mutoscope and Biograph Company, led to a cross-licensing arrangement through the Motion Picture Patents Company they created in 1908. By this time, Porter's film style was seen as outmoded and lacking a coherent narrative flow, particularly in contrast to the work being done by directors such as D. W. Griffith at the Vitagraph Company. In 1909 Porter was demoted from his role as studio chief at the Edison company's Bronx Studio, and he soon left the company.

While the managers of the Edison company sought to improve the aesthetic quality of their films, Edison focused the work of his laboratory, which had undertaken almost no significant work on motion picture technology during the decade, on two innovations that they hoped would put the company into the forefront of picture making. Several researchers were hired to develop a process for producing color film, and Daniel Higham was hired specifically to work on a longtime interest of Edison's, the linking of motion pictures with the phonograph to produce sound film. The color film project ultimately failed, and the Edison kinetophone for talking pictures proved to be a commercial failure after its introduction in 1913. Edison's connection with these projects was primarily as research director. One of his few personal efforts to improve motion picture technology, on which he received a patent in 1910, was intended to reduce flicker when films were projected, but this device never came into commercial use.[7]

Although Edison devoted little of his own attention to his phonograph and motion picture businesses during the first decade of the twentieth century, they provided him a sizeable income that he would use as investment capital for his inventive work. After the commercial failure of the Ogden Works, Edison had begun to look for new fields for innovation that were more promising commercially. The first of his new endeavors was a direct outgrowth of the ore-milling venture. The most successful product of the Ogden Works had turned out to be the waste sand produced by the crushing and separation process. Although it sold for only twenty or twenty-five cents a ton, whereas ore concentrate generally went for $3.50 to $5.00 per ton, income from sand sales often exceeded those from ore. The sand was used for a variety of purposes. Initially, Edison sold it primarily to railroads for engine boxes and to some extent for building construction and asphalt paving, and in 1893 he began to screen the sand with different meshes for these purposes. To expand the market for this byproduct, he had Francis Upton make a survey of the suppliers of sand for cement building construction in the area around New York City. In August 1895 Upton reported that most of the readily available sand in the region was wet, whereas the Edison sand was dry, thus providing "an opening in N.Y. for sand of a definite mixture that will economize lime and cement and ship so that it will make a firm cement and mortar [while in] Elizabeth, Newark and Jersey City there is a ready market for sand at 60-70 cents per yard." In 1897–1898, as Edison tried to get the Ogden Works operating on a full-time basis, he found a ready market for his sand among several cement companies in New York and Pennsylvania.[8]

Portland cement was just emerging as a major building material in the 1890s and the industry was growing rapidly. Artificial cement had been developed in England earlier in the century and had gotten its name from its color, which was similar to that of Isle of Portland building stone. In the United States, the Portland cement industry did not emerge until after the Civil War, and natural cement continued to enjoy a better reputation and larger market through the 1890s until it became evident that Portland cement manufacturers could maintain more uniform quality and produce a cement that set harder and with more strength and durability than natural cement. By 1898, when Edison decided to investigate the possibility of manufacturing Portland cement, it was becoming the preferred building material and its production was on the verge of overtaking that of natural cement.

As it became apparent that they would be unable to raise the necessary funds for rebuilding the Ogden Works, Edison and Walter Mallory decided in late 1898 to explore the possibility of applying the expertise and machinery they had developed at Ogden to the production of Portland cement. The crushing and material handling machinery for ore milling could be readily adapted for this purpose, and Edison hoped as well that the cement plant would provide a testing ground for some of the improvements he believed necessary for the iron works. By the beginning of 1899 Edison had begun to study up on the cement industry, and accompanied by Mallory and Upton he visited several cement plants in the nearby Lehigh Valley, at that time the industry center. He also began to conduct several hundred assays of cement rock and limestone in New Jersey and Pennsylvania and soon settled on land near Stewartsville, New Jersey, about five miles northeast of Easton, Pa., on the Delaware, Lackawanna & Western Railroad, as offering the best site for his cement plant.[9]

Much of the money for the new venture came in part from a group of Philadelphia investors brought in by Pilling and Crane. In April 1899 they agreed to form the Edison Portland Cement Company with a capital stock of $11 million. The investors initially contributed $1 million, which was issued as preferred stock and was used to fund the erection and operation of the cement plant. In exchange for his patents and expertise, Edison received a majority share of the $9 million in common stock (there was another $1 million of preferred stock). William Shelmerdine, who along with Harlan Page was among the largest investors from Philadelphia, became the company's president, Mallory was appointed vice president, and William Pilling was named secretary-treasurer. Edison served as the company's general manager.[10]

From his investigations of the cement industry Edison concluded that "the quality of a cement depends upon two things. 1st The proper proportioning of the ingredients and burning. 2nd to fine grinding." He already had what he believed to be the best crushing and grinding technology in the world, and he selected the Stewartsville site to take advantage of it. The limestone and cement rock deposits at Stewartsville were in vertical shafts rather than flat as they were elsewhere in the region, and this allowed him to use the same methods as at Ogden to work the rock cheaply and in large quantities by blasting it with dynamite, loading it with steam shovels, and crushing it with his giant rolls. At the time, cement manufacturers ground to a fineness sufficient for passing 75 percent of the rock through a 200-mesh screen. Edison, however, believed that the standard should be 85 percent, and he redesigned his three-high rolls and screening process so that the requirement for such a fine grind would be "more than met."[11]

Although most of the technology for cement production could be adapted from his iron-concentrating plant, Edison quickly realized that the most crucial element of cement production was the roasting of the ground mixture of cement rock and limestone into a material known as clinker. At the time roasting usually was done in sixty-foot-long rotary kilns. From his investigation of the cement industry, however, Edison had concluded that "the sixty foot kiln is a rotten proposition. . . . I believe I can invent a kiln which will be very much more efficient in economy and have a much larger output."[12] The standard kiln produced about 150 to 200 barrels in twenty-four hours, and Edison planned to build one capable of producing 1,000 barrels in that time with much greater fuel efficiency. He planned to build a kiln twice the size of the standard one and to use two high-pressure coal guns to throw fuel and air into the kiln cylinder to produce overlapping areas of combustion and a larger roasting zone in which the clinkering could take place. In this way he could reduce the amount of coal consumed relative to the area of combustion while increasing the amount of material that could be burned. This design also allowed him better control of the temperature of the clinkering process.

Because the kiln was to be so long, Edison decided to make sections of cast rather than wrought iron, as was standard practice. He sketched out his ideas in January, and by March his staff had constructed a wooden model of a ten-foot-long section at the laboratory. Edison understood the value of starting small. As he explained, "many inventors try to develop things life-size, and thus spend all their money, instead of first experimenting on a small scale."[13] Scaling up, of course, always presented additional problems, but the knowledge he gained from model tests proved invaluable in solving these new difficulties. Edison used his model kiln to experiment with rotation speeds and lining materials and to study the flow of material through it before ordering a full-scale kiln in November. When the large kiln was finally ready in May 1900, after delays caused by difficulties in obtaining material, Edison and his staff found several problems that required design changes. These included the mechanism used to rotate the kiln, the paddles that fed raw material into it, and the coal guns that fired the kiln. Finally, before shipping it to the cement plant in October 1901, Edison decided to lengthen the kiln to 150 feet and ordered additional sections as well as a second kiln for the plant.

The cement works, too, began as a one-sixth scale wooden model built at the laboratory to Edison's specifications during the summer of 1899. Edison designed it so that most of the operations were carried out by automatic machinery. Like many other engineers and managers, Edison recognized that the costs of materials processing could be greatly reduced by designing a "rational factory." This was a lesson he had learned during the years of work at Ogden and that he applied at Stewartsville. Most of the machinery and processes he used in his cement works were the same as in his ore-milling plant: quarrying, crushing, drying, roasting, fine crushing, screening, and storage of materials. But Edison improved on many of them, notably the fine crushing rolls, the screening of the rock, and the conveyors used to move the material from the stockhouse. Furthermore, to ensure the proper mixture of rock and limestone that was so crucial to cement production, he also arranged for automatic machinery to sample, average, and mix the bulk materials.[14]

Erecting the cement plant began at the end of 1900 under the supervision of Mallory and chief engineer Edward Darling, a Columbia University mechanical engineer. Because of delays in acquiring steel and Edison's decision to increase the plant's capacity from 4,000 to 10,000 barrels per day, the last of the reinforced concrete buildings was just being completed at the time he shipped the first kiln from the laboratory in October 1901. Full-scale testing did not begin until the following summer, when Edison began to spend much of his time at the site, which had become known as New Village. It would be another year after the kiln arrived, however, before they finally began testing it.[15]

This photograph shows one of the first giant rotary kilns at Stewartsville and the mechanism used to turn it.

Getting the kiln to work properly at the mill required considerable additional testing and modification because of problems posed by its added length. Nonetheless, Edison's faith in his design was reinforced when he discovered that it had additional unanticipated advantages over standard rotary kilns. Because of the increased size of the clinkering zone, which exposed the cement material to heat for a longer time, he actually could reduce the temperature in the kiln. This effected a further savings in fuel costs, so that the kiln required only about seventy-five pounds of coal per barrel of clinker compared with about 120 pounds of coal in the standard sixty-foot kiln. Furthermore, Edison found that the added pressure on the cylinder lining from using five to seven times more material with only a slight increase in diameter from that of a standard kiln caused a protective coating to form, "several inches in thickness, which almost continuously covers the lining for that portion of the kiln that is subjected to the higher temperature" when the material was heated sufficiently to become "plastic and sticky," thus helping to reduce the maintenance costs of his kiln.[16]

Edison was convinced of the advantages of his long kiln, but he and Mallory had great difficulty in getting it to work to its full theoretical capacity. Plant testing was completed by the end of 1902, but workers were unable to produce more than 450 to 500 barrels of cement per day from the kiln during much of 1903. Mallory later recalled that "Edison was more than disappointed at this result. His terse comment on my report was: 'Rotten. Try it again.'" Although Mallory got production up to 650 barrels per day, Edison remained dissatisfied.

Mallory told Edison that he "would be very glad to have him tell us how to do it, and that we would run it any way he directed. He replied that he did not know what it was that kept the output down, but he was just as confident as ever that the kiln would make one thousand barrels per day, and that if he had time to work with and watch the kiln it would not take him long to find out the reasons why."[17]

Edison's comments pointed to one of the difficulties that he faced in making his cement mill a commercial success. Because it was such a radical departure from the industry practice, the best conditions for operating it could not be extrapolated from standard practice. Although Edison made suggestions throughout the trials, he was often occupied with other matters, particularly the development of the new storage battery, and Mallory and his staff had to learn from experience how best to operate the kilns. It took them about three years to reach Edison's desired capacity of 1,000 barrels per day.

The effort to increase kiln capacity encountered a major setback in early March 1903 when a fire broke out in the coal-grinding plant, resulting in the death of several workmen, including Darling. As a result of the fire, Edison, who had been in Fort Myers at the time, decided not only to close the mill and redesign the coal plant but also to make other changes in the cement works to simplify its operation. To carry this out, he had to convince the stockholders, who felt that further delay might endanger the financial health of the company, to increase the capital stock. Several of the stockholders, who were beginning to express "doubts as to the ultimate successful operation of [Edison's] innovations in the manufacture of cement," urged him to take a conservative approach and buy standard coal-grinding machinery rather than suffer additional expenses and delay while he redesigned the plant. Edison, as he had done often in the past, was able to convince his investors to rely on his judgment regarding technical matters.[18]

Edison saw the size, scale of the plant, and its extensive use of automatic machinery as long-term advantages. He believed that "large works can afford to experiment & keep up to date."[19] In the short-term, however, the scope of the undertaking caused immense problems. As he explained to the stockholders,

> The Engineer not only has great difficulty in adjusting it to the work to be done, but must teach the operators a new trade, substituting for instance, a highly organized machine worked by one man, to do the work of forty men and forty wheelbarrows, is not easy. It requires a lot of testing at full capacity to adjust this or that; to make changes here and there, and, moreover, it requires time.
>
> The time has not yet arrived when we can produce men so highly endowed that they can plan, make and put in operation machinery of this character and have it work the first time without a hitch.[20]

If some of the stockholders were dismayed by the delays and rising costs of the plant, the principal investors who sat as directors of the company agreed with Robert Thompson, who declared that even with all the delays he was not discouraged as to the eventual outcome. I have never changed my opinion, that if our quarry has the right stuff (and I am assured that it has) we have more than an ordinary business chance of great success, but we must make up our minds that no limit can be set as to the time. As it appears to me, the broad, comprehensive plans of Mr. Edison are everywhere in evidence in this undertaking, and I believe it has great merit and is as capable of great success as many other great enterprises originating with him, have had. I do not know of any of his enterprises (the iron mine proposition probably excepted) that, when backed by loyalty, sufficient means, and *business* management, has not been an unusual success.[21]

Edison's reputation helped to keep his investors in line, but as the delays and expenses mounted, even these men began to waiver and Edison himself took on more of the financial burden of the cement works.

The next three years were a continual struggle to get the cement works operating to full capacity. A host of minor and major troubles plagued the plant and required additional modifications, and Edison also continually looked for ways to reduce costs by improving the machinery. As he explained to William Mason, who had replaced Darling as chief engineer, "the only way to keep ahead of the procession is to experiment. If you don't, the other fellow will. When there's no experimenting there's no progress. Stop experimenting and you go backward. If anything goes wrong, experiment until you get to the very bottom of the trouble." Edison received regular reports from the works and frequently suggested small changes to save costs. For example, he discovered that they were spending considerable sums on the brushes used on the conveyors and suggested testing a less expensive fiber for them. In another instance he suggested a modification in the oiling system at the plant that might "save a mill per barrel based on your regular daily output."[22] A pencil note to Emil Herter, one of Edison's draftsmen who was a key assistant at both Ogden and New Village, provides a typical example of his suggestions. Learning from Mallory that oil was leaking out of the bearings of a new roller, he wrote,

> I can tell you what we can do in the event that we *cant* stop the oil coming out & that is a supplemental chamber with an extra overflow pipe to drain it & a scraper of shaft to cause oil to fall off into the supplemental chamber which can be small— Thus this oil biz is important, you better go down & see Mason show him this sketch & try & learn cause & write me about proposed remedy— I will also think it over & write you anything I can think of— With the sketch, we would never get dirt into the inner oil chamber—perhaps a bit of canvas over the supplemental chamber put on same as we had at Edison & on main shafts at Cement would even keep the oil free of grit & only allow float to get into the supplemental chamber.

As he finished describing this modification, Edison became excited that it might prove a permanent solution and added a postscript: "The more I think of this supplemental chamber the more I like it."[23]

As was so frequently the case during his career, Edison seemed to be able to find solutions to problems that stumped his experts on the scene. One of the key difficulties with cement manufacture was to produce a finished product with the proper hygroscopic qualities. Cement was tested by boiling it, and any cement that did not pass this test had to be aged for several months to absorb enough moisture. However, this increased costs. After a series of poor boiling tests in early 1906 the cement works hired a new chemist who seemed to solve the problem by increasing the amount of lime used in the cement. However, when the problem recurred the following December, Mallory and the chemist, Dr. H. E. Kiefer, were forced to turn to Edison, who soon solved the problem by developing a method to artificially season the cement in a matter of hours. This prompted Mallory to call Edison's improvement "the greatest one since the present fine grinding rolls were developed. . . . We will have absolute control of our cement at all seasons of the year and be able to ship the most reliable and uniform cement going from any plant in the country."[24]

By 1907 the cement works was regularly producing fine cement, and Edison's most important innovation—the long rotary kiln—had been shown to be such a significant advance that other companies began to adopt it. Although the Edison Portland Cement Company soon became one of the nation's largest producers of cement, it struggled to make a sufficient profit to pay off the large fixed costs of the plant and of the research and development that had gone into designing the technology it employed. Although the long kiln reduced the costs of production for cement manufacturers, it also exacerbated a problem of overproduction in the industry, which helped to keep prices low. The Edison cement business, because of its seasonal nature and highly competitive business environment, never became a large profit maker and often lost money. Edison joined with other eastern manufacturers in the Portland Cement Association to prevent ruinous competition and encourage cooperation within the industry. To stimulate the use of cement they promoted its use in all types of buildings, and Edison himself attempted to develop a process for making low-cost cement houses. The industry continued to suffer throughout the 1910s, particularly during World War I, and it only really revived after the war. The Edison Portland Cement Company did not become profitable until 1922, but throughout most of the 1920s it was moderately successful and remained one of the country's largest producers of cement.[25]

The high cost of innovation caused Edison's own cement business to struggle for many years, but the technology he developed for it was quickly adopted by other manufacturers. His kiln was regarded as a major technical breakthrough in the cement industry. From his experience in ore milling Edison had also introduced quarrying methods, fine grinding, and the idea of reducing costs by processing large amounts of raw material with automatic machinery. His quarrying techniques were soon adopted, but there was more resistance to his crushing and grinding technology. The manager of the Lehigh Portland Cement Company, for example, complained to Edison in 1905 "at the bad precedent you are making in calling to the attention of the public that you are grinding finer than any one else. All manufacturers of course will have to follow in line, it is not going to give you a cent more for your cement, nor do Architects and Engineers ask for such a fineness, and therefore we should have thought it would have been better for you to have made a cement similar to our own, and thus be the gainer in the cost of manufacture."[26] Nonetheless, finer grinding became common and Edison also received royalties from licensing his crushing technology, which was marketed for several years by the Edison Crushing Roll Company, for use in mines and by producers of rock products, including cement manufacturers.

Edison's innovative effort in cement manufacturing was largely a continuation of the line of development he had begun with his ore-milling venture. Most of the work involved building and testing machinery and designing the cement plant itself. Although Edison was responsible for designing this machinery and for the innovations they embodied, he did not spend most of his time in the day-to-day work of the plant. Instead, during the development years, he devoted his own time primarily to another experimental endeavor, his attempt to produce a revolution in personal transportation by developing a new storage battery that would make electric cars cheap and feasible alternatives to gasoline-powered automobiles. In 1895 the first practical gasoline-powered cars began to appear, and Americans started their romance with the automobile. Edison joined the craze, declaring that "the horse is doomed . . . the horseless vehicle is the coming wonder," and he even conducted some experiments with a motorized tricycle. At the time he expressed doubts that they could be run by electric batteries, although he did think it possible that "an electrical storage battery will be discovered which will prove more economical" than gasoline. Four years later he was devoting his own energies to making this possible.[27]

Edison had long been skeptical about the commercial prospects of rechargeable storage batteries. He had investigated them extensively in the early 1880s, particularly to use in isolated electric lighting plants where the generator could be run during the day to store electricity in the batteries that would then run lamps at night. In both isolated and central station plants batteries could also be used to even out fluctuating current and prolong lamp life. Edison's own experiments and investigations of existing storage batteries convinced him that they were "a catch-penny, a sensation, a mechanism for swindling by stock companies."[28] Most American electrical engineers agreed with him, and storage batteries played little role in the early lighting industry in the United States, although they were used to a greater extent in Britain where small installations for private residences were common. In the late 1880s and early 1890s, storage batteries began to be used in central stations to balance the load factor between day and night as a way of increasing operating efficiency, and by 1895 they appeared in increasing numbers in American central stations. Four years later Edison changed his mind about storage batteries and their feasibility for powering vehicles. In May of that year, when several electric automobiles were exhibited at the annual Electrical Exhibition in New York, newspapers reported that Edison planned to develop his own inexpensive electric automobile. In fact, he was not working on an automobile but on a storage battery to power it.[29]

The design of storage batteries relied on a phenomenon of electrochemical polarization that occurred when ions in the battery electrolyte migrated to the electrodes and impeded the passage of the current. Standard wet cell primary batteries, such as those Edison had used in telegraphy, utilized two different materials so that current flowed when chemical oxidation, caused by a reaction between the positive electrode and the chemical electrolyte, produced positively charged ion particles that migrated to the negative electrode, where another reaction known as chemical reduction caused them to adhere to the negative electrode, which became positively charged. These chemical reactions exhausted the active properties of the electrolyte and eventually destroyed the electrodes. As a result, both the electrodes and the electrolytes had to be frequently changed. Storage batteries rely on a passive system of polarization that generates electric current without consuming the electrodes and exhausting the electrolyte. When a storage battery is charged, a chemical reaction oxidizes the positive pole and reduces the negative pole. This chemical reaction is reversed during discharge and the positive plate gives up its oxygen while the negative pole becomes oxidized. Because the chemical reaction can be reversed without exhausting the electrodes and electrolyte, storage batteries can be charged and discharged many times. The problem facing automobile battery designers was to prevent the battery from losing its electrical capacity after being charged and recharged several times, to find a way to maintain the charge for a sufficient period of time, and to rapidly recharge the battery while at the same time producing enough power so that the size and weight of the battery did not become drawbacks.

The first commercial storage batteries used acid electrolytes like those employed in primary batteries, but they required electrodes that would not readily corrode. Lead proved to be the most inert and inexpensive electrode material for use in acid-electrolyte storage batteries, but it had serious drawbacks when used for automobile batteries. The most obvious disadvantage was due to the density of lead, which made the batteries extremely heavy. The weight of lead-acid batteries relative to their electrical output made them significantly less economical than gasoline as a power source for automobiles and also required more sturdily built and expensive vehicles. Furthermore, these batteries required frequent and careful charging and recharging. As he set out to develop a storage battery that would make electric automobiles competitive with those powered by gasoline, Edison determined that he had to design one that would be cheap, have a "large storage capacity" relative to its weight, require "no attention" from users and be capable of "withstanding careless treatment," not deteriorate during use, and be rapidly recharged. Aware of the problems with lead-acid batteries, Edison decided to experiment with alkaline electrolytes to develop a lightweight and long-lasting battery.[30]

Edison was already familiar with alkaline primary batteries, which had emerged during the 1880s for consumer electric appliances such as doorbells, fans, and sewing machines. He had experimented with copper-oxide batteries to power his new electric phonograph and eventually acquired American rights to a zinc and copper-oxide battery developed by French inventors Felix de La-lande and Georges Chaperon for this purpose. It turned out that customers preferred lead storage batteries for the phonograph because they did not have to change the electrodes and replenish the electrolytes. However, the Edison Manufacturing Company did manufacture and sell the Edison-Lalande battery for its electric fans and other small electrical devices, including telephones. Two former employees of the Edison Machine Works saw the potential of the Lalande-Chaperon battery and formed the Waddell-Entz Manufacturing Company, which produced a rechargeable zinc and copper-oxide storage battery for electric trolleys. Ultimately, this battery proved inadequate for the task. It was not sufficiently lighter than lead, was no more durable, and often could not be recharged when it was discharged at too high a rate. Finally, zinc proved to be too soluble and often failed to replate properly during charging. Nonetheless, the Waddell-Entz battery provided a starting point for other researchers, including Edison.[31]

When he began his research on a storage battery for electric vehicles in 1899, Edison conducted extensive experiments with zinc-copper batteries. He directed this research toward reaching a deeper understanding of the chemical and mechanical design of alkaline batteries. Like so much of Edison's work, ranging from automatic telegraphy to electric lamps to phonograph cylinders, this involved testing a variety of materials and compounds to find out how they acted under the particular operating conditions created in a storage battery and to determine the optimal conditions in an alkaline cell. He therefore had his researchers test a variety of copper compounds, mix additives with the copper and zinc, and try different methods of packing them into plates for use as electrodes.[32] After six months they also began to experiment with silver oxide as a depolarizer and to use potassium hydroxide, which would serve as the basic electrolyte in all of Edison's batteries, in place of sodium hydroxide. Edison arrived at the same conclusion as other experimenters working on alkaline batteries: zinc was too soluble for use in a storage battery.

Edison was certainly aware that the problem of replating zinc had been "met in practice by other experimenters with batteries of this type and ha[d] so far been insurmountable."[33] In one of his first patent applications on a reversible storage battery, filed in October 1900, Edison suggested the use of magnesium as a support for the zinc electrode as a way of solving this problem, but his own research had already led him in a different direction. He decided to replace the zinc with more insoluble materials. In making this shift, Edison was probably influenced by the work of the man who would prove to be his closest rival. Swedish chemist Waldemar Jungner had begun by working on zinc-copper batteries in the mid-1890s, but he had given up the use of zinc by 1897. In his 1899 patent, which included the use of silver oxide as a depolarizer, he had indicated that both cadmium and iron were good conductors of electricity, porous, insoluble in the electrolyte, and formed hydroxides on discharge. In his own tests of over fifty metals and minerals in alkaline solutions during the summer of 1900, Edison also found cadmium to be among the most insoluble, and he filed an application in October for a cadmium-copper design that he believed would prove to be "be a good solution to the light storage battery."[34]

Edison's cadmium-copper battery proved to have one crucial drawback that prevented him from moving it into commercial production. With a raw material cost of about $1.20 per pound for cadmium he could not compete with lead battery manufacturers who paid only about 4¢ a pound for lead. Having found what he believed to be a good technical solution, Edison initially tried an old solution to overcome its economic drawbacks: he began searching for large deposits of cadmium ore as he had once searched for plentiful and cheap supplies of platinum for his lamps. Unable to find a cheap supply of cadmium, Edison was soon forced to abandon its use.

As he turned away from cadmium in December 1900, Edison also abandoned the use of copper oxide as a depolarizer. Edison and other researchers had discovered that the copper oxide produced a small amount of copper salt that was soluble in the electrolyte and produced local action on the electrode and caused it to deteriorate. Although his application for the cadmium-copper battery included what he believed to be a solution to this problem, Edison could not overcome it entirely. Silver oxide presented a similar problem for Jungner, and he abandoned it at about the same time as Edison turned away from copper oxide.

Edison soon designed another promising alkaline battery. He had "discovered by experiment" that both nickel and cobalt oxide were basically insoluble in an alkaline electrolyte and that both "gave nearly the same voltage in use." However, he considered cobalt not "as desirable for use as nickel, owing to its greater cost and to the fact that it is slightly soluble." For the other pole of his new battery Edison used iron because it too had cost advantages. However, as he explained in his patent application, his "attempts to utilize iron as the oxidizable element in an alkaline reversible battery were for a long time frustrated" and "only after exhaustive experiments" did he arrive at a way to use finely divided iron so that it was converted into insoluble ferric oxide during electrolytic oxidation.[35] In turning to iron and nickel Edison followed a path similar to Jungner's, but he considered the design shown in Jungner's patents as worthless "because they are based on theory & actual experiments will prove his patents bad in every particular." Edison would eventually prevail over Jungner in their crucial U.S. and German patent battles.[36]

Convinced that he had found the right materials for his battery by the beginning of February 1901, Edison arranged with Herman Dick, the son of

A. B. Dick, to form a company. They incorporated the Edison Storage Battery Company at the end of May with a capital stock of $1 million. Wanting to retain control of the company and still obtain the necessary funds to continue development work and manufacture the battery, Edison arranged to have all of the company's stock issued to him in exchange for his patents while the company raised its working capital by issuing $500,000 worth of 6 percent mortgage bonds. Edison would then give bond purchasers stock equal to 50 percent of their par value (that is, $250,000 worth of his shares) while he retained the voting power on this stock until they subscribed the remaining 50 percent. Among the principal investors in the battery company were several men who had already invested in the Edison Portland Cement Company, including Mallory, Pilling, Theron Crane, and Shelmerdine. Edison also gave Dick the power to negotiate foreign rights, and Dick soon left for Europe. There he initiated discussions with powerful financial interests, including the Morgan banking houses, regarding English and French rights. In the fall of 1902 Dick and Edison arranged with Sigmund Bergmann to organize a German company backed by the Deutsches Bank, and Bergmann began to establish a factory to manufacture the battery there.[37]

While Dick brought together investors for the battery, Edison and Jonas Aylsworth continued to refine its design and to plan for its production. In July 1901 Edison asked his trusted assistant Emil Herter, who had been involved in the design of the iron ore and cement works, to "take charge of the placing and arranging of the Silver Lake Chemical Works" where the battery would be manufactured.[38] Two years would go by before regular production of the batteries began at the new works, because Edison found it necessary to make changes in the mechanical construction of his battery and to further reduce its weight. He and his staff also designed special machinery to automate production and reduce manufacturing costs. Concerned about the cost of nickel, Edison once again conducted a search for cheap and plentiful supplies that led him to form the Mining Exploration Company, which conducted magnetic surveys and drilling operations in the Sudbury district of Ontario under the direction of his brother-in-law John V. Miller. Because Edison had to get the machinery operating properly and coordinate production at the battery plant at the same time he was engaged in a similar campaign at the cement works, both plants suffered delays and neither began regular production on time.

Battery manufacturing finally started in January 1903, but production problems plagued the plant until August when Edison reported to Dick, "We have had a —— of a time getting our iron filling machine to work, but at last we have got it doing 85% which is commercially perfect this removes the last obstacle to progress— We are mfg at rate of 20 cells daily and are getting things in shape so that within 2 or 3 weeks we shall turn out 50 soon 100."[39] Regular production and delivery of cells apparently did not begin until 1904. By October the factory was producing over two hundred cells per day, and Edison planned to install additional machinery to further reduce manufacturing costs and increase production to over three hundred cells a day. By late November the factory had produced about 37,000 cells in three sizes, designated E-18, E-27, and E-45, each with a different weight and power output as well. Placed in trays holding two to eight cells each, several cells together made up the battery for a vehicle and the type and number used depended on the size and weight of the vehicle.

Edison had begun his publicity campaign nearly three years before he started regular battery production. In May 1901 he talked about it in newspaper interviews, and his former assistant Arthur Kennelly read a technical paper on the battery before a meeting of the American Institute of Electrical Engineers in New York City. Edison had drafted this paper for Kennelly, but as always he shied away from making the public presentation himself. He was always more comfortable chatting up reporters, who almost invariably came away from their encounter to write glowing reports of the wizard's newest wonder. Edison continued to use the press to maintain interest in his new battery while manufacturing problems delayed its commercial introduction. Part of his publicity campaign centered around rigorous road tests—sending automobiles powered by his batteries over poor roads and up the steep hills near the laboratory—and dropping the batteries out of second- and third-story windows. In the spring of 1902 he planned an even more extensive and widely publicized set of road tests, after which he expected to begin offering them for sale to the public. As the Edison Storage Battery Company informed one prospective customer:

> We are about to start a test of batteries by operating them in several types of automobiles, ranging in size from a small runabout to a three ton truck. We propose to run these automobiles over average New Jersey roads and shall continue the tests until the batteries have each made 5,000 miles. We shall expect the batteries to go through these tests and be in as good condition at the end as they are at the beginning of the run. We shall operate them daily, both day and night until the tests are completed. When we have accomplished this, our factory will probably be in such shape that we can turn out daily a reasonable number of batteries for the market and the output will thereafter be rapidly increased. We will place your name on our mailing list and send you catalogues and printed matter as soon as we are ready.[40]

Edison's battery fared very well in these road tests, which led him to make typically bold claims for his new invention. "These batteries," he told reporters, "will run for 100 miles or more without recharging. They can be charged in a few hours. They require no attention for all that is needed to replenish the liquor is to pour in a little water now and then to take the place of that which has evaporated. I do not know how long it would take to wear out one of the batteries, for we have not yet been able to exhaust the possibilities of one of them. But I feel sure one will last longer than four or five automobiles." In the July 1902 issue of the *North American Review*, Edison claimed that he had achieved the "final perfection of the storage battery" that would mark the advent of the electric automobile.[41]

Once his batteries reached the market in 1903, Edison continued his media campaign by focusing on their technical advantages over the lead batteries of his competitors, which he believed would offset the higher price of the Edison battery. In particular, he claimed that his battery, unlike those using lead, was practically maintenance free and did not use hazardous and foul-smelling acids. Encouraged by positive road tests, and Edison's claims, and in the hope that the inventor's reputation would help boost their own sales, several car and truck manufacturers worked with him to adapt their vehicles to fit the larger Edison battery.

Not everyone was convinced that Edison had achieved the major breakthrough that he claimed. The leading automobile journals, *Outing*, *Overland Monthly*, and *Motor World*, all expressed considerable skepticism that the day of the electric automobile was now at hand. They certainly would have agreed with the conclusion of an article in a German technical journal that "a revolution in the making of Accumulators [batteries], has not been caused by the Edison Apparatus, as it is wished for in the interest of the Automobile Industry." In October 1902 the British *Electrician* commented that "English engineers have read in the lay press so many ridiculous stories of 1,000-mile runs and of unnecessarily strenuous tests and records that they are beginning to grow skeptical." This issue of the journal contained the summary of a favorable report on the Edison battery by W. Hibbert of the London Polytechnic, considered one of the leading experts on storage batteries, but as the *Electrician* pointed out the Edison battery's output of 11.8 watt-hours per cell was "nothing extraordinary and has been exceeded by numerous lead cells." In fact, the energy-to-weight ratios of the three types of Edison batteries were about the same or only slightly better than that of the leading iron battery, the Exide, sold by the Electric Storage Battery Company. The *Electrician* concluded, in a statement that would prove prophetic, that "we still have to learn how the [Edison] cell will stand the wear and tear of the road" after it was "run under working conditions for six months or a year."[42]

As it turned out, the Edison battery did not fare at all well under those conditions. After several months of service consumers discovered two serious defects. The first evident problem was that the batteries leaked because the caustic electrolyte ate through the outer can's soldered seams. Even more seriously, customers began to complain that the Edison battery lost much of its electrical capacity after being charged and discharged several times. Although Edison quickly found that he could bring these batteries "back to their original capacity by [heating and] reversing the current . . . for 15 hours," he recognized that "this is not convenient for the public."[43] Just as he had begun making plans to expand production in November 1904, Edison decided instead that it would be best to shut down production of new batteries while he solved the problems plaguing the old ones and redesigned the tools used in their manufacture.

Edison and his staff thought they had solved the leakage problem by welding the cans instead of soldering them, but as Edison explained to Bergmann in November, "the welded cans in Wagons outside developed entirely too many leaks, pretty near every can showed exceedingly fine hair like holes which was so small that no liquid showed but what came though came so slowly that the potash evaporated as fast as liquid leaked & left the side seam with little white patches some seams would show 6 to 8 white spots others only one. We are experimenting to get best way to solder the welded seam, as 99 percent is welded good & strong we think that by soldering in addition that they will hold for years." By January, one of his machinists had designed a machine for this purpose, and by the end of February, after making and testing several hundred welded batteries, Edison was convinced that "our welded cans now are perfect."[44]

The other problem was an unexplained loss of capacity in some of the cells. In late November 1904 Edison had two of the laboratory's rooms specially "fitted up" for this purpose, and working with a staff of eighteen men and boys "day & night" he experimented to find a solution. Edison told Bergmann in January, "I hope to write you shortly that we have found the reason for the loss of capacity," but he found this to be a difficult problem to resolve. By March he had finally determined that the deterioration in the battery's electrical capacity was due to the nickel-oxide plates, and he set about redesigning the electrode. William Gilmore reported to Bergmann in June that "Mr. Edison has made over 10,000 different experiments on these last changes and is still continuing to make other experiments, so that you can readily appreciate that the combined work of Aylsworth and himself has been anything but a small job." Edison was optimistic, however, "that the battery is going to be a great deal better than he or Aylsworth ever supposed it would be."[45]

Edison and Aylsworth had discovered that the active material in the electrode tended to change its contact with the conducting shells of the pocket during charge and discharge, which caused its resistance to increase and thus lower the capacity of the battery cell. Therefore, they designed a new pocket "in the form of small perforated tubes with closed ends and containing the active material under pressure" to ensure better contact.[46] Their experiments also suggested that cobalt flakes would help maintain better contact between the active material and the conducting shells than had the graphite flake they had been using. Cobalt, however, was more susceptible to destruction by the electrolyte, and Edison developed a spongy composite of nickel and cobalt that prevented this. At the end of July 1905 he jubilantly informed Bergmann that the new battery design appeared to be a complete success: "The weight per horsepower has been greatly reduced. The new cell I speak of gives 48.8 pounds per horse power at 5 hour charge & 37 pounds on the long charge— This beats anything on record with the addition that there is a certainty that the battery will last for years."[47]

Unfortunately, cobalt was an expensive material that was not readily available in commercial quantities. Nonetheless, Edison optimistically expected that his new battery would be a commercial success, telling Bergmann that even though the battery used more expensive materials, with its "increased capacity we shall have very much more profit."[48] He soon discovered, however, that finding a plentiful supply of cobalt for the battery would not be as easy as he thought, and he once again conducted an extensive search for mines containing the metal. As he had done years before during his search for platinum, he sent circular letters to telegraph operators in mining districts telling them where to find the metal and asking them to collect ore samples in their spare time and send them to him for assay. Late in 1905 he acquired a Canadian cobalt mine and made arrangements to purchase the metal from other mines in the region. He also began to establish a chemical works for processing it. After becoming frustrated with his Canadian sources Edison began to look at mines in the southern United States, and during the summer of 1906 he personally made an extensive journey there to prospect for cobalt. In the fall, convinced that he had finally found abundant supplies of the material, Edison began construction of a new storage battery factory directly across from the laboratory where he planned to soon begin turning out 1,000 per day. By the following February, however, Edison had grown so disgusted with the difficulty of obtaining cobalt "at a price I could use it & make a cent, that I have stopped constructing & abandoned Cobalt Works & will not in the future use it. I am progressing towards accomplishing results by other means."[49] By this time he had discovered that he could use nickel flake rather than the nickel-cobalt alloy, and he developed a process for making the flakes exceedingly thin so that they would not displace too much nickel hydroxide from the small tube pockets. In addition he found that by adding a small amount of lithium hydroxide to his potassium hydroxide solution the capacity of the nickel hydroxide could be substantially increased and maintained for a longer time.

In July 1907, confident that he had finally developed a superior, long-lasting battery, Edison informed the directors of Bergmann's Deutsche Edison Accumulator Company that "the new battery is now entirely commercial & if made correctly will be satisfactory & advise that you go ahead with a small output and gradually increase it after [attaining] the proper familiarity with the construction of good cells." He also agreed to allow the company to sell batteries in England and France until he could arrange for factories there. This was a relief to Bergmann, who had written Edison in April, "I have made up my mind to take a run over to America and find out what chances there are about the new battery. I cannot any longer pacify the [company's] shareholders."[50]

After Edison developed his nickel-cobalt plate, production of E-cells with the new plate resumed at his Glen Ridge plant and Bergmann also began to manufacture them at his German factory. No production figures are available for Bergmann's plant, but the Glen Ridge factory produced nearly 19,000 cells. In the United States Edison batteries continued to be used in over 300 delivery trucks operated by firms such as Tiffany & Company of New York, the Central Brewing Co. of East St. Louis, and Montgomery & Ward of Chicago. The Adams Express Company, whose president was a good friend of Edison's, used about 100 vehicles powered by Edison batteries, and reported in October 1906 that "from their previous experience [these] cells are very much cheaper to operate in the long run, and they would not use the lead battery at any price."[51] By replacing old batteries with new ones using the new electrode, Edison was able to test it under actual operating conditions. He also kept loyal customers for the day when his new, improved battery finally became available.

Edison had hoped to begin manufacturing the nickel-flake battery in early 1908, but he found it necessary to conduct further experiments and to design new production machinery that delayed manufacturing for over a year. Full-scale production did not begin until 1910. Increasingly conscious of the role of manufacturing as a crucial element of innovation, Edison took great care in designing the battery factory at West Orange and the special-purpose machinery used in it as well as developing new techniques to process the nickel and iron powder at his chemical works in Silver Lake. These would prove crucial to ensuring the quality and durability of the battery and reducing its production costs.[52]

As a result of the manufacturing delays, Bergmann's shareholders again became restless. Unwilling to ask them for the money needed to build the new machine for producing nickel flake, and unable to begin production of the improved battery without it, Bergmann wrote Edison in July 1910, "They are getting very 'ugly' now, and talking about sueing me for getting them to subscribe for the Stock for the Deutsche Edison Akkumulatoren Company under false pretenses, and I know if you will help me that we can quiet them down, and probably show them that they have not spent their money in vain." Edison, however, suggested that Bergmann spend his own money for this purpose. To which Bergmann replied, "I want to tell you that I have only a certain amount of money to spend, and I have already invested over one million marks in your battery out of my own pocket, not counting the money I have paid, before I made the contract with you, to Dick and yourself. I am not squealing, but I cannot do any more and invest any more money than I have already done. I cannot pacify my stockholders as easily as you could yours at the time when you had to take over this whole business and fight it out with your own money."[53]

Edison, unlike Bergmann, did not have to answer to restless stockholders. In fact, he had not even called a stockholders' meeting until October 1908. By keeping control of the Edison Storage Battery Company in his own hands Edison remained free to halt manufacturing until he was satisfied that he had found the answer to the problems plaguing the battery. This meant, however, that he spent $1.5 million of his own money out of a total of $2.5 million to develop the battery and build manufacturing facilities; $43,000 of this he wasted prospecting for nickel and cobalt. Bergmann's shareholders finally agreed to raise additional capital after they were reassured by Heinrich Kammerhoff, a company director who had visited Edison's plant, and by a letter from Edison about the potential profits to be made from the new battery.[54]

Edison's delay in bringing the battery to market had unfortunate consequences. In 1904–1905, the Morgan banking houses in England and France were both prepared to back manufacturing companies in those countries and even went so far as to draft contracts. By the time Edison was finally manufacturing his improved battery in 1910, the British firm decided that because of "improvements in Gasolene Engines on the one hand, and the cheapness of horse traction in London and other large cities here, we have felt doubtful of the special adaptability of your Battery to conditions in this country. Whereas we understand that in the United States and elsewhere the Battery has conclusively proved its usefulness, we do not feel certain that the same success could be expected here."[55] Edison agreed that there seemed little prospect for the battery business in England. The following year the French firm also declined to take up the battery, and Edison instead made arrangements with John F. Monnot of Paris to market batteries made at the West Orange plant in both England and France. In the meantime matters were not progressing well at all in Germany and Bergmann decided to sell out his interest in the German company.

The new battery cells, designated as type A, were a decided improvement over the old E-cells. They produced a higher output, and with roughly comparable weights they were considerably more efficient and economical even at a slightly higher price. Although the average charging time of the new cells was considerably higher than the old ones, they actually improved their performance in use. Furthermore, if they were charged for ten hours the A-cells increased their output by as much as 30 percent, although this did require more charging current and caused excessive heating, which meant that distilled water had to be added to the cells more frequently than when they were charged normally.[56]

Once he had a reliable battery, Edison struggled to gain market share from the lead batteries that had been powering electric vehicles since the beginning. Furthermore, in response to Edison's new battery, the Electric Storage Battery Company of Philadelphia, the most important of Edison's lead battery competitors, brought out a new version of its well-regarded Exide battery, which it called the "Ironclad" even though it contained no iron. A fierce battle for the electric vehicle market ensued. Electric Storage Battery had a significant head start in the pleasure vehicle market, which it continued to dominate through its relationships with the major vehicle manufacturers and because of the lower cost of its batteries. The main advantage of the Edison alkaline battery was its greater durability, which even at higher cost (about twice that of a lead battery) produced long-term savings for businesses using electric trucks. Owners of pleasure vehicles were much less concerned with amortizing their investment over time and tended to focus on the initial cost of their automobiles. Furthermore, pleasure vehicle manufacturers were reluctant to redesign their vehicles to hold the larger Edison battery and to protect it from cold weather, which reduced the battery's efficiency. The Edison battery had only about a 25 percent share of the pleasure vehicle market by 1914, but it powered over half of all electric trucks. Edison, in fact, attempted to design and manufacture an electric truck specially designed for his battery, although he eventually gave up this project. He also supported the work of engineer Ralph Beach to develop streetcars using the Edison battery, but after a promising start this venture failed as well.[57]

The competition to provide batteries for electric vehicles took place in a market that was losing ground to gasoline vehicles. Although Edison blamed the lead battery, the real cause was a failure on the part of both vehicle and battery manufacturers to recognize that they could not compete with gasoline vehicles for touring or for rural communities. Perhaps if their makers had focused on the urban market, the use of electric vehicles might not have declined so precipitously and might even have grown. However, Henry Ford's introduction of the Model T at the end of 1908, which made available a low-priced, high-quality, gas-powered automobile and worked a revolution in the industry, marked the beginning of the end for electric automobiles. After the appearance of the self-starter for gasoline engines in 1912, electrics lost one of their greatest advantages over gasoline vehicles, which caused the number of electric trucks to begin a rapid decline as well. Because self-starters required the higher voltage produced by the lead battery, Edison was never able to compete for the immense market that developed in starter batteries, although he spent a decade attempting to develop a suitable alkaline battery with extensive funding from Ford, a great admirer who became his closest friend during the last two decades of Edison's life.[58]

The alkaline battery never saw much use in the market for which Edison had originally designed it, consumer automobiles. Instead, Edison set to work "creating new uses for the battery" and within a short time was selling them for a variety of industrial applications, including railroad signals and switches, lighting for ships and railway cars, submarines, ship radios, backup power for central stations, isolated house lighting, miner's lamps, and electric trucks. Over the years the Edison Storage Battery Company, which was earning about $25,000 per month by the end of 1912, continued to prosper in these markets.[59] The battery, in fact, would soon replace the phonograph as the foundation of Edison's business empire. However, the decade-long effort required to introduce his new methods of cement manufacture and the new battery had taken a heavy toll not only on Edison's finances, which led to a corporate reorganization, but also on his health, which caused him to retire from the business of innovation.

CHAPTER 22

Edison Incorporated

Two decades devoted to major innovations in ore milling, cement, batteries, and sound recording finally wore Edison down, and his health began to suffer. On February 11, 1907, his sixtieth birthday, he announced his intention to "give up the commercial end . . . and work in my laboratory as a scientist."[1] He planned to study electrical and chemical phenomena that he had encountered during his years as an inventor but had never found the time to investigate fully. Two years earlier Edison had undergone an ear operation, and in February 1908 he underwent two serious operations for an acute abscess in the same ear. He also suffered from damage to his eyes and stomach caused by X-ray research that had caused the death of his assistant Clarence Dally, who had had both arms amputated in an effort to slow the effects of the X-rays before he died in 1904. Another longtime Edison employee, his private secretary and one of the old Menlo Park boys, John Randolph, driven by the stress of juggling Edison's financial and other business affairs, committed suicide a few days before the first of Edison's ear operations in 1908. Edison himself was the one who prevented Randolph's widow from taking her own life when he arrived at the Randolph house after hearing of his secretary's suicide.

The stresses in Edison's personal life were compounded by his international celebrity. Although it had helped him immensely in his inventive and business efforts, by the end of the first decade of the twentieth century, the fame he had achieved from his inventive accomplishments was beginning to give way to a more uncertain celebrity. Increasingly, he and other members of his family appeared in the newspapers simply because Edison himself was well-known and often in the news. By the teens Edison's children were so used to being the subjects of press notice that when Charles passed a mathematics examination, a subject in which he did poorly at MIT, he joked that he was "astonished that the papers have not published the result of my examination."[2] This shift from fame to celebrity was part of a more general phenomenon affecting other well-known people as well.

During the nineteenth century those who achieved renown were regarded generally as models for emulation, but by the beginning of the twentieth century the rise of media-made celebrities caused famous people to be viewed more ambiguously. The growing disparity between rich and poor in the late nineteenth century made fame and fortune something to be envied as much as emulated. The rise of ransom kidnapping during this era was a symptom of this shift, and Edison was not immune. In 1901 his daughter Madeleine was threatened by a kidnapping plot. Although this did not progress beyond threatening letters Edison was concerned enough to hire Pinkerton detectives, and the family remained apprehensive for several months until the culprit was caught and confessed. Madeleine's governess became so distraught at the threat that she left the family's employ and later committed suicide. A sense of public envy was also apparent in threats against Edison himself. In 1901 the night watchman at the laboratory was attacked by a man who threatened the inventor, and in 1905 Frank Dyer, Richard Dyer's brother, reported that Edison was "continuously being annoyed by letters from cranks and lunatics from all over the world," several of whom made threats against him for perceived wrongs. By 1908 Dyer, acting as Edison's personal and corporate attorney, became sufficiently concerned about this problem to hire "a personal attendant to safeguard [Edison] from possible cranks and other people who might annoy him."[3]

Recovering from his operations during the summer of 1908, Edison reiterated his intention to "devote his remaining years to investigate anything that strikes his fancy, without regard to its financial productiveness" and he told reporters that he planned "to take life more easy." He also "promised his family and friends to give up slaving night and day, Sundays and holidays, in his laboratory. Not only that, but he is going to take some jaunts about and see something of the rest of the world." Edison had actually begun to take more time for family vacations following his return to the laboratory in 1899. In 1903, for example, the family had traveled by automobile through New England into Canada and in 1906 through New York State to Canada. In the summer of 1908 Edison took his family on a vacation to the Pacific coast, and in 1911 they traveled to Europe. Edison and his family also began to resume their yearly visits to their winter home in Fort Myers, a place where his son Charles could not picture his father "without a fish pole some of the time." He later recalled that his father "always used to say that fishing off the end of the dock [or going out in a boat] was the greatest relaxation he knew of." In 1915 Edison and Mina traveled with Henry Ford and his wife to the expositions in San Francisco and San Diego celebrating the opening of the Panama Canal. And beginning in 1916 Edison began to go on yearly automobile "camping" trips with Ford, rubber manufacturer Harvey Firestone, and naturalist John Burroughs; on one occasion they were even accompanied by President Warren Harding.[4]

Edison hardly slowed down when he was at the laboratory, and whenever he was away on vacation he still received regular reports on laboratory work and often sent instructions to his assistants. He also continued to play a major role in developing key improvements designed to keep the existing Edison companies competitive. However, he no longer sought out new technologies to innovate, and this shift explains his continued insistence "that I have retired from commercial work & dont want take up anything new."[5] One indication of Edison's changing role was that he moved his cot from his second-floor workroom to the library and office where he began to spend more of his time. As Edison stepped away from his role as innovator, the West Orange laboratory also changed from a center for the innovation of new technologies and the incubator of new industrial enterprises to a service organization for the existing Edison businesses.

But Edison was too much the practical inventor to devote his attention full-time to the scientific investigation of interesting phenomena. His curiosity about them might have generated a flurry of experiments, but he remained primarily interested in finding out how they might be practically applied. Furthermore, all of the technologies that he had pioneered in his laboratory during the first half of the decade faced crucial challenges that required his attention. The storage battery still needed further development work before Edison could put it into commercial production, and both the cement works, which was finally beginning to turn out cement on a regular basis, and the phonograph business were deeply affected by the banking crisis that became the Panic of 1907 and caused a national downturn in the economy.

The crisis facing the phonograph was particularly crucial because that business had supported much of Edison's work on cement and storage batteries. But around 1907 Edison cylinder phonographs and records, which had dominated the industry, began to face strong competition from the gramophone produced by the Victor Talking Machine Company. Both companies suffered from the 1907 depression as record and machine sales fell from a high of $7,104,628 in 1907 to $4,831,131 in 1908 for National Phonograph and from $6,015,240 to $3,631,285 for Victor, but National Phonograph's sales continued to fall over the next several years, reaching a low of $2,217,547 in 1912, whereas Victor quickly recovered and exceeded its 1907 total only three years later.[6] Victor continued to grow strongly while National Phonograph struggled. The reason for this shift in fortunes was in large part a product of important advantages that the Victor disc records provided to consumers: at four minutes they had a playing time that was twice as long as the cylinder, they were easier to store, they were generally more durable, and they were less expensive because of lower manufacturing costs for both records and machines.

Edison had produced the first disc phonographs back in 1877–1878 in his efforts to develop a dictating machine on which records could be easily re-aligned for playback. However, he was unable to design an adequate disc machine, and when he resumed development work on the phonograph in the mid-1880s he focused on cylinders. This left the development of the disc to German immigrant Emile Berliner. Berliner had developed a carbon telephone transmitter in 1877–1878 that the Bell Telephone Company used in competing with Western Union and the Edison carbon transmitter. Like Edison, Berliner also lay claim to being the inventor of the microphone. Ten years later, following the development of the wax-recording graphophone by Tainter and Bell, Berliner developed his disc-record gramophone. Berliner duplicated recordings by covering a metal disc with a fatty film and then using acid to etch the grooves in the film. The etched metal master was electroplated with copper to make a matrix that could then be stamped onto a blank wax disc. Berliner began selling 7-inch records made by this process in 1893, but the records did not sell well because of their poor sound quality; the acid used to etch the master discs removed part of the recording and surface noise could be heard when the steel needle played in the grooves of the wax records.

Sound quality and other problems plaguing the early disc phonographs were solved by Eldridge Johnson, a Camden, New Jersey, machinist whom Berliner had commissioned to design a new spring motor for the gramophone in 1896. Johnson then went into the business of manufacturing the machines and also began to work on improving the quality of the disc records. Instead of etching a metal master Johnson decided to record on a wax master that was electroplated in a manner similar to that used by Edison. Johnson was probably familiar with the Edison laboratory's work on electroplating cylinders, and he certainly took advantage of its research on wax compounds; rather than develop his own compound Johnson melted down Edison cylinders to get the wax. In 1901 Johnson and Berliner founded the Victor Talking Machine Company, and the next year they opened their new record factory. Because stamped discs were easier to manufacture than molded cylinders, they were able to begin mass production a year before Edison.

Besides its ease of manufacture and the advantages that the disc format offered consumers, another factor gave Victor a crucial edge during the 1907 downturn. Its record catalog offered a greater variety of artists, particularly its Red Label catalog, which featured prominent opera stars such as Enrico Caruso. These records appealed to the upper-middle-class urban market that had been much less affected by the economic downturn than the small-town and rural customers of the National Phonograph Company. In addition, Victor sold more expensive gramophones to these customers that generated a larger profit per machine. Its best machine was the Victrola, which sold at $200 and came in an attractive cabinet with a hidden horn that made the record player an elegant piece of furniture. After visiting the Victor Company's factory in January 1909, Joseph McCoy, who served the Edison interests as a kind of industrial spy, pointed out the great advantage this gave to Victor:

> They were explaining to me the difference between the recording done by the Victor company and the recording done by the Edison Company. They said that the

Edison Company was selling a number of phonographs and records in the small towns and country places, as they were making records of the popular selections and catering to that trade, but when the hard times struck the country, a year ago, the Edison Company had nothing in the way of records to offer other than their popular selections, and the business must have fell off considerably in the large cities when a number of people were out of work and others working but half time.

McCoy also noted that whereas Victor's sales of low-priced machines had fallen off, it was unable to meet the demand for its high-priced machines. Furthermore, Victor was confident of the future because "they were doing more than 65% of the business now done in the cities in the country, as the wealthy people, who are educated, have acquired a taste for high class musical and operatic selections, and are now purchasing Victor machines and records. they have records by renowned musicians, and the greatest operatic stars, which no other Talking Machine Company, or Phonograph Company, are putting on the market." He concluded that "as most all the famous artists are now under contract with the Victor Company, they do not see whom they could get to make records for [the cylinder record companies] that would compete with the famous operatic stars who are now under contract with their Company."[7]

In 1906, concerned over the growing threat of the four-minute Victor discs and the introduction of four-minute cylinders by other phonograph manufacturers, including Columbia Phonograph, Edison and Aylsworth had begun to develop a four-minute cylinder. Because Edison wanted the new cylinder to be playable by existing machines, they decided to alter the standard sized cylinder to hold 200 instead of 100 threads. The finer number of threads per inch required Aylsworth to develop a new, harder wax composition. Aylsworth, who received $25,000 for his patents on the new record, and Walter Miller were once again given the task of working out the process for manufacturing the cylinders, and each of them received $10,000 for their efforts. In the meantime Edison designed a new reproducer with a smaller reproducing point. So that existing machines could play the new cylinder, Edison and his staff of phonograph engineers also constructed attachments for the new reproducer and for the gearing necessary to run the record at the proper speed. They also developed a new machine to compete with the "hornless" Victrola. Designed to play both standard and Amberol cylinders, it was placed in a cabinet resembling the Victrola and given a name that mimicked it as well—the Amberola. Although the Amberol Record was introduced with much fanfare in late 1908 and the Amberola phonograph followed a year later, they failed to produce the expected revival of the Edison phonograph business.[8]

While Edison and his staff were working to meet Victor's challenge, the business of the National Phonograph Company was further disrupted by the outcome of a lawsuit that had been filed several years earlier by the New York Phonograph Company, one of the local companies that had been established by the North American Phonograph Company. The courts ruled that Edison, as the purchaser of the bankrupt North American, had to uphold New York

Phonograph's contracts with the company. As a consequence, National Phonograph could not sell phonographs and records in New York State that were covered by several of Edison's patents. Although a settlement was subsequently reached, for over a year the company had to use another method to duplicate records and its engineers had to modify several parts of the phonograph to get around Edison's own patents.[9]

Besides these challenges the Edison phonograph business was further distressed by the discovery that William Gilmore had arranged a much too favorable and exclusive printing contract for the company's printing business with Essex Press, a company in which he owned an interest. In 1908 Frank Dyer, Edison's lawyer and the head of the legal department established in 1904 to serve all of the Edison businesses, replaced Gilmore as manager of these enterprises. As general counsel, Dyer was already familiar with much of the day-to-day operations of the businesses, and with the legal issues becoming ever more important to their smooth operation, particularly for the motion picture and phonograph businesses, he proved a fortuitous choice. Dyer soon set about bringing greater cohesion and efficiency to the operations of Edison's business ventures to place them in a better position to meet challenges from competitors and to deal with the debts of the cement and battery companies.

By the beginning of 1910 Dyer had begun discussing plans with Edison "to consolidate all of your interests here in one concern." Dyer thought the new firm should be called "Thomas A. Edison Incorporated" although Edison objected to the name as "not sufficiently dignified." Dyer argued successfully that "because you have always called yourself an inventor and manufacturer . . . it would be perfectly natural for you to carry on your own business under your own name."[10] In February 1911, the National Phonograph Company changed its name to Thomas A. Edison Incorporated (TAE Inc.), and consolidated with the Edison Manufacturing Company, the Edison Business Phonograph Company, and the New Jersey Patent Company (an Edison patent-holding company). As with his other companies, TAE Inc. was "substantially owned by Mr. Edison, and the corporate form of doing business was adopted by him largely because of commercial convenience."[11] The Edison Portland Cement and Edison Storage Battery Companies remained independent. However, TAE Inc., designed to be a financial umbrella for the Edison enterprises, provided financial support for these companies and carried out certain administrative functions such as advertising and purchasing.

Even before the formal organization of TAE Inc., the Edison enterprises had grown administratively close. By 1900 Gilmore had consolidated the administration of the companies that made up TAE Inc. and organized their foreign business under a single department. In 1908 Dyer formed an executive committee that was responsible for major decisions affecting these businesses, and in 1909 he tried an experiment in which National Phonograph's sales force handled other Edison products as well. Although this practice proved unsatisfactory, except for the business phonograph, it indicated the extent to which management considered the various enterprises to be a single organization.

In 1910 the laboratory also became more closely linked to this incipient organization. In January, Edison "decided to install at the laboratory an Engineering and Experimental Department which will have charge of the entire developments of new machines," which would be approved for manufacture by the executive committee.[12] A few months later Dyer formed a manufacturing committee "for the purpose of passing on all matters pertaining to the issuing of shop orders or requisitions, or the expenditure of monies, for experimental work, tools, machinery, equipment, new buildings or additions thereto, improvements to plant, &c."[13] This general laboratory department was formed out of an existing nucleus developed to oversee work on phonographs. The seeds for this phonograph engineering department may have been sown in 1905 when Arthur Mundy, a cable telegraph inventor who had worked with Elisha Gray just prior to Gray's death, wrote to Edison that he had "three separate and distinct principles" that he thought could be applied to the phonograph to "improve *the quality* of the tones delivered." Although Mundy did not join the West Orange staff, Edison thought that "it would pay us to give such a man the facilities of the Lab to work up improvement on the phonog[rap]h recording etc we agreeing to pay him liberally if he gets anything good [as] we are poorly provided in this connection."[14] The following year he hired Charles Hibbard specifically to improve the business phonograph. By 1909 an engineering department had been established under the direction of Peter Weber, who as general superintendent for the Edison phonograph business had been responsible for several improvements to the Edison phonographs. At the beginning of the year Weber, who was also a member of the executive committee, appointed an assistant, Charles Schiffl, a skilled toolmaker who was a foreman at the Phonograph Works, with instructions that "Hereafter all designs of articles manufactured will be made under his supervision in the Engineering Dept." Weber required that experimental work "be done in strict accordance with drawings or other instructions supplied by Mr. Schiffl or myself, and under no circumstances should changes be made in experimental work until such changes have been recorded by him and approved by me."[15] When Edison established the general Engineering and Experimental Department a year later the phonograph engineering department became its nucleus.

In 1911, Edison appointed Donald Bliss as the first chief engineer at the laboratory. Bliss, who had originally come to the laboratory to work on motors and other electrical devices, proved to be an ineffectual administrator and was fired the following year. He was replaced by Miller Reese Hutchison, whose invention of the Klaxon horn and the Acousticon hearing aid had given him a minor reputation as an inventor before he became connected with the Edison storage battery business in 1910. Hutchison developed an intimate personal relationship with Edison as he worked to build up the battery business and to extend its use by promoting the use of the batteries in military submarines. At various times in 1910 and 1911, he and Edison spent some late nights together conducting battery experiments and discussing business plans. In some ways Hutch, as he became known to Edison, may have reminded the Old Man of the trusty Batch (Charles Batchelor). In November 1911, nine months before he replaced Bliss as chief engineer, Edison asked Hutchison "to be his Ch[ief] Engr & pers[onal] representative & represent him" at the laboratory.[16] Hutchison's informal position as Edison's representative made Bliss's job even more difficult and seems to have caused some jealousy among the laboratory staff, although the bad feelings had begun to ease before Hutchison's formal appointment as chief engineer in August 1912. Hutchison's role was not the only reason that "everyone looks on [Bliss] as a figure head." Bliss also had to contend with Edison's formidable presence. Edison may have stepped aside to some extent from the routine affairs of the laboratory, but he nonetheless continued to play a very active role, as is evident from his statement in December 1911 that "I have 250 experimenters who depend on me daily for directions and when I go away it greatly disturbs the organization."[17] And Edison continued to be the final authority over the work of the laboratory.

Edison gave his new Engineering and Experimental Department primary responsibility for engineering refinements on existing products and the development work necessary to turn experimental devices into commercially manufactured products. The department played a major role in the effort to revive the Edison phonograph business. One of the first important projects undertaken by the engineering staff was to alter the Amberola phonograph so that it could play a new cylinder record that had been developed by Aylsworth and Miller. The fine threads of the original Amberol cylinder had proved too fragile, causing records to wear out quickly. Although Edison, Aylsworth, and Miller conducted extensive experiments, they were unable to develop a harder material suitable for phonograph records. Unfortunately, Edison was unable to use celluloid, which was already known to be the best substance for this purpose. In 1902 he had received a patent for molding record cylinders made from celluloid, but a judge, misunderstanding the nature of the nine years of laboratory experiments undertaken to produce a commercially practicable celluloid cylinder, had ruled in an infringement case that these experiments constituted prior use. He therefore voided Edison's patent in favor of one Thomas Lambert had filed a year later. It was decisions such as this that created Edison's cynicism regarding the patent system. Although the Lambert Company soon failed, National Phonograph solved the problem of poor records only after acquiring patent rights for the use of celluloid from the Indestructible Record Company. Two key figures connected with Indestructible Record, Ademor N. Petit, an inventor with several patents, and Albert Philpott, an expert on making celluloid records, also came to work at the West Orange laboratory. With rights to the use of celluloid assured, Edison and his chemists, led by Aylsworth, developed the Blue Amberol, an extremely durable and practically unbreakable celluloid record. This record together with the improved Amberola phonograph developed by the engineering staff marked the high point of cylinder phono-graph technology.[18] Unfortunately, even though the Blue Amberol was able to revive cylinder sales, it arrived too late to prevent the preponderance of the phonograph market from switching to discs, a change that Edison probably could not have prevented even if he had introduced his new product earlier.

Dyer had been urging him to develop a disc machine for some time and had "hired a man on my own responsibility to experiment on the Disc ma-chine in a room in New York where no one would know about it, and when those experiments were finished they were brought to [Edison's] attention by making the demonstration behind a curtain."[19] When the sales of Victor gramophones and records began to surpass Edison cylinders, Edison finally rec-ognized the importance of introducing his own disc design, and in mid-De-cember 1909 he launched an experimental campaign. Aylsworth attacked the problem of developing a new material for disc records, and Miller and Edward Aiken, a laboratory experimenter with several phonograph and record patents, moved into the top floor of the Edison factory in nearby Glen Ridge to devise methods for making master disc molds and manufacturing records; Miller also conducted disc recording experiments at the National Phonograph's New York recording studio. Edison focused his own attention on recorder and reproducer technology, especially the ongoing effort to use diamond instead of sapphire needles, but he gave primary responsibility for the mechanical design and the cabinet for the disc phonograph to Weber and his engineering staff.

Always aware of his reputation for innovation, Edison wanted his disc pho-nograph to surpass the Victrola in sound quality. The most important research therefore focused on developing a higher-quality record surface and on record-ing and reproducing music with greater fidelity. To surpass the technical per-formance of Victor, Edison continued to use the vertical cut he employed in his cylinder machines instead of the lateral cut used by the disc manufacturers. He was less concerned with those aspects of the machine that played no role in producing high fidelity and willingly borrowed cabinet and mechanical design elements from the Victrola. Because the mechanical design primarily involved engineering refinements, the Engineering Department was able to produce the first model by the following July. The research on improved record mate-rials, recording and reproducing technology, and record duplicating took much longer, continuing into 1911. And as the disc phonograph and record moved from research into development, Edison and his staff had to solve a host of problems before they were ready for commercial production.

Aylsworth's work on new record materials proceeded relatively quickly, but the process of manufacturing the new record was fraught with difficulties. At the time the disc research began, Aylsworth had been experimenting with phe-nol resins to develop a better material for the four-minute Amberol records. These resins were unsuitable for cylinders but they proved to be just the answer for the disc record. Aylsworth's research paralleled that of Leo Bakeland, who produced Bakelite, the first commercially successful hard and heat-resistant phenol resin material. Aylsworth developed a purer resin that he called Con-densite; the name was derived from the condensation of phenol and formalde-hyde that occurred when it was processed. Aylsworth and Dyer formed the Condensite Company of America to market the new substance, which was li-censed to TAE Inc. for use in phonograph records. As early as 1911, Conden-site Company advertising claimed that Edison records made with this material were "hard, practically unbreakable, can be played from ten to twelve times as often as any other form of record without deterioration in the quality of the sound, and none of the quality is lost in the production of duplicates."[20] How-ever, quality recording and manufacturing of the records proved to be no sim-ple task. Aylsworth, Miller, Aiken, and Edison conducted extensive experiments before they actually produced high-quality commercial records.

The other key innovation introduced with the Edison disc phonograph was the diamond needle and floating-weight recorder assemblies for reproducers and recorders. Concerned that harder record materials would cause the sap-phire needles used in the Edison phonograph reproducers to wear too quickly Edison had begun to experiment with alternative materials in early 1909, and by August he began focusing on a diamond needle. The following spring a pro-totype of the new reproducer was ready, but the final result required, according to a 1914 advertisement, "three years of continuous research by Mr. Edison himself, during which he built, tested and discarded 2,300 different types of re-producers."[21] This extraordinary number was typical of the claims Edison liked to make to demonstrate the effort and thoroughness with which he attacked a problem, but it is not entirely clear what it represented in the case of the de-velopment of the diamond reproducer. The new reproducer and recorder as-semblies used a refinement of the floating-weight diaphragm Edison had first introduced in 1903. In the new design he used a larger diaphragm and weight to achieve louder reproduction. To prevent the extreme vibrations of the larger diaphragm from obliterating the sibilant sounds he suspended it in a semivis-cous substance called "goo" in order to dampen it.

This new design produced very high-quality recordings and playback. MIT engineering professor Dugald Jackson commented in a 1916 letter to Charles Edison that he had concluded "the Edison phonograph is really a reproducer of music, and has largely overcome the traditional suggestion of what is known as 'canned' music." He asked Charles whether his father had "an adequate the-ory to explain the difference between the apparent quality of the tones which come from the new Edison phonograph and the several other types of phono-graph made." Charles gave as his father's reply "that the results on Edison Disc is [the] result of many things—recording apparatus, materials for recording on, the technique of preparing the masters to preserve the overtones, the material used in the Disc, and to some extent the Reproducer diaphragm, most all at-tained by many years of empirical experimentation."[22]

The Edison Disc Phonographs, as they became officially known in Octo-ber 1911, were first made public in July of that year at the annual convention of the National Association of Talking Machine Jobbers. At the same time, production orders were given for the manufacture of the first 3,600 machines. In August, before leaving on his European vacation, Edison also left instructions to start disc record production at a small pilot plant where the manufacturing process could be refined prior to setting up the large-scale facility, which began to be equipped in late February 1912. As he had done with the storage battery, Edison paid considerable attention to the design of machinery used in manufacturing records and phonographs even though this slowed production. When TAE Inc. finally did begin to sell Edison Disc records and machines they continued to be plagued by a host of difficulties. Over the next three years several parts of the phonograph were redesigned, including the motor, governor, stop mechanism, and reproducer. Much of this work was done by the Engineering Department, while Edison focused his attention on quality control of record manufacturing, which continued to be a source of concern to him for many years.[23]

The effort to improve the disc phonograph and bring it to market was further complicated on December 9, 1914, when a fire broke out in a wooden shed containing inflammable motion-picture film. The original wooden Phonograph Works building was soon in flames, and by morning thirteen buildings surrounding the laboratory had been badly damaged or destroyed, although the laboratory buildings themselves were saved. Edison immediately began to plan the rebuilding campaign and predicted that he would begin manufacturing phonograph records again within ten days. On December 15 the company issued a press release announcing heroic progress in the fire's wake with "Edison, personally directing a force of over 2000 men to which he is adding daily [who were] inspired to the limit of human endurance by his example." Although Edison's prediction proved a little optimistic, when the manufacture of Blue Amberol records resumed on the last day of the year, Edison was pleased to report to his phonograph dealers that "Getting back in the ring in twenty-two days is going some." The first discs were produced in the battery plant across from the laboratory by the end of January 1915.[24]

Edison's response to the fire highlights a key element of his character. Where others might see disaster and failure he was always optimistically looking for opportunities and seeing the possibility of new directions for improvements. He rebuilt all the manufacturing plants out of reinforced concrete to make them more fireproof. And to take advantage of the latest improvements in factory design developed by Henry Ford, who was at the forefront of the rational factory movement, he wrote to Ford's assistant E. G. Liebold asking him to "loan me one of his Efficiency Engineers for a little while . . . I am repairing my concrete buildings and wish to arrange my machinery properly in order to take advantage of Mr. Ford's methods as far as possible." Ford, who greatly admired Edison, was happy to oblige his friend in this matter. Edison used the opportunity created by the fire to further streamline his manufacturing operations by consolidating the designs of cylinder and disc phonographs into a few basic models with standardized parts. For example, three days after the fire Edison approved the A-100 disc phonograph, which became known as the standard because its mechanism was also used "for the 150, 200 and 250 types, with changes in barrels, springs, horns and cabinets."[25]

As the work of the laboratory shifted from the innovation of new technology to product improvement and production efficiency, Edison's role changed as well. He continued to supervise the work of the Engineering and Experimental Department at the laboratory, but he was less personally involved in the day-to-day tests and experiments that took place there. Instead, the laboratory became just one of several divisions that reported to Edison through reports, although he personally approved experimental and production models as he began to play a larger role in TAE Inc. operations than he had in any of his previous companies.

Following the organization of the Engineering Department in 1910, Edison started to pay greater attention to business matters. Previously he had been largely content to leave the administration of the business to William Gilmore and then to Frank Dyer. The instructions left by Gilmore when he visited the Edison European operations in 1907 indicate the limited involvement that Edison played in the business operations of his companies. Gilmore told his department heads to consult together and only

> if a decision cannot be reached then the matter should be taken to Mr. Edison. I particularly do not want Mr. Edison brought into any questions of business policy, or in fact any other matters, unless it is absolutely necessary that he be approached on the subject, my idea being that with the combined judgment you should in nine out of ten cases be able to act intelligently and wisely without disturbing or bothering Mr. Edison with matters with the details of which he is not familiar. It is not to be considered, however, on the part of any of the Managers of the departments that they shall not see Mr. Edison and inform him as to conditions in their relative departments, as of course I desire the same course to be pursued in my absence as has been the case in the past. I want it distinctly understood that Mr. Edison should be informed as to how business is progressing and all information given him that he may require, so as to keep him conversant with the general conditions.[26]

This situation continued under Dyer as he and his executive and manufacturing committees made most of the day-to-day decisions. By November 1911, however, Edison's growing involvement in business operations had so undermined Frank Dyer's authority as president of TAE Inc. that he resigned. In a long letter to Edison he detailed his complaints:

> My present position is quite untenable. Many subordinates are reporting directly to you, and I have reason to believe that in a number of cases you have indicated to them that you have lost confidence in my ability or capacity. Rumors of this sort naturally spread very rapidly and destroy all possible authority. I cannot remain in a position where I might be held responsible for conditions over which I have no control. . . . In addition to the worries incidental to a business of this size, both in

a commercial and a legal sense, there are the additional worries of trying to please you and of trying to carry your ideas into effect. Furthermore, and by no means least, there are the worries and anxieties due to disorganization resulting from gossip and rumors of all sorts, which are gradually undermining the entire organization and reducing the efficiency of the force. . . . In my recent talk with you, you criticized me quite severely, but I do not think that your criticisms were fair or just. I believe that you do not appreciate the amount of work I have done and what I have accomplished.

The official notice of Dyer's resignation, however, claimed that his other interests outside of TAE Inc. "have grown so extensive of late that he has felt for some time that he was unable to do full justice to the multitudinous duties which his various connections involved, and, as a duty to himself, to Mr. Edison, and to the enterprises with which he was connected, decided that he must curtail his numerous responsibilities." Rather than appoint someone else to run his business, Edison decided to assume the presidency himself with Carl H. Wilson, the vice president, continuing as general manager of the business.

Among the areas that Edison had begun to manage personally in 1911 was a key aspect of record quality that he had previously ignored—the selection of music and recording artists. Following his return from Europe in September 1911 he had begun to go "over all our records at my house . . . to get a broad idea of the whole and to draw some general conclusions." With the "aid of several people who are opera goers and are familiar with the music and are themselves musicians" he then "selected 230 tunes to be put on the new disc." From that point on Edison began "to dictate to our record department just what they are to record and how I want it." Edison's involvement with "the musical end of the new disc" marked an important departure in his role with the phonograph business.[27]

Edison had always believed that superior technology was the key to competition in the phonograph business. As he took over control of the musical direction of the phonograph business he declared that he would "depend upon the quality of the records and not on the reputation of the singers. There are, of course, many people who will buy a distorted, ill-recorded and scratchy record if the singer has a great reputation, but there are infinitely more who will buy for the beauty of the record, with fine voices, well instrumented and no scratch." When the disc phonographs were finally ready to challenge the Victrola in 1915, Edison company advertising promoted the technical quality of machine and record—the products of the great inventor's art—rather than the musical quality of its recording artists. Edison's campaign "to produce a disc machine free from a mechanical tone, distortion of the original sounds & free from those irritating scratchy sounds now in all disc machines" was the subject of most advertising. When the artists were featured in promotional activities they were used to highlight "Edison's New Art." A key element of the Edison advertising campaign were the "Tone Tests" in which an artist performed with an Edison phonograph playing a recording of him or herself. At some point, of-

ten after the lights had been dimmed, the artist would stop performing, allowing the phonograph to continue on alone and amaze the audience, which was
unable to distinguish between the live and recorded performances.[28]

The tone tests were popular and successful forms of advertising and helped
to demonstrate the technical superiority of the Edison disc phonograph. But
even though Edison disc phonographs sold reasonably well, the Edison company lost over $1 million on disc records between 1915 and 1917 and contin-
ued to lag well behind Victor in sales of machines and records. Fidelity was
only one aspect of the battle for supremacy in the recording business. The catalog of Edison recording artists failed to match the variety and quality of those
offered by Victor. As the manager of the Edison Shop in New York explained in
1915, "the machine first sells on its own merits," but owners soon wonder
"Why *don't* you have the artists?"[29] The consequence of this limited selection
of artists was that they reverted to buying Victor records and using adaptors to
play them on the Edison disc phonograph. After Edison decided to stop manufacturing an adaptor, purchasers of his machines were limited to the catalog of
Edison records. Victor's more extensive and higher-quality catalog gave it an
important advantage not only over Edison but over its other competitors as
well. The limited quality of the Edison catalog was still apparent in a 1919 report on the turntable test developed by Edison engineers to enable phonograph
dealers to compare the Edison disc with the machines of other manufacturers.
The author of the report noted that "in almost every store . . . I heard the same
comment when I referred to the Edison, 'Why the Edison?' They are not even
considered a competitor. . . . They always ended their argument by calling my
attention to the superiority of the Victor artists and number of record selections
listed by them over the Edison list."[30]

Edison himself was primarily responsible for his company's catalog. It is
striking that a man who had become extremely hard of hearing would set himself up as the sole arbiter of the artists and music to be recorded for his discs
and cylinders. The explanation can be found in a 1913 interview in which he
detailed his plans to standardize music by placing it on a scientific basis. Edison claimed that his deafness actually allowed him to "hear better than anybody else." As he explained, "Part of every sound wave is lost before it reaches
the inner ear." Edison listened by placing his head against the phonograph and
by biting into the wood with his teeth to hear faint sounds. "The sound-waves
thus come almost directly to my brain. They pass through only my inner ear.
And I have a wonderfully sensitive inner ear . . . [that] has been protected from
the millions of noises that dim the hearing of ears that hear everything." As a result, he felt that "no one who has a normal ear can hear as well as I can" because they could not distinguish the "little sounds," such as a squeaky flute key,
"that do not belong in music" and spoiled it. Pianist Ernest Stevens, who became music director of the Edison recording studio, related how Edison could
tell the exact vibration of any note played on the piano. However, Stevens felt
that when Edison bit into the wood of the piano "to get the conduction

Edison listening to a disc recording and making notes about it in one of his notebooks.

through his teeth . . . the higher the pitches . . . the fainter it would be to his ear." Although he could hear a four-octave range above and below middle C quite well, his hearing rapidly tapered off, especially in the higher ranges. This may be why he considered Rachmaninoff to be a "pounder."[31]

Besides his unique style of hearing recordings, Edison also determined what he considered to be sonic defects by visual examination of a record with a microscope. He and his staff had been examining records this way for many years and Edison claimed that he could "tell a soprano from Basso Baritone or Tenor & each from another also every instrument in the orchestra when played alone by looking at record thru a microscope," although he did concede that it was "difficult to tell compound tones from several instruments." Samuel Gardner, a violinist whom Edison used for recording tests, recalled that Edison "made decisions not by the ear very much, because he was pretty deaf, but by looking at the record through a magnifying glass." Gardner related how Edison didn't like vibrato and demonstrated to him why it was bad by showing him the shakes in a record groove.[32]

Although Gardner believed that Edison's "deafness had nothing to do with his musicality, because he didn't have any," his odd way of hearing music must have affected his musical tastes.[33] Certain notes and instruments hurt his ears and probably contributed to his notion that songs should be written only in thirds and sixths with simple melodies. It also led him to dislike vibrato and to perceive most singers as having excessive tremolo. His views on singing were particularly important for the Edison catalog of opera stars and other singers. By 1919 he had tested some 3,800 singers but found only "22 who sing pure notes, without extraneous sounds and the almost universal tremolo effect." Most singers he believed could not pass the "acid test" of his disc phonograph, which caused "the defects in a singer's voice [to] become very apparent, because we reveal his voice, exactly as it is. . . . There are no realistic stage settings and no dramatic action to key our emotions to a pitch that renders us tolerant of imperfect singing. . . . I have every admiration for the peculiar gifts of the singer, whose stage presence, or physical charm, enables him, or her, to achieve a great reputation, despite the handicap of an inferior voice, but I hope no one will expect me to record such voices." Record sellers, however, found "that many a pleasing and saleable 'performance' is thrown in the discard because of defects that are largely imaginary, or not noticed by the public," while others were passed "when they never had a chance with the public."[34] By 1921, as TAE Inc. fell "from 3rd to 5th or 6th position as regards the record business," an exasperated Walter Miller told Edison that "a one man opinion on tunes is all wrong. Last year when you were the only picker of tunes, you refused to let us record the four biggest successes of the year. . . . I am convinced that the policy is not sound, other wise we would make a better showing in the Phonograph industry."[35]

Edison's stubborn insistence on being the sole judge of talent and music for the phonograph was only partly about his belief that his disc phonograph provided such incredible fidelity that it made readily apparent the flaws of singers and other musicians that would otherwise be overlooked. Just as important was the special attachment he felt toward the invention he called "my baby." In 1899 he had remarked that "commercial reasons when it comes to the phonograph dont count with me. Its the only invention of mine that I want to run myself."[36] When he took over as president of TAE Inc. in 1912 Edison established his role as that of "dictat[ing] the policies of the company and determin[ing] by the reports" he received that others in the company were acting in accord with those policies, passing on all contracts, and setting the company's plans for each fiscal year.[37] The phonograph was the only part of the business in which he played such a significant day-to-day role involving the selection of recording artists and the quality control of record manufacture. By 1915 he had even begun to turn over some of his presidential duties to his son

Charles and to Steven Mambert, Charles's assistant, who became the company's "Efficiency Engineer" and was responsible for its financial affairs.

Charles Edison and Mambert probably were responsible for the 1915 reorganization of TAE Inc. into a divisional structure, although this was presented as Edison's plan. The divisional policy was typical of a growing pattern in American industry as product diversification became a way for companies to ensure their long-term profitability by moving into new markets. As Edison noted in a 1923 interview: "If you have five lines of business, any two of them will carry you through a bad period; but if you have only one or two kinds and they both go bad, then you are in the soup."[38] Diversification also enabled a company to make more efficient use of its manufacturing facilities and other resources. As a result of the diversification of products that led to the formation of TAE Inc. in 1911, the enterprise had become too complex for personal administration. Charles and his father therefore agreed that they should integrate the various products under a centralized management, with Edison setting the general policy but division managers having considerable authority to determine how those policies would be carried out. In this regard TAE Inc. was like other family-owned firms in which the owner continued to be responsible for general corporate policy while the daily operations of each product division were under the control of a management team that could respond more quickly to changes in the market. Edison's failure in the phonograph business resulted from his not listening to the managers of the record division when they complained that he was out of touch with the market. Nonetheless, the diverse products and divisional structure helped TAE Inc. to prosper even as the phonograph and record divisions, which had long been the mainstay of the Edison industries, continued to lose money.

The organization of TAE Inc. and of the laboratory Engineering Department in 1910–1911 marked a shift in Edison's role from inventor to head of a large industrial enterprise and a director of research and development. He had already made the choice for personal reasons to stop innovating, and the new institutional structure reinforced that decision. But the corporation that took Edison's name was unable to institutionalize innovation. The diversity of Edison products marketed by TAE Inc. had not been a consequence of corporate strategy but rather of Edison's own interests as an independent inventor. He had introduced each new product through a separate independent company. When Edison and Dyer had formed TAE Inc. they did not consciously adopt a strategy of diversification even though Edison had long used his more successful products to support research and development of others. This had been the role of his phonograph business for a decade. After the formation of TAE Inc. the storage battery provided the profits to help the company as the phonograph business declined in the face of new competitors. Yet, even though Edison had to come out of retirement to develop the new disc phonograph, neither he nor others in his company took this as a sign that they needed to institutionalize innovation as part of a larger diversification strategy. Instead, Edison and his managers took a more conservative approach that focused on the improvement of existing products to lower manufacturing costs as a way of increasing profits. It was at other companies, such as General Electric and DuPont, that corporate managers would design new strategies to protect the long-term vitality of their businesses by using research and development to diversify their product lines.

Edison also failed to replace himself at TAE Inc. because he was unwilling to relinquish his control over laboratory work involving new products. He may have told Hutchison in 1911 "that he is getting old & wants me to prepare to step into his shoes if he ever passes out," but he did nothing to make such a succession possible. In 1918 Hutchison left Edison's employ, ostensibly "to devote his entire time to war work," but he had probably grown frustrated by the fact that his research budget was less than half the budget for research initiated by Edison. Furthermore, Hutchison found his research confined to that "of routine character and little, if any, of it being connected with work personally directed by Mr. Edison." Others in TAE Inc. viewed the laboratory as "a place where sundry mysterious experiments are carried on by Mr. Edison and charged to other Edison functions arbitrarily without any corresponding advantage to them . . . [and] performed at high cost, due to inefficient management; against all of which no redress is to be had because the Laboratory is under the special protection of Mr. Edison." In 1920 Edison would establish new procedures to eliminate these complaints, but in fact he and the laboratory already had become more responsive to the larger organization. Most of the research he carried out involved new products intended to supplement those offered by existing company divisions, such as a "more Elementary Dictating Machine," high-voltage storage batteries, and the Ford self-starter.[39] There was, however, another significant group of experiments directed by Edison that had nothing to do with the needs of his company. This was his war research for the U.S. government, which arose out of his role as the nation's inventor-philosopher.

CHAPTER 23

Inventor-Philosopher

Edison's "retirement" prompted him to begin thinking about his place in history. He made plans for an official biography to be written by Frank Dyer and T. C. Martin, editor of the *Electrical World*, and between 1908 and 1909 he filled several notebooks with personal reminiscences for the book, which was published in 1910. During these same years Edison began to take on a new role as the nation's inventor-philosopher. The inventor who always prided himself on having "besides the usual inventor's make-up, the bump of practicality as a sort of appendix, the sense of business, money value of an invention," now began to consider developing inventions from which he would not profit but that might provide technical solutions to social problems.[1] Reporters responded to his growing interest in social issues by seeking his opinion on any and all subjects, from the role of inventions in the Great War and the technologies of the future to questions of diet and the existence of God.

Edison's low-cost cement house for working-class families is the best known example of his efforts to find technological solutions to social problems. He was not alone in thinking that such houses were not only technically feasible but also a possible way to lighten the burden of the poor and working classes. Typically, Edison's speculations about low-cost cement houses prompted considerable interest among would-be homeowners and contractors. This interest encouraged Edison to develop plans for a system of casting a house in twelve hours from iron molds. He was spurred in part by the need to boost the sales of Portland cement, but his goal was not to make money from the design or sale of the houses themselves. In October 1907, after his plans were well under way he released a statement in which he explained: "I have not gone into this with the idea of making money from it, and will be glad to license reputable parties to make molds and erect houses without any payments on account of patents, the only restrictions being that the designs of the houses be satisfactory to me and that they shall use good material."

Edison expected the set of molds for each house to cost about $25,000, the rest of the equipment for erecting them to be about $15,000, and the buildings themselves to cost about $1,000. The low construction costs made possible by his system would enable working people to live in "small palaces renting for about ten dollars a month." Impressed by Edison's plans, philanthropist Henry Phipps met with the inventor to discuss the possibility of using his system to solve the tenement problem in New York City by building "a city" of "beautiful nine room house[s], suitable for two families" to be rented for as little as $7.50 a month. "Mr. Phipps thinks as I do," Edison told reporters, "that my house will solve this problem. It is for me to build one of these houses, to create the unit. Some one else must build the city, and Mr. Phipps seems to be the proper man to put it up."[2]

Although Edison applied for patents on his system of constructing cement houses in August 1908 and had a model designed by the New York firm of Mann & MacNeille, he encountered a great deal of difficulty in making the molds and determining the proper formula for the cement. Edison found the original model to be too ornate and had his draftsmen design a smaller and less complex house that would simplify the molds. By the summer of 1910, he had prepared a circular about his plans and announced that his molds were about 60 percent completed. Although Edison's research enabled him to develop an appropriate cement mixture and he cast two experimental two-story buildings on the grounds of Glenmont—a gardener's cottage and a garage—he ended up abandoning the project because of the demands of his various business enterprises, especially the effort to develop the disc phonograph. The projected concrete city never materialized, but a few concrete buildings based on Edison's ideas were later cast by Frank Lambie and Charles Ingersoll in Union, New Jersey.[3]

The cement house was not Edison's only idea for new technologies that could make life more pleasant and affordable for the working class, although it was the only one that he actively pursued. As early as 1902 he had proposed a combination stove and light, using the Welsbach mantle, "for poor people in Cities."[4] And in 1910, as he was working on the cement house, he conceived the idea of developing automatic vending machines to supply such necessities as coal and vegetables to the urban poor. Edison proposed to design a shop that would automatically retail goods in five cent lots through nickel-in-the-slot machines. "In the walls of the shop there will be dozens and dozens of small openings. Above each opening will be a sign telling in half a dozen languages just what parcels that particular opening will deliver. . . . The upper part of the store will be merely an adaptation of machines already in use. There will be rows of bins in which produce is dumped as it is received from the farmers. Machines attached to the lower end of these bins will weigh or measure out the goods, wrap and tie it and deliver it to the chute from which it drops into the customer's hand. All the storekeeper need do is to keep the bins filled and the machinery oiled" and, of course, "collect the nickels at night."[5] Although A. H. Jaeger of the Jaeger Automatic Machine Company in Philadelphia and W. J. Paul of the Barlow Foundry Company in Newark both proposed working with Edison to develop this idea, his other enterprises prevented him from finding the time to work it out.

One project that Edison did find time for in the midst of his efforts to develop the disc phonograph was the promotion of motion picture technology for classroom use. This had become a subject of public interest in 1907, and Edison expressed his enthusiasm for it in a 1909 letter to Burnett Hamm, Public Health Commissioner of Queensland, Australia, in which he stated that "the introduction of Kinetoscope pictures in schools would be an epoch in the common school." Although Edison later claimed that he had always been more "interested in the educational and not the entertainment" use of motion pictures, he clearly was influenced by the Progressive Movement's interest in educational reform that would deemphasize rote and passive learning and make school more interesting and stimulating. Edison and other film producers involved in the Motion Picture Patents Company were engaged in an effort to improve the moral content of films to counter the bad reputation of the nickelodeons and encourage the patronage of the middle class. Edison had been involved in this effort since at least 1907, when he stated that "nothing is of greater importance to the Success of the motion picture interests than films of good moral tone." By 1910 there was a growing catalog of educational and moral uplift films, including a series of Edison films produced for the National Association for the Study and Prevention of Tuberculosis (now the Lung Association). The following year Edison announced his plan to begin producing films for schools. As he told a reporter for *Harper's Weekly*, these films could "teach children everything from mathematics to morality by little dramas acted out before the camera, and reproduced in the school-room at very low cost. Sort o' swing the education on them so attractively that they'll *want* to go to school."[6]

In 1910 Edison had set his Engineering Department to work developing a small motion picture apparatus for use in homes, schools, and churches that became known as the Home Projecting Kinetoscope (or Home P.K.). They also developed a special film for the projector that contained three separate rows of pictures in a smaller-than-standard frame (5.7 mm) that were shown by moving the position of the projector's aperture and running the middle row in reverse. This enabled the equivalent of a 1,000 foot standard one-reel film running about sixteen minutes to fit on a 77-foot reel. The stock for these films was a nonflammable safety film that had recently been developed by Eastman Kodak, and Edison made sure that the projector also was fireproof. The Engineering Department finished the model of the Home P.K. in early 1911 and by December Edison told B. L. Singly of the Keystone View Company that "we are now making 10000 small machines for teaching in schools by moving pictures & will soon have several hundred films to start the course."[7] The machine was not introduced to the public for several more months because of manufacturing delays caused by several design problems, including the need to make the instrument easier to operate. Work on the Home P.K. was charged to TAE Inc., but Edison himself funded the development of educational films by the laboratory staff. They made several experimental films, including some on such scientific subjects as crystals, insects, and trout eggs, which they filmed using a special tripod and microscope. Edison planned to produce these types of films for regular release by the motion picture division of TAE Inc. A majority of the Edison educational films did have commercial releases, but many of them were commercial films that were subsequently reduced to fit the Home P.K.

Late in 1912 Edison expressed his frustration over the expense and delays experienced by the educational film project: "Up to date school pictures have cost $20000. I dont see that we have much for this money or getting things better."[8] Although Edison's educational films received much favorable publicity and the film catalog grew during 1913 from 50 to about 160 subjects, neither the films nor the Home P.K. proved profitable. Edison's enthusiasm for the application of motion picture technology to education was not widely shared by the educators themselves. The initial responses by education leaders brought to West Orange in 1913 by the magazine *Survey* was generally favorable, but they expressed concern that motion pictures were not a panacea and could easily be misused. They all agreed that motion pictures were capable of providing a superior learning experience for some subjects, "especially those in the field of microscopic life and industrial processes," but several educators at the symposium cautioned that films were merely another tool to be "used in connection with good teaching, which includes reading on the subject, laboratory work, and writing up the results of observations and deductions."[9]

Most schools were ill prepared to incorporate motion pictures into their curriculum, particularly because projectors and films added to the cost of education. It is not surprising that a catalog of Edison educational films distributed to 16,000 school superintendents throughout the United States in 1913 generated little demand. The selection of subjects and the development of pedagogical techniques to incorporate films into the curriculum required a different kind of innovation from Edison than merely having his laboratory staff experiment with the production of films about industrial processes and scientific subjects and releasing historical dramas, travelogues, and other commercial movies in the Home P.K. format. As one of the participants in the *Survey* symposium pointed out, "it will be at great sacrifice of his own time and money and of the welfare of children if Mr. Edison is forced to learn what films are of most value to children by the method of experiment alone." Edison was not prepared to keep spending his own money on this project, and in August of 1913 he told Hutchison "I think we better quit on school film all together until we get outside money." The project was finally abandoned because

Edison "could not get up enough interest among teachers etc to make them pay the cost."[10]

Unlike the cement house and educational films, most of Edison's ideas about the application of technology to social problems never became anything more than a subject for discussion in newspapers and magazines. Reporters seemed fascinated by his speculations on a range of subjects. Some of them were natural subjects for Edison to address, particularly those related to the future of electricity and of technology in general, but others were topics to which he had given little attention and on which he offered poorly considered opinions. Whatever the issue he usually ruminated on its possible social impact. One subject that Edison addressed on several occasions was the future of work itself. Not surprisingly, he expressed the view that machinery would liberate people. "The machine," he argued, "has been the human being's most effective means of escape from bondage. Too many people, even now, remain bond-slaves to laborious hand processes. . . . Man will progress in intellectual tasks according to his release from the mere motor tasks."[11] He predicted that "There will be no manual labor in the factories of the future. The men in them will be merely superintendents, watching the machinery to see that it works right . . . it will be work with the brain, something that man will be interested in, and done in wholesome, pleasant surroundings. Less and less man will be used as an engine, or as a horse, and his brain will be employed to benefit himself and his fellows."[12] Industrial workers were not the only ones he expected to extend their intellectual capabilities when liberated from manual labor. Women of the future, freed from household work by machinery, would be able to "more generally exercise their mental force . . . and thus insure a brain development in them such as has been prevented in the past."[13] The social consequences of machine labor replacing human labor would, he believed, be immense, solving the labor and servant problems that perplexed contemporary society and enabling the human race to reach its full potential.

As his views on labor suggest, Edison believed that environment played a crucial role in the development of human potential. These views also may explain why he believed in racial and ethnic stereotypes even though in his relations with employees and others whom he knew well he often acted in disregard of those same stereotypes. His clearest statement in this regard concerned Jews:

> The Jews are certainly a remarkable people, as strange to me in their isolation from all the rest of mankind as those mysterious people called Gypsies— While there are some "terrible examples" in mercantile pursuits, the moment they get into art, music, science, & literature the Jew is fine— The trouble with the Jew that he has been persecuted for centuries by ignorant malignant bigots & forced into his present characteristics and he has acquired a 6th sense which gives him an almost unerring judgment in trade affairs— Having this natural advantage over his fellows he has taken too great an advantage of it & got himself disliked by many as I saw in Europe= I believe that in America where he is free that in time he will cease to be so clannish, & not carry to such extremes his natural advantages.[14]

Edison also argued that the "almost supernatural business instincts of the Jew" could be attributed to the necessity for women in the face of severe persecutions to share in the pursuits of Jewish men, particularly "in business management. The result is that the Jewish child receives commercial acumen not only from the father's but from the mother's side." Edison was hopeful that "This may be taken as an evidence of what may come in future when womankind in general is equally developed with men along all lines," although he criticized Jews for not intermarrying, which he considered one of the strengths of American culture. Although Edison may have had some notion that ethnic characteristics were influenced by cultural and social contexts, he nonetheless thought that Jews as a group couldn't be trusted, and he held similar prejudices against other ethnic groups, such as Sicilians, whom he believed "You can't trust. . . . They'll stick a knife in your back."[15]

Edison may have treated some general racial and ethnic characteristics as environmentally determined, but he also believed that certain personal genetic characteristics were markers of behavior. Although usually he was most concerned with whether someone was capable of doing a job and working hard, Edison sometimes did draw on phrenological theories that claimed that the contours of the skull were indicative of mental faculties and character when he considered a new hire. He sometimes asked a prospective employee for a photograph because he thought that the head shown could determine what kind of work its owner was best suited for. Thus, he believed that "a pear shaped skull is the best type," but that a "pin head [was] not good for inspector."[16] In general, however, Edison was more concerned with the willingness of his employees to work hard and do the job than he was with their ethnic or racial background or physical appearance.

Following his "retirement," interviews with Edison increasingly focused on his speculations about the future and proposals for dealing with important issues of the day rather than his current inventive work. Although he occasionally made statements that generated some controversy, notably the heated debate provoked by his comments in the October 2, 1910, issue of the *New York Times* in which he denied the immortality of the human soul (see Chapter 1), most of his statements, no matter how speculative, seem to have been well regarded by most reporters and by the general public. Nonetheless, there were occasions when even a seemingly innocuous prediction about future inventions could cause a bit of trouble. After an article appeared in *Cosmopolitan* filled with Edison's predictions about the future, including the idea that books could be made from thin sheets of nickel "one twenty-thousandth of an inch thick . . . cheaper, tougher, and more flexible than an ordinary sheet of paper," Frank Dyer suggested to the head of TAE Inc. advertising that "Mr. Edison's prediction as to the use of sheet nickel as a substitute for paper is a very long look into the future, and I believe it would be unwise for us to say anything about it."[17]

Edison not only thought that technology could provide an answer to vexing social problems, but he also believed that the methods used to develop new technology were themselves applicable to these problems. He argued that in the city of the future "time saving will be of prime importance and traffic congestion will be solved by the mathematician, who will supplant the traffic policeman; crime will decrease before the advent of the scientific policeman and taxes will become astonishingly low with government of the cities by experts." Edison was very much in the mainstream of Progressive Era city reform movements as he called for the complete elimination of politics from city management, "turning it over to real experts," such as a "highly trained mayor, educated as a specialist in municipal management."[18]

Edison also criticized what he saw as unscientific attempts to regulate business, such as the Sherman Antitrust Act, which he contended had been conceived "as a sort of experiment, and instead of conducting all the experiments beforehand they then try it on business while it is still an experiment. . . . It is a hopeless task for lawyers to try to make such a law unassisted by the industrial experts of the country." Edison made his own attempt to translate the approach he took to technical problems to those of economics. During the early 1920s, after reading extensively on banking and finance he worked out an idea he had long held about replacing the gold standard by a system of commodities exchange based on "an international index of value for exchangeable necessaries of life. . . . A great amount of research and other work would need to be done before this system could be established. . . . But what is better money than that based on certified commodities in government warehouses and merchants notes for goods actually sold and discounted by a bank taking currency issued by the Federal Reserve Bank, with notes as security." In essence Edison proposed replacing gold reserves with commodity reserves. In part, this idea would have been a way for Ford to finance his proposed Muscle Shoals power project, and Ford had provided support for Edison's research on commodity money. Edison proposed that notes for the funding of the project be issued by the government to pay the workmen and suppliers. These notes would serve as government currency but they would be retired by the earnings of the dam. The published version of Edison's plan, entitled A Proposed Amendment to the Federal Reserve Banking System, primarily focused on the plight of farmers. As William Trufant Foster, the director of the Pollack Foundation for Economic Research, noted in his address on "Edison-Ford Commodity Money" before the Academy of Political Science, Edison and Ford "have long been distrustful of the gold standard, distressed over fluctuations in the purchasing power of the dollar, eager to aid farmers to obtain loans easily, 'to divorce agriculture from the banking system,' and to abolish speculation in farm products." Because Edison was "the most distinguished of the numerous advocates of what is called commodity money," Foster focused his critique on Edison's plan, which enjoyed a brief notoriety but was never seriously considered for adoption.[19]

The most influential interview that Edison gave on a great public question appeared in the May 31, 1915, issue of the New York Times. Responding to concerns about American military preparedness raised by war in Europe, Edison described how the United States could prepare without raising taxes or militarizing the country. Rather than a standing army, he advocated raising "a great surplus of trained men, then send[ing] them back to industry, with payment of a small annual retainer." Not surprisingly, Edison saw modern war as "more a matter of machines than men." He thought it would be possible to raise a well-equipped volunteer army in a relatively short time by organizing a system of armory factories and state militias and by constructing an enormous fleet of airplanes, submarines, and other naval vessels "to be kept ready in drydock, practically in storage, and fully up to date, until needed." Perhaps most significantly, Edison proposed the establishment of "a great research laboratory, jointly under military and naval and civilian control" to develop "great guns, the minutiae of new explosives, all the technique of military and naval progression. . . . When the time came, if it ever did, we could take advantage of the knowledge gained through this research work and quickly manufacture in large quantities the very latest and most efficient instruments of warfare."[20]

Edison's statements prompted Josephus Daniels, the Secretary of the Navy, to write Edison on July 7: "I think your ideas and mine coincide if an interview with you recently published in the New York Times was correct. There is a very great service that you can render the navy and the country at large, and which I am encouraged to believe from a paragraph in Mr. Marshall's interview, you will consent to undertake, as it seems to be in line with your own thoughts." Daniels was referring specifically to Edison's proposal for the establishment of a military laboratory:

> One of the imperative needs of the navy, in my judgment, is machinery and facilities for utilizing the natural inventive genius of Americans to meet the new conditions of warfare as shown abroad, and it is my intention if a practical way can be worked out . . . to establish at the earliest moment a department, to which all ideas and suggestions, either from the service or from civilian inventors, can be.

Daniels told Edison that his plan for organizing such a department "is still very hazy as to details," but that he thought it met "with your ideas of such a department for the Government," which would undertake experimental and investigative work. Explaining that the prospects for "getting the public interested and back of this project will be enormously increased if we can have, at the start, some man whose inventive genius is recognized by the whole world," he asked Edison "if you would be willing, as a service to your country, to act as an adviser to this board, to take such things as seem to you to be of value, but which we are not, at present, equipped to investigate, and to use your own magnificent facilities in such investigation."[21]

When they met at Glenmont on the evening of July 15 to discuss Daniels's ideas, Edison agreed to head the Naval Consulting Board and to help choose its members. He suggested that instead of picking out a few well-known inventors "who would represent themselves alone," they should "enlist the scientific and engineering and inventive organizations."[22] They therefore decided to ask the eleven largest engineering societies to select two members each for the advisory board. In drawing up the list, Edison omitted both the National Academy of Sciences and the American Physical Society because "it was his desire to have this Board composed of *practical* men who are accustomed to *doing* things, and not *talking* about them." However, he did include members from the American Mathematical Society because "*very few really practical men* are . . . expert mathematicians, and [he] thought it advisable to have one or two men on the Board who could figure to the 'nth' power, if required."[23] Edison's ideas regarding the role of mathematicians arose from his own lack in this regard and his appreciation for the work that men such as Francis Upton, Charles Clarke, and Arthur Kennelly had done to make up for his deficiencies. However, most of the men appointed by the engineering societies were of a new generation that was college educated and quite capable at mathematical analysis. Members of the scientific community, including those on the Naval Consulting Board, objected to their lack of representation. In 1916 the National Academy of Sciences, which had advised the government on scientific and technical issues since the Civil War, convinced President Woodrow Wilson to create a National Research Council. Made up of leading scientists and engineers from universities, industry, and the military, the Council's role was to encourage both pure and applied research and to promote cooperation among the country's research institutions.

The key difference between the Council and the Board, and even among members of the Board, related to the role of pure research and was the result of an important shift that was taking place in the American industrial research community. This was apparent to the Naval officer who wrote the official history of the Naval Consulting Board, published in 1920. In contrast to the Naval Consulting Board, which was advisory, the National Research Council "under the modern method of organization . . . was in a position to do a specific thing. . . . After war was declared, comparatively large sums were placed at the disposal of the council for scientific experiments. . . . As most inventions in modern warfare are based upon highly technical data and information, it was not long before the activities of the National Research Council led it into the field of the scientific subjects upon which naval inventions were founded." It was the Council rather than the Board, he concluded, that "helped to build up the scientific departments of the Army and Navy."[24] Although individual members conducted the research, the primary work of the Board involved the effort to mobilize the nation's independent inventors. The formal results of the Board's work were disappointing; only about 100 of the more than 100,000 inventions suggested to the Board merited further investigation, and only one device was actually built.

The contrast in research methods between inventors like Edison and the university-educated scientists and engineers who were working in the nation's leading industrial and academic laboratories was apparent within the Board and spurred a vigorous debate over plans for a naval laboratory. This was a debate that Edison would eventually lose because his methods, which had been at the forefront of industrial research in the United States during the nineteenth century, now seemed increasingly outmoded. Edison explained both his mode of working and his plans for the laboratory to the House Committee on Naval Affairs in March 1916: "The object of the laboratory is to perfect all the different details, or one unit of all the war machinery, and do it quickly. My methods are probably a little different from anybody else's in laboratory work. When I want to make a thing quickly, I put everybody in the shop on it. If the longest thing takes ten hours, then in 15 hours I have got my machine, because I put a man on every part."

Shedding further light on his own techniques, Edison claimed that "in all laboratories like this we have no system; we have no rules, but we have a big scrap heap." He also modeled the physical layout of the proposed naval facility on his own laboratory. It would contain "all universal machinery, the same as they use in the great tool shops for making tools for manufacturing. I can do almost anything in that shop. We have a foundry, a forge shop, and a pattern shop, with all kinds of things, and with men who have had experience, and we can build anything, and we can build it quickly." The laboratory would design and test a working model of a machine and then produce the drawings and gauges necessary for the manufacturers who would fabricate it. Another member of the Naval Consulting Board, mining engineer William Saunders, called the facility an "experimental station and laboratory" when he testified in favor of Edison's plan. Edison's plans astounded the chemists and physicists on the Board. Chemist Leo Bakeland noted that he, Willis Whitney, the director of General Electric's research laboratory, and Robert Woodward, president of the Carnegie Institution, "took into consideration primarily the chemical and physical departments of the projected laboratory, and it was very interesting to see that although we had prepared the recommendations independently, we very closely agreed as to [its] cost and operation." However, they "felt like small fry" when Edison and other inventors and engineers on the Board "began to show what could be done. . . . We realized that the needs for such a laboratory are much vaster than anything which we chemists or physicists could accomplish."[25]

Although the full Board supported Edison's plans for a $5 million laboratory, the House appropriated less than half this amount for construction and only $500,000 for the first year's operating expenses. The Board decided to submit a revised plan, and a committee, which included Edison, submitted a report in December 1916 that called for a laboratory that focused on basic research, experimental testing, and quality control. Instead of the extensive shop facilities originally proposed by Edison, which were capable of constructing full-scale prototypes, it would be equipped only for building small-scale experimental models. The committee also recommended that it be located in Annapolis, Maryland, on the site of a small experimental station operated by the Navy's Bureau of Steam Engineering and near the Naval Academy. Edison, however, opposed this plan and submitted a minority report in which he continued to argue for his original idea of the laboratory as a "works" capable of rapidly building and testing experimenting devices. Regarding the role of basic research, he argued that "Research work in every branch of science and industry, costing millions of dollars . . . has been [going] on for many years . . . only a ridiculously small percentage has yet been applied. . . . It is therefore useless to go on piling up more data." He also argued that Sandy Hook, New Jersey, provided a more suitable location for the laboratory because of its proximity to New York, because "the very heart of such a laboratory [as he proposed] is rapid construction, and there is no place in this country where this can be done successfully, except within one hour's journey of New York City, the market from which everything can be obtained quickly." Edison also opposed the new plan and the Annapolis site because he believed, "whether right or wrong, that the public would look to me to make the Laboratory a success, and that I would have to do 90% of the work. Therefore, if I cannot obtain proper conditions to make it a success, I would not undertake it nor be connected with it in the remotest degree."[26] Elmer Sperry, a noted electrical inventor and designer of gyroscope stabilizers, who was a great admirer of Edison, hoped to affect a compromise by suggesting that the laboratory be built at the New York navy yard where there were machinists and shops that could supplement its facilities, but Edison remained adamant in his opposition and Daniels was unwilling to act without the inventor's approval. Edison reiterated his position prior to the Board's final report on the laboratory in June 1918. In a letter to Daniels he explained that the laboratory in his proposal

is to build anything from a submarine to a microscope and is not a research laboratory; it is a constructing laboratory—more properly a universal machine shop—whose specialty is rapid construction by special tools and system of working.

Of course the board can do what in their judgment they think best, but they cannot expect me to agree to recommend what I firmly believe will be a failure to give rapid production. I am so deaf that I have seldom attended meetings of this consulting board and am so entirely out of touch with it that it seems to be a species of deception for me to continue as its head, so I think I had better disconnect and work direct for the Navy, the board electing a young and aggressive man in my place.[27]

Edison continued to press unsuccessfully for his plan and did not resign from the Board until January 1921, following the decision to establish the Naval Research Laboratory in Washington under the direction of naval officers instead of civilians as he advocated.

In January 1917, several months before the United States entered the war, Edison had begun to devote nearly all his time to experiments for the Navy. Over the next two years he devised some forty-five inventions and plans, including methods for detecting submarines, torpedoes, and airplanes, detecting the location of guns, blinding submarines and periscopes, and camouflaging ships. Two ideas that he thought particularly important were a sea anchor for turning ships quickly to avoid torpedoes and a plan for night shipping to avoid submarines. He also worked out several minor ideas, such as an extension ladder for lookouts, a telephone system for ships, and a method of protecting observers from smoke-stack gas. Edison conducted experiments at the laboratory in West Orange, on a ridge overlooking the laboratory, and in the waters of New Jersey, Long Island Sound, and Key West, Florida, on a yacht fitted up for his use by the Navy. Daniels also provided Edison with an office in Washington, D.C., and Mina accompanied him during the time he was there compiling data on ship sinkings that he used in devising his plan for night shipping.

None of Edison's inventions or plans were adopted by the Navy, which Edison called a "close corporation" whose officers "seem to resent ideas for the betterment of the Navy rather than welcome them."[28] He also complained that they obstructed his experiments by failing to provide or delaying his use of ships and other equipment. It is possible that some of the opposition to Edison's ideas was caused in part by the ongoing investigation into a submarine explosion that had occurred in December 1915. The Navy blamed the Edison storage battery that they had been using for the explosion, while the Edison company charged the ship's crew with negligence. However, Edison was not the only prominent inventor to have his ideas rejected. In December 1917, when Reginald Fessenden complained about "being turned down by the Navy people," Edison told him "this is true of all others."[29] At least some of Edison's ideas were turned down because he failed to understand the Navy's needs. Even Elmer Sperry, whose work on gyroscopes had given him insights into naval vessels, had his plan for a system using antisubmarine nets turned down after tests demonstrated several difficulties and it was found that the allies had already investigated the system.

In fact, Naval engineers and officers did not turn down all research efforts. What they did support fully was research that they considered more up-to-date than Edison's. As proponents of a research-oriented facility and opponents of Edison's proposed works laboratory, they may have felt that his approach lacked the mathematical rigor and theoretical basis that their university training had taught them were the foundations of modern research. This may explain why Edison was frustrated in his efforts to develop a submarine detector. His work on this problem was not inconsequential. He conducted extensive experiments and developed a listening device that he later claimed was "given practical tests" that showed it fulfilled "all requirements" and worked "perfectly even when the ship was plowing at full speed through the roughest seas." On at least one occasion "a submarine bell 5 1/2 miles away" could be heard during a storm and the device "had no difficulty whatever in hearing a torpedo more than 4,000 yards away."[30] Nonetheless, the Navy recalled the vessel Edison was using for his tests before they were completed.

The Navy gave much greater support to two other research efforts concerned with submarine detection. The first of these was led by Willis Whitney, head of the Naval Consulting Board's submarine-detection subcommittee, who set up a research team consisting of industrial scientists and engineers from General Electric and AT&T. The team worked in an experimental station in Nahant, Massachusetts, that was supported by the Navy's Bureau of Steam Engineering. Although the Nahant researchers ended up developing a simple acoustic device that was in effect an underwater stethoscope, their general approach to the problem probably seemed more scientific and modern to the naval engineers, as did their continuing effort to develop electronic versions of the detector. The other research program, which was supported by the Navy even after the Nahant group developed its detector, was undertaken by a group of academic physicists at a facility in New London, Connecticut, that had been established by the National Research Council. The physicists actually succeeded in developing a superior detector, but it proved more difficult to manufacture than the Nahant device. From the standpoint of the Navy, these detectors outclassed not only Edison's, but also those developed by the British, who had been working on the problem since before the war.[31]

Edison was well aware of these other research efforts, and at Whitney's request he even wrote in support of the New London laboratory, although he did not approve of Whitney's idea that it should become the basis for the naval laboratory. Edison may have urged Daniels to extend the research work at New London, but he continued to press for his own plan for a large works laboratory in Sandy Hook, New Jersey. When the Naval Research Laboratory was finally established after the war, it drew on the industrial and academic scientific research models of New London and Nahant rather than the older style of research symbolized by Edison's original plans for the naval laboratory.[32]

Edison's most important war work took place long before Daniels asked him to assist the Navy. When war broke out in Europe in the summer of 1914, the English government put an embargo on carbolic acid, which Edison used in his phonograph records and that was also an ingredient in several other industrial products, including explosives. Unable to obtain it from domestic suppliers and faced with the prospect of having to shut down his phonograph record plant, Edison decided to start his own carbolic acid plant. His success in accomplishing this within a very short time could only have reinforced his ideas about the naval laboratory. According to newspaper and magazine accounts from November 1914:

> He spent three days and nights looking up and examining the different known processes of making synthetic carbolic acid. There are some half a dozen of them. He narrowed these down to one or two, took them into this laboratory and did some experimenting. Finally, at the end of the third day, he had fixed on a certain one, known as the sulphonic acid process, as most satisfactory. This was early in August. . . . He detailed 40 men, draftsmen and chemists, and told them what he wanted; divided them into three eight-hour shifts, and gave the command to start. In a week, 163 consecutive hours of work for 40 men in three shifts and Edison in one, the plans were finished. . . . Seventeen days afterward his plant delivered its

first day's output of product, which other chemists assured him would take at least six months.[33]

Edison was soon besieged by other producers who needed carbolic acid, and he decided to erect a second plant to meet the demand. As he increased production of carbolic acid, Edison discovered a shortage of benzol, which was used in manufacturing it. Benzol, one of several useful chemical byproducts produced by the burning of coal in coke ovens during the process of manufacturing steel, also was used in producing aniline, another crucial ingredient in his records. Edison therefore erected a benzol plant in Johnstown, Pennsylvania, and contracted with several Pennsylvania steel companies to deliver the chemicals to the plant. He erected a second plant in Woodward, Alabama, and arranged an aniline plant in New Jersey, which also began to sell aniline oil to textile manufacturers who used it for dyeing. Pressed by the demands of manufacturers and the U.S. government, Edison soon established other plants and began producing several other crucial chemicals. In each case he applied the same technique, studying the problem to determine the best manufacturing methods and then using teams of men to design the works for their production. When he entered the business of manufacturing chemicals, Edison drew on what had become one of his strong suits as an innovator. He was a very capable production engineer, skilled at developing improved methods of production and directing a team to design, build, and work out the bugs of large-scale manufacturing plants.

Edison began manufacturing chemicals as a temporary expedient, and within three years, as other manufacturers entered the field, he had shut down most of his chemical plants. By November 1917 TAE Inc. was mainly producing aniline, and rather than go into the production of new chemicals Charles Edison, who was running TAE Inc. while his father devoted his time to war research, thought that it was time to "wind up and sell out our apparatus." Writing to his father in Washington, he remarked:

> You once told me that more money is lost by not knowing when to stop than in almost any other way. Our Chemical Plants were designed to last three years, and your guesses are usually right. . . . It is the business that is constantly changing and unstable that requires the most attention from the executive heads, and in this respect the Chemical business, as far as we are concerned, is very similar to the Motion Picture business. In other words, even though it were possible to start on some product that would net us a nice profit, it would not be very long before we would have to change from this to something else, and from that something else to something else, and so on indefinitely, and each change will mean prolonged discussions and meetings and reorganizations, for which at this time we cannot afford to spend the time.[34]

Like most American companies, TAE Inc. had converted much of its productive capacity to war work and lost much of its administrative staff and labor force to the armed services. Neither Charles nor his father was willing to commit many resources to the company's film business, which had begun a steady decline following the breakup of the Motion Picture Patents Company as an illegal trust in 1915. The Edison motion picture had long ceased to be at the forefront of the motion picture industry. Although Edison and his company focused on technical innovations such as sound and color as a way of regaining market share, competitors focused on ultimately more significant innovations in the dramatic arts. Faced with rising costs due to increased movie length, higher production standards, and the emergence of the star system, as well as the loss of its European markets due to the war, TAE Inc. was faced with the prospect of either committing more resources to effectively compete with its competitors or selling out. With the U.S. entry into World War I, it became apparent that resources would be better spent on products with wartime uses, such as batteries, dictating machines, and even phonographs (Edison and his engineers designed a special field model for the armed forces). Even though phonograph production did decline during the war there was every expectation that the business would revive afterwards, and the company kept the Phonograph Works busy by producing bombsights, gas masks, and other military products. Based on this assessment, TAE Inc. sold its motion picture business in early 1918.

As expected, there was a postwar economic boom that benefited the phonograph industry. However, by the end of 1920 the boom had come to an end and the nation's economy suffered a serious downturn as the government pursued deflationary policies. The phonograph business in particular was affected by the postwar depression, and during the 1920s the industry as a whole suffered a decline in production relative to the previous decade. TAE Inc. was also slow to meet the challenge of increased competition and the rise of radio.

By the end of 1920 Edison had become so concerned over the effects of the downturn that he reasserted his authority and began an "economy campaign" that greatly downsized the Edison industries. Edison was guided in this by his experience of past depressions as well as by his belief that most businesses, including his own, suffered from too much overhead, "too much supervision of supervision, from too many executives, in short, from too many nonproductive additions to both manufacturing and selling." Much to Charles Edison's chagrin, his father wanted him to cut management personnel so drastically "that I started worrying about the fact that he wanted me to destroy this magnificent organization that I had built." This led to "several battles" between them, but Charles finally conceded and later became convinced that his father had been right. Nonetheless, several top managers left the company, and in the long run this may have affected the company's ability to meet new problems.[35]

Edison cut his factory force even more dramatically. In a time of rising wages, he argued, the best way to increase profits was to introduce new production machinery that would make it possible to double output while reducing the number of workers by half. Edison focused his own efforts on improving production methods, particularly in record manufacturing. The Engineering

Department, too, focused its efforts on "lower[ing] production costs, without lowering quality, or making fundamental changes in design." By February 1922 Edison had reduced employment in the company's plants from 10,000 to 3,000.[36] Edison's downsizing appeared to many, particularly those on the factory floor, as completely arbitrary. Karl Ehricke, whom Edison hired as a chemist in 1920, recalled "stories about sometimes he'd feel he had too many people and walk up and down the production lines saying 'you're fired,' [to] every other one or something." While Edison clearly could be quite arbitrary in his hiring and firing practices, it does appear that his downsizing in the early 1920s was generally based on careful analysis of the work force. Nonetheless, the manner in which he let people go, combined with his anti-union stance and tightfisted wage policies, led to hard feelings on the part of the factory workers. In 1972, A. E. Johnson, whom Edison had hired as a record tester in July 1920, observed that "the people who worked very closely with Mr. Edison, as the years go by, have all very fond memories. However, its been my experience here in West Orange that every one of the folks who worked in the factory, weren't next to the right hand men, I haven't found one person who expressed a good opinion of him. . . . Even today you find around here in West Orange people who say, 'Oh he was rotten, he was an S.O.B.' "[37]

By the time downsizing came to an end in 1922 Edison had reduced not only the number of managers and workers in his plants but even the personnel of the Engineering Department, which was only one-sixth as large as it had been at its peak in October 1920. He also sought other savings apart from lower labor costs as part of his economy campaign. He and Mambert collided over issues related to what Edison termed "mere 'bookkeeping,'" which included reducing the number of bookkeepers and ending the practice of making cost accounts, which Edison believed "never did us any good."[38] In 1924, Mambert, too, would leave the company. As he attempted to gain control over his company's expenditures Edison began supervising all advertising expenses and put an end to those he considered wasteful. For example, he thought phonograph advertising in newspapers would be better "expended *directly* with dealers to increase sales" and that "advertising an artical which is made obsolete by a subsequent advertisement like phonograph records is an absolute waste of money." Edison also ended the use of the musical scouts the company had begun to use in an effort to "beat the other fellow to it in the matter of dance music and comic opera hits." Personnel and other decisions made by Edison may have left the company in better immediate financial shape, but they probably weakened its ability to respond to future challenges.[39]

The most important of these challenges came from phonograph competitors. Besides the continuing complaints over the quality of the artists and songs released on Edison records, TAE Inc. had the additional problem of facing a shift in the market toward lower priced phonographs. At the end of the war the best-selling Edison machine was its most expensive, the Official Laboratory Model, which sold for $285. Furthermore, the work of the company's laboratory and engineers was aimed at "the improvement of the product rather than the lowering of its cost."[40] To increase sales Edison experimented with a number of different sales campaigns. He also developed a loud reproducer for "Restaurants, Movies & small dance halls" to meet a growing demand, and in an effort to trump the competition he produced long-playing records of 20 minutes and 40 minutes (one- and two-sided), which the company promoted as providing more music at only a small increase in price although they required a special reproducer. Advertising campaigns for Edison phonographs, however, suggested that Edison and his managers still had little appreciation for how much the phonograph business had changed. Once again the focus was on Edison's technical accomplishments: "Edison has at last perfected the phonograph" read one typical advertisement. Furthermore, in an era of cheap phonographs, potential customers were told that "Every Edison phonograph in use today is a perfect example of individual craftsmanship" and even about the "tremendous cost of maintaining this ideal."[41]

Edison continued to focus on the technical qualities of reproduction in his phonograph and records and rejected any changes that he considered deleterious to this. Thus, he rejected repeated pleas by others in the Edison company for a shift to lateral cut records or the adoption of an adaptor to allow the records of other manufacturers to be played on Edison machines. And he rejected the most important potential innovation being adopted by his competitors, combined radio-phonograph sets. Since 1922 phonograph dealers had been imploring Edison to go into radio. Over the next few years "every Edison Distributor" was "obliged to add radio to his line to keep his head above water and his books out of the red." Edison continued to object that "there are several laws of nature which cannot be overcome when attempts are made to make the radio a musical instrument," and he was convinced that the improvements he was making on the phonograph "will make it very much more desirable in competition with the radio."[42] Edison was not alone among phonograph manufacturers in his objection to radio; Victor too delayed introducing radios in its machines until its own sales declined precipitously and the company neared bankruptcy. Although Edison considered radio to be a "craze," Victor found that consumers were demanding "the radio timbre of electric recording" and the company also introduced its new Orthophonic line with electrical pickup in 1926.[43] After considerable difficulty Charles and his brother Theodore finally convinced their father to introduce an electrical pickup and radio-phonograph sets in 1928. By then it was too late. At the end of October 1929 TAE Inc. announced that it would discontinue its phonograph and record businesses. Ironically, the reason given was "the fact that we are greatly handicapped in the expansion of our Radio Business because of limited factory space, [which] led Mr. Edison, The Executive Board, and Mr. Walsh to the opinion that our wisest course would be to devote the Record Plant to the production of Radio and kindred new developments in the radio and home entertainment field." However, a year later, as the Great Depression worsened, Charles told his father that he and Theodore had decided to quit the radio business, "the last of our products to carry the name Edison into the home." It turned out that his father had been right when he told Charles, "In three years it'll be such a cutthroat business that nobody will make any money . . . you'll get busted if you get into it."[44]

By 1927 Edison had essentially retired from business to begin his last major research campaign—finding an alternative source of natural rubber. He had some time before given up the task of listening to recording artists, having "become almost totally deaf." As Charles, who had assumed the presidency of TAE Inc. in 1926, noted, his father "want[ed] to concentrate on rubber and not bother much with the details of the business."[45] Edison used rubber for insulation in his storage batteries, and like many other manufacturers he grew concerned when the British rubber monopoly, which controlled nearly 70 percent of worldwide rubber production, raised prices dramatically in 1925–1926. The rise in prices caused a more general American concern over British dominance of the market to give way to a state of near panic and led to an investigation of the problem by Secretary of Commerce Herbert Hoover. The United States was particularly vulnerable because it consumed more than 70 percent of the total rubber output, much of it used in the rapidly expanding automobile industry. Many American manufacturers recalled the chemical shortages of World War I and were particularly concerned over the dangers arising from over reliance on foreign suppliers of crucial materials. Among them were Edison and his friends Henry Ford and Harvey Firestone, who needed plentiful and cheap supplies of rubber for automobile tires. As Edison later told a reporter for *Popular Science Monthly*, "[we] were considering what this country would do in case of a war which cut off our rubber supply. . . . We decided that the thing for us to do was to find a source of rubbers, so that we can produce it quickly right here at home."[46]

To free themselves from reliance on the British monopoly, Firestone and Ford both attempted to exploit rubber plantations in Liberia and Brazil and to experiment with growing rubber trees at their winter homes in Florida; Firestone tried recycling rubber as well. Beginning about 1922 Edison had begun to read extensively in the literature on rubber as he made plans to erect a plant for making the hard rubber used in his storage battery (hard rubber was also used in the electroplating process for phonograph records) to reduce his costs. He also experimented with a process for manufacturing chlorinated rubber that he considered using in the manufacture of his disc records. His conversations with Firestone about the cost of rubber led him to begin conducting botanical experiments on rubber plants at Fort Myers in 1923. Two years later Firestone suggested to Ford and Edison that they form a $1 million corporation to produce rubber domestically, but instead they agreed to a more modest proposal to fund Edison's research on the production of rubber from domestic plants. In 1927 they each put up $25,000 to form the Edison Botanic Research Corporation, and they each contributed an additional $25,000 the following year.

During the years of Edison's most intensive work on the problem, between 1927 and 1930, the research cost $168,844.70.[47]

As usual, Edison began by thoroughly investigating rubber cultivation and manufacture and then laid out a research strategy to solve the problem at hand. As he explained to the reporter for *Popular Science Monthly*, "we can't compete with the tropics in commercial rubber" because the "American workingman can't and should not be asked to work for the low wages necessary to make commercial rubber cultivation possible." He was, however, aware of an alternative strategy for the production of domestic rubber that was already in place. A limited amount of rubber was being produced in California from the gum of the guayule shrub, a plant that grew readily in the southwest. Mechanized harvesting and processing of this shrub made it possible to compete with imported rubber, but as Edison noted the plant took five years to mature sufficiently for this purpose and "all the guayule rubber grown in the United States will not provide a large enough supply in case of war." To solve the problem he wanted to "find something which will produce enough rubber, within a year after the beginning of war, to replace the year's supply which we normally have on hand; something which won't be occupying valuable land meantime, or tying up capital, or requiring a continuous expenditure of money without any return. . . . An annual crop, something which the farmer can sow in the field, by machinery, which will come to maturity in eight or nine months, which can then be harvested by machinery, and from which rubber can be obtained by processes almost entirely mechanical, with the least amount of hand labor."[48]

By the summer of 1927 Edison had nine acres at Fort Myers devoted "to the growth and cultivation of a great number of latex-bearing vines, plants, and shrubs, as well as several species of Ficus." He also hired several field men, including a number of university botanists, to collect latex-bearing plants in the southern states and as far north as New Jersey. Edison frequently went on local collecting expeditions himself, and as he had done so famously in the past, he once again launched a national and international search for rubber-producing plants. He was assisted in this effort by the New York Botanic Gardens and the Arnold Arboretum in Boston as well as by station agents of the Union Pacific Railroad and private collectors. Edison eventually received over 17,000 plant samples representing 2,222 species "classified in 977 genera and 186 natural plant families."[49] The plants and seeds were sent to Edison at West Orange and Fort Myers, where he and his staff tested them for rubber content and experimented with cultivation and processing methods.

By March 1929 Edison had reached some important conclusions about the types of plants best suited for his purposes:

It seems that most of the wild plants collected and transplanted were for the quality of their rubber and not their quantity. Last year at may-June period we didn't know that the viscous tar-like substance from plants was really a partially polymerized rubber. Nearly every high-yield plant gave this viscous sticky stuff, hence we only put on the list plants that gave good rubber. Subsequently the discovery that this viscous stuff, if dispersed in benzol, could be coagulated into good rubber has caused us to change our kind of plants desirable for transplanting. We now want high-yielding plants. Also the realization that shrubs, even if perennial, are not so desirable as herbs which are also perennial. Shrubs in many cases cannot stand 100% pruning, many die and others are weakened; whereas an herb perennial is cut just as the seeds are ripe and plant stems and tops have started to die . . . which is only what it would do by itself—hence no injury.[50]

He searched through his gardens "to pick out plants that probably give one ton of leaves per acre" and became particularly enamored of the genus *Solidago*, known commonly as goldenrod.

Goldenrod proved to have several potential advantages over other plants. It could "be mowed like wheat and the rubber obtained by chemical solvents with very little machinery." Furthermore, whereas many plants took years to reach maturity, "Goldenrod only requires three months. Once planted it is perennial and, like sugarcane, comes up after cutting. After planting it need not be planted again for several years." Finally, Edison found the rubber in goldenrod to be "entirely in the leaf" and he devised a machine for stripping the leaves from the stem. While he focused on goldenrod, Edison continued to collect and test other plants as well. He also had Firestone make two sets of tires from guayule rubber so he could test them on automobiles because he was worried "that if results are unfavorable it is probable that my rubber will on tests be the same or worse." It is apparently these guayule tires that have led to the belief that Firestone made a set of tires from goldenrod for Edison.[51]

By the fall of 1930 Edison was planning to begin extracting rubber in quantity, and he expected that "there will be plenty of it if war cause[s] the introduction of Golden rod as a source of Rubber." A year later, however, it was much less clear that this would occur. As Mina's brother John Miller reported to the stockholders of the Edison Botanic Research Corporation in December 1931, "From articles appearing in the trade papers during the Fall . . . synthetic rubber undoubtedly will become a factor in rubber supply. . . . Should this rubber become a practicable commercial product possibly the need of an emergency supply from Golden Rod will end." Edison had rejected research on synthetic rubber from the beginning "as it would require years of work." His estimation of the difficulty of developing commercially acceptable synthetic rubber turned out to be quite accurate. Nonetheless, when war did come the government supported a crash program to move synthetic rubber from the laboratory to the market.[52]

At the age of eighty Edison clearly did not feel that he had a lot of time to develop synthetic rubber, but there were other reasons for his focusing on alternative plant sources. This involved a kind of materials research that Edison had undertaken on many of his major projects, including lamp filaments, recording surfaces, and storage battery elements. Furthermore, his approach involved a traditional kind of organic chemistry. Research on synthetics relied on the development of colloid chemistry and on new theoretical knowledge regarding the structure of long-chain macromolecules, which had revolutionized the field of polymer chemistry. Although Aylsworth's earlier work on phenol resins and the development of natural rubber both had involved colloid chemistry and polymerization, by the 1920s Edison had no chemists on his staff who were prepared to undertake the kind of research necessary to take advantage of the new research in polymer chemistry.

Edison's lack of chemists familiar with the most recent research had grown out of the frustrations he experienced in his relations with university-educated chemists, particularly those who had studied in Germany. In 1903, when Edison fired Martin Rosanoff, a young chemist who had graduated from New York University and then studied in Germany and France, he complained that Rosanoff was "all talk & not a practical Chemist—I have made up my mind that he is the last foreigner in the chemical line that I shall hire, I prefer bright young Americans." These were just the sort of chemists he employed in the 1920s. The experience of A. E. Johnson, one of the college questionnaire men hired by Edison in 1920, was typical. Johnson recalled that upon meeting Edison the first thing the inventor said was "You like chemistry?" When Johnson replied that he did "but I don't know anything about it," Edison said "I'm going to make a chemist out of you. . . . Trouble with these damn graduate chemists, they think they know everything. I can't tell them anything." Karl Ehricke, another of Edison's college hires, gave a similar account of his becoming a chemist. He also noted that Edison preferred men whom he considered generalists: "He didn't want to hire technical training, he wanted to train them himself, and evidently he wanted to pick men . . . that were observant and generally interested in things and were able to observe things." The questionnaires he designed were intended to test for general knowledge and what he considered clear thinking rather than specific scientific or technical knowledge.[53]

By the 1920s the increase in scientific and technical knowledge had begun to make generalists such as Edison increasingly outmoded. This became evident during his last major experiment—his effort to improve his own declining health. During 1931, after returning from Fort Myers, where he spent the winter experimenting, Edison's health had reached a point where, his brother-in-law reported, he was "unable to do much experimental work."[54] As a consequence, John Miller took charge of the rubber research while Mina helped her husband by screening his correspondence. At the beginning of August Edison suffered a serious collapse, and by early October his condition had become critical as his kidneys began to fail from uremic poisoning. Ironically, as it turned out, Edison's final illness was a consequence of his own experimental methods.

Edison had been troubled by diabetes and stomach disorders for years, and as was his habit he had read extensively in the medical literature on these subjects to determine a course of self-treatment. According to his doctor, Edison "had a profound knowledge of medicine. He had for many years always read everything pertaining to diabetes and stomach disorders. His interest in chemistry was not limited to his industrial experiments, but included an unusual knowledge and understanding of physiological chemistry and of pharmacy." Edison had long taken an interest in medical matters, and this was not the first time that he had tried to treat himself. As early as 1878 he had developed the patent medicine polyform to treat his neuralgia. When he was diagnosed with diabetes in the early 1890s, a doctor from his insurance company reported that "Mr. Edison in [his] usual way has started a wholesale experiment, every man woman and child in the laboratory is to be tested for sugar by all know[n] tests, I presume we will soon hear from him on the subject." And during an illness in 1891 he reportedly told friends worried about his health that "my ailment is not serious, if properly treated. If I were to follow your advice, take all the drugs you suggest or all that the physician you advise me to call in would prescribe, I would become worse. The fact is my liver is out of order and my kidneys are not in just the condition they should be. I will remedy that very speedily. My cure will be a change in diet."[55]

As a follower of Luigi Cornaro (see Chapter 1), Edison had been experimenting with his diet all of his life, and it is not surprising that he also took this path in treating his later stomach troubles. To relieve his gastric discomfort during the late 1920s Edison studied the subject, "even to the determination of the kind of gases formed during digestion," and "experimented with different diets to determine the effect of food on his stomach pain." Discovering that milk relieved his gastric pain, he began to increase the milk in his diet and to reduce his consumption of other foods until he gave up other food entirely. For three years he consumed nothing more than a pint of milk every three hours. He also rarely drank water because he disliked its taste. In May 1931 he further reduced his intake of milk from fourteen to seven glasses a day. Not surprisingly, to the doctor who treated him in the last year of his life, this diet proved insufficient in both nutrients and fluid. Edison lost both weight and strength. The lack of fluids also meant, according to his doctor, that "his kidneys were unable to carry off the waste products which they ordinarily eliminate, and these substances accumulated in the blood in sufficient concentration to become alarming." His doctor modified his diet to include some solid food, increased his intake of water, and reduced further the amount of milk. To get Edison to drink water it had to be flavored with peppermint or other extracts. Edison's milk diet had also exacerbated his diabetes. The diabetes was controlled by insulin and better diet, but "the kidney impairment continued to become more acute."[56]

For a time Edison's condition stabilized and even improved to some extent. As he gained strength he took great interest in discussing his treatment with his doctor and even asked for charts on his twice-weekly blood examinations, and he read a major work on insulin. By the middle of August he was well enough to plan a return to his rubber experiments, but within a short time his condition worsened as his kidneys became unable "to reduce urea and other nitrogenous waste products in his blood below three times their normal concentration."[57] On September 12, Mina's secretary reported to Henry Ford, "There has been no material change in Mr. Edison's condition other than the fact that his strength seems poorer from day to day." During the following weeks he weakened further. On September 28, according to Mina's secretary, Edison's doctor found him "somewhat depressed by the lack of improvement in his condition." Then his eyesight began to fail, and his hearing, long impaired, became nearly nonexistent. According to the *New York American,* "The voice of Mrs. Edison alone, by reason of its long familiarity and a peculiar timbre, was the only one he seemed to recognize or understand."[58] He became increasingly drowsy and eventually sank into a coma. Even before this occurred, Mina was aware that her husband was dying and began to make preparations for the funeral. She knew that there would be great public interest in paying tribute to him. Finally, in the early morning hours of October 18, 1931, with his family gathered around him, he quietly passed away.

The world had followed the news of his illness, and during the last ten days of his life kept vigil with the family through newspaper reports filed by reporters for whom it "was a twenty-four-hours-a-day assignment." Each day "hundreds of inquiries" on Edison's condition came from prominent men and women and from the "anonymous public."[59] The public reacted in the same way to his death by sending hundreds of letters, cards, poems, and other expressions of sorrow and sympathy to the family. These messages arrived from all over the world, from heads of state, government bodies, business and civic organizations, and schoolchildren. Many of them spoke about the meaning of his work to their own lives and of its significance to their country and the world. During the days between his death and his burial on October 22, newspapers ran special features and sections with photographs of the inventor. They told the story of his life and death, recounted anecdotes by those who knew him, and published tributes by world leaders. The National Broadcasting Service broadcast memorial services and played his favorite song, "I'll Take You Home Again Kathleen," as a special musical tribute.

For two days after his death Edison's body remained in an open casket in his library at the West Orange laboratory, as thousands of men, women, and children filed past. President Herbert Hoover, unable to attend the funeral because of a conference with the premier of France, sent his wife as his representative. On the afternoon of October 21 she joined the Edison family and Edison's close friends Henry Ford and Harvey Firestone and their wives in an upstairs room at Glenmont, where they listened to the hour-long memorial service held downstairs broadcast to them over a set of speakers. Following the service the house was cleared and they came downstairs to accompany the casket to nearby Rosedale Cemetery, where six state troopers maintained an honor guard for forty-eight hours. Finally, at 10 P.M. Eastern time, in response to a request from the president, the nation extinguished its electric lights for one minute while the broadcast networks observed a minute of silence and even suspended their programs to pay tribute to the "Inventor of the Age."

Epilogue

Edison's death seemed to many to mark the passing of an era. Writing in the *New York Times Magazine*, Waldemar Kaempffert, the editor of a two-volume *Popular History of Invention*, expressed what would become common wisdom about Edison's empirical methods:

> Always a point was reached where empiricism came to an abrupt halt. He saw the organized industrial laboratory, directed by a scientific captain, invading the kingdoms he had opened but could not enter, partly because age was creeping upon him, partly because there were too many problems for a lone Titan to solve.
>
> So it comes about that he was the last and greatest of a long line of experimenters who followed only the dictates of their inner selves and who were as willful and unrestrained as poets. With him the heroic age of invention probably ends. The future belongs to the organized, highly trained physicists and chemists of the corporation research laboratory.[1]

A few days later, the journal *Science* published an obituary of the inventor that featured short statements by several prominent members of the scientific community that echoed these sentiments. So, too, did the authors of four longer and more considered appraisals of Edison's contributions to science and industry that appeared in the journal's January 15 issue the following year. Although they were universal in their praise for Edison as a man and inventor, the authors of these articles had great difficulty in assessing his relationship to science. Two of the longer pieces, by physicists F. B. Jewett of AT&T and Robert Millikan of Caltech, which were intended to address this issue specifically, ended up tiptoeing around the question. Millikan, however, recognized that part of the problem arose from the fact that "the relative importance of pure science and applied science has undergone change since Edison was born." Furthermore, as Jewett pointed out, in his later years, as a consequence of his willingness to give interviews on any subject, Edison's name had become "associated with inconsequential things or with personal idiosyncracies." While these "subtracted nothing from the judgment of men who knew Edison's real worth, they did unquestionably portray a great man in a somewhat false and belittling light to vast numbers of a younger generation." Jewett concluded that Edison's great achievements were made in the 1870s and 1880s and that "as science itself developed, the practical application of new knowledge came to require a type of training which Edison did not possess."[2]

Indeed, much had changed in the relationship between science and technology since the beginning of Edison's career. The journal *Science* itself represented many of those changes. Its earliest incarnation had, in fact, been funded by Edison in the early 1880s, when he was clearly part of the scientific community. Over the course of his life *Science* had become even more closely identified with that community, whereas by the 1920s Edison seemed very marginal to it. *Science* was started by journalist John Michels, who had been an editorial writer for the *New York Times* and had contributed to scientific journals such as *Popular Science Monthly*. Michels planned to model his new journal on the British weekly scientific journal *Nature*. As was typical of many general scientific journals at the time, Michels proposed a mix of items about recent scientific research or discoveries with discussions of new inventions and other technologies and "to give the Journal a hold on the general public, current social subjects connected with Science . . . such as Public health, Sanitary science &c." When the new journal began publication in July as *Science, a Weekly Record of Scientific Progress,* it met with an enthusiastic reception from the American scientific community and the list of subscribers soon included "all the leading universities and colleges" as well as several prominent scientists, including Spencer Baird, Joseph Henry's successor as Secretary of the Smithsonian Institution, who wanted to publish the Institution's weekly reports in the journal. *Nature* welcomed its American cousin and expressed the hope that "it may be a means of spreading a wide interest in Science on the other side of the water."[3] The journal primarily consisted of reprints of papers delivered before the American and British Associations for the Advancement of Science, the Royal Society, and other scientific institutions, occasional original papers, and reports on items of scientific or technical interest, including some new inventions.

Edison's own role in the new journal seems to have been mainly as a patron who wanted to contribute to the larger scientific community. He played almost no role in determining content and failed to respond to Michels's desire for more details about his own inventive work, which made only token appearances in the journal. By October 1881 he had decided that he was unwilling to provide all the funds needed to put the journal on firmer financial footing and decided to end his support.

Michels soon found another prominent inventor to provide backing—Alexander Graham Bell. Unlike Edison, who identified himself as an inventor, Bell saw himself foremost as a scientist. Yet the journal that appeared under his patronage was substantially the same as the one funded by Edison, even though biologist Samuel Scudder replaced Michels as editor. The lead editorial on the first page of the revived journal could have appeared in the July 1880 issue:

> The leading feature of American science, however, and that which most distinctly characterizes it, is its utilitarianism. True, there are in our country able investigators working in scientific fields which do not offer the promise of material reward;

but notwithstanding this, it remains still true that those sciences whose principles are capable of useful application are the most zealously cultivated among us, and attract the largest number of students. . . . It may readily be conceded that the man who discovers nothing himself, but only applies to useful purposes the principle which others have discovered stands upon a lower plane than the investigator. But when the investigator becomes himself the utilizer; when the same mind that made the discovery contrives also the machine by which it is applied to useful purposes—the combined achievement must be ranked as superior to either of its separate results.

This view that invention was more than merely applied science helps to explain why the scientific community was so interested in Edison's work during the 1870s and 1880s and why he was invited to appear and enthusiastically received by the National Academy of Sciences and the American Association for the Advancement of Science:

> Becoming restive at the slow progress of discovery, the inventor has himself assumed the *rôle* of investigator; and the results of his researches appear in the records of the patent-office. . . . In consequence, the discoveries upon which many of the most important scientific investigations of the day rest, will be searched for in vain in scientific literature. The telegraph, the telephone, and the electric light are inventions which illustrate the fact now stated, in an eminent degree.[4]

The work of Edison and of other inventors on these technologies was not just of interest to scientists but sometimes became the subject of their own investigations. Charles Young and Cyrus Brackett of Princeton, for example, conducted tests on the efficiency of Edison's generator in 1880, and Henry Rowland of Johns Hopkins University and George Barker of the University of Pennsylvania tested the efficiency of Edison's lamp. Rowland's earlier researches on electromagnetism led Edison to discuss with him the possibility of using it to defeat a patent of William Siemens. And Rowland, who presented a paper on dynamo design at the 1884 Electrical Exhibition in Philadelphia, established one of the first electrical engineering programs in the nation.

For all his interest in electrical technology, Rowland responded to the *Science* editorial at the August 1883 meeting of the American Association for the Advancement of Science by making what would become a famous "Plea for Pure Science." Rowland objected to calling "telegraphs, electric lights, and such conveniences, by the name of science. I do not wish to underrate the value of all these things," he told the physical section of the Association,

> the progress of the world depend on them, and he is to be honored who cultivates them successfully. . . . And yet it is not an uncommon thing, especially in American newspapers to have the *applications* of science confounded with pure science; and some obscure American who steals the ideas of some great mind of the past, and enriches himself by the application of the same to domestic uses, is often lauded above the great originator of the idea, who might have worked out hundreds of

such applications, had his mind possessed the necessary element of vulgarity. I have often been asked which is more important to the world, pure or applied science. To have the applications of a science, the science itself must exist.[5]

Rowland's view that invention was merely the application of science was shared by other leading members of the scientific community and echoed earlier writings by Joseph Henry about the dependence of technology on science. Both scientists argued that only through science could inventors, in Henry's words, "predict that certain proposed inventions are impossible as well as declare that others are in accordance with established principles." Rowland, who would soon begin training engineers, argued that scientific training would enable an engineer or inventor "to evolve a [perfect] dynamo-electric machine, or any other machine of this kind, out of his mind before he had tried a single experiment." These scientists assumed that methods of mathematical analyses suitable for developing new technology could simply be derived from fundamental scientific principles. Yet Rowland's own work demonstrates the problems with this formulation. Historian Edwin Layton, writing about Rowland's work on magnetic permeability during the early 1870s, noted that the physicist had "'discovered' a key to the design of electric dynamos without realizing it." It was not until after British electrical engineer John Hopkinson independently made the same discovery several years later while working out the engineering parameters of dynamo design that the significance of Rowland's work became apparent to electrical engineers.[6]

Not surprisingly, therefore, the engineers who helped to found engineering science rejected the idea that it "could be reduced to the application of the laws of basic science." As Layton has noted, engineering science involves "idealizations of machines, beams, heat engines, or similar devices. And the results of engineering science are often statements about such devices rather than statements about nature." It therefore had to be "less abstract and idealized" because of "the complex interactions of physical factors which take place in machines." Furthermore, as Westinghouse engineer B. G. Lamme argued in a 1916 paper, new designs often required an engineer to work "far ahead of his available data. He is obliged to plot his existing data and experience and then [extrapolate] for the new points which he finds necessary in his work." And, as Lamme pointed out, analytical skill in engineering was not merely mathematical ability but rather the "ability to analyze and draw correct conclusions from the data and the facts available." As a result, the best engineers were those who could "develop a mental picture or a 'physical conception' of what is going on in a machine, in distinction from a purely mathematical conception."[7]

Constrained in his own research by a lack of resources for laboratories and assistants, Rowland's argument that science was the basis of both new invention and engineering design was prompted in part by a reaction against the democratic ethos of American society that gave pride of place to commercial application over fundamental scientific discovery. His plea was in part an argument for increasing the status and resources devoted to science in the United States. During the first decades of the twentieth century, his view that technology depended on scientific theory began to win out not only in the pages of *Science*, which in 1895 became the official journal of the American Association for the Advancement of Science, but also among many of those responsible for developing new technologies. Engineers educated in the nation's universities, who were taught to incorporate analytical techniques from theoretical physics, began to emulate their professors and model their own profession on science. In certain technical fields, notably electricity and chemistry, new discoveries helped to spur the development of technology and led to a redefinition of industrial research. The new industrial research laboratories established by companies such as General Electric, AT&T, and DuPont differed from earlier laboratories such as Edison's, which grew out of traditional shop invention. Rather than emphasize practical knowledge combined with reading in technical and scientific literature and experimental research, the new laboratories drew on academic models of research and employed researchers whose specialized scientific education prepared them to investigate the fundamental science behind the technologies they were developing. The early successes of these new laboratories gave rise to support for fundamental research in the belief that it would lead to new technologies. This shift was evident in the debate over the Naval Research Laboratory in which an institution devoted to basic research won out over Edison's idea for a works laboratory.

Edison was a proponent of engineering education because he appreciated the value of scientific training for engineers and recognized its importance for deriving design principles. He also recognized that scientific knowledge was crucial for his research on new inventions. However, he distinguished the work of the inventor from that of the scientist: "The inventor discovers things and then the scientist steps in and tells or tries to tell what it is that has been discovered. The telephone is an invention. Its principle was discovered. Scientists are still endeavoring to tell how it works. We all know it works—that is all an inventor cares to know; but a scientist wants to know why and how it works."[8]

As industrial research and engineering came to emulate academic science, Edison's approach to science seemed increasingly anachronistic. This was most evident in his rubber research. His method of reading extensively in scientific and technical literature to determine the parameters for a materials search stood in stark contrast with the research on synthetic rubber that relied on new theoretical approaches regarding the nature of molecules. Both involved the use of scientific knowledge, but Edison's approach harked back to an older tradition of American science in which the gathering of facts took precedence over the development of theory, and theory often lagged well behind the technology. Now, however, the increasing specialization of scientific research was beginning to alter the equation. The pace of scientific research was pushing it beyond the reach of a generalist like Edison and also making it harder for him to incorporate knowledge about a field gained by reading and experiment. In 1891 Edison could claim, "There is as much difference between an inventor and a scientist as there is between a explorer and a geographer. . . . Of course, scientists may be inventors and inventors may be scientists. And explorers may write geographies, but they seldom do."[9] Although Rowland had objected that telegraphs, telephones, and electric lights were no longer seen as fit subjects for basic scientific research, by the end of Edison's life the growing importance of scientific education and research to the development of these technologies meant that scientists and scientifically trained researchers were increasingly becoming inventors. Yet in practice their research often differed little from Edison's because materials and devices put to new uses often react in ways that cannot be predicted from known scientific facts or theory.

The growing power and prestige of scientific research altered the relationship of inventors such as Edison to the scientific community. This became apparent in the effort to elect Edison a member of the National Academy of Sciences. In the 1870s Edison had been feted by the Academy, but in 1911 his nomination as a member received only three votes "because of the profound prejudice amongst our academic colleagues against any kind of work not done in their characteristic ways." Physicist Robert Woodward, who was then president of the Carnegie Institute, complained that "the prejudice against men who follow the profession of engineering is especially strong unless they have been redeemed by that modicum of classical learning. . . . We ought in our day to be entirely free of the notions which determine a man's standing by means of his early education or lack of it, and seek to measure men by their actual accomplishments." The engineering and scientific communities disagreed about Edison because they emphasized different aspects of the scientific enterprise. This was apparent in 1915, when the president of MIT, Richard McLaurin, who was also a physicist, gave a talk on "Mr. Edison's Service for Science" that was subsequently published in *Science*. McLaurin argued that Edison "has proved himself a great force in education by giving so brilliant an exhibition of the *method* of science, the method of experimentation. When we get to the root of the matter we see that nearly all great advances are made by improvement in method." To McLaurin, Edison was "an institute of technology or a school of applied science" who "more than any one else in this country has taught men to see something of what science can do."[10]

The effort to make Edison a member of the National Academy, according to scientist Charles Greeley Abbot's later account, was renewed in 1926 after "the engineers had persuaded a prominent physicist to second the nomination. [A prominent physicist] rose and made an eloquent speech of recommendation, saying at length: 'I am sure there is no physicist who would not be glad to second the nomination to Academy membership of this great inventor.' Albert A. Michelson, perhaps at that time the greatest in the world, rose and said quietly: 'I am such a physicist.'"[11] Michelson's speech ended the debate, although Edison was finally elected the following year.

Michelson might have had a very different sense of Edison as a contributor to American science if he had gone to Menlo Park to carry out his experiments on the velocity of light as had been proposed in 1880. But Edison's self-identification as an inventor had increasingly set him apart from the scientific community. In this he was unlike other notable inventors, such as Alexander Graham Bell and Elihu Thomson, who identified themselves at least in part as scientists. Furthermore, because Edison disliked formal writing for technical and scientific journals, he presented his work and ideas largely through intermediaries or, more commonly, through the press, which further distanced him from the conventions of scientific publication. And because of his increasingly poor hearing, he did not participate in meetings of scientific or technical societies. [12]

Edison did, however, seek the respect of scientists. This was most evident in his various disputes over priority of invention and discovery, such as the microphone controversy of 1878. Although Edison seems to have played little role in the dispute over his election to membership in the National Academy, another dispute over his contributions to science suggests just how important such recognition was to him. In 1923 P. B. McDonald, a professor of engineering at New York University, wrote to Edison that he was "gathering the opinions of prominent authorities on who have been America's greatest pure scientists." In the process he had became interested in finding out about "the fundamental theories advanced by Edison, and incidentally of the opposition that his theories aroused from conservative physicists." Responding to McDonald's inquiry, Edison attempted to stake his claims as a scientific investigator. "I have made a number of scientific discoveries," he wrote, "most of which are scattered through my note books and never have been published. These arose in connection with the work on my inventions, but none were due to investigations in pure science, disconnected from invention." He noted five in particular. The first of these, and the one scientific contribution for which Edison is given credit today, was the "Edison Effect." During his work on the problem of lamp-blackening in 1880 Edison had inserted an extra electrode into the lamp and demonstrated the emission of electrons, although the effect remained a laboratory curiosity until it was explained and exploited by J. A. Fleming twenty years later. The second was his electromotograph effect, which had been the first work he presented to the National Academy of Sciences. Third was the etheric force, which he now knew to be "the phenomenon afterwards investigated by Herz"—radio waves. Fourth was his "discovery of a combination and conditions" necessary to developing an alkaline storage battery. Last was his "investigation in the direction of finding substances which would vary their resistance under pressure." Interestingly, he noted the importance of this work to the telephone but not to the microphone, perhaps not wishing to revive the old controversy.[13]

McDonald told Edison that he had "found in talking to various scientists about your discoveries in pure science, the greatest confusion and lack of precise knowledge" and asked him to respond directly to Columbia University physicist Michael Pupin's critical evaluation. Pupin, it should be pointed out, had obtained the fundamental patent for loaded line telephone circuits even though his practical understanding of loading was less sophisticated than that of AT&T engineer George Campbell, who was the one who reduced the idea to practice. Pupin's patent was judged to be stronger than Campbell's application, in part because it contained a great deal of mathematical analysis. After it became apparent that the lack of such an analysis was a problem, Campbell explained that he had followed the advice of his lawyer, who thought that "mathematical formulae should be entirely omitted from the specifications, and that they should be made in a language which would be at once understood by telephone engineers" (and by Campbell's lawyer).[14] As a physicist who gained fame and fortune from a patent based on his mathematical analysis of an engineering problem, Pupin not surprisingly was critical of Edison's claims about his contributions to pure science. He was willing to credit Edison only for the electromotograph effect. Pupin argued that the Edison Effect had been discovered earlier by someone else, that the etheric force had been observed thirty-three years earlier by Henry and that no one had understood what he had observed until Hertz's experiments years later, that Edison's work on the storage battery was not science at all, and that the variability of the electrical resistance of carbon under pressure had been discovered by David Hughes. Edison responded by defending his claims to these contributions and adding some additional ones, including his work on X-rays, various experiments he conducted on dynamos, and his research to find the most sensitive metal (tellurium) for automatic recording. Surprisingly, he seems not to have objected to Pupin's giving Hughes credit for the discovery of the variable resistance of carbon. Edison's arguments failed to sway Pupin from his original conclusion that the inventor's "achievements in pure science are very small in comparison with his achievements in applied science."[15]

In an era when the development of new technology was increasingly seen as the mere application of science and science itself elevated theory over experiment, Edison's work seemed to the scientists who evaluated it to be less scientific than it had fifty years earlier. Furthermore, as researchers with extensive scientific education took a larger role in the nation's industrial laboratories Edison himself seemed antiquated. As Karl Compton acknowledged in his appraisal for the January 1932 issue of *Science,* "There are some who think that the day of the inventor of Mr. Edison's type has passed because of the continually greater and greater degree of specialization and scientific background which is demanded." This was apparent even in Compton's generally positive appraisal of Edison's war research in which he had personally assisted. Compton found that "Edison was not ignorant of what others had done, even though he often appeared to pay little attention to it." However, because "he would not let his own or any one else's preconceived ideas stand in the way of making a test" Edison ended up conducting "many futile experiments." Compton, like the other scientists who appraised Edison in 1932, acknowledged that "it is equally true that [this method] led to some successful discoveries which caused scientists to revise their earlier ideas." Nonetheless, Compton would have agreed with Jewett that these discoveries dated from Edison's early career. Furthermore, the examples Compton presented from the inventor's war research suggest that Edison would have been better off relying on other research on materials or using mathematical analysis in building apparatus rather than testing a whole series of chemicals or conceivable variations in the design of a device, no matter how "thorough and systematic" he was in making these tests.[16]

Edison's method of research had proved productive when he was working at or beyond the cutting edge of scientific knowledge of a subject. Even when he conducted long series of tests of materials or alternative designs of devices, he used the best science of the day. Such tests often served as a kind of basic research that gave him a deeper knowledge of such things as materials or electromagnetic effects that proved essential to his inventive work. Thus, as he explained to McDonald, "I made extensive investigations in the constructive principles of dynamo machines, which led to the introduction of the low internal resistance armature and powerful fields." Likewise, the "alkaline storage battery was based on original research because there was nothing known at the time I started that would permit of such a battery." But Edison ultimately was an inventor, not a scientist. He was concerned with making things and did not consider it his place to develop theory or add to the scientific literature by publishing his data and tests, as did Elihu Thomson, although Edison did make some minor contributions to the scientific literature in the 1870s. Furthermore, Edison had grown up in an era when American science focused on collecting facts rather than on developing theory. Thus, the scientific character of his research looked very different in an era that emphasized theory over facts.[17]

Edison's empiricism was what seemed to set him apart from modern researchers. Most members of the scientific community were in full agreement with the editor of *Science,* who wrote in 1931 that Edison had succeeded by making "trial and error combined with industrial organization a method of research." But they failed to recognize his legacy. In the United States Edison had been the pivotal figure responsible for transforming the domain of invention into organized industrial research. As historian Thomas Hughes noted in his seminal article on "Edison's Method," "the words 'invention' and 'inventor' had fallen into disuse by the time of Edison's death to be replaced by 'research,' 'development,' and 'industrial scientist.' "[18] But it was Edison who created the first industrial research laboratory in the United States by taking traditional shop-based invention and grafting onto it modern chemical and electrical laboratories. In the process he devised a method of team research that made invention more regular and predictable and demonstrated to corporate leaders that support for research could be of long-term benefit to their companies. Edison's laboratories became models for other inventors and for the early research organizations established at corporations such as Bell Telephone and General

Electric, which would in turn help to create the new style of science-based industrial research during the first decades of the twentieth century. Edison never recognized how profoundly industrial research had changed by the end of his career as a growing body of technical and scientific knowledge made specialization a necessity. Perhaps if he had hired specialists to aid him in his later years Edison might have remained a significant figure in industrial research by meshing their talents and knowledge with his abilities as a generalist to define critical problems and judge among various solutions. But he failed even to build on his own experience and create a corporate research organization that could survive him and provide new inventions to assure the long-term health of his own company. As a consequence, the man who might have been remembered as the founder of American industrial research became instead a symbol of a mythic American past in which an unschooled empirical genius could astound the world through hard work and persistence.

Notes

Chapter 1: Childhood and Education

1. J. J. Brown, *Ideas in Exile: A History of Canadian Invention* (Toronto: McClelland and Steward Ltd., 1967), 342; see also Bruce Sinclair, Norman R. Ball, and James O. Peterson, eds., *Let Us Be Honest and Modest: Technology and Society in Canadian History* (Toronto: Oxford University Press, 1974).

2. William A. Simonds, *Edison: His Life, His Work, His Genius* (New York: Blue Ribbon Books, 1940), 21–31; Gregory Palmer, *Biographical Sketches of Loyalists of the American Revolution* (Westport, Conn.: Meckler, 1984), 249. On settlement in Upper Canada, see C. O. Ermatinger, *The Talbot Regime—Or the First Half Century of the Talbot Settlement* (St. Thomas: Municipal World Ltd., 1904); G. P. de T. Glazebrook, *Life in Ontario: A Social History* (Toronto: University of Toronto Press, 1968); Edwin C. Guillet, *Early Life in Upper Canada* (Toronto: University of Toronto Press, 1963); Fred Coyne Hamil, *Lake Erie Baron: The Story of Colonel Thomas Talbot* (Toronto: Macmillan, 1955); and Colin Read, *The Rising in Western Upper Canada, 1837–38: The Duncombe Revolt and After* (Toronto: University of Toronto Press, 1982).

3. Quoted in George Lathrop, "Edison's Father," *Once A Week*, 30 Jan. 1894, 7.

4. Read, *Rising in Western Upper Canada*, 50. Read is the best work on the political conflict and rebellion in which Samuel Edison participated. See also S. D. Clark, *Movements of Political Protest in Canada, 1640–1840* (Toronto: University of Toronto Press, 1959); Gerald M. Craig, *Upper Canada: The Formative Years, 1784–1841* (London: Oxford University Press, 1963); Edwin C. Guillet, *The Lives and Times of the Patriots* (Toronto: Thomas Nelson, 1938); Fred Landon, *Western Ontario and the American Frontier* (Toronto: The Ryerson Press, 1941); David Mills, *The Idea of Loyalty in Upper Canada, 1784–1850* (Kingston and Montreal: McGill-Queen's University Press, 1988); Colin Read and Ronald J. Stagg, eds., *The Rebellion of 1837 in Upper Canada: A Collection of Documents* (Toronto: The Champlain Society, 1985). On British radicalism, see Edward Royle and James Walvin, *English Radicals and Reformers, 1760–1848* (Lexington: University Press of Kentucky, 1982); Gareth Stedman Jones, *Studies in English Working Class History, 1832–1982* (Cambridge: Cambridge University Press, 1983), chap. 3; Frank Thistlethwaite, *The Anglo-American Connection in the Early Nineteenth Century* (Philadelphia: University of Pennsylvania Press, 1959); and D. G. Wright, *Popular Radicalism: The Working-Class Experience, 1780–1880* (London: Longman, 1988).

5. Read, *Rising in Western Upper Canada*, 116, 122, 128, 223–24, 249; Copy of Notice of Warrant of Attachment against the Estate of Samuel Edison, 1 Mar. 1838, Cat. 114,588, Edison National Historic Site (hereafter ENHS).

6. *Milan Tribune*, 5 Dec. 1844, quoted in Charles E. Frohman, *Milan and the Milan Canal* (Sandusky, Ohio: Charles E. Frohman, 1976), 43.

7. All accounts indicate that Samuel was a shinglemaker. For the family property, see deed of Lydia Cummings to Nancy Edison, 4 Aug. 1841, Erie County Record of Deeds, which also contains other deeds and leases related to Samuel's real estate dealings. For his brother's lumber enterprise, see *J. Merrill v. Samuel, Thomas, and Amos Edison*, Erie Country Common Pleas Record, and Grace Goulder, *Ohio Scenes and Citizens* (Cleveland: World, 1964), 84–85, which also discusses Samuel's shingle business. In 1843 Samuel also served as county auctioneer for one year (auction license in Erie Country Common Pleas Record). Among those associated with the Edisons were the prominent Lockwood family (George Lockwood was the childhood friend of Thomas's who drowned), James Merrill, and Zenas King who supported Samuel's license as county auctioneer. Merrill, who built a large shingle factory and warehouse in 1846, was also connected in the lumber trade with Samuel's brother Thomas. Zenas King was a prosperous contractor who later became a noted iron bridgebuilder. On the Edisons' status in Milan, see Reese Jenkins, Robert Rosenberg, et al., *The Papers of Thomas A. Edison* (Baltimore: Johns Hopkins University Press, 1989–), 1:19, n. 3 (hereafter cited as *TAEB*).

8. William McDonald to Thomas Alva Edison (hereafter TAE), 16 Sept. 1919, Document File, ENHS (hereafter DF), on which Edison noted, "Say I remember all the things he writes about." On his health, see Joseph McCoy's notes of an interview with Mary Barney, 26 July 1926, DF. TAE wrote a letter to Maria Taylor Ottis [Mary Taylor], 5 June 1910, in which he recalled that "we played together a great deal I think I can even draw a map of the houses" (DF).

9. Frank Dyer and T. C. Martin, with William Meadowcroft, *Edison: His Life and Inventions* (New York: Harper Brothers, 1929), 17–18; Frohman, *Milan and the Milan Canal*, 83–84; TAE to Ruth Thompson, 23 June 1922, DF.

10. Lee Soltow and Edward Stevens, *The Rise of Literacy and the Common School in the United States: A Socioeconomic Analysis to 1870* (Chicago: University of Chicago Press, 1981), 65–68. On the schooling of Edison's brother and sisters, see Goulder, *Ohio Scenes and Citizens*, 86.

11. Quoted in Caroline Farrand Ballantine, "The True Story of Edison's Childhood and Boyhood," *Michigan History Magazine* 4 (1920): 177. A table published in the *Port Huron Commercial* of 3 July, 1852 indicated that the town had ten lumbermills, all but the smallest of which operated with steam power. Their fifteen saws produced 18.6 million boardfeet, or, 20 percent, of the total from the state's Saginaw region.

12. Ibid., 179–80, 182–83. See also Richard B. Stamps, Bruce Hawkins, and Nancy E. Wright, *Search for the House in the Grove: Archaeological Excavation of the Boyhood Homesite of Thomas A. Edison in Port Huron, Michigan, 1976–1994* (Rochester, Mich.: Richard B. Stamps, Bruce Hawkins, and Nancy E. Wright, 1994). On Fort Gratiot, see William L. Bancroft, "A History of the Military Reservation at Fort Gratiot, with Reminiscences of Some of the Officers Stationed There," *Michigan Pioneer and Historical Society Collections* 11 (1887–88): 249–61.

13. R. G. Dun & Co. credit reports, 25 Nov. 1856, 5 Feb. and Dec. 1857, 15 Feb. 1858, 69:61, Baker Library, Harvard University. Samuel's legal problems resulted from a real estate venture undertaken with his son-in-law Samuel Bailey (*People of the State of Michigan vs. Samuel Edison & Samuel Bailey* and *Peter Sanborn & John Sanborn vs. Samuel Bailey & Samuel Edison*, Circuit Court Minutes 2:299-300, 308, 5:4, Michigan Historical Commission, State Archives Library, Lansing, Mich.).

14. Edison's reminiscences, *TAEB* 1:628–29. For Samuel's real estate dealings, see indexes to the Register of Deeds and the Register of Mortgages, and for his ventures in the timber business, see Register of Deeds 1266, all St. Clair County Building, Port Huron, Mich. Ambrose Robinson boarded in 1858–59, Elder Brown began to board with the family about the same time and continued to board while Thomas was a newsboy on the Grand Trunk Railroad. Captain Cyrus H. Sinclair also boarded with the family while Edison worked on the train. Robinson to TAE, 13 Apr. 1923; Brown to TAE, 1 July 1878; Sidney Morris to TAE, 23 Oct. 1929 (all DF).

15. *Port Huron Commercial*, 18 Aug. 1855.

16. Engle to TAE, 13 Aug. 1885, DF. Edison sent $17 to help Miss Edson, his "old music teacher," after receiving a request from Engle's daughter Mary (Mary Engle to TAE, 4 Oct. 1886, DF), and in a 1926 interview he recalled that the family had a piano, although he did not remember taking music lessons (*Musical Observer*, Aug. 1926, clippings). Advertisements for Engle's school provide information about the subjects offered and the cost of tuition (*Port Huron Commercial*, 6 Apr. 1854 and 18 Aug. 1855).

17. P. L. Hubbard to TAE, 23 Dec. 1911; N. W. King to TAE, 9 Nov. 1914; Ambrose Robinson to TAE, 23 Apr. 1923, all DF. Another boyhood friend recalled that Edison went to the school "in the years around 1855–1860" (Eugene O. Fechet to TAE, 13 Feb. 1924, DF).

18. J. S. C. to Editor, *Port Huron Commercial*, 25 Aug. 1855. On the Union School, see *TAEB* 1: 23–25, and the Annual Report of the School Inspectors of the City of Port Huron, County of St. Clair, microfilm, Michigan Historical Commission, State Archives Library, Lansing, Mich. On the Michigan rate bill system, see Sol Cohen, ed., *Education in the United States: A Documentary History* (New York: Random House, 1974), 2:1030; on the state school system, see Charles R. Starring and James O. Knauss, *The Michigan Search for Educational Standards* (Lansing: Michigan Historical Commission, 1969).

19. TAE to Pupils of the Grammar Schools of New Jersey, 30 Apr. 1912, DF. Nancy's religious background no doubt influenced his education. His mother had been a member of the Congregational (later Presbyterian) Church in Milan in 1843 and transferred her church membership to the Congregational Church in Port Huron in 1858, Church Records, 2:42, First Presbyterian Church, Milan, Ohio. For Thomas Edison's attendance at Sunday school see his marginal comment, Mary O. Hoyt to TAE, 9 Feb. 1921, DF. For information about Sunday school education, see Anne M. Boylan, *Sunday*

School: The Formation of an American Institution, 1790–1880 (New Haven: Yale University Press, 1988), chap. 2.

20. Dagobert Runes, ed., *The Diary and Sundry Observations of Thomas Alva Edison* (New York: Philosophical Library, 1948), 154; a similar account is found in Edison's introduction to an edition of Paine's works (William M. Van der Weyde, *The Life and Works of Thomas Paine* [New Rochelle, N.Y.: Thomas Paine National Historical Association, 1925], vii). On Gibbon, Hume, and Paine, see Gregory Claeys, *Thomas Paine: Social and Political Thought* (Boston: Unwin Hyman, 1989); Patricia B. Craddock, *Movements of Political Protest in Canada, 1640–1840* (Toronto: University of Toronto Press, 1989), chap. 17; Henry F. May, *The Enlightenment in America* (New York: Oxford University Press, 1976); Nicholas Phillipson, *Hume* (New York: St. Martin's Press, 1989), Epilogue; George Spater, "The Legacy of Thomas Paine," in Ian Dyck, ed., *Citizen of the World: Essays on Thomas Paine* (New York: St. Martin's Press, 1988), 129–48; John M. Werner, "David Hume in America," in Donald Livingston and Marie Martin, eds., *Hume as a Philosopher of Society, Politics and History* (Rochester, N.Y.: University of Rochester, 1991), 151–68; and David A. Wilson, *Paine and Cobbett: The Transatlantic Connection* (Kingston and Montreal: McGill-Queen's University Press, 1988). For the appearance of these works in Upper Canada during the period when Samuel Edison was living there, see Glazebrook, *Life in Ontario*, 63, and Charles Lindsey, *The Life and Times of Wm. Lyon Mackenzie* (Toronto: P. R. Randall, 1862), 2:304.

21. Edison's marginal note in F. M. Clough, *Blasting the Rock of Ages* (Boston: The Roxburgh Publishing Co., Inc., 1925), 71. On free thought, see John Robertson, *A History of Freethought in the Nineteenth Century* (New York: G. P. Putnam's Sons, 1930), and Sidney Warren, *American Freethought, 1860–1914* (London: P. S. King & Staples, 1943). For Paine's scientific deism, see Harry Hayden Clark, "Toward a Reinterpretation of Thomas Paine," *American Literature* 5 (1933): 140–43.

22. Edison's marginal note on G. W. Curtis of the Ingersoll Memorial Association to TAE, 20 Mar. 1911, DF; see also *New York Daily Graphic*, 13 July 1878, Thomas E. Jeffrey et al., *Thomas A. Edison Papers Microfilm Edition* (Frederick, Md.: University Publications of America, 1985–), reel 94: frame 288 (hereafter cited as, e.g., *TAEM*, 94:288).

23. Runes, *Diary and Sundry Observations*, 157.

24. TAE to H. Toyer, 15 Oct. 1910, DF. In another letter Edison commented that "As far as my observations extend I am compelled to believe in the existence of a supreme intelligence & that while man is im[m]ortal through propagation of the species if not interferred with by a catastrophe I cannot see that his personality is immortal" (TAE to Joseph P. Smithers, 9 Nov. 1910, DF).

25. Draft of TAE to M. C. Williams, 3 May 1911, DF. When attacked by one clergyman who claimed that the "Bible has in it every form of literature, and it is the greatest nature book in all the world," Edison scribbled to an associate "This is the limit We better use it for our chemical, Biological, & physical Expts as Text book—its so informing about nature." He wrote his comment on a copy of the 14 April 1913 issue of the *Brooklyn Eagle*, which reported the Reverend Dr. Schofield's sermon criticizing Edison's views.

26. Warren, *American Freethought*, 227.

27. Draft of TAE to S. H. Norton, 21 Feb. 1911, DF.

28. TAE to Geo. W. Barton, 15 Jan. 1923, DF.

29. Louis Cornaro, *The Art of Living Long* (Milwaukee: William F. Butler, 1903), 48.

30. A. L. Benson, "Edison on How to Live Long," *Hearst's Magazine* 23 (Feb. 1913): 267.

31. Cornaro, *Art of Living Long*, 48, 57.

32. TAE to Elmer Landes, 2 Oct. 1908, and TAE to Robert Hugh Rose, 15 July 1926, both DF; see also Edison's marginal notes on Irving Fisher to TAE, 29 Mar. 1906, and Joseph H. Thoms to TAE, 11 Dec. 1925, both DF, and Louise Fox Connell, "Feeding Your Husband: Mrs. Edison's Study of the Inventor's Diet Suggests How to Keep Men Fit," *Charm* (Jan. 1924): 15–17, 80–81.

33. Edison's marginal note on A. G. Gehman to TAE, 26 June 1930, DF; see also TAE to Irving Fisher, c. 1930, DF.

34. Edison's marginal note on Louis R. Huber to TAE, 11 Feb. 1920, DF. In 1878 Clancy wrote Edison that he "helped to pay for and built the first telegraph line in your life—the one from your House to mine. You remember we had a office underground in your Fathers garden [probably in the cellar] and one in my house" (Clancy to TAE, 22 Feb. 1878, DF); see also Edison's reminiscences, *TAEB* 2:786.

35. William H. Bishop, "A Night with Edison," *Scribner's Monthly* 17 (Nov. 1878): 90; Dyer and Martin, *Edison*, 37. On Fresenius, see Ferenc Szabadvàry, translated by Gyula Svehla, *History of Analytical Chemistry* (Oxford: Pergamon, 1966), 166–81.

36. Clancy to TAE, 3 Mar. 1889 (*TAEM* 125:178).

37. Hubbard to TAE, 23 Dec. 1911, DF.

38. Dyer and Martin, *Edison*, 28; Edison's reminiscences, *TAEB* 1:652, 2:786; Stamps, Hawkins, and Wright, *Search for the House in the Grove*.

39. Waldo P. Warren, "Edison on Invention and Inventors," *Century Magazine* 82 (1911): 415–16, 418.

40. Robinson to TAE, 13 Apr. 1923, DF.

41. H. S. Palmer to TAE, 11 Mar. 1898 (*TAEM* 137:21); Mrs. Harrison [Clara Spalding] Wood to TAE, 7 Feb. n.d., with Edison's marginal comments, DF.

42. *George W. Hawes' Michigan State Gazetteer and Business Directory for 1860* (Detroit: F. Raymond & Co., 1860).

43. "Sunday 1 Mr. Edison's Interview," galley copy in Edison Biographical Collection, ENHS.

44. Quoted in Matthew Josephson, *Edison: A Biography* (New York: McGraw-Hill, 1959), 23.

45. Anthony Rotundo, "Boy Culture: Middle-Class Boyhood in Nineteenth-Century America," in Mark C. Carnes and Clyde Griffen, *Meanings for Manhood: Constructions of Masculinity in Victorian America* (Chicago: University of Chicago Press, 1990), 23; see also Rotundo's *American Manhood: Transformations in Masculinity from the Revolution to the Modern Era* (New York: Basic Books, 1993), chap. 2.

46. "Sunday 1 Mr. Edison's Interview."

47. John Talbot to TAE, 26 Nov. 1920, DF; on the fight with the Canadian boys, see Edison's reminiscences, *TAEB* 1:632, and N. W. King to TAE, 9 Nov. 1914, DF.

48. James Clancy to TAE, 3 Mar. 1889 (*TAEM* 125:178).

49. Edison's reminiscences, *TAEB* 2:785.

50. Edison's marginal note, Carrie Buchanan Harrington to TAE, c. 1888, DF; see also Mrs. Harrison [Clara Spalding] Wood to TAE, 7 Feb. n.d., DF; Rotundo "Boy Culture," 28–29.

51. John Talbot to TAE, 26 Nov. 1920, DF.

52. James Clancy to TAE, 3 Mar. 1889 (*TAEM* 125:178).

53. Edison's reminiscences, *TAEB* 2:785.

54. Rotundo, "Boy Culture," 31; "The Only Person He Obeys," *The Literary Digest* 47 (1913): 976.

55. Andre Millard, *Edison and the Business of Innovation* (Baltimore: Johns Hopkins University Press, 1990), 127.

56. "The Only Person He Obeys"; also see "Mrs. Thomas A. Edison as the Wife of a Genius Has a Full-Time Job," *Delineator* 3 (1927): 8, 74, 77.

57. Edison's reminiscences, *TAEB* 1:629.

58. James Symington to TAE, 23 Feb. 1891 (*TAEM* 130:988).

59. Edison's reminiscences, *TAEB* 1:629.

60. Edison's reminiscences, *TAEB* 1:630.

61. Edison's reminiscences, *TAEB* 1:652; 2:786.

62. *TAEB* Doc. 2, 1:25–26; 2:786; Edison's marginal note, Hoke Smith to TAE, 20 Nov. [no year], DF.

63. Edison's reminiscences, *TAEB* 2:786.

64. Dyer and Martin, *Edison*, 37.

65. William Meadowcroft to E. G. Liebold, 24 Feb. 1932, Historical Reference File, ENHS; summary of 1940 interview with Dr. Linn Emerson in Subject Card File, Archives Office, ENHS.

66. Wright to TAE, 10 Oct. 1878, and 29 June 1900, both DF; Edison's reminiscences, *TAEB* 1:651.

67. John Thomas's account is in the *Detroit Free Press*, 15 Sep. 1901; Raper to TAE, 5 Apr. 1878, and Betts to TAE, 12 Feb. 1931, both DF; Edison's reminiscences, *TAEB* 1:631. The son of another operator wrote Edison that his father and John Thomas worked at the telegraph office in Detroit and that Edison "used to stop over between trains and spend the night with them. It was during this time that they taught you telegraphy" (Robert Wagner to TAE, 24 July 1928, and TAE to Wagner, 1 Aug. 1928, both DF). Another of the Grand Trunk newsboys remembered learning telegraphy together with Edison (John Allyn to TAE, 31 Mar. 1878 [*TAEM* 15:431]).

68. Edison's reminiscences, *TAEB* 1:631; Walker to O. M. Carter, 31 Mar. 1908, DF, stated that "only a small portion of the eastern news came through our offices. It came West via Detroit."

Chapter 2: Itinerant Telegrapher

1. The following discussion of operator culture is drawn from Edwin Gabler, *The American Telegrapher: A Social History, 1860–1900* (New Brunswick, N.J.: Rutgers University Press, 1988), chaps. 3–4, and Paul Israel, *From Machine Shop to Industrial Laboratory: Telegraphy and the Changing Context of American Invention, 1830–1920* (Baltimore: Johns Hopkins University Press, 1992), chap. 3.

2. Gabler, *American Telegrapher*, 52. On tramping workers in the United States, see Eric Monkkonen, *Walking to Work: Tramps in America, 1790–1935* (Lincoln: University of Nebraska Press, 1984), especially the articles by Jules Wygiel ("Tramping Artisans: Carpenters in Industrial America, 1880–90," 87–117) and Patricia A. Cooper ("The 'Traveling Fraternity': Union Cigar Makers and Geographic Mobility, 1900–1919," 118–38).

3. Milton Adams quoted in Dyer and Martin, *Edison*, 73–74. Itinerancy may also have provided a kind of vacation from the intense physical demands telegraphy placed on operators, which made it predominantly a young man's profession. Operators could also leave behind an office manager or chief operator with whom they had fallen out (operators considered favoritism by management to be a serious problem).

4. Edison's reminiscences, *TAEB* 1:659. Some of the lore and anecdotes were collected together in the following works: F. M. Huntington, *The Telegrapher's Souvenir. A Work Comprising Compilations and Original Articles . . . Intended to Be Instructive, Interesting and Amusing. Not Only to the Fraternity, But to Strangers as Well* (Paterson, N.J.: Lyon and Halsted, 1875); William John Johnston, *Telegraphic Tales and Telegraphic History* (New York: William J. Johnston, 1877); and Walter Polk Phillips, *Oakum Pickings: A Collection of Stories, Sketches, and Paragraphs Contributed from Time to Time to the Telegraphic and General Press* (New York: W. J. Johnston, 1876).

5. Rotundo, *American Manhood*, chap. 3.

6. Edison's reminiscences, *TAEB* 1:637.

7. Richard T. Perrin to TAE, 31 Aug. 1913, DF; Edison wrote on this letter, "The operators in those days were certainly a funny lot."

8. Edison's reminiscences, *TAEB* 1:662–63.

9. Gilliland is quoted in "Thomas Alvey Edison," *Cincinnati Commercial*, 18 Mar. 1878 (*TAEM* 94:126); Edison's reminiscences are in *TAEB* 1:655.

10. Edison's reminiscences are in *TAEB* 1:635, 661; John Longeran to William A. Simonds, 1 Aug. 1932, Edison Papers & Related Items, Henry Ford Museum Archives, Dearborn, Mich. (hereafter cited as EP&RI).

11. Edison's account of his role as an "Alcoholometer" is in his reminiscences, *TAEB* 1:655; James Smith, president of the NTU, argued against drunken operators in his report published in the *Telegrapher* 1 (1864–65): 2. Gabler, *American Telegrapher*, 86, is the source for the other quotation from the *Telegrapher*.

12. Edison's reminiscences in *TAEB* 1:635. In chaps. 3 and 4 of *The American Telegrapher*, Gabler discusses the evolution of operator culture as self-consciously middle-class and white-collar during the 1870s and 1880s, as well as the role of women in the craft, but see also Melodie Andrews, "'What the Girls Can Do': The Debate over the Employment of Women in the Early American Telegraph Industry," *Essays in Economic and Business History* 8 (1990): 109–20.

13. I detail the technical self-education of telegraph operators in *From Machine Shop to Industrial Laboratory*, especially in chap. 3, as part of a larger discussion of the practice of invention in the American telegraph industry.

14. Edison's marginal notes on David E. Heinman to TAE, 3 Aug. 1909, and A. D. Wilt to TAE, 28 June 1909, DF.

15. Edison's reminiscences, *TAEB* 1:631, and Dyer and Martin, *Edison*, 55; the original biographical account of the device is in George Bliss, "Thomas A. Edison," *Chicago Tribune*, 8 Apr. 1878 (*TAEB* 4, App. 3).

16. Edison's reminiscences, *TAEB* 1:631.

17. Edison's reminiscences, *TAEB* 1:658; Dyer and Martin, *Edison*, 56–57.

18. Edison's reminiscences, *TAEB* 1:658.

19. *Indianapolis Daily Journal*, 2 Dec. 1864.

20. Edison's reminiscences, *TAEB* 1:659.

21. Edison's reminiscences, *TAEB* 1:659, and Doc. 10. In the fall of 1876 Edison began developing an embossing recorder-repeater on which he applied for a patent the following February (*TAEB* Doc. 857; U.S. Pat. 213,554).

22. *TAEB* 1:659; Ed Parmalee to TAE, 9 Mar. 1891 (*TAEM* 130:778).

23. George Parmalee to TAE, 7 Jan. 1891, and Ed Parmalee to TAE, 9 Mar. 1891, *TAEM* 130:738, 778.

24. George Parmalee to TAE, 7 Jan. 1891 (*TAEM* 130:738); George Ohmer to TAE, 22 Jan. 1912, DF; Edison's reminiscences, *TAEB* 1:659. On Edison's appearance, see also "Tom Edison's Operating Days," *Operator* 9 (1 Apr. 1878): 4. The valise is mentioned in a letter to his parents dated 30 Sept. 1867 (*TAEB* Doc. 25).

25. An anonymous article in the 1 June 1878 issue of the telegraph journal *Operator* (p. 10) claimed that "When Edison was a telegraph operator in Cincinnati in 1865, his ambition was to be a tragedian." Joshua Spencer to TAE, 8 Apr. 1878; "Thomas Alvey Edison," *Cincinnati Commercial*, 18 Mar. 1878 (*TAEM* 94:126); Nat Hyams to TAE, 11 Feb. 1912, DF; *Cincinnati Daily Gazette*, 12 June 1865, lists Hyams's performance; Edison's reminiscences, *TAEB* 1:650, 660. On Cincinnati, see Steven J. Ross, *Workers on the Edge: Work, Leisure, and Politics in Industrializing Cincinnati, 1788–1890* (New York: Columbia University Press, 1985).

26. Adams is quoted in Dyer and Martin, *Edison*, 70–71. Cincinnati newspapers from the period of Edison's time in the city reveal a significant amount of Shakespearean drama being performed, but do not contain references to performances by either Forrest or McCullough. Edwin Adams appeared in *Richard III* in March 1865 and Junius Brutus Booth, Edwin and John Wilkes Booth's brother, appeared in the play the following month. Booth was giving his last performance in the city as Iago in *Othello* the same night his brother John assassinated Lincoln (*Cincinnati Daily Enquirer*, 2 Mar., 3 Apr., and 13 Apr. 1865).

27. *Operator*, 1 June 1878, 10.

28. Quoted in Warren, "Edison on Invention and Inventors," 418.

29. Edison's reminiscences, *TAEB* 1:660.

30. "More Edisonian Reminiscences," *Operator*, 15 Aug. 1880, 7.

31. Edison's reminiscences, *TAEB* 1:660–61; "Sunday Night Dispatches," *Cincinnati Daily Enquirer*, 18 Sept. 1865; see also "Telegraphic Miscellanea," *Telegrapher* 1 (1864–65): 114; "District Proceedings: Cincinnati District," ibid., 172. Edison's account of his fellow operator's drunken spree may be corroborated in a letter from J. W. Doan to TAE, Mar. 1878 (*TAEM* 15:439), who recalled "the Time Geo Pendleton was so anxious for the nomination that he donated the champagne to the operators for nearly the whole day," although Pendleton is not listed in the *Telegrapher's* account of the meeting and Doan may be recalling another election.

32. Edison's name is also found in the *Memphis City Directory* published in 1866, but it is unclear when he would have needed to be in the city for it to appear. The publisher of the city directory was in the same building as the telegraph office and might easily have added Edison's name at the last moment; Edison's entry appears on p. 110. Edison's account is from his reminiscences, *TAEB* 1:661; for his stay in Nashville, see Lonergan to W. A. Simonds, 1 Aug. 1932, EP&RI, and William A. Simonds, *Edison: His Life, His Work, His Genius* (New York: Blue Ribbon Books, 1940), 60, 338, n. 4. According to Simonds, Edison had a copy of George Tucker's *Life of Thomas Jefferson*, which he had inscribed "Thomas A. Edison, Telegraph Operator, Memphis, Tenn., March 11, 1866"; at the Edison National Historic Site is a copy of the 1865 edition of E. A. Andrews and S. Stoddard's *A Grammar of the Latin Language* with the inscription "Thomas A. Edison Telegraph operator Memphis Tenn Mch 29 1866."

33. Edison's reminiscences, *TAEB* 1:661–62; Edison's marginal note, Clyde Grissam to TAE, 7 Apr. 1919, DF; draft of TAE to A. W. Dealy, c. 12 Jan. 1909, DF. On the situation in Memphis, see Jack D. L. Holmes, "The Underlying Causes of the Memphis Race Riot of 1866," *Tennessee Historical Quarterly* 17 (1958): 195–221.

34. Simonds 1934, 60, indicates that Edison had a Spanish dictionary. He also shipped a box of books from Memphis when he left the city (*TAEB* Doc. 4). Stewart is quoted in "Tom Edison's Operating Days," *Operator* 9 (1 Apr. 1878): 4. Ed Gilliland claimed that Edison had begun his duplex experiments in Cincinnati in 1865 ("Thomas Alvey Edison," *Cincinnati Commercial*, 18 Mar. 1878 [*TAEM* 94:126]).

35. Edison's account of his repeater is in his reminiscences, *TAEB* 1:653, and Dyer and Martin, *Edison*, 74; his relief at being dismissed is in his reminiscences, *TAEB* 1:661. Edison also was very complimentary of the Memphis office manager in a letter to Mrs. A. S. Church, 21 Sept. 1921, DF. The article about connecting New York and New Orleans is found in the *Telegrapher* 2 (1865–66): 27. On the riot and rising tensions in the city during March and April, see Holmes, "Underlying Causes," and James G. Ryan, "The Memphis Riots of 1866: Terror in the Black Community during Reconstruction," *Journal of Black History* 61 (1977): 243–57.

36. Dyer and Martin, *Edison*, 75; *Louisville Daily Courier*, 9 and 10 Apr. 1865; Edison's reminiscences, *TAEB* 1:653–54; "Western Union Telegraphs," *Louisville Daily Journal*, 5 Aug. 1867.

37. *Louisville Daily Courier*, 4 Dec. 1866, 17 Jan., 19 Apr., and 27 Apr. 1867, describes these lectures, the beerhalls, and notes a performance of *The Dumb Boy of Manchester* at the Louisville Theater. Edison's copy of Pitman's 1860 edition of *A Manual of Phonography*, located at the Edison National Historic Site, is inscribed "A. Edison Louisville Ky April 4 1867."

38. C. J. McGuire to TAE, 12 Feb. 1912, DF; *TAEB* Doc. 5.

39. Edison's reminiscences, *TAEB* 1:657; *TAEB* Doc. 6. Another operator, whom Edison knew in Cincinnati, "went to Central America to build telegraphs in '67 and made a nice little fortune," although he later lost it "through bad business and hard times" (Charles H. Billings to TAE, 30 Mar. 1878 [*TAEM* 15:424]).

40. "Why Edison Is a Republican," *Canton (Ohio) Repository*, 22 Feb. 1892, "Edison for Harrison," *New York Express*, 6 Nov. 1892, and "Edison Will Vote," *New York Evening Advertiser*, 6 Nov. 1892 (*TAEM* 146:737, 831).

41. *TAEB* Doc. 39.

42. Dyer and Martin, *Edison*, 79–80; Edison's reminiscences, *TAEB* 1:654, 657.

43. Edison's reminiscences, *TAEB* 1:655–56.

44. A former operator who shared boardinghouse quarters with Edison also referred to him as "Victor Hugo" (E. W. Clowes to TAE, 21 Jan. 1912, DF). Richard T. Perrin to TAE, 31 Aug. 1913, and C. J. McGuire to TAE, 12 Feb. 1912, both DF; Edison's reminiscences, *TAEB* 1:658.

Chapter 3: From Operator to Inventor

1. Israel, *From Machine Shop to Industrial Laboratory*, chap. 4, discusses the urban telegraph community.

2. Edison's reminiscences, *TAEB* 1:662.

3. Ibid. A list of operators who were at Cincinnati in 1867 is found in William Lawler to TAE, 2 Mar. 1908, DF.

4. James Gamble to W. A. Robinson, n.d., DF; articles about Gamble, *Cincinnati Times-Star*, 20 Oct. 1931, 2 July 1932; E. L. Bernays to William Meadowcroft, 27 July 1931, DF; Alfred Lief, *"It Floats": The Story of Procter & Gamble* (New York: Rinehart & Co., 1958), 37.

5. Lonergan makes this claim in a quotation found in Simonds, *Edison*, 60. The following discussion of the notebook is drawn from *TAEB* 1:29–32 and Docs. 7–24, as well as my work on telegraph invention, *From Machine Shop to Industrial Laboratory*, chap. 4.

6. Robert Conot, *A Streak of Luck: The Life and Legend of Thomas Alva Edison* (New York: Seaview Books, 1979), 43.

7. *History of St. Clair County* 1883, 630; O. M. Carter to T. C. Martin, 14 Dec. 1907, Meadowcroft Collection, ENHS (hereafter Meadowcroft Collection).

8. Gilliland described the chief operator's claim in "Thomas Alvey Edison," *Cincinnati Commercial*, 18 Mar. 1878 (*TAEM* 94:126).

9. *TAEB* Doc. 9.

10. David B. Grandy to the Editor, *Telegraph Age* 14 (1894): 42.

11. Franklin Pope, *Modern Practice of the Telegraph* (New York: Russell Bros., 1869), 107–08, reprinted in *TAEB* Doc. 59.

12. *TAEB* Docs. 47 and 49; Edison's reminiscences, *TAEB* 1:663.

13. *TAEB* Docs. 26 and 28.

14. Edison's *Telegrapher* articles are *TAEB* Docs. 28, 30, 32, 34, 40–41, and 44; he did sign two of these "T.A.E."

15. Edison offered this advice in correspondence with Mary E. Odell, 19 and 25 Aug. 1883, and L. Pulliam, 2 Jan. 1884 (*TAEM* 64:413, 1202; 71:390).

16. *TAEB* Doc. 31. For Edison's relationship with Roberts, see also *TAEB* Docs. 43, 51, 90, 192 and Roberts to TAE, 28 May 1877 (*TAEM* 14:63).

17. *TAEB* Doc. 43.

18. *TAEB* Docs. 35, 51, and 54.

19. Newton to TAE, 7 May 1878 (*TAEM* 15:615); *TAEB* Docs. 36–38.

20. *TAEB* Docs. 45, 48, 61, and 65.

21. *TAEB* Docs. 42 and 46.

22. *TAEB* Doc. 46.

23. NS-74-002 (*TAEM* 7:231–34).

24. Edison's reminiscences, *TAEB* 1:639. For the "Boston" printer and the stock-and-gold quotation business, see *TAEB* Docs. 52–54, 56, 60 and Hills to TAE, 29 Dec. 1879. For the private-line business, see *TAEB* Docs. 57, 62, 65–71, 73.

25. *TAEB* Doc. 55. Even before he resigned his position at Western Union, Edison had been paying other operators to take his shift (*TAEB* Doc. 56).

26. For a discussion of urban telegraph markets see Israel, *From Machine Shop to Industrial Laboratory*, chaps. 4–5. For customers' responses to Edison's printer, see *TAEB* Docs. 66–67, 70–71.

27. *TAEB* Doc. 63.

28. *TAEB* Doc. 68.

29. *TAEB* Docs. 70, 72.

Chapter 4: A Leading Electromechanician

1. William Orton to Anson Stager, 24 Jan. 1870, Letterbook 8:317–21, Western Union Collection, Smithsonian Institution (hereafter Western Union).

2. *TAEB* Doc. 74.

3. *TAEB* Doc. 77.

4. *TAEB* Docs. 75, 79, 84.

5. *TAEB* Docs. 78 and 80.

6. *TAEB* Doc. 86, see also Docs. 76, 85.

7. Edison's reminiscences, *TAEB* 1:641 and Doc. 85.

8. *TAEB* Docs. 91 and 164. The May 1871 agreement also settled the claims for this and other printing telegraph inventions made by Edison and acquired by Gold and Stock.

9. *TAEB* Doc. 92.

10. *TAEB* Doc. 68.

11. Jesse H. Bunnell was one of the many operators who worked on repeaters after the Civil War. His patented design of 1868 was manufactured by the Philadelphia firm of Partrick and Carter, who invited him to become a partner in 1871. The following year he opened a New York City branch office of Partrick, Bunnell and Company. In 1875 he joined the firm of Tillotson & Company, and three years later, he established J. H. Bunnell and Company, which became one of the largest electrical manufacturing concerns in the United States (John B. Taltavall, *Telegraphers of To-Day* [New York: Taltavall, 1893], 223–24). Telegraph inventor Elisha Gray had formed Gray and Barton in 1868 with former operator Enos Barton. In 1872 they joined Anson Stager in forming Western Electric Manufacturing Company. The company became a subsidiary of Western Union.

12. *TAEB* Docs. 96–97.

13. Gold and Stock Minutebook (1867–1870), 141–45, Western Union.

14. Israel, *From Machine Shop to Industrial Laboratory*, chap. 5; *TAEB* Docs. 94–95, 100.

15. *TAEB* Docs. 107 and 130.

16. Edison's reminiscences, *TAEB* 1:642.

17. *TAEB* Doc. 492 and headnote; Henry Van Hoevenbergh to Ralph Pope, 24 July 1908, Meadowcroft Collection.

18. Henry Van Hoevenbergh to Ralph Pope, 24 July 1908, Meadowcroft Collection.

19. *TAEB* Docs. 110–23 and headnote, 1:196.

20. For Craig's arguments regarding automatic telegraphy, see Daniel H. Craig, *Machine Telegraph of Today* (New York: n.p., 1888), his numerous letters and articles in the *Telegrapher*, and *TAEB* 1 between 1870 and 1872. For the history of automatic telegraphy in the United States, see Israel, *From Machine Shop to Industrial Laboratory*.

21. At the time, Little's system was operating at speeds as high as 100 to 130 words per minute, whereas Wheatstone ink recorders were achieving 60 to 120 words per minute. Chemical recorders had much higher potential speeds; Edison's later designs easily worked over 500 words per minute, and he sought to achieve speeds of 1,500 to 2,000.

22. Agreement between The National Telegraph Company and George Little and Daniel H. Craig, 9 September 1869, "Respondents' Exhibit No. 4," *Harrington et al. vs. Atlantic and Pacific et al.*, Federal Archives and Record Center, New York. The Company also agreed to solicit Lefferts's cooperation and make him a member of the Executive Committee and general superintendent at a salary commensurate with that being paid by Western Union. Little was to be made company electrician at a salary of "not less than two hundred dollars per month."

23. *TAEB* Doc. 101 (U.S. Patent 114,656).

24. *TAEB* Doc. 103.

25. *TAEB* Docs. 104 and 137.

26. *TAEB* Doc. 106; Docs. 104–05, 140, 147, 163.

27. Edward Johnson to Uriah H. Painter, 9 Aug. 1878, Uriah H. Painter Papers, Pennsylvania Historical Society, Philadelphia (hereafter cited as Painter Papers). On the phonograph, see Chapter 9.

28. *TAEB* Doc. 109; Certificates of Incorporation of the Automatic Telegraph Co., 28 Nov. and 2 Dec. 1870, New York County Hall of Records, New York.

29. *TAEB* Doc. 129.

30. Doc. 133. Contrary to Robert Conot's claims and Edison's own reminiscences about his bookkeeping methods, there are careful accounts for all his manufacturing operations. Payroll records of the American Telegraph Works indicate that by December the work force numbered around forty-five (Conot 1979, 44; Edison's reminiscences, *TAEB* 1:644). Manufacturing accounts are found in *TAEM*, reels 20–22; for the December payrolls, see *TAEM* 20:197–204.

31. Docs. 132–33.

32. Ibid.

33. Ibid.

34. *TAEB* Docs. 131 and 136.

35. William Orton to Anson Stager, 12 Nov. 1870, Letterbook 8:161–70, Western Union. On the universal private-line printer, see *TAEB* Docs. 115, 126, 128, 165.

36. *TAEB* Docs. 138–39.

37. William Orton to Anson Stager, 24 Jan. 1870, Letterbook 8:317–21, Western Union.

38. William Orton to Anson Stager, 22 Mar. 1871, Letterbook 9:35–39, Western Union.

39. Originally Orton and Lefferts considered establishing a separate company to develop business outside of New York City, which was reserved to Gold and Stock. Orton, however, expressed concern over the time and money required to develop a new company for this purpose and proposed that Gold and Stock carry on the business itself, doubling its capital stock and issuing half to Western Union in exchange for that company's printing telegraph patents and its cooperation in developing the business. After extensive negotiation, this was agreed to, and Gold and Stock also acquired the Commercial News Department business. Although Lefferts wished to retain a degree of autonomy for his company, Western Union's ability to threaten its New York market if competition ensued probably convinced him to agree to Orton's offer. William Orton to Anson Stager, 24 Feb., 22 Mar., 30 Mar. 1871, Letterbook 8:428–39, 9:35–39, 57–61, Western Union; James D. Reid, *The Telegraph in America* (New York: Derby Bros., 1879), 611–13; Marshall Lefferts to stockholders, 27 May 1871 (*TAEM* 12:614); Gold and Stock Minutes 1870–79, 27–77, Western Union.

40. Gold and Stock Minutebook 1870–79, 51, Western Union.

41. *TAEB* Docs. 126 and 164, and Edison's reminiscences, 1:642.

42. *TAEB* Docs. 149, 153, 155, 159.

43. Josephson, *Edison*, 85.

44. *TAEB* Doc. 144.

Chapter 5: Competing Interests

1. Quoted in E. C. Baker, *Sir William Preece: Victorian Engineer Extraordinary* (London: Hutchinson & Co, 1976), 157.

2. The notebook introductions quoted are *TAEB* Docs. 179, 181, 183, and 187; the other quotation is from Doc. 188.

3. Warren, "Edison on Invention and Inventors," 418.

4. E. N. Dickerson's argument, *Quadruplex Case*, 17 (*TAEM* 10:734).

5. *TAEB* Docs. 184, 189, 193–94.

6. *TAEB* Doc. 140.

7. Notebook of telegraph escapements drawn in February 1872, Box 13, Item 1, EP&RI.

8. The quote on analogies comes from an interview conducted by French Strother, "The Modern Profession of Inventing, *World's Work* 10 (1905): 6295. According to this article, Edison considered persistence and imagination, along with analogic thinking, to be the three major qualities of the inventor. The table of contents and preface of Edison's book are *TAEB* Docs. 408 and 409. See n. 3 in the headnote preceding Doc. 408 for the location of chapter drafts and notes.

9. Reid, *Telegraph in America*, 644–45. On the electromechanical style of telegraph invention see Israel, *From Machine Shop to Industrial Laboratory*.

10. *TAEB* Doc. 158.

11. *TAEB* Doc. 220.

12. *TAEB* Doc. 224.

13. *TAEB* Doc. 195.

14. *TAEB* Doc. 211.

15. The general superintendent of Exchange Telegraph was Edward Calahan, who had resigned from his position as superintendent of Gold and Stock. On Edison's involvement with Exchange Telegraph, see *TAEB* 2:153 and Docs. 227, 296, 379, 462, 490–91, and 622.

16. *TAEB* Doc. 205.

17. *Christian Herald and Sign of Our Times*, 25 July 1888 (*TAEM* 146:286).

18. On women in telegraphy, see Gabler, *The American Telegrapher*, chap. 4, especially pp. 112–26.

19. *TAEB* Docs. 241 and 248.

20. *TAEB* Doc. 166.

21. *TAEB* Doc. 143.

22. *TAEB* Doc. 167

23. *TAEB* Doc. 177. Although Harrington had found someone to take over the financial end of the business, when Edison wrote this letter he had not yet begun work.

24. Edison's reminiscences, *TAEB* 1:644. On Edison's accounting practices, see Andre Millard, "Machine Shop Culture" in William Pretzer, ed., *Working at Inventing: Thomas A. Edison and the Menlo Park Experience* (Dearborn, Mich.: The Henry Ford Museum & Greenfield Village, 1989): 63–64.

25. On Edison's shops, see *TAEB* 1:515, n. 5, 501, n. 2, and Docs. 254 and 264–66.

26. Doc. 203. Typical of most inventors, Little wanted due credit for his inventions, and in September Harrington had agreed to mollify Little by giving him half of his interest in Edison's automatic patents "in order to avoid all difficulties, as to the relative value of Edison's invention as compared with Little's inventions." Perhaps hedging his bets as his relationship with Edison cooled, Harrington also acquired a half interest in Little's inventions (*TAEB* Doc. 199).

27. *TAEB* Doc. 261.

28. Israel, *From Machine Shop to Industrial Laboratory*, 135–38.

29. *TAEB* Docs. 282 and 284.

30. Testimony of Thomas A. Edison, *Quadruplex Case* (*TAEM* 9:496).

31. William Orton to Joseph B. Stearns, 2 Dec. 1874, Letterbook 14: 34–38, Western Union. Also see Orton's testimony in *Quadruplex Case* (*TAEM* 10:58–154).

32. Orton's testimony, *Quadruplex Case* (*TAEM* 10:63).

33. Orton's testimony, *Quadruplex Case* (*TAEM* 10:63).

34. *TAEB* Docs. 285 and 292

35. *TAEB* Doc. 303.

36. *TAEB* 1:556–57 and Docs. 304–05, 308–11, and 314–15.

37. Orton's testimony, *Quadruplex Case* (*TAEM* 10:64).

38. The advantages of the Morse key and sounder system led the British Post Office Telegraph Department to adopt it for most ordinary messages in the late 1870s. Previously, the department had relied largely on the Wheatstone automatic. William Preece, *Recent Advances in Telegraphy* (London: Society for the Encouragement of Arts, Manufactures, and Commerce, 1879), 20–21.

39. William Orton to James D. Reid, 21 September 1869, Letterbook 6: 405–10, Western Union. For a more extensive discussion of the merits of multiple telegraph systems, such as the duplex, and automatic systems, see Israel, *From Machine Shop to Industrial Laboratory*, chap. 5.

40. *TAEB* 1:328, n. 1, 492. It is not known whether the company actually used a typewriter for transcribing messages, and it may have used one devised by Christopher Sholes for which Craig acquired rights in 1871 (*TAEB* Doc. 142).

41. *TAEB* Docs. 298–99, 317.

42. *TAEB* Doc. 274.

43. Edison's continuing friendship with Reiff can be followed through their correspondence in the archives at the Edison National Historic Site (see *TAEM Guides*, s.v. "Reiff, Josiah"). Also located there is an accounting of Reiff's estate following his death, which shows over $61,000 in loans from Edison (Kellow File).

44. James Brown, Edison's assistant on his duplex experiments, also may have accompanied them on the voyage. Brown arrived in England sometime in 1873 and assisted with subsequent tests of Edison's automatic in that country.

45. *TAEB* Docs. 318–19.

46. See *TAEB* 1, chap. 12; 2, chaps. 1–3; and "Automatic Telegraph" folder, British Post Office Archives, London.

47. Dyer and Martin, *Edison*, 151–52; Willoughby Smith, *The Rise and Extension of Submarine Telegrahy* (New York: Arno Press, 1974; reprint of London: J. S. Virtue & Co, 1891), 317–18; *TAEB* 2, chaps. 2–3; Doc. 350.

Chapter 6: From Shop to Laboratory

1. *TAEB* Doc. 379.

2. *TAEB* Doc. 379.

3. Henry C. Fischer and William H. Preece, "Joint Report upon the American Telegraph System," pp. 341–45, British Post Office Archives, London. This did not mean that scientific theory and higher physics were an integral part of telegraph engineering in Great Britain, but rather that telegraph engineers there were attempting to develop an engineering science. See Bruce Hunt, "'Practice vs. Theory': The British Electrical Debate, 1881–1891," *Isis* 74 (1983): 341–55.

4. Crosbie Smith and M. Norton Wise, *Energy and Empire: A Biographical Study of Lord Kelvin* (Cambridge: Cambridge University Press, 1989); Brian Bowers, *Sir Charles Wheatstone FRS, 1802–1875* (London: Her Majesty's Stationery Office, 1975). In his report to Orton, Cromwell Fleetwood Varley urged the company to adopt regular testing to ensure the standardization of wire, battery and insulation quality, and relay resistance ("Report on the Condition of the Lines of the Western Union Telegraph Company," Western Union).

5. Smith, *The Rise and Extension of Submarine Telegraphy*, 317–18.

6. For Edison's plans regarding cable telegraph experiments, see *TAEB* Docs. 321–36, 341–45, 351.

7. *TAEB* Docs. 426 and 418. On the tests of Edison's automatic, see also *TAEB* Docs. 350, 381, 383–85, 390–91, 405, 407, 413, 416, 418, 420, 426–27, 429–30.

8. *TAEB* Doc. 357. Notebook entries on Edison's cable, automatic, and multiple telegraph experiments influenced by his British trip are in *TAEB* 2, chaps. 1–4.

9. *TAEB* Doc. 334.

10. *TAEB* Docs. 342, 362, 392. See Edison's annotated copy of Elliott Bros. "Catalogue of Electrical Tests Instruments" in *Catalogues, Electrical and Telegraph Instruments*, Library, ENHS.

11. *TAEB* Docs. 400–01, 403. Edison's copies of these books are found in the Library, ENHS.

12. The original article mistakenly printed the equation as "L x N x R." *TAEB* Doc. 28.

13. Dyer and Martin, *Edison*, 620–21.

14. *TAEB* Doc. 354.

15. He also seems to have read through the standard telegraph texts in his library to see what they said about chemical solutions developed by earlier experimenters in automatic telegraphy.

16. *TAEB* Docs. 419, 424–25, 459, n. 1.

17. Edwin M. Fox, "Edison's System of Fast Telegraphy," *Scribner's* 18 (1879): 844.

18. *TAEB* Doc. 410.

19. Fox, "Edison's System of Fast Telegraphy," 845.

20. *TAEB* Doc. 352.

21. *TAEB* Doc. 368–69.

22. *TAEB* Docs. 411, 490A, n. 4.

23. *TAEB* Docs. 408–09, 293.

24. NS-74-012 (*TAEM* 7:289–90). On Edison's work for the *Operator*, see *TAEB* Docs. 478, 479, 489, 495, and 505.

25. Dyer and Martin, *Edison*, 620.

26. Smith and Wise, *Energy and Empire*, 463–71.

27. L. Pearce Williams, *Michael Faraday: A Biography* (New York: Simon & Schuster, 1971), 27; Dyer and Martin, Edison, 101.

28. David Gooding, "Geometry and Genius: Mathematics and Method in Faraday's Experiments," and Ryan Tweney, "Stopping Time: Faraday and the Creation of Perceptual Order," both papers presented at Society for the History of Technology and History of Science Society, Madison, Wisc., 1991.

29. Dyer and Martin, *Edison*, 623.

30. NS-Undated-005, Lab (*TAEM* 8:410); see also NS-74-001, Lab. (*TAEM* 7:21–22).

31. Laboratory notebook, Cat. 287:12(2) (*TAEM* 5:478); U.S. Patent 146,311.

32. *TAEB* Doc. 267.

33. *TAEB* Doc. 285. For Edison's subsequent quadruplex research, see *TAEB* Docs. 348, 441–42, 444, 446, 449–50, 453–54, 467–73, 477, 485, 488.

34. *TAEB* Docs. 432, 441–42, 444–45, 451, 453, 466, 477.

35. *TAEB* Docs. 454, Docs. 466–73, and headnote preceding them.

36. Western Union Annual Report 1874, 13–14, Western Union. Edison filed four caveats on 4 December and another six on 18 January that describe changes made to the system during and as a result of the Boston and Chicago tests (*TAEB* 2:347–48 and Docs. 512–13, 531–34).

37. Regarding Edison's financial situation, see Edison's reminiscences, *TAEB* 2:787 and his affidavit in the *Quadruplex Case*, *TAEB* 2:812–13; on his house, see *TAEB* Doc. 504; regarding outside contracts, see *TAEB* 2:313 and Doc. 501.

38. *TAEB* Docs. 434–35, 423.

39. *TAEB* Doc. 428, 438.

40. Warren, "Edison on Invention and Inventors," 418.

41. *TAEB* 1:122–23, 227, 228, n. 9, and Docs. 415, 443, 447, 545, 553, 582, 614–15, 640, 653–54.

42. *TAEB* Doc. 452; see also Docs. 264, 429–30, 516, 520.

43. *TAEB* Doc. 515; see also Docs. 516, 519, 521.

44. *TAEB* Doc. 522. On Gould's effort to compete with Western Union, see Israel, *From Machine Shop to Industrial Laboratory*, 146–49.

45. Edison's testimony, *Harrington and Edison v. Gould and A&P*, 3:37, Box 17, National Archives, Northeast Region, New York; *TAEB* Docs. 526–29, 535–38.

46. *TAEB* Doc. 528. The *Tribune* is quoted in n. 5.

47. *TAEB* Doc. 530; PN-75-01-05 (*TAEM* 20:28–36). "A Quadruplex Telegraph," *Newark Evening Courier*, 16 Apr. 1878 (*TAEM* 27:278).

48. Regarding Edison's work for Atlantic and Pacific and the roman letter automatic, see *TAEB* Docs. 349, 373–74, 394, 457, 529, 539, 546, 555–60, 566, 571, 596, 598, 618, 648, 853.

49. Edison's reminiscences, *TAEB* 2:789. Regarding Edison's advice and proposals to Gould, see *TAEB* Docs. 528, 590, 596, 598, 606.

50. The *Quadruplex Case*, as it became known, was in fact a series of judicial and patent office proceedings. The records of these proceedings are found on *TAEM*, reels 9–10.

51. *TAEB* Docs. 561–62, 606, 618, 676, 740, 750, 823, 983. See also Chapter 7.

52. *TAEB* Doc. 585.

53. *TAEB* Docs. 574, 593–94.

Chapter 7: New Directions

1. *TAEB* Doc. 579.

2. *TAEB* Docs. 461, 574, 593–94.

3. *TAEB* Doc. 595; see also Docs. 568, 580, 587–88, 608, 620.

4. *TAEB* Docs. 620, 622–23.

5. *TAEB* Doc. 625

6. *TAEB* Docs. 629, 632.

7. *TAEB* Docs. 647, 661. See also Docs. 642–44, 646, 649, 720–21.

8. William Orton to T. B. A. David, 22 Dec. 1875, Letterbook 15:384, Western Union. On the agencies, see *TAEB* Docs. 624–25, 632, 636–37, 639.

9. *TAEB* 2:706 and Docs. 687, 711, 723–24, 731.

10. *TAEB* Docs. 599, 671; William Orton to George M. Phelps, 8 Sept. 1875, Letterbook 14:462, Western Union; Western Union Executive Minutebooks B:433 and C:288, Western Union; Elisha Gray testimony, *Telephone Interferences*, U.S. Patent Office, RG-241, National Archive, College Park, Md. See also David Hounshell, "Elisha Gray and the Telephone: On the Disadvantages of Being an Expert," *Technology and Culture* 16 (1875): 133–61.

11. *TAEB* Doc. 606; see also Docs. 590, 596, 598, 867.

12. *TAEB* Doc. 676; see also Docs. 740, 750, 823, 983 and the record of *Harrington, Edison and Reiff v. Atlantic and Pacific, and George Gould et al.*, National Archives, Northeast Region, New York.

13. *TAEB* Doc. 516. The suit is *Seyfert v. Edison* (*TAEM* 46:407).

14. *TAEB* Docs. 853, 1042, 1075.

15. *TAEB* Docs. 694–95.

16. Edison's testimony, *Telephone Interferences*, 4 (*TAEM* 11:23).

17. Edison's marginal comment in Hermann von Helmholtz, *On the Sensations of Tone as Physiological Basis for the Theory of Music* (London: Longmans, Green, and Co., 1875), 605.

18. *TAEB* Doc. 664; see also Docs. 658–59, 662.

19. George Prescott, *Electricity and the Electric Telegraph* (New York: D. Appleton and Co., 1877), 103–04.

20. *TAEB* Doc. 665. The remainder of the etheric force experiments are detailed in Docs. 666, 668–70, 673, 679–81, 686, 690, 693, 701, 710, 718, 726, 764 and in Cat. 1317:16–25 (*TAEM* 90:665–69).

21. *TAEB* Doc. 499; undated clipping of items 8256-27, probably from the *English Mechanic*, Cat. 1143, and *Newark Morning Register*, Cat. 1144 (*TAEM* 27:237, 282).

22. Henry Olcott, *Old Diary Leaves: The True Story of the Theosophical Society* (New York: G. P. Putnam's Sons, 1895), 467; *TAEB* Doc. 499.

23. *TAEB* Docs. 579, 581.

24. *TAEB* Docs. 669–70, 678.

25. *TAEB* Doc. 678. Clippings from the Newark and New York papers, as well as brief reports in Cincinnati and Albany papers are found in Cat. 1144 (*TAEM* 27:282, 290–91, 297–300).

26. "Edison's New Moonshine," *Telegrapher* 11 (4 Dec. 1875); the *Evening Post* is quoted in "The 'Etheric Force,'" *New York World*, 4 Dec. 1875 (*TAEM* 27:298).

27. Beard to the Editor of the *New York Tribune*, 9 Dec. 1875, "Mr. Edison's New Force" (*TAEM* 27:291); see also *TAEB* 675, n. 4, 690, n. 3.

28. An excellent account of Thomson's and Houston's role is in W. Bernard Carlson, *Innovation as a Social Process: Elihu Thomson and the Rise of General Electric, 1870–1900* (Cambridge: Cambridge University Press, 1991), 56–64.

29. *TAEB* Doc. 764.

30. *TAEB* Doc. 687. The draft caveat is in NS-Undated-001 (*TAEM* 8:2–4).

31. Edison described the various instruments he used in his five January 1876 caveats. See *TAEB* Docs. 708–09 and 715 and their related headnote on pp. 709–10.

32. *TAEB* Docs. 674–75; see also Docs. 681, 683, 686.

33. *TAEB* Doc. 699.

34. Edison's testimony, *Telephone Interferences*, p. 16 (*TAEM* 11:29).

35. *TAEB* Doc. 702.

36. *TAEB* Docs. 703–04.

37. *TAEB* Docs. 706–07.

38. Vol. 10:11 (*TAEM* 3:826); *TAEB* Doc. 713.

39. *TAEB* Doc. 728. See also TAE to William Orton, 24 Jan. 1876 (*TAEM* 13:1253); *TAEB* Docs. 715, 719, 725.

40. "The Telegraphic Situation," *Telegrapher* 11 (1875): 34.

41. Edison's reminiscences, *TAEB* 2:790, see also p. 780. On the purchase of the land and the building of the laboratory, see *TAEB* Doc. 737; deed, mortgage, bond, and agreement between Edison and George Goodyear, 29 Dec. 1875 (*TAEM* 28:1180); "Edison's Newark Expense Book, 1875–1878," EP&RI.

Chapter 8: The Invention Factory

1. Josephson, *Edison*, 136–37. Matthew Josephson appropriately credited Norbert Wiener with this observation, but it was the biographer who brought this idea to a wide audience and who has influenced subsequent research on Edison. For statements regarding the importance of Edison's laboratory in the historical transition from lone inventors to modern industrial research, see Kendall Birr, "Industrial Research Laboratories," in Nathan Reingold, ed., *The Sciences in the American Context: New Perspectives* (Washington, D.C.: Smithsonian Institution Press, 1979), 198; David A. Hounshell, "The Modernity of Menlo Park," in Pretzer, *Working at Inventing*, 128–29; Thomas P. Hughes, "Edison's Method," in Willaim B. Pickett, ed., *Technology at the Turning Point* (San Francisco: San Francisco Press, 1977), 5–22; idem, *American Genesis: A Century of Invention and Technological Enthusiasm, 1870–1970* (New York: Viking, 1989), 29–34; David W. Lewis, "Industrial Research and Development," in Melvin Kranzberg and Carroll W. Pursell Jr., *Technology in Western Civilization* (New York: Oxford University Press, 1967): 624–25; John Rae, "The Application of Science to Industry," in Alexandra Oleson and John Voss, eds., *The Organization of Knowledge in Modern America, 1860–1920* (Baltimore:

Johns Hopkins University Press, 1979), 259–60; Leonard S. Reich, *The Making of American Industrial Research: Science and Business at GE and Bell, 1876–1926* (Cambridge: Cambridge University Press, 1985), 44–45.

2. The term "invention factory" first appears in "A Visit to Edison," *Philadelphia Weekly Times,* 29 Apr. 1878 (*TAEM* 25:189); the rest is quoted in Josephson, *Edison,* 133–34.

3. *TAEB* Doc. 34.

4. *Catalogue of Western Electric Manufacturing Company* (Chicago: Jameson & Morse, printers, 1876), 5 (ENHS). For Edison's work at Bradley's shop, see *TAEB* 1:641–42 and Doc. 85.

5. "At Home with Edison," *Scientific American* 94 (13 July 1878): 256; "A Visit to Edison," *Philadelphia Weekly Times,* 29 Apr. 1878 (*TAEM* 25:189). A reporter for the *Boston Daily Evening Traveler* thought it "gives the idea externally of a country shoe factory" ("The Phonograph Etc," 23 May 1878 [*TAEM* 94:211]).

6. G. M. Shaw, "Sketch of Thomas Alva Edison," *Popular Science Monthly,* 13 (Aug. 1878), 489–90.

7. William H. Bishop, "A Night with Edison," *Scribner's Monthly,* 17 (Nov. 1878), 95.

8. "A Call upon the Phonograph," *Newark Daily Advertiser,* 3 May 1878 (*TAEM* 94:191). On Newark see Stuart Galishoff, *Newark: The Nation's Unhealthiest City, 1832–1895* (New Brunswick: Rutgers University Press, 1988); for suburbanization, see Kenneth T. Jackson, *Crabgrass Frontier: The Suburbanization of the United States* (New York: Oxford University Press, 1985), and John R. Stilgoe, *Borderland: Origins of the American Suburb, 1820–1939* (New Haven: Yale University Press, 1988).

9. Bishop, "Night with Edison," 95.

10. Insurance policy, 7 Apr. 1876 (*TAEM* 13:918).

11. Marion later remembered that the house was "run by three servants, either all black or all white." A photograph that probably dates from 1877 shows black servants (Marion Edison Oser reminiscence, Edison Biographical Collection, ENHS, hereafter cited as Marion Edison Oser reminiscence). On the Menlo Park staff, see "Charles F. Stilwell" and "Charles Nicholaus Wurth," Edison Pioneers Collection biographical folders, ENHS (hereafter cited as Edison Pioneers); Jehl, *Menlo Park Reminiscences,* 28.

12. Edison to Frank Royce, June 1876, quoted in Josephson, *Edison,* 134.

13. Batchelor to Thomas Batchelor, 9 May 1876 (*TAEM* 93:63).

14. Marion Edison Oser reminiscence. Just before the move to Menlo Park, Mary's family and friends threw her a surprise party (*TAEB* Doc. 733).

15. Donna R. Braden, "Sarah Jordan's Boarding House: Research Report," Henry Ford Museum and Greenfield Village, Dearborn, Mich.; Jehl, *Menlo Park Reminiscences,* 25–29.

16. David T. Marshall, *Recollections of Edison* (Boston: Christopher Publishing House, 1931), p. 56. Charles Wurth remembered that Samuel Edison brought the bear from Port Huron ("Charles Nicholaus Worth," Edison Pioneers); on its death, see Charles Batchelor's journal, Cat. 1233:96 (*TAEM* 90:101). On fishing, see Batchelor's and Charles Mott's journals (Cat. 1233: 254–56 [*TAEM* 90: 180–81]; N-80-03-14, p. 249–50 [*TAEM* 33:808–09]).

17. *TAEB* 3:27–29 and Docs. 745, 749, 754.

18. *TAEB* Doc. 756; *TAEB* 3:159, n. 10. Batchelor to Thomas Batchelor, 9 May 1876 (*TAEM* 93:63); electric pen pamphlet of George Caldwell, Agent, Centennial Exhibition (*TAEM* Supp. III); electric pen copies, Cat. 593 (*TAEM* 27:623, 625, 628, 634, 641). "A Visit to the Centennial Exhibition," *Telegrapher* 12 (1876): 160. For Edison's exhibit, see *TAEB* Docs. 601, 657, 730, 732.

19. *TAEB* 3:60–61, n. 9–10, and Docs. 741, 746, 748, 925.

20. *TAEB* Doc. 804.

21. Dodgson is quoted in Morten N. Cohen, "The Electric Pen," *Illustrated London News,* Christmas number (1976): 33; Breckon to TAE, 3 Mar. 1880 (*TAEM* 54:344). On the electric pen in Great Britain, see *TAEB* Docs. 779, 796, 803–04, 815, 893, 899, 925, 965.

22. Edward Johnson to TAE, 3 May 1880, DF (*TAEM* 54:347). For Western Electric's and George Bliss's management of the electric pen business, see *TAEB* Docs. 817, 861–62, 883, 892, 912, 1019, 1032, 1037, 1124, 1138, 1143, and Document File folders D-78-022, D-79-023, D-80-027 (*TAEM* 18:257, 50:359, 54:343). On Edison's relationship with A. B. Dick, see manuscripts listed in *TAEM Guide,* Part III, s.v. "Dick (A. B.) Co." and "Dick, Albert Blake."

23. *TAEB* Doc. 833.

24. *TAEB* Docs. 765 and 784.

25. *TAEB* Docs. 782, 800, 802, 829.

26. Edison's testimony, pp. 3006–07 and 3041, *Sawyer and Man v. Edison* (TAEM 48:10, 27); see also Johnson's and Batchelor's testimony in that case, pp. 100, 3164–69 (TAEM 46:235; 48:92). For the products and operation of the American Novelty Company in which Edison was president and Johnson was secretary and general manager, see *TAEB* Docs. 825, 829, 831, 836, 837, 865; stock certificate, 15 Dec. 1876 (TAEM 13:791); Cat. 1233:104, 141 (TAEM 90:113, 114); Cat. 1240, item 4 (*TAEM* 94:7).

27. *TAEB* Docs. 758, n. 2, 770, 774, 775–78, 780–81, 783–85, 787.

28. *TAEB* Doc. 789; U.S. Patent 200,994.

29. *TAEB* Doc. 819; see also *TAEB* Docs. 789, 792, 806, 809, 819–20, 857.

30. *TAEB* Docs. 833, 850, 876.

31. On Bell's telephone, see Robert B. Bruce, *Bell: Alexander Graham Bell and the Conquest of Solitude* (Boston: Little, Brown, 1973) and George Prescott, *Bell's Electric Speaking Telephone* (New York: D. Appleton & Co., 1884; reprint Arno Press, 1972).

32. Gray to A. L. Hayes, 12 Nov. 1876, quoted in David Hounshell, "Elisha Gray and the Telephone: On the Disadvantages of Being an Expert," *Technology and Culture* 16 (April 1876): 157; Hounshell's article (pp. 133–61) is an excellent account of the arguments regarding the commercial possibilities of the telephone; see also W. Bernard Carlson, "Entrepreneurship in the Early Development of the Telephone: How Did William Orton and Gardiner Hubbard Conceptualize This New Technology?" *Business and Economic History* 23 (Winter 1994): 161–92.

33. On Bell's work, see Bruce, *Bell*; Michael E. Gorman and W. Bernard Carlson, "Interpreting Invention as a Cognitive Process: The Case of Alexander Graham Bell, Thomas Edison, and the Telephone," *Science, Technology, & Human Values* 15 (Spring 1990): 131–64; and Michael Gorman, Matthew Mehalik, W. Bernard Carlson, and M. Oblon, "Alexander Graham Bell, Elisha Gray and the Speaking Telegraph: A Cognitive Comparison," *History of Technology* 15 (1993): 1–56.

34. Edison's testimony, *Telephone Interferences*, 9 (TAEM 11:25). In their studies of Edison's work in telephony, W. Bernard Carlson and Michael E. Gorman misunderstand Edison's use of the Reiss telephone. They argue that his basic approach represented a modification of this device and that he and his staff "would return to the Reiss telephone to review their mental model and get ideas for new experiments." In fact, Edison immediately realized that the Reiss was a make and break and that, rather than modify it, he had to devise an alternative design capable of producing variable resistance. When he did return to the Reiss telephone it was to explore the use of a make-and-break design as an alternative to his variable resistance approach (see, for example, *TAEB* 2:524–26, 3:230, n. 1, and Docs. 599, 981, 1057, 1079). Edison even argued that "Bell has done absolutely nothing new over Reuiss [sic] except to turn Reuiss [sic] from a Contract Breaking Telephone into a *magneto* Non Contact Breaking Telephone; with permanent magnet & worked the thing up to a success" (*TAEB* Doc. 1083). W. Bernard Carlson and Michael E. Gorman, "Thinking and Doing at Menlo Park: Edison's Development of the Telephone, 1876–1878," in Pretzer, *Working at Inventing*, 89; see also Carlson and Gorman, "A Cognitive Framework to Understand Technological Creativity: Bell, Edison, and the Telephone," in R. J. Weber and D. N. Perkins, eds., *Inventive Minds: Creativity in Technology* (New York: Oxford University Press, 1992), 48–79.

35. *TAEB* Doc. 759.

36. "Gray's Electro-Harmonic System," *Operator* 5 (1 July 1876): 7.

37. *TAEB* Doc. 1083. In another letter, Edison said "Bell had a very easy job compared to what I have had . . . all he had to ascertain was if well known means would do it . . . where as I had to create new things and many obscure defects in applying my principle" (*TAEB* Doc. 1025).

38. *TAEB* Doc. 863.

39. NS-74-002 (TAEM 7:102); *TAEB* Doc. 799.

40. Edison's testimony, *Telephone Interferences*, 46 (TAEM 11:44); *TAEB* Doc. 351.

41. *TAEB* Doc. 863; see also Doc. 860.

42. *TAEB* Doc. 1025.

43. *TAEB* Doc. 873; Edison's Exhibit 29-11, *Telephone Interferences* (TAEM 11:243).

44. *TAEB* Doc. 882.

45. *TAEB* Doc. 887; see also Docs. 885, 926.

46. *TAEB* Doc. 881; see also *TAEB* 3:280–83 and documents mentioned on those pages.

47. Cat. 1233:183–84 (TAEM 90:144–45); *TAEB* Doc. 1030; *TAEB* 3:248–50.

48. *TAEB* Docs. 920, 924, 928, 932, 937, 941, 945, 948.

49. *TAEB* Doc. 873; *TAEB* 3:314, n. 1; see also Docs. 888–89, 908, 917, 932, 962.

50. *TAEB* Doc. 907.

51. Cat. 1233:137, 139 (TAEM 90:121–22).

52. *TAEB* Doc. 932.

53. *TAEB* Docs. 921, 948; see also Docs. 921, 944, 966, 968, 972–73.

54. *TAEB* Doc. 968.

55. *TAEB* Doc. 968.

56. *TAEB* Docs. 986–87; see also Docs. 997, 1000, 1005, 1013, 1016, 1034–35, 1041, 1054.

57. *TAEB* Doc. 1033.

58. *TAEB* Docs. 1050, 1054.

59. *TAEB* Docs. 1079, 1081. For T. B. A. David and Franklin Badger, see *TAEB* Docs. 963, 1006–09, 1021–23, 1025, 1050, 1052, 1054, 1058–59, 1061, 1063–65, 1069, 1073, 1083.

60. *TAEB* Doc. 1097.

61. *TAEB* Docs. 1062, 1066–68, 1079, 1081, 1091, 1095, 1100, 1107.

62. *TAEB* Doc. 1112, 1121–22; George Prescott, *The Speaking Telephone, Electric Light, and Other Recent Electrical Inventions* (New York: D. Appleton and Co., 1879), 225.

63. *TAEB* 3:644, n. 1.

64. *TAEB* Doc. 1173.

65. *TAEB* Doc. 1241.

66. *TAEB* Doc. 1241; see also Docs. 1194, 1204, 1223, 1225–26, 1235, 1239, 1240, 1247.

67. George Prescott, *The Speaking Telephone, Electric Light, and Other Recent Electrical Inventions* (New York: D. Appleton and Co., 1879), 226–27. See also *TAEB* Docs. 1247, 1252, 1254.

68. *TAEB* Doc. 1256. On negotiations for rights to the new telephone, see also *TAEB* Docs. 1257–58, 1261, 1279–80, 1290, 1295–96, 1302, 1332, 1342. The agreement between Edison and Western Union was signed on May 31 (*TAEM* 28:1105).

69. *TAEB* Doc. 1117.

Chapter 9: The Wizard of Menlo Park

1. "The Inventor of the Age," *New York Sun*, 29 Apr. 1878 (*TAEM* 94:186).

2. Letter quoted in ibid. Dr. J. W. S. Arnold of the University of the City of New-York (now New York University) gave a lecture in late March in which he described the phonograph as "probably the greatest inventions in acoustics, or the greatest acoustical phenomenon of this century." In the lecture he explained the complexity of human speech and hearing (*New York Tribune*, 25 Mar. 1878, Cat. 1240, item 457 [*TAEM* 143]).

3. *TAEB* Doc. 1175.

4. *TAEB* Doc. 1260.

5. *TAEB* Docs. 969, 972.

6. *TAEB* Docs. 991, 1004, 1013, 1039. The term *phonograph* was then used in reference to shorthand. Edison envisioned his speaking phonograph primarily as an intermediary between speech and text that would do away with stenographers or in his initial conception skilled telegraph operators.

7. *TAEB* Docs. 1040, 1102, 1109, 1119, 1133–34, 1137, 1140, 1144–45.

8. *TAEB* Doc. 1150; see also Docs. 1147, 1164.

9. Towns where Edison worked as a telegrapher wanted to claim him as their own, and the newspapers published accounts by those who had known him as an operator. Ezra Gilliland's account appeared in the *Cincinnati Gazette* ("Thomas Alvey Edison," 18 Mar. 1878, p. 5). George "Fatty" Stewart published his account of Edison in Boston as "The Napoleon of Science" in the *New York Sun* (10 Mar. 1878 [*TAEM* 94:119]). George Bliss published a biographical sketch with reference to his telegraph days in the *Chicago Tribune* that became the basis for many of the subsequent biographical sketches that appeared in the following months, as well as a source for later book-length biographies (*TAEB* 4, Appendix 3).

10. The following discussion of Edison's growing fame is based on the extensive collections of clippings contained in scrapbooks kept by Charles Batchelor and the Menlo Park staff. Cat. 1029–31, 1240–41 (*TAEM* 26:161, 255, 27:732; 94:4, 345). See also the headnote "Edison and the Press" preceding *TAEB* Doc. 1266.

11. Apparently Dana himself did not originally believe Cummings's article on the phonograph until he read about the invention in *Scribner's* and *Popular Science Monthly* (Cummings to TAE, 23 Mar. 1878, DF [*TAEM* 17:30]). On the New York newspaper business, see James L. Crouthamel, *Bennett's New York Herald and the Rise of the Popular Press* (Syracuse, N.Y.: Syracuse University Press, 1989); Frank M. O'Brien, *The Story of the Sun, New York, 1833–1918* (New York: George H. Doran Co.,

1918); Sidney Kobre, *Development of American Journalism* (Dubuque, Iowa: Wm. C. Brown Co., 1969); Frank Luther Mott, *American Journalism: A History of Newspapers in the United States through 260 Years: 1690–1950* (New York: Macmillan, 1950); Michael Schudson, *Discovering the News: A Social History of American Newspapers* (New York: Basic Books, 1978).

12. *TAEB* Doc. 1513.

13. On competition between reporters for exclusive rights to new Edison inventions, see Fox to TAE, 20 Oct. 1878, and Croffut to TAE, 1 June and 28 Oct. 1878 (*TAEM* 15:732, 17:206, 212). On the hoax, see "A Food Creator," *New York Daily Graphic*, 1 Apr. 1878 (*TAEM* 94:150), and *TAEB* Doc. 1282; Doc. 1277 is another Croffut article, "The Papa of the Phonograph."

14. On Edison's relationships with various reporters, see his correspondence with them in the *TAEM Guides* Parts 1–3, s.vv. "Croffut, William," "Cummings, Amos," "Fox, Edwin," and "Maguire, Thomas."

15. *TAEB* Docs. 1164, 1166.

16. *TAEB* Doc. 1277. Thomas A. Edison, "The Phonograph and Its Future," *North American Review* 126 (June 1878): 527–36.

17. *TAEB* Doc. 1190.

18. Drafts of the toy and clock agreements and a proposed list of toys are in *TAEM* 18:898; 19:31, 33, 35, 146; copies of the actual contracts and drafts of the two James contracts are in *TAEM* 28:1064, 1068, 1072, 1074, 1078. For experimental work, see *TAEB* Docs. 1188, 1191, 1216, 1321, 1448.

19. *TAEB* Doc. 1153; TAE agreements with Theodore Puskas and George Bliss, 17 Dec. 1877 (*TAEM* 15:316; 28:1080, 1195, 1204).

20. *TAEB* Doc. 1237; TAE agreements with George Nottage and Howard Kennard, 22 Mar. 1878 (*TAEM* 15:316; 28:1080–89).

21. *TAEB* Doc. 1285. Regarding Edison's relationships with Gouraud and Puskas, see *TAEM Guides* Parts 1–3, s.vv. "Gouraud, George" and "Puskas, Theodore."

22. *TAEB* Docs. 1317, n. 2, 1328, n. 6, 1372, and 1536; Document File folders D-79-039, D-80-047, D-81-047, D-81-048 (*TAEM* 52:170; 55:771; 59:667, 988).

23. *TAEB* Doc. 1198.

24. *TAEB* Docs. 1195, 1199, 1234.

25. Edison Speaking Phonograph Co. circular, Form 502, n.d., Painter Papers.

26. Charles Batchelor to Sigmund Bergmann, 20 Apr. 1878 (*TAEM* 93:191).

27. Thomas Watson to Gardiner Hubbard, 20 Apr. 1878, Box 1205, AT&T Archives, Warren, N.J.

28. Charles Batchelor to Frank MacLaughlin, 16 July 1878 (*TAEM* 93:215). On Edison's disk phonographs and an alternative dictating phonograph design, see *TAEB* 3, chap. 5, headnote n. 5, and Docs. 1161, 1174, 1203, 1227, 1341, 1481.

29. Gardiner Hubbard to Charles Cheever, 20 Mar. 1878, AT&T. On the exhibitions, see *TAEB* Doc. 1308, n. 5.

30. James Redpath to E. [or C.] Barnes, 3 June 1878, Painter Papers. For the new phonograph, see *TAEB* Doc. 1369.

31. Edward H. Johnson, *Instructions for the Management and Operation of Edison's Speaking Phonograph* (Philadelphia: Burk & McFetridge, 1878) (*TAEM* 96:509). For the standard exhibition phonograph, see *TAEB* Doc. 1417. For Johnson's parlor phonograph, see Document File folder D-79-032 (*TAEM* 51:681); TAE to Brehmer Brothers, 17 and 25 Nov. 1879 (*TAEM* 80:185, 195); and "Edison's Parlor Speaking Phonograph" circular (*TAEM* 96:516).

32. *TAEB* Docs. 1210, 1228, 1298, 1314, 1326, 1388, n. 10. Edison's acoustic researches even led the Metropolitan Elevated Railway Company to ask for his assistance after a group of doctors complained to the New York grand jury that the noise of the railway was a public nuisance. The railway directors turned to Edison in the hope he could discover the cause and offer a solution to this problem. Edison and Batchelor conducted experiments with a phonoautograph, a well-known device for recording (but not reproducing) sound that he adapted for use in this research (see *TAEB* Docs. 1371, 1446).

33. *TAEB* Doc. 1298; clipping in Cat. 1240, item 598 (*TAEM* 94:197). Regarding the interest in Edison's efforts to develop a hearing aid, see also Document File folder D-78-001 (*TAEM* 15:3).

34. William Carman's marginal note on John Shinn to TAE, 21 Mar. 1878; Edison's marginal note on J. H. Edwards to TAE, 4 Apr. 1878 (*TAEM* 15:11, 14).

35. *TAEB* Doc. 1288.

36. *TAEB* Doc. 1117.

37. Charles Ponce de Leon, "Idols and Icons: Representations of Celebrity in American Culture, 1850–1940" (Ph.D. dissertation, Rutgers University, 1992), 34. See also *TAEB* Docs. 1293, n. 3, 1297, n. 3, 1299, n. 7, and 1308, nn. 1–2, regarding Edison's trip to Washington and the Brady photograph.

38. "The Phonograph" in the 17 January 1878 issue of the *London Times* (p. 4) was subsequently reprinted in other British papers (one copy is in Cat. 1031:4 [*TAEM* 27:734]).

39. *TAEB* Docs. 1259 and 1248 enclosure; George L. Beetle to TAE, 6 Sept. 1878 (*TAEM* 17:590); see also "Edison's Phonograph in Paris," *New York Daily Graphic*, 8 June 1878 (*TAEM* 94:228).

40. David Rodgers to TAE, 24 July 1878; F. Haug to TAE, 12 Nov. 1878, E. T. Graham to TAE, 13 Apr. 1878 (*TAEM* 16:711, 870; 15:26).

41. John Decker to TAE, 6 Mar. 1878 (*TAEM* 16:604).

42. "Edison's Inventions," *New York World*, 12 Jan. 1878; "A Wonderful Discovery" and "The Inventor of the Age," *New York Sun*, 22 Feb. and 29 Apr. 1878 (*TAEM* 94:98, 115, 186). The wizard theme has been emphasized by cultural historians Wyn Wachhorst in *Thomas Alva Edison, an American Myth* (Cambridge, Mass.: MIT Press, 1981), and David Nye, *The Invented Self: An Anti-biography from Documents of Thomas A. Edison* (Odense, Denmark: Odense University Press, 1983). However, what stands out in the articles and seemed to most capture the public imagination was the representation of Edison as a man of the people.

43. *TAEB* Doc. 1272.

44. "A Call upon the Phonograph," *Newark Daily Advertiser*, 3 May 1878 (*TAEM* 94:191).

45. Unidentified clipping in Cat. 1240, item 607; "The Bores of Science," *Sentinel of Freedom, and Weekly Advertiser*, 21 May 1878; *New Brunswick Weekly Fredonian*, 18 June 1878 (*TAEM* 94:199–200, 235).

46. "William Orton's Career," *New York World*, 23 Apr. 1878, 1.

47. *TAEB* Doc. 1300.

48. *TAEB* Doc. 1297.

49. *TAEB* Doc. 1331.

50. "The Hughes Telephone," *Engineering*, 10 May 1878 (*TAEM* 94:243).

51. David Hughes, "On the Sonorous Vibrations in Varying the Force of an Electric Current," *Engineering* 25 (17 May 1878): 384–85, a reprint of his paper read before the 9 May meeting of the Royal Society of London.

52. Extract copy of Preece to TAE, 22 May 1878, William H. Preece Papers, Institute of Electrical Engineers, London.

53. *TAEB* Doc. 1346–47.

54. *TAEB* Doc. 1348; Edison's draft to William Barrett, 7 Oct. 1878 (*TAEM* 16:194).

55. *TAEB* Doc. 1350.

56. The debate can be followed in the pages of Charles Batchelor's scrapbook, Cat. 1240 (*TAEM* 94:22–329, passim).

57. TAE to the Editor, 11 July 1878, *English Mechanic* (*TAEM* 94:314).

58. *TAEB* Doc. 1338.

59. *TAEB* Doc. 1231; Thomson to the Editor, 30 July 1878, *New York Daily Tribune*, 12 Aug. 1878 (*TAEM* 94:317), a copy of which Thomson sent to Edison and which is an enclosure with *TAEB* Doc. 1398.

60. William Thomson to William Preece, 12 June 1878, Preece Papers; Gouraud sent a copy of this letter to Edison on 18 July (*TAEM* 15:952, 961).

61. "The Telephone Relay or Repeater," *Nature*, 20 June 1878 and "The Microphone Relay," *English Mechanic*, 26 July 1878, Cat. 1240, items 740, 813 (*TAEM* 94:259, 313); Edison to the Editor, 8 July and 29 Sept. 1878, *Chemical News*, 38 (26 July and 18 Oct. 1878): 45, 198; Houston to the Editor, 22 Aug. 1878, ibid. 38 (13 Sept. 1878): 138–39. Edison's letters to the *Chemical News* are *TAEB* Docs. 1374 and 1460.

62. "Edison's Latest Inventions," *New York Daily Graphic*, 19 July 1878 (*TAEM* 94:286).

63. "The Eclipse," *New York Herald*, 30 July 1878 (*TAEM* 94:305). Edison's account of the eclipse is found in Doc. 1401. For his relationship with Draper see *TAEB* Docs. 967, n. 6, 989–90, 992, 998, 1010, 1018, 1380; for Langley see Docs. 1095A, 1135, 1367, and Langley to TAE, 7, 11, 22 June and 5 July 1878 (*TAEM* 15:760, 776, 823, 889).

64. John A. Eddy, "Thomas A. Edison and Infra-Red Astronomy," *Journal of the History of Astronomy* 3 (1972): 165–87.

65. TAE reminiscences, *TAEB* 4, Appendix 1.A5.

66. Edison's reminiscences, *TAEB* 4, Appendix 1.A4; *TAEB* Docs. 1393, n. 2 and 1395, n. 1; Washoe Club invitation, 9 Aug 1878 (*TAEM* 15:1046); bill of Louis Miller to Ed. Dickinson, 20 July 1878 (*TAEM* 17:287).

67. "Edison's Trip and Inventions," *New York Daily Graphic,* 28 Aug. 1878; "Four Hours with Edison," *New York Sun,* 29 Aug. 1878 (*TAEM* 94:338–39).
68. *TAEB* Docs. 1394, 1398.
69. *TAEB* Doc. 1401.
70. Laboratory notebook Cat. 297:85(4), (*TAEM* 5:785).
71. "Science at St. Louis," *New York Daily Tribune,* 24 Aug. 1878, "National Academy of Sciences," *Washington Star,* 19 Apr. 1878 (*TAEM* 94:337, 171).
72. "The Scientists," *Chicago Tribune,* 24 Aug. 1878, 3.
73. "Science at St. Louis," *New York Daily Tribune,* 24 Aug. 1878, (94:337); *TAEB* Docs. 1407–08.
74. Charles Batchelor's reminiscences, *TAEB* 4, Appendix 2.
75. *TAEB* Docs. 970 and 1031; *Iron,* 30 June 1877 (*TAEM* 94:63); W. James King, "The Development of Electrical Technology in the Nineteenth Century: 3. The Early Arc Light and Generator," in *United States Museum Bulletin* 228 (Washington, D.C.: Smithsonian Institution, 1962), 393–96.
76. Batchelor's and Edison's testimony, pp. 3149, 3018, *Sawyer and Man v. Edison* (*TAEM* 48:81, 16).
77. Edison's testimony, pp. 3020–21, *Sawyer and Man v. Edison* (*TAEM* 48:17).
78. The September 10 *New York Sun* article, "A Great Triumph," was reprinted the same day in the *New York Mail* (*TAEM* 94:349).
79. "Edison's Electric Light," *New York Sun,* 20 Oct. 1878 (*TAEM* 94:382).

Chapter 10: Inventing a System

1. On the electric light as metaphor, see Bernard S. Finn, "The Incandescent Electric Light," in Margaret Latimer, Brooke Hindle, and Melvin Kranzberg, eds., *Bridge to the Future: A Centennial Celebration of the Brooklyn Bridge* (New York: New York Academy of Sciences, 1984), 247–63. This chapter draws extensively on Robert Friedel and Paul Israel, *Edison's Electric Light: Biography of an Invention* (New Brunswick, N.J.: Rutgers University Press, 1986), and *TAEB* 4 and 5 (the latter forthcoming).
2. Stephen Jay Gould, *The Panda's Thumb: More Reflections in Natural Philosophy* (New York: Norton & Co., 1980), 66. For other interesting research on creativity, see Kenneth A. Brown, *Inventors at Work: Interviews with 16 Notable American Inventors* (Redmond, Wash.: Tempus Books of Microsoft Press, 1988); Mihaly Csikszentmihalyi, *Creativity: Flow and the Psychology of Discovery and Invention* (New York: Harper Collins, 1996); Howard E. Gruber, *Darwin on Man: A Psychological Study of Scientific Creativity* (Chicago: University of Chicago Press, 1981); Vera John-Steiner, *Notebooks of the Mind: Explorations of Thinking* (New York: Harper & Row, 1985); and Robert W. Weisberg, *Creativity: Genius and other Myths* (New York: Freeman, 1986).
3. Hughes, "Edison's Method," 18.
4. E. N. Dickerson's argument, *Quadruplex Case,* 17 (*TAEM* 10:734).
5. *TAEB* Doc. 1433. See also *TAEB* Docs. 1424, 1429, 1427, 1432.
6. *TAEB* Doc. 1439.
7. *TAEB* Doc. 1427. See also Docs. 1454–56.
8. *TAEB* Docs. 1098 and 1590.
9. Edison had grown familiar with the basic laws of electric circuits during his work on telegraphy. His copy of Latimer Clark and Robert Sabine, *Electrical Tables and Formulae for the Use of Telegraph Inspectors and Operators* (London: E. & F. N. Spon, 1871), has annotations by both Edison and Francis Upton, who helped him with formal calculations on electric light circuits, on the pages containing these and other electrical laws.
10. "Edison's Light," *New York Herald,* 30 Jan. 1879; "Edison's Electric Light," ibid., 12 Oct. 1878; "Edison's Electric Light," *New York Sun,* 20 Oct. 1878 (*TAEM* 94:455, 375, 382).
11. The edition that Edison had at Menlo Park can still be found in the chemical laboratory of his West Orange laboratory. For examples of Edison's use of Watts, see *TAEB* Doc. 1543 and Vol. 16:417–19 (*TAEM* 4:852–54).
12. Friedel and Israel, *Edison's Electric Light,* 115; Arthur A. Bright, *The Electric-Lamp Industry: Technological Change and Economic Development from 1800 to 1947* (New York: Arno Press, 1972), 35–55.

13. *TAEB* Doc. 1455.

14. *TAEB* Doc. 1577; see also Doc. 1491.

15. *TAEB* Doc. 1445.

16. *TAEB* Docs. 1459 and 1471.

17. *TAEB* Doc. 1477.

18. *New York Herald*, 20 Oct. 1878 (*TAEM* 94:382).

19. J. Pierpont Morgan to Walter H. Burns, 30 Oct. 1878, J. S. Morgan Co. Letterbook 12:457–59, Morgan Library, New York.

20. *TAEB* Doc. 1520; Grosvenor Lowrey to TAE, 25 Jan. 1879 (*TAEM* 50:232). The agreement with Drexel Morgan is in *TAEB* Doc. 1649.

21. *TAEB* Doc. 1490.

22. *TAEB* Docs. 800, 802, 1427, 1547, 1620; U.S. Patents 200,032 and 218,166.

23. "The Genie of Menlo Park," *New York Sun*, 19 Dec. 1878 (*TAEM* 94:436).

24. Doc. 1636.

25. Edison to Johnson, 23 Nov. 1881 (*TAEM* 81:111); Friedel and Israel, *Edison's Electric Light*, 42–46.

26. *TAEB* Doc. 1611.

27. Cat. 1304:25 (*TAEM* 91:27).

28. *TAEB* Doc. 1570.

29. *TAEB* Docs. 1586 and 1612.

30. *TAEB* Doc. 1639. On the issue of electric light accounts, see *TAEB* Doc. 1562, n. 1.

31. Lowrey to TAE, 31 Oct. 1878 (*TAEM* 18:56); *TAEB* Doc. 1542. See also *TAEB* Docs. 1535 and 1537–38.

32. *TAEB* Doc. 1546.

33. Francis Upton to TAE, 22 Nov. 1878 (*TAEM* 18:72).

34. *TAEB* Doc. 1651.

35. These experiments are found in Menlo Park Notebook N-79-01-19, pp. 27–68 (*TAEM* 31:134–72).

36. N-79-01-19, pp. 61–62 (*TAEM* 31:165–66).

37. Grosvenor Lowrey to TAE, 25 Jan. 1879 (*TAEM* 50:232).

38. N-78-12-31, p. 97 (*TAEM* 30:424).

39. Edison also coated the wires with infusible oxides, especially magnesium oxide, in the belief that this made the wire harder, and also experimented with rolling the platinum wire on bobbins made of infusible oxides. Brit. Pat. 2402 (1879).

40. Charles Batchelor to Adams, Cat. 130:47 (*TAEM* 93:261).

41. TAE to Theodore Puskas, 8 Apr. and 10 May 1879, Puskas Papers; draft patent application, 1 Mar. 1879, N-79-02-24.2:51 (*TAEM* 31:1018); "Edison's Electric Light," *New York Herald*, 27 Mar. 1879 (*TAEM* 94:464).

42. Edison likely had read accounts of these experiments, but the notebooks seem to indicate that he came to this conclusion independently. On Thomson's and Houston's experiments, see Carlson, *Innovation as a Social Process*, 86–87.

43. Francis Upton, "Methods for Testing Faradic Machines," *Proceedings of the AAAS* (1880): 178–80; Menlo Park Notebook N-80-03-29, pp. 7–9 (*TAEM*, 33:5–6).

44. TAE to Edward Johnson, 6 Mar. 1882 (*TAEM* 81:409).

45. Francis Upton to Elijah Wood Upton, 6 July 1879 (*TAEM* 95:543).

46. Thomas A. Edison, "On the Phenomena of Heating Metals in Vacuo by Means of an Electric Current," *Proceedings of the AAAS* (1880): 173–77.

47. Little is known of the background of either man. Haid's university education is inferred from references to him as Dr. Haid. The platinum search correspondence is in Document File folder D-79-028 (*TAEM* 50:580).

48. For Charles Edison's experiments, see *TAEB* Docs. 1440, 1495, 1529, 1591, 1650; N-79-01-014:4–17, N-79-01-014:18–29, N-78-12-04.1:235–49b (*TAEM* 31:263–69, 31:270–75, 29:550–58). For the British telephone business, see Document File folders D-79-041 and D-80-049. Francis Upton describes how Edison spent the money from the British company in a 24 May 1879 letter to his father, Elijah Wood Upton (*TAEM* 95:529).

49. For Charley's relationship with Murray, see Murray's 22 October 1879 letter to TAE (*TAEM* 49:963). For the telephone school, see Jehl, *Menlo Park Reminiscences*, 277–80, which also quotes George Bernard Shaw's amusing account of the American telephone experts in Britain.

50. "Edison's Eureka—The Electric Light at Last," *New York Herald*, 21 Dec. 1879 (*TAEM* 94: 537).

51. N-79-07-31, p. 105 (*TAEM* 33:594).

52. N-79-07-31, p. 117 (*TAEM*, 33:599). Cards with these carbonized materials on them still exist at ENHS.

53. Francis Upton to Elijah Wood Upton, 2 Nov. 1897 (*TAEM* 93:568).

54. Francis Upton to Elijah Wood Upton, 9 Nov. 1879 (*TAEM* 95:570).

55. Francis Upton to Elijah Wood Upton, 16 Nov. 1879 (*TAEM* 95:572).

56. "A Night with Edison," *New York Herald*, 31 Dec. 1879 (*TAEM* 94:557).

57. Francis Upton to Elijah Wood Upton, 21 Dec. 1879 (*TAEM* 95:584).

58. The *New York Herald* reports are in Jehl, *Menlo Park Reminiscences*, 1:410–27, the quotes are on pages 414, 422, 427.

59. Lamps made according to Sawyer's patents would all have had low resistance. Sawyer's testimony, *Edison Electric Light Co. v. United States Electric Lighting Co.* p. 984 (*TAEM* 47:303). Sawyer's and Albon Man's testimony in this case (*TAEM* 47:8–304) provides the basis for my discussion of Sawyer's work.

60. TAE to Benjamin Butler, 17 Feb. 1879, Benjamin Butler Papers, Library of Congress. Thomas P. Hughes, *Networks of Power: Electrification in Western Society, 1880–1930* (Baltimore: The Johns Hopkins University Press, 1983); Hughes, "Edison's Method."

61. Man's testimony, *Edison Electric Light Co. v. United States Electric Lighting Co.*, p. 501 (*TAEM* 47:58).

Chapter 11: From Research to Development

1. Edison's testimony, p. 39, *Boehm v. Edison*, Pat. Int. 7943, U.S. Patent Office Records, RG-241, Washington National Records Center, College Park, Md. (hereafter cited as U.S. Patent Office). The following discussion of research and development at Menlo Park is largely based on the Menlo Park Notebooks (*TAEM*, reels 29–41), which include a daily record of work at the laboratory kept by Charles P. Mott, a member of his office staff (N-80-03-14 and N-80-07-10 and PN-81-01-19 [*TAEM* 33:683; 37:302; 43:1115]). Specific notebooks are usually cited only when quoted from. See also the reminiscences in the Edison Pioneers; Jehl, *Menlo Park Reminiscences*; Friedel and Israel, *Biography of an Invention*, chaps. 5–6; and the forthcoming *TAEB* 5.

2. "Electric Light," *New York Herald*, 17 Jan. 1879 (*TAEM* 94:450).

3. Francis Upton to Elijah Wood Upton, 27 Apr. 1879 (*TAEM* 95:527).

4. Edison's testimony, p. 50, *Boehm v. Edison*, Pat. Int. 7943, U.S. Patent Office.

5. Wilson Howell's reminiscences, typescript, p. 4, Edison Pioneers.

6. Quoted in Jehl, *Menlo Park Reminiscences*, 2:858. Though unreliable concerning some of the technical work at Menlo Park in which he was not involved and self-aggrandizing in discussing his own role, Jehl nonetheless provides a good sense of the working atmosphere at Menlo Park.

7. Millard, "Machine Shop Culture and Menlo Park," 62–64.

8. Edison's testimony, *Telephone Interferences*, p. 11 (*TAEM* 11:26). Originally these notebooks were large tablets, but in November 1878, as the work on the electric light intensified, he began to use the 4 x 6 hardcover notebooks that became the laboratory standard through the rest of his career. Besides the notebook records kept by experimenters, Edison also had Charles P. Mott, a member of his office staff, keep a detailed record of the work at the laboratory (N-80-03-14 and N-80-07-10 and PN-81-01-19 [*TAEM* 33:683; 37:302; 43:1115]). Besides Edison's own account books, a separate set of statements was kept detailing the electric light research (Electric Light Statement Books [*TAEM* 88: 412–587].).

9. Edward G. Acheson, *A Pathfinder* (Port Huron, Mich.: Acheson Industries, 1965), 17–18, and Jehl, *Menlo Park Reminiscences*, 2:497. Regarding statements about their work as merely carrying out Edison's directions and ideas, see testimony from any of the contemporary patent interference cases such as *Sawyer and Man v. Edison*, some of which is in *Edison Electric Light Co. v. U.S. Electric Lighting Co.* (*TAEM* 46:228–45; 48:9–135). See also *Edison v. Siemens v. Field; Keith v. Edison v. Brush; Mather v. Edison v. Scribner; Edison v. Sprague; Sprague v. Edison* (*TAEM* 45:5–202, 290–30), and *Boehm v. Edison*, Pat. Int. 7943, U.S. Patent Office. Reminiscences referring to Edison as the source of all inventive ideas at the laboratory can be found throughout the Edison Pioneer files and Jehl, *Menlo Park Reminiscences*.

10. J. H. Howe (an attorney) to TAE, 7 Sept. 1885, and enclosure (*TAEM* 78:878); Anthony William Deller, *Walker on Patents* (New York: Baker, Vorrhis and Co., 1937), 1:407–09; J. N. Claybrook, *Patents* (Charlottesville, Va.: The Michie Co., 1927): 154–55.

11. Wilson Howell, reminiscences, manuscript, pp. A–B, Edison Pioneers. The Otto Moses literature search is in Menlo Park Notebooks N-80-00-05, N-80-00-06, and N-80-00-07 (*TAEM* 37:969, 38:2, 39:1064). On the bamboo search, see Document File folder D-80-020 (*TAEM* 53:552) and John Fredericks Collection, photocopies in Thomas A. Edison Papers search file.

12. N-80-03-14, p. 202 (*TAEM* 33:785).

13. Thomas A. Edison, "The Success of the Electric Light," *North American Review* 131 (1880): 298.

14. Hornig's testimony, p. 7, *Edison v. Siemens v. Field* (*TAEM* 46:8).

15. Israel, *From Machine Shop to Industrial Laboratory*, 144–45, discusses the problems of urban electric wires.

16. A good summary of Edison's work on electric railways from this period can be found in the testimony from *Edison v. Siemens v. Field*; the quote is from Edison's testimony, p. 74 (*TAEM* 6:42). The Charles Mott journals also provide a description of this work. On the effort to commercially develop the railway, see Document File folders D-80-39, D-81-043, D-82-049, D-83-072, D-84-070 (*TAEM* 55:300, 59:418, 63:585, 70:1089, 76:825) and Cat. 2175 (*TAEM* 89:248).

17. R. G. Dun Credit Report, 7 Feb. 1881, N.J. 52:399, R. G. Dun Records, Baker Library, Harvard University; TAE agreement with Edison Elec Light Co., 8 Mar. 1881 (*TAEM* 86:384); draft agreement between TAE, Bergmann, and Johnson, April 1881 (*TAEM* 57:7); Edison and his manufacturing partners to Sherbourne Eaton, 1 Feb. 1883 (*TAEM* 66:714); Samuel Insull to Charles Batchelor, 5 Nov. 1883 (*TAEM* 65:393); Insull was Edison's private secretary. See also agreements and exhibits regarding the shops, Sept. 1884 (*TAEM* 86:801); Jehl, *Menlo Park Reminiscences*, 2:743–45, 3:987.

18. John Ott's testimony, *Mather v. Edison v. Scribner*, 15 (*TAEM* 46:185).

19. Martin Force's testimony, *Mather v. Edison v. Scribner*, 22 (*TAEM* 46:189). Edison described his patent policy in a letter to Sherbourne Eaton of 12 June 1882 (*TAEM* 80:602).

20. For work at the Menlo Park laboratory during 1881–82, see Logan's reports to Edison in Document File folder D-81-037, John Ott's Menlo Park notebook N-82-06-21 (*TAEM* 41:2940) and his personal notebook owned by Charles Hummel, Wayne, N.J.; and Charles Hughes's Menlo Park notebooks regarding vacuum preservation and electric railroads, N-81-04-30 and N-82-03-12 (*TAEM* 41:860, 1155). For the closing of the Menlo Park laboratory, see Insull to Batchelor, 28 Sept. 1882; Insull to John Randolph, 12 Oct. 1882; and Ott to TAE, 26 Oct. 1882 (*TAEM* 63:167, 205, 212).

21. There is a set of eight Machine Works Testing Department notebooks that were copied for Charles Clarke in 1936. Four of these are concerned with research on electric meters, and four are labeled "Electrical Experiments and Tests" and range from work on dynamos to fuses and switches. They are located in Boxes 28 and 30, EP&RI. The following discussion of experimental work at the shops is based on those notebooks and the following material: Edison's notes to his patent attorneys from the 1880s, Cat. 1147–53 beginning in *TAEM* 44:224; technical notes and drawings in some of the later Menlo Park notebooks covering the years 1881–1884 in *TAEM* reels 38–44 and in the Unbound Notes and Drawings for those years beginning in *TAEM* 44:1010; reminiscences found in Jehl, *Menlo Park Reminiscences* and the Edison Pioneers biographical files; summaries of the defect reports sent to Edison in Document File folders D-82-002 and D-83-028 (*TAEM* 60:932, 66:811); reports from Charles Clarke, chief engineer, and other technical personnel connected with the Edison Electric Light Company in Document File folders D-82-027, D-83-029, D-83-030 (*TAEM* 61:426, 66:873, 934); correspondence and test reports from the shops in Document File folders D-81-023, D-81-025, D-81-029, D-81-031, D-82-030, D-82-032, D-82-033, D-82-035, D-82-036, D-83-032, D-83-033, D-83-034, and D-83-035 (*TAEM* 57:756, 1090; 58:203, 374; 61:720, 955, 1000; 62:25, 90; 67:90, 299, 353, 442); and Edison's numerous U.S. patents on electric lighting from this period in *TAEM* reels 1–2; see the list that precedes them at the beginning of reel 1.

22. Upton to TAE, 19 June 1884 (*TAEM* 73:427).

23. TAE to Batchelor, 31 Aug. 1882 (*TAEM* 81:841).

24. Upton to TAE, 7 Feb. 1881 (*TAEM* 57:772).

25. Batchelor to Edison, 5 July 1883 (*TAEM* 67:796).

26. Upton to TAE, 4 May 1881 (*TAEM* 57:871).

27. TAE to Richard Dyer, 28 Oct. 1882, Cat. 1148 (*TAEM* 44:398).

28. TAE marginal note on Upton to TAE, 21 July 1882 (*TAEM* 61:787); U.S. Pat. 438,299.

29. "A History of the Development of the Incandescent Lamp," typescript, c. 1910–12, p. 31, photocopy, ENHS. Other discussions of technical changes in lamp design and production are found in

John W. Howell and William Schroeder, *History of the Incandescent Lamp* (Schenectady, N.Y.: The Maqua Co., 1927), and Jehl, *Menlo Park Reminiscences* 2, chaps. 67–69, 81–83.

30. Francis Upton to TAE, 18 Apr. 1881; TAE to Johnson, 23 Nov. 1881; TAE to Batchelor, 31 Dec. 1881 (*TAEM* 57:853; 81:111,178).

31. TAE to Edward Johnson, 27 Nov. 1881 (*TAEM* 81:134).

32. TAE to Société Electrique Edison, 21 Nov. 1882 (*TAEM* 81:1021.2).

33. N-81-04-06, p. 37 (*TAEM* 41:52).

34. Charles Clarke to TAE, 1 Aug. 1882 (*TAEM* 61:520).

35. Jehl, *Menlo Park Reminiscences*, 3:986, see also the rest of chap. 97.

36. Jehl, *Menlo Park Reminiscences*, 653, see also Chaps. 70–71; Menlo Park Notebooks N-81-04-06, N-81-08-30, N-81-03-18, N-81-09-03, and N-81-03-11 (*TAEM* 41:36, 253, 390, 509, 537); and Edison's note to Dyer on the thermal regulator, 16 May 1881, Cat. 1147 (*TAEM* 44:280).

37. The cost of the station can be found in a statement on *TAEM* 66:700. The progress of the Pearl Street station can be followed in the Edison Electric Light Company *Bulletins* beginning on *TAEM* 96:667. See also Jehl, *Menlo Park Reminiscences*, 3:1041–88.

38. "Edison's Illuminator," *New York Herald*, 5 Sept. 1882 (*TAEM* 24:82); the *New York Sun* quote is in Friedel and Israel, *Biography of an Invention*, 222.

39. Alexander Bell to TAE, 25 May 1879 (*TAEM* 49:238).

40. Simon Newcomb to TAE, 19 Jan. 1880 (*TAEM* 49:238). On the influence of Menlo Park, see also Bruce, *Bell*, 341; Israel, *From Machine Shop to Industrial Laboratory*, 79–80; David O. Woodbury, *A Measure for Greatness: A Short Biography of Edward Weston* (New York: McGraw-Hill, 1949), 150–53; Paul Israel, "Telegraphy and Edison's Invention Factory," and David Hounshell, "The Modernity of Menlo Park," both in William S. Pretzer, *Working at Inventing: Thomas A. Edison and the Menlo Park Experience* (Henry Ford Museum and Greenfield Village, 1989), 80–83, 128–33.

Chapter 12: Inventing an Industry

1. I consider Edison's electric railway patent applications and those on storage batteries to be directly related to his work on electric light and power. It should also be noted that Edison filed many additional unsuccessful patent applications during these years, the claims for many of them are found in Patent Application Casebook E-2536–2538 (*TAEM* 45:698–817). Edison applied for 90 successful applications in 1881, 106 in 1882, and 65 in 1883.

2. TAE to George Bliss, 8 Nov. 1882 (*TAEM* 81:998); TAE to Sherbourne Eaton, 3 Nov. 1882 (*TAEM* 81:989); see also TAE to Edison Electric Light Company Ltd., undated draft (*TAEM* 68:214); George Bliss to TAE, 29 May 1884 (*TAEM* 74:495); Edison Company for Isolated Lighting, Annual Report, 1884 (*TAEM* 96:266).

3. TAE to Edison Electric Light Company Ltd., undated draft (*TAEM* 68:214); TAE to Edward H. Johnson, 2 Jan 1882 (*TAEM* 81:223).

4. TAE to Sherbourne Eaton, 13 Dec. 1883 (*TAEM* 65:809).

5. TAE, Edward Johnson, and Francis Upton to Sherbourne Eaton, 1 Feb. 1883 (*TAEM* 66:714); Samuel Insull to George Bliss, 7 May 1883 (*TAEM* 82:389); see also the Annual Reports to the Stockholders in the *Edison Electric Light Company Bulletins*, 15:37–39, 19:41–50 (*TAEM* 96:784–85, 887–93).

6. This undated letter is unsigned; it was probably written by Edward Johnson, but Edison would certainly have approved it. TAE, Edward Johnson, and Francis Upton to Sherbourne Eaton, 1 Feb. 1883 and the draft that follows (*TAEM* 66:714).

7. Insull Memoirs, 27, Samuel Insull Papers, Loyola University Archives, Chicago (hereafter Insull Papers). See also TAE to Edward Johnson, 23 Nov. 1881 (*TAEM* 81:111); receipt for the sale of 286 $^1/_2$ shares of telephone stock and notes for loans with Drexel, Morgan & Company and receipt for sale of stock to Spencer Trask & Company (*TAEM* 86:403, 477, 480, 499, 509, 549); Personal Account Ledger 8:226 and Private Ledger 2:88–98 (*TAEM* 88:99, 242–43).

8. Francis Upton to TAE, 19 June 1884 (*TAEM* 73:427); see also Upton to TAE, 15 Jan. and 31 Aug. 1883 and (*TAEM* 67:107, 243). On the affairs of the Edison Electric Lamp Co., see the following Document File folders: D-80-021, D-81-023, D-82-030, D-82-031, D-83-032, D-84-029 (*TAEM* 54: 2–32; 58:69–201; 61:720–954; 67:299–352; 73:359–485).

9. Francis Upton to TAE, 15 Jan. 1884 (*TAEM* 73:364).

10. Annual Report to the Stockholders of the Edison Electric Light Company, 23 Oct. 1883, *Edison Electric Light Company Bulletin* 19:48 (*TAEM* 96:892).

11. Sherbourne Eaton to TAE, 2 Nov. and 31 May 1882 (*TAEM* 61:101, 213).

12. TAE to Owen Gill, 29 Jan. 1881 (*TAEM* 80:493).

13. Annual Report to the Stockholders of the Edison Company for Isolated Lighting, 21 Nov. 1882, *Edison Electric Light Company Bulletin* 15:43–44 (*TAEM* 96:787).

14. Samuel Insull to Charles Batchelor, 30 Apr. 1882; Samuel Insull to Sherbourne Eaton, 15 Nov. 1882 (*TAEM* 81:534, 1009).

15. Samuel Insull to Charles Batchelor, 28 Sept. 1882 (*TAEM* 63:167); TAE to Edward Johnson, 23 Nov. 1882 (*TAEM* 81:111). In 1883, the Machine Works earned over $12,000 on $176,800 in sales, and credited an additional $18,450 to experimental expenses that Edison wanted to charge to the Edison Electric Light Company (summary account [*TAEM* 67:436]). Monthly reports on the numbers and types of dynamos that were built and sold by the Machine Works can be found in the following Document File folders: D-82-034 and D-83-034 (*TAEM* 62:2, 67:353).

16. James Harrison to Edison Company for Isolated Lighting, 11 Feb. 1882, *Edison Electric Light Company Bulletins* 4:3 (*TAEM* 96:677). The progress of the Isolated Company's business can be followed through the *Bulletins* and in Document File folders D-81-021, D-82-021, D-83-025, D-84-025 (*TAEM* 57:702, 60:844, 66:484, 73:96).

17. Originally published in the London *Journal of the Society of Arts*, 16 Dec. 1881, Preece's remarks were reprinted in the *Edison Electric Light Company Bulletin* 2:1 (*TAEM* 96:672); see also William Preece to TAE, 10 Feb. 1882 (*TAEM* 60:67).

18. TAE to Charles Batchelor, 13 Sept. 1881 (*TAEM* 58:476). For the Edison Electric Light Company of Europe, see the following Document File folders: D-80-024, D-81-027, D-82-028, D-83-031 (*TAEM* 54:138, 58:69, 61:587, 67:2). The best account of Edison's European light businesses is found in Hughes, *Networks of Power*, chap. 3.

19. Batchelor to TAE, 26 June 1882 (*TAEM* 62:441). See also Reports of Messrs. Puskas and Bailey to the Edison Electric Light Company of Europe Ltd., 25 Aug. 1882 (*TAEM* 61:643, 658); Report of the Board of Directors of the Edison Electric Light Company of Europe Ltd., to the Stockholders, May 1883, and Sherbourne Eaton statement regarding the unpaid claims of the Edison Electric Light Company of Europe Ltd. against the *Compagnie Continentale*, 14 Sept. 1883 (*TAEM* 67:41, 58). For the French electric light companies, see also the following Document File folders: D-81-032, D-82-038, D-83-037 (*TAEM* 58:417, 62:198, 67:591).

20. Charles Batchelor to TAE, 16 Mar. 1883 (*TAEM* 67:163). See also Batchelor to TAE, 20 Aug., 31 Oct., 25 Dec. 1883; 8 and 22 Feb., 3 Mar. 1884 (*TAEM* 67:841, 936, 967; 74:80, 116, 599); Report of the Board of Directors of the Edison Electric Light Company of Europe Ltd. to the Stockholders, May 1883, and Sherbourne Eaton statement regarding the unpaid claims of the Edison Electric Light Company of Europe Ltd. against the *Compagnie Continentale*, 14 Sept. 1883 (*TAEM* 67:41, 58); Bailey to the Directors of the Edison Electric Light Company of Europe Ltd., 28 Nov. 1884 (*TAEM* 73:337); Memoranda on the Proposed International Edison Company (*TAEM* 96:312); Report to the Stockholders of the Edison Electric Light Company of Europe Ltd., n.d. (*TAEM* 73:298).

21. Samuel Insull to Charles Batchelor, 30 Oct. 1882 (*TAEM* 89:467).

22. *London Daily News*, 19 Mar. 1882, quoted in Hughes, *Networks of Power*, 53.

23. For the British Edison Electric Light Company Ltd., see the following Document File folders: D-81-033, D-82-039, D-83-038 (*TAEM* 58:594, 62:625, 68:2). See also Hughes, *Networks of Power*, 52–66; idem, "British Electrical Industry Lag: 1882–1888," *Technology and Culture* 3 (1962): 27–44; and Friedel and Israel, *Biography of an Invention*, 215–18.

24. N-79-07-12, p. 5 (*TAEM* 40:283); TAE to E. H. Johnson, 23 Nov. 1881 (*TAEM* 81:111); Grosvenor Lowrey to TAE, 23 Oct. 1883 (*TAEM* 58:1098). See also TAE to Johnson, 9 Oct. 1881 (*TAEM* 81:60). On the issue of Edison getting the idea of carbon from Swan, see Friedel and Israel, *Edison's Electric Light*, 234. On Swan's work, see George Wise, "Swan's Way: A Study in Style," *IEEE Spectrum* 19 (1982): 66–70.

25. Theodore Waterhouse to TAE, 7 July 1883 (*TAEM* 68:88); Edison's quotes on the British patent system are from TAE to D. V. Lynch, 4 Dec. 1878, and TAE to E. H. Johnson, 2 Jan 1882 (*TAEM* 18:830, 81:223).

26. Arnold White to TAE, 15 June 1883 (*TAEM* 68:63). On the squirted cellulose lamps, see Upton to TAE, 20 July 1883 (*TAEM* 67:229); John W. Howell and Henry Schroeder, *History of the Incandescent Lamp* (Schenectady, N.Y.: The Maqua, 1927), 81–83.

27. TAE to E. H. Johnson, 5 Mar. 1883 (*TAEM* 81:777).

28. TAE to Sherbourne Eaton, 29 May 1882 (*TAEM* 81:748); see also Eaton to TAE, 8 Aug. 1882 (*TAEM* 61:362).

29. "Edison and His Light" (*TAEM* 66:21), a clipping dated by an archivist as March 13, 1883; TAE to Edward Johnson, 5 Mar. 1883 (*TAEM* 81:777).

30. *Edison Electric Light Company Bulletin* 17:5 (*TAEM* 96:811); Jehl, *Menlo Park Reminiscences*, 3:1092–94.

31. U.S. Patent 274,290.

32. TAE to Edward Johnson, 5 Mar. 1883 (*TAEM* 81:777). A good description of Edison's work on distribution systems is found in Appendix XI and XII of Dyer and Martin, *Edison*; see also Hughes, *Networks of Power*, 83–84, and W. J. Jenks, "The Edison Three-Wire System of Distribution," *Electrical World* 14 (20 July 1889): 39–43.

33. Ballou to TAE and TAE to Ballou (*TAEM* 66:20, 82:223); Johnson to TAE, 20 June 1883 (*TAEM* 68:70); Power of attorney to Samuel Insull, 3 May 1883 (*TAEM* 86:562). The only significant historical study of the Construction Department is Maryann Hellrigel, "Creating an Industry: Thomas A. Edison and His Electric Light System" (Master's Thesis, University of California, Santa Barbara, 1989), esp. chap. 3. The extensive records of this business can be found in *TAEM*, reels 68–70, 74–76, and 97:134–206.

34. Insull memoirs, 28, 32–33, Insull Papers; TAE to Charles E. Rocap, 10 February 1883 (*TAEM* 67:360). On Insull's role, see Forrest MacDonald, *Insull* (Chicago: University of Chicago Press, 1962), 21–32, and Millard, *Edison and the Business of Innovation*, 54.

35. Alfred Tate, *Edison's Open Door* (New York: E. P. Dutton & Co., 1938), 264.

36. Jehl, *Menlo Park Reminiscences*, 987.

37. Insull's memorandum for T. C. Martin, 10 Feb. 1909, Insull Papers.

38. Samuel Insull to Charles Brown, 26 May 1883 (*TAEM* 82:499); TAE to W. W. Chamberlaine, 14 Feb. 1884 (*TAEM* 71:972); Hellrigel, "Creating an Industry," 88–89.

39. Samuel Insull to J. N. Culbertson, 13 May 1883 (*TAEM* 82:413).

40. Samuel Insull to Spencer Borden, 25 June 1883 (*TAEM* 64:813).

41. Extract of Philip A. Lange's address to the Engineering Club, Manchester, England, printed in *Electrical Journal* of May 1907, Box 1, Sprague Papers, New York Public Library (hereafter Sprague Papers); Sherbourne Eaton to Charles Clarke, 14 Nov. 1883 (*TAEM* 66:906).

42. Frank Sprague's 2 March 1883 letter to Edward Johnson concerning the three-wire system was sent to Edison and may well have arrived before he executed his patent on March 20 (*TAEM* 66:5).

43. *New York Times*, 1 Apr. 1883, quoted in Bob Rosenberg, "Academic Physics and the Origins of Electrical Engineering in America" (Ph.D. dissertation, Johns Hopkins University, Baltimore, 1990), 34. Rosenberg provides the best discussion of the need of the early electrical industry for trained engineers. See also Jehl, *Menlo Park Reminiscences*, 3:962–65.

44. Samuel Insull to C. H. Campbell, 8 Dec. 1883 (*TAEM* 69:2620).

45. Frank Sprague to TAE, 10 Sept. 1883 (*TAEM* 69:121); TAE per Insull to Sprague, 8 Sept. 1883 (*TAEM* 65:71).

46. Samuel Upton to TAE, 8 November 1883 (*TAEM* 67:264); see also Insull to C. H. Campbell, 8 Dec. 1883 (*TAEM* 69:262); Alfred Tate to Samuel Insull, 18 and 26 Dec. 1883 and 29 Jan. 1884 (*TAEM* 65:876–936; 71:918); Insull to W. D. Rich, 4 Mar. 1884 (*TAEM* 72:51).

47. TAE to Samuel Insull, 8 Mar. 1884 (*TAEM* 74:439).

48. Although it canvassed much of the northeast and Midwest, the Construction Department built stations only in Pennsylvania (5), Ohio (4), Massachusetts (3), and New York (1). The largest city was Fall River, Massachusetts, with a population of almost 49,000, and the smallest was Mt. Carmel, Pennsylvania, with a population under 2,400. Four of the installations used underground conductors and had a capacity of 1,600 lights each. The overhead system at Shamokin, Pennsylvania, also had this capacity. The other overhead stations included 4 of 1,000 lights, 1 of 800, and 3 of 500, including Sunbury. The cost of these plants ranged from $14,500 to $41,800. The failure of some companies to make final payment apparently stemmed from disagreement with Edison over what constituted "an adequate plant" under the terms of the contract (Sherbourne Eaton to Executive Committee of Edison Electric, 24 May 1884, DF [*TAEM* 73:215]). Construction Department accounts, 30 November 1883, DF (*TAEM* 68:607); Hellrigel, "Creating an Industry," 70, 72–73, 97; Alfred Tate to Samuel Insull, 29 Jan. 1884 (*TAEM* 71:918); Insull to Eaton, 10 Mar. 1884 (*TAEM* 72:101); Insull to TAE, 11 Mar. 1884 (*TAEM* 72:123); Insull to A. A. Cowles, 1 Aug. 1884 (*TAEM* 82:746); Insull to Edward Johnson, 3 June 1885 (*TAEM* 83:179).

49. TAE to William Andrews, 26 Apr. 1884 (*TAEM* 72:579).

50. TAE to Sherbourne Eaton, 24 Apr. 1884 (*TAEM* 73:188).

51. Eaton's memo to Edison Electric Executive Committee, 24 May 1884 (*TAEM* 73:215). See also TAE to Andrews, 26 Apr. 1884; Eaton to Edison, Insull, Johnson, and Upton, 26 Apr. 1884; F. S. Hastings to Thomas A. Edison Construction Department, 29 Apr. 1884; Edison to Eaton, 15, 21, 22, and 24 May 1884 (*TAEM* 72:579, 696, 729, 738, 771; 73:215; 74:464).

52. Eaton to Edison Electric Directors, 29 Jan. 1884, DF (*TAEM* 73:159).

53. Annual Report to the Stockholders of the Edison Electric Light Company, 24 Oct. 1882 (*TAEM* 61:86).

54. Unsigned letter from Edison and his manufacturing partners to Eaton, 1 Feb. 1883 (*TAEM* 66:714).

55. Francis Upton to TAE, 4 Jan. 1883 (*TAEM* 67:97); see also Eaton memoranda, 19 and 24 Jan. 1883 (*TAEM* 67:116; 66:395).

56. Unsigned letter from Edison and his manufacturing partners to Eaton, 1 Feb. 1883 (*TAEM* 66:714).

57. Grosvenor Lowrey to TAE, 19 Oct. 1884 (*TAEM* 73:240); see also Edison to Henry Villard, 24 Apr. 1884 (another version of this letter was probably sent by Edison's manufacturing partners but is incorrectly identified as being from the Isolated Company) (*TAEM* 73:191, 270); report of the Committee of Three, 18 June 1884 (*TAEM* 73:225); agreements between Edison Electric and Edison Machine Works, Bergmann & Co., and Electric Tube Co., 1 Sept. 1884 (*TAEM* 86:801, 818, 883).

58. Grosvenor Lowrey to TAE, 19 Oct. 1884 (*TAEM* 73:240). Lowrey was probably referring to those provisions relating to restrictions on the profits allowed the shops and those stating the conditions under which Edison Electric could license other manufacturers.

59. Samuel Insull to Alfred Tate, 27 Oct. 1884, DF (*TAEM* 73:250); see also TAE to Uriah Painter, 16 Oct. 1884, Painter Papers.

60. Samuel Insull to Alfred Tate, 27 Oct. 1884, DF (*TAEM* 73:250). Regarding the issue of experimental expenses and Eaton's criticisms of Insull, see TAE to Eaton, 13 Mar. 1884 (*TAEM* 65:809); Eaton to Insull, 18 Feb., 1 and 17 Mar. 1884 (*TAEM* 74:413, 418; 73:172, 180); Insull to Eaton, 18 and 19 Feb., 10, 11, and 19 Mar. 1884 (*TAEM* 74:416, 419–20; 72:99, 125, 73:180); F. S. Hastings to Insull 3 May 1884 (*TAEM* 73:198).

61. "Edison on the Warpath," undated clipping from c. October 1884 (*TAEM* 89:667).

62. Samuel Insull to Alfred Tate, 27 Oct. 1884 (*TAEM* 73:250).

63. TAE to Edward Johnson (*TAEM* 81:351).

Chapter 13: Family Matters

1. Marion Edison Oser reminiscences.

2. Rufus R. Wilson, "Edison on Invention," *Monthly Illustrator* 11 (Nov. 1895): 344 (*TAEM* 146:657); Marion Edison Oser reminiscences; "Edison as a Pianist," *Electrician* 11 (1885): 44.

3. Leslie Ward to TAE, 18 Jan. 1882 (*TAEM* 50:698).

4. Marion Edison Oser reminiscences. In his 1995 biography, *Edison: Inventing the Century* (New York: Hyperion, 1995, 134), Neil Baldwin mistakenly says that Edison did not go with his wife to Florida in 1882. However, he was unaware of correspondence from Edison's secretary, Samuel Insull, noting Edison's absence in Florida as well as the telegram and letter from the Palatka taxidermists, Hoyt and Dickson, who shipped Edison two birds he had probably killed while hunting there (Insull to Charles Batchelor, 7 and 24 Mar. 1882 [*TAEM* 81:429, 460]; Hoyt & Dickson to TAE, 8 Apr. 1882 [*TAEM* 60:111–12]). Insull to Benjamin Hardwick, 3 Apr. 1882, indicates Mary and Edison had returned (*TAEM* 81:502). On the 1883 trip see TAE to Insull, 13 and 15 Feb. 1883 (*TAEM* 64:75, 109). On the weather and Edison's hunting and fishing in 1884 see Mary Edison to Insull, 27 Feb. 1884 (*TAEM* 71:605); Insull to Clarendon Hotel, 6 Feb. 1884 (*TAEM* 71:999).

5. Samuel Insull to Charles Batchelor, 28 Sept. 1882 (*TAEM* 63:167). Other letters relating to the closing of the Menlo Park Laboratory include Insull to John Randolph, 12 Oct. 1882, and Ott to TAE, 26 Oct. 1882 (*TAEM* 63:205, 212). For the move back to Menlo Park following Edison's Florida vacation, see Insull to Batchelor, 10 Apr. 1882, and TAE to Charles Young, 11 May 1882 (*TAEM* 81: 534, 645).

6. Regarding the Gramercy Park apartment, see correspondence, lease, and inventory listed in *TAEM Guide*, Part III, s.vv. "Pryor, James. W." On Gramercy Park, see Stephen Garmey, *Gramercy Park:*

An Illustrated History of a New York Neighborhood (New York: Balsam Press, 1984), and Carole Klein, *Gramercy Park: An American Bloomsbury* (Boston: Houghton Mifflin, 1987).

7. TAE to Samuel Insull, 7 Apr. 1884 (*TAEM* 71:611); see also Edison's marginal note on Keith to TAE, 11 Apr. 1884 (*TAEM* 71:104). In his 1979 biography, *Streak of Luck,* Robert Conot mistakenly transcribes Edison's telegram as "Send trained man nurse who is not afraid of person out of her mind— send as soon as possible" (p. 218). However, the following day, Mary was lucid enough to ask Insull for some money and at the end of the month was asking him to send a wagon to the Clarendon Hotel to move some boxes to Menlo Park. Neil Baldwin also assumes that the man nurse was for Mary, because she had become "hysterical with grief," but he almost certainly was for her father (Baldwin, *Edison,* 142).

8. Mary Edison to Samuel Insull, 30 Apr. 1884, and Robert Lozier to John Tomlinson, 9 Aug. 1884, DF (*TAEM* 71:615, 627). See also Mary Edison to Insull, 8 and 29 May, DF (*TAEM* 71:613–14); Marion Edison Oser reminiscences.

9. TAE to Samuel Insull, 9 Aug. 1884 (*TAEM* 71:628); Insull to Mary E. Wicker, 15 Sept. 1884 (*TAEM* 82:835); Edison's rental agreement with George W. Folsom, 1 Sept. 1884 (*TAEM* 71:250). Regarding Eugenia Stilwell's education, see William C. Bowen to TAE, 19 and 25 Aug. 1884 (*TAEM* 71:663, 666); for assistance to the family, see *TAEM Guide,* Part III, s.vv. "Stilwell, Eugenia" and "Stilwell, Margaret."

10. *Seyfert v. Edison* (*TAEM* 46:607); *TAEM Guide,* Part II, s.vv. "Schenck, Abraham," and "Strong (Woodbridge) & Son"; George W. Vroom to Josiah Reiff, 8 Apr. 1884; John Tomlinson to TAE, 23 Apr. and 3 Oct. 1884; Vroom to Tomlinson, 3 and 13 May 1884; Tomlinson to Vroom, 13 May 1884, with affidavit of same date; Reiff to TAE, 17 May 1884; accounting from suit, June 1884; Tomlinson to Insull, 21 July 1884; warrant of attachment (*TAEM* 71:100, 119, 131, 148, 152, 162, 196, 217, 282, 350).

11. Marion Edison Oser reminiscences.

12. "Producing Electricity Directly from Coal," *Operator* 15 (1 Oct. 1884): 181. The original conception of Edison's direct conversion process is found in a description given to his patent attorney Richard Dyer on 7 September 1883 (*TAEM* 44:584–89); see also U.S. Patent 490,953. The July experiments are found in N-82-05-15, pp. 104–81 (*TAEM* 40:514–51).

13. Michael Faraday, *On the Various Forces of Nature* (New York: Thomas Y. Crowell Co., 1957), 141.

14. Notebooks N-80-08-09, pp. 13, 57, 218 (*TAEM* 38:433, 454, 459). Marion's presence in the laboratory was also marked by an October 8 notebook entry in her hand regarding telephone experiments being conducted by her father and John Ott (N82-05-15, p. 196 [*TAEM* 40:558]). Regarding Marion's schooling, see *TAEM Guide,* Part II, s.v. "Mears, A. L"; prior to attending this school she had attended the Misses Graham's school for young ladies on Fifth Avenue, and she and her cousin Eugenia both attended Mademoiselle de Janon's English and French school for young ladies in Gramercy Park (*TAEM* 57:539, 60:722).

15. Gilliland's testimony, *Edison & Gilliland v. Phelps,* p. 3, Pat. Int. 10,369–72, U.S. Patent Office.

16. Samuel Insull to Dillwyn Parrish, 23 Nov. 1885 (*TAEM* 78:901). For Edison's relations with American Bell, see also TAE to Theodore Vail, 12 and 29 Oct. 1884, Vail to American Bell Executive Committee, 9 May and 15 Oct. 1885, and agreement between TAE and American Bell, 16 Feb. 1886, all President's Files, AT&T; Vail to TAE, 25 Oct. 1884 and 9 May 1885 (*TAEM* 76:972, 78:855); John Tomlinson to TAE, 5 Jan. 1885 (*TAEM* 78:822); Gilliland to TAE, 11 Feb. and 28 Apr. 1885 (*TAEM* 78:840, 854); TAE undated 1884 memorandum and draft agreements with American Bell. (*TAEM* 76:1030–33; 86:841).

17. The importance of Edison's new carbon telephone transmitter is discussed in M. D. Fagen, *A History of Engineering and Science in the Bell System: The Early Years, 1875–1925* (n.p.: Bell Telephone Laboratories, 1975): 74–75.

18. N-82-05-15, p. 199; see also pp. 104–217 and N-80-08-09, pp. 13–29 (*TAEM* 40:514–68; 38: 433–55).

19. Ezra Gilliland to Theodore Vail, 9 Dec. 1884, President's Files, AT&T; Gilliland's testimony, *Edison & Gilliland v. Phelps,* p. 5, Pat. Int. 10,369–72.

20. Theodore Vail to TAE, 9 May 1885 (*TAEM* 78:855); Vail to American Bell Executive Committee, 9 May 1885, President's Files, AT&T.

21. Gilliland's testimony, *Edison & Gilliland v. Phelps,* pp. 8–10, Pat. Int. 10,369–72, *New Orleans Picayune,* 8 Feb. 1885, Theodore Whitney, to TAE, 9 Feb. and 6 Apr. 1885 (*TAEM* 77:42, 72); TAE to Insull, 24 and 28 Feb., 6 Mar. 1885 (*TAEM* 77:53, 60–61); receipt for property from Huelsenkamp & Cranford, 21 Mar. 1885 (*TAEM* 78:325). In an undated typescript of an interview, possibly from 1917, Edison stated, "I had all the houses framed in Maine, loaded on a vessel called the 'Edna,' and had them sent down by sea to Fort Myers" (DF).

22. Thomas A. Edison, "The Air-Telegraph," *North American Review* 142 (March 1886): 286.

23. For early work on the railway telegraph, see the testimony and exhibits in *Edison & Gilliland v. Phelps*, Pat. Int. 10,369-72; for the organization of the company, see Railway Telegraph & Telephone Co. Incorporation and Association Papers, 1885 (*TAEM* 58:246); Agreement between TAE, Gilliland, and Railway Telegraph & Telephone Co., 23 Feb. 1885 (*TAEM* 86:901); Wiley W. Smith to TAE, 18 Feb. 1885 (*TAEM* 78:541); TAE to Smith, 25 Feb. 1885 (*TAEM* 83:97); Railway Telegraph & Telephone Co., List of Stockholders, 21 Nov. 1885 (*TAEM* 78:719). Edison Electric president Eugene Crowell also became a major stockholder and was later president of the Railway Telegraph & Telephone.

24. Thomas A. Edison, "The Air-Telegraph," *North American Review* 142 (1886): 287.

25. Gilliland's testimony, *Edison & Gilliland v. Phelps*, pp. 10–11, Pat. Int. 10,369-72. The draft caveat is in NS-Undated-001 (*TAEM* 8:2–4).

26. Although Edison later claimed that he successfully transmitted up to two and one-half miles, by 1886 he had succeeded in transmitting only as far as 580 feet. He also incorrectly remembered that "I did not think of using the results of my experiments on 'etheric force' that I made in 1875. I have never been able to understand how I came to overlook them. If I had made use of my own work I should have had long-distance wireless telegraphy" (Dyer and Martin, *Edison*, 578). However, it is clear from his 1886 article, "The Air-Telegraph," (pp. 285–86), that he did in fact draw on his earlier experiments. On the air telegraph system, see U.S. Patent 465,971; TAE to Richard Dyer, 6 May 1885 (*TAEM* 44:684); Ezra Gilliland to TAE, 27 Apr. 1885 (*TAEM* 77:84); Martin Force to Samuel Insull, 6,8, and 21 July, 1 Aug. 1885 (*TAEM* 78:577–78, 581, 583); Force to TAE, 9 July 1885 (*TAEM* 78:579); bill, 3 Sept. 1885 (*TAEM* 78:599).

27. These experiments were conducted by new Edison employees W. T. King and S. K. Dingle with assistance from John Ott and Martin Force, who had conducted the laboratory experiments. All of these men were rewarded with stock in Railway Telegraph & Telephone. Gilliland, Edison, Ott, and Force testimony, pp. 13–14, 21, 39–43, 45–47, 52–55, *Edison & Gilliland v. Phelps*, Pat. Int. 10,369-72; N-85-10-01, pp. 13–61 (*TAEM* 42:254–78); John Ott notebook, p. 52 and loose page, Charley Hummel, Wayne, N.J.; "The Edison System of Railway Telegraphy," *Scientific American* 54 (20 Feb. 1878): 119–20. Regarding the arrangement of tests on the Staten Island Rapid Transit Railroad, see Ott to TAE, 20 July 1885 (*TAEM* 77:130); TAE to Samuel Insull, 20 July 1885 (*TAEM* 77:132); C. F. Cutler to TAE, 4 Aug. 1885 (*TAEM* 78:584); Insull to Erastus Wiman, 5 Oct. 1885 (*TAEM* 83:307); Insull to Eugene Crowell, 8 Oct. 1885 (*TAEM* 83:309).

28. Railway Telegraph & Telephone Co. Resolutions 30 Apr. 1886 (*TAEM* 79:1134).

29. TAE to C. H. Rudd, 13 May 1886 (*TAEM* 83:619); S. K. Dingle to TAE, 5 June 1886 (*TAEM* 79:1152); see also Samuel Insull to Ezra Gilliland, 1 and 13 Mar. 1886 (*TAEM* 83:433, 470); Insull to TAE, 13, 18, 23, and 29 Mar., 22 Apr. 1886 (*TAEM* 83:476, 514, 521, 528, 603); Alfred Tate to TAE, 15 Mar. 1886 (*TAEM* 83:500); Insull to Rudd, 22 April 1886 (*TAEM* 83:603), Rudd to TAE, 3 May and 21 June 1886 (*TAEM* 79:1135, 1163); Dingle to TAE, 29 and 31 May, 4 and 12 June 1886 (*TAEM* 79:1144, 1148, 1150, 1160); Dingle to Eugene Crowell, 9 June (*TAEM* 79:1175).

30. "Exhibition of Train Telegraphy," *Scientific American* 57 (15 Oct. 1887): 240. The interference was *Edison & Gilliland v. Phelps*, Pat. Int. 10,369-72, U.S. Patent Office. For the Phelps system, see Phelps Induction Telegraph Co. circular (*TAEM* 78:544) and "Recent Progress in Electricity— The Phelps System of Telegraphing from a Railway Train while in Motion," *Scientific American* 52 (21 Feb. 1885): 118–19. Regarding the merger and the formation of Consolidated Railway Telegraph, see *TAEM Guide*, Parts II–III, s.vv. "Consolidated Railway Telegraph Co.," "Phelps Induction Telegraph Co.," "Railway Telegraph & Telephone Co.," "International Railway Telegraph Co."

31. Phonoplex pamphlets (*TAEM* 96:498); U.S. Patents 333,290, 333,291, 422,072; the 1878 design is *TAEB* Doc. 1415 and U.S. Patent 217,782. The technical and business development of the phonoplex system is detailed in N-84-05-22, pp. 35–63; N-85-10-01, pp. 115–45; N-85-10-03, pp. 1–55; N-86-03-18, pp. 11, 67–73, 97–101, 117 (*TAEM* 42:95–109, 301–13, 353–80, 819, 847–50, 862–64, 871); John Ott notebook, pp. 50–51, 53, Charley Hummel, Wayne, N.J.; TAE to Dyer, 18 Sept. and 22 Oct. 1885 and 28 Feb. 1886 (*TAEM* 44:690, 696, 712); TAE to Wiman, 14 May, 19 Sept. 1885 (*TAEM* 78:559; 83:263); Wiman to TAE, 7 Aug., 17 Sept. 1885 (*TAEM* 78:586, 602); George Hamilton to TAE, with Edison's marginal comment, 10 July 1885 (*TAEM* 78:850); TAE to H. P. Dwight, 11 May 1886 (*TAEM* 83:614); Samuel Insull to TAE, 17 Dec. 1885, 1, 13, and 29 Mar., 18 Oct. 1886 (*TAEM* 83:386, 437, 476, 528, 763); Insull to E. T. Gilliland, 1 and 13 Mar. 1886 (*TAEM* 83:433, 470); correspondence to and from Alfred Tate between September 1885 and December 1886 in *TAEM* reels 78, 83–84; Document File folders D-87-53, D-83-53, D-89-66, D-3, 1997-90-63, D-91-56, D-92-47, D-93-47 (*TAEM*

120:322, 124:877, 128:874, 130:619, 132:256, 133:746, 134:1008); and letterbook LM-025 (*TAEM* 160:122).

32. TAE to Wiman, 14 May 1886 (*TAEM* 78:559).

33. Alfred Tate to Samuel Insull, 23 Oct. 1885 (*TAEM* 78:668).

34. TAE to Alfred Tate, 19 Nov. 1885 (*TAEM* 83:348).

35. Alfred Tate to TAE, 17 Dec. 1885, (*TAEM* 78:786).

36. Samuel Insull to TAE, 29 Mar. 1886 (*TAEM* 83:528).

37. TAE to Richard Dyer, June 1885 (*TAEM* 44:659).

38. TAE to Samuel Insull, 20 July 1885 (*TAEM* 77:132).

39. Draft agreement, c. 1885, between TAE, Sigmund Bergmann, Edward Johnson, and Zalmon Simmons; TAE's undated memorandum regarding proposed agreement (*TAEM* 78:884, 923); see also other 1885 draft agreements with Zalmon Simmons (*TAEM* 78:926, 941, 954); James H. Howe to TAE, 21 and 24 Aug., 1, 8, 22, and 28 Sept., and 16 Oct. 1885 (*TAEM* 78:873, 875, 877–78, 600, 882, 883, 891); TAE to Howe, 21 Sept. 1885 (*TAEM* 83:289); TAE's statement, 16 Sept. 1885 (*TAEM* 78:506); Johnson's patent application, 24 Jan. 1883 (*TAEM* 70:934).

40. *New Orleans Picayune*, 8 Feb. 1886 (*TAEM* 89:706); "Lucky Edison Draws a Prize," undated clipping, "Marriage" folder, Edison Biographical Collection, ENHS; Edison's 1885 diary, Cat. 117 (*TAEM* 90:28).

41. TAE to Lewis Miller, 30 Sept. 1885, facsimile in Josephson, *Edison*, plates; TAE to Samuel Insull, 27 June 1885 (*TAEM* 77:117); Edison's 1885 diary, Cat. 117 (*TAEM* 90:21, 28).

42. Edison's 1885 diary, Cat. 117 (*TAEM* 90:29).

43. TAE to Samuel Insull, July 1885 (*TAEM* 77:137).

44. Edison's 1885 diary, Cat. 117 (*TAEM* 90:29).

45. Edison's 1885 diary, Cat. 117 (*TAEM* 90:38).

46. Jennie Miller to Mina, 17 Dec. 1885 (*TAEM* 161:837).

47. Edison's 1885 diary, Cat. 117 (*TAEM* 90:10).

48. Edison's 1885 diary, Cat. 117 (*TAEM* 90:46–47).

49. Ellwood Hendrick, *Lewis Miller: A Biographical Essay* (New York: Putnam's, 1925), v.

50. Lewis Miller to Mina, 26 Apr. 1887 (*TAEM* 161:486).

51. Mary Valinda Miller to Mina, 25 Nov. 1892, Family Correspondence (15-8080), ENHS.

52. Runes, *Diary and Sundry Observations*, 54; Marion Edison Oser reminiscences.

53. TAE to Lewis Miller, 30 Sept. 1885, facsimile in Josephson, *Edison*, plates.

54. Jennie Miller to Mina, 21 Nov. and 17 Dec. 1885, 26 Feb. 1886 (*TAEM* 161:835, 837, 845).

55. Mary Miller to Mina, n.d., Family Correspondence (3-2082), ENHS.

56. Mary Valinda Miller to Mina, 18 Feb. 1888 and 18 Nov. 1892 (*TAEM* 161:629, 751).

57. TAE to John and Theodore Miller, 24 Dec. 1885 (*TAEM* 77:480).

58. Mina Miller interview with Associated Press reporter, 10 Jan. 1947, typescript in Edison Biographical Collection, ENHS; "The Most Difficult Husband in America," *Collier's*, 18 July 1925, 11; Edwd. P. Hamilton & Co. to TAE, 12 Jan. 1886 (*TAEM* 79:50); H. Hudson Holly to TAE, 12 Jan. 1886, with enclosure (*TAEM* 78:347–48); Samuel Insull to Miss Clara H. Warner, 23 Nov. 1885 (*TAEM* 83:388). TAE drawings of proposed lab, c. Jan.–Feb. 1886, N-85-10-01, pp. 63–68, (*TAEM* 42:279–82); Insull to A. D. Pickering, 13 May 1886 (*TAEM* 22:121).

59. Cat. 1335, items, 23, 25 (*TAEM* 90:320).

60. Clippings in "Marriage" folder, Edison Biographical Collection, ENHS; Jennie Miller to Mina, 26 Feb. 1886 (*TAEM* 161: 845); Samuel Insull to Ezra Gilliland, 1 Mar. 1886 (*TAEM* 83:433).

61. Ezra Gilliland to Samuel Insull, 7 Mar. 1886 (*TAEM* 79:86); see also dispatch to the *New York World* from Atlanta, Ga., 27 Feb. 1886 (*TAEM* 89:703); TAE to Samuel Insull, 10 and 18 Mar. 1886 (*TAEM* 79:89, 92); Insull to Ezra Gilliland, 13 Mar. 1886 (*TAEM* 83:470).

62. TAE to Samuel Insull, 11 Mar. 1886 (*TAEM* 79:90).

63. TAE to Edward Johnson, 21 Mar. 1886 (*TAEM* 79:90, 331); the notebooks are N-86-03-18, N-86-04-03.3, N-86-07-07, and N-86-08-03 (*TAEM* 42:813; 43:2; 43:169; 43:299).

64. N-85-12-08, p. 1 (*TAEM* 42:469).

65. "Edison's Latest Ideas," [*Cairo?*] *Ill. Gazette*, 25 July 1885 (*TAEM* 89:647).

66. N-86-08-17, pp. 23, 31 (*TAEM* 43:311, 315).

67. N-86-04-28, pp. 79–81 (*TAEM* 590–91).

68. N-86-04-07, pp. 197–99 (*TAEM* 43:262–63). Edison's atomic theory also seems to have influenced his ideas regarding the XYZ force experiments. See also *TAEB* Doc. 1315, axiom 6.

69. N-86-03-18, p. 57 (*TAEM* 42:842). The book of instructions and plans for the plantings at Fort Myers is N-86-04-05 (*TAEM* 43:142).

70. Marion Edison Oser reminiscences; the story is found in N-86-04-03.1, pp. 162–63 (*TAEM* 42:1028).

71. Jennie Miller to Mina, 12 and 23 May 1886 (*TAEM* 161:872, 881). See also Jennie to Mina, 9, 20, and 27 May 1886 (*TAEM* 161:868, 876, 885), and Mary Valinda Miller to Mina, 9, 16, 23, and 30 May 1886 (*TAEM* 161:518, 520), and family correspondence, ENHS.

72. Cat. 1336:33–71, 79–87, 153, items 71, 74, 78–79, 82, 84–86, 89, 94, 96, 107, 113, 126, 271, 272, and clippings pp. 35, 84 (*TAEM* 90:331–48, 352–56, 389).

73. "Edison's Men on Strike," *New York World*, 30 May 1886, Cat. 1336:35 (*TAEM* 90:332). TAE is quoted in Baldwin, *Edison*, 178, the source is apparently "Walks and Talks in the Grove," *Chautauqua Assembly Herald*, 16 Aug. 1886.

74. TAE to Edward Johnson, 11 June 1886 (*TAEM* 83:664).

75. Edison marginal note to Francis Upton on Western Edison to Edison Lamp Co., 26 Jan. 1886 (*TAEM* 95:746).

76. Cat. 1336:103, item 167 (*TAEM* 90:364). See the Lamp Factory notebooks N-86-06-28, N-86-07-07, N-86-08-03, N-86-08-24, N-86-10-05, N-86-10-08 (*TAEM* 43:430, 532, 670, 769.1, 808, 842, 855).

77. "Billy" may be derived from Wilhelmina, which is most likely Mina's given name, although there is no evidence she ever went by it. See notebooks N-86-08-03, PN-86-03-04, Miscellaneous Notebook of 1887, PN-87-05-08 (*TAEM* 43:670; 44:155; 106:657, 667).

78. "The Woman of the Future," *Good Housekeeping* 55 (1912): 436–44.

79. Mary Valinda Miller to Mina, 3 Jan. 1887 (*TAEM* 161:551).

80. "The Most Difficult Husband in America," *Collier's*, 18 July 1925, 11.

81. Cat. 1336, items 147, 153 (*TAEM* 90:387, 389).

82. Mary Valinda Miller to Mina, 27 Oct. and 17 Nov. 1886 and 26 Jan. 1887 (*TAEM* 161:541, 545, 562); Lewis Miller to Mina, 26 Apr. 1887 (*TAEM* 161:486).

83. Mary Valinda Miller to Mina, 1 Mar. 1887, and Lewis Miller to Mina, 26 Apr. 1887 (*TAEM* 161:568, 486); see also Cat. 1336:163–65, 169, 173–75, items 284, 290, 301, 308 (*TAEM* 90:394–95, 397, 399–400).

84. Cat. 1336:179–89, 195, items 322–24, 330, 336, 350 (*TAEM* 90:402–07, 410).

85. Lewis Miller to Mina, 26 Apr. 1887, and Marion Edison to TAE, 24 Apr. 1887 (161:484, 5).

86. Jennie's letter suggests that Mina may have thought she was already pregnant. Jennie Miller to Mina, 8 Mar. 1887 (*TAEM* 161:907).

87. On Bradford Academy, see Jean Sarah Pond, *Bradford, A New England Academy* (Bradford, Mass.: Bradford Academy Alumnae Association, 1930).

88. The boys had been going to school at the Dearborn-Morgan School in Orange (tuition bill 24 June 1887, DF [*TAEM* 119:561]). On St. Paul's, see Arthur Stanwood Pier, *St. Paul's School, 1855–1934* (New York: Charles Scribner's Sons, 1934).

Chapter 14: A New Laboratory

1. Draft of TAE to J. Hood Wright, c. Aug. 1887, N-87-11-15 (*TAEM* 98:671). This letter is identified in the *TAEM* index as November 1887. However, it is clear from Batchelor's diary, Cat. 1336: 277–78, item 454, and from Wright's letter to Edison dated 17 August that this letter must date from early August 1887 (*TAEM* 90:453–54; 119:100).

2. The quotes about Weston are from the *Newark Call*, 7 Nov. 1886, and *Daily Herald*, 28 Oct. 1887, both quoted in Millard, *Edison and the Business of Innovation*, 330, n. 11–12; Millard's book is the first detailed study of the West Orange laboratory. Weston's laboratory is described in Woodbury 1949, 151. Regarding their mutual dislike see Weston's, Edison's, and Francis Upton's letters to the Editor of *Scientific American* 41 (1879): 270, 308, also reprinted in Edison Isolated Company Bulletin No. 12, 15–18 (*TAEM* 97:98–100); Edison's comments on Henry Morton to TAE, 5 July 1883, (*TAEM* 64:221); and David O. Woodbury, *A Measure for Greatness: A Short Biography of Edward Weston* (New York: McGraw-Hill, 1949), 206.

3. Millard, *Edison and the Business of Innovation*, 7. Although undated, Edison's drawings for his proposed laboratory appear between notebook entries of 30 Jan. and 3 Feb. 1886 (N-83-10-01, pp. 63–68 [*TAEM* 42:279–82]).

4. Regarding Batchelor's role in the design see TAE to Batchelor, 4 Apr. 1887 (*TAEM* 119:121), and Cat. 1336:187–88, 191, 195, 199, 203, 209, items 336, 341, 350, 356, 360, 367 (*TAEM* 90:406–08, 410, 412, 414, 417).

5. Draft of TAE to Wright, c. Aug. 1887, N-87-11-15 (*TAEM* 98:671).

6. Notebook E-4294:31, 34–38 (*TAEM* 108:961, 963–64); undated drawings and notes in D-87-55 (*TAEM* 120:553, 603, 612–15); Cat. 1336:253–54, item 422 (*TAEM* 90:439–40); laboratory building plans (*TAEM* 108:1066–78); N-87-00-00.3:3 (*TAEM* 98:87).

7. Jeff Waldron's inspection notebook, PN-87-07-16 (*TAEM* 108:917). See also correspondence listed in *TAEM Guide*, Part III, s.vv. "Holly, Henry Hudson" and "Taft, Joseph J."

8. Samuel Insull to Alfred Tate, 1 Sept. 1887 (*TAEM* 119:698). See also Ledger #5:423–35, 460, 598 (*TAEM* 618–23, 630, 699); "Edison's New Laboratory," *Scientific American* 57 (1878): 184; TAE to Henry Villard, 19 Jan. 1887 (*TAEM* 119:168). Regarding the order of machinery see Notebooks 87-06-00 and E-4294 and Scrapbooks E-4295 and E-6726-6 (*TAEM* 108:691, 945, 969, 1015); and Document File folders D-87-56, D-87-57, D-88-56 (*TAEM* 120:640, 912, 124:1028).

9. "Edison's New Laboratory," *Scientific American* 57 (1878): 184. For Edison's own lists of materials see N-88-06-01.1 and N-88-06-01.2 (*TAEM* 99:422–70, 503–22).

10. Horace Townsend, "Edison, His Work and His Work-Shop," *Cosmopolitan Magazine* (April 1889), 604 (*TAEM* 146:445).

11. Townsend, "Edison, His Work and His Work-Shop," 604.

12. *Scientific American*, n.s. 57 (1878): 184.

13. For the library holdings and their use, see N-88-01-30 and N-90-02-15 (*TAEM* 108:825, 882); on the Kunz mineral collection, see W. K. L. Dickson and Antonia Dickson, *The Life and Inventions of Thomas A. Edison* (New York: Thomas Y. Crowell & Co, 1892), 283–84.

14. Dickson and Dickson, *Life and Inventions*, 283, 287–88; "Edison's Birthday," clipping dated 11 Feb. 1889 (*TAEM* 95:243); "Historic Furnishings Report" 1:17–18; W. Bernard Carlson, "Building Thomas Edison's Laboratory at West Orange, New Jersey: A Case Study in Using Craft Knowledge for Technological Invention, 1886–1888," *History of Technology* 13 (1991): 150–67.

15. Edison's marginal note on Edward Johnson to TAE, 6 July 1887 (*TAEM* 120:29).

16. Draft of TAE to J. Hood Wright, c. Aug. 1887, N-87-11-15 (*TAEM* 98:671); Batchelor's diary, Cat. 1336:277–78, item 454 (*TAEM* 90:453–54); Wright to TAE 17 Aug. 1887, TAE to Garrison, 13 Aug. 1887, and Garrison to TAE, 19 Aug. 1887 (*TAEM* 119:100, 172, 177).

17. Draft agreements between TAE and Henry Villard, 1887 and 1888; drafts of prospectus and agreements, Edison Industrial Co., 1887 (*TAEM* 145:124, 276; 119:367, 372, 380, 384); TAE to Villard, 19 Jan. 1887 (*TAEM* 119:168).

18. Exhibit A of the draft 1888 agreement with Henry Villard (*TAEM* Supp. IV) and Edison's draft of this exhibit (121:180–97); TAE to Villard, 19 Jan. 1888 (*TAEM* 121:168); *TAEM Guide*, Part III, s.vv. "Burrell, David Hamlin" and "Richardson, J.S."; *TAEB*, Doc. 579; abandoned patent applications (*TAEM* 114:7, 32); N-85-10-01, p. 113 (*TAEM* 42:300); Ledger #5, pp. 529, 539, 555, 569, 572, 574 (*TAEM* 87:664, 670, 677, 684, 686, 687).

19. He listed these as Edison Lamp Co. $10,000, Edison Electric Light Co. $5,000, Edison Machine Works $6,000, Edison Phonograph Co. $3,000, and Edison Ore Milling Co. $3,000. TAE to Villard, 19 Jan. 1887 (*TAEM* 119:168).

20. The expenses were broken down as interest on investment ($9,200), insurance ($1,100), depreciation ($9,200), supplies ($7,000), and payroll ($62,400). It is unclear what these figures are based on as monthly accounts suggest a much higher operating expense for the laboratory. The money to be paid from existing contracts was not broken down but now included Edison's experiments on the mimeograph for the A. B. Dick Novelty Co. Draft agreement between TAE and Henry Villard, dated only 1888; TAE to Villard, 19 Jan. 1887 (*TAEM* 145:276; 119:168); U.S. Pats. 506,215 (plate glass) and 563,462 (drawing wire) and abandoned patent applications for ornamental pearl and wrought iron (*TAEM* 114:7, 32); Journal #5, pp. 1, 15–16, 35–36, 46–47, 57–58, 70–71, 147 (*TAEM* 87:335, 342–43, 352–53, 358, 363–64, 370, 408).

21. TAE to Sigmund Bergmann, 30 Jan. 1888 (*TAEM* 122:60). Edison's negotiations with the light companies are detailed in Chapter 16.

22. Agreement between TAE and Edison Ore Milling Co. Ltd., 14 Oct. 1887 (*TAEM* 144:67); agreement with Edison Phonograph Co., 28 Oct. 1887, and incorporation papers, 30 Sept. 1887 (*TAEM* 118:6, 55); *TAEM Guide* Parts II–III, s.vv. "Dick (A.B.) Co.," "Dick, Albert Blake," "Sims-Edison Electric Torpedo Co."; Journal #5, pp. 21, 37, 52, 62, 73, 108 (*TAEM* 87:345, 353, 361, 366, 371, 389).

23. *TAEM Guide*, Part III, s.v. "Carr, S.P." and "Carr & Dickinson"; David Trumbull Marshall, *Recollections of Edison* (Boston: The Christopher Publishing House, 1931), 62; N-88-02-17 and N-88-

03-30 (*TAEM* 102:75, 85–86; 248–94). Edison spent $355 on the tobacco experiments (Journal #5, p. 147 [*TAEM* 408]).

24. TAE to Alfred Tate, n.d. (*TAEM* 130:703). On using the accounting records to estimate the commercial cost of an invention see Reginald Fessenden to Tate, c. 1888–89 (*TAEM* 124:1079); see also the laboratory accounts on *TAEM*, reels 110–13.

25. Notebook E-4294:32 (*TAEM* 108:962). The actual size and makeup of the staff can be followed through the laboratory timesheets found at ENHS and the Distribution of Labor Books (*TAEM* 112:468, 113:1, 155).

26. Alfred Tate to G. H. Jordan, 12 Feb. 1889 (*TAEM* 138:868). Information on the staff can be found in the Edison Pioneers Collection, ENHS, and Document File folders D-87-13, D-88-14, D-88-15, D-89-14, D-90-13, D-91-11 (*TAEM* 119:464; 121:840, 1030, 125:775; 128:879, 130:962).

27. Arthur Kennelly to Dr. Muirhead, 26 Dec. 1888 (*TAEM* 109:227); see also Vannevar Bush, "Biographical Memoir of Arthur Edwin Kennelly, 1861–1939," *National Academy of Sciences, Biographical Memoirs* 22 (1943), 5th memoir; and Kennelly's notebooks and letterbooks in *TAEM*, reels 104–06, 109.

28. On Aylsworth see L. H. Sperling, "Jonas W. Aylsworth: Leif Erickson of Interpenetrating Polymer Networks," *Polymer News* 12 (1987): 332–34.

29. Reginald Fessenden to TAE, 18 July 1887 (*TAEM* 119:468).

30. Reginald Fessenden, "The Inventions of Reginald Fessenden," *Radio News* (Aug. 1925): 158, 237; see also TAE to Alfred Tate, 21 Mar. 1889 (*TAEM* 125:790); TAE to Henry Wurtz, 21 Mar. 1889 (*TAEM* 138:1083); TAE letter of recommendation for Erwin Wilmowsky, 13 May 1889 (*TAEM* 139:260).

31. The best biographical information on Dickson is found in Appendix A of Gordon Hendricks's highly partisan *The Edison Motion Picture Myth* (Berkeley: University of California Press, 1961). Unfortunately, Hendricks is given to interpreting all facts to fit his interpretation. Thus, after noting that Dickson was superintendent of the testing room at Goerk Street in 1884 and did not go to work at Edison's laboratory, then located in the Edison Lamp Works, until early 1887, Hendricks nonetheless asserts that it is probable that Dickson had become Edison's official photographer by September 1884. He bases this assertion on Tate's statement that by that time Edison had "a man in his Laboratory who does all the photographing he requires." Besides the inherent contradictions between Hendricks's chronology and Tate's statement regarding a photographer at the laboratory, when Edison listed his staffing ideas for the West Orange laboratory he included the statement "photographer—Parrish will do," suggesting that he hardly had an official photographer at that time. A list of experimental projects that Edison drew up on 15 November 1887, however, shows that he put Dickson in charge of those involving photography. Hendricks, *Edison Motion Picture Myth*, 150–51; Notebook E-4294:32; N-87-11-15, pp. 39, 47 (*TAEM* 108:962; 98:688, 692).

32. Typescript of an 1888 interview (*TAEM* 121:793).

33. Edison's marginal notes on Francis Upton to TAE, 18 Apr. 1888 (*TAEM* 123:363).

34. Charles H. Heely to Alfred Tate, 11 Feb. 1888; Tate to Charles E. Renshaw, 16 June 1888 (*TAEM* 123:332; 122:368).

35. TAE to Sigmund Bergmann, 14 Dec. 1910, Letterbook 85:74, ENHS.

36. Marshall, *Recollections of Edison*, 58–59, 61. When he began work at his new laboratory, Edison drew up instructions for his assistants in one of his notebooks (N-87-11-15, pp. 39–197 [*TAEM* 98:668–767]). These included several notes for "chemist Marshall" and a number of items on which Edison noted "entered in Marshall's book," referring to Donald's brother John, who had come with Edison from the Lamp Works laboratory.

37. Fessenden, "The Inventions of Reginald Fessenden," 276.

38. Fessenden, "The Inventions of Reginald Fessenden," 276; Fessenden to TAE, 15 June 1915, DF.

39. Fessenden, "The Inventions of Reginald Fessenden," 276.

40. Marshall, *Recollections of Edison*, 57–58.

41. Marshall, *Recollections of Edison*, 88–89.

42. Fessenden, "The Inventions of Reginald Fessenden," 157, 277.

Chapter 15: Inventing Entertainment

1. Runes, *The Diary and Sundry Observations*, 77.

2. On changes in the workplace and the emergence of consumer culture see Stuart M. Blumin, *The Emergence of the Middle Class: Social Experience in the American City* (Cambridge: Cambridge University Press, 1989); Stuart and Elizabeth Ewen, *Channels of Desire: Mass Images and the Shaping*

of American Consciousness (Minneapolis: University of Minnesota Press, 1992); David Nasaw, *Going Out: The Rise and Fall of Public Amusement* (New York: Basic Books, 1993); Kathy Peiss, *Cheap Amusements: Working Women and Leisure in Turn-of-the-Century New York* (Philadelphia: Temple University Press, 1986); Daniel T. Rodgers, *The Work Ethic in Industrial America, 1850–1920* (Chicago: University of Chicago Press, 1978); Roy Rosenzweig, *Eight Hours for What We Will: Workers and Leisure in an Industrial City, 1870–1920* (Cambridge: Cambridge University Press, 1983); Alan Trachtenberg, *The Incorporation of America: Culture and Society in the Gilded Age* (New York: Hill and Wang, 1982).

3. N-86-08-25, pp. 19–26 (*TAEM* 43:828–35); Ezra Gilliland to Samuel Insull, 18 June 1886 (*TAEM* 79:913).

4. Charles Sumner Tainter wrote an account of Volta Laboratory phonograph experiments entitled "The Talking Machine and Some Little Known Facts in Connection with Its Early History," located in the Tainter Papers, National Museum of American History Archives, Smithsonian Institution. See also Leslie J. Newville, "Development of the Phonograph at Alexander Graham Bell's Volta Laboratory," *United States National Museum Bulletin 218* (Washington, D.C.: Smithsonian Institution, 1959), 70–79.

5. Edward Johnson to Uriah Painter, 17 Sept. 1885, Painter Papers. On the negotiations between the Edison and Bell interests see Ray Wile, "Edison and Growing Hostilities," *ARSC Journal* 22 (1991): 13–16; 1885–1887 Correspondence files of the Painter Papers; and Document File folder D-87-50 (*TAEM* 120:228).

6. Cat. 1336:197 (*TAEM* 90:355). Charles Sumner Tainter, "The Graphophone," *Electrical World*, 14 July 1888, copy in Tainter Papers.

7. Cat. 1336:201, 205, 207, items 358, 363, 365 (*TAEM* 90:413, 415–16); TAE to Richard Dyer, 21 May 1887, Lab. (*TAEM* 44:824); Brief for Defendant, pp. 2–3, *American Graphophone Co. v. National Phonograph Co. (MacDonald Patent No. 606,725)* (*TAEM* 116:481).

8. Cat. 1336:211–15, 221, 223, 229, 232–33, 236–37, 243–45, 247, items 370, 374, 376, 381, 387, 396–97, 408, 413 (*TAEM* 90:418–20, 423–24, 427, 429, 431, 434–36).

9. TAE to George Gouraud, 21 July (*TAEM* 120:277); TAE to George Gould, 21 July (*TAEM* 138:185); Cat. 1137:17, 19, items 486, 490 (*TAEM* 90:466–67); PN-87-09-24 and 1887 Notebook, p. 19 (*TAEM* 106:190–93, 666).

10. Uriah Painter to Edward Johnson, 9 Oct. 1887, Painter Papers.

11. TAE to Edward Johnson, c. 24 Oct. 1887, Painter Papers.

12. Edison to Edward Johnson, 22 Nov. 1887, DF (*TAEM* 120:243); Edison to Uriah Painter, 5 Dec. 1887, Painter Papers. Regarding the breakup with Painter see Wile, "Growing Hostilities," 17–19, and correspondence between Edison, Painter, and Edward Johnson listed in *TAEM Guide*, Part III, and the 1887 Correspondence files of the Painter Papers.

13. Ezra Gilliland to TAE, 16 Dec. 1887 (*TAEM* 119:265); "The Phonograph Patents, *New York Evening Post*, 5 Jan. 1887; *Scientific American* 57 (1887): 273, 328, 415, 422; Mark E. Ham, "Edison and the Phonograph, 1877–1889," pp. 5–7, typescript dated 19 May 1986, ENHS; Allen Koenigsberg, compiler and editor, *The Patent History of the Phonograph, 1877–1912* (Brooklyn, N.Y.: APM Press, 1990), xxvi.

14. Sigmund Bergmann to Uriah Painter, 15 Jan. 1888, Painter Papers.

15. Considered one of the most learned men at the laboratory, Schulze-Berge was placed in charge of the laboratory library. For Schulze-Berge's work see testimony and exhibits in *American Graphophone Co. v. National Phonograph Co. (MacDonald Patent No. 606,725)* (*TAEM* 116:478) and *Edison v. Lambert* (*TAEM* 117:270); his letter of recommendation from Hermann von Helmholtz is found in *TAEM* 79:240.

16. Edison's testimony, pp. 142, 150, *National Phonograph Co. v. American Graphophone Co. (Edison's Patent 667,662)* (*TAEM* 117:145, 149). This case details the experiments on phonograph cylinder duplicating processes.

17. N-87-01-01, pp. 3–113 (*TAEM* 101:444–502); U.S. Pat. 382,462. Aylsworth did experiment for a short time "to produce a wax-like material from chloride of lead, which was described in Watt's Dictionary, as a horn-like substance." However, this proved too "brittle and harder than horn and consequently not adapted for the use anticipated for it." Aylsworth's testimony, *American Graphophone Co. v. National Phonograph Co. (MacDonald Patent No. 606,725)*, p. 14; N-78-01-01, pp. 101, 111 (*TAEM* 116:560; 101:496, 501).

18. Aylsworth's testimony, *American Graphophone Co. v. National Phonograph Co. (MacDonald Patent No. 606,725)*, p. 19 (*TAEM* 116:570); N-87-01-01, pp. 115, 143–44 (*TAEM* 101:503, 517–18); U.S. Pat. 430,274.

19. "The Phonograph Patents, *New York Evening Post*, 5 Jan. 1887.

20. See U.S. Pats. 393,466; 393,966; 393,967; 394,105; 394,106; 400,646; 400,647; 437,423; 448,780; 448,781; 450,740; 488,189; 488,190; 499,879.

21. U.S. Pat. 393,966; N-88-06-06.1 (*TAEM* 99:471–90); Unbound Notes and Drawings, 20 July 1888 (*TAEM* 107:652).

22. *TAEB* Doc.1265.

23. TAE to George Gouraud, 30 May 1889 and 1 Oct. 1888 (*TAEM* 139:239; 124:779). On the American system of manufacture see David Hounshell, *From the American System to Mass Production, 1800–1932: The Development of Manufacturing Technology in the United States* (Baltimore: Johns Hopkins University Press, 1984), and Otto Mayr and Robert Post, eds., *Yankee Enterprise: The Rise of the American System of Manufactures* (Washington, D.C.: Smithsonian Institution Press, 1981).

24. Edison Phonograph Works Minute Book, pp. 1–38 (*TAEM* 154:795–814); Edison Phonograph Works General Ledger 1:25, 29, 33, 57, 67, 97, 115 (*TAEM* 155:40, 44, 56, 61, 76, 85); notes enclosed by Edison to Villard, 19 Jan. 1888, Villard Papers; Alfred Tate to TAE, 21 Sept. 1888; Alfred Tate to Jesse H. Lippincott, 24 Oct. 1888; TAE to George Gouraud, 30 May 1889 (*TAEM* 121:460; 124:439; 139:239).

25. Ezra Gilliland to TAE, 19 and 31 Mar. and 24 May 1888 (*TAEM* 124:298, 301–02, 306, 334), Gilliland's 24 May letter is misidentified as 24 March in *TAEM*; see also Alfred Tate to A. J. Lawson, 22 May 1888 (*TAEM* 122:319), and notes enclosed by Edison to Henry Villard, 19 Jan. 1888, Villard Papers.

26. Ezra Gilliland to TAE, 6 June 1888, with Edison's marginal comment, and enclosed draft circular letter of 5 June (*TAEM* 124:345–48); see also TAE to Gilliland, 13 June 1888 (*TAEM* 122:359).

27. TAE to George Gouraud, 30 May 1889 (*TAEM* 139:239).

28. Thomas A. Edison, "The Perfected Phonograph," *North American Review* 146 (1888): 646.

29. George Frow, *Cylinder Phonograph Companion* (Woodland Hills, Calif.: Stationery X-Press, 1970), chap. 2

30. George Lathrop to Alfred Tate, 12 and 27 June and 19 July 1888 (*TAEM* 124:354, 371, 385); see also Tate to A. A. Cowles, 24 April 1888 (*TAEM* 122:277); Ezra Gilliland to TAE, 27 June 1888 (*TAEM* 124:374); Tate to Gilliland, 2 July 1888 (*TAEM* 122:413).

31. The negotiations are described by Edison's, Gilliland's, and Tomlinson's affidavits and appended documents, including the agreement between Lippincott and Edison, *Edison v. Gilliland and Tomlinson*, Equity Case No. 4652, U.S. Circuit Court, Southern District of New York, National Archives, Northeast Region, New York, N.Y.; and in Edison's and Lippincott's affidavits (*TAEM* 144:405; 145:196, 247). See also Wile, "Growing Hostilities," 21–29.

32. TAE to Ezra Gilliland, 11 Sept. 1888; Gilliland to TAE, 13 Sept. 1888 (*TAEM* 124:410).

33. See Chapters 16 and 17 regarding differences over electric lighting.

34. George Lathrop to Alfred Tate, 19 July 1888; see also Gaston and Marsh to TAE, 21 Sept. 1888 (*TAEM* 124:385, 211).

35. North American Phonograph Co. Minutebook, pp. 1–32; North American Phonograph Co. circulars, 1889, 20 Jan. 1890, *New York Phonograph Co. v. National Phonograph Co.* (*TAEM* 157:481–97; 117:315, 358).

36. Thomas Lombard's testimony, p. 153; Edison's testimony, pp. 160–63, *American Graphophone v. Edison Phonograph Works*, Equity Case No. 3500, U.S. Circuit Court, District of New Jersey, p. 153; U.S. Pats. 397,280, 430,278, 465,972, 484,583, 484,584; Raymond R. Wile, ed., *Proceedings of the 1890 Convention of Local Phonograph Companies* (Nashville, Tenn.: Country Music Foundation Press, 1974).

37. Thomas Lombard's testimony, p. 153, *American Graphophone v. Edison Phonograph Works*; Edison to Gouraud, 1 Oct. 1888 and 30 May 1889 (*TAEM* 124:779; 139:239).

38. Oliver Read and Walter L. Welch, *From Tin Foil to Stereo* (Indianapolis: Howard W. Sams & Co., 1976), 50; North American Phonograph Co. reports of machines for January–March and June 1892 (*TAEM* 133:593, 596–97, 613).

39. Quoted in Roland Gelatt, *The Fabulous Phonograph, 1877–1977* (New York: Collier Books, 1977), 45.

40. TAE to Samuel Insull, 30 June 1891 (*TAEM* 132:148). See also North American Phonograph Co. price list of supplies, 28 May 1889, North American to Edison Phonograph Works, 12 Dec. 1889; Eaton to TAE and Edison's marginal note, 9 Dec. 1890; Thomas Lombard to the Phonograph Companies, 24 Feb. and 19 June 1890 (*TAEM* 128:7, 37; 130:127, 324, 331).

41. Wile, *1890 Convention*, 163–84; Read and Welch, *From Tin Foil to Stereo*, 105–15; *TAEM Guide*, Part III, s.v. "Automatic Phonograph Exhibition Co."

42. Caveat 110, 8 Oct. 1888 (*TAEM* 113:236). The following discussion of Edison's experimental work on motion pictures is largely derived from W. Bernard Carlson and Michael E. Gorman, "Understanding Invention as a Cognitive Process: The Case of Thomas Edison and Early Motion Pictures, 1888–91," *Social Studies of Science* 20 (1990): 387–430; Charles Musser, *Before the Nickelodeon: Edwin S. Porter and the Edison Manufacutring Company* (Berkeley: University of California Press, 1991), and idem, *The Emergence of Cinema: The American Screen to 1907* (Berkeley: University of California Press, 1990), chap. 2. Also useful for detail, though rather polemical in its interpretation is Hendricks, *Edison Motion Picture Myth*.

43. Quoted in Musser, *Emergence of Cinema,* 62.

44. Caveat 117, 2 Nov. 1889, figs. 46–48 (*TAEM* 113:670).

45. W. K. L. Dickson, "A Brief History of the Kinetograph, the Kinetoscope, and the Kineto-Phonograph," in Raymond Fielding, ed., *A Technological History of Motion Pictures and Television* (Berkeley: University of California Press, 1967), 13.

46. *New York Sun* and *New York Herald* quoted in Hendricks, *Edison Motion Picture Myth,* 114–16.

47. The following discussion of Edison's motion picture business is primarily derived from Musser, *Emergence of Cinema,* chaps. 2–3, and *Before the Nickelodeon,* chaps. 3–4; and W. Bernard Carlson, "Artifacts and Frames of Meaning: Thomas A. Edison, His Managers, and the Cultural Construction of Motion Pictures," in Wiebe E. Bijker, ed., *Shaping Technology — Building Society: Studies in Sociotechnical Change* (Cambridge: MIT Press, 1992); 175–98.

48. TAE to Edison United Phonograph Company, 16 June 1893 (*TAEM* 134:740).

49. TAE to Julius Block, 19 May 1894 (*TAEM* 135:456).

50. The *Electrical Review,* 8 Apr. 1896, announcement of Edison's new spring-motor phonograph is quoted in Frow, *Cylinder Phonograph Companion,* 83; see also United States Phonograph Co. circular (*TAEM* 147:526); "Phonograph Improved," *New York Times,* 5 Apr. 1896 (*TAEM* 146:1013); and Edison's U.S. Patent 604,740. The development of spring-motors is described in Brief for Appellant, pp. 32–33, 216–18, and testimony of James Adem and Cleveland Wolcott, pp. 583–87, 1703–1757; *New York Phonograph Co. v. National Phonograph Co.* (*TAEM* 117:412, 504–05, 927–69; 118:435–59); Koenigsberg, *Patent History of the Phonograph,* xxxvii–xlii; and Frow, *Cylinder Phonograph Companion,* 61–65, 83–85. For the Columbia Phonograph Company see Read and Welch, *From Tin Foil to Stereo,* 59–65.

51. Frow, *Cylinder Phonograph Companion,* 98–99, 114–17 128–29; Read and Welch, *From Tin Foil to Stereo,* 83–89; Gelatt, *The Fabulous Phonograph,* 69–71; National Phonograph Co., *Catalogue,* c. 1898 (*TAEM* 147:329); see also Document File folder D-98-26 (*TAEM* 137:398) regarding the competition over small, cheap phonographs and Edison's efforts to design and manufacture them.

52. TAE to Mina, dated "8th," sold at auction by Swann Galleries, 14 Feb. 1990, lot 64. Production figures are in "Brief for Appellant," *New York Phonograph Co. v. National Phonograph Co.* (*TAEM* 117: 505).

53. George Morison to Stephen Moriarty, 8 Feb. 1898 (*TAEM* 137:472).

54. Musser, *Before the Nickelodeon,* 56.

55. Quoted in Musser, *Emergence of Cinema,* 105.

56. This argument is made by Charles Musser in *Emergence of Cinema, Before the Nickelodeon,* and in his book with with Carol Nelson, *High-Class Moving Pictures: Lyman H. Howe and the Forgotten Era of Traveling Exhibition, 1880–1920* (Princeton: Princeton University Press, 1991).

57. Quoted in Musser, *Emergence of Cinema,* 104.

58. Norman Raff and Frank Gammon to Armat, 5 Mar. 1896, quoted in *Edison v. American Mutoscope Co. & Keith,* pp. 116–17 (*TAEM* 116:75).

59. Norman Raff and Frank Gammon to Armat, 5 Mar. 1896, quoted in *Edison v. American Mutoscope Co. & Keith,* pp. 116–17 (*TAEM* 116:75).

60. Alfred Tate to Walter Miller, 2 May 1892 (*TAEM* 133:413).

Chapter 16: Industrial Research

1. TAE to Edison Lamp Co. (*TAEM* 122:77); see also TAE to Sigmund Bergmann, 28 and 30 Jan. 1888; TAE to Samuel Insull and TAE to Edison Lamp Co., both 30 Jan. 1888; TAE to Edison Electric Light Co., 7 Feb. 1888; Francis Upton to West Orange laboratory, 31 Jan. and 3 Feb. 1888 (*TAEM* 122:57, 60, 62, 65, 95; 123:327, 330).

2. Edward Johnson to TAE, 21 Feb. 1888, with Edison marginal notes (*TAEM* 123:22).

3. TAE to Samuel Insull, 2 Feb. 1888 (*TAEM* 122:73); see also Insull to TAE, 31 Jan. 1888 (*TAEM* 123:463).

4. Samuel Insull to TAE, 3 Feb. 1888 (*TAEM* 123:469). On Bergmann & Co. see Sigmund Bergmann to TAE, 11 Feb. 1888 (*TAEM* 121:61).

5. Samuel Insull to Edison Laboratory, 6 Apr. 1888; Insull to Alfred Tate, 5 July 1888 (*TAEM* 133:506; 123:545). See also TAE to Edison Machine Works, 29 Mar. 1888; Tate to Edison Machine Works, 19 Apr. 1888; Insull to Tate, 20 Apr. and 28 June 1888, (*TAEM* 122:224; 138:416; 123:515, 544).

6. W. J. Jenks to TAE, 19 Dec. 1887 (*TAEM* 119:865); see also Johnson to officers of the Edison lighting companies, 14 Dec. 1887 (*TAEM* 119:864).

7. James Hayes to Charles Batchelor, 23 Jan. 1887; Batchelor to F. H. Underwood, 21 Oct. 1887 (*TAEM* 124:973; 120:772); "The Dynamo Room of Edison's Laboratory," *Electrical World* 15 (1890): 237; "Edison Laboratory Historic Furnishings Report. Volume 1: Historical Data and Furnishing Plan," Edison National Historic Site, 1995, pp. 26–27.

8. Charles Wirt to W. J. Jenks, 18 Aug. 1888 (*TAEM* 123:73). See also Edward Johnson to TAE, 20 Aug. 1888; Arthur Kennelly to Johnson and report on meter tests, c. Jan. 1889; Kennelly to Jenks, 29 Jan. 1889; Kennelly report on meters, 4 Feb. 1889; Kennelly to Henry Seely with draft patent specification, 30 Jan. 1888; Kennelly to Jenks, 20 Feb. and 13 Mar. 1888; Jenks to Kennelly, 19 Feb. 1888; Jenks to Edison Laboratory, 10 July and 22 Aug. 1888; Kennelly to J. H. Vail, 4 July 1888; J. H. Vail to TAE, 3 Feb. 1888, with report on underground conductors; Jenks to TAE, 12 May 1888 and 3 May 1889; Jenks to Kennelly, 18 July 1889; Kennelly to Jenks, 22 Apr. 1889 (*TAEM* 123:70; 109:229–69, 267–68, 270–79, 281, 285; 126:252, 279, 286; 123:57, 6, 27; 126:260, 280, 283; 109:295).

9. Batchelor's work can be followed through his journals (Cat. 1336 and Cat. 1337 [*TAEM* 90: 316; 457) and through correspondence with Henry Walter, who had charge of this work at the Machine Works (*TAEM Guides*, Parts II–III, s.v. "Walter, Henry E"); see also Document File folder D-87-37 (*TAEM* 119:1197). For the transition from Batchelor to Kennelly see Cat. 1337 and notebook N-87-12-00 (*TAEM* 90:457; 101:604). For Kennelly's role and galvanometer room research on which the following discussion of electrical work at Edison's laboratory is based see his notebooks and letterbooks (N-88-01-19, N-88-04-18, N-88-06-06, N-88-06-10, N-88-08-28, N-88-09-28, Kennelly Notebooks 1–7, Kennelly Letterbooks 1–7 [*TAEM* 101:843; 102:308, 451, 548, 751, 856; 104:251.1–106:116; 109: 107–end]).

10. Ronald Kline, "Engineering R&D at the Westinghouse Electric Company, 1886–1922," paper presented at the annual meeting of the Society for the History of Technology, Pittsburgh, October 1986.

11. "A Chat with Edison," *East Saginaw [Mich.] Herald*, 4 Jan. 1889, reprinted from the *Philadelphia Press* (*TAEM* 146:372).

12. N-87-11-15, p. 77, N-87-12-10.2, N-88-01-19; N-87-00-00.3, p. 9 (*TAEM* 98:707, 905–07; 101: 942–52; 98:96). The following discussion of electric lighting research relies extensively on an examination of the Lamp Factory notebooks from 1886–1887, beginning on *TAEM* 43:430, along with a set of Edison's instructions for lamp experiments from May 1, 1886, in N-86-08-17, pp. 195–285 (*TAEM* 43:382–427); Edison's notes to his patent attorneys from July 1886 through 1888 in Cat. 1151–53 (*TAEM* 44:720–969); West Orange laboratory notebooks and letterbooks on *TAEM* reels 98–109; Edison's caveats and abandoned patent applications on *TAEM* reels 113–15; and his issued patents on *TAEM* reels 1–2.

13. N-87-12-10.2, N-88-02-02, N-90-01-04.7, N-92-04-16 (*TAEM* 98:936–41; 99:241; 100:377–78, 385–96).

14. TAE to Arthur Kennelly, 27 Jan. 1896 (*TAEM* 136:499). A fine account of Edison's X-Ray work is found in George Tselos, "'Start Up at the Top and Work Down': Thomas A. Edison and the Fluoroscope," paper presented at Interpreting Edison Conference, Newark, N.J., June 1997.

15. TAE marginalia on Richard Stockton to TAE, 14 Feb. 1896, Document File folder D-96-31.

16. Edwin Houston and Arthur Kennelly, "Mr. Edison's Researches on Roentgen Rays," *Electrical Engineer* 21 (18 Mar. 1896): 282.

17. TAE to John Pender, 13 Mar. 1896 (*TAEM* 136:559).

18. "Edison Will Not Secure a Patent," *New York Journal*, 28 Mar. 1896, Cat. 1246, item 3404, Batchelor Collection, ENHS.

19. Thomas A. Edison, "On a Pyromagnetic Dynamo: A Machine for Producing Electricity Directly from Fuel," *Proceedings of the American Association for the Advancement of . . .* (Mar. 1888): 94–98; U.S. Pat. 476,983; N-87-03-01, p. 11 (*TAEM* 98:408). See also U.S. Patents 380,100, 434,586; N-87-12-10.2 (*TAEM* 98:904); abandoned patent applications (*TAEM* 114:73, 78, 302); TAE to Richard Dyer, 27 Feb. 1888 (*TAEM* 114:303) and Chapter 13 regarding Edison's earlier work on the direct conversion of coal to electricity.

20. TAE to Richard Dyer, 4 Jan. 1888 (*TAEM* 44:920); Edison, "On a Pyromagnetic Dynamo."

21. N-87-12-10.2 (*TAEM* 98:905).

22. Quoted in Millard, *Edison and the Business of Innovation*, 98; see also Samuel Insull to TAE, 5 Nov. 1887 (*TAEM* 119:1170) and Alfred Tate to Insull, 10 Jan. 1888 (*TAEM* 138:435). Millard mistakenly identifies the insulation research as focused on underground conductors. Some research on conductor insulation did take place at the laboratory, but most of the work was on house wire insulation.

23. U.S. Pat. 470,924. In a 1905 interview Edison regretted the invention of the electric chair and reaffirmed his opposition to capital punishment (James S. Evans, "Edison Regrets Electric Chair Was Ever Invented," *New York American*, 10 Feb. 1905, Clippings).

24. Fessenden, "The Inventions of Reginald Fessenden," 158.

25. PN-88-00-00 (*TAEM* 106:227). See also PN-88-04-13, PN-88-08-16 (*TAEM* 106:234–36, 285–86, 305); N-87-11-15 (*TAEM* 98:681); N-88-00-00.1, N-88-11-02 (*TAEM* 99:1, 822). Edison was still opposing high voltage twenty years later ("Edison Condemns High Voltages," *Newark Advertiser*, 26 Dec. 1907, Clippings).

26. Dyer and Martin, *Edison*, 605.

27. Fessenden, "The Inventions of Reginald Fessenden," 158.

28. Samuel Insull to TAE, 2 May and 4 1888 (*TAEM* 123:527–28).

29. Samuel Insull to Tate, 12 June 1888 (*TAEM* 123:537); Charles Batchelor to Insull, 19 May 1888 (*TAEM* 122:311).

30. Cat. 1337:55–56, item 555, see also pp. 54, 56–57, items 554, 556 (*TAEM* 90:486–87); N-87-12-26 (*TAEM* 101:790–93); Charles Batchelor to John Kruesi, 27 Aug. 1888 (*TAEM* 122:525).

31. Samuel Insull to Alfred Tate and Marshall to Insull, both 19 Dec. 1888 (*TAEM* 123:594, 597). See also John Kruesi to Charles Batchelor, 22 Oct. 1888; Kruesi to TAE, 20 Nov. 1888; Insull to Tate, 12 Dec. 1888; Insull to TAE, 12 and 19 Dec. 1888 (*TAEM* 123:577, 591, 593, 595, 598); TAE to Insull, 20 Dec. 1888; TAE to Kruesi, 31 Dec. 1888 and 13 Mar. 1889; Tate to Kruesi, 2, 4–5, 11 Jan., and 12 Feb. 1889; Edison Laboratory to Kruesi, 10 Jan. and 11 May 1889; TAE to Kruesi, 13 Mar. 1889; Edison Laboratory to Insull, 5 June 1889 (*TAEM* 138:641, 1037, 667–68, 671, 676, 701, 869, 693); Insull to TAE, 19 Mar. 1889; Insull to Edison's Laboratory, 15 and 25 Jan., 28 Mar., and 3 June 1889; Marshall to Kruesi, 4 June 1889 (*TAEM* 125:1009, 991–93, 1000, 1013–14, 1015).

32. Thomas Maguire to John Kruesi, 14 Dec. 1891; Maguire to W. E. Gilmore, 18 Feb. 1892 (*TAEM* 142:1088, 143:104). See also Fessenden "The Inventions of Reginald Fessenden," 158; Marshall, *Recollections of Edison*, 67–69; Alfred Tate to Samuel Insull, 26 Oct. 1891 (*TAEM* 142:993).

33. On Edison's general patent policy, see Chapter 11. U.S. Pat. 438,309; Fessenden, "The Inventions of Reginald Fessenden," 276.

34. Regarding the assignment of researchers see John Randolph to Alfred Tate, 5 Aug. 1890 (*TAEM* 128:906); the laboratory notebooks on lamp experiments; Distribution of Labor #6–7 (*TAEM* 112:468, 113:1), and laboratory timesheets, ENHS. H. de Coursey Hamilton, who had assisted with lamp experiments at the Lamp Works at West Orange for a time, but on phonograph cylinder research.

35. Francis Upton to TAE, 1 Aug. 1888 (*TAEM* 122:921).

36. N-86-06-28 (*TAEM* 43:481); U.S. Pat. 490,954; see also Bright, *Electric-Lamp Industry*, 122.

37. TAE to Samuel Insull, 18 June 1890 (*TAEM* 141:160). On Edison's earlier experiments with hydrocarbon flashing, see Chapter 11. On the Sawyer-Man process, see Howell and Schroeder, *History of the Incandescent Lamp*, 79–80, and "A History of the Incandescent Lamp," c. 1910–1912, 46–49, typescript, ENHS. Regarding Edison's experiments and tests at the Lamp Works and the West Orange laboratories, see TAE to Samuel Flood, 13 July 1888 (*TAEM* 122:469).

38. On Swan and Powell, see Brian Bowers, *A History of Electric Light & Power* (New York: P. Peregrinus in association with the Science Museum, 1982), 123–24; Howell and Schroeder, *History of the Incandescent Lamp*, 81–83; "History of the Development of the Incandescent Lamp," 49–50.

39. TAE to George Bliss, 12 May 1888 (*TAEM* 121:332); TAE to Edison Electric Light Co., 12 Sept. 1888 (*TAEM* 12:557).

40. Fessenden's account is in "The Inventions of Reginald Fessenden," 237. For the municipal cutout see Sherbourne Eaton to Samuel Insull, 23 June 1891, and his reports on meetings of the Edison General Electric Patent Litigation Committee, 31 July 1891 and 1 Mar. 1892 (*TAEM* 131:693, 719; 133:182); John Ott to Dyer & Seely, 8 Oct. 1891, with attached note received 29 Sept. 1891 (*TAEM* 131:773–74). Regarding Westinghouse see Harold C. Passer, *The Electrical Manufacturers, 1875–1900: A Study in Competition, Entrepreneurship, Technological Change, and Economic Growth* (Cambridge: Harvard University Press, 1953), 142–43, 160–61, and Bright, *Electric-Lamp Industry*, 90–91.

41. Transcription of a phonograph interview with Edison for the *Cincinnati Inquirer*, c. 1888 (*TAEM* 121:793).

42. Sherbourne Eaton's report on the meeting of the Edison General Electric Patent Litigation Committee, 13 Oct. 1890 (*TAEM* 129:1096); see also Richard Dyer to TAE, 17 May 1890, with en-

closed draft of law; Eaton to TAE, 21 May 1890; Eaton's report on the meeting of the Patent Litigation Committee, 30 July 1890 (*TAEM* 129:1022–23, 1037, 1064). Regarding Edison's request to launch the series of suits, see his undated 1890 memorandum listing these suits (*TAEM* 129:1146–55).

43. "About Patents," *New Haven, Conn. Palladium*, 7 Jan. 1888 (*TAEM* 89:208). See also Thomas E. Jeffrey, *Thomas Lanier Clingman: "Fire Eater" from the Carolina Mountains* (Athens: University of Georgia Press, 1998), chap. 18.

44. Edison's marginalia on Dyer & Seely to TAE, 30 Dec. 1890, and TAE to A. T. Leith, 7 Oct. 1886 (*TAEM* 129:1140; 87:731).

45. Alfred Tate to George Henry Knight, 12 June 1890 (*TAEM* 141:139).

46. Edison's marginalia on Arthur Steuart to TAE, 2 July 1888; Edison's marginalia on E. N. Hatcher to TAE, 29 Mar. 1893; TAE to Charles Kintner, 20 June 1893 (*TAEM* 141:139; 124:34; 134: 461; 105).

47. TAE to Samuel Insull, 21 July 1891 (*TAEM* 142:428); Tate to Insull, 6 Feb. 1892 (*TAEM* 143: 80); see also TAE to Edison & Swan United Electric Light Co, 4 Jan. 1892 (*TAEM* 143:7).

48. TAE draft to Insull, 4 Mar. 1891 (*TAEM* 31:228, the letterbook version is 142:305). On Brown, see TAE notes for letter to Brown, c. 27 Mar. 1891 (*TAEM* 131:234, letterbook version is 142:98) and Edison's instructions in N-90-01-04.7 (*TAEM* 100:363–67). For another effort to translate improvements at the laboratory to production at the factory see TAE to James Hipple, n.d. (*TAEM* 95:927).

49. TAE to Edward Johnson, 27 Feb. 1887 (*TAEM* 148:22). See also J. H. Vail to TAE, 24 Aug. 1887, and Johnson to Vail, 29 Aug. 1887 (*TAEM* 148:26–27); Francis Upton to TAE, 19 Nov. and 2 Dec. 1887; 24 and 26 Apr. and 7 May 1889, with enclosures (*TAEM* 119:989; 95:832; 126:519–25); Stern & Silverman to Edison Lamp Co., 30 Nov. 1887 (*TAEM* 95:833).

Chapter 17: Competition and Consolidation

1. Dietrich G. Buss, *Henry Villard: A Study of Transatlantic Investments and Interests, 1870–1895* (New York: Arno Press, 1978), 196–210; undated memorandum regarding consolidation (*TAEM* 123: 305).

2. TAE to Henry Villard, 8 Feb. 1890, Villard Papers, Baker Library, Harvard University (hereafter Villard Papers).

3. Samuel Insull's memorandum of Edison's 10 Dec. 1888 meeting with Villard (*TAEM* 144:165).

4. Edison's marginal note on William Marks to TAE, 4 Sept. 1888 (*TAEM* 121:850).

5. TAE to Edward Johnson, c. 1888 (*TAEM* 123:313). Edison also reiterated his complaints about Johnson's role in the phonograph business.

6. Sigmund Bergmann to TAE, 11 Feb. and 20 Nov. 1888; TAE to Bergmann, c. 26 Sept. and 23 Nov. 1888; (*TAEM* 121:61, 98, 119, 116).

7. TAE to Edward Johnson, n.d. 1888 (*TAEM* 123:313). See also Johnson to TAE, 30 Aug. 1888; Samuel Insull to TAE, 18 Aug. 1888 (*TAEM* 121:471, 272); papers relating to Edison General Electric in the Miller file (*TAEM* 144:162, 222). For the Edison General Electric Company, see *TAEM Guide*, Part IV, s.v. "Edison General Electric Co."

8. Edison's 1 April 1889 reply to Thomson-Houston memorandum of 23 Mar. 1889, Villard Papers (draft in *TAEM* 144:205); see also TAE to William Marks, 7 Apr. 1891; undated Edison memoranda (*TAEM* 131:145; 123:313, 315).

9. For the development of alternating current systems, see Passer, 1953, chap. 9; Hughes, *Networks of Power*, chaps. 4–5; Carlson, *Innovation as a Social Process*, 249–61.

10. TAE to Edward Johnson and Siemens & Halske report, both c. Nov. 1886 (*TAEM* 148:5; 79: 383); N-86-04-28, pp. 261–65 (*TAEM* 42:632–34).

11. For Edison's work on alternating current and high-voltage systems, see U.S. Patents 365,978, 524,378, 382,415, 483,308, 470,298; N-86-04-28, pp. 261–65; N-87-11-15, p. 69, 79; N-88-09-13, pp. 5–6 (*TAEM* 46:632; 98:703, 708; 99:622–23); Caveat 117 (*TAEM* 113:667); abandoned patent applications (*TAEM* 114:159, 212); TAE to Richard Dyer, 25 Oct. and 20 Dec. 1887 (*TAEM* 114:159, 214).

12. "The Edison System of Incandescent Lighting as Operated from Central Stations," 2d ed. 1885, 7 (*TAEM* 96:30).

13. TAE to Edward Johnson, c. Nov. 1886 (*TAEM* 148:5).

14. TAE to Edward Johnson, c. Nov. 1886 (*TAEM* 148:5); see also Johnson to TAE, 13 Nov. 1886; W. J. Jenks to J. H. Vail, 12 Nov. 1887; Charles Chinnock to TAE, 1 Dec. 1887 (*TAEM* 79:325; 119: 849; 120:26); U.S. Patent 380,101.

15. "Edison Municipal System Rules for Installation, 1887" (*TAEM* 147:836).

16. TAE to Edward Johnson, c. Nov. 1886 (*TAEM* 148:5).

17. "Memorandum of Mr. Edison's Work during the Year 1891" (*TAEM* 143:16); TAE to the Duke of Marlborough, 4 Sept. 1891 (*TAEM* 142:757); see also J. H. Vail to TAE, 28 Dec. 1886; TAE to Francis Upton, 15 May 1890 (*TAEM* 79:429; 141:12).

18. Alfred Southwick to TAE, 8 Nov. and 5 Dec. 1887 (*TAEM* 119:294, 321).

19. TAE to Alfred Southwick, 19 Dec. 1887 (*TAEM* 138:355).

20. Alfred Tate to Henry Bergh, 2 May 1888 (*TAEM* 122:288). The following discussion draws extensively on Thomas Hughes, "Harold P. Brown and the Executioner's Current: An Incident in the AC-DC Controversy," *Business History Review* 32 (1058): 143–65; Terry Reynolds and Theodore Bernstein, "Edison and 'The Chair'," IEEE *Technology and Society Magazine* 8 (1989): 19–28; idem, "The Damnable Alternating Current," *Proceedings of the IEEE* 64 (1976): 1339–43; W. Bernard Carlson and A. J. Millard, "Defining Risk within a Business Context: Thomas A. Edison, Elihu Thomson, and the A.C.-D.C. Controversy, 1885–1900," in B. B. Johnson and V. T. Covello, eds., *The Social and Cultural Construction of Risk* (Boston: Reidel Publishing, 1987): 275–93.

21. Brown's letter to the *New York Evening Post* and some of the responses to it are reprinted in "The Admission of Alternating Currents into New York City," *Electrical World* 12 (1888): 40–46; for Brown's background see his testimony in *Kemmler v. Durston* (*TAEM* 115:861–63).

22. Kennelly to the *New York World*, 20 Aug. 1888 (*TAEM* 109:124); "Electricity as a Life Taker," *New York Morning Sun*, 2 Nov. 1888; Kennelly Notebook 2:113–14 (*TAEM* 146:353; 104:552–53). The 1970s studies are cited in Reynolds and Bernstein, "Edison and 'The Chair'," p. 28, n. 74.

23. Reynolds and Bernstein, "Edison and 'The Chair'," 26.

24. F. S. Hastings to TAE, 21 Jan. 1889 (*TAEM* 126:11).

25. Thomas A. Edison, "The Dangers of Electric Lighting," *Electrical World* 149 (Nov. 1889): 632.

26. Carlson, *Innovation as a Social Process*, 249–63; Carlson and Millard, "Defining Risk within a Business Context."

27. W. J. Jenks to J. H. Vail, 12 Nov. 1887 (*TAEM* 119:849); memorandum enclosed with William Meadowcroft to Francis Upton, 21 Mar. 1890 (*TAEM* 95:868).

28. "Annual Convention of Edison Illuminating Companies," *Electrical World* 24 (1889): 136; see also W. J. Jenks to TAE, 8 and 22 Apr. 1889; Jenks to Charles Batchelor, 4 Sept. 1889 (*TAEM* 126:259, 265, 322).

29. TAE to Jacob H. Herrick, 30 Oct. 1889 (*TAEM* 139:825).

30. TAE memorandum, 14 May 1890 (*TAEM* 130:679).

31. Samuel Insull to TAE, 16 July 1890 (*TAEM* 129:228). See also John Kruesi to Insull, 31 July 1890 (*TAEM* 129:236).

32. For work on the alternating current system see Kennelly's Notebook #2, pp. 46, 151, 159, and Kennelly's Notebook #3, pp. 2, 10, 138–39, 148 (*TAEM* 104:79, 590, 598, 622, 632, 786–87, 800); "Interview with Dr. A. E. Kennelly on May 19th," Kennelly folder, Edison Pioneers Collection; see also Samuel Insull to TAE, 8 Sept. and 31 Oct. 1890; Insull to Alfred Tate, 6 Nov. 1890; Tate to Insull, Nov. 1890; Insull to J. C. Henderson, 5 Nov. 1890; J. D. Greene to TAE, 10 Oct. 1890 (*TAEM* 129:245, 275–78, 263); Tate to J. D. Greene, 14 Oct. 1890; Tate to Insull, 1 Nov. 1890 (*TAEM* 141:638, 700).

33. J. C. Henderson to Henry Villard, 27 June 1890, and TAE to Villard, 5 and 6 Oct. 1891, Villard Papers; U.S. Patent 509,581; "Memorandum of Mr. Edison's Work during the Year 1890" (*TAEM* 143:16); TAE with Edison General Electric Co. and North American Co. Railway Agreement, 1 Oct. 1890 (*TAEM* 144:574).

34. TAE and Edison General Electric Co. Laboratory Agreement, 1 Oct. 1890 (*TAEM* 144:543).

35. TAE to Henry Villard, 8 Feb. 1890, Villard Papers.

36. Samuel Insull to Henry Villard, 2 July 1890, Villard Papers.

37. TAE to Henry Villard, 8 Feb. 1890, and Henry Villard to TAE, 3 Feb. 1890, Villard Papers.

38. Chas Fairchild to Henry Villard, 23 and 25 Feb. 1890, Villard Papers; Sherbourne Eaton to TAE, 10 June 1890; Eaton to Villard, 10 June 1890; draft agreement between Edison Electric Light Co. and Thomson-Houston Electric Co., 10 June 1890 (*TAEM* 128:636, 1041, 1044). Regarding patent litigation in 1890–1891, see Eaton to TAE, 13, 15, 23 Oct. 1890; Samuel Insull to TAE, 17 Oct. 1890 (*TAEM* 129:1105, 1112, 1115, 1120); Eaton's reports of Edison General Electric Patent Litigation Committee, March 1891, 31 July 1891, 13 Jan. 1892, 1 Mar. 1892 (*TAEM* 131:625, 720; 131:139; 138:182).

39. Henry Villard to Drexel Morgan, 13 Mar. 1890, quoted in Carlson, *Innovation as a Social Process*, 287. On the negotiations that finally formed General Electric see Carlson's book (pp. 271–301)

as well as "Competition and Consolidation in the Electrical Manufacturing Industry, 1889–1892," in William Aspray, ed., *Technological Competitiveness: Contemporary and Historical Perspectives on the Electrical, Electronics, and Computer Industries* (New York: IEEE Press), 287–311, and Passer, *Electrical Manufacturers*, 321–27.

40. "Mr. Edison Is Satisfied," *New York Times*, 21 Feb. 1892 (*TAEM* 146:753).

41. Insull's memoirs, pp. 52–53, Insull Papers. See also Alfred Tate, *Edison's Open Door*, (New York: E. P. Dutton, 1938), 261–62; "Edison Makes Objection," *New York Tribune*, 20 Feb. 1892, and "Electric Disappointments," *Newark Call*, 28 Feb. 1892 (*TAEM* 146:752–53).

42. Agreement between TAE, General Electric, and Edison General Electric, 1 Oct. 1895 (*TAEM* 144:814); Frederick P. Fish to TAE, 27 Jan. 1897, with Edison's marginal note (*TAEM* 136:733).

43. U.S. Pats. 626,460, 865,367; Notebook N-94-12-11, N-95-12-04, and Lamp Test Notebooks #1–4 (*TAEM* 100:895; 101:1; 107:1, 170, 348, 353); Edison's marginalia on F. Dippel to TAE, 11 Mar. 1898; TAE to Frederick Fish, 15 Dec. 1896 and 1 Feb. 1897 (*TAEM* 137:185; 143:516, 539). For Edison's earlier work see *TAEM Guide*, Part III, s.v. "Powell, John B."

Chapter 18: Innovation and Enthusiasm

1. Millard, *Business of Innovation*, 124; Theodore Waters, "Edison's Revolution in Iron Mining," *McClure's Magazine* (Nov. 1897): 79.

2. *Webster's Ninth New Collegiate Dictionary*, s.v. "folly."

3. Tate, *Edison's Open Door*, 278–81.

4. Dyer and Martin, *Edison*, 504–05.

5. Rotundo, *American Manhood*, chap. 10.

6. *TAEB* Docs. 579, 959; see also Docs. 437, 480, 650, 952, 954, 1475, and *TAEB* 4, chap. 4 introduction.

7. U.S. Pat. 248,432. The first patent is U.S. Pat. 228,329, and the claims and drawings of Edison's other applications can be found in Patent Application Casebooks E-2536 and E-2537 (*TAEM* 45:710, 734). For Edison's experimental work, see entries from the spring and summer of 1880 in Charles Mott's journals N-80-03-14 and N-80-07-10 (*TAEM* 33:683, 37:302). For the Edison Ore Milling Company, see *TAEM Guide*, Part II–III, s.v. "Edison Ore Milling Co Ltd."

8. Samuel Insull to George Gouraud, 11 June 1881 (*TAEM* 57:139).

9. On the Rhode Island operation, see the Edison Ore Milling Co. Minutes, which include annual reports (*TAEM* 97:384); Edison Ore Milling Co. Letterbook (*TAEM* 97:384, 84:210); Report to the Stockholders, 16 Jan. 1883 (*TAEM* 70:802); and Document File folders D-81-039, D-81-040, D-82-046, D-82-047 (*TAEM* 59:160, 213, 63:263, 301); for Conley and the Ocean Magnetic Iron Co., see also *TAEB Guides*, Parts II–III, s.vv. "Conley, M. R.," "Ocean Magnetic Iron Co.," and "Bell (Wm) & Co."

10. On Edison's proposed reorganization of Edison Ore Milling Co., see Alfred Tate to William S. Perry, 27 June 1887 and "Proposed Plan for Reorganizing the Edison Ore Milling Company, Limited" (*TAEM* 120:191, 78:475).

11. Dickson's experiments are in Notebook E-2610 (*TAEM* 106:673). See Edison's U.S. Pats. 476,991 and 474,591 as well as his 1884 caveat draft (*TAEM* 44:630) and 1887 abandoned patent applications for "Extracting Gold from Sulphide Ores," 27 July 1887, and "Separating Metals from Their Ores," 20 Apr. 1888 (*TAEM* 114:101, 309) for his gold separation processes.

12. Witherbees Sherman to TAE, 4 and 7 Oct., 14 Nov., 14 Dec. 1887; TAE to John Birkinbine, 9 June 1888 (*TAEM* 120:147, 149, 158, 169; 122:355); Notebook E-2610:39–63 (*TAEM* 106:692–704).

13. Regarding Birkinbine's introduction to Edison and his arrangement, see Witherbees Sherman to TAE, 12 Apr., 14 and 24 May 1888, and Birkinbine to TAE, 30 July 1888 (*TAEM* 123:893, 902, 909, 942); for Birkinbine's efforts on behalf of Edison, see *TAEM Guide*, Part III, s.v. Birkinbine, John; see also Birkinbine, "Prominent Sources of Iron-Ore Supply," and Birkinbine and Edison, "The Concentration of Iron-Ore," both *AIME Transactions* 17 (1888–89): 715–44. For other information about the Eastern ore industry and the concentration of low-grade ores, see Ferd. S. Ruttman, "Concentrating Magnetite with the Conkling Jig at Lyon Mountain, N.Y.," ibid. 16 (1887–88): 609–22; Robert Anderson Cook, "The Wenstrom Magnetic Separator," ibid. 17:599–606; John Smock, "A Review of the Iron-Mining Industry of New York for the Past Decade," ibid., 745–50; and Henry E. Armitage, "Concentration of Low-Grade Ores," ibid. 18 (1889–90): 257–61.

14. Birkinbine and Edison, "The Concentration of Iron-Ore," 741–42; TAE to Charles Chandler, 17 July 1890 (*TAEM* 141:304).

15. John Birkinbine, "The Iron-Ore Supply," *AIME Transactions* 27 (1897): 524–26.

16. W. Bernard Carlson, "Edison in the Mountains: The Magnetic Ore Separation Venture, 1879–1900," History of Technology 8 (1983): 43. Birkinbine and Edison seemed to have differed primarily over whether Edison should go into mining himself or only sell his separator (Birkinbine to TAE, 13 July 1889, with Edison's marginal notes [*TAEM* 126:1022]).

17. Bruce Seely, "Experts, Enthusiasm, and 'Failure': Iron Making in the Adirondacks, 1830–1980," p. 30, paper presented at the Annual Meeting of the Society for the History of Technology, Lowell, Mass., 1994.

18. Walter Mallory to TAE, 7 July, 8 and 13 Aug., 13 Oct., 14 Dec. 1888, 3 and 24 Jan. 1889 (*TAEM* 123:931, 952, 954, 1002, 1092; 126:1075–76); proposal for Edison Ore Milling Co. (*TAEM* 126:1071); preliminary agreement between Edison Ore Milling Co. and Mallory, 25 July 1888 (*TAEM* 129:781; 148:37); Mallory, "Edison Could Take It," manuscript in "Mallory, Walter S.," Biographical Collection, ENHS; *TAEM Guide*, Part III, s.v. "Edison Iron Concentrating Co."

19. Mallory to TAE, 2 Feb. 1889 (*TAEM* 126:1083).

20. Ira Miller to TAE, 10 Apr. 1889; Mallory to TAE, 12 Apr. 1889 (*TAEM* 126:1097, 1099); TAE to Mallory, 13 Apr. 1889 (*TAEM* 139:36).

21. Walter Mallory to Ira Miller, 21 Oct. 1889 (*TAEM* 148:530). For Edison's technical work see N-88-01-03.2, N-88-06-01.1, N-89-05-18 (*TAEM* 99:157–59, 167–68, 172, 492–93, 981–82); U.S. Patent 430,280; Caveats 115 and 116 (*TAEM* 113:494, 590); abandoned patent application files, 29 July 1889 and 1 Aug. 1889 (*TAEM* 114:691, 719). For Kennelly, see Notebook #1:163, 166; Notebook #2:15, 21, 42, 45 (*TAEM* 104:419, 422, 448, 454, 475, 478). For Batchelor, see Cat. 1337:69, item 581 (*TAEM* 90:493).

22. U.S. Patent 434,588; Cat. 1137:81, 83, 85–86, 88, 96–97, 1104–07, 128, items 596, 598, 600, 604, 616, 627, 629, 658 (*TAEM* 90:499–503, 507, 511–12, 523); Document File folder D-89-50 (*TAEM* 126:1074); Letterbook LM-261 (*TAEM* 148:49).

23. "Unsolved Problems That Edison Is Studying," *Scientific American* 69 (8 July 1893): 25.

24. Samuel Insull to Alfred Tate, 30 July 1889, Lbk. 31:451 (*TAEM* 139:594). The records of the NJPCW, which provide the basis for the rest of this chapter, are in *TAEM*, reels 149–54; another crucial source is the testimony of Emil Herter and Walter Mallory in *Edison v. Allis-Chalmers, et al.* (*TAEM* 118:904, 929).

25. TAE to W. H. Walbaum & Co., 20 June 1889 (*TAEM* 139:391); Edison memorandum, probably for Villard, c. 1889 (*TAEM* 125:538); Edison memorandum, c. 1894, American Society for Metals; Theodore Waters, "Edison's Revolution in Mining," *McClure's Magazine* (Nov. 1897): 77–78; TAE to H. C. Demming, 7 Nov. 1889 (*TAEM* 138:971). The capital stock of the company was raised to $150,000 in November, instead of $100,000 as they had originally decided in July when only the Bechtelsville plant needed funds (NJPCW Minutes, 23–24, 28–29 [*TAEM* 152:607–08, 610]).

26. Alfred Tate to A. Blue, 21 Dec. 1889 (*TAEM* 140:92); Harry Livor to TAE, 23 Jan. 1890 (*TAEM* 149:74). Regarding Bechtelsville, see also Livor to TAE, with Edison's marginal note, 13 Oct. 1890 (*TAEM* 149:191); Livor to P. F. Gildea listed in *TAEM Guide*, Part III, under "Gildea, P. F.," and the entries for "Hartzell, H. K."

27. TAE to Harry Livor, 27 Jan. 1889; TAE to H. K. Hartzell, 3 Feb. 1890 (*TAEM* 140:364, 451).

28. Ira Miller to TAE, 23 Aug. 1890 (*TAEM* 129:758). See also Document File folders D-90-45 and D-91-35 (*TAEM* 129:690, 131:485) and Letterbook LM-261 (*TAEM* 148:49) regarding the fate of the Iron Concentrating Company venture.

29. Edison's draft memoranda, c. 1893, American Society for Metals.

30. "Report of Mr. Edison on Mill and property at Ogden," 16 July 1890, NJPCW Minutes, 41–49 (*TAEM* 152:616–20).

31. William Dickson to TAE, 2 Sept. 1890 (*TAEM* 129:937); see also Dickson to TAE, 24 July, 25, 26, 28, and 29 Aug., 3, 4, 5, 7, and 12 Sept. 1890 (*TAEM* 129:917, 923–24, 926, 929, 941, 943, 947, 949, 953). Walter Mallory to TAE, 1 Aug. 1890 (*TAEM* 129:737); TAE to Harry Livor, 24 July, 15 Aug. 1890 (*TAEM* 149:143, 146); Livor to TAE, 23 and 24 July, 4 and 8 Aug. 12 Sept., 1890 (*TAEM* 149:143, 151, 156, 158, 169, 178); Alfred Tate to William Dickson, 20 Sept. 1890; Tate to Livor, 9 Oct. 1890 (*TAEM* 141:567, 621); NJPCW Minutes, pp. 59–62 (*TAEM* 152:625–67).

32. TAE to Walter Mallory, 5 May 1891 (142:211). See also Abraham S. Hewitt to TAE, 17 Apr. 1891 (*TAEM* 149:230); Harry Livor to TAE, 10 and 14 Apr. 1891 (*TAEM* 149:232, 239); TAE to Livor, 16 Apr. 1891 (*TAEM* 149:156); TAE to James J. Fronheiser, 16 Apr. 1891 (*TAEM* 142:157); William S. Perry to Arthur W. Howe, 24 Apr. 1891 (*TAEM* 152:780); Bethlehem Iron Co. to TAE, 14 May 1891 (*TAEM* 149:265).

33. TAE to Harry Livor, 10 June and 24 June 1891 (*TAEM* 149:316, 369); TAE to Samuel Insull, 29 June 1891 (*TAEM* 149:383). See also TAE to Livor, 13 and 18 June 1891 (*TAEM* 142:330, 349); Livor to TAE, 11 June 1891 (*TAEM* 149:318, 323); Bethlehem Iron Co. to TAE, 9 June 1891 (*TAEM* 149:313); TAE to Bethlehem Iron Co., 10 June 1891 (*TAEM* 142:311). On the problems at Ogden and criticism of Livor's management, see TAE marginal note on Perry to TAE, 27 June 1891; Henry Hart to William Perry (*TAEM* 149:383, 388); TAE to Harry Livor, 18 June 1891, Lbk. 50:58 (*TAEM* 142:349); Dickson's Odgen Report, 25 June 1891 (*TAEM* 99:1018); Henry W. Hart to Robert L. Cutting Jr., 30 June 1891 (*TAEM* 149:385, 388); TAE to Postmaster General, 10 July 1891 (*TAEM* 149:393).

34. TAE marginal note on Stephen R. Krom to TAE, 14 Oct. 1891 (*TAEM* 149:415); Batchelor's journal Cat. 1337:173–74 (*TAEM* 90:541).

35. TAE to Erastus Wiman, 16 July 1891 (*TAEM* 142:415).

36. Batchelor journal Cat. 1337:173–84 (*TAEM* 90:541–47); NJPCW Experiment Book, pp. 53–63 (*TAEM* 151:508–13).

37. Cat. 1337:173 (*TAEM* 90:541).

38. Cat. 1337:185–210 (*TAEM* 90:547–60); NJPCW Experiment Book, pp. 65–77 (*TAEM* 151:514–19); Charles Batchelor to TAE, 11 and 13 Feb. 1892; TAE to Batchelor, 10, 13, and 19 Feb. 1892; Owen Conley to TAE, 23 and 25 Feb., 17, 21, and 24 Mar. 1892; (*TAEM* 149:456, 459–60, 455, 460, 461, 462, 462–63, 476, 479–880) TAE to Conley, 17 and 23 Mar. 1892 (*TAEM* 143:152; 149:479).

39. Walter Mallory to TAE, 1 July 1889 (*TAEM* 126:1101); Samuel Insull to Mallory, 6 July 1889 (*TAEM* 139:494). See also Cat. 1337:210–17 (*TAEM* 90:560–63); Alfred Tate to Owen Conley and TAE to Conley, both 17 Mar. 1892 (*TAEM* 149:473–74).

40. William Perry to Arthur W. Howe, 5 Oct. and 14 Nov. 1892 (*TAEM* 152:874, 880); see also William Perry to Robert L. Cutting Jr., 5 Oct. 1892 (*TAEM* 149:512); Perry to Howe (*TAEM* 152:884).

41. "Unsolved Problems That Edison Is Studying," *Scientific American* 69 (1893):25; NJPCW Minutes, 91–92 (*TAEM* 152:641–42).

42. Walter Mallory's deposition, *Edison v. Allis-Chalmers et al.*, 641 (*TAEM* 118:930); NJPCW Experiment Book, pp. 233, 244–47, 251–301 (*TAEM* 151:591, 597–623).

43. William Perry to Charles Batchelor, 17 Mar. 1893 (*TAEM* 92:894).

44. William Perry to Charles Batchelor, 17 Mar. 1893 (*TAEM* 92:894); "The Edison Concentrating Works," *Iron Age* 59 (1897): 7.

45. Constitution of the Muckers of the Edison Laboratory, c. 1902, Muckers, ENHS.

46. N-93-05-22 (*TAEM* 152:134); this notebook contains a record of the extensive bricking experiments made during 1893 and the first months of 1894; see also N-93-08-01 and N-93-11-20 (*TAEM* 103:846, 929).

47. Pilling & Crane to TAE, 31 Mar. and 5 Apr. 1894 (*TAEM* 149:624, 629). See *TAEM Guide*, Part III, s.vv. "Pilling, William Stockman" and "Pilling & Crane," and "Wharton, Joseph." For Wharton see also W. Ross Yates, *Joseph Wharton: Quaker Industrial Pioneer* (Bethlehem, Pa.: Lehigh University Press, 1987), 315–19.

48. Walter Mallory to Morton McMichael, 16 Mar. 1896 (*TAEM* 154:529). On Perry see, for example, William Perry to Charles Batchelor, 17 Mar. and 18 Apr. 1893 (*TAEM* 92:894, 900); Perry to Mallory, 21 Mar., 16 Aug., 13 Nov. 1893, 7 June 1894 (*TAEM* 152:910, 957, 980, 1039); Perry to Samuel Insull, 23 Oct. 1893 (*TAEM* 152:974).

49. "Edison Will Vote," *New York Evening Advertiser*, 4 Nov. 1892 (*TAEM* 146:831); Edison's draft of the statement that accompanied this article is in *TAEM* 132:433. A transcription of Edison's notebook on government regulation is found in Israel Rubin, "Thomas Alva Edison's 'Treatise on National Economic Policy and Business,'" *Business History Review* 59 (1985): 433–64.

50. Mallory's testimony, p. 643, *Edison v. Allis-Chalmers et al.* (*TAEM* 118:931).

51. NJPCW Minutes, 103, 105–06, 112–13 (*TAEM* 152:658–60, 665–66); Walter Mallory to John Fitz, 11 Nov. 1895 (*TAEM* 152:393); Mallory's testimony, pp. 648, 655, *Edison v. Allis-Chalmers et al.* (*TAEM* 118:934, 937).

52. Herter's and Mallory's testimony, pp. 558–59, 648, 676–77, *Edison v. Allis-Chalmers et al.* (*TAEM* 118:911, 934, 948); Walter Mallory to William Perry, Sept. 1896 (*TAEM* 154:365); see also Edison's notices to workers, 22 Aug. 1896 (*TAEM* 153:437–38); Mallory to James C. Parrish, 9 Sept. 1896 (*TAEM* 152:68).

53. Herter's testimony, p. 568, *Edison v. Allis-Chalmers et al.* (*TAEM* 118:916).

54. Herter's and Mallory's testimony, 547, 550, 552, 556, 580, 652–53, 668, *Edison v. Allis-Chalmers et al.* (*TAEM* 118:905, 907–08, 910, 922, 936, 944); W. H. Mason, "The Edison Roll Crushers," reprint

from *American Society of Mechanical Engineers Transactions*, pp. 411–13, Historical Reference File, ENHS.

55. "The Edison Concentrating Works," *Iron Age* 59 (1897): 6.

56. Mallory testimony, p. 677, *Edison v. Allis-Chalmers et al.* (*TAEM* 118:948).

57. TAE to Frederick P. Fish, 15 Dec. 1896; Mallory to Stuart A. Coats, 29 Jan. 1897 (*TAEM* 143:516; 154:413).

58. Leonard Peckitt to TAE, 22 Jan. 1897 (*TAEM* 149:740).

59. Mallory to Samuel Flood Page, 23 Aug. 1897 (*TAEM* 154:460).

60. "Mr. Edison's Iron Ore-Milling Work in New Jersey," *Electrical Engineer* 24 (28 Oct. 1897): 402; other articles included "The Edison Concentrating Works," *Iron Age* 59 (28 Oct. 1897): 1–8; "Magnetic Ore Separation at Edison, New Jersey, U.S.A.," *Engineering* 12 (Nov. 1897): 579–82; "Edison Ore Mines," *Electrical Review* 31 (27 Oct. 1897): 202–03; and Waters, "Edison's Revolution in Mining" (*TAEM* 146:1118–47).

61. Walter Mallory to Samuel Flood Page, 28 Aug. 1898 (*TAEM* 154:460) discusses the operating expenses and expected income. The administrative system is described in "Edison Concentrating Works," *Iron Age* 59 (1897): 7.

62. Walter Mallory to Ira Miller, 29 Jan. 1898; Mallory to Stuart Coats, 28 Apr. 1898; Mallory to James Cutting, 1 May 1898 (*TAEM* 154:579, 602, 607).

63. TAE to Richard Bowker, 6 Aug. 1897 (*TAEM* 154:454); see also TAE to Bowker, 7 Oct., 12 Nov., and 31 Dec. 1897; Henry Villard to Bowker, 11 Nov. 1897; "Confidential Statement of Mr. Edison to Mr. Bowker; and Edison's handwritten proposal regarding the syndicate, all in the Bowker Papers, New York Public Library.

64. Walter Mallory testimony, pp. 647–58, *Edison v. Allis-Chalmers et al.* (*TAEM* 118:933–34); Mallory to Ira Miller, 29 Jan. 1898; Mallory to Stuart Coats, 28 Apr. 1898; Mallory to Pilling & Crane, 13 Apr. 1898 (*TAEM* 154:579, 602; 153:248).

65. TAE to Alexander Elliott, 13 Dec. 1898 (*TAEM* 149:933); TAE to A. N. Brady, 21 Dec. 1898 (*TAEM* 143:958).

66. Mallory to General Electric Co., 25 Sept. 1900; Mallory to W. S. de Camp, 21 Dec. 1900 (*TAEM* 154:14, 78); Mallory's testimony, p. 669, *Edison v. Allis-Chalmers et al.* (*TAEM* 118:944); Mallory to William Meadowcroft, 15 June 1932, DF; Dyer and Martin, *Edison*, 502.

67. For the Edison Ore Milling Syndicate Ltd. and the Dunderland Iron Ore Company, see Edison Ore Milling Syndicate Ltd. and Related Companies Records, ENHS; a "Statement of Facts," Aug. 1910, provides a nice overview. For the gold mining ventures, see Document File folders D-98-20, D-99-14, D-00-14, D-01-25, D-01-27, D-02-24, D-03-23, D-04-23. For the New Jersey Zinc Company, see Mallory's testimony, pp. 658–60, 672–75 (*TAEM* 118:939–40, 946–47), and *TAEM Guide*, Parts III and IV, s.v. "New Jersey Zinc Co."

Chapter 19: A Modern Legend

1. I have used Robert Martin Adams's translation of *Tomorrow's Eve*, which was published by University of Illinois Press in 1982. It should be noted that Adams shows his unfamiliarity with even the basic Edison literature by translating Edison's most common nickname "The Wizard of Menlo Park" as "The Sorcerer of Menlo Park." Furthermore, a more appropriate translation of the title would be *The Future Eve*. On Villiers and his novel, see Paul K. Alkon, *Science Fiction before 1900: Imagination Discovers Technology* (New York: Twayne Publishers, 1994): 84–88; Daniel Gerould, "Villiers de l'Isle-Adam and Science Fiction," *Science-Fiction Studies* 2 (1984): 318–23; Linda Wheat, "L'Eve Future (The Future Eve)," in Frank N. Magill, ed., *Survey of Science Fiction Literature* (Englewood Cliffs, N.J.: Salem Press, 1979), 2:735–38; A. W. Raitt, *The Life of Villiers de l'Isle-Adam* (Oxford: Oxford University Press, 1981).

2. Villiers, *Tomorrow's Eve*, 61; Allen L. Benson, "Edison's Dream of New Music," *Cosmopolitan* 54 (1913): 799. On science fiction in the nineteenth century, see Alkon, *Science Fiction before 1900*.

3. Villiers, *Tomorrow's Eve*, 18.

4. Lloyd Bryce to TAE, 18 Dec. 1890; L. S. Metcalf to TAE, 28 Jan. 1889 (*TAEM* 128:739; 125:583); Jules Verne, "In the Year 2889," *The Forum* 6 (Feb. 1889): 662–77. On Bellamy, see Everett W. MacNair, *Edward Bellamy and the Nationalist Socialist Movement 1889 to 1894* (Milwaukee, Wisc.: The Fitzgerald Co., 1957), and Daphne Patai, ed., *Looking Backward 1988–1888: Essays on Edward Bellamy* (Amherst, Mass.: University of Massachusetts Press, 1988).

5. George Lathrop, "Talks with Edison," *Harper's Magazine* 80 (Feb. 1890): 435. An even earlier interview containing Edison's ideas regarding atoms is found in "Edison's Religious Beliefs," *Salt Lake City Democrat*, 16 July 1885 (*TAEM* 89:661), see also *TAEB* Doc. 1315, axiom 4.

6. George Lathrop to TAE, 10 Aug. 1891 (*TAEM* 130:845); "Of Thomas A. Edison. The Electrical Inventor and His Electrical Novel," *Lynchburg Virginian*, 19 Nov. 1891 (*TAEM* 146:728); see also Lathrop to TAE, 30 June, 10 July, 13 Oct. and 22 Nov. 1890; Tate to Lathrop, 7 Jan. 1891 (*TAEM* 128:650, 659, 706, 727–28; 141:909).

7. Edison's notes for Lathrop, n.d. (*TAEM* 128:747).

8. Alfred Tate to George Lathrop, 27 Aug. 1891 (*TAEM* 142:734); Lathrop to Tate, 29 Aug. 1891 (*TAEM* 130:856).

9. George Lathrop to TAE, 5 Oct. 1891 (*TAEM* 130:866); Alfred Tate to Lathrop, 8 Oct. 1891 (*TAEM* 142:844); see also Lathrop to TAE and TAE to Lathrop, both 25 Jan. 1892 (*TAEM* 132:333–34).

10. E. F. Bleiler, "From the Newark Steam Man to Tom Swift," *Extrapolation* 30 (1989): 108; see also Sam Moskowitz, *Strange Horizons: The Spectrum of Science Fiction* (New York: Charles Scribner's Sons, 1976): 160–66. Eight Tom Edison Jr. stories appeared in the *Nugget Library*: "Tom Edison, Jr.'s Sky-Scraping Trip" (No. 102), "Tom Edison, Jr.'s Prairie-Skimmer Team" (No. 110), "Tom Edison, Jr.'s Sky-Courser" (No. 115), "Tom Edison, Jr.'s Air-Frigate" (No. 119), "Tom Edison, Jr.'s Steam Four-in-Hand" (No. 124), "Tom Edison, Jr.'s Electric Mule (No. 128), "Tom Edison, Jr.'s Electric Sea-Spider" (No. 134), "Tom Edison, Jr.'s Chillian Explorer" (No. 144).

11. TAE to Arthur Brisbane, 14 Jan. 1898; Brisbane to TAE, 14 Jan. 1898, enclosing the 14 Jan. installment of "Edison Conquers Mars" (*TAEM* 137:11–15); TAE to Garrett Serviss and TAE to Brisbane, both 15 Jan. 1898 (*TAEM* 143:609, 612). Edison's letter to the Editor of the *New York Sun*, 11 Jan. 1898 (*TAEM* 143:601), was reprinted in the *Electrical Review* of 19 Jan. 1898. For newspaper comments on Edison's work on the novel with Lathrop see "Edison as a Novelist," clipping from unknown Milwaukee newspaper, 30 Sept. 1891; notice in the *Dispatch*, 29 Sept. 1891; and "Of Thomas A. Edison: The Electrical Inventor and His Electrical Novel," *Lynchburg Virginian*, 19 Nov. 1891 (*TAEM* 146:702, 713, 728). On Serviss and his story see Sam Moskowitz, "Edison's Conquest of Mars" in Frank N. Magill, ed., *Survey of Science Fiction Literature* (Englewood Cliffs, N.J.: Salem Press, 1979), 2:698–702; "Garrett P. Serviss," *Science Fiction Writers* (New York: Charles Scribner's Sons, 1982): 39–44; "Serviss, Garrett P[utnam]," in Everett F. Bleiler, *Science Fiction: The Early Years* (Kent, Ohio: The Kent State University Press, 1990): 665; Alkon, *Science Fiction before 1900*, 108–09; H. Bruce Franklin, *War Stars: The Superweapon and the American Imagination* (New York: Oxford University Press, 1988): 66–69.

12. "The American Mechanic," *New York Evening Telegram*, 25 Apr. 1878 (*TAEM* 94:170).

13. "An American Abroad," *New York Daily-Tribune*, 18 Aug. 1889 (*TAEM* 146:476)

14. "Edison Goes Abroad," *Brooklyn Citizen*, 3 Aug. 1889 (*TAEM* 146:470). The press reports of his trip are found in Clippings (*TAEM* 146:469–539).

15. Margaret Upton to her Mother, [13 Aug. 1889?], Upton Papers, New Jersey Historical Society, Newark, N.J.; Mina Edison to Mary Valinda Miller, 28 Aug. 1889 (*TAEM* 161:650); "Edison at Home Again," *Newark News*, 7 Oct. 1889 (*TAEM* 146:539).

16. "Edison Talks about Paris," *New York World*, 8 Sept. 1889; "Events in Paris," *London Standard*, 12 Sept. 1889 (*TAEM* 146:477, 503).

17. Quoted in David Cahan, *An Institute for Empire: The Physikalisch-Technische Reichsanstalt, 1871–1918* (Cambridge: Cambridge University Press, 1989), 38; "Mr. Edison at Home Unspoiled by Glory," *New York Herald*, 7 Oct. 1889 (*TAEM* 95:244).

18. "Honors for Edison," *New York Herald*, 27 Sept 1889 (*TAEM* 146:520).

19. "Edison Could Whip Chili," *New York World*, 17 Jan. 1892, quoted in Franklin, *War Stars*, 69; Samuel Insull to J. F. Morrison, 7 Mar. 1881, Letterbook 9:53 (*TAEM* 81:32).

20. "A Talk with Edison," *Scientific American* 66 (2 Apr. 1892): 216, which reprints an interview from the January 17 *New York World*.

21. W. K. L. Dickson and Antonia Dickson, *History of the Kinetograph, Kinetoscope and Kineto-Phonograph*, reprint edition (New York: Arno Press, 1970): 4, 55; Edison to Raff, 5 Feb. 1895; Alfred Tate to John Birkinbine, 3 May 1892 (*TAEM* 143:725, 214).

22. Musser, *The Emergence of Cinema*, 116.

23. Frank Sprague to TAE, 25 April 1884, Sprague Papers, New York Public Library (hereafter Sprague Papers).

24. Frank Sprague to Board of Trustees, Sprague Railway & Motor Co., 7 June 1890, see also his letter to the Board of 26 Apr. 1890 and Sprague to the President and Board of Directors of Edison General Electric, 2 Dec. 1890, all Sprague Papers.

25. Frank Sprague to the President and Board of Directors of Edison General Electric, 2 Dec. 1890, Sprague Papers.

26. Frank Sprague to President and Board of Directors, Edison General Electric Co., 2 Dec. 1890; see also Sprague to Edison General Electric, 26 Apr. 1890; Sprague to Eickemeyer, 22 July 1890; and the pamphlet *Edison System of Electric Railways*, extensively annotated by Mrs. Sprague; all Sprague Papers.

27. Henry to Sprague, 22 Nov. 1928, Sprague Papers; Frank Sprague, "Electric Railway Not Creation of One Man," *New York Times*, 23 Sept. 1928, 9; Harriet Sprague, *Frank J. Sprague and the Edison Myth* (New York: William-Frederick Press, 1947). See also Frank Sprague, "Early Steps in the Development of Electric Traction," *AERA* (Sprague Papers) for another important article. For other correspondence about this issue, see Sprague to General Electric and Patent Departments, 20 Mar. 1928; Sprague to T. E. Mitten, 29 Oct. 1928; G. Pantaleoni to Sprague, 30 Jan. 1929; Sprague to Pantaleoni, 25 Feb. 1929; Sprague to S. H. Libby, 10 Oct. 1931; Sprague to James Lawson Crane, 4 Sept. 1934; G. S. Bryan to Harriet Sprague, 11 October 1941; all Sprague Papers.

28. Edward Thomson to Sprague, 29 Sept. 1928, Sprague Papers; see also Thomson's "Memo Relating to the Work of Mr. Thomas A. Edison," 3 May 1915, Dugald Jackson Papers, MIT.

29. Edward Thomson to Charles Coffin, 29 Oct. 1891, Thomson File, Hall of History, Schenectady, N.Y. Thomson's letter to Coffin was in response to an article in the *New York Herald* of 25 October 1891 (supplement p. 12) entitled "Exit the Locomotive! 'Tis Edison Who Says It."

30. TAE to Raff, 5 Feb. 1895 (*TAEM* 143:726).

31. George Gouraud to TAE, 29 Feb. 1888; TAE to Gouraud, 21 Mar. 1888; Gouraud to TAE, 3 Mar. 1888, with Edison's marginal notes (*TAEM* 121:696; 122:199; 124:677).

32. On Barnum see Neil Harris, *Humbug: The Art of P. T. Barnum* (Boston: Little, Brown, 1973); A. H. Saxon, *P. T. Barnum: The Legend and the Man* (New York: Columbia University Press, 1989); and Leo Braudy, *The Frenzy of Renown: Fame and Its History* (New York: Oxford University Press, 1986): 491–506.

Chapter 20: Fame in the Family

1. Edison's letters to Mina are quoted in Neil Baldwin, *Edison, Inventing the Century* (New York: Hyperion, 1995): 250; "Theodore Waters, "Edison's Revolution in Iron Mining," *McClure's Magazine* (Nov. 1897): 80.

2. Edison's letters to Mina from the 1890s are among those sold at auction by the Swann Galleries, photocopies of which are located at the Edison National Historic Site. The quoted letters are from catalogues of autographs sold on 14 Feb. 1990, lots 63–64; 17 Sept. 1992, item 91; and 11 Oct. 1990, items 87–88; 21 Sept. 1989, item 93. Mina's view of the home is in Martha Coman and Hugh Weir, "The Most Difficult Husband in America," *Collier's* (18 July 1925): 11, 42.

3. "'If My Daughter Were Going to College': Mrs. Thomas A. Edison Tells What She Would Hope For," *Charm* (Sept. 1930): 21, 56.

4. Marion to Mina, n.d.; Jennie Miller to Mina, 21 Mar. 1889 (*TAEM* 161:27, 33, 41, 935). For Marion's letters to Mina, which are mostly undated, see *TAEM* 11:9–237. These are part of the Family Correspondence Files in the Charles Edison Fund Collection. This material is located at the Edison National Historic Site and the Edison-Ford Winter Estates in Fort Myers, Florida. There is also a microfilm copy of this material that is organized by correspondent but not by date, as much of this material is undated. This chapter is largely based on the Family Correspondence from the Charles Edison Fund Collection, and other family materials found at ENHS, which will appear in *TAEM*. Where possible for quoted letters I give *TAEM* reel and frame or date citations to the materials not yet in *TAEM*. In many cases a document number has been written on the letters from the Charles Edison Fund Collection, and those numbers will be cited, preceded by the designation F.C. for Family Correspondence.

5. Jennie Miller to Mina, 18 June 1889 (*TAEM* 161:939).

6. Marion to TAE, 24 Apr. 1887 and n.d.; Marion to Mina, 2 Nov. 1889 and n.d. (*TAEM* 161:5, 20, 61, 94).

7. Marion to Mina, n.d. and 9 Feb. 1892 (161:94, 118, 141).

8. Marion to Mina, c. 1 Mar. 1890 (*TAEM* 161:148).

9. S. W. Bingham to Mina, 7 Apr. 1890 (*TAEM* 161:160).

10. Marion to Mina, c. Summer–Fall 1891 (*TAEM* 161:208).

11. Mary Valinda Miller to Mina, [24?] July and 18 Sept. 1892, F.C. (*TAEM* 161:747)

12. Marion to Henry Ford, 17 Feb. 1932, Box 8-29, EP&RI; TAE Jr. to Mina, 19 May 1897 (*TAEM* 161:257).

13. TAE Jr. to Mina, 23 Nov. 1892 (*TAEM* 161:249).

14. William to Mina, n.d. (*TAEM* 161:382, 366, 413, 411); Edison is quoted in Warren, "Edison on Invention and Inventors," 418.

15. William to Mina, n.d. (*TAEM* 161:444); regarding the issue of his course of study, see John Hawkins to Mina, 2 Mar. 1894 (*TAEM* 161:418).

16. John Hawkins to Mina, 2 Mar. 1894 and 25 Feb. 1896 (*TAEM* 161:418, 435).

17. William to TAE, n.d. (*TAEM* 161: 455, 453).

18. *New Haven Record*, 12 Mar. 1898 (*TAEM* 146:1168).

19. William to TAE, 25 Apr. 1898, with TAE marginal note to Gilmore (*TAEM* 137:83); *New York Evening Journal*, 17 June 1898 (*TAEM* 146:1168); the Photoscope is described in a brochure, "The Edison-Rogers Company," enclosed with William to TAE, 11 Oct. 1899, DF.

20. William to TAE, Fall 1899 and 6 Feb. 1900 (F.C. 4-3759, 4-3779); William to TAE, 11 Feb. 1903 (F.C.). On the marriage and falling out see also "Edison's Son Has Stormy Season of Love," *New York Evening Journal*, 26 Sept. 1899; "Edison, Wizard, Not Matchmaker," *New York Press*, 11 Nov. 1899; "Gossip of New York," *Chicago Inter-Ocean*, 12 Nov. 1899; all Clippings, ENHS (hereafter cited as Clippings).

21. TAE Jr. to TAE, 14 Jan. 1897 (F.C. 5-4402).

22. TAE Jr. to TAE, 14 Jan. 1897 (F.C. 5-4402); TAE Jr. to Mina, 8 Oct. 1897 (F.C. 5-4390); TAE Jr. to Mina, 4 Nov. 1897 (F.C. 5-4412).

23. TAE Jr. to Mina, 15 May and 12 Nov. 1897 (F.C. 5-4384, 5-4405).

24. TAE Jr. to Mina, 12 Nov. and 17 Oct. 1897 (F.C. 5-4405, 5-4413); see also TAE Jr. to Ed Redington, 18 Jan. 1898, DF (*TAEM* 137:108); TAE Jr. to Mina, 10 Jan. 1898 (F.C. 5-4397); TAE Jr. to Ed Redington, 29 May 1898, DF (*TAEM* 137:135); "Edison Jr. Wizard," *New York Herald*, 6 Dec. 1897 (*TAEM* 146:1150, see also clippings on 1137, 1150); "Young Tom Edison," *Cincinnati Commercial Tribune*, 3 July 1899, Clippings.

25. TAE Jr. to Ed Redington, 22 June, 18 Apr., and 29 May 1898, DF (*TAEM* 137:147, 125, 135); TAE Jr. to Mina, 11 Sept 1898 (F.C. 5-4378).

26. William to TAE Jr., Dec. 1898; TAE Jr. to TAE, 17 Dec. 1898; both DF.

27. William to TAE, 21 Nov. 1900, DF; see also "Young Edison's Marriage," *New York Tribune*, 3 July, 1899; "Young Tom Edison," *Cincinnati Commercial Tribune*, 3 July 1899, "Young Edison's Bride May Reconcile Father and Son," *Chicago Chronicle*, 13 July 1906, all Clippings.

28. "Young Tom Edison," *Cincinnati Commercial Tribune*, 3 July 1899, Clippings.

29. For the Thomas A. Edison Jr. and Wm. Holzer Steel and Iron Process Company, see F. D. Palmer to TAE, 14 Mar. 1899; L. Barton Case to TAE, 28 Feb. 1901; Brown, Bruns & Co to TAE, 1 Mar. 1901; Josephine Crist to TAE, c. 1902; Laura Pease to TAE, 28 Jan. 1909, all DF; Harry F. Miller to Thomas J. Carew, 15 Aug. 1908, Letterbook 77:449; Abram Soper to TAE, 14 Feb. 1906; John A. Thompson to Soper, 6 May 1903, 9 and 14 Jan. and 8 Feb. 1904, Frank Dyer to Abram Soper, 22 Feb. 1906, all General Correspondence, Edison's Name Files, Legal Department Records, ENHS; "To Test New Steel Process," *Chicago Times-Herald*, 3 Mar. 1899; "A New Method of Hardening Steel," *New York Tribune*, 3 Mar. 1899; "Its Merit Doubted," *Philadelphia Inquirer*, 3 Mar. 1899, all Clippings.

30. TAE Jr. to TAE, 29 Dec. 1902, DF. On the International Bureau see A. A. Friedenstein to TAE, 8 May 1900, and L. Barton Case to John Randolph, 14 May 1900, DF. On the Edison Chemical Company see General Correspondence, *Thomas A. Edison v. Edison Chemical Company*, and *Thomas A. Edison v. Thomas A. Edison, Jr., Chemical Company*, Edison's Name Files, Legal Department Records, ENHS, and *TAEM Guide* Part IV s.v. "Edison Chemical Company" and "Thomas A. Edison, Jr., Chemical Company."

31. TAE Jr. to TAE, 21 July 1903, with Edison's marginal note, DF.

32. TAE Jr. to TAE, 17 Dec. 1898, DF; see also TAE Jr. to John Randolph, 17 Dec. 1903, and C. F. Stilwell to Randolph, 18 Dec. 1903, both DF; TAE Jr. to Frank Dyer, 18 Oct. 1904, 23 and 26 Feb., 4, 7, and 23 Mar. 1906; William to TAE, 9 Feb. 1906; Dyer to TAE, 7 Mar. 1906; Dyer to TAE Jr. 9 Mar. 1906, all General Correspondence, and *Thomas A. Edison v. Thomas A. Edison, Jr., Chemical Company*, Edison's Name Files, Legal Department Records, ENHS; "Young Edison's Bride May Reconcile Father and Son."

33. U.S. Trademark 34,806; "Inventor Edison after Bogus Agents," *Newark News*, 5 Jan. 1899, Clippings; Gilmore to John Searles, 9 June 1898; G. N. Morison to S. F. Moriarity, 15 June and 6 July 1898;

(*TAEM* 137:763, 773, 836); see also the material listed under Edison's Name Files, Legal Department Records, ENHS.

34. TAE to William, 13 Oct. 1903; William to TAE, with Edison's marginal note, 17 Oct., both DF. See also William to TAE, 11 and 19 Feb. 1902; 12 and 18 Aug., 6, 9, and 26 Sept., 12, 14, 16, 18, 21 Oct., 14 Nov. 1903; TAE to William, 14 Oct. 1903; Edward Duvall to TAE, 17 Oct. 1903; Howard Hayes to John Randolph, 21 Oct. 1903; Hayes to TAE, with draft assignment, 20 Nov. 1903, all DF.

35. Blanche Edison to TAE, "Monday" and 12 Dec. 1903; TAE draft to Blanche Edison, n.d. Dec. 1903, all DF.

36. William to TAE, 16 Dec. 1903; William to Mina, "Saturday"; Blanche Edison to TAE, 23 Oct. 1907, all DF. See also Samuel Scoggins to TAE, with Edison's marginal note, 27 Dec. 1903; William to Randolph, 12 Feb. 1904; William to TAE, n.d. 1904, all DF.

37. Richard Dyer to William, 4 May, 1909; William's circular "Removal Notice and Change of Name," c. Apr. 1909; William to Dyer, 2 May 1909, all DF. See also William to TAE, 20 Mar., 7 June, 3 Oct., 13, 16, 17 and 22 Nov. 1907, 24 Nov. 1908, Sunday 21 1909; William to Dyer, 17 Feb. and 18 Apr. 1909; Dyer to William, 30 Apr. 1909; James P. Whelan to TAE, 13 Nov. 1907, all DF.

38. William to Richard Dyer, 2 May 1909; Dyer to William, 4 May 1904, both DF. The later careers of both sons are detailed in letters from the 1910s and 1920s in the Document File at ENHS, the Family Correspondence Files of the Charles Edison Fund Collection, and the Edison Papers & Related Items, Henry Ford Museum, Dearborn, Mich.

39. William to Richard Dyer, 2 May 1909, DF.

40. Warren, *Edison on Inventions and Inventors*, 415–16, 418; TAE in Lyman Abbott, ed., "How to Succeed as an Inventor," *How to Succeed* (New York: G. P. Putnam's Sons, 1882): 98.

41. Charles Edison oral biography, pp. 36, 97, Oral History Research Office, Columbia University, copy at ENHS. On Charles see also John D. Venable, *Out of the Shadow: The Story of Charles Edison* (East Orange, N.J.: Charles Edison Fund, 1978).

42. "Young Edison an Inventor," *Rockport, Ind., Journal*, 18 Apr. 1913, Clippings.

43. Theodore to Charles, 1 Apr. 1931 (F.C. 11-5843); Ann Edison to Mina, 31 May 1931 (11-5827); Theodore to TAE, 5 Apr. 1931 (11-5820); see also Theodore to Mina, 5 and 21 Apr. 1931 (F.C. 11-5821 and F.C. 11-5823). Theodore's wife Ann wrote in her May 31 letter, "It is an equal disappointment to Ted (and of course to me too) that he could not continue at the Laboratory, and it was the realization of what a marvelous team he and Father Edison and Charles could have been, were their dispositions and ideas more sympathetic, that kept him for years trying to find his place among them." Theodore's papers, including records of the Calibron Company, are now at ENHS.

44. Quote is from TAE to Madeleine on Madeleine to TAE, 4 Apr. 1923 (Bart Cox donation, ENHS); Madeleine to TAE, 11 Apr. 1923 (F.C. 1-360); Madeleine to Mina, n.d. (F.C. 1-357); "Tom Edison's Daughter Prince in School Play," *Akron Press*, 11 June 1906, 1.

45. "The Edison Questionnaire—Its Aim, Its Results, and Its Collateral Significance," *Scientific American* 125 (Nov. 1921): 16.

Chapter 21: The Business of Innovation

1. Millard, *Edison and the Business of Innovation*, 159.

2. For Edison's work on a telephone message system see "Edison's Testimony and Exhibits," *Edison v. Macdonald*, Patent Office Interference No. 25,677, Box 112, Legal Dept. Files, ENHS. In this effort he again experimented with his phonograph and his electromotograph in combination with a telephone. On the radium and XYZ experiments, see correspondence from William Hammer in Document File folder D-03-31 and notebooks N-01-01-02.02, N-02-03-08, N-02-03-18, N-02-05-01, N-03-01-22, N-03-02-26, N-03-02-27.1, N-03-02-27.2, N-03-12-12.1, N-06-11-18, N-07-03-19, N-08-02-13.

3. The mechanical duplicating method and experiments on Edison's gold mold process are discussed in Albert Wurth's, Jonas Ayslworth's, and Edison's testimony, *National Phonograph Co v. American Graphophone Co.* (*TAEM* 117:90–103, 129–54); Edison's and Charles Wurth's testimony, *Lambert v. Edison*, (*TAEM* 117:285–99); U.S. Patents 484,582, 648,935, 713,209; W. B. Northrop, "Edison Achieves a New Inventive Triumph," 1902 Clippings; Read and Welch, *From Tin Foil to Stereo*, 80–90.

4. Edison's testimony, p. 247, *Lambert v. Edison* (*TAEM* 117:286). See also laboratory notebooks N-91-11-24 and N-97-12-15 for work by Charles and Albert Wurth carried out between 1891 and 1902.

5. Miller's, Aylsworth's, and Edison's testimony, *National Phonograph Co v. American Graphophone Co.* (*TAEM* 117:114–24, 129–54); National Phonograph Co. circular, 13 Jan. 1902, ibid. (*TAEM* 117:255–57); U.S. Patents 667,662, 683,615, 663,676; W. B. Northrop, "Edison Achieves a New Inventive Triumph," 1902 Clippings.

6. Miller's testimony and National Phonograph Co. circular, 13 Jan. 1902, *National Phonograph Co v. American Graphophone Co.* (*TAEM* 117:124, 255–57); Wurth's testimony, *Lambert v. Edison* (*TAEM* 117:294); "Brief for Appellant," *New York Phonograph Co. v. National Phonograph Co.* (*TAEM* 117:505).

7. On the Edison film business and the Motion Picture Patents Company see Musser, *Before the Nickelodeon*, 433–77, and Robert J. Anderson, "The Motion Picture Patents Company (Ph.D. dissertation, University of Wisconsin, 1983); see also the Motion Picture Patents Company Records, ENHS. On Higham see Millard, *Business of Innovation*, 226; on Powrie see folder "Color Photography—Powrie, John H.," Legal Dept. Files, ENHS; on Edison's 1910 (U.S. Patent 964,097) see Richard Dyer to Gaumont Co., 23 June 1911, DF.

8. It may not be a coincidence that the first cement company to become a major purchaser of Edison sand was the Atlas Portland Cement Company of New York; the company's founder, Jose de Navarro, had earlier formed the Edison Spanish Colonial Electric Light Company. Sand Sales Book (1892–1902); John Walsh to I. D. Barton, 12 Feb. 1892; William Perry to D. C. Houston, 30 Jan. 1893; Perry to Walter Mallory, 14 Aug. 1893; Perry to E. H. Vreeland, 2 Sept. 1893; Upton sand report, Aug. 1895 (*TAEM* 154:679; 152:843, 901, 955, 962; 151:678).

9. Robert W. Lesley, *History of the Portland Cement Industry in the United States* (New York: Arno Press, 1972); Complainant's Record on Final Hearing, 846–47, and Mallory's testimony, *Edison and North American Portland Cement Co. v. Alsen's American Portland Cement Works*, Box 30, Legal Dept. Records, ENHS; TAE to Herman Dick, 12 Jan. 1899; Walter Mallory to Stuart Coats, 20 Feb. 1901; and Mallory to Josiah Reiff, 7 May 1902 (*TAEM* 143:965; 154:99, 241); Charles Matcham to TAE, 17 Dec. 1899 (*TAEM* 1437:268); Francis Upton Memorandum, 2 Jan. 1899, Edison Portland Cement Company Records, ENHS (hereafter EPCC); TAE to Henry Kummel, 23 Nov. 1900, DF.

10. See 1899 agreements and assignments in Edison Portland Cement Co. folder, Kellow File, ENHS. The development of Edison's cement technology and the operations of the company are detailed in Edison Portland Cement Company Records and in the testimony and exhibits from *Edison and North American Portland Cement Co. v. Alsen's American Portland Cement Works*, Box 30, Legal Department Records, ENHS.

11. TAE to Theron Crane, 8 Mar. 1899 (*TAEM* 154:628); see also TAE to Herman Dick, 12 Jan. 1899 (*TAEM* 143:965); [Walter Mallory?] to Dick, 11 May 1900, EPPC; U.S. Patents 648,934 and 727,116.

12. Edison's comments were recalled by Walter Mallory, who also described the experimental work on the long kiln, during his testimony in *Edison and North American Portland Cement Co. v. Alsen's American Portland Cement Works*, pp. 847–56, 868, 874; see also Emil Herter's testimony, pp. 900–05, and U.S. Patents 759,356 and 759,357 regarding the design of the long kiln.

13. Dyer and Martin, *Edison*, 616.

14. The term *rational factory* comes from Lindy Biggs, *The Rational Factory: Architecture, Technology, and Work in America's Age of Mass Production* (Baltimore: Johns Hopkins University Press, 1996), which provides an excellent introduction to the ideas regarding factory design that would have influenced Edison.

15. Herter's testimony, *Edison and North American Portland Cement Co. v. Alsen's American Portland Cement Works*, pp. 902–06; Walter Mallory to William Shelmerdine, 1 May 1901; Mallory to W. S. de Camp, 21 Dec. 1900; and Mallory to Josiah Reiff, 29 July 1902 (*TAEM* 148:90; 154:78, 255); U.S. Patents 660,845, 662,063, 758,432, 832,046.

16. Herter's testimony, *Edison and North American Portland Cement Co. v. Alsen's American Portland Cement Works*, pp. 902–06; U.S. Patent 802,631.

17. Mallory's testimony, *Edison and North American Portland Cement Co. v. Alsen's American Portland Cement Works*, pp. 878–81, 892; Dyer and Martin, *Edison*, 514.

18. Edison Portland Cement Co. Minutes, 6 and 19 Mar. 1903 (from microfilm copy at ENHS); TAE to Walter Mallory, 3 and 5 Mar. 1903, EPPC; TAE to Edison Portland Cement Co Stockholders, 14 Apr. 1903, EPPC; Edison's undated notes on repairs and improvements to plant, EPPC.

19. TAE to Charles Matcham, 20 May 1905, DF.

20. TAE to Edison Portland Cement Co. Stockholders, 14 Apr. 1903; William Pilling, secretary-treasurer to the Edison Portland Cement Co. Stockholders, 18 Feb. 1908; and William Shelmerdine, president, to the Edison Portland Cement Co. Stockholders, 8 June 1904; all EPPC.

21. Robert Thompson to Thomas Thompson, 22 Jan. 1903, EPPC. For Edison's increased financial involvement relative to the other investors, see, for example, William Pilling to TAE, 7 and 22 July and 21 Nov. 1904; Walter Mallory to TAE, 2 Mar., 15 June, 23 Aug., and 17 Dec. 1906; all EPPC.

22. Quoted in Dyer and Martin, *Edison*, p. 618; Mallory to Mason, 6 Apr. 1906, EPPC. Mason would go on to apply some of the lessons he learned at Stewartsville in the development of masonite (*National Cyclopedia of American Biography* 37:224).

23. TAE to Emil Herter, c. June 1906, EPPC.

24. Walter Mallory to John Randolph, 14 Mar. 1907, EPPC; U.S. Patents 941,630, 944,481.

25. In his biography of Edison, *Streak of Luck* (pp. 347–48), Robert Conot paints a very negative picture of the financial history of the Edison Portland Cement Company. However, he fails to place his discussion in the larger context of the cement industry's own financial history and relies on a few retrospective accounts of the business for his interpretation. Financial statements found in the company's minute books, however, show that, except for the year 1927, between 1922 and 1928 the company was financially sound and made a profit. The heavy debt of the company continued to be a problem, but most of this debt was in the form of debenture notes owned by Edison himself. Regarding the financial status of the company, see agreements between TAE and the Edison Portland Cement Co., 15 May 1906 and 15 Feb. 1909, Edison Portland Cement folder, Kellow File; financial and other data folders, especially Answers to Questions of Counsel dated February 9, 1922, by Edison Portland Cement, *United States v. Cement*, Box 16, and minutes in folder 1, Box 18, both Legal Department Records; Edison Portland Cement Co. Minutebook No. 5; and Preliminary Plan for Settling Estate of Thomas A. Edison, 8 Oct. 1932, Edison Estate Records. See also Lesley, *History of the Portland Cement Industry*, and Henry Parker Willis and John R. B. Byers, *Portland Cement Prices: Their Basis, Character, and Present Position* (New York: The Ronald Press, 1924).

26. Charles Matcham to TAE, 19 May 1905, EPCC; Agreement between TAE, Edison Portland Cement Co., and North American Portland Cement Co., 8 Jan 1908, Box 13, Legal Dept. Files, ENHS; Edison Crushing Roll Company folder, DF, ENHS; Edison Crushing Roll Co., royalty account book, 1911–16, Accounts, ENHS.

27. "Edison on the Horseless Carriage," *Electrical Review* 27 (27 Nov. 1895): 307. Nothing is known of Edison's "motor tricycle" experiments, although they are listed as laboratory shop order number 825 in N-87-11-24 (*TAEM* 108:809) and among the June–September 1896 experimental accounts in Journal #8, pp. 64, 69, 73, 77 (*TAEM* 112:212, 214, 216, 218). For an interesting perspective on the history of the electric automobile, see Michael Brian Schiffer, *Taking Charge: The Electric Automobile in America* (Washington, D.C.: Smithsonian Institution Press, 1994).

28. "Mr. Edison on Storage Batteries," *Boston Herald*, 28 Jan. 1883, reprinted in *Edison Electric Light Co. Bulletins* 16, pp. 31–36 and 20, pp. 44–53 (*TAEM* 96:804–07, 915–19). The history of storage batteries is told in Richard H. Schallenberg, *Bottled Energy: Electrical Engineering and the Evolution of Chemical Energy Storage* (Philadelphia: American Philosophical Society, 1982). The following discussion of Edison's work on storage batteries and electric vehicles draws in particular on Schallenberg's book and W. Bernard Carlson, "Thomas Edison as a Manager of R&D: The Case of the Alkaline Storage Battery, 1898–1915," *IEEE Technology and Society Magazine* (Dec. 1988): 4–12, as well as documents in the Edison Storage Battery Company Records, ENHS (hereafter ESBC) and Document File folders under the headings Battery—Storage and Automobile.

29. "Edison on the Automobile," *Philadelphia Press*, 22 June 1899; "Edison and the Automobile," *New York Sun*, 24 June 1899; "It Will Be Run by Electricity," *New York Morning Journal*, 25 June 1899, "Edison on Automobiles," *New York Tribune*, 4 Aug. 1899; Cyrus P. Jones, "Edison and the Automobile," *Dry Goods Economist (New York)*, [16?] Sept. 1899; all Clippings, ENHS.

30. Edison described his analysis of the requirements for a storage battery in a paper delivered to the May 21, 1901, meeting of the American Institute of Electrical Engineers by Arthur Kennelly ("The New Edison Storage Battery," *AIEE Transactions* 18 [1901]: 219–30); Edison's draft of this paper is in N-01-04-23.

31. Regarding Lalande, see U.S. Patent 430,279; agreements with Felix de Lalande, 24 Aug. 1889 and 8 Apr. 1890 (*TAEM* 144:313, 145:487); TAE to Lalande, 1 Mar. 1894 (*TAEM* 135:152); and advertising pamphlets of the Edison Manufacturing Co. (*TAEM* 147:572–605). Schallenberg, *Bottled Energy* (pp. 338–41) discusses the efforts of Waddell and Entz; see also Dyer, Edmands & Dyer to TAE, 19 June 1899, enclosing their patents.

32. In "Thomas Edison as a Manager of R&D," W. Bernard Carlson argues that Edison's research on storage batteries marked a new style for the inventor. He calls this "convergent" research, in which "Edison assigned a specific material or arrangement to each experimenter who then conducted a long

series of standard experiments until he secured the best possible results." Carlson contrasts this with a "divergent" approach in which Edison and his assistants worked on several components of a system simultaneously. As a result, he argues, "Edison had altered the creative process from hands-on ingenuity and skilled observation to persistence and careful record-keeping." However, this fails to account for Edison's earlier research, which often involved just this sort of careful series of experimental tests of materials.

33. U.S. Patent 684,204; see also U.S. Patent 871,214.

34. Quoted in Schallenberg, *Bottled Energy*, p. 357, for the relative prices of cadmium and lead, see p. 358. For Jungner, see Schallenberg, *Bottled Energy*, 344–50, 356–58, 366–68, and *Edison v. Junger*, Storage Battery Files, Legal Department Records, ENHS.

35. U.S. Patents 701,804, 684,205, 678,722; see also U.S. Patents 692,507, 704,304, 700,136.

36. TAE draft to Willis Stewart, 15 July 1901, DF.

37. Agreement between Edison and Herman Dick, 1 Feb. 1901; Dick to Pilling and Crane, 1 Feb. 1901; agreement between Dick and Cary and Whitridge, 6 Feb. 1901; memorandum of agreements between TAE and the Edison Storage Battery Co., 11 and 17 July 1901, all Kellow File, ENHS.

38. TAE to Emil Herter, 19 July 1901, ESBC. For the development of the battery and some of the special manufacturing processes, see U.S. Patents 721,682, 723,450, 721,870, 727,117, 754,859, 754,858, 727,118, 852,424, 723,449, 873,220, 831,269, 857,041, 898,633, 766,815, 817,162, 821,625, 821,623, 821,032, 797,845, 827,297, 948,542, 861,242, 879,612, 821,622, 767,554, 785,297, 821,624; TAE draft to Louis A. Ferguson, 3 Sept. 1903; TAE drafts to Sigmund Bergmann, 9 Nov. and c. 7 Dec. 1903; all DF; A. H. Whiting to National Motor Vehicle Co., 13 June 1904, ESBC. On the price of nickel, see the proof of "The Wonders of a Wizard," enclosed by Francis Chrisman to TAE, 4 Aug. 1903, DF; and B. K. Jamison to TAE, 15 Oct. 1903, with clipping from *Scientific American*, DF. On the Sudbury mining operation and the Mining Exploration Company, see that company's records at ENHS.

39. TAE draft to Herman Dick, 24 Aug. 1903, DF; "The Edison Storage Battery" (1903), Primary Printed, ENHS. According to a 1911 report by Edison to the Edison Storage Battery Company's stockholders (ESBC), the company had manufactured "the equivalent of 37,068 E-18 cells."

40. ESBC to J. T. Mann, 10 June 1902, ESBC.

41. Arthur Kennelly, "New Edison Storage Battery"; "Good-By to the Horse," *Chicago Record-Herald*, one of several clippings enclosed with Herman Dick to TAE, 31 May 1902, DF; Thomas A. Edison, "The Storage Battery and the Motor Car," *North American Review* (1902): 1–4.

42. Translation of "Criticisms on the Edison Accumulator," *Technische Rundschau* 31:392, DF; "Notes" and "Tests of the Edison Battery," *Electrician* 51 (2 Oct. 1930), enclosed with Herman Dick to TAE, 19 Oct. 1903, both DF.

43. Draft of TAE to Sigmund Bergmann, 29 Nov. 1904, DF.

44. TAE drafts to Sigmund Bergmann, 8 Nov. 1904 and 27 Feb. 1905, both DF; see also U.S. Patent 847,746.

45. TAE drafts to Sigmund Bergmann, 11 Jan. 1905, 29 Nov., and 29 Dec. 1904; William Gilmore to Sigmund Bergmann, 9 June 1905, all DF.

46. U.S. Patent 976,791; see also U.S. Patents 914,343, 827,717, 857,929, 854,200, 860,195, 936,433, 967,178, 914,342.

47. TAE draft to Sigmund Bergmann, 26 July 1905, DF.

48. Ibid.

49. TAE to Horace M. Wilson, 12 Feb. 1907, Mining Exploration Company Records, ENHS. For the cobalt search see D-05-23, D-06-21, D-07-26. Regarding the shift from cobalt to nickel, see U.S. Patents 865,688, 936,525, 865,687, 876,445, 896,811, 880,978.

50. TAE draft to Deutsche Edison Accumulatoren Co., 22 July 1907; Sigmund Bergmann to TAE, 30 Apr. 1907, both DF.

51. TAE to Sigmund Bergmann, 26 Oct. 1906, DF; see also William G. Bee's correspondence regarding his battery inspections in DF and ESBC, particularly his letter to William E. Gilmore, 26 Sept. 1905, DF.

52. Some of the special-purpose machinery is illustrated in "Useful Information about the Edison Storage Battery in Practical Use" (1910), Primary Printed, ENHS.

53. Sigmund Bergmann to TAE, 12 July and 15 Sept. 1910, DF.

54. Frank Dyer to TAE, 26 Oct. 1908; Dyer to the Stockholders of Edison Storage Battery Co., 9 May 1910; Dyer memo, 9 May 1910, all ESBC; William E. Gilmore to Alphons Westee, 2 Jan. 1908; TAE draft to Sigmund Bergmann, 1 Oct. 1910; Deutsche Edison Accumulatoren Co. Minutes, 6 Oct. 1910, both DF.

55. Morgan, Grenfell & Co to TAE, 10 May 1910, DF; on the Morgan interests, see H. E. Dick, John H. Harjes, 11 Sept. 1903, and TAE to Sigmund Bergmann, 31 Oct. 1904, both DF; and Document File folders D-05-04, D-06-04, D-10-07. On Monnot and Bergmann, see Dyer to Paul Cromelin, 6 Nov. 1911, and TAE to Herman Harjes, 15 Nov. 1911; John F. Monnot to TAE, 11 June 1912 and 7 July 1914; Bergmann to TAE, 9 Jan. and 11 May 1911, 17 Apr. and 26 Sept. 1912; TAE draft to Bergmann, 24 Mar., 31 May, 20 Nov. 1911; TAE draft to Emil Rathenau, 27 May 1911, all DF.

56. "The Edison Storage Battery" (1903) and "Useful Information about the Edison Storage Battery in Practical Use" (1910–11), both Primary Printed, ENHS.

57. Regarding the Electric Storage Battery Company and the Exide battery, see comparison between Edison and Exide batteries, n.d., DF; "Facts Concerning the New 'Ironclad=Exide' Battery for Electric Vehicles," Primary Printed Collection, ENHS; and Schallenberg, *Bottled Energy*, 202–21, 256–71, 284–86. On Lansden and Beach, see *TAEM Guide*, Part IV, s.vv. "Lansden Co.," "Lansden, John, Jr.," and "Beach, Ralph H."

58. On the fate of electric vehicles and the starting battery, see Gilbert P. A. Mom, "The Miracle Battery: Edison and the Electric Vehicle, 1895–1915," paper presented at Interpreting Edison Conference, Newark, N.J., June 1997; Schallenberg, *Bottled Energy*, chap. 4; on Edison and Ford, see TAE to Stockholders, 4 Nov. 1912; TAE marginal note on A. I. Clymer to William Meadowcroft, 19 Dec. 1912; Harry F. Miller to Clymer, 27 Dec. 1912, all ESBC; and Edison-Ford Office Correspondence, Boxes 4–5, EP&RI.

59. TAE draft to Clymer attached to Clymer to Harry F. Miller, 17 Nov. 1911. The Edison Storage Battery Company Records contain much correspondence regarding other uses of the battery, which are described in the company's advertising and sales literature in Primary Printed, ENHS. On the battery and its other applications, see standard storage battery textbooks, such as Morton Arendt, *Storage Batteries: Theory, Manufacture, Care and Application* (New York: D. Van Nostrand, 1928); Cyril Methodius Jansky, *Elements of Storage Batteries* (New York: McGraw-Hill, 1923); and the various editions of George Wood Vinal, *Storage Batteries: A General Treatise on the Physics and Chemistry of Secondary Batteries and Their Engineering Applications* (New York: John Wiley & Sons, 1924), the fourth and last edition was 1955.

Chapter 22: Edison Incorporated

1. "Edison Sixty To-Day," Meriden Journal, 11 Feb. 1907; see also "Thomas A. Edison and His Recent Investigations," *Dallas Times-Herald*, 7 July 1908; "Thos. Edison Worth $25,000,000 Retires," *Albany Times-Union*, 6 Aug. 1908; all Clippings, ENHS (hereafter cited as Clippings); TAE marginal note on F. T. Callow to TAE, 7 Oct. 1907, DF. Regarding his health see "Edison Weak; Wife with Him in Hospital," *New York Mail Express*, 24 Feb. 1908; "Thomas A. Edison's Condition Critical—Family Is Summoned to His Bedside," *New York Herald*, 28 Feb. 1908; "Edison Not out of Danger," *Boston Record*, [29?] Feb. 1908; all Clippings; "Edison Is Failing," clipping enclosed in G. B. Farmer to TAE, 1 Nov. 1904, DF. Regarding Randolph see "Edison's Secretary Takes Own Life Today," *Elmira Gazette*, 17 Feb. 1908; "Edison's Secretary Takes Own Life," *St. Paul Pioneer Press*, 17 Feb. 1908; "A Private Secretary Who Desired to Quit," *Bradford Era*, 18 Feb. 1908; "Edison Plant Is Stilled during Randolph Burial," *Newark Advertiser*, 19 Feb. 1908; all Clippings.

2. Charles Edison to Mina, n.d. (F.C. 5-4624). About this same time his younger brother Theodore was in the news, see "Edison's Son Is Now an Edison," *Greenville, S.C. News*, 10 Sept. 1912; "Young Edison an Inventor," *Rockport, Ind., Journal*, 18 Apr. 1913; "Theodore Edison a Speeder," *New York Herald*, 24 Oct. 1913, both Clippings. On shifts in the nature of fame and celebrity, see Leo Braudy, *The Frenzy of Renown: Fame and Its History* (New York: Oxford University Press, 1986); Ponce de Leon, "Idols and Icons"; Richard Schickel, *Intimate Strangers: The Culture of Celebrity* (New York: Fromm International Publishing Corp., 1986); and "The Most Useful Americans," *The Independent* 74 (11 May 1913): 956–58, which published the results of a poll naming the ten most useful Americans, in which Edison was named on nine-tenths of the ballots and led his nearest competitors by nearly 200 votes; see also George Ethelbert Walsh, "With Edison in His Laboratory," *The Independent* 75 (4 Sept. 1914): 557.

3. Frank Dyer to Chief of Police, Glasgow Scotland, 17 May 1905, Dyer to Harry F. Miller, 16 Nov. 1908; both DF; see also "Edison's Watchman Assaulted by Crank," *New York World*, 31 Aug. 1901; "Desires to Kill Edison," *New York Morning Telegraph*, 1 Sept. 1901, Clippings. On the prospective kidnapping, see Pinkerton reports in Document file folder D-01-11; numerous clippings, among

them "Edison Threatened by Kidnapping" and "Threat to Kidnap Edison's Daughter," *New York Evening Journal*, both c. 25 May 1901; "Edison's Daughter's Kidnapping a Joke" and "Edison Plotter Is Living Here," *Hoboken, N.J. Observer*, 25 and 27 May 1901; "Arrest in Edison 'Kidnapping' Case to-Day," "Found Writer of Kidnapping Letters," and "Gratitude Moved Kinni to Confess," *New York Herald*, 27 May, 31 Aug. and 1 Sept. 1901; "Clew in Kidnaping Case Leads to a Prominent Society Man," *Chicago Herald*, 28 May 1901; "Edison Governess a Suicide," *New York Sun*, 15 Aug. 1904, "Edison Governess Driven to Suicide," *New York World*, 15 Aug. 1904; all Clippings; and Ernest Kahlar Alix, *Ransom Kidnapping in America, 1874–1974: The Creation of a Capital Crime* (Carbondale: Southern Illinois University Press, 1978).

4. "Mr. Edison's New Plans," *London Daily Mail*, n.d. 1908, Clippings; Charles Edison to TAE, n.d., (F.C. 5-4633); Charles Edison oral biography, p. 76. See also 1903 and 1906 diaries of Madeleine Edison, Lot 100, Swan Galleries Catalog of Autographs, 21 Sept. 1989; "Thos. Edison Worth $25,000,000 Retires." "Wizard Edison on a Vacation Visits Seattle," *Seattle Post-Intelligencer*, 12 Sept. 1908, both Clippings; Typescript of Mina Edison interview by Milton Mamor, Associated Press, 10 Jan. 1947, Edison Biographical Collection. On the camping trips, see Dorothy Boyle Huyck, "Over Hill and Dale with Henry Ford and Famous Friends," *Smithsonian* (June 1978): 88–95; Mary B. Mullett, "Four Big Men Become Boys Again," *American Magazine* 87 (Feb. 1919): 34–37; Harvey Firestone's memoirs with Samuel Crowther, "My Vacations with Ford and Edison," and "Was There Another Vacation Like This?" *System* 49 (May–June 1926): 643–54, 722–24, 791–94; Edward Renehan, *John Burroughs: An American Naturalist* (Post Mills, Vt.: Chelsea Green, 1992), 273–75.

5. Edison's marginal note on Philip Cavanaugh to TAE, 21 Feb. 1910, DF; "In the Interpreter's House: A New View of Thomas A. Edison," *American Magazine* 67 (Nov. 1908): 101–04.

6. Sales figures are found in Millard, *Edison and the Business of Innovation*, 195 (Table 9.1).

7. Joseph McCoy to Frank Dyer, 31 Jan. 1909. This letter, formerly in the Document File, has been moved to the National Phonograph Company Records. Many other twentieth-century documents are in the process of being moved from the Document File to more appropriate archival series. Readers should be aware that many of the items listed in this and the following chapter as DF may have been moved. Most of these will be accessible through the *TAEM Guides*. The Edison Papers is also making its index available through a web site currently located at http://edison.rutgers.edu.

8. William Gilmore to John Randolph, 16 Jan. 1908; National Phonograph Co. to Edison Dealers, 5 and 19 Oct. 1908; Frank Dyer to Walter Miller, 12 May 1909; M. J. [Laidlaw?] to Frank Dyer, 2 July 1909; all DF.

9. Frank Dyer to William Gilmore, 7 Feb. 1908; Gilmore to F. K. Dolbeer, 4 Mar. 1908; memorandum of "Changes Necessary in Machines for New York State," n.d.; Dyer to TAE, 4 Apr. 1909; all DF.

10. Frank Dyer to TAE, 20 Feb. 1910; see also Dyer to TAE, 13 Apr. 1910, both DF; *Newark News*, 2 Mar. 1911, Clippings; Ernest J, Berggren to R. G. Dun Co., 31 June 1911, DF.

11. Frank Dyer to Charles Howard Williams, 14 Jan. 1911, DF.

12. Frank Dyer to Alphons Westee, 26 Jan. 1910; Westee to Dyer, 27 Jan. 1910, both DF.

13. Frank Dyer to Peter Weber, Schiffl, C. H. Wilson, and George Scull (all members with Dyer of the Manufacturing Committee), 4 June 1910, DF.

14. Arthur Mundy to TAE, 4 July 1905; TAE to William Gilmore, c. 1 Aug. 1905, both DF.

15. Peter Weber to All Foremen, 29 Jan. 1909, DF.

16. Hutchison's diary, 11 Nov. 1911, ENHS; see other entries in the diary for his role in the storage battery. See also Hutchison to Charles Edison, 15 Apr. and 2 May 1905, both DF, regarding the issue of jealousy; and biographical information in Charles Federick Carter, "Invention Plus Advertising Equals Success," *Printers Ink Monthly* (Oct. 1921): 23, 113–16 and "Miller Reese Hutchison, Edison Associate," *Newark News* 18 Feb. 1944; both Biographical File, ENHS. On Bliss, see Hutchison to TAE, 12 Aug. 1912; Frank Dyer to TAE, 26 Aug. 1912; Dyer to Bliss, 29 Aug. 1912, all DF; Andre Millard, *Edison Laboratory Historic Furnishings Report*, 1:68.

17. Hutchison to TAE, 12 Aug. 1912, DF; TAE to H. M. Byllesby, 2 Dec. 1911, quoted in Millard, *Business of Innovation*, 217.

18. Regarding the celluloid record controversy, see Dyer to P. C. Dyrenforth, 19 Aug. 1904 and 21 Oct. 1905, both DF, *National Phonograph Co. v. Lambert*, Legal Department Records, ENHS; also see Read and Welch, *From Tin Foil to Stereo*, chap. 8. Regarding Petit, see Petit patent folders, Box 107, Legal Department Records; memorandum of payment for Petit patents, 27 Nov. 1908; Petit to Frank Dyer, 4 and 13 Dec. 1908; Dyer to Petit, 11 and 14 Dec. 1908; all DF.

19. Frank Dyer to TAE, 9 Nov. 1912; Dyer to Weber, 15 Dec. 1909, both DF.

20. Condensite Company of America, *Condensite for Plastic Molding* (New York: Press of Willis McDonald & Co., 1911), Primary Printed, ENHS; TAE to James Aylsworth, n.d. (c. 1911), DF, regarding the patenting of condensite records.

21. TAE Inc. Phono Sales Dept. to Canadian Jobbers, 12 Oct. 1914, DF. See also TAE to W. R. Wills, 13 and 20 Aug., 30 Oct., 3 Nov. 1909; TAE to George Kunz, 4 Dec. 1909; Frank Dyer to Peter Weber, 15 Dec. 1909; Dyer to TAE, 18 Feb., 14 Mar., and 5 Apr. 1910; Dyer to Dyer Smith, 3 June 1910, all DF; N-09-02-07, N-10-02-11, N-10-04-10, N-10-09-23; Read and Welch, *From Tin Foil to Stereo*, 192–93; Millard, *Business of Innovation*, 214.

22. Dugald Jackson to Charles Edison, 3 July 1916, and Edison's reply quoted in Charles Edison to Jackson, 18 July 1916, both Dugald Jackson Papers, MIT Archives. Preserving the overtones had been a subject of particular interest to Edison, as attested to by his annotations from this period in the 1875 edition of Helmholtz's *Sensations of Tone*, which he had first used in his acoustic telegraph experiments.

23. George L. Frow, *The Edison Disc Phonographs and the Diamond Discs: A History with Illustrations* (Sevenoaks, Kent, Great Britain: George L. Frow, 1982), 6–24, 209–31; C. H. Wilson to Wetzel and Hird, 19 October 1911; Wilson to F. K. Dolbeer, L. C. McChesney, and Peter Weber, 22 July 1911; TAE to [Albert?] Petit, 1 Aug. 1911; TAE to [Sam?] Moore, 1 Aug. 1911; Weber to Donald Bliss, 17 Aug. 1911; Wilson to Hird, 18 Aug. 1911; William Meadowcroft to TAE, 13 and 27 Mar. 1912; Wilson to TAE, 5 Oct. 1912; Wilson to Wetzel, 27 Dec. 1912; William Meadowcroft to Miller Reese Hutchison, 17 July 1913; TAE marginalia on W. Ritcher Crawford to TAE, 16 Feb. 1914; TAE draft answer to Paul Lovewell to TAE, 23 Feb. 1914; Meadowcroft to TAE, 12 Mar. 1914; TAE marginalia on John U. Wood to TAE, 27 Apr. 1914; [Charles Edison ?] to TAE, 16 May 1914, all DF; Statement showing cost of development work now being done for TAE Inc. at the laboratory to 1 Sept. 1914 and the following folders in the Engineering Department Files (Boxes 2-3): Disc Record–Special; Engineering Dept. Work List, Engineering Committee Minutes, Halpin Reports, Phonograph Engineering Committee, Phonograph–Lubrication, Phonograph–Special Tests; on the continuing need for inspection to maintain record quality see Karl Ehricke interview, 13 Mar. 1973, Columbia University Oral History Research Office, copy at ENHS.

24. TAE Inc. Press Release, 15 Dec. 1915; TAE and C. H. Wilson telegram to Phonograph Dealers, 31 Dec. 1914, both DF.

25. TAE to E. G. Liebold, 23 Feb. 1915, and other correspondence regarding the efficiency engineer, Box 4, EP&RI; C. H. Wilson to H. T. Leeming, C. A. Nicolai, Frank Waterman, Peter Weber, and Parkhurst, 12 Dec. 1914, DF. See also H. T. Leeming to TAE, 14 Nov. 1914; Charles Edison memorandum, 15 Dec. 1915; TAE to Robert Bachman, 2 Jan. 1915; H. T. Leeming to Wetzel, 13 Jan. 1915, all DF; "Report of the Committee on Edison Fire," *Journal of the American Concrete Institute* 11 (Aug. 1915), Clippings; Millard, *Business of Innovation*, 230–33; Frow, *Edison Disc Phonographs*, 37–38.

26. William E. Gilmore to Westee, Weber, et al., 3 May 1907, DF.

27. TAE to Thomas Graf, 20 Nov. 1911; William Meadowcroft to Frank Dyer, 7 June 1912, both DF; see also "Edison's Dream of a New Music," *Cosmopolitan* 54 (May 1913): 797–800; John Harvith and Susan Edwards Harvith, eds., *Edison, Musicians, and the Phonograph: A Century in Retrospect* (New York: Greenwood, 1987), Introduction. Regarding Edison's role, see the Voice, Song and Recording Selection files, Boxes 25–34, Recording Division and Related Records, ENHS.

28. "Mr. Edison's New Art" and "Edison's Musical Miracle," both Primary Printed, ENHS. See also Emily Thompson, "Machines, Music, and the Quest for Fidelity: Marketing the Edison Phonograph in America, 1877–1925," *Musical Quarterly* 79 (Spring 1995): 131–71; Marsha Siefert, "Aesthetics, Technology, and the Capitalization of Culture: How the Talking Machine Became a Musical Instrument," *Science in Context* 8 (Summer 1995): 417–49; Harvith and Harvith, eds., *Edison, Musicians, and the Phonograph*, 11–13.

29. L.S.M of Edison Shop, New York, to Walter Miller, 4 Jan. 1915, quoted in Harvith and Harvith, *Edison, Musicians, and the Phonograph*, 16. See also George J. Lenth to TAE, 17 Nov. 1915, DF; sales and profit and loss statements are from Millard, *Business of Innovation*, 195, and H. Musk to Steven Mambert, 21 May 1917, DF.

30. New York Investigator X-5 Report, 11 Sept. 1919, DF.

31. "Edison's Dream of a New Music," 798; Stevens interview in Harvith and Harvith, eds., *Edison, Musicians, and the Phonograph*, 26; TAE marginalia on William Maxwell to F. E. Nixon, 16 Sept. 1920, DF.

32. TAE marginalia on A. S. Abell Co to TAE, 1 Jan. 1914, DF; Gardner interview in Harvith and Harvith, eds., *Edison, Musicians, and the Phonograph*, 48.

33. Gardner interview in Harvith and Harvith, eds., *Edison, Musicians, and the Phonograph*, 49; see also Stevens interview in ibid., 27, 29, 31.

34. "An Interview with Thomas A. Edison Regarding the Imperfections of the Human Voice," Primary Printed Collection, ENHS; "Edison on Music," *Music* (May 1917), Clippings; Goodwin of the Phonograph Co., Chicago, to C. B. Hayes, 2 Oct. 1914, DF.

35. Walter Miller to TAE, 1921, Walter Miller File, ENHS.

36. *TAEB* Doc. 1277; TAE to Wm. D. Marks, 22 Nov. 1899, Letterbook 64:218, ENHS.

37. "Key to Office Organization Chart," 6 Dec. 1912. On Mambert see Millard, *Business of Innovation*, 233–38.

38. Thomas A. Edison, "How I Would Double the Volume of a Business," *System* 44 (Sept. 1923): 330. See also Charles Edison, "Round Table Letter," 26 Apr. 1920, DF; Charles Edison oral biography, pp. 128–31; Millard, *Business of Innovation*, 233–38; Alfred Chandler, *The Visible Hand: The Managerial Revolution in American Business* (Cambridge: Harvard University Press, 1977); idem, *Scale and Scope: The Dynamics of Industrial Capitalism* (Cambridge: Harvard University Press, 1990).

39. "Dr. Hutchison Resigns," *New York Times*, 8 July 1918, Clippings; R. W. Kellow to the Executive Committee of the Laboratory of Thomas A. Edison, Personal, 12 May 1920; "Laboratory Monthly Payroll Analysis," 23 Apr. 1920; "Work in Process Balances" Dec. 1918 to Dec. 1920; Engineering Department Files.

Chapter 23: Inventor-Philosopher

1. Strother, "Modern Profession of Inventing," 6293. On Edison's autobiographical notes, see Frank Dyer to TAE, 23 Feb. and 8 Mar. 1909; Dyer to Frank Marshall White, 31 Mar. 1910; all DF; and the William H. Meadowcroft Collection, ENHS. Edison's autobiographical notes relevant to each volume of *TAEB* can be found in that volume's Appendix 1, which also contains a discussion of their creation.

2. "Concrete Dwellings," *New York Insurance Press*, 30 Oct. 1907; "Concrete Houses for Working Men," *Concrete Review* 2 (15 Sept. 1907): 4–8; "Phipps May Build City of Concrete," *New York Herald*, 14 Nov. 1907, all Clippings; see also Dyer and Martin, *Edison*, 519–26.

3. U.S. Pats. 909,167, 909,169, 1,123,261, 1,219,272, 1,326,854; "Edison Cast Concrete House," circular, and documents in "Cement House" folder, DF; H. Ward Jandl et al., *Yesterday's Houses of Tomorrow: Innovative American Homes, 1850–1950* (Washington D.C.: Preservation Press, 1991), chap. 4; Michael Peterson, "Thomas Edison's Concrete House," *Invention and Technology* 11 (Winter 1996): 50–56; on Lambie's earlier relationship with Edison, see Lambie to TAE, 28 Feb. 1910, DF, and "Popularity of Concrete," *New York Tribune*, 11 June 1911, Clippings.

4. Entry dated 1 Nov. 1902 in Notebook N-02-05-01.

5. "Five and Ten Cent Store Will Be the New Automatic Shop," *Detroit News*, 22 May 1910, Clippings; see also "Edison Has Solution," United Press, 22 Jan. 1910, Clippings; A. M. Jaeger to TAE, 24 Jan. and 19 Apr. 1910; W. J. Paul to TAE, 19 May and 30 Nov. 1910; all DF.

6. TAE to Burnett Hamm, 7 Dec. 1909, quoted in Ben Singer, "Early Home Cinema and the Edison Home Projecting Kinetoscope," *Film History* 2 (1988): 65, n. 54; Runes, ed., *Diary and Sundry Observations*, 65; Edison's 1907 quote is from an advertisement in the *Moving Picture World*, 21 Dec. 1907, quoted in Singer, "Early Home Cinema," 66, n. 64; William Inglis, "Edison and the New Education," *Harper's Weekly* 55 (4 Nov. 1911): 5, 8; see also Martin S. Pernick, "Thomas Edison's Tuberculosis Films: Mass Media and Health Propaganda," *Hastings Center Report* (June 1978): 21–27. Singer's article in *Film History* (pp. 37–69) provides an excellent account of Edison's Home Projecting Kinetoscope and educational films.

7. TAE marginalia on B. L. Singly to TAE, 12 Dec. 1911, DF. See also "Engineering Department Work List, Beginning January 1st, 1911," item No. 11; "Statement Showing Cost of Development Work Now Being Done for Us at the Laboratory," 1 Sept. 1914; both Engineering Dept.; design problems are discussed in J. Farrell to Donald Bliss, 15 Nov. 1911; C. H. Wilson to J. Farrell and others, 18 Jan. 1912; Wilson to Bliss and Willard Greene, 30 Jan. 1912; Wilson to Peter Weber, 26 Aug. 1912; F. E. Madison to Dyer, 29 Aug. 1912; Miller Hutchison to TAE, c. 4 Sept. 1912; and Hutchison to Wilson, 6 Sept. 1912; all DF; for experiments on film subjects and the production of educational films, see Willard Green to Frank Dyer, 13 Nov. 1911; TAE marginalia, Harry Miller to S. G. Warner, 4 Nov. 1911; TAE marginalia; C. T. Kilbourne to TAE, 28 Nov. 1911; Edward Bigelow to Hutchison, 17 Feb. 1913; S. G. Warner to TAE, 22 Apr. 1912; Dyer to Horace G. Plimpton, 2 May and 13 Aug. 1912; William Maxwell to TAE, 24 Oct. 1912; W. W. Dinwiddie to TAE, 25 Nov. and 30 Dec. 1912; "Minutes of the First

Meeting of the Educational Committee," 24 Dec. 1912; Wilson to Plimpton, 27 Dec. 1912; and L. W. McChesney to Hutchison, 5 Oct. 1914; all DF; "Home 'Movie' is Exhibited," *Elizabeth N.J. Journal,* 5 Apr. 1912, Clippings.

8. TAE to Miller Hutchison, n.d. 1912, DF.

9. "Edison vs. Euclid, Has He Invented a Moving Stairway to Learning: A Symposium with an Introduction by Winthrop Lane," *Survey* (6 Sept. 1913): 681–95, quotes are from Henry W. Thurston (p. 692) and Arthur D. Dean (p. 691).

10. Henry W. Thurston in "Symposium," *Survey* (6 Sept. 1913): 692; TAE to Hutchison, 19 Aug. 1913, quoted in Singer, "Early Home Cinema," 61; TAE to George Iles, 17 May 1916, DF. On the poor sales of the Home P.K. and an effort to redesign the films from three to two rows, see C. H. Wilson to A. F. Gall and L. W. McChesney, 22 July 1914; W. McChesney to Wilson, 25 Jan. 1915; Gall to Wilson, 27 Jan. 1915, with pencil memorandum by I. W. Walker, 30 Jan. 1915; Gall to TAE, 1 Feb. 1915; McChesney to Walter Stevens, 4 Feb. 1915; McChesney to Wilson, 6 Mar. 1915; all DF.

11. Runes, *Diary and Sundry Observations,* 171–72.

12. "The Kingdom of Labor Is at Hand, Declares Edison," *Seattle Star,* 14 Jan. 1910, Clippings.

13. "The Woman of the Future," *Good Housekeeping* 55 (1912): 440; Allan L. Benson, "Mr. Edison Says: Electricity and Machinery Can Make Household Drudgery a Thing of the Past," *The Delineator* (Jan. 1911): 7, 67. Regarding the servant problem, see David Katzman, *Seven Days a Week: Women and Domestic Service in Industrializing America* (New York: Oxford University Press, 1978), chap. 6; on the failure of machinery to free the time of housewives for other pursuits, see Ruth Schwartz Cowan, *More Work for Mother: The Ironies of Household Technology from the Open Hearth to the Microwave* (New York: Basic Books, 1983).

14. TAE draft to Isaac Markins, 15 Nov. 1911, DF.

15. "The Woman of the Future," 441; A. L. Shands, "The Real Thomas A. Edison," *Haldeman-Julius Monthly* 8 (Aug. 1928): 85–86. The *Cedar Rapids Republican* (n.d., Clippings) noted that "Mr. Edison thinks that this beauty of American women is largely due to 'our cross breeding,' the mixing of many bloods and nationalities into one composite type."

16. Shand, "The Real Thomas A. Edison," 85; TAE marginalia on Mark Jones memoranda to TAE, c. 1920, Mark Jones Collection, ENHS; see also Edison's comments in the 1908 Edison, T.A.— Employment folders, DF, and "Edison's Laboratory Tests for Human Nature," *Literary Digest* 56 (Mar. 1918): 55.

17. Allan L. Benson, "The Wonderful New World ahead of Us," *Cosmopolitan* 50 (Feb. 1911): 299; Frank Dyer to Leonard McChesney, 2 Oct. 1911.

18. "Inventor Says City of Today Has Outgrown Its Usefulness," *Raleigh News & Observer,* 15 Nov. 1926, Clippings; Edward Marshall interview of TAE, "The Scientific City of the Future," *Forum* 76 (Dec. 1926): 829.

19. "Edison on the Sherman Anti-Trust Law and Industrial Regulation," *Electrical World,* 16 Dec. 1911; "What Edison Thinks of Gold," *The Mentor* 9 (1 Jan. 1922): 29; William Trufant Foster, *Edison-Ford Commodity Money* (New York: Academy of Political Science, 1922), 2–3; TAE, *A Proposed Amendment to the Federal Reserve Banking System: Plan and Notes* (West Orange, N.J.: Thomas A. Edison, 1922); "Thomas A. Edison on the Money Subject," *New York Money Leaflet No. 1,* all "Edison on Money" file, Edison Biographical Collection.

20. Edward Marshall, "Edison's Plan for Preparedness," *New York Times,* 31 May 1915, 5:6–7.

21. Josephus Daniels to TAE, 7 July 1915, reprinted in Lloyd N. Scott, *Naval Consulting Board of the United States* (Washington, D.C.: Government Printing Office, 1920), 286–88, and in "Edison Will Head Navy Test Board," *New York Times,* 13 July 1915, 1.

22. Quoted in Josephus Daniels, *The Wilson Era: Years of Peace, 1910–1917* (Chapel Hill, N.C.: The University of North Carolina Press, 1944): 491–92; see also "Daniels to Confer with Edison Today," *New York Times,* 15 July 1915, 1; "Daniels and Edison Pick Navy Board," *New York Times,* 16 July 1915, 1, 4.

23. Miller Reese Hutchison to Josephus Daniels, 6 Nov. 1915, quoted in Daniel J. Kevles, *The Physicists: The History of a Scientific Community in Modern America* (New York: Vintage Books, 1979), 109; see also "Daniels Names Naval Advisers," *New York Times,* 13 Sept. 1915, 1, 3. Kevles's book is one of several works containing excellent accounts regarding the roles of the Naval Consulting Board and the National Research Council in World War I. See also Scott, *Naval Consulting Board;* Thomas P. Hughes, *Elmer Sperry: Inventor and Engineer* (Baltimore: The Johns Hopkins University Press, 1971), 244–70; idem, *American Genesis: A Century of Invention and Technological Enthusiasm* (New York: Viking, 1989), 118–37; and A. Hunter Dupree, *Science in the Federal Government: A History of Policies and Activities* (Baltimore: The Johns Hopkins University Press, 1986), chap. 16.

24. Scott, *Naval Consulting Board,* 119.

25. Edison's, Saunder's, and Bakeland's testimony in U.S. Congress, House of Representatives, Committee on Naval Affairs, *Hearings on Estimates Submitted by the Secretary of the Navy, 1916* (Washington, D.C.: Government Printing Office, 1916): 3344, 3374, 3392.

26. Scott, *Naval Consulting Board,* 231; TAE to Josephus Daniels, 4 Mar. 1918, Naval Consulting Board Files, ENHS; TAE to Daniels, 22 Dec. 1916, quoted in Hughes, *Elmer Sperry,* 253.

27. TAE to Daniels, 4 Mar. 1918, Naval Consulting Board Files, ENHS; see also other correspondence between Edison and Daniels in these files.

28. Clippings titled "Turned Down Edison" and "Lists 45 Edison War Inventions," Reginald Fessenden Papers. Division of Archives and History, North Carolina Dept. of Cultural Resources. Edison's work on naval experiments is detailed in Scott, *Naval Consulting Board,* chap. 11; Naval Consulting Board Files, ENHS, including a "List of War Subjects upon which Mr. Edison worked in 1917 and 1918"; and Edison's reminiscences dated 30 Sept. 1919; also see Thomas Robins's reminiscences in the Historical Reference File, ENHS.

29. TAE to Reginald Fessenden, 7 Dec. 1917, Fessenden Papers; see also Leonard De Graaf and Edward Wirth, "Thomas A. Edison and the Exploding Submarine," *Seaport* (Winter–Spring 1991): 38–41.

30. Scott, *Naval Consulting Board,* 163; see also "What Did Edison Do during the War?," attached to William Maxwell to F. E. Nixon, 16 Nov. 1921, DF; "How Edison Won the War," *Literary Digest* 67 (23 Oct. 1920): 26; "Lists 45 Edison War Inventions," *Boston Herald,* 17 Feb. 1923, Reginald Fessenden Papers. Edison's reminiscences dated 30 Sept. 1919, are in the Naval Consulting Board Files, ENHS.

31. Kevles, *The Physicists,* 117–26; George Wise, *Willis Whitney and the Origins of U.S. Industrial Research* (New York: Columbia University Press, 1985), 187–94.

32. Willis Whitney to TAE, 19 July 1918, and TAE to Whitney, 22 July 1918, both Naval Consulting Board Files, ENHS.

33. "How Edison Meets Exigency Problem," *Bridgeport, Conn. Standard,* 11 Nov. 1914; see also "Men and Methods," *System* 26 (Nov. 1914): 522–24; "Edison, Bogardus and Carbolic Acid," *Electrical Review and Western Electrician* 75 (Nov. 1914): 965–66. Dyer and Martin, *Edison,* 790–98, provides the best overview of Edison's work on the production of chemical products.

34. Charles Edison to TAE, 26 Nov. 1917, DF.

35. R. W. Kellow to TAE, 10 Dec. 1920, DF; Edison, "How I Would Double the Volume of a Business," 268; TAE marginalia on William Maxwell to TAE, 6 Nov. 1921, DF; Charles Edison oral biography, pp. 158–60; see also "Edison Vice President Joins Executives Who Are to Quit Tomorrow," *Newark News,* 28 Feb. 1922, Clippings; W. E. Sanborn to TAE, 14 Apr. 1921, DF; Charles Edison to Mark Jones, 10 May 1920, Mark Jones Collection, ENHS; Millard, *Business of Innovation,* 294–95.

36. William Maxwell to TAE, 6 Oct. 1920, DF. See also Maxwell to TAE, 8 Oct. 1920; R. R. Karch to J. W. Robinson, 11 Sept. 1920; Stephen Mambert to All Managers, 9 Jan. 1920; George E. Clark to Mambert, 10 Jan. 1920; TAE to Engravers & Printers Machinery Co., 26 Oct. 1921; E. E. Jones to Charles Edison, 24 July 1922; [J.A.G.?] to TAE 2 Oct. 1922; all DF.

37. Karl Ehricke interview (1973), 24; A. E. Johnson interview (1974), 19; Edward Cary interview (1973), 181; all Columbia University Oral History Research Office. On the analysis of the work force see, for example, 1920 Reports of the Personnel Service Department on various divisions of TAE Inc.; TAE to Mark Jones, 20 Aug. 1920; Jones memoranda to TAE; all Mark Jones Collection, ENHS; [Stephen Mambert?] to Charles Luhr and Howard Eckert, 8 Nov. 1920; Osborn to TAE, 20 July 1922, DF; [Lamb?] to TAE, 4 Feb. 1922; undated (c. 1922) memorandum on personnel of Edison Storage Battery Co.; both ESBC; and TAE to Alex Moore, 25 Dec. 1920, Lot 78, Charles Hamilton Auction No. 165.

38. J. W. Robinson to Stephen Mambert, 31 Mar. 1922, DF; see also Robinson to Eckert, 23 Jan. 1922; J. V. Miller to Robinson, 2 Mar. 1922, both DF.

39. TAE marginalia on A. L. Walsh to TAE, 6 Feb. 1923; TAE to Charles Edison, 11 Feb. 1923; [Bill Hayes?] to TAE, 19 Mar. 1920; see also TAE marginalia on Mambert to Executive Committee, 1 April 1921; J. W. Robinson to Stephen Mambert, [22?] Aug. 1921, both DF.

40. William Maxwell, "'Advertising Hop' Meaning Artificial Stimulus," *New York Advertising and Selling* (14 Dec. 1919): 6.

41. C. S. Williams to TAE, 10 May 1925; advertising copy attached to A. L. Walsh to TAE, 31 Jan. 1927, both DF; see also undated (c. 1926) TAE draft of advertising copy for 40-minute record and A. L. Walsh to Charles Edison, 25 Apr. 1927, both DF.

42. Harger & Blish, Inc., to TAE, 24 Oct. 1924; TAE marginalia on H. Philips to TAE, 12 Dec. 1925, both DF.

43. Millard, *Business of Innovation*, 308, see also pp. 301–07.

44. Charles Edison memorandum, 30 Oct. 1929, DF; Charles Edison to TAE, 16 Oct. 1930, Lot 99, Swann Auction, 21 Sept. 1989; Charles Edison Oral Biography, 154. See also A. L. Walsh to Charles Edison, 14 June 1929; Walsh and Allen to Charles Edison, 14 Oct. 1929; Walter Miller memorandum, 21 Oct. 1929; Charles Edison to TAE, 1 Nov. 1929; all DF; "Edison Drops Phonograph to Make More Radio Sets," *New York Post*, 9 Nov. 1929, Clippings.

45. William Meadowcroft to Anna Ziegler, 23 Nov. 1928; Charles Edison to TAE, 21 June 1927; both DF.

46. Frank Parker Stockbridge, "Rubber from Weeds—My New Goal—Edison," *Popular Science Monthly* 111 (Dec. 1927): 9–10. See also William Orton, "Rubber: A Case Study," *American Economic Review* 17 (Dec. 1927): 617–35; "How the British Rubber Monopoly Trims Us," *Literary Digest* 88 (9 Jan. 1926): 5–7; "Synthetic Rubber Again," idem. 95 (31 Dec. 1927): 46–47; "Synthetic Rubber, Is There Anything in It?" *Scientific American Digest* 135 (1926): 51–52. The best accounts of Edison's rubber research are Tom Carroll, "The Search for Domestic American Rubber, 1923–1931: A Case Study of Edison's Inventive Method in His Later Years," and Stephen S. Anderson, "The Story of Edison's Goldenrod Rubber," manuscripts in Historical Reference File, ENHS; Byron M. Vanderbilt, *Thomas Edison, Chemist* (Washington, D.C.: American Chemical Society, 1971), chap. 9; Loren G. Polhamus, compiler, *Plants Collected and Tested by Thomas A. Edison as Possible Sources of Domestic Rubber*, Agricultural Research Service Bulletin 34–74, U.S. Department of Agriculture, July 1967.

47. Edison's work on rubber can be followed through the records of the Edison Botanic Research Corporation Records (hereafter cited EBRC) and through over 500 rubber plant collection and experiment notebooks. On the formation and funding of the company, see Harvey Firestone to TAE, 13 June 1925; TAE to Henry Ford, 5 Aug. 1927; TAE to Firestone, 16 Aug. 1927; Lybrand, Ross Bros. & Montgomery, Accountants to John Miller, 30 July 1928; Miller to Ford, 9 Jan. 1929; Miller to TAE, 1 Mar. 1929; Miller to Firestone, 9 Feb. 1931; financial statement of 17 July 1931; all EBRC; Austin Coates, *The Commerce in Rubber: The First 250 Years* (Oxford: Oxford University Press, 1987): 232–35.

48. Stockbridge, "Rubber from Weeds," 10–11.

49. TAE to Fresno Nursery Co., 10 June 1927, EBRC; Polhamus, *Plants Collected and Tested by Thomas A. Edison*, 11.

50. Notebook entry of March 1929, quoted in Anderson, "Story of Edison's Goldenrod Rubber," p. 14.

51. TAE to Ellwood Ivins, 24 June 1930; TAE marginalia on G. H. Carnahan to TAE, 7 Mar. and 13 Dec. 1930; all EBRC; Anderson, "Story of Edison's Goldenrod Rubber," 14–15. Matthew Josephson (*Edison*, 473) states that Firestone made tires in 1929 out of goldenrod. However, it is clear that the Firestone chemists did not even produce a full analysis of the goldenrod rubber until after Edison's death (E. B. Babcock to John Miller, 28 Oct. 1931; Miller to Edison Botanic Research Corporation Stockholders, 31 Dec. 1931; both EBRC).

52. TAE marginalia on Paul D. Lamson to TAE, 23 Oct. 1930; Miller to Edison Botanic Research Corporation Stockholders, 31 Dec. 1931, both EBRC; Dr. A. J. Edwards to TAE, 4 Oct. 1927, EBRC. On the development of synthetic rubber, see Peter Morris, *The American Synthetic Rubber Research Program* (Philadelphia: University of Pennsylvania Press, 1989); idem, *Polymer Pioneers: A Popular History of the Science and Technology of Large Molecules* (Philadelphia: Beckman Center for the History of Chemistry, 1990); Raymond B. Seymour, ed., *Pioneers in Polymer Science* (Dordrecht: Kluwer Academic Publishers, 1989).

53. TAE to Gilmore, c. 1 Mar. 1904, DF; A. E. Johnson (1974) and Karl Ehricke (1973) interviews, Oral History Research Office, Columbia University; see also Gilmore to TAE, 29 Feb. 1904, DF; Rosanoff testimony, *National Phonograph Co. v. American Graphophone Co.* (TAEM 117:198); and M. A. Rosanoff, "Edison in His Laboratory," *Harper's Magazine* 165 (Sept. 1932): 402–17. The problems inherent in Edison's technique of having his chemists learn on the job was apparent to Karl Compton during the war. Compton had been among the young scientists that the president of Princeton sent at Edison's request to assist in his war research. Compton's first task involved developing a better fuel for torpedoes. As was his practice, according to Compton, when Edison was working on a problem that he did not understand well himself he liked to put two men to work on it independently to see if they agreed. In this case the other researcher was a Columbia University scientist. Compton found that he and the Columbia scientist "agreed entirely as to method but disagreed radically as to conclusions." It turned out that the Columbia researcher, who was "a mathematician and not a chemist" had gone into the library to look up a formula for alcohol but failed to realize that he was using an old book with an

incorrect formula and was thus basing all of his calculations on a formula for sugar. Compton, "Edison's Laboratory in War Time," *Science* 75 (15 Jan. 1932): 70.

54. John Miller to *Illustrated Mechanics*, 112 Nov. 1931, EBRC.

55. Dr. Hubert S. Howe, "Doctor Says Edison Preferred Death to Being a Family Burden," *New York American*, 19 Oct. 1931, 1, Clippings; Theo. W. Harvey to George Raymond, 19 May 1893, Mutual Life Insurance Company of New York microfilm, ENHS; "Edison His Own Doctor," *New York Sun*, 10 May 1891, Clippings. Edison also undertook other medical investigations unrelated to his own health. For example, in 1888–1889 he investigated the cause of yellow fever and after concluding that it was spread by germ microbes that crawled along the ground, he experimented with the use of gasoline and other disinfectants to stop their spread. In 1890 he presented a paper to the International Medical Congress in Berlin on the use of electrical endosmosis to treat gouty deposits more rapidly with lithium salts. And in 1896 during his work on X-rays he experimented with the rays as a way of relieving certain kinds of blindness as well as an aid to surgery. As late as 1920 he wrote Dr. Simon Flexner of the Rockefeller Institute regarding "a suggestion for fighting skin diseases produced by germs." Yellow Fever Scrapbook, Cat. 1077 (*TAEM* 146:167); TAE, "An Account of Some Experiments on the Application of Electrical Endosmose to the Treatment of Gouty Concretion" (*TAEM* 146:75); 1896 Clippings file (*TAEM* 146:998); TAE to Flexner, 18 June 1920 and Flexner to TAE, 16 Aug. 1920, American Philosophical Society.

56. Howe, "Doctor Says Edison Preferred Death"; "People," *Time* 10 Aug. 1931, 22.

57. Howe, "Doctor Says Edison Preferred Death."

58. M. E. Given to Frank Campsall, 12 and 28 Sept. 1931, Box 7-4, Ford-Edison Office Correspondence, EP&RI; "Thomas A. Edison Dead at 84," *New York American*, 18 Oct. 1931, 6. Regarding the funeral preparations see William Nichols to Mina, 18 Sept. 1931 (F.C. 3-3016).

59. "World Followed News of Illness," *New York Times*, 19 Oct. 1931, 23. The letters, cards, and other tributes and expressions of sympathy and sorrow sent to the Edison family are preserved in several boxes at the Edison National Historic Site along with complete editions of the New York and Newark papers for the week following Edison's death.

Epilogue

1. Waldemar Kaempffert, "Titan of the Heroic Age of Invention," *New York Times Magazine*, 25 Oct. 1931, 22.

2. TAE Obituary, *Science* 74 (23 Oct. 1931): 404–05; C. L. Edgar, "An Appreciation of Mr. Edison Based on Personal Acquaintance"; F. B. Jewett, "Edison's Contributions to Science and Industry"; R. A. Millikan, "Edison as a Scientist"; and K. T. Compton, "Edison's Laboratory in War Time," idem 75 (15 Jan. 1932): 59–71.

3. Edison's relationship to Science is detailed in the 1881–1882 Document File folders *"Science"* (*TAEM* 55:360, 59:451, 63:661); bound copies of the journal are at ENHS. Quotes are from an 1880 and an 1881 prospectus and from Michel to Stockton Griffin, 9 Aug. 1880 (*TAEM* 55:368, 59:607, 55:424).

4. "The Future of American Science," *Science* 1 (9 Feb. 1883): 1. On Bell's patronage of *Science* see Robert V. Bruce, *Alexander Graham Bell and the Conquest of Solitude* (Boston: Little, Brown, 1973): 376–78.

5. Henry Rowland, "A Plea for Pure Science," *Science* 2 (1883): 242.

6. Joseph Henry is quoted in Arthur P. Mollella, "The Electric Motor, the Telegraph, and Joseph Henry's Theory of Technological Progress," *Proceedings of the IEEE* 64 (1976): 1277; Henry Rowland is quoted in David Hounshell, "Edison and the Pure Science Ideal in 19th-Century America," *Science* 207 (1980): 616; Edwin Layton, "Mirror-Image Twins: The Communities of Science and Technology in 19th Century America," *Technology and Culture* 12 (1971): 577. Hopkinson's work was further refined by others; see D. W. Jordan, "The Magnetic Circuit Model, 1850–1890: The Resisted Flow Image in Magnetostatics," *British Journal for the History of Science* 23 (1990): 131–73.

7. Edwin Layton, "American Ideologies of Science and Engineering," *Technology and Culture* 17 (1976): 691, 693, 695; B. G. Lamme, "Engineering by Analysis," *Electrical Engineering Papers* (East Pittsburgh, Pa.: Westinghouse Electric & Mfg. Co., 1919): 756, 759.

8. "Arrival of Thomas A. Edison," *Chicago Daily Globe*, 13 May 1891, Clippings (*TAEM* 146: 696); Daniel J. Kevles, *The Physicists*, 43–44.

9. "Arrival of Thomas A. Edison," *Chicago Daily Globe*, 13 May 1891, Clippings (*TAEM* 146: 696).

10. Richard McLaurin, "Mr. Edison's Service for Science," *Science* 31 (1915): 813–15.

11. Woodward to T. C. Mendenhall, 15 Nov. 1911, American Institute of Physics; Charles Greeley Abbot, *Adventures in the World of Science* (Washington, D.C.: Public Affairs Press, 1958): 76–77.

12. Abbot, *Adventures in the World of Science*, 77; W. Bernard Carlson, "Elihu Thomson: Man of Many Facets," *IEEE Spectrum* (Dec. 1983): 74.

13. P. B. McDonald to William Meadowcroft, 12 Oct. 1923; Meadowcroft to McDonald, 31 Oct. 1923, also see TAE's draft of this response, all in folder "Edison on Pure Science," Edison Biographical Collection.

14. Campbell is quoted in Neil H. Wasserman, *From Invention to Innovation: Long-Distance Telephone Transmission at the Turn of the Century* (Baltimore: The Johns Hopkins University Press, 1985); 96.

15. Michael Pupin to P. B. McDonald, 8 Nov. 1923. This and other correspondence related to Edison's claims is in folder "Edison on Pure Science," Edison Biographical Collection.

16. Karl Compton, "Edison's Laboratory in War Time," *Science* 75 (15 Jan. 1932): 71

17. TAE Obituary, *Science* 74 (23 Oct. 1931): 405; TAE to P. B. McDonald, 19 Nov. and 30 Nov. 1923, in folder "Edison on Pure Science," Edison Biographical Collection.

18. Hughes, "Edison's Method," 5–6.

Index

A. B. Dick Novelty Co., 269
Abbot, Charles Greeley, 468
Academy of Political Science, 446
Academy of Sciences (France), 155, 371
Acheson, Edward, 195
Acoustic telegraphy: *See* Telegraphy, acoustic
Acoustic transfer system: *See* Telegraphy
Acousticon, 428
Adams, James: and acoustic telegraphy, 116,
    118, 124; becomes experimental assistant,
    105; death, 185; and electric lighting, 185;
    and electric pen, 106; royalty shares, 105,
    108, 195; and telephony, 131–34, 159
Adams, Joseph, 42
Adams, Milton, 23, 29, 40–41, 43
Adams Express Co., 419
Adrian, Mich., 25–26, 237
Aerophone, 152
Agreements: with Andrews, 52; with Ansonia
    Clock Co., 148; with Bell Telephone Co.,
    269; with Birkinbine, 342; with Caldwell,
    136; with Craig, 58–59; with Drexel Mor-
    gan, 174; with Edison (Charley), 136; with
    Edison Electric Light Co., 212; with Edi-
    son General Electric, 334; with Edison
    Speaking Phonograph, 148; with Field, 52;
    with General Electric, 337; with Gold and
    Stock, 52–56, 63; with Gould, 102–3; with
    Gouraud, 149; with Harrington, 60, 64,
    82–83, 103; with Hills, 43; with Lane, 43;
    with Lefferts, 125; with Lippincott, 289;
    with Murray, 104; with Plummer, 43; with
    Prescott, 98, 101; with Puskas, 148; with
    Reiff, 81, 83, 103; with Roberts, 42; with
    TAE Jr., 391; with Welch, 43; with Western
    Electric, 126; with Western Union, 79, 109,
    115, 129–30, 132, 135, 140–41; with
    Yeaton, 125
Aiken, Edward, 402, 430–31
Akron, Ohio, 246–48, 250, 253
American Association for the Advancement of
    Science (AAAS), 162–64, 183, 310,
    464–65, 467
American Automatic Telegraph Co., 104, 108–9
American Bell Telephone Co., 243
American Burglar Alarm Co., 75
American District Telegraph Co., 100, 372
American Graphophone Co., 280, 286, 289–90,
    298
American Institute (New York City), 54
American Institute of Electrical Engineers, 415

American Institute of Mining Engineers,
    343–45
American Mathematical Society, 448
American Mutoscope and Biograph Co., 402
American Novelty Co., 128, 165
American Philosophical Society, 114
American Physical Society, 448
American Printing Telegraph Co., 54–55, 61, 63
American Society for the Prevention of Cruelty
    to Animals, 328
American Speaking Telephone Co., 139
American Swedes Iron Co., 341
American Telegraph Co., 53
American Telegraph Works, 60, 64, 75–77, 86
American Theosophical Society, 111
Ampére, André, Marie, 182
Amusement Phonograph Co., 288, 290
Anders, George, 43, 47, 50
Anderson, James, 84
Andrews, Elisha, 52, 73
Andrews, William, 205, 223, 225
Annapolis, Md., 449–50
Anschütz, Ottomar, 296, 300
Ansonia Clock Co., 148
Armat, Thomas, 301, 374
Armington and Sims steam engine, 205
Armstrong, E. C., 36
Arnold Arboretum, 458
Arnoux and Hochhausen dynamo, 175, 189
Artificial materials: celluloid substitute, 105;
    ivory, 268; mother of pearl, 268–69, 366;
    silk, 251, 268
Ashley, James: and American Printing Telegraph
    Co., 54; TAE, opinion of, 51; TAE, rela-
    tionship with, 54–55, 66, 103–4, 113, 118;
    and Financial and Commercial Telegraph
    Co., 51, 53; and Pope, Edison & Co.,
    50–51, 54; as *Telegrapher* editor, 24, 40
Associated Press, 34, 56, 58
Association of Edison Illuminating Companies,
    307, 332–33
Association of Railway Telegraph Superinten-
    dents, 240
Astronomy: solar eclipse, 161–62; solar system,
    251–52; sunspots, 251
Atlanta, Ga., 250
Atlantic and Pacific Telegraph Co.: and auto-
    matic telegraphy, 102–4, 108–9, 124–25;
    and district telegraphy, 372; TAE as
    electrician, 101–2, 109; TAE's double trans-
    mitter test, 43, 48